The Complete
American-Jewish
Cookbook

The Complete
AMERICAN-JEWISH
COOKBOOK

In accordance with the Jewish Dietary Laws

Edited by ANNE LONDON, *Director,*
Homemakers Research Institute
and BERTHA KAHN BISHOV, *Home Economics Consultant,*
Jewish Family and Community Service

ASSOCIATE EDITORS: *Ethel I. Ugelow, Eugenia J. White,*

Leona Shapiro, Pascha Phillips

Harper & Row, Publishers, New York
Cambridge, Philadelphia, San Francisco, London
Mexico City, São Paulo, Singapore, Sydney

America's
Most Complete
Jewish
Cookbook
A Publication of
HOMEMAKERS
RESEARCH
INSTITUTE
®

A hardcover edition of this book was published in 1971 by Harper & Row, Publishers.

First PERENNIAL LIBRARY edition published 1989.

LIBRARY OF CONGRESS CATALOG CARD NUMBER 88-45726
ISBN 0-06-091590-0 (pbk.)

89 90 91 92 93 RRD 10 9 8 7 6 5 4 3 2 1

contents

introduction

MODERN JEWISH COOKERY

The cookery of a people, like all other aspects of its culture, is a reflection of its history—and, like the rest of the culture, it does not develop overnight. It is thus not surprising that Jewish cookery has developed characteristics of its own which make it different from other cookery. Probably in no other religious or ethnic tradition do diet and food occupy a more important place. The Jewish dietary laws (*kashruth*), which prohibit the use of certain foods entirely and the mixing of some foods at the same meal, foster the imaginative use of available foods. It is such inventiveness that creates great artistry in cooking.

For many centuries, influenced originally by Biblical prohibitions and mandates, the art of food preparation by the Jews was developed and expanded, and in time certain dishes became associated with particular holidays and festivals as well as with the Sabbath. The day when the Jews, in their haste to escape from Egyptian oppression, unable to leaven their bread properly, held the dough up to the sun to bake and ate the resultant "matzo," was the forerunner of a Jewish dietary pattern which has lasted nearly 3,500 years. Now, during Passover, because of the commandment to abstain from all leaven, there has been a truly amazing development of innumerable cakes, torten, puddings, dumplings, and other unusually rich and flavorsome dishes utilizing matzos and matzo meal. This is an outstanding example of the innumerable ways in which history and tradition have influenced Jewish cookery. And it is no wonder that the prohibition against cooking on the Sabbath developed the "cholent," which was simmered all night in brick ovens, and which to this day recalls nostalgic memories at the mere mention of this savory dish.

The true gourmet has also become interested in the international flavor of Jewish foods—the dishes of many lands adopted and varied by Jewish homemakers over the years. It must be remembered that the Jewish people, without a homeland for almost 2,000 years, were scattered over all parts of the world. They were forced to wander from country to country, often suffering privations, prejudice, and poverty, compelled to make the most of whatever food was available to them—and at the same time they have always been confined by dietary commandments and rituals which are observed by many to this very day.

It was natural for the Jews of Lithuania, forced to subsist for days on the lowly herring, to devise delectable ways of preparing this fish, as it was natural for Jews in many lands to learn ways to extend other fishes by chopping them and adding fillers and seasonings, as in "gefilte fish." Undoubtedly, too, Jewish cooks developed their special skills in the preparation of fish dishes because of the many prohibitions regarding the preparation and eating of meats. Fish was readily available when ritually slaughtered meat was unobtainable, and there is no prohibition against preparing or serving it with milk or milk products.

While the Jews in their travels in the Diaspora (exile) have left behind in each country their own ideas for the preparation of foods, they have gathered up from each land the best that that country had to offer. Thus what is usually designated "Jewish Cookery" is the preparation of dishes peculiar to the Jewish people supplemented by the most delectable, and often the most economical, dishes from the best of each nation in which the Jewish people have lived.

In the United States it is a gastronomically exciting experience to prepare Jewish foods, recognizing that these dishes are the culmination of the wanderings of a people through varied lands and climates. The Jewish people have migrated to our country from many nations, including almost all the nations of Europe and the Near East. Each of those countries, and areas within the countries, contributed favorite dishes. The names and terms for foods of different nations have become part of their culinary vocabulary just as the adopted dishes have become an accepted part of Jewish cookery. The foods which they have brought to our country were prepared here with necessary variations in accordance with prevailing tastes and the availability of seasonings.

From Spain and Portugal have come a fondness for olives and oil, sharp peppers and spices, and the custom of frying fish and other foods in oil. From Germany have come the sweet-and-sour stews. Hospitable Holland contributed pickled cucumbers and herring and dainty butter cakes and coffee cakes. From Poland have come a variety of soups, stuffed fish, stewed fish and sour cream dishes, as well as a variety of meat dishes. From Russia have come blintzes, buckwheat groats (kasha), a variety of borshts, fermented dark breads, pickled red cabbage, smoked fishes, and rich fruit compotes. Rumania added distinctive meat dishes, such as carnatzlach, and eggplant in many forms. In Hungary the Jews learned to use paprika and make strudel. America has added corn, sweet potatoes, turkeys, and other foods.

It must, then, never be forgotten that it was impossible for any other era, period or land to have reached as great a height of development in the art of cooking as has been attained in the United States. The abundance of numerous spices, varieties of foods imported from all over the world, our own diverse climate and the resultant refinements of foods through processes of growth plus the relatively low cost of flavoring agents which are unobtainable in many countries—all tend to make America the natural home of the gourmet—the lover of fine food.

We must also remember that America has been the melting pot for emigrants of all nations. Our country has served as the meeting place for peoples of many religions and folkways. All of these have contributed to make America stand at a pinnacle of progress in the culinary arts. American-Jewish cookery would seem to be symbolic of that development. A careful study of that cookery will reveal a blend of the flavors and methods of many nations all embodied in it—with certain distinctive additions. It combines a mixture of the best the East has to offer in spices and flavors plus the variety and quality in foods of the West.

The development of a cookery is a continuous and unending process. In this book we offer not only the traditional Jewish dishes of many lands but also the great variety of distinctly American foods. We hope it will serve as an inspiration to the homemakers of America—both Jewish and Gentile—to continue with the experimentation and development that have made cooking into a great art.

KOSHER FOODS AND THE KOSHER KITCHEN

One of the first thoughts that arises in relation to Jewish cookery is the puzzling question of the dietary laws. It's puzzling because so few people really know the laws—and that includes a remarkably large number of modern Jews. Frequently people are astonished to learn that they can read the laws given by God to Moses in Leviticus, the Third Book of Moses. Specifically the basis for the selection of prohibited and approved foods is very simply set forth in Leviticus XI.

Orthodox Judaism affects the way in which Jewish food is prepared and served in any country. If the religious precepts are followed, the Jew eats only that which is *kosher* and properly prepared. The Table of Prepared Law (*Shulkhan Aruch*) is the recognized guide to food observances and is used as a means for directing the dietary habits of Orthodox Jews.

A few obvious questions concerning the origin and reasons for certain prohibitions occur to almost everyone and will be considered here because there is so much misinformation and speculation about them. The editors of this book believe that while these speculations are of value to the student, in the last analysis, the main importance of laws and rites is in what they signify. To the pious Jew the prohibited mixing of meat and milk foods and the necessity of two sets of dishes have a strong religious significance derived from Biblical command. The same is true of other prohibitions, such as those against eating pork, certain fish and shellfish, and certain fowl. The Orthodox Jew considers his prescribed method of slaughtering animals and fowl for food as the most humane method of killing, one causing the least pain.

There are a relatively limited number of specific prohibitions set forth in the Bible. As previously mentioned the basis for most specific prohibitions is given in Leviticus XI. In Exodus XXIII, 19, Exodus XXXIV, 26, and again in Deuteronomy XIV, 21 there is an additional injunction: "Thou shalt not seethe (cook) a kid in its mother's milk." Later commentaries on the Bible enlarged and expanded this concept to forbid the use of milk or milk products and meats in the same meal. In addition to the specific or implied Biblical prohibitions, distinctions between clean and unclean animals, birds, and seafood seem further in some respects to be based on hygiene. These are sanitary measures promulgated by the rabbis through the ages as measures for health protection. Many of the early laws are directly traceable to measures for the preservation of health in ancient Palestine.

A question that frequently arises concerns the prohibition of pork. There have been a number of theories advanced, particularly that the pig, like certain other animals and seafoods, is a carrier of disease. The prohibition in the Bible is specific and the reason given is similar to the reasons for forbidding the flesh of other animals. Although the pig has cloven hooves, it does not chew the cud (Leviticus XI, 7).

A number of theories are advanced by various authorities about the ancient prohibition which requires the thorough removal of blood from the meat of animals or fowl before cooking. Perhaps the most common theory proclaims the belief that it was intended to wean man away from any spirit of violence by implanting in him the horrors of bloodshed. There are specific prohibitions in the Bible which account for the process of *kashering* (soaking and salting of meat). Blood is regarded as the life of the flesh, and only meat from which blood has been removed is approved as food. "For the life of the flesh is in the blood."—Leviticus XVII, 11 and in Leviticus XVII, 12—"Therefore I said unto the children of Israel, No soul of you shall eat blood, neither shall any stranger that sojourneth among you eat blood."

Frequently the non-adherent or Reform Jew is aware of the dietary prohibitions, their Biblical basis, and their relation to health protection but apparently he has decided that with modern sanitary measures adherence is no longer necessary in any greater measure than for the Gentile in the same environment. The observation of these laws, more than anything else, distinguishes the Jew as orthodox. Obedience to the Law is of vital importance because the Law is truth set forth in terms of action in this world. The Orthodox Jew considers his dietary adherence an effective symbol of disciplined loyalty to his religion which stresses good conduct and character. He considers strict adherence to *kashruth* as much a contribution to Judaism as attendance at the synagogue—perhaps even more since his primary concern in a new community is the question of obtaining *kosher* food rather than the location of the synagogue. He can always pray at home if necessary. In following the tenets governing diet, however, he proclaims and lives the teachings of the Bible in his everyday activities.

RULES FOR KOSHER FOOD

Permitted food and meat must be slaughtered according to rabbinical specifications and processed for human consumption according to a code of law (laws of *shekhitah*). Permitted meat or other food is called *kosher* (fit). Forbidden food is called *t'refah*. Animals or birds must be killed by a man trained to slaughter in accordance with ritual (a *shokhet*). A knife (*khaluf*) is specifically made and sharpened for the purpose so that little pain is suffered by the animal or fowl when the jugular vein is severed. This method of slaughter (*shekhitah*) causes the maximum effusion of blood in the animal or fowl. The remaining blood is extracted as explained below by soaking and salting the meat (*kashering*). Only the forequarters of permitted animals which include deer, goats, sheep, and cattle may be used.

There is a costly process called "treibern" by which a trained man can remove certain veins and fatty portions of the hindquarter and in that way make it kosher. The method was used in small communities in other lands that were so highly populated by Jews that it wasn't possible or perhaps economically advisable to sell the hindquarter to non-Jews. The limited amount of available meat made it a necessity to use the entire animal. The flesh of an animal or fowl on the permitted list becomes impure if it is not slaughtered in the prescribed manner. Each slaughtered animal must be examined by an expert and if it shows any signs of disease or lesions it must be considered impure and discarded. If the flesh of a permitted animal or fowl has been mutilated in any way, as by being torn by a wild beast, it must be considered impure. It should be noted that prohibited birds are usually scavengers and birds of prey.

In this modern world, with so much food processed away from the home, many specific questions arise in regard to *kashruth* regulations. Many of them regarding foods are answered by the *hekhsherim* (certificates of *kashruth*) that are sometimes placed on labels of the processed foods. When in doubt about a question of *kashruth* consult rabbinical authority. Below are fundamental regulations that must be observed by the homemaker who wants to conduct a kosher kitchen.

Kashering. Even though meat and poultry is purchased in a kosher market it must still be *kashered* to thoroughly remove all blood from the meat before it is cooked. This does not apply to the blood in the flesh of a fish. Meat and poultry must be soaked for a half hour in cold water in a container used only for that purpose. The meat is then rinsed, placed on a perforated board, and sprinkled with coarse salt. If the board is not perforated then it should be tilted so as to permit the blood to flow off. The salted meat must remain on the board for one hour and is then washed. Hearts of animals and poultry must be cut open, veins removed and blood permitted to flow before soaking and salting.

Liver. Liver from permitted animals or poultry must be prepared separately from other meat because it contains so much blood. It does not have to be soaked and salted; however, it may be prepared only by broiling. After it has been broiled it may be eaten that way or used in any manner in liver recipes which require additional cooking.

Broiled meats. Meats used for broiling need not be salted, since the broiling process permits the free flow of blood from the meat.

Poultry. The neck vein of a fowl must be removed by cutting lengthwise along the neck between the tendons. The claws and skin of the feet must be removed. The feet may be used. The cleaned fowl must be *kashered* as explained above.

Meat and milk. Meat may not be cooked in milk or with a milk derivative or otherwise prepared and served together with milk or a milk derivative. Foods containing milk or milk derivatives may not be served for 6 hours after meats. Meats may be served after milk dishes.

Fish and seafood. Only fish that have scales and fins are acceptable. For example, mollusks and eels are prohibited. Permitted fish may be cooked and served together with dairy dishes. Fish may not be cooked together with meat or eaten from the same dishes. Fish may be served before the meat course; however, it must be served on a neutral (*pareve*) dish or dairy (*milchig*) dish which is kept separate from meat (*fleishig*) dishes.

Eggs. There are no prohibitions against the use of eggs with milk or meat dishes. The only prohibition regarding eggs is that the egg be free of blood. If an egg is found in a slaughtered fowl, the egg cannot be cooked with milk dishes.

Dishes and utensils. Orthodox Jews must of necessity have at least two sets of dishes, utensils, and tableware, because meat and milk products may not be prepared or served in the same pots or dishes. Dairy products may not be served on a dish which contained meat, or vice versa. In fact, some Orthodox Jews will not eat at a table where meat and milk products are served simultaneously. It is believed that the restrictions on the utensils originated at a time when porous metals, unglazed porcelain, and wooden bowls were used. Glass was usually exempted from this prohibition. The prohibition is still regarded as prevailing, although nonporous utensils are now in general use. The use of the same towels for wiping meat and dairy dishes and utensils is forbidden. Kosher soap, soap powder, and scouring powders must be used for cleaning dishes and utensils. During Passover additional sets of dishes and utensils are used unless certain specified processes are followed. Those are explained in detail in the Passover section.

glossary of special yiddish terms

The list below includes an explanation of the Jewish calendar, all major holidays, and traditional foods for the holidays, as well as general names for popular dishes and related terms. Detailed recipes for the dishes listed here can be found in the recipe section of this book. An attempt has been made to normalize all transliteration of Hebrew words to the phonetic patterns of Sephardic, or Palestinian, usage. The exceptions are certain terms that have become fully naturalized in Yiddish. Where two alternative spellings exist in fairly equal frequency, both have been given. Where certain inconsistencies in transliteration appear, these result from the prevailing usage for some common terms. Thus, for example, although *kh* is normally used to indicate the uvular fricative *ch* of German *Nacht*, certain terms that occur frequently in print are entered here with the commoner *ch* spelling.

afikoman: The middle *matzo* of the three which are set aside and over which the benediction is pronounced at the beginning of the Passover *seder*. Part of this middle *matzo* is hidden during the service, and traditionally the child who finds it requests a prize for its "ransom." See seder symbols.

arba kosot: The four cups of wine which each person drinks during the course of the *seder*. See seder symbols.

Asseret Yeme Teshuvah: Ten Days of Penitence starting with the first day of Rosh Hashana and ending with Yom Kippur.

balabusta: An efficient housewife.

bar mitzvah: Literally, a "son of the commandment," a Jewish boy who has reached the age of responsibility, thirteen years. The term is also used for the ceremony celebrating this event on the Sabbath nearest his thirteenth birthday. On this occasion the youth is symbolically accepted into the community of adult Jews and becomes eligible for a *minyan* and for participation in the reading of the Torah. In most Reform Synagogues a Confirmation Service, celebrating graduation from a religious school, is substituted for the *bar mitzvah*, and it is conducted for boys and girls alike. Cakes, wines, and liquors are customarily served on this festive occasion, although a complete meal, including a number of holiday dishes, may be served.

b'dikas khametz: The search through the house for the last remnants of leaven on the night preceding the first evening of Passover.

bagel or begel: A variety of bread roll, made of yeast dough formed into a small doughnutlike shape, cooked in simmering water, and then baked in the oven.

bentshen: The act of blessing or a benediction; specifically, the reciting of grace after a meal.

ben zochor: A male child. The term is also used for the ceremony celebrating the birth of a newborn male child on the Friday evening following the birth. Wine and cakes are served as well as other foods. *Nahit* are also traditionally served.

beryah: A "jewel" of a homemaker.

beth-din: A court of law formerly resorted to by orthodox Jews to settle controversies.

biur khametz: Burning of the leaven. A traditional ceremony carried out, following the *b'dikas khametz*, on the day before the first *seder*.

blintzes: Very thin pancakes rolled and filled with a variety of fillings, most popularly with cheese.

bob: Broad beans, or favah beans. It is customary to eat these on Khamishah Asar b'Shevat.

bokser: The carob, traditionally eaten on Khamishah Asar b'Shevat.

borsht: Basically, any of a variety of soups originating in Russia, but popularly, a beet soup made with or without meat and served hot or cold. Cabbage or spinach borshts are popular variations of this dish. On Passover it is customary to make a hot meat borsht from soured beet juice (*russel*).

bosor kosher: Kosher meat. This is the phrase that appears in Hebrew letters on the windows of kosher meat markets.

brith millah: The rite of circumcision, which usually takes place on the eighth day after birth. Wine and cakes are the traditional refreshment; sometimes, however, an elaborate meal is served.

calendar: The Jewish year is based on lunar computations. The ordinary year consists of 12 months, 355 days. Some of the months have 29 days; others have 30 days. The Hebrew calendar is periodically brought into conformity with the solar year of 365.24 days by adding a 13th month, *Adar Sheni* (Second *Adar*). This 13th month falls between *Adar* and the following month, *Nisan*. Such a "leap year" is introduced seven times in every 19 years.

Jewish holidays, therefore, do not fall on the same days in the calendar of the Common Era every year. In the early days, the Sanhedrin fixed the dates of holidays and sent out the news by messengers from Jerusalem. Later these dates were fixed by astronomical calculation. The Jewish religious year commences with New Year's Day (*Rosh Hashana*), which normally occurs in September or October. The months are as follows:

1.	*Tishri*	September to October
2.	*Kheshvan*	October to November
3.	*Kislev*	November to December
4.	*Teveth*	December to January
5.	*Shevat*	January to February
6.	*Adar*	February to March

(In leap years *Adar Sheni* follows *Adar*)

7.	*Nisan*	March to April
8.	*Iyar*	April to May
9.	*Sivan*	May to June
10.	*Tammuz*	June to July
11.	*Ab*	July to August
12.	*Elul*	August to September

carnatzlach: A highly seasoned, ground-meat dish of Rumanian origin. The meat is formed into small sausagelike shapes and broiled.

chalif: See khaluf.

challah or **hallah:** Twisted loaves of white bread prepared for the Sabbath. They are also made in a variety of forms for the various holidays of the year.

chametz: See khametz.

Chamishah Asar b'Shevat: See **Khamishah Asar b'Shevat.**

Chanukah: See Hanukkah.

charoses: See Seder Symbols.

chassana: A wedding. Wine is used in the wedding ceremony and, of course, the foods served may include an elaborate festive menu.

cholent or **chunt:** A Sabbath dish prepared on Friday and cooked over night in a very slow oven. Some variation of this dish was developed by Jews in almost every country of Europe because of the prohibition against cooking on the Sabbath. Some scholars believe the name is a corruption of *schul ende*, referring to the fact that it would be ready when the synagogue service was over on Saturday morning. Others believe it is derived from French *chaud*, meaning warm. In some communities it was customary to use the local baker's brick oven as a community oven for baking the Sabbath *cholent*.

chupah: The wedding canopy under which marriages are traditionally solemnized. One theory of its origin is that it is intended as a reminder of the ancient tent life of Israel.

chol hamoed: The four days intervening between the first two days of Passover and the last two days, or the corresponding period of *Sukkoth*. These days are lesser holidays.

chremsel (pl. **chremslach**): A Passover fritter.

dolma: An oriental combination of meat, rice, vegetables, and spices, popular with Jews in Turkey, Syria, and other Near Eastern countries.

eierkichel: Egg wafers, also made without sweetening and used as a *canapé* base.

einbren: A thickening for stews, tzimmes, and other dishes, made by lightly browning flour in melted fat and stirring in some of the liquid from the stew.

erev yomtov: The day or days immediately preceding a holiday.

essig fleish: Literally, vinegar meat, a potted meat which has vinegar added for seasoning. It is a popular dish with Eastern European Jews.

farfel: Noodle dough chopped into fine grains.

fleishigs: Meat or meat derivatives, or dishes made with these.

forshpeis: An appetizer.

galuptze: Russian term for chopped meat rolled in cabbage leaves. Also called prokes, holishkes.

gebrattens: Roasted meat.

gefilte fish: Literally, stuffed fish. Some variation of this fish is prepared by Jews in every country of Central and Eastern Europe.

gehakte: Chopped.

g'milas chesed: An act of loving kindness or charity. Such acts are continually incumbent, as a matter of course, upon all Jews.

griebenes or grieben: Cracklings which are strained from rendered chicken fat or goose fat. They are very popular among the Jews of Eastern Europe and are frequently added to mashed potatoes and other dishes.

haggadah: Literally, a telling. The narration of the Passover, which is read at each *seder*.

halke: A potato dumpling. Also called **knaidel**.

hamantaschen: Triangular cakes filled with honey and poppy seed, or other filling, and eaten at Purim. The word derives from the Biblical Haman (see **Purim**), and, possibly, from German *taschen* (pockets), probably with reference to the manner in which the cakes are filled. The triangular shape of the cakes traditionally recalls the triangular hat Haman is supposed to have worn.

Hanukkah or Chanukah: The Feast of Lights, celebrated for eight days. It commemorates the heroic victory of the Maccabees in the year 165 B.C.E. (Before the Common Era) and the rededication of the Temple in Jerusalem. In the year 168 B.C.E., King Antiochus of Syria commanded the Jews to worship idols. The Jews revolted under the leadership of the Maccabees and drove the Syrians out of Jerusalem and the Temple. According to legend, in the search for oil to rekindle the Eternal Light, a cruse was found with enough oil to burn for only one day. It lasted, however, the full eight days that it took to secure a fresh supply. Today the eight days are commemorated by lighting eight candles, one the first day, two the second day, etc. A ninth candle, the *shammes*, is used to light the others. Among the traditional foods served on Hanukkah are potato *latkes*. Gifts are traditionally given to children.

hekhsherim: Certificates of *kashruth*.

helzel: A neck, especially with reference to the neck skin of a chicken, duck, etc., filled with various stuffings.

holishkes: See galuptze.

Hosh'ana Rabba: Literally, the great hosanna. The name of the seventh day of Sukkoth. It is one of the three holidays on which it is customary to eat *kreplach*.

ingberlach: A variety of ginger candy.

kabbalah: A certificate issued to a prospective *shokhet* by a rabbi who has examined him to test his knowledge of *shekhitah*.

karpas: See seder symbols.

kartoffel kloese: Potato dumplings or potato croquettes.

kasha: Mush, especially a mush made of cooked buckwheat groats.

kasher: To soak and salt meats and poultry before cooking, in accordance with the laws of *kashruth*.

kashruth: The Jewish dietary laws.

kastenee: A chestnut.

Khag Hamatzot: The Feast of Unleavened Bread. Another name for Passover.

khaluf: A knife of specified length and sharpness, used for slaughtering animals or fowl in accordance with the laws of *shekhitah*.

khametz: Leavened bread, or any food or utensil regarded as not *kosher* for Passover use.

Khamishah Asar b'Shevat: Literally, the 15th day of the month of *Shevat*, the New Year of the Trees. A special day observed by planting trees in Israel and eating fruits that grow there, such as dates, figs, and carob (*bokser*).

kharoses: See seder symbols.

kichel (pl. **kichlach**): A cooky or wafer.

kiddush: The benediction pronounced over wine on the Sabbath and holidays.

kishke: A large beef intestine, stuffed with various savory fillings and roasted. The most common filling is made of flour and fat seasoned with onions, salt, and pepper.

knaidel (pl. **knaidlach**): A dumpling.

knish: A baked or fried dumpling or patty, frequently served with soup. Among the most popular *knishes* are those made of a thinly rolled or stretched dough with fillings of chopped, seasoned meat, mashed potatoes, or *kasha*.

koch kaese: German boiled cheese.

Kol Nidre: The prayer of atonement recited at the beginning of the Yom Kippur eve services.

kosher: Literally, fit; used to designate foods that have been selected and prepared in accordance with the Jewish dietary laws.

kosher l'Pesach: Fit for Passover use.

kreplach: Noodle dough cut into small squares, filled with meat, cheese, or other fillings and cooked in soups. It is a particular favorite of Eastern European Jews. *Kreplach* are traditionally eaten at least three times a year: on Purim, on the day preceding Yom Kippur, and on Hosh'ana Rabba.

kuchen: Cake; specifically, a coffee cake.

kugel: A pudding, especially one made of potatoes or noodles and baked.

Lag l'Omer: Literally, the 33d day of the *omer* (the count of 49 days from the second day of Passover to the first day of Shevuoth). It commemorates the cessation of the massacre of over half a million Jews by the Romans after the unsuccessful uprising under Bar Kochba about 132 C.E., and is usually celebrated with outings and games.

latkes: Pancakes, especially pancakes made of grated raw potato or of *matzo* meal.

l'chayim: Your health!—a toast.

leckach: Honey cake.

linzen: Lentils, or lentil soup.

lox: A variety of smoked salmon.

lukshen or lokshen: Noodles.

mandelbrot: An almond-flavored pastry baked in a long roll, then cut into thin slices, which are browned in the oven.

mandlen or mandlach: Soup nuts.

maos khitim: Literally, funds for wheat. Money contributed to provide for the Passover needs of the poor.

mashgiakh (pl. mashgikhim): An inspector employed by the community to see that *kosher* meat markets, etc., conform to the laws of *kashruth*.

matzo (pl. matzoth): Unleavened bread eaten during Passover. The custom of eating unleavened bread grew out of the Biblical narrative about the Exodus from Egypt. In their haste to depart, the Israelites carried with them dough which was still unleavened. As a yearly reminder of this "bread of affliction," the people were commanded to eat only unleavened bread for one entire week.

mazeltov: Good luck!—an expression of congratulation.

med: Mead, a fermented drink made of honey, hops, and water.

megillah: Literally, a scroll. Any of the five books of the Hagiographa, especially, the Book of Esther, read at Purim.

meichel (pl. meicholim): A tasty or savory dish.

mekhiras khometz: Literally, the "selling of leaven." All leaven in the home must be disposed of during the Passover festival. It was traditional to "sell" all leaven to a non-Jewish friend for a nominal sum and then to repurchase it after the festival.

menorah: A candelabrum; specifically, the eight-branched candelabrum used during Hanukkah.

mevin: A connoisseur, expert, or gourmet.

milchigs: Dairy products, or dishes made with these.

miltz: A spleen.

minyan: The minimal group of ten adult men required for the holding of congregational services.

Mishnah: The first part of the Talmud, containing traditional oral interpretations of scriptural ordinances, compiled by the rabbis about 200 C.E.

mitzvah (pl. mitzvoth): A commandment or precept, as in the Bible, or an act fulfilling such a command or the spirit of such commands.

Mogen Dovid: Literally, the Shield of David, a six-pointed star formed of two interlaced equilateral triangles, regarded as a historical symbol of Judaism.

mohn: Poppy seed.

moror: See seder symbols.

nahit: Chick-peas.

nevelah: The carcass of an animal not slaughtered in accordance with the laws of *shekhitah*.

orech: A guest. It is a traditional and prescribed custom to invite at least one *orech*, especially a traveler or stranger in the city, for the Sabbath and holiday meals.

parve or pareve: Neither *milchig* nor *fleishig* (i.e., neither a dairy nor meat dish), as fish, fruit, and vegetables.

Passover (Pesach): A holiday commemorating the deliverance of the Israelites from slavery in Egypt, as told in the Book of Exodus. For a detailed explanation of the holiday and its special foods, see the section containing Passover recipes.

Pentateuch: The first five books of the Bible, the Five Books of Moses. See Torah.

Pesach: Passover.

Pesachdig: For Passover use.

pidyon haben: The redemption of the first-born son of one who is not a *kohen* (priest) or *levi* (Levite). In a joyful home ceremonial, taking place thirty days after the birth of the child, a *kohen* is summoned, and the child is symbolically redeemed from God by giving the *kohen* five silver dollars (representing five shekels). Cakes and wine are then served, along with other festive foods.

piroshki or **pirogen**: Baked or fried dumplings made of yeast dough or pastry dough, with various fillings. They are served as a soup accessory or, in some forms, as canapés or desserts.

prokes: See galuptze.

Purim: The Feasts of Lots, commemorating the deliverance of the Jews by Esther from a general massacre inspired by Haman, as recounted in the Book of Esther. When the *Megillas Ester* (Book of Esther) is read in the synagogue on the eve of Purim, children traditionally swing noisemakers known as "gragers" at every mention of Haman's name. Traditional foods include *hamantaschen* and a variety of sweetmeats.

rabbi: Literally, my master. An ordained teacher of the Jewish law, authorized to decide questions of law and ritual and to perform marriages, etc., now usually the spiritual head of a congregation.

Rosh Hashana: The festival of the New Year, the first day of the Jewish religious year. Traditional foods associated with the holiday are *lekach*, carrot *tzimmes*, and apple slices dipped in honey.

russel: A soured beet juice, used especially to make Passover borsht.

Sanhedrin: The highest court and council of the ancient Jewish nation until the destruction of Jerusalem in 70 C.E. It was composed of 71 members and had religious and civil functions.

schav: A cold borsht made of sorrel grass, spinach, etc.

schmaltz: Rendered chicken fat or goose fat.

shalachmonos: An alteration of the Hebrew *mishloah manoth*, a sending of gifts. Gifts, especially platters of cakes and sweetmeats, exchanged at Purim.

seder: Literally, order, or arrangement. The feast commemorating the Exodus of the Jews from Egypt, observed in the home on the eve of the first day (and by orthodox Jews also the eve of the second day) of Passover.

seder symbols:

bitter herbs (moror). These herbs, usually horseradish, are a reminder of the bitter lot of the Israelites under bondage in Egypt.

charoses (kharoses): A mixture of nuts, apple, and wine symbolizing the mortar used by the Israelite slaves in the erection of the pyramids in ancient Egypt.

cup of Elijah: A cup of wine set aside for the prophet Elijah, who was expected to come bearing glad tidings—the word of the coming of the Messiah. With the setting aside of the cup of wine there are the accompanying customs of opening the door and leaving a vacant chair during the *seder* to welcome the prophet.

matzoth: The three whole *matzoth* set aside at the beginning of the *seder*. These *matzoth*, called the *Kohen*, *Levi*, and *Yisroel*, symbolize the three main groups of Israelites: the Priests, the Levites, and the laymen. See afikoman.

parsley (karpas): This vegetable, as well as other green vegetables, is used as a relish, symbolizing the festive nature of the meal.

roasted egg: A symbol of the freewill festival offering brought to the Temple, supplementing the Paschal lamb.

roasted meatbone (zeroa): A symbol of the Paschal lamb which was sacrificed on Passover eve during the days of the Temple.

wine: Each person at the *seder* is expected to drink four cups (*arba kosot*) of wine at specified points in the service. The first follows the *kiddush*, as on other festive occasions and on the Sabbath. The second is drunk at the end of the first half of the *seder*. The third follows the grace at the end of the meal. The fourth is after the praises to God recited toward the end of the *haggadah*.

Shabbos: The Sabbath. Traditional foods are: challah, chicken soup, gefilte fish, chopped liver, cholent, helzel, poultry, and tzimmes.

Shabuoth: The Feast of Weeks, or Pentecost, originally celebrating the spring harvest, but now also associated with the revelation of the Law at Mount Sinai. In recent times it has become customary to hold youth Confirmation services on Shabuoth. Dairy dishes, such as cheese blintzes, are traditionally eaten on this holiday.

shekhitah: The method of slaughtering animals or fowl in accordance with the Jewish dietary laws.

shofar: A ram's horn. In ancient times, the *shofar* was blown as a military alarm or for the purpose of signaling an important announcement. It is now sounded in the synagogue to announce the New Year and as a summons to repentance on Yom Kippur.

shokhet: A man trained and authorized to slaughter animals or fowl in accordance with the laws of *shekhitah*.

Shulchan Aruch: Literally, a prepared table, the authoritative code of Orthodox Judaism, first formulated in the 16th century.

Simchas Torah: Literally, Rejoicing in the Law, a festival occurring on the last of the nine days of Sukkoth, celebrating the completion of the yearly cycle of reading the Torah. On this day, the last verses of Deuteronomy are read, followed by the first verses of Genesis, to symbolize the eternal cycle of the Law. This is a joyous festival observed with singing, drinking, and processions through the synagogue with the scrolls of the Torah.

strudel: A pastry of stretched or rolled dough, with various fillings.

sukkah: A hut, or tabernacle, built for observance of the Sukkoth festival. Traditionally the family eats, or even lives, in the *sukkah* for the entire week of the festival. The roof is usually made of branches or other foliage so as to be partially open to the sky. The *sukkah* is generally decorated with fruits of all sorts.

Sukkoth: The Feast of Tabernacles, celebrating the fall harvest. It is also associated with the wandering through the wilderness after the Exodus. Among traditional foods served might be *kreplach* and *strudel*.

synagogue: A local assembly of Jews organized for public worship, or the place of assembly used for religious worship by a Jewish community.

tahar: Clean or pure, with reference to *kosher* meat or other foods.

tallith: The prayer shawl, with fringes (*zizith*) on each corner, worn over the shoulders or head by Jewish men during morning prayer.

Talmud: The collection of writings constituting the Jewish civil and religious law. It consists of two parts, the *Mishnah* (text) and the *Gemara* (commentary), but the term is sometimes restricted to the *Gemara*.

Talmud Torah: An elementary Hebrew school, offering instruction in the Bible, liturgy, and Jewish history.

tam: Taste, especially a savory taste.

teiglach: A confection made of pieces of dough cooked in honey.

Tishah b'Ab: The Ninth (day) of *Ab*, a fast day commemorating the destruction of the Temple and the exile of the people of Israel.

t'noyim: The marriage contract written on the engagement of a couple. Wine and cake and other sweets were customarily served on this occasion.

Torah: Literally, the Law. The word embraces several concepts; specifically (1) the whole body of Jewish religious literature, including the Scripture, the Talmud, etc.; (2) the Pentateuch, or the first five books of the Bible; (3) a parchment scroll containing the Pentateuch, kept in an ornamental ark in the synagogue. It is divided into fixed weekly portions, which are read every Sabbath and holy day in the year.

t'refah: Not *kosher*, that is, not in accordance with Jewish dietary laws.

tzimmes: A composite dish of meat, sweetening, and vegetables, prepared especially for the Sabbath, Rosh Hashana, or before the Yom Kippur fast. There are many varieties, the most popular of which is the carrot *tzimmes* (*mehren tzimmes*).

verenikes: Filled rounds of noodle dough, similar to *kreplach*.

Yom Kippur: The Day of Atonement, a solemn day of fasting marking the end of the ten Penitential Days, which begin with the judgment of God on Rosh Hashana.

Z'man Kherusenu: The Period of Our Emancipation, another name for Passover.

zwiebel: An onion.

The Complete
American-Jewish
Cookbook

passover recipes

Passover (Pesach) is the spring festival, observed for 8 days, which recalls the Exodus from Egypt and the liberation of the Israelites from slavery. The name is derived from Exodus XII telling of the "passing over"—the sparing of the houses of the Israelites when the first-born of Egyptian homes were smitten by the Angel of Death. Over the years elaborate customs have developed in preparation for the holiday because Passover is primarily a home festival. The house is completely cleaned of all khametz (leaven). Year 'round dishes and kitchen utensils are put away and replaced by those especially reserved for Passover—or if utensils used throughout the year have to be used they are "kashered"—made fit for Passover. Pots and pans, dishes and silverware, must be scalded in boiling water. Metal baking utensils are passed through fire. Spits and broilers must be heated red hot before they may be used for Passover.

On the night before Passover (prior to the First Seder) the father performs the traditional final act of cleansing—the search for the last crumbs of leaven (B'dikas Khametz). This consists of gathering up a few crumbs with a goose quill and a wooden spoon and making the prescribed blessing.

The first two nights are celebrated with the family in an elaborate feast, called the Seder, in which the story of the Exodus is read from the Haggadah, and with ritual, song, and food the liberation story is recalled.

The word "Seder" in Hebrew means "order" and refers to the traditional order of the Passover ceremony. At the head of the table the following symbolic foods are placed: three whole matzos on a dish covered with a napkin, a roasted egg, a roasted meatbone, charoses, bitter herbs, a dish of salt water, and a vegetable to be dipped in the salt water during the service. These symbols are explained, during the service. For details see "Seder Symbols" in Glossary of Special Yiddish Terms on p. xvii. A glass of wine is placed before each person present and everyone is expected to drink wine during the ceremony.

PASSOVER FOODS

Foods eaten during the eight days of Passover differ from those of the rest of the year because of the prohibition of all leaven. Foods containing baking powder, baking soda, and yeast are forbidden, as well as such legumes as dried peas and dried beans, and grains. The usual flours are replaced with matzo meal, matzo meal cake flour (finely ground matzo meal), and potato flour. The Passover recipe section contains traditional Passover recipes as well as numerous recipes using matzo meal, matzo cake meal, and potato flour. Recipes in other sections of this book may be used for Passover as long as they do not contain the prohibited foods.

BEET SOUR (Russel)

Wash and scrape 12 pounds of beets and cut into large pieces. Place in a 12-quart earthenware crock. Cover with cold water almost to the top. Place a cover over the crock, allowing a small opening. Then cover with a clean cloth to keep out dust. Let stand in a warm spot about 1 week to ferment. A white foam forms on

3

top which is removed, and the beet mixture is stirred thoroughly. In about 3½ weeks the mixture will be ready to use as russel.

RUSSEL BORSHT

Dip out required russel, using 1 cup per serving, and strain. If too sour dilute with a little water. Season with onion and sugar to taste. Boil 10 to 15 minutes. Strain and stir in beaten egg yolks (1 per quart) or sour cream. Serve each portion garnished with chopped hard-cooked egg, minced parsley, and chopped cucumber. Serve hot or cold with boiled potatoes. Do not reheat after adding egg yolks or sour cream.

Russel borsht with meat: Add a 2-pound piece of brisket of beef and marrow bones (if desired) with the seasoning. Beets from the russel may be chopped and added with the meat. Dilute to taste with additional water. Simmer until the meat is tender (about 1½ hours). Serve hot with beaten egg yolk stirred in liquid as above. Garnish with chopped, hard-cooked egg and minced parsley.

CHAROSES

1 cup chopped apples	Grated rind of ½ lemon
¼ cup chopped nuts	1 teaspoon cinnamon
1 teaspoon sugar or honey	2 tablespoons red wine (about)

Mix all ingredients. Add enough of the wine to bind the mixture.

MATZO BRIE (Fried Matzo)

3 matzos	1 teaspoon salt
2 eggs	1 tablespoon butter or other fat
½ cup milk	

Soak matzos in water and drain. Mix with beaten eggs, milk, and salt. Fry on both sides until brown. Serve as main dish, or as dessert with cooked fruit, or sprinkled with sugar and cinnamon, or honey. Serves 2 to 3.

MATZO ZWIEBEL (Onion Matzo)

Rub matzo with the cut side of a raw onion. Sprinkle lightly with salt. Place in a hot oven for a few minutes to dry. Spread with butter or chicken fat and serve hot.

MATZO AND SCRAMBLED EGGS

4 matzos	Salt and pepper to taste
4 eggs	4 tablespoons butter

Break matzos in small pieces into a colander. Pour boiling water over them and drain. They should be moist but not soggy. Beat eggs well with salt and pepper and fold in the matzos lightly. Heat butter in a frying pan. Add the mixture and fry over moderate heat. Serve hot with or without sugar, or sugar-cinnamon mixture sprinkled on top. Serves 4 to 6.

Variation: Brown 1 medium-size chopped onion in hot fat. Fold in with the eggs.

SPICED MATZOS

Beat 3 eggs well. Brush 3 matzos with melted butter, then with beaten egg. Sprinkle liberally with mixture of cinnamon, nutmeg, and sugar. Bake in moderate oven (350°F.) until crisp (5 to 10 minutes). Serves 2 to 3.

FRENCH TOASTED MATZOS

Beat an egg with 1 tablespoon milk and salt to taste. Break a matzo in 3 or 4 pieces. Dip each piece into the egg mixture. Fry in hot, buttered pan until brown. Turn and brown other side. Serve hot with sugar and cinnamon, syrup, or honey. Serves 1.

FARFEL PANCAKES

Pour 1 cup water over 2 cups matzo farfel. Add 2 well-beaten eggs, 1 teaspoon salt and mix well. Fry on well-greased hot skillet. Serve with syrup or honey. Serves 4 to 6.

MATZO MEAL OMELET

Beat 3 eggs until light. Add ¾ cup water, ½ cup matzo meal, ¼ teaspoon salt and pepper to taste. Mix well. Melt 2 tablespoons chicken fat in a large skillet. Pour in the mixture. Fry over moderate heat until brown on one side. Turn and brown the other side. Serve hot. Serves 2 to 3.

MATZO OMELET

Break 2 matzos into small pieces. Scald with boiling water and drain immediately Add 2 well-beaten eggs, salt and pepper to taste. Fry in hot melted butter until brown on both sides. Turn only once while frying. Serve hot. Serves 2.

BAKED MATZOS AND CHEESE

1 pound dry cottage cheese	½ teaspoon cinnamon
½ teaspoon salt	Dash of nutmeg (optional)
5 eggs	1 teaspoon sugar
6 matzos (whole)	2 tablespoons butter

Combine cheese with salt and 3 eggs. Mix well. Dip whole matzos in remaining 2 eggs, beaten lightly. Place layer of matzos in a buttered dish. Cover with a layer of cheese. Sprinkle with mixture of cinnamon, nutmeg, and sugar. Alternate layers of matzos and cheese until all is used. Bake in moderate oven (350°F.) 30 minutes. Serves 6.

MATZO EIR KUCHEN

½ cup water	1 teaspoon salt
¼ cup matzo meal	4 eggs, separated

Pour water on meal, add salt and well-beaten yolks. Let stand 5 minutes. Gently fold in stiffly beaten whites. Drop by spoonfuls on greased pan. Brown both sides, turning only once. Serve hot with sugar and cinnamon, honey, or preserves.

TOASTED FARFEL FOR SOUP

1 cup matzo farfel
2 egg yolks

½ teaspoon salt
2 tablespoons oil or chicken fat

Combine and mix together all ingredients. Spread out in a flat baking pan. Separate the particles and brown in moderate oven (350°F.). Serve in hot soup.

MATZO MEAL MANDELACH

3 eggs
⅔ cup cake meal

½ teaspoon potato flour
⅛ teaspoon salt

Beat eggs and add cake meal, potato flour, and salt. Knead and roll out ¼ inch thick. Cut into ¼-inch squares. Fry in deep hot oil (375°F.) until brown. Remove and drain on absorbent paper. Serve in hot soup.

PASSOVER EGG NOODLES

4 eggs
4 tablespoons cold water

1 tablespoon matzo cake flour
⅛ teaspoon salt

Combine all ingredients and beat until thoroughly blended. Heat some vegetable oil in a skillet. Pour in a small amount of the egg mixture. Tilt pan to spread evenly into very thin sheet. Fry until set. Turn out on a kitchen towel bottom side up. Continue in this manner until all batter is used. Cool and roll up each sheet. Cut into thin strips for noodles. To serve, drop into boiling soup and cook 1 minute. Store remainder in refrigerator.

EGG DROPS

2 eggs
¼ teaspoon salt
½ cup water

10 tablespoons cake meal
    or matzo meal

Combine well-beaten eggs with salt, water, and cake meal. Mix thoroughly until mixture is smooth. Drop by spoonfuls into boiling soup and cook 2 or 3 minutes.

SOUP NUTS

½ cup chicken fat
1 cup water
2 teaspoons salt

3 cups matzo meal
½ teaspoon pepper
8 eggs

Combine fat, water, and seasoning. Bring to a boil. Gradually add mixture to matzo meal, stirring constantly with a fork until well blended. Beat in eggs and knead thoroughly. Roll dough into marbles about ½ inch in diameter. Bake on a greased sheet in a hot oven (400°F.) until brown (about ½ hour). Serve in hot soup.

FLUFFY KNEIDLACH

3 eggs, separated

¾ cup matzo meal
½ teaspoon salt

Beat egg whites until stiff. Add yolks and continue beating. Fold in matzo meal and salt. Let stand 5 minutes. Form into small balls. Drop into boiling soup or boiling salted water. Cover and cook at a slow boil for 20 minutes. Serves 4 to 6.

Variations of fluffy kneidlach
1. Add a dash of ginger to the mixture.
2. Add 1 tablespoon finely chopped nuts and a dash of cinnamon, or ginger.
3. Add 2 tablespoons finely chopped parsley to mixture, with or without 1 tablespoon uncooked or cooked beef marrow.
4. Add 2 tablespoons chopped liver to mixture.
5. Add 1 cup cooked, strained vegetables to mixture.

MATZO BALLS (Knoedel)

4 eggs, beaten	1 teaspoon salt
½ cup water	Dash of pepper
⅓ cup melted shortening	1 cup matzo meal

Combine eggs with water, melted shortening, salt and pepper. Mix well. Add matzo meal and stir thoroughly. Let stand 20 minutes. Form into balls and drop into soup, or into 1½ quarts boiling water to which 1 tablespoon salt has been added. Cook 20 minutes. Serves 6.

Variations: Chopped parsley, chopped liver, chopped nuts, or marrow may be added to the mixture.

ALMOND BALLS FOR SOUP

2 eggs, separated	¼ teaspoon salt
¼ pound ground almonds	1 teaspoon grated lemon rind

Beat egg yolks and add almonds, salt, and lemon rind. Mix well. Fold in stiffly beaten egg whites. Heat oil 1 inch deep in a skillet. Drop batter in from teaspoon. Fry until golden brown. Drain on absorbent paper. Serve in hot soup.

MASHED POTATO KNEIDLACH

2 cups mashed potatoes	2 eggs, slightly beaten
1 teaspoon salt	⅔ cup matzo meal (about)

Add salt and eggs to cooled mashed potatoes and mix well. Add just enough matzo meal to hold mixture together. Form into balls the size of walnuts. Drop into boiling salted water and cook 20 minutes. Drain well and spread with chicken fat Brown in hot oven (400°F.). Serves 4 to 6.

GRATED POTATO KNEIDLACH

3 large raw potatoes	⅛ teaspoon pepper
1½ cups matzo meal	½ teaspoon salt
¼ cup chicken fat	½ cup water
3 eggs	

Pare and grate potatoes. Squeeze out as much liquid as possible. Combine with rest of ingredients and mix thoroughly. Let stand about 1 hour. Form into balls the size of walnuts. Drop into boiling salted water or boiling soup. Cook about 1 hour. Serves 6 to 8.

FILLED POTATO KNEIDLACH

1 pound potatoes (cooked in jackets)	¼ cup matzo meal
2 eggs	1 onion, minced
½ teaspoon salt	4 tablespoons cooking fat
¼ teaspoon pepper	1 cup finely chopped cooked meat

Peel and mash potatoes. Add eggs, seasoning, and matzo meal. Mix thoroughly. Divide in 8 pieces. Brown onion in 2 tablespoons fat and add meat. Make large, flat cakes of potato mixture. Put 1 tablespoon meat mixture in center of each cake. Fold edges over mixture and press together tightly so filling is completely covered. Brush tops with remaining fat. Bake in well-greased pan in moderate oven (375°F.) about 30 minutes, or until well browned. Serves 6.

HUNGARIAN POTATO JAM KNEIDLACH

8 medium-size potatoes	1 cup melted cooking fat or
1 teaspoon salt	chicken fat
4 eggs	Prune jam
1 cup matzo meal	Sugar and cinnamon

Pare and dice potatoes. Cook in water to cover until tender. Drain. Turn into a large bowl and mash with a fork. Beat eggs with salt and add alternately with matzo meal to potatoes. Stir in 2 tablespoons melted fat. Cool and form into moderate size balls. Make a depression in each ball. Fill hole with a tablespoon of prune jam, bringing dough over to smoothly cover the hole. Drop into boiling salted water 1 or 2 at a time so that boiling does not stop. Cover, leaving enough opening for escape of steam. Cook 10 to 12 minutes. Remove dumplings with a slotted spoon as they rise to the top. Serve with melted fat, and sugar and cinnamon to taste. If desired, dust dumplings with sugar-cinnamon mixture. Baste with remaining melted fat and brown in moderate oven (350°F.) about 10 minutes. Serves 6 to 8.

FRUIT KNEIDLACH

1 pound prunes	3 tablespoons melted cooking fat
2 slices lemon	¾ cup matzo meal
3 eggs, separated	Raisins and almonds
½ teaspoon salt	

Wash prunes and soak overnight in water to cover. Next day simmer prunes in the same water with lemon slices. In the meantime prepare the kneidlach. Beat egg whites until stiff. Add beaten egg yolks, salt, melted fat, and matzo meal. Mix well. Form into balls about the size of a walnut, inserting 1 raisin and 1 almond in the center of each. Sweeten prunes to taste. Place the kneidlach in a casserole. Pour the prunes and juice over them. Bake in moderate oven (350°F.) 30 minutes. Serves 4 to 6.

PASSOVER CHEESE BLINTZES

3 eggs	¾ cup matzo cake flour
½ teaspoon salt	1½ cups water (about)

Beat eggs and add salt, flour, and water alternately to make a thin batter. Put 3 tablespoons of batter in a hot greased skillet, spreading out as thin as possible. Fry brown on one side. Turn out on a towel browned side up. Cool and spread with filling. Fold sides in and roll up. Fry again, turning once to brown both sides. Serve with sour cream or plain. Yield: 6 blintzes.

Cheese filling: Mix 1 pound cottage cheese with 1 egg, ½ teaspoon salt, ½ teaspoon sugar, and 1 tablespoon thick sour cream.

Blintzes with preserves: Spread a thin layer of preserves over each pancake. Roll up and brown lightly.

Meat blintzes: Fry pancakes in chicken fat. Fill with any seasoned cooked, chopped meat, or chicken moistened with beaten egg.

Prune blintzes: Spread a tablespoonful of chopped raw prunes, sweetened to taste, on each pancake.

VERENIKAS

2 cups mashed potatoes
¼ cup matzo cake meal
1 teaspoon salt
⅛ teaspoon pepper

3 eggs, well beaten
1 cup chopped cooked meat
½ cup matzo meal

Combine potatoes, cake meal, salt, pepper, and 2 well-beaten eggs. Form into balls. Make a depression in center of each. Fill with chopped meat and enclose smoothly with potato-meal mixture. Flatten slightly and dip in beaten egg and then in matzo meal. Fry in hot chicken fat, turning only once to brown both sides. Serves 4 to 6.

BEOLAS

6 eggs
¼ cup cake meal (about)

Deep hot fat
Syrup

Beat eggs until very light. Add enough cake meal to give firmness and stir well. Drop from teaspoon into deep, hot fat (375°F.). When light brown, remove and drain on absorbent paper. Serve cold with syrup. Serves 4 to 6.

FILLED MATZO MEAL PANCAKES

5 potatoes (cooked in skins)
1 cup matzo meal
3 eggs
2 teaspoons salt

¼ teaspoon pepper
½ pound boiled beef, chopped fine
½ pound broiled beef liver,
    chopped fine

Peel and mash hot potatoes. Add matzo meal, eggs, and seasoning. Make a soft dough. Divide into 10 small pieces. Mix chopped beef and liver. Season to taste. Roll out the pieces of dough. Cover half of each piece with a spoonful of meat and liver mixture. Fold dough over filling. Press edges together firmly. Fry in hot fat until golden brown on both sides. Serves 6 to 8.

MATZO MEAL PANCAKES

½ cup matzo meal
½ teaspoon salt
1 teaspoon sugar

3 eggs, separated
¾ cup water or milk

Mix dry ingredients. Beat egg yolks and add water. Combine the 2 mixtures. Let stand 15 minutes, then fold in stiffly beaten egg whites. Drop by spoonfuls on a well-greased griddle. Brown on 1 side. Turn and brown other side. Serve hot with syrup, or sugar and cinnamon. Serves 4 to 6.

MATZO PANCAKES

6 matzos
8 eggs, beaten
½ cup sugar
1 teaspoon cinnamon

½ cup melted butter
½ teaspoon lemon extract or
   juice of ½ lemon
1 cup matzo meal

Soak matzos in water. Press out all excess moisture when soft. Add beaten eggs, sugar, cinnamon, butter, and lemon extract or juice. Beat thoroughly. Add matzo meal and mix well. Drop by spoonfuls on hot, greased griddle. Fry until brown on both sides, turning once. Sprinkle with sugar. Serve hot. Serves 6 to 8.

POTATO MATZO MEAL PANCAKES

2 cups mashed potatoes
4 eggs, well beaten
1 cup cake meal

½ teaspoon salt
1 cup water
Cooking fat

Mix all ingredients except fat. Fry in hot fat until brown on both sides. Serves 6.

CHEESE PANCAKES

Mix ½ pound dry cottage cheese with 4 well-beaten eggs. Slowly stir in 1 tablespoon sugar, 1 teaspoon melted butter, ½ cup matzo meal, and ½ teaspoon salt. Mix well. Fry as above. Serve, sprinkled with powdered sugar and cinnamon, or syrup. Serves 6.

POTATO KNISHES

4½ cups mashed potatoes
3 eggs
½ cup matzo meal
¼ teaspoon pepper

3 teaspoons salt
3 large onions
4 tablespoons cooking fat

Mix potatoes, beaten eggs, meal, pepper, and 2 teaspoons salt. Brown onions in hot fat, and add 1 teaspoon salt. Flatten small pancakes of the potato mixture in the hand. Cover with brown onions. Press another pancake on top. Roll in matzo meal. Fry in hot fat or bake in hot oven (400°F.). Serves 6 to 8.

Variations: Meat or liver mixture can be used instead of onions.

APPLE FRITTERS

1 cup matzo meal
3 eggs, beaten
2 tablespoons melted cooking fat

½ teaspoon salt
½ cup water
3 tart apples, thinly sliced

Mix ingredients in order given. Drop by tablespoonfuls into deep, hot fat (375°F.) and fry until golden brown, or fry in a skillet as for pancakes. Drain on absorbent paper. Sprinkle with sugar and cinnamon. Serves 6.

PRUNE FRITTERS

4 matzos
1 cup sugar
4 eggs

½ teaspoon salt
1 cup matzo meal
½ pound cooked prunes, pitted

Soak matzos in cold water until soft. Squeeze out excess water. Add sugar, beaten eggs, salt, and meal. Flatten a little of this dough in palm of hand. Place a prune in center and cover with another oval of dough. Press edges together and roll in matzo meal. Fry in deep hot fat (375°F.) until brown. Drain on absorbent paper; sprinkle with powdered sugar. Serves 6.

MATZO FRITTERS

3 matzos	1½ tablespoons brown sugar
1½ cups milk	½ teaspoon salt
2 eggs, separated	½ teaspoon cinnamon, if desired
¾ cup matzo meal	3 tablespoons vegetable oil

Pour warm water over matzos. Dry in hot oven for 1 minute. Combine milk with beaten egg yolks; add matzo meal, sugar, salt, and cinnamon. Fold in stiffly beaten egg whites. Spread mixture on one side of each matzo. Fry in hot oil on the batter side until brown. Spread batter on other side and fry again until brown. Serve hot sprinkled with sugar. Serves 6.

BOSTON CHREMSLACH (Basic Recipe)

6 eggs	½ cup finely cut sour beets
1½ cups matzo meal	½ cup honey
6 tablespoons water	¼ teaspoon ginger
3 tablespoons melted cooking fat	¼ cup chopped nuts
½ teaspoon salt	⅓ cup cold sweetened tea or "Med"

Beat eggs and add meal, water, melted fat, and salt. Let dough stand ½ hour. Combine beets, honey, ginger, and nuts; brown in skillet. Remove from fire and add tea or Med. Place triangles of dough on greased baking sheet. Spread with beet mixture. Cover each with another triangle of dough. Brush a little fat on each chremsel. Bake in hot oven (400°F.) ½ hour. Turn once to brown other side. Sprinkle with sugar and cinnamon. Top with spoonful of beet mixture. Serves 6 to 8.

STUFFED CHREMSLACH (Basic Recipe)

4 eggs	1½ teaspoons salt
¾ cup warm water	1½ tablespoons melted cooking fat
⅛ teaspoon pepper	⅛ teaspoon ginger
1½ tablespoons potato flour	1¾ cups matzo meal (about)

Beat eggs. Add remaining ingredients and enough matzo meal to make a very thick batter. Chill until firm enough to shape (several hours). Add more meal if necessary. Form into flat patties, allowing a heaping tablespoon for each. Spread filling between 2 layers. Flatten slightly to make round cakes. Fry in deep hot fat, or pan fry until golden brown on both sides. Serve with jelly, or cinnamon and sugar. Serves 6.

Meat chremslach filling: Mix 1 pound ground cooked meat, ½ ground onion, 1½ tablespoons chicken fat, salt, pepper, and cinnamon to taste.

Prune and nut chremslach filling: Combine 1 cup pitted, chopped prunes, ¼ cup chopped nuts, ⅓ cup chopped raisins, ¼ cup sugar, and juice of ½ lemon. Mix well.

Jelly or stewed fruit filling: Use drained, mashed, stewed fruit or any jam or jelly.

Apple and nut filling: Combine 1½ cups grated apples, ½ cup finely chopped nuts, ¼ cup sugar, ½ teaspoon cinnamon, dash of nutmeg (optional), and 3 tablespoons matzo cake meal. Mix well.

MATZO STUFFING

4 matzos
½ cup water
1 medium-sized onion, chopped
2 tablespoons cooking fat

½ teaspoon salt
Dash of pepper
¼ teaspoon sugar
2 eggs, beaten
1 tablespoon chopped parsley

Crumble matzos. Sprinkle with water. Brown onion in hot fat. Add salt, pepper, sugar, and eggs to matzos. Mix well. Turn into pan with onions. Stir lightly over a low flame until mixture is slightly dry. Cool. Add parsley. Use to stuff steaks, veal birds, chops, or poultry.

With cracklings: Add 2 to 3 tablespoons chopped cracklings (greben).

With almonds: Add ¼ cup chopped, blanched almonds.

With prunes: Add ½ cup diced, soaked, pitted prunes and ¼ teaspoon cinnamon.

APPLE SPONGE PUDDING

4 apples
⅛ cup raisins
½ teaspoon cinnamon
⅛ cup blanched almonds, chopped
1 tablespoon white wine

1 cup sugar
4 eggs, separated
Grated rind of ½ lemon
½ cup sifted cake meal
⅛ teaspoon salt

Pare apples. Cut off tops. Reserve as covers for apples. Hollow out insides, being careful not to break apples. Chop and mix apple with raisins, cinnamon, almonds, wine, and 1 tablespoon sugar. Fill apples with mixture. Cover with tops. Place apples in greased casserole. Add a few tablespoons water. Simmer 10 minutes. Beat egg yolks and remaining sugar until light and fluffy. Blend in lemon peel and cake meal. Beat egg whites with salt until stiff; fold into batter. Pour over apples. Bake in moderate oven (350°F.) 45 minutes. Serve with a wine sauce or any fruit sauce. Serves 4.

MOCK NOODLE PUDDING

4 matzos
3 eggs, well beaten
½ teaspoon salt
4 tablespoons sugar

5 tablespoons butter, melted
1 cup walnuts, chopped
3 apples, pared and sliced very thin
½ teaspoon cinnamon

Break matzos into thin strips. Pour boiling water over them in a colander, drain, let cool. Stir in beaten eggs, salt, 3 tablespoons sugar, and butter. Pour half this mixture into a well-greased casserole. Cover with walnuts and apples. Sprinkle with cinnamon and remaining sugar. Cover with remaining matzo mixture. Dot with butter. Bake in moderate oven (350°F.) ½ hour. Serve plain or with desired fruit sauce. Serves 6 to 8.

MATZO SHALET

6 matzos
1 tablespoon onion, minced
4 tablespoons chicken fat
3 eggs, well beaten
3 tablespoons cracklings (greben)

1 teaspoon salt
⅛ teaspoon pepper
3 tablespoons sugar
Paprika (optional)

Soak matzos in water until soft. Drain off excess water. Fry onions in a little fat until brown and add to matzos with remaining ingredients. Turn mixture into a baking pan with 2 tablespoons melted chicken fat. Bake in moderate oven (375°F.) until brown (about 45 minutes). Serves 8.

MATZO APPLE PUDDING

3 matzos
3 large apples
½ cup currants
¾ cup raisins
2 teaspoons cinnamon
¼ teaspoon salt

Dash of nutmeg (optional)
Grated rind of 1 lemon
¾ cup firmly packed brown sugar
4 tablespoons melted cooking fat
6 eggs, well beaten

Soak matzos until soft. Press out as much of water as possible. Pare and cut apples in small pieces. Add apples, currants, raisins, cinnamon, salt, nutmeg, lemon rind, sugar, and melted fat. Mix well. Add eggs, mixing thoroughly. Pour into a greased casserole. Bake in moderate oven (350°F.) about 45 minutes, or until apples are tender. Serves 6 to 8.

MATZO NUT PUDDING

4 eggs, separated
⅔ cup confectioners' sugar
2 cups grated apples

Grated rind of ½ lemon
½ cup matzo meal
¼ teaspoon salt
4 tablespoons almonds, chopped

Beat egg yolks until light. Sift in sugar and beat until fluffy. Add apples, lemon rind, and matzo meal. Mix well. Beat egg whites with salt until stiff but not dry and fold lightly into mixture. Pour into a spring form or pan lined with waxed paper. Sprinkle nuts over the top. Bake in moderate oven (350°F.) 45 minutes. Serve plain, or with wine or fruit sauce. Serves 6 to 8.

MATZO KUGEL

3 matzos
2 tablespoons chicken fat
1 cup matzo meal
5 eggs, separated
¼ cup blanched chopped almonds

Grated rind of ½ lemon
½ teaspoon salt
1 large apple, pared and grated
Dash of nutmeg (optional)
½ cup hot chicken fat

Soak matzos in water until soft. Press out excess water. Melt 2 tablespoons chicken fat in frying pan. Add matzos and fry until they are somewhat dry. Remove to bowl when fairly dry and stir in matzo meal. Beat egg yolks and stir in with almonds, lemon rind, salt, grated apple, and nutmeg. Beat egg whites until stiff. Fold lightly into mixture. Turn into well-greased casserole. Pour over hot chicken fat. Bake in moderate oven (350°F.) until brown (about 45 minutes). Serve with wine sauce. Serves 6.

MATZO CHARLOTTE

1 matzo
3 tablespoons sugar

2 eggs, separated
¼ cup chopped almonds
¼ cup chopped raisins

Soak matzo in water until soft, and press out well. Add beaten egg yolks, sugar, chopped almonds, and raisins. Mix thoroughly. Fold in stiffly beaten egg whites. Bake in greased baking dish in moderate oven (350°F.) until top is golden brown (about 30 minutes). Serves 4.

BANANA NUT FARFEL PUDDING

2 cups matzo farfel
2 eggs
½ teaspoon salt
⅓ cup sugar

3 tablespoons chicken fat
1 banana, sliced
¼ cup walnuts, chopped

Pour cold water over farfel in a colander. Drain at once, leaving farfel moist but not soggy. Beat eggs. Blend into farfel. Add salt, sugar, and chicken fat. Stir well. Add banana and nuts. Mix and pour into a greased casserole. Bake in moderate oven (350°F.) until brown (about ½ hour). Serves 6.

Variation: One large sliced apple may be substituted for banana.

CARROT NUT PUDDING

8 eggs, separated
1½ cups confectioners' sugar
½ cup matzo meal
2 cups grated raw carrots

½ cup blanched almonds, ground
Grated rind of ½ lemon
1 tablespoon wine
¼ teaspoon salt

Beat egg yolks until light. Sift in sugar, beating until light and fluffy. Add matzo meal, carrots, almonds, lemon rind, and wine; mix thoroughly. Beat egg whites with salt until stiff and fold lightly into batter. Pour into a well greased, floured baking pan. Bake in slow oven (300°F.) 1 hour. Serve plain or with any fruit sauce. Serves 6.

MATZO CHEESE PUDDING

3 eggs
1 pound dry cottage cheese
½ teaspoon salt

1 tablespoon sugar
2 tablespoons butter
3 matzos

Beat 1 egg and combine with cottage cheese, salt, sugar, and melted butter. Spread this mixture on the matzos about ¼ inch thick. Beat remaining eggs well and spread over cheese mixture. Bake in moderate oven (350°F.) until brown (about 10 minutes). Serve hot. Serves 6.

DATE PUDDING

¾ cup sugar
1 cup matzo meal
3 eggs, separated

¼ teaspoon salt
½ cup nuts, chopped
¼ pound dates, cut in pieces

Combine sugar and matzo meal. Blend in well-beaten egg yolks. Beat egg whites with salt until stiff. Fold into mixture. Gently stir in nuts and dates. Pour into a greased pan. Set it in a pan of hot water. Bake in moderate oven (350°F.) 45 minutes. Serve cold with fruit sauce. Serves 8.

ALMOND MACAROONS

4 teaspoons cake meal
1 pound blanched almonds,
    finely ground

4 cups confectioners' sugar
Grated rind of 2 lemons
5 egg whites

Combine cake meal, almonds, sugar, and lemon rind. Fold in egg whites, beaten until stiff but not dry. Dust a greased cookie sheet thickly with cake meal. Drop mixture from a teaspoon, allowing 1 inch between cookies. Bake in slow oven (300°F.) 15 minutes, then increase heat to 350°F. for about 10 to 15 minutes to brown the macaroons. Let cool before removing from sheet. Yield: about 36 cookies.

ALMOND COOKIES

½ cup cake meal
¼ cup potato flour
⅛ teaspoon salt

¼ cup almonds, chopped
½ cup sugar
2 eggs, beaten

Mix and sift cake meal, potato flour, and salt 2 times. Add remaining ingredients. Mix thoroughly. Roll out on a floured board (use potato flour mixed with sugar). Cut into desired shapes. Bake on greased cookie sheet in hot oven (400°F.) 8 to 10 minutes. Yield: about 4 dozen cookies.

MOCK OATMEAL COOKIES

2 cups matzo meal
2 cups matzo farfel
1½ cups sugar
1 cup raisins
1 cup nuts, chopped

1 teaspoon cinnamon
½ teaspoon salt
⅔ cup vegetable oil
4 eggs

Combine dry ingredients. Beat in eggs and oil. Drop by teaspoonfuls on a greased cookie sheet. Bake in moderate oven (350°F.) about ½ hour. Yield: about 4 dozen cookies.

NUT COOKIES

3 eggs
½ cup sugar
½ cup cake meal

½ cup finely chopped nuts
½ teaspoon salt
⅛ teaspoon spice

Beat eggs until light. Add sugar and continue beating until mixture is smooth and creamy. Fold in remaining ingredients. Drop mixture by teaspoonfuls on well-greased cookie sheet. Allow room for mixture to spread. Bake in hot oven (400°F.) 15 minutes. Yield: 2 dozen cookies.

Nut raisin cookies: Add ½ cup raisins to mixture.

COCONUT COOKIES

5 eggs, beaten
1½ cups sugar
1 cup matzo meal

2 cups shredded coconut
2 lemons, juice and grated rind
¼ teaspoon salt

Beat eggs well. Gradually sift and beat in sugar until creamy. Add remaining ingredients and mix well. Drop by spoonfuls on a greased cookie sheet sprinkled with matzo meal. Bake in slow oven (325°F.) ½ hour, increasing heat to 350°F. for last 10 minutes of baking to brown the cookies. Yield: about 24 cookies.

RAISIN BARS

4 eggs, separated	1 teaspoon vanilla
½ cup sugar	½ cup blanched almonds, chopped
2 tablespoons water	½ cup raisins, cut fine
½ cup cake meal	½ teaspoon salt

Beat egg yolks until light. Sift in sugar and beat until light and fluffy. Add water, cake meal, and vanilla. Mix well. Add almonds and raisins; blend thoroughly. Beat egg whites with salt until stiff and fold in lightly. Turn into greased pan to about ¼-inch thickness. Bake in slow oven (325°F.) until browned (about 10 minutes). Cut into 4 x 1-inch strips. Return to pan, placing them on one cut side. Brown again and roll in powdered sugar.

WALNUT PATTIES

3 cups powdered sugar	½ teaspoon salt
3 eggs	¾ cup cake meal
3 cups finely ground walnuts	

Cream sugar and eggs until light. Add walnuts, salt, and cake meal. Mix thoroughly. Drop by teaspoonfuls on a greased cookie sheet, allowing room for spreading. Bake in slow oven (325°F.) 20 minutes. Yield: about 4 dozen cookies.

KANISH BREAD

2 cups chopped nuts	½ teaspoon salt
2 cups sugar	6 eggs, well beaten
Juice of ½ lemon	2 cups matzo meal
1 tablespoon vegetable oil	1 teaspoon potato starch

Mix all ingredients to make a stiff dough; place in greased pan and brush top with beaten egg yolk. Bake in moderate oven (350°F.) 1 hour.

NUT AND RAISIN COOKIES

3 eggs	½ teaspoon cinnamon
½ cup sugar	½ cup chopped nuts
½ cup cake meal	½ cup raisins
½ teaspoon salt	

Beat eggs well, add sugar gradually while beating. Add cake meal, salt, cinnamon, nuts, and raisins. Drop by spoonfuls onto a greased cookie sheet, allowing room for cookies to spread. Bake in hot oven (400°F.) 15 minutes.

QUICK NUT BARS

Break matzos along the grooves into strips. Make 4 strips to the matzo. Mix sugar, chopped nuts, and spices. Butter matzos lightly. Press buttered side into sugar and nut mixture. Place on broiler under moderate flame; broil until butter bubbles and nuts are toasted. Serve hot.

PASSOVER PUFFS

1 cup water
⅓ cup shortening
1 cup matzo meal

½ teaspoon salt
4 eggs

For shortening use vegetable or salad oil, or butter. Bring water and shortening to a boil. Then pour in meal and salt all at one time and continue cooking and stirring until the dough no longer sticks to sides of pan. Remove from flame and add unbeaten eggs 1 at a time, beating thoroughly after each addition. Drop by tablespoonfuls on a lightly greased baking sheet. Bake in hot oven (450°F.) 25 minutes. Then reduce heat to 325°F. and bake 45 minutes longer or until browned. When cool, slit along 1 side. Insert about 1 tablespoon of filling and sprinkle with powdered sugar. Yield: about 12 large puffs. For the filling, use preserves, stewed, dried fruits, or flavored, sweetened whipped cream. Nuts may be added to the filling.

CHEESE CAKE

6 matzos
6 tablespoons butter
1 pound cottage cheese
3 eggs, beaten

¼ teaspoon salt
½ cup sugar
Juice of ½ lemon

Dip matzos in water and drain. Grease a baking dish with 4 tablespoons melted butter. Fit bottom and sides of dish with matzos. Mix cheese, eggs, salt, sugar, and lemon juice. Spread half the mixture over layer of moistened matzos. Repeat with cheese filling and then another layer of matzos. Brush top with 2 tablespoons melted butter. Bake in moderate oven (350°F.) until golden brown (about 1 hour). Sprinkle with powdered sugar and cut in squares. Serve hot or cold.

With nuts and berries: Mix ¼ cup each of chopped nuts and dried currants with the cheese.

MATZO MEAL MUFFINS

3 eggs, separated
¼ teaspoon salt

2 tablespoons cold water
½ cup matzo meal

Beat egg whites with salt until stiff. Beat egg yolks with water until light. Fold into whites. Fold in matzo meal. Bake in lightly greased muffin tins in moderate oven (350°F.) until browned (about 30 minutes). Yield: 8 muffins.

POTATO FLOUR MUFFINS

4 eggs, separated
¾ cup potato flour
2 tablespoons cold water

2 tablespoons sugar
½ teaspoon salt
Grated rind of ½ lemon

Beat egg yolks until light. Add sugar gradually, beating until light and creamy. Add water, sugar, and rind. Slowly sift in potato flour. Beat egg whites with salt until stiff. Fold into batter. Fill greased muffin tins half full. Bake in moderate oven (350°F.) 20 minutes. Yield: 12 muffins.

POTATO CUPCAKES

2 tablespoons matzo meal
1½ cups cold mashed potatoes
3 eggs, well beaten

3 tablespoons melted fat
½ teaspoon salt
⅛ teaspoon pepper

Combine all ingredients, and mix well. Fill heated custard cups half full. Bake in moderate oven (350°F.) 15 to 20 minutes. Turn out immediately; serve hot. Yield: 12 cupcakes.

MATZO MEAL BISCUITS

½ cup matzo meal
¼ cup potato flour
¼ teaspoon salt

½ cup sugar
¼ cup almonds, ground
2 eggs, beaten

Sift together matzo meal, potato flour, and salt 2 times. Add sugar, almonds and beaten eggs. Blend well. Roll out dough to ¼-inch thickness on a board floured with potato flour mixed with sugar. Cut out with a cutter or a floured glass. Bake on greased sheet in hot oven (425°F.) 10 to 12 minutes. Yield: about 12 biscuits.

MATZO FARFEL MUFFINS

2 cups matzo farfel
3 tablespoons matzo meal
3 eggs, beaten

1 teaspoon salt
1 tablespoon chicken fat
¼ teaspoon cinnamon
⅓ cup seedless raisins (optional)

Soak farfel in cold water 5 minutes; drain well. Add remaining ingredients and mix thoroughly. Bake in greased muffin tins in hot oven (425°F.) 30 minutes. Yield: 12 muffins.

MATZO PIE CRUST

4 matzos
2 tablespoons shortening or
  vegetable oil
½ cup matzo meal

4 eggs
4 tablespoons sugar
¼ teaspoon salt
½ teaspoon cinnamon

Soak matzos in cold water 5 minutes. Drain and squeeze dry. Heat shortening or oil. Add matzos and heat until dry in the same pan. Add remaining ingredients and mix well. Pat mixture over bottom of pie plate about ¼ inch thick. Fill with desired fruit filling. Bake in moderate oven (350°F.) about 30 minutes. Yield: crust for 2 open-faced pies.

SPONGE CAKE (6 eggs)

6 eggs, separated
1⅓ cups sugar
½ cup hot water
  Grated rind and juice of 1 lemon

½ cup potato flour
½ cup matzo cake meal
½ teaspoon salt

Beat egg yolks and sugar together until light. Stir in hot water and lemon rind and juice. Mix and sift potato flour and cake meal, and add to egg mixture. Beat egg whites with salt until stiff. Fold into batter. Turn into pan lined with moistened paper. Bake in moderate oven (350°F.) 1½ hours. Invert on wire rack and cool in pan before removing.

VARIATIONS OF SPONGE CAKE

Nut sponge cake: Add ½ cup very finely chopped walnuts before folding in egg whites.

Strawberry sponge cake: Bake sponge cake in 2 layers. Sweeten strawberries or use frozen strawberries and place between layers. Spread whipped cream over top and sides. Chill in refrigerator.

Cupcakes: Follow sponge cake recipe with or without nuts. Bake in greased cupcake tins in moderate oven (350°F.) 30 minutes.

SPONGE CAKE #1 (8 eggs)

8 eggs, separated	Grated lemon rind
1½ cups sugar	1 cup cake meal

Beat egg yolks, sugar, and lemon rind together until very light to about thickness of custard. Then add cake meal, stirring without beating. Fold in stiffly beaten egg whites. Bake in a moderate oven (350°F.) 1 hour.

SPONGE CAKE #2 (8 eggs)

8 eggs, separated	1 teaspoon vanilla
1½ cups sugar	½ teaspoon almond extract
½ cup cake meal	¼ teaspoon salt
½ cup potato flour	

Beat egg yolks until light; gradually add sugar, beating until fluffy. Mix and sift cake meal and potato flour; fold into creamed mixture with flavoring. Beat egg whites with salt until stiff but not dry; fold lightly into batter. Turn into ungreased pan. Bake in slow oven (325°F.) 1¼ hours. Invert on cake rack and allow to cool in pan.

SPONGE CAKE (12 eggs)

1 cup cake meal	12 eggs, separated
¼ cup potato starch	1 lemon rind
1½ cups sugar	½ glass orange juice

Sift together cake meal and potato starch. Add sugar to well beaten yolks. Add grated lemon rind and orange juice. Fold in sifted meal. Mix well. Fold in stiffly beaten egg whites. Bake 1 hour in slow oven (325°F.).

SPONGE CAKE (Pulverized Sugar)

9 eggs, separated	½ cup cake meal
1½ cups pulverized sugar	½ cup potato flour
1 tablespoon lemon juice	Dash of salt

Beat egg yolks until light. Sift in sugar, beating until light and fluffy. Add lemon juice and blend well. Mix and sift cake meal and potato flour 3 times and stir into creamed mixture. Beat egg whites with salt until stiff but not dry and fold lightly into batter. Turn into ungreased spring form, or use a square or round pan with bottom lined with wax paper. Bake in slow oven (325°F.) 1½ hours. Remove from oven and invert on cake rack. Allow to cool in pan.

POTATO FLOUR SPONGE CAKE

8 eggs, separated
1¼ cups sugar
¼ teaspoon salt

Juice and grated rind of 1 lemon
¼ teaspoon cinnamon
1 cup potato flour (scant)

Beat yolks and sugar until light and fluffy. Beat in lemon juice, rind, and cinnamon. Beat egg whites with salt until very stiff and fold into the mixture. Sift potato flour and fold in very lightly, but thoroughly. Bake in an ungreased tube pan in moderate oven (350°F.) 50 minutes. Invert pan on a wire rack. Allow to cool completely before removing from pan.

CHOCOLATE CAKE

7 eggs, separated
¼ teaspoon salt
1 cup sugar
½ cup cake meal

3 tablespoons cocoa
2 tablespoons water
½ cup nuts, chopped
1 teaspoon vanilla

Beat egg whites with salt until stiff but not dry and gradually beat in sugar. Beat egg yolks 5 minutes then gently fold in beaten egg whites. Mix and sift cake meal and cocoa, and fold in a little at a time. Gradually add water and fold in nuts and vanilla. Turn into an ungreased pan. Bake in slow oven (325°F.) 45 minutes. Invert on cake rack and allow to cool in the pan.

SPICE CAKE

¾ cup matzo meal
8 eggs, separated
1½ cups confectioners' sugar
Grated rind of 1 lemon
2 squares chocolate, grated

1 teaspoon allspice
2 teaspoons cinnamon
Juice of 1 orange
3 tablespoons wine
1 cup blanched almonds, chopped
¼ teaspoon salt

Sift matzo meal 4 times. Beat egg yolks until light and slowly sift in sugar and beat until creamy. Add grated lemon rind, chocolate, spices, orange juice, wine, and nuts, blending well after each addition. Add sifted meal. Beat egg whites with salt until stiff but not dry and gently fold into batter. Turn into waxed paper lined pan. Bake in slow oven (325°F.) about 1 hour.

WALNUT CAKE

9 eggs, separated
1⅓ cups confectioners' sugar
½ cup cake meal

1 teaspoon vanilla
1½ cups walnuts, ground
¼ teaspoon salt

Beat egg yolks until light and sift in sugar, beating until light and creamy. Sift meal 3 times and blend into creamed mixture. Add vanilla and walnuts. Mix well. Beat egg whites with salt until stiff but not dry and fold lightly into creamed mixture. Turn into spring form or waxed paper lined pan. Bake in slow oven (325°F.) 50 minutes. Remove from oven. Invert and allow to cool in pan before removing.

ORANGE NUT CAKE

½ cup cake meal
2 tablespoons potato flour
6 eggs, separated
1 cup sugar

½ cup nuts, ground
1 teaspoon orange extract
¼ teaspoon salt

Mix and sift cake meal and potato flour. Beat egg yolks until light. Sift in sugar and beat until creamy. Add sifted cake meal and mix thoroughly. Stir in nuts and flavoring. Beat egg whites with salt until stiff but not dry and fold in gently. Turn into waxed paper lined pan. Bake in slow oven (325°F.) 45 to 60 minutes.

ALMOND NUT CAKE

½ cup cake meal
¼ cup potato flour
1 cup sugar
½ teaspoon salt
1 cup blanched almonds, chopped

1 tablespoon melted butter
2 eggs
⅓ cup milk
1 teaspoon vanilla

Mix and sift cake meal, potato flour, sugar, and salt 3 times. Add nuts, butter, eggs, and milk. Beat thoroughly. Beat in flavoring. Turn into a greased cake pan. Bake in moderate oven (350°F.) 45 minutes.

APPLE TORTE

8 eggs, separated
¼ teaspoon salt
¾ cup sugar
1 teaspoon cinnamon

¼ cup almonds, ground
1 cup matzo meal
1 tablespoon orange juice
8 apples, pared and grated

Beat egg whites with salt until stiff and gradually fold in sugar. Mix in beaten egg yolks. Combine and add cinnamon, nuts, and matzo meal, then the orange juice and grated apples. Turn into pan lined with waxed paper. Bake in moderate oven (325°F.) 1¼ hours. Serve with wine sauce.

WINE CHOCOLATE CAKE

8 eggs, separated
1½ cups sugar
¾ cup cake meal

2 tablespoons cocoa
1 orange (juice and grated rind)
¼ cup wine

Beat yolks with sugar until thick and creamy. Sift cake meal with cocoa and stir in. Add grated orange rind, orange juice, and wine; mix well. Fold in stiffly beaten egg whites. Bake in slow oven (325°F.) for 50 minutes.

PASSOVER BEET PRESERVES

2 pounds beets
1½ pounds sugar
¾ cup water

1 lemon, peeled and sliced thin
2 ounces blanched almonds, chopped
1 teaspoon ginger

Use fresh beets or beets from the *RUSSEL*. If fresh beets are used, boil until tender. Drain, cool, and peel. If the beets from the *RUSSEL* are used, peel off the slippery film which has formed, slice, and rinse in several waters. Cut beets into thin strips or dice. Bring sugar and water to a boil. Add beets and cook 1 hour.

Add lemon slices and simmer 1 hour longer until jellied and the beets become transparent and slightly brown. Add nuts and ginger. Stir well and continue cooking 15 minutes longer. Cool and store in jars or stoneware crock away from light to prevent loss of color.

PASSOVER CARROT CANDY

1½ pounds carrots, cooked
1 pound sugar
½ cup orange juice
½ tablespoon grated orange rind
½ teaspoon salt

2 ounces almonds, ground
1 ounce bitter almonds, ground
1 teaspoon ginger
1 teaspoon vanilla

Mash carrots and press off all juice through a strainer. To mashed carrots add remaining ingredients. Cook in sauce pan on low flame ½ hour or more until very thick, stirring often to prevent scorching. Sprinkle a little ginger and sugar on a board. Spread carrot mixture evenly over this to about ¼ inch thickness. Sprinkle sugar and ginger over the top. Let cool slightly. Cut into 1-inch diamonds or squares before completely hardened.

PASSOVER INGBERLACH

1 cup sugar
¾ cup honey
2 eggs, well beaten

1 cup matzo meal
2 tablespoons powdered ginger
½ cup ground almonds

Bring sugar and honey to a boil in a deep saucepan. Cook until it turns a reddish, golden color (about 10 minutes). Remove from fire. Combine other ingredients and add to sugar-honey mixture. Cook on low heat until thick, stirring constantly (about 10 minutes more). Turn out on a wet board and pat out to ½ inch thickness with palm of hand which is dipped in cold water. Sprinkle with sugar and a little ginger. Cut into squares or diamond shapes.

MEAD (OR MED)

1 ounce hops
1 gallon honey

4 gallons water
1 large lemon, sliced thin

Tie hops in a piece of cheesecloth. Combine water and honey in a large pot and add lemon and hops. Bring to a boil, stirring often. Reduce the heat and cook gently for ½ hour, skimming as necessary during cooking. Let cool in the pot, then strain through a double thickness of cheesecloth into a small wooden barrel. Fill the barrel about ⅔ full in order to allow for fermentation without overflowing. Let it remain in a moderately cool room until fermentation is completed (about 3 weeks). Then bottle it, if desired, and keep in a cool, dark place until ready to use it. If a dark amber mead is desired, caramelize ½ cup sugar over low heat until dark brown. Add to mead when fermentation is completed. Yield: about 4 gallons.

PASSOVER RAISIN WINE

2 pounds seedless raisins
1 pound sugar

1 lemon, sliced
6 quarts boiling water

Chop raisins fine and place in an earthenware crock. Add other ingredients. Cover and stir once each day for a week. Store in a cool, dark place. Ready for use in about 2 weeks. Yield: about 1½ gallons.

CONCORD GRAPE WINE

Wash and stem 10 pounds Concord grapes. Mash well. Measure and place in a large jar. For each 2 cups of grapes add 2 cups sugar. Keep in a warm place for 2 weeks, then strain and bring to boiling point. Pour into sterilized bottles and seal. Keep in a cool place. Yield: about 2 gallons.

PASSOVER SALAD DRESSING

1 teaspoon salt	3 tablespoons RUSSEL
½ teaspoon pepper	Juice of 2 lemons
2 teaspoons sugar	1 cup vegetable oil

Pour all ingredients into a jar. Cover tightly and shake to blend well.

ORANGE SAUCE

2 egg whites	½ cup orange juice
½ cup sugar	1 tablespoon grated orange rind

Beat egg whites until stiff. Add sugar gradually alternating with a few drops of the orange juice, beating constantly. Mix in grated orange peel just before serving. If desired, garnish with candied orange peel.

WINE SAUCE

½ cup cold water	Grated rind of 1 lemon
1 teaspoon potato flour	2 eggs, separated
1 cup Concord grape wine	Dash of salt

Blend water and flour to a smooth paste. Add wine and lemon rind. Cook over low heat, stirring constantly, until thick and smooth. Remove from heat and slowly pour over beaten egg yolks. Return to heat and beat thoroughly 1 minute. Remove from heat. Fold in stiffly beaten egg whites. Serve at once.

TEIGLACH FOR PASSOVER

¼ cup oil	1 cup honey
6 tablespoons water	½ cup sugar
½ teaspoon salt	1½ teaspoons ground ginger
1 cup matzo meal	½ cup chopped walnuts
2 eggs	

Combine oil, water, and salt in a saucepan; bring to a boil. Add matzo meal and blend over low heat until mixture forms a ball and pulls away from the sides of the pan. Remove from heat; beat in eggs, one at a time, very thoroughly until dough is smooth. Oil hands lightly and shape dough into several ½-inch thick ropes. Cut into ½-inch pieces. Place on well greased cookie sheets; bake in hot oven (400°F.) 20 minutes, or until golden brown. Combine honey, sugar, and ginger in a saucepan; bring to a boil over moderate heat. Add baked teiglach; cook 15 minutes, stirring occasionally. Stir in nuts; pour onto a wet board or platter to cool.

appetizers

Appetizers are served preceding a meal and, as the name suggests, are intended to tempt the appetite. They should, therefore, be very colorful, bright, and attractive. Hot or cold, they include canapés, hors d'oeuvres, cocktails, soups, and small salads. Canapés and hors d'oeuvres are made to eat with the fingers and are generally served before your guests have been seated. Canapé is the French word describing a small piece of fried or toasted bread, spread or topped with appetizers. Hors d'oeuvre is a French term which means literally "outside of work," hence served before a meal. The term is commonly accepted as the French word for relish. Served as hors d'oeuvres are the almost endless varieties of tidbits on cocktail picks, as well as a colorful array of deviled eggs, stuffed celery, pickles, olives, pickled onions, and the like.

Fish cocktails, fruit cups, small salads, and clear soups, as well as some large canapés and hors d'oeuvre, are served at the table as a first course. The suggestions for canapés and hors d'oeuvres offered include so many of our favorite flavors that anyone, with the application of a little imagination, can make a delectable array of these dainties. A beautiful tray of appetizers may display ingenuity and will create just the right note of informality when served on many different occasions. They offer you endless combinations and should be served with beverages in the living room before dinner and for parties.

For rolled canapés use fresh bread. For others use day-old bread. Use a variety of breads as well as pastry cakes, crackers, potato chips, canapé puffs, cocktail crêpes, etc. Make them small, and garnish each simply but include a variety of colors. The serving of appetizers is simple. When served in the living room they should be decoratively arranged on large trays or platters, along with small-sized cocktail napkins, and should be accompanied with beverages. After they are passed around once or twice they should be placed so the guests may help themselves. Before planning appetizer trays be sure to look also in the salad and sandwich sections for additional varieties in textures and flavors.

CANAPE BASES

Cut round or fancy shapes from thin bread slices with cookie cutter or sandwich cutters. Place on broiler rack. Preheat broiler oven. Place rack about 3 inches from flame. Toast bread on one side, and brush toasted side with melted butter or butter substitute. Spread appetizer mixture on untoasted side. Savory butters add flavor to canapé bases.

SAUTEED BREAD BASES

Cut bread into desired shapes. Sauté on one side in a little butter, or butter substitute, over low heat. Spread and garnish untoasted side.

PASTRY CANAPE BASES

Use plain pastry recipe or any of its variations. Roll very thin (about ⅛ inch). Cut into fancy shapes and bake until lightly browned. For variety, sprinkle, before baking, with allspice, cardamom, caraway seed, coriander, cayenne, curry powder, mace, mustard, paprika, or grated cheese. Use with desired canapé spreads.

PUFFED CRACKER BASES (Basic Recipe)

Soak soda crackers in ice water 8 minutes. Drain on absorbent paper. Place on greased cooky sheet with a spatula. Brush with melted butter. Bake in a hot oven (450°F.) for 10 minutes, or until crisp and delicately browned.

Caraway seed: Sprinkle seeds over crackers just before baking.

Cheese: Sprinkle with grated cheese just before baking.

Curry: Before brushing, season the melted butter with paprika, curry powder, and salt.

Nut: Sprinkle finely minced nuts over crackers before baking.

VARIETY CRACKER BASES

Use crisp, savory crackers. Brush lightly with melted butter and place in a moderate oven until delicately browned. For variations, sprinkle with caraway seed, celery salt, garlic salt, grated cheese, or paprika before toasting.

PUFF PASTRY BASES

Use recipe for *PUFF PASTRY*. Roll very thin (about ⅛ inch). Cut into small rounds and put 2 together to form patty cases and bake. Fill with any canapé filling, such as cheese, fish, or fruit. Or roll puff pastry slightly thicker and cut into small, fancy shapes. Bake, and use with desired spreads.

Puff shells: Use puff pastry recipe and prepare tiny puff shells. Fill with desired canapé spread.

CANAPE BUTTERS

To prepare any of the following savory butters, mix the ingredients into ¼ cup of creamed butter. Store in covered container in refrigerator until ready to use. If they harden, cream them enough to soften before spreading on canapés.

Anchovy butter: Use 1 tablespoon anchovy paste, or mashed anchovy filets, and ½ teaspoon lemon juice.

Cheese butter: Use ¼ cup soft snappy cheese.

Chili butter: Use 2 tablespoons chili sauce.

Chives butter: Use 1 tablespoon finely minced chives and 1 teaspoon lemon juice.

Chutney butter: Use 1 tablespoon chutney.

Egg butter: Use 2 mashed hard-cooked eggs, ½ teaspoon lemon juice, a dash of tabasco sauce, salt and cayenne to taste.

Garlic butter: Use 1 small clove of garlic, minced fine.

Green savory butter: Use 3 tablespoons spinach purée, 1 tablespoon anchovy paste, a dash of paprika, 1 teaspoon capers, and salt to taste.

Honey butter: Use ¼ cup honey.

Horseradish butter: Use 2 to 3 tablespoons drained horseradish.

Ketchup butter: Use 2 to 3 tablespoons ketchup.

Lemon butter: Use ½ teaspoon grated lemon rind and 1 tablespoon lemon juice. (Lime and orange rind and juice may be substituted for lemon.)

Mint butter: Use 2 tablespoons minced mint leaves and 1 teaspoon lemon juice.

Mustard butter: Use 1 tablespoon prepared mustard.

Nut butter: Use 2 tablespoons finely chopped, salted nuts.

Olive butter: Use ⅛ cup finely chopped green or stuffed olives and a few drops onion juice.

Onion butter: Use 1 teaspoon onion juice.

Parmesan butter: Use 2 tablespoons Parmesan cheese.

Parsley butter: Use 2 tablespoons minced parsley.

Peanut butter: Use ¼ cup peanut butter, 1 teaspoon honey, and salt to taste.

Pimiento butter: Use 2 tablespoons mashed pimiento and 1 teaspoon finely chopped pickles.

Roquefort butter: Use 1 tablespoon of Roquefort cheese.

Salmon butter: Use 1 tablespoon salmon paste, or mashed smoked salmon (1 ounce), and 1 teaspoon lemon juice.

Sardine butter: Use 1 tablespoon sardine paste, or mashed sardines, and ½ teaspoon each of lemon and onion juice.

Watercress butter: Use 2 tablespoons of finely chopped watercress, 1 teaspoon lemon juice, and a few drops of Worcestershire sauce.

Worcestershire butter: Use ¼ teaspoon of Worcestershire sauce.

CHEESE CANAPE SPREADS

Cheese-caviar: Soften cream cheese with cream. Spread on small crackers. Dot with caviar.

Cheese-green pepper: Blend 1 cake (3 ounces) cream cheese with 4 tablespoons minced green pepper, 2 tablespoons minced onion, 1 teaspoon French dressing, and a few grains cayenne.

Cheese-nut: Blend cream cheese with chopped nuts. Sweeten to taste with confectioners' sugar.

Cheese-olive: Combine ¼ cup grated soft sharp cheese with ¼ cup butter. Add ¼ cup finely chopped green or stuffed olives. Season to taste with salt and pepper.

Cheese-onion: Soften cream cheese with cream. Add a few drops onion juice or minced onion. Season with salt and pepper. Sprinkle with paprika or minced parsley.

Cheese-pickles: Mix finely chopped sweet pickles with cream cheese. Garnish with slices of stuffed olives.

Cheese-sour cream: Blend cream cheese with sour cream. Season with salt and pepper.

Cheese-watercress: Cream 1 cake (3 ounces) cream cheese. Dry and chop 1 cup watercress. Blend together with 1 teaspoon Worcestershire sauce and ¼ teaspoon salt.

Chili-cheese: Combine 1 package (3 ounces) cream cheese or ½ cup grated American cheese with enough chili sauce to moisten.

Orange-cream cheese spread: Mix 1 package (3 ounces) cream cheese, grated rind of 1 orange, ¼ teaspoon salt, and ⅛ teaspoon paprika. Spread on buttered bases. Top with chopped, toasted pecan meats.

Parmesan-tomato: Place thin slices of tomato on toasted canapé bases. Sprinkle with grated Parmesan cheese. Garnish with parsley.

Roquefort: Combine ¼ cup Roquefort or blue cheese with 2 tablespoons cream cheese and 1 tablespoon mayonnaise. Season with a few drops of Worcestershire sauce.

Roquefort-chives: Mix Roquefort cheese with enough French dressing to moisten. Season with chopped chives.

Yellow cheese: Spread soft yellow cheese on canapé bases cut into rounds. Decorate with minced parsley or sliced stuffed olives.

FISH CANAPE SPREADS

Anchovy-cheese: Combine 1 part anchovy with 2 parts cream cheese. Spread and garnish with minced egg yolk.

Anchovy-egg: Mash and blend 4 hard-cooked egg yolks and 4 anchovies. Moisten to spreading consistency with mayonnaise. Season with grated onion and black pepper. Spread and garnish with chopped egg white.

Caviar: Flavor caviar with onion juice and lemon juice. Spread and decorate with tiny pearl onions.

Caviar-egg: Spread sides of toasted round bases with mayonnaise. Roll sides in sieved egg yolk. Spread top with caviar. Place thin slice of cooked egg white over caviar.

Chopped herring: Wash, clean, bone, and chop herring which has been soaked in cold water for several hours. For each herring use 1 onion, 1 tart apple, 1 slice of toast soaked in vinegar or lemon juice. Chop all together very fine. Add 1 teaspoon salad oil, a dash each of cinnamon and pepper. Serve garnished with finely chopped hard-cooked egg.

Kippered herring: Combine 1 cup mashed, kippered herring with 1 chopped hard-cooked egg, ¼ cup minced cucumber, enough mayonnaise to moisten, and 2 drops lemon juice.

Sardine: Mash and blend together 3 sardines and 1 cake (3 ounces) cream cheese. Season with lemon juice to taste.

Smoked fish: Arrange thin strips of smoked salmon and smoked herring on bases. Decorate edge with chopped egg yolk. Sprinkle with minced parsley.

Smoked salmon-egg: Chop or grind ½ pound smoked salmon. Add and blend 1 tablespoon olive oil, a dash of paprika, and ½ teaspoon lemon juice. Mince yolks and whites of 2 hard-cooked eggs. Spread salmon mixture on canapé bases. Sprinkle with yolks, then with whites in circles.

Smoked salmon and caviar: Roll thin slices of smoked salmon into cornucopias. Mix riced hard-cooked eggs with caviar. Season with lemon juice and paprika. Fill the salmon rolls.

Smoked salmon and mayonnaise: Chop smoked salmon and combine with chopped, hard-cooked eggs. Add mayonnaise and paprika.

Tuna or salmon: Make a paste from cooked or canned salmon or tuna. Moisten with mayonnaise and add lemon juice to flavor. Spread and decorate with minced parsley.

FRUIT AND VEGETABLE CANAPE SPREADS

Avocado: Pare avocados and mash pulp with a fork. Season with lemon or lime juice and salt. Spread on canapé base. Garnish with minced parsley.

Avocado-egg: Mash and blend equal parts of avocado pulp and hard-cooked egg yolk. Season with lemon juice and salt to taste.

Avocado-olive: Mix 1 cup mashed avocado pulp with ¼ cup finely chopped ripe or green olives. Season with lemon or lime juice. Spread on canapé base. Garnish with paprika, curled anchovies, pimiento strips, or red radish rounds.

Avocado-onion: Season mashed avocado pulp with minced onion, salt, and a dash of Tabasco sauce. Place a slice of tomato on canapé base. Cover with spread.

Guava-cheese: Spread cream cheese over canapé bases. Then spread with guava jelly. Sprinkle chopped nuts over top.

Mushrooms: Wash and chop or grind mushrooms fine. Fry lightly in butter for 5 minutes. Cool and season to taste with lemon juice, salt, and pepper.

Onion-egg: Chop 1 large onion fine. Add 1 hard-cooked egg. Chop together until fine. Add about 4 tablespoons melted chicken fat and salt and pepper to taste.

MEAT CANAPE SPREADS

Chicken livers: Combine ½ cup cooked chicken livers, 1 or 2 hard-cooked eggs, and ½ small onion. Chop together until fine. Season to taste with salt and pepper. Moisten with chicken fat.

Chicken or turkey: Chop or grind cooked chicken or turkey. Moisten with mayonnaise. Add finely chopped celery. Season to taste. Garnish with watercress.

Chopped liver and egg: Grind or chop very fine ½ pound cooked chicken livers, 1 hard-cooked egg, ½ cup chopped celery, and 1 small onion. Moisten with melted chicken fat. Add salt and pepper to taste. Mix to a smooth paste.

Chopped liver and mushrooms: Chop fine ½ pound of cooked chicken or calves liver. Sauté ½ cup fresh mushrooms for 5 minutes in 3 tablespoons chicken fat. Chop fine and add to the liver both mushrooms and the fat in which they were fried. Season to taste with salt, pepper, and onion juice.

Roast beef or veal: Moisten finely ground cooked meat with mixture of horseradish and mayonnaise. Season to taste.

Tongue, corned beef, bologna, or salami: Moisten finely ground cooked meat with mayonnaise. Add a little finely chopped sweet pickle and pimiento. Season to taste.

STUFFED CELERY

Wash tender celery stalks and crisp in ice water. Trim leaves. Cut large stalks in 2-inch lengths. Fill grooves with any of the following fillings, pressed through pastry tube or spread with knife.

Avocado: Mash avocado pulp. Sprinkle with lemon juice. Season to taste with salt and pepper. Moisten slightly with mayonnaise. Stuff, and garnish with bits of pimiento.

Cottage cheese: Season cheese with salt, and spread into grooves. Garnish with thin slices of radish with red edge showing.

Cream cheese: Mix cheese with finely chopped nuts. Spread in celery grooves. Or mix cheese with finely chopped, stuffed olives.

Egg: Chop hard-cooked eggs fine. Moisten with mayonnaise. Season with salt and pepper. Stuff, and sprinkle with paprika or minced parsley.

Roquefort or blue: Combine Roquefort style or blue cheese with a little butter or cream cheese. Season with grated onion.

Seafood: Combine tuna fish or other flaked, cooked, or canned seafood with a little lemon juice to flavor and mayonnaise to moisten.

CELERY PINWHEELS

Cut base from celery bunch. Separate, wash, and dry stalks. Fill each stalk with tangy cheese spread. Press stalks together in shape of original bunch and tie with string. Chill. To serve, cut into ¼-inch to ½-inch slices.

FLAKED FISH CANAPES

Cook, cool, and flake fish filets or use canned flaked fish. Serve in any of the three following ways:

1. Mix equal quantities of flaked fish and chopped pearl onions. Mix with mayonnaise and chili sauce. Serve on whole-wheat crackers.
2. Mix equal quantities of flaked fish and chopped mustard pickle. Serve on crackers or toast strips.
3. Moisten flaked fish with cream and horseradish. Serve on crackers or toast strips, garnished with green pepper.

CHICKEN LIVER AND GIZZARD SPREAD

4 chicken gizzards
8 chicken livers
1 medium onion, minced

3 tablespoons chicken fat
2 hard-cooked eggs
Salt and pepper
1 teaspoon parsley, minced

Simmer gizzards, in enough water to cover, until tender. Broil livers under moderate heat 3 to 5 minutes. Fry chopped onion in chicken fat until lightly brown. Add and sauté livers and cooked gizzards. Chop eggs, gizzards, liver, and onions. Add seasoning, parsley, and some chicken fat. Press through sieve. Serve cold.

DEVILED TONGUE CANAPES

1 cup ground cooked smoked
  beef tongue
1 tablespoon grated horseradish
1 tablespoon pickle relish

1 teaspoon Worcestershire sauce
2 tablespoons salad dressing
Pimiento-olives

Combine tongue, horseradish, pickle relish, and Worcestershire sauce. Add salad dressing for spreading consistency. Trim crusts of bread. Cut in strips and toast lightly on one side. Spread untoasted side with tongue mixture. Garnish with lengthwise cuts of stuffed olives. Yield: 24 canapés.

SALAMI CANAPES

½ pound salami
3 hard-cooked eggs
½ cup salad dressing

Thin-sliced bread
Parsley
Pimiento

Put salami and eggs through food chopper 2 or 3 times. Blend with salad dressing. Trim crusts. Cut into small squares. Toast on one side, spread untoasted side with salami mixture. Sprinkle with chopped parsley and garnish with pimiento strips. Yield: 30 canapés.

EGG APPETIZER

3 hard-cooked eggs
1 tablespoon anchovy paste
½ teaspoon Worcestershire sauce
1 tablespoon parsley, finely chopped

Dash of paprika
6 slices bread, cut in ¼-inch slices
½ cup Russian dressing

Cut hard-cooked eggs in halves, lengthwise, and remove yolks. Blend yolks, anchovy paste, seasoning, and parsley to smooth paste. Refill whites and chill. Cut bread with 3-inch round cutter. Toast on one side only. Spread with butter. Cut out centers with 1¼-inch cutter. Place chilled egg in each circle so that it sets firmly. Pour on Russian dressing. Garnish with water cress.

MARINATED HERRING CANAPES

Cut squares of marinated herring. Place on small slices of raw onion. Arrange on crackers or toast. Garnish with tiny pickled red peppers.

POTATO CHIP CANAPES

Combine ½ cup Roquefort or blue cheese with 1 teaspoon minced onion. Just before serving, spread on potato chips.

SAVORY CHEESE CANAPES

Mash ¼ cup soft American cheese and blend with 1 tablespoon cream. Season with ⅛ teaspoon chili powder. Sprinkle crackers with chopped nut meats. Spread cheese mixture onto crackers with a pastry tube.

RAINBOW CANAPE WHEEL

Cut thin slices of pumpernickel or steamed brown bread. Spread with softened butter. Place a slice of hard-cooked egg in center. Spread red caviar around the egg slice in a narrow strip. Soften cream cheese with mayonnaise, and color half of it green with vegetable coloring. Spread around caviar. Add a circle of black caviar, then a circle of white cream cheese. Edge with red caviar, chill, and serve cut into pie-shaped wedges.

DEEP-SEA CANAPE

Make a paste by mashing kippered herring with lemon juice, moistening with mayonnaise. Spread on toasted bread cut in diamond shape. Edge with mayonnaise to which sifted hard-cooked egg yolks have been added. Cross each canapé diagonally with tiny strips of herring.

CANAPE RUSSE

1½ tablespoons caviar	1 package (3 ounces) cream cheese
10 toast rounds	3 egg yolks, hard-cooked
8 olives, chopped	1 teaspoon prepared mustard
1 tablespoon Russian dressing	1 pimiento, chopped fine
3 tablespoons anchovy paste	Cream

Place a small mound of caviar in the center of each toast round. Next place a circle of chopped olives mixed with enough Russian dressing to hold them together. Outside this, put a layer of anchovy paste that has been mixed with ⅓ of the cream cheese, then a circle of egg yolk mashed very fine and mixed with the mustard. Chop pimiento very fine. Mix with ⅔ of the cream cheese and moisten with enough cream to put through a pastry tube around the edge of toast rounds. Garnish edge with finely chopped parsley, if desired. Yield: 10 canapés.

CHEESE CARROTS

1 teaspoon plain gelatin	¼ teaspoon Worcestershire sauce
2 tablespoons cold water	2 medium size carrots, grated
½ cup smoked cheese spread	Parsley

Soften gelatin in cold water 5 minutes. Melt over hot water. Cool slightly. Blend with cheese and Worcestershire sauce. Place in refrigerator until of pliable consistency. Divide into 1 teaspoon portions. Shape into cones. Roll in grated carrots, and stick sprig of parsley in large end to represent carrot top. Yield: about 30.

ROQUEFORT CHIPS

6 ounces cream cheese	3 ounces Roquefort cheese
6 tablespoons milk	Potato chips

Whip cheese with milk until soft and creamy. Crumble Roquefort cheese and stir into mixture. Blend thoroughly. Prepare a day in advance and store in refrigerator to blend flavors. Remove from refrigerator 2 hours before serving. Let guests dip potato chips into cheese mixture.

ANCHOVY ROUNDS

10 melba toast rounds	1 2-ounce tin rolled
1 tablespoon cream cheese	anchovy filets
1 hard-cooked egg, sliced	

Spread melba toast with cream cheese. Cover with slice of hard-cooked egg and top with anchovy. Yield: 10.

ANCHOVY CURLS

Place anchovy curls on toast fingers. Dip edges in mayonnaise, then in sieved egg yolks. Garnish with strips of pimiento.

ANCHOVY-CHEESE CANAPES

Mash soft American cheese. Season with Tabasco or Worcestershire sauce. Spread on toasted canapé bases or crackers. Top each with a rolled anchovy.

ANCHOVY PECANS

Toast pecan nut meat halves in moderate oven (350°F.) for 5 minutes. Spread flat side of each with thin layer of anchovy paste. Press 2 halves together. Serve at once.

PORCUPINE BALL

Use a large grapefruit, a big red apple, or one of the wooden or metal figures made to hold hors d'oeuvres on toothpicks. Any sort of toothpick may be used, but the colored ones are most attractive. On the ends of the toothpicks place stuffed olives, little sweet pickles, rolled anchovy filets, little cocktail sausages, or any other desired tidbits. Stick the other ends of the toothpicks into the grapefruit, apple, or other holder, porcupine fashion, and place on a serving dish or tray.

TIDBITS TO BE SPEARED ON COCKTAIL PICKS

Anchovy pickles: Wrap each small pickle with a strip of anchovy. Secure with toothpicks.

Apples: Cut raw apples into ½-inch cubes. Cover all sides with a nippy cheese spread.

Button mushrooms: Sauté mushrooms. Chill and marinate in lemon juice. Top with slice of stuffed olive.

Cauliflower: Marinate cooked sections in a thin, sharp French dressing.

Cheese: Marinate tiny cubes of American cheese in chili sauce.

Cheese balls: Roll cream cheese balls in chopped nuts or poppy seed. Place a cocktail pick in each.

Cocktail mushrooms: Use small mushrooms. Remove skin and stems. Cover with sherry and soak several hours. Drain and fill with Roquefort cheese or caviar. Serve each on a cocktail pick.

Hot cocktail sausages: Broil or sauté cocktail-size sausages. If larger ones are used cut into 1-inch lengths.

Hot codfish balls: Shape canned codfish cakes into very small balls. Fry in deep, hot fat.

Olive and onion kabobs: Alternate small stuffed olives with small pickled onions on toothpick.

Prunes: Remove pits from small prunes, steamed until almost tender, and fill with a tangy cheese.

Salami: Spear bite-size cubes along with small olives.

Salami cornucopias: Roll thin slices of sausage into cornucopias and fasten with a toothpick. Place either a small pickle or a stuffed olive in the center as a filling.

Smoked salmon pickles: Wrap each small pickle with a thin strip of smoked salmon.

Stuffed olives in anchovy filets: Roll each large stuffed olive in an anchovy filet. Secure with a cocktail pick.

Stuffed pecans: Put pecan halves together with any cream cheese spread. Chill before inserting picks.

Stuffed radishes: Hollow out radishes with a sharp-pointed knife. Crisp in ice water. Stuff with a mixture of caviar, minced parsley, mayonnaise, lemon juice, and onion juice, seasoned to taste.

Swiss and dill kabobs: Cut Swiss cheese into ½-inch cubes. Put between 2 thin slices of dill pickle, and skewer with toothpick.

Tongue pickles: Wrap thin slices of cooked tongue around small gherkins.

CHEESE ROLLS

6 ounces cream cheese	Dash of pepper
⅛ pound Roquefort cheese	Salad dressing
2 tablespoons celery, chopped fine	1½ cups walnut meats,
1 tablespoon onion, chopped fine	chopped fine

Blend the two cheeses. Add celery, onion, pepper, and salad dressing. Form into tiny rolls. Roll in nutmeats. Chill. Yield: about 18 rolls.

STUFFED CHEESE OLIVES

Cut large stuffed olives into halves lengthwise. Cut American cheese into ½-inch squares about ¼ inch deep. Place 1 cheese square between every 2 halves of olive and press firmly together.

OLIVES IN FRENCH DRESSING

Place green or ripe olives in a bowl. Cover with a well-seasoned French dressing to which a cut clove of garlic has been added. Let stand several hours or overnight in a cold place. Drain and serve.

LETTUCE ROLLS

Combine ½ cup mashed sardines, ¼ cup chopped sweet pickle, ½ teaspoon minced onion, and 2 tablespoons mayonnaise. Spread small amount on each small lettuce leaf. Roll tightly and fasten with cocktail picks.

STUFFED SLICED CUCUMBER

Remove center of pared cucumber with vegetable corer. Stuff with a mixture of 1 cup flaked tuna or salmon, 2 tablespoons mayonnaise, ½ teaspoon each of onion and lemon juice, a dash of Worcestershire sauce, and salt and pepper to taste. Chill and cut into ½-inch slices.

EGGPLANT CAVIAR

1 eggplant	1 ripe tomato, peeled and minced
2 small onions, minced	Salt and pepper
2 cloves, minced	Vinegar
1 clove garlic, minced	Olive oil

Broil the whole eggplant over direct flame, or in a broiler for 15 to 20 minutes, turning to cook evenly on all sides. Remove the inside pulp and mix with the onions, cloves, and garlic. Add the tomato, and season to taste with salt, pepper, vinegar, and oil. Serve on greens, garnished with quartered tomatoes and black olives.

SMOKED SALMON

Thin-sliced bread	⅛ pound smoked salmon
Mayonnaise	1 hard-cooked egg
Parsley	

Stack 4 slices of bread. Trim crusts. Cut in strips. Toast on one side and spread un-toasted side with *LEMON-BUTTER*, brush edges with mayonnaise and dip in chopped parsley. Place wafer-thin slice of smoked salmon on toast. Garnish with cooked egg white and parsley. Yield: 12 canapés.

Variation: Chop 2 egg whites very fine. Mix with ½ teaspoon grated onion, salt and pepper, and enough mayonnaise for spreading consistency. Spread on buttered toast. Place sliced olive in center and strips of smoked salmon at each end.

DUNKING TRAYS

Dunking trays are among the most popular of drink accompaniments, and they can be relatively simple or they may be very elaborate. Arrange one or two dunking bowls in the center of the tray. Around them place alternate layers of vegetable hors d'oeuvres such as celery, raw carrot cut in strips or very long slices curled in ice water, cauliflower broken and sliced in flowerets, asparagus tips, white and red radishes, green onion, tiny cherry or plum tomatoes, paper thin slices of turnip, cucumber, and zucchini. In addition to the suggestions that follow for dunking bowls you may want to choose one of the cocktail sauces, or a salad dressing like green mayonnaise or Russian dressing. They are especially good with seafood or cubes of avocado. You'll find a bowl of thick sour cream with chopped chives or red caviar in it especially welcome with vegetable hors d'oeuvres or squares of pumpernickel or rye bread.

DUNKING BOWLS

Combine the enumerated ingredients, mix thoroughly and heap into a bowl.

Curried cheese dunk
  2 cups cottage cheese
  6 tablespoons mayonnaise
  4 tablespoons cream
  3 teaspoons curry powder
  1 teaspoon salt

Vegetable-cheese dunk
  2 cups cottage cheese
  ¼ cup heavy cream
  ¼ cup grated raw carrot
  ½ cup finely cut green onions
  ¼ cup chopped green pepper
  6 radishes, sliced very thin

Sour cream dunk
  2 cups sour cream
  1 cup finely chopped green pepper
  ¼ cup chopped chives
  ¼ cup chopped parsley
  ¼ cup thinly sliced radishes
  Salt and pepper to taste

Pink mayonnaise dunk
  1 cup mayonnaise
  ½ cup chili sauce or ketchup
  Juice of 1 lemon
  About 5 drops onion juice

TUNA FISH COCKTAIL

1½ cups flaked, canned tuna fish	Lettuce and parsley
¾ cup cocktail sauce	Lemon wedges

Flake and chill the tuna fish. Arrange ¼ cup in cocktail glasses which have been lined with lettuce leaves. Pour 2 tablespoons *COCKTAIL SAUCE* over each. Garnish with parsley and lemon wedge. Yield: 6.

AVOCADO AND TUNA FISH COCKTAIL

Use equal amounts of flaked tuna fish and cubed avocado. Serve in cocktail glasses with 2 tablespoons *COCKTAIL SAUCE.*

AVOCADO COCKTAIL

Chill avocado thoroughly. Cut in cubes. Serve in cocktail glasses after pouring *COCKTAIL SAUCE* over cubes.

COCKTAIL SAUCES

Standard cocktail sauce: Mix 1 cup ketchup, 4 teaspoons prepared horseradish, ¼ cup lemon juice, 1 teaspoon Worcestershire sauce, a dash of Tabasco sauce, and 1 teaspoon salt. Chill. Yield: about 1 cup.

Cocktail dressing: Mix ½ cup mayonnaise, 1 tablespoon lemon juice, 1 tablespoon ketchup, 1 tablespoon horseradish, ¼ teaspoon paprika, 3 drops Worcestershire sauce, 2 drops Tabasco sauce, and salt to taste. Chill. Yield: about ¾ cup.

Piquant cocktail sauce: Mix ⅓ cup ketchup, 1 teaspoon onion juice, ½ teaspoon Tabasco sauce, and salt and pepper to taste. Chill. Yield: about ⅓ cup.

Celery cocktail sauce: Mix ¾ cup ketchup or chili sauce with 2 tablespoons lemon juice, 1 teaspoon Worcestershire sauce, ¼ cup chopped celery, and a dash each of salt and cayenne. Chill. Yield: about 1 cup.

Cucumber cocktail sauce: Mix ½ cup chili sauce with 1 teaspoon onion juice, 1 teaspoon lemon juice, ½ cup pared and grated cucumber, and a dash each of pepper, salt, and Tabasco sauce. Chill. Yield: about 1 cup.

TURKISH CHEESE APPETIZERS (Beureks)

Cut ½ pound Gruyère cheese into small pieces. Place in a saucepan with ¼ cup thick white sauce. Stir until cheese is melted and mixture is thick. Spread on a platter to cool. Chill if necessary. Shape into small sausages. Wrap each sausage in a thin piece of plain pastry and fry in deep hot fat (385°F.) until golden brown. Drain. Serve hot or cold.

HOT CHEESE-PIMIENTO CANAPE

6 large canned pimientos
  Salt
  Pepper
  Cayenne

¼ pound sliced sharp American
  cheese
Flour
Buttered toast rounds

Sprinkle inner surface of pimientos with salt, pepper, and cayenne to taste. Cut the cheese slices into rectangles the same size as the pimientos. Place cheese rectangles on pimientos and roll up. Skewer with toothpicks, roll in flour, and sauté in hot butter for 3 minutes, or until the cheese melts. Serve hot on the toast rounds.

HOT RED PEPPER CANAPE

2 hard-cooked eggs, minced
1 tablespoon canned red peppers, minced
¼ teaspoon salt
⅛ teaspoon dry mustard

2 tablespoons grated sharp American cheese
Melted butter
6 rounds rye bread

Mix together the eggs, red peppers, salt, mustard, cheese, and enough melted butter to make a paste. Fry the bread rounds in deep, hot fat (390°F.). Drain and cool. Spread them evenly with the paste. Place in a very hot oven (500°F.) for 3 minutes. Garnish with watercress and serve hot.

HOT CHEESE BALLS

2 teaspoons flour
Dash of paprika
½ teaspoon salt
1 cup grated American cheese

2 teaspoons minced pimiento
1 egg white
¼ cup finely chopped salted peanuts

Mix flour, paprika, and salt with grated cheese. Add pimiento. Fold egg white, beaten until stiff, but not dry, into cheese mixture until well-blended. Form into small balls and roll in chopped peanuts. Fry in deep hot fat (375°F.) until golden brown. Serve hot. Yield: 12 to 15 balls.

HOT SALAMI AND EGG CANAPE

1 cup ground hard salami
4 to 6 eggs

1 onion, minced
Salt and pepper

Beat all ingredients together until frothy. Drop by spoonfuls into a well-greased hot skillet. Serve on canapé bases spread with mustard.

TOASTED CHEESE SQUARES

Spread toasted square bread cubes on 5 sides with butter. Roll in grated cheese. Arrange unbuttered side down on a rack. Place rack on a flat pan and broil about 2 minutes, or until cheese is melted and delicately browned.

HOT TUNA CANAPES

Mix flaked canned tuna fish with chopped stuffed olives and mayonnaise or salad dressing. Season with Worcestershire sauce. Spread on small squares, strips, or rounds of toast. Sprinkle with grated American cheese. Place under moderate broiler until cheese is melted. Serve hot.

HOT MUSHROOM CANAPES

½ pound mushrooms
2 canned pimientos
1 small slice onion
2 tablespoons butter
2 tablespoons flour

½ teaspoon salt
Few grains cayenne
1 loaf bread
¼ cup soft butter

Clean the mushrooms. Drain liquid from pimientos. Chop the mushrooms, onion, and pimientos. Place in a saucepan with 2 tablespoons butter. Cook over low heat, stirring occasionally until the mushrooms are tender (about 5 minutes). Sprinkle the flour over the mushroom mixture and stir vigorously until the mixture thickens. Season with salt and cayenne. Remove from stove. Toast strips of bread on one side only. Butter untoasted side and spread with the mushroom paste. Place in a shallow pan or baking sheet. Heat in a hot oven (400°F.) for 5 to 10 minutes. Garnish with 2 thin strips of canned pimiento. Serve hot.

CHEESE CANAPES

1 recipe *PLAIN PASTRY*	Salt
½ cup grated cheese	Pepper
½ cup chopped onion	

Roll pastry into thin sheet and cut strips 4 inches long and ½ inch wide. Sprinkle with cheese, onion, salt, and pepper. Roll as for jelly roll, fasten with toothpicks and place on baking sheet, cut side down. Bake in hot oven (450°F.) 15 minutes, or until done. Yield: about 4 dozen.

FRUIT COCKTAILS

Fruit cocktails may be made from mixtures of almost any fruits, canned or fresh. As a rule, combinations of a sweet and sour fruit are most piquant in flavor. All fruit appetizers should be chilled before serving.

Avocado cocktail: Chill avocados thoroughly. Peel, slice, and marinate for about 5 minutes in chilled French dressing. Serve in lettuce-lined cup. Sprinkle with chopped parsley or chopped mint.

Berry-melon cup: Cover fresh raspberries or strawberries with sugar. Chill thoroughly. Force through coarse sieve. Put diced, chilled watermelon in cocktail cups and pour the crushed berries over it.

Broiled grapefruit: Sprinkle each half with 1 tablespoon (or more, to taste) sugar. Place fruit under moderate heat in broiler. Pour a tablespoon of sherry over each half when fruit is hot. Serve at once.

Citrus fruit cup: Combine equal amounts of diced orange sections, diced grapefruit sections, and diced fresh pineapple. Flavor with lime juice, rum, brandy, or sherry. Sweeten with thin sugar syrup.

Fruit-sherbet cup: Fill sherbet cup half full with combined diced orange and grapefruit sections. Top with scoop of lemon or other fruit sherbet. Arrange fruit sections around sherbet. Garnish with mint leaves.

Ginger ale fruit cup: Pour small amount of chilled ginger ale over any combination of canned fruits.

Grape-melon cup: Mix equal amounts seedless grapes, diced honeydew melon, and diced orange sections. Flavor with lemon juice. Sweeten with sugar.

Melon-ball cup: Cut balls from watermelon, cantaloupe, and honeydew melons with melon ball cutter or teaspoon. Add lime juice and thin sugar syrup to flavor. Garnish with a sprig of mint.

Orange-mint cup: Sweeten diced orange sections with thin sugar syrup. Add minced mint to flavor. Garnish with mint leaves.

Pineapple boats: Trim ⅔ from leafy top of large pineapple and chill. Cut into 8 lengthwise wedges. Cut out cores. Pare skin in one piece, leaving it in place. Cut pulp downward into 5 or 6 slices, retaining shape. Serve each portion garnished with whole berries and powdered sugar.

Pineapple-strawberry cup: Combine equal amounts fresh diced pineapple and sliced fresh strawberries. Sweeten with thin sugar syrup.

BRAZILIAN GRAPEFRUIT COCKTAIL

Cut grapefruit into halves. Remove seeds and pulpy center. With a sharp knife remove membrane between segments. Sprinkle tops with ground Brazil nuts and finely cut fresh mint. Add light cover of powdered sugar. Chill. Just before serving, pour a teaspoonful of sherry in the center of each half. If fresh mint cannot be obtained, take a little of the grapefruit juice which will form in the hollow of the fruit and flavor with a few drops of oil, or essence, of peppermint. Pour this over the fruit before adding the powdered sugar. Sherry may be omitted.

BANANA FRUIT CUP

Put sliced banana in serving cups. Cover with a mixture of chilled orange and grapefruit juice.

LOGANBERRY CUP

Peel and section out oranges and grapefruit. Remove membranes. Add loganberry juice and chill thoroughly. Serve in sherbet glasses.

MINTED STRAWBERRY CUP

Wash and hull strawberries. Combine orange juice and chopped mint. Pour over berries and sprinkle with powdered sugar. Chill thoroughly.

FROZEN GINGER ALE MELON CUP

Cut out 2 cups melon balls with a ball cutter or teaspoon. Sprinkle with a few grains salt. Freeze 2 cups ginger ale in refrigerator tray to mush-like consistency, stirring once. Turn into a chilled bowl and combine with melon balls. Serve in sherbet cups. Serves 6.

CHILLED JUICE COCKTAILS

Serve the following suggested combinations over cracked ice. Chill before combining.

1. 1 part grape juice and 2 parts unsweetened pineapple juice.
2. Equal parts grape juice and unsweetened grapefruit juice.
3. Equal parts orange juice and unsweetened pineapple juice, with a dash of fresh lime juice.
4. Season chilled tomato juice with Worcestershire sauce, lemon juice, and a bit of onion, if desired.
5. Equal amounts of unsweetened grapefruit juice and apricot juice.
6. 2 cups sweet cider, ½ cup pineapple juice, and ½ cup orange juice.
7. 2 parts grape juice, 1 part ginger ale, and lemon juice to taste.
8. Cranberry juice, dash of lemon juice, sweetened to taste.
9. Canned or fresh berry juice, or other fruit juice, with charged water or ginger ale.

To frost glasses for chilled juice cocktails: To frost edge, rub with a piece of lemon, then dip into confectioners' sugar. Or dip glass edge into unbeaten egg white, then into granulated sugar. Let glasses dry before serving.

FROZEN GRAPE FRUIT JUICE

Combine 2 cups grape juice and 1 tablespoon lemon juice. Turn into freezing tray of refrigerator. Freeze to mush, stirring once. Turn into a chilled bowl and beat with a fork. Serve at once.

MINTED FRUIT JUICE

Combine 1 cup each of pineapple juice and orange juice. Chill. To serve, flavor with a few drops of peppermint extract.

SAUERKRAUT JUICE COCKTAIL

Combine 3 cups canned sauerkraut juice with ½ teaspoon Worcestershire sauce, ¼ teaspoon prepared mustard, and a dash of pepper. Serves 6.

TOMATO JUICE COCKTAIL

Served chilled tomato juice, seasoned as desired with any of the following: salt, pepper, cayenne, celery, garlic or onion salt, lemon juice, onion juice, Tabasco or Worcestershire sauce.

FROZEN TOMATO JUICE

Season tomato juice as desired. Turn into freezing tray of refrigerator. Freeze to mush, stirring once. Turn out into a chilled bowl and beat with a fork. Serve at once.

TOMATO AND SAUERKRAUT JUICE COCKTAIL

Combine equal amounts of tomato and sauerkraut juice. Season to taste with Worcestershire sauce.

TOMATO AND CELERY COCKTAIL (Basic Recipe)

1 cup grated celery	1 tablespoon sugar
4 cups tomato juice	⅛ clove garlic, crushed
1 teaspoon salt	Salt to taste
⅛ teaspoon cayenne	Minced parsley

Combine all ingredients except parsley. Bring to steaming point over low heat and steam 5 minutes. Strain. Cool and chill in refrigerator. Serve in cocktail glasses garnished with minced parsley.

Tomato-cucumber cocktail: Omit grated celery and add 1 cucumber, grated with peeling.

beverages

DECORATIVE ICE CUBES

To add a touch of color and interest to cool summer beverages, color the ice cubes which you use. To make ice cubes with the decorations in the center, fill a freezing tray half full of water, freeze slowly, and add decorations. These may be small flowers, such as rose buds, green and red cherries, mint leaves, or sections of orange and lemon slices. A tablespoon more of water may be added and frozen to keep the decorations in place, before the tray is filled with chilled water. In making colored cubes, be careful not to use too much coloring matter, so cubes will be a delicate color.

Coffee ice cubes: Prepare strong black coffee, let cool, and freeze in ice-cube tray.

Tea ice cubes: Prepare hot tea, cool, and freeze.

Berry ice cubes: Add 1 strawberry, raspberry, or blackberry to the water in each section of ice-cube tray. Freeze.

Ginger ale cubes: Freeze ginger ale in ice-cube trays.

Half-n-half cubes: Freeze ½ part ginger ale and ½ part loganberry juice.

HOW TO MAKE PERFECT COFFEE

1. Measure the coffee and water accurately, using 2 level measuring tablespoons of coffee to 1 measuring cup of water for each serving.
2. Use fresh coffee of the correct grind for your coffee maker.
3. Start with freshly drawn water from the cold-water faucet.
4. Serve as soon as possible after brewing.
5. Keep coffee maker immaculately clean. Air the parts, disassembled, between each use.

Drip method: Scald coffee maker with boiling water. Measure coffee into filter section. Measure boiling water into upper section. Cover. When all of the water has dripped through, remove the upper container and stir brew slightly, or beverage will be of uneven strength.

Percolator method: Measure freshly drawn cold water into percolator and place on heat. When water boils, remove from heat. Measure coffee into basket and place in percolator. Cover and return to heat. Percolate slowly for 6 minutes after water is straw colored. Remove basket before serving.

Vacuum method: Measure cold water into lower bowl and set on heat. Place filter and coffee in upper bowl. When water boils, lower heat. Insert upper bowl, twisting slightly to make an air-tight seal. When all but a small quantity of water below tube is in upper bowl, stir mixture. Remove from heat. Allow brew to return to lower bowl. Remove upper bowl just before serving.

Old-fashioned boiled method: Measure cold water into coffee maker and bring to boil. Measure coffee into the freshly boiling water. Stir well. Cover tightly and let stand on asbestos pad over low heat 7 to 10 minutes. Strain brew immediately. Pour into heated serving pot.

Coffee for large groups: Mix coarsely ground coffee with an egg and a little cold water to moisten. Use 1 pound of coffee for 2 gallons of water. Place mixture in cheesecloth or muslin bag large enough to allow for expansion. Place coffee bag in rapidly boiling water. Cover tightly. Reduce heat and let stand 7 to 10 minutes. Lift bag up and down a few times to extract full flavor. Remove bag. Keep coffee hot over low heat until serving time.

Extra strength coffee: Follow any method, using 3 level measuring tablespoons for each measuring cup of water.

Café au lait: Make coffee double strength by any method. Heat some milk to scalding point. Pour coffee and milk together into serving cups in proportions to suit individual tastes—usually equal amounts. Serve topped with whipped cream.

Viennese coffee: Prepare strong black coffee. Serve with sugar and whipped cream.

After dinner coffee (*café noir*): Make double-strength coffee by any method. Serve black, with or without sugar.

ICED COFFEE

Method 1: Prepare double-strength coffee by any method. Pour over cracked ice in tall glasses.

Method 2: Freeze regular-strength coffee in refrigerator trays. To serve, pour freshly made regular strength hot coffee over coffee cubes in tall glasses. Serve iced coffee with plain or whipped cream and confectioners' sugar.

Spiced iced coffee: Pour 3 cups hot, double-strength coffee over 2 cinnamon sticks, 4 cloves, and 4 allspice berries. Let stand 1 hour. Strain. Pour over ice in tall glasses. Serve with sugar and cream. Serves 4.

Mint iced coffee: Pour precooled regular-strength coffee over ice in glass. Top with whipped cream into which a drop or two of mint has been added.

Oriental iced coffee: Pour double-strength hot coffee into glass filled with ice. Before serving, add a few drops of oil of clove to a whipped cream topping.

Mocha iced coffee: Combine freshly made double-strength coffee with an equal amount of cooled cocoa. Pour into tall glass filled with ice. Add powdered sugar and cream to taste.

Rum iced coffee: Pour precooled regular-strength coffee over ice in glass. Serve with whipped cream topping to which rum flavoring has been added.

Iced coffee Angostura: Combine an equal amount of double-strength coffee and sugar syrup in a saucepan. Simmer 5 minutes. Cool. Add a few drops of vanilla and Angostura bitters. Pour over ice cubes in tall glass ¾ full. Fill with ice-cold water.

Viennese iced coffee: Half fill tall glass with cracked ice. Sprinkle with confectioners' sugar to taste. Add 1 tablespoon whipped cream. Fill with hot double strength coffee.

Iced chocolate-café: Combine and beat thoroughly 1 cup double-strength coffee, 1 tablespoon chocolate syrup, 2 tablespoons whipped cream, and 3 tablespoons crushed ice. Serve immediately.

CAFE SPECIAL

½ lb. (32) marshmallows
1½ cups strong coffee
1½ cups heavy cream

2 teaspoons vanilla extract
Few grains salt

Cut marshmallows into pieces. Add hot coffee and melt over low heat, stirring occasionally. Cool. Whip cream until partially stiff. Add vanilla and salt. Fold cream into coffee mixture. Pour into freezing tray of refrigerator. When half frozen, beat vigorously. Finish freezing.

To serve café special: Fill tall glass ¾ full with chilled regular-strength coffee. Add cream and ice-cold water. Top glass with generous scoop of frozen mixture.

To serve as dessert: Top frozen mixture with a swirl of whipped cream, and garnish with pecans.

ARMENIAN COFFEE

Cold water
6 teaspoons powdered sugar
6 teaspoons powdered coffee

1 or 2 cardamom seeds, slightly
    cracked
2 drops orange flower water

Into a racquie* pour cold water to within 2 inches of top. Place over chafing-dish flame or electric table stove. Add powdered sugar. Bring to brisk boil. Add coffee and cardamom seeds. Boil to a froth. Remove from heat and tap pot once or twice to settle brew. Return to fire instantly. Bring to a quick boil again and tap again. Repeat procedure twice again. Dip foam from the top into 12 cups. Add orange flower water to pot and about 1 teaspoon of cold water to settle coffee. Pour into cups.

COFFEE ROYAL

4 2-inch cinnamon sticks
6 cups hot, strong coffee
⅓ cup sugar

1 cup whipping cream
Almond flavoring

Let cinnamon stand in hot coffee 1 hour. Remove cinnamon and add sugar and ½ cup of cream. Chill. Pour into 6 tall glasses and fill with crushed ice. Add a little sugar and almond flavoring to remaining cream after whipping it stiff. Top each glass of coffee with a large helping of this cream. Serve immediately. Serves 6.

ARABIAN COFFEE

8 tablespoons powdered burnt
    mocha coffee
4 cups boiling water

Pinch of saffron
6 whole cloves
Sugar

Place coffee in a small saucepan and pour boiling water over it. Cover and simmer 4 to 5 minutes. Add saffron and cloves. Let stand 2 minutes and pour into a copper kettle. Serve in demitasses. Sweeten to taste. Serves 4.

FRENCH FLAMING COFFEE (Café Brulot)

In a flameproof bowl place 4 lumps of sugar, 4 pieces of lemon peel, 4 whole cloves (heads removed), 2 small cinnamon sticks, and a small glass of brandy. Blend well,

* NOTE: A racquie is a special Syrian or Armenian pot. It is sold by Syrian and Armenian importing stores. It is made of copper, lined with nickel and urn shaped, and has a long handle at the side.

set a match to the mixture and let burn for about a half minute, stirring constantly with a metal spoon. Slowly add 1½ cups strong, fresh coffee and strain into heated demitasses. Serve at once. Serves 4.

TURKISH COFFEE

6 rounded tablespoons powdered
    coffee
6 tablespoons sugar

3 cups cold water
Rosewater (optional)

Place coffee, sugar, and water in a lidless coffee pot or pan. Heat until mixture comes to a brisk boil, stirring constantly. Remove from flame and let the froth subside. Replace pot on very hot flame and repeat process 3 more times. Add a little cold water to pot just before serving to settle brew. Add a few drops of rosewater, if desired, to each cup. Serve in demitasses.

HOW TO MAKE PERFECT TEA

Use teapot made of glass, china, or earthenware. Scald teapot with boiling water and drain. Measure tea into teapot, using one teaspoon tea leaves, or one teabag, for each measuring cup of water, plus one extra teaspoon or bag "for the pot." Bring measured cold water to a galloping boil and pour over tea leaves. Let steep 4 to 5 minutes to develop full flavor. Dilute to the desired strength with clear, boiling water.

Variations: Serve tea with sugar, honey, fruit preserves, cream, lemon or orange slices, crystallized ginger, or cloves.

ICED TEA

Method 1: Prepare double-strength tea. Pour hot over crushed ice in tall glasses.

Method 2: Prepare regular-strength tea. Freeze in refrigerator trays. To serve, pour freshly made regular-strength hot tea over tea cubes in tall glasses.

Method 3: Cool regular-strength tea to room temperature and place in refrigerator to chill. Serve over crushed ice in tall glasses.

ICED SPICED TEA

3 tablespoons tea leaves
4 cups boiling water
12 whole cloves

12 allspice berries
1 2-inch cinnamon stick
Lemon wedges

Put tea leaves in a heated pot and add water. Add spices and let stand 5 minutes. Pour through a strainer into tall glasses filled with ice. Serves 4.

RUSSIAN TEA

Scald an earthenware teapot with boiling water and drain. Put in 2 teaspoons of tea leaves for each cup of water. Pour boiling water over the tea leaves. Cover tightly and keep warm for 5 minutes. Strain into another scalded pot. To serve, pour ¼ cup of tea infusion into each cup. Fill with boiling water and serve with lemon and sugar.

COCOA SYRUP

½ cup hot water
6 tablespoons cocoa
1½ cups corn syrup or
    8 tablespoons sugar

⅛ teaspoon salt
1 teaspoon vanilla

Pour hot water over cocoa and stir until smooth. Add corn syrup, or sugar, and salt. Simmer 10 minutes, stirring constantly. Add vanilla. Serve hot or cold over ice cream or other dessert. Syrup may be covered and stored 4 to 6 weeks in refrigerator.

Chocolate syrup: Substitute 2 squares unsweetened chocolate for cocoa.

To make cocoa or chocolate: Add 1½ to 2 tablespoons of cocoa syrup or chocolate syrup to each cup hot or cold milk. Serve iced drinks over chipped ice in tall glass. Top with whipped cream.

Variations: Flavor with cinnamon, ginger, a drop of peppermint extract, or crushed mint leaves.

COCOA (Basic Recipe)

¼ to ⅓ cup sugar to taste
6 tablespoons cocoa
    Dash of salt

1 cup water
5 cups milk

Combine sugar, cocoa, and salt in a pan. Add water slowly and boil 2 minutes, stirring until thickened. Add milk and heat slowly to just below boiling point. Before serving, beat with rotary beater until frothy. Serve topped with whipped cream or marshmallow. Serves 6.

Iced mint cocoa: Follow basic recipe, increasing sugar to 1 cup. Add 3 sprigs crushed mint with sugar. Strain hot cocoa and chill. Add 1 teaspoon vanilla extract. Serve over crushed ice. Top each portion with whipped cream.

SPICED HOT COCOA

¼ cup cocoa
¼ cup sugar
    Few grains salt
⅛ teaspoon cinnamon

2 cups water
1 tall can evaporated milk
½ teaspoon vanilla
    Whipped cream

Mix cocoa, sugar, salt, and cinnamon. Add water and bring to boiling point. Cook 3 minutes. Add milk and heat. Beat with rotary beater until frothy. Add vanilla. Serve topped with whipped cream. Serves 4 to 6.

QUICK HOT CHOCOLATE

Combine 2 cups hot milk with ½ cup chopped semisweet chocolate. Beat with rotary beater until chocolate is dissolved. Serves 2.

BANANA COFFEE FROST

3 ripe bananas   1 teaspoon vanilla
3 cups coffee, precooled   1 pint coffee ice cream
1 cup milk

Mash bananas through a sieve. Add coffee, milk, and vanilla. Chill. Just before serving add ice cream and beat until frothy. Serves 4 to 5.

MALTED MILK

Cold: For each serving, measure and add 2 to 3 tablespoons malted milk powder to 1 cup milk. Beat with a rotary beater until well blended.

Hot: For each serving, measure and add 2 to 3 tablespoons malted milk powder to ¾ cup hot milk. Stir until dissolved. If desired, beat slightly with rotary beater.

COFFEE MALTED

Mix together with a rotary beater 1½ cups strong, precooled coffee, ½ cup light cream, 4 tablespoons malted milk powder, and ⅓ cup sugar syrup. Serve in chilled glasses. Serves 2.

COFFEE BROADWAY FROSTED

Combine 1½ cups cold, double-strength coffee, 1 cup chilled milk, and ½ cup chilled light cream. Add ½ pint of chocolate ice cream. Beat with rotary beater until foamy. Pour into tall glasses. Serves 4.

PINEAPPLE FLOAT

1 quart ginger ale   1 pint pineapple ice
½ pint coffee cream

Combine ginger ale and cream. Pour into 8 tall glasses and drop into each several spoonfuls of pineapple ice. Serve at once. Serves 8.

FRUIT MILK SHAKES

Use thoroughly chilled milk, fruit juice, or fruit pulp. Shake or beat with fruit or syrup until well blended. Sweeten to taste. Garnish with whipped cream if desired. Evaporated milk diluted with an equal amount of water may be used instead of fresh milk. Each of the following makes 4 generous servings.

Banana shake: Combine 3 mashed ripe bananas with 3 cups milk.

Fruit juice shake: Combine 4 cups milk with ½ cup fruit syrup from cooked or canned fruit. Use apricot, peach, plum, pineapple, prune, or fruit nectar.

Grape juice shake: Combine 2½ cups milk, 1½ cups grape juice, and 1 teaspoon lemon juice.

Orange shake: Combine 2 cups milk, 2 cups orange juice, and ¼ teaspoon almond extract.

Prune shake: Combine 2 cups milk, 2 cups prune juice, and 1 teaspoon lemon juice.

Strawberry shake: Combine 4 cups of milk and 1 cup crushed sweetened strawberries.

CHOCOLATE MILK SHAKES

Use 2 tablespoons chocolate syrup or cocoa syrup for each cup of milk. Shake or beat well. Garnish with whipped cream if desired.

Chocolate frosted: Beat dip of vanilla or chocolate ice cream into chocolate milk shake.

Minted chocolate shake: Flavor each chocolate milk shake with 3 drops of peppermint extract. Garnish with whipped cream and sprig of fresh mint.

Chocolate-mocha shake: Mix ¼ cup hot, double-strength coffee, 1 cup milk, and 2 tablespoons chocolate syrup. Cool, and pour over cracked ice in glasses. Top with whipped cream. Serves 2.

EGGNOG

Few grains salt	¼ teaspoon vanilla
1 egg	1 cup cold milk
1 tablespoon sugar	Dash nutmeg

Beat egg, salt, and sugar. Add vanilla and milk. Beat thoroughly. Pour into glass and sprinkle lightly with nutmeg. Serves 1.

Almond eggnog: Omit vanilla and flavor eggnog with 6 drops almond extract.

Chocolate eggnog: Omit sugar. Add 1½ tablespoons chocolate syrup and 1 tablespoon malted milk (optional). Beat well. Top with whipped cream.

Fruit juice eggnog: Flavor eggnog with 2 tablespoons fresh or canned fruit juice.

Honey eggnog: Substitute 2 tablespoons honey for sugar.

Malted milk eggnog: Add 1 to 2 tablespoons malted milk to eggnog.

Sherry eggnog: Flavor eggnog with 2 tablespoons sherry wine or other favorite wine.

PRUNE NOG

1½ cups evaporated milk	1½ cups cold water
3 cups prune juice	

Chill milk and prune juice. Mix milk and water. Stir in prune juice. If desired, add a dash of cinnamon or nutmeg. Serves 6.

ORANGE NOG

1½ cups orange juice	1 cup evaporated milk
1 tablespoon lemon juice	1 cup cold water
3 tablespoons sugar or	
4 tablespoons white corn syrup	

Mix together the orange juice, lemon juice, and sugar. Stir slowly into diluted milk. Serve at once with cracked ice. Serves 6.

ELIXIR OF GOLD

Few grains salt	1 egg, well beaten
⅔ to 1 cup orange juice	

Add salt and orange juice to egg. Beat or shake. Serves 1.

MINT TINKLE

1½ cups water
½ cup granulated sugar
6 tablespoons lemon juice

⅛ teaspoon mint extract
Green vegetable coloring
1 quart ginger ale

Combine water and sugar. Bring to a boil, stirring constantly. Remove from heat, and cool. Add lemon juice, mint extract, and enough coloring to tint mixture a very delicate green. Just before serving, add ginger ale, and serve over chopped ice or ice cubes, garnished with thin slice of lemon and sprig of mint in each glass. Makes 1½ quarts.

CURRANT FIZZ

2 8-ounce glasses of currant jelly
2 cups boiling water
2½ cups orange juice

⅔ cup lemon juice
1 quart ginger ale

Beat currant jelly until frothy. Add boiling water and continue beating until jelly is dissolved. Add fruit juices and stir well. Chill. Just before serving, add ginger ale. Makes over 2 quarts.

LEMONADE

1 cup SUGAR SYRUP
  (or to taste)

Juice of 6 lemons
1 quart water

Combine SUGAR SYRUP, juice, and water. Chill. Pour over cracked ice in tall glasses.

Variations: Substitute carbonated water, ginger ale, grape juice (reduce SUGAR SYRUP to taste), or orange juice. To serve, garnish with lemon or orange slices, mint leaves, fresh berries, crushed fruit, etc.

Spiced lemonade: Combine 1 cup SUGAR SYRUP with 12 whole cloves and 1 3-inch cinnamon stick. Cook 5 minutes. Strain. Add juice of 6 lemons and 1 quart water. Chill. Serve over crushed ice.

Limeade: Use 1 cup lime juice, 1 cup SUGAR SYRUP, and 1 quart water.

Orangeade: Use juice of 5 oranges, juice of 1 lemon, 1 cup SUGAR SYRUP, and 1 quart water.

BASIC TEA PUNCH

2 cups hot tea infusion
  (pour 1 pint boiling water over
  1 teaspoon tea leaves)

6 cups fruit juice
4 cups ginger ale or carbonated water
Sugar

Just before serving, combine, sweeten to taste, and pour over ice block in punch bowl. Serves 25.

California punch: Use 3 cups loganberry juice, 2½ cups orange juice, ½ cup lemon juice as the fruit juice.

Golden punch: Use 1 cup lime juice, 2 cups orange juice, and 3 cups pineapple juice as the fruit juice.

Royal punch: Use 4 cups grape juice and 2 cups grapefruit juice as the fruit juice.

LIGHT PUNCH

½ cup orange juice
¼ cup lemon juice
1 cup pineapple juice
½ cup grapefruit juice

½ cup strong tea
1½ cups water
½ cup SUGAR SYRUP

Combine ingredients. Stir and chill. Serve with mint cubes. Serves 6 to 8.

DARK PUNCH

1 cup strong tea
½ cup lemon juice
1 cup orange juice
2 cups water

1 cup pineapple juice
½ cup blackberry juice
½ cup raspberry juice
¾ cup SUGAR SYRUP

Combine ingredients. Stir and chill. Serve over TEA ICE CUBES. Garnish with slices of orange and lemon, berries, and mint leaves. Serves 8 to 10.

COUNTRY CLUB PUNCH

3 cups sugar
3 quarts water
1 cup strong tea
Juice of 12 lemons

Juice of 12 oranges
1 quart grape juice
1 small can crushed pineapple
2 quarts ginger ale

Boil sugar and water together for 8 minutes. Add tea and chill. Add juice of oranges and lemons to grape juice and pineapple. Place in refrigerator for about 2 hours. Before serving, add 2 quarts of ginger ale and ice cubes. If served in a punch bowl, add quarter slices of orange and lemon and 1 small bottle of maraschino cherries. Serves about 50.

PIQUANT PUNCH

Strain juice of 6 lemons. Combine with 1 pint grape juice and ½ cup SUGAR SYRUP. Add 2½ cups chilled water. Chill. Serve over ice. Serves 6.

MULLED CIDER

1 gallon sweet cider
6 cinnamon sticks, broken in
    1-inch pieces
1 tablespoon whole cloves

1 tablespoon whole allspice
2 pieces whole mace
3 cups brown sugar
2½ cups canned, spiced crabapples

Put cider in kettle. Add cinnamon. Tie other spices in cheesecloth bag, and drop into cider. Stir in sugar. Heat slowly and simmer 20 minutes. Add apples 5 minutes before serving. Remove spice bag before serving. Serve hot in earthen mugs with an apple in each mug. Yield: 3½ quarts.

MULLED WINE

1 cup sugar
1 cup water
3 cinnamon sticks
12 whole allspice

2 lemons, sliced thin
20 whole cloves
3 cups red wine

Combine sugar, water, cinnamon, and allspice in a saucepan. Bring to boiling point over low heat and simmer 5 minutes. Stud the lemon slices with whole cloves and pour the heated mixture over these. Let stand about 30 minutes. Add wine and heat slowly to just under boiling point. Serve hot. Serves 6.

SPICED CIDER

1 quart sweet cider	8 short pieces stick cinnamon
¼ cup sugar	12 whole cloves
⅛ teaspoon salt	8 whole allspice

Mix all ingredients and bring to boiling point. Cool, and let stand several hours. Reheat, remove whole spices, and serve hot with sandwiches or cookies. Serves 6.

SPICED GRAPE JUICE

1 quart grape juice	12 whole cloves
½ cup sugar	⅛ teaspoon salt
2 short pieces stick cinnamon	

Mix all the ingredients and bring to boiling point. Cool, and let stand several hours. When ready to serve, reheat, remove spices, and add lemon juice if desired. Serve hot with sandwiches or cookies. Serves 6.

alcoholic beverages

COCKTAILS AND OTHER ALCOHOLIC BEVERAGES

In the average home cocktails are usually mixed in the kitchen and brought to the room where they are served with various accompaniments. Whether they are prepared in the kitchen or at a home bar, a certain minimum of functional tools are necessary. All of these given in the list that follows will be required for the kitchen or the home bar. All the basic drinks are easy to prepare with this equipment. A professional barman uses only a few essential tools and that should be kept in mind when equipping your own bar.

1 metal mixing cup.
1 mixing glass which may be inverted in the metal mixing cup for a shaker.
1 long handled bar spoon for stirring.
1 measuring spoon.
1 cocktail strainer (rounded and perforated, or flat with flexible spring around the edge).
1 hard-wood muddler.
1 1-ounce measuring glass with lip (the kind used by chemists).
2 squeezers (regular type for lemons and oranges; pincer type for limes and lemon sections).
1 sharp small-bladed knife (stainless steel).
1 bottle opener.
1 corkscrew (lever type or double action French corkscrew).
1 ice pick or crusher.
1 canvas bag and mallet for pounding ice.

HOW TO MEASURE

Measuring terms differ in various localities. Most of the recipes which follow are for one cocktail. They are given in specific quantities. In this book the cocktails are based on the table of measurements given below. By using these measurements, it's easy to compute the requirements for greater quantities. To compute the number of drops required where they are called for in a recipe, use the following figures based on 3 drops per dash:

For 6 cocktails . . . . ⅕ teaspoon
For 10 cocktails . . . . ⅓ teaspoon
For 25 cocktails . . . . ¾ teaspoon
For 100 cocktails . . . . 3⅓ teaspoons

STANDARD MEASUREMENTS

Dash . . . . 3 drops
3 teaspoons . . . . 1 tablespoon (½ oz.)
1 pony . . . . 1 ounce
1 jigger . . . . 1½ ounces
1 large jigger . . . . 2 ounces
1 wine glass . . . . 4 ounces
2 cups granulated sugar . . . . 1 pound
1 cup (milk or water) . . . . . 8 ounces
16 ounces . . . . 1 pint
⅕ gallon . . . . 25 ounces
32 ounces . . . . 1 quart
4 quarts . . . . 1 gallon
Split . . . . ½ pint or 1 cup
A twist or curl of lemon . . A thin slice of outer rind.

About glasses: Avoid novelty shapes and colored glass. Proper glasses should be selected because they do enhance a drink. For example: Cocktail glasses should preferably have stems because a drink is warmed by the hand, and a cocktail should remain cold. Old Fashioneds are traditionally served in broad, almost straight, tumblers, usually measuring 6 ounces. Highballs are served in tumblers measuring 8 to 10 ounces. Collins and rickeys in 10 to 14 ounce glasses. Glasses as well as the shaker should be thoroughly chilled before using.

Cocktails for a crowd: When preparing cocktails for a large party, the arithmetic is as follows: A 3½-ounce glass will hold 3 ounces. Allow 1 ounce for melted ice if mixed thoroughly. If there are 25 people, this demands 50 ounces of the mixture. A Martini, therefore, would call for 32 ounces or 1 quart of gin and 16 ounces or 1 pint of vermouth, giving you 48 ounces of Martini mixture. The ice would bring it up to the correct amount.

In order to save time, the liquors may be mixed in advance for a crowd; however, if cocktails containing fruit juice are to be served, the final mixing should not be done until serving time. Sugar syrup may be prepared in advance. Fruit juices should be prepared at the last moment and added just before serving.

Shaking or stirring: Some cocktails are stirred while some are shaken. If shaking is called for, add the ice and shake vigorously. Strain and serve promptly. If a recipe calls for stirring, then stir it and do not shake. Specific instructions are given with each recipe. Usually cocktails containing wine as a principal ingredient are stirred, but there are exceptions to this rule, too. Never shake or stir a carbonated water vigorously because this releases the gas and leaves the drink flat in a very short time.

SUGAR AND SYRUP FOR COCKTAILS

Many cocktails require a sweetener of sugar in some form. For convenience it pays to prepare simple bar syrup and store it in advance in the refrigerator. It keeps almost indefinitely. If sugar is to be used in the cocktails, avoid powdered sugar because it contains some cornstarch. Use as fine a grain as possible of granulated sugar. The fine granulated sugar known as fruit or berry sugar serves the purpose very well.

BAR SYRUP

Combine 4 cups sugar and 1 cup water in a saucepan and place over heat. Stir until sugar is dissolved. Reduce heat until mixture simmers. Simmer until liquid is clear. Bottle and keep either in the refrigerator or in an airtight container. If you wish to clarify syrup further, add 1 well-beaten egg white. Skim until perfectly clear.

WHISKEY

Whether it is rye, bourbon, Scotch, or Irish, whiskey is the product obtained from the aging of the distillate of fermented grain. The grain may be corn, rye, barley, or oats. Age may be anything from a few weeks to many years. Aging may take place in charred oak barrels, as in American whiskey, or in sherry casks as with Scotch or Irish whiskey. Some whiskies may be bottled "straight" while others may be blended from several types of whiskey with or without neutral grain spirits added. All of these factors create the different types of whiskey and influence both the taste and the cost of the finished liquor.

Proof: It is the measurement of the alcoholic strength. Each degree of proof equals ½ of 1% alcohol. Therefore 100 proof whiskey contains 50% alcohol. Most blended whiskies are sold at 86 proof, containing, therefore, 43% alcohol. Bonded straight whiskies are sold at 100 proof, containing, therefore, 50% alcohol.

Grain neutral spirits: They may be distilled from grains and other products such as potatoes, sugar, rice, sugar cane, etc. American distillers usually use carefully chosen grains and the distillation is carried out at a very high proof (over 190) which will result in a final product that is almost completely odorless, tasteless, and colorless. For mixing with straight whiskey neutral spirits are cut with water and sometimes colored with a little caramel.

Straight whiskey: Although the name may be applied to any whiskey whether made of rye, bourbon, corn, wheat, or malt, nevertheless only two have become important commercially in the United States—rye and bourbon. Both whiskies are generally made from several kinds of grains but rye must have at least 51% rye in the mash and bourbon must have at least 51% corn in the mash. Both whiskies are made in the same way. The grain is first cleaned and ground to a meal. The meal is mixed with malt and water and the mash is cooked. After it has cooled it is mixed with a yeast and allowed to ferment. At this point it is essentially similar to beer. It is then distilled and the result is a spirit of about 160 proof. It is then reduced to 100 proof by the addition of distilled water and placed in charred oak barrels to mature. This aging process takes place in government bonded warehouses where the liquor must remain at least 2 years to be legally classified as rye or bourbon whiskey. Most straight whiskies are aged 4 to 8 years.

Blended whiskey: It is a mixture of at least 20% straight 100 proof whiskey and grain neutral spirits. Most of the better known blends contain 35% to 40% straight whiskey and 65% to 60% neutral spirits. By law the maker is required to state the amount and approximate age of the whiskies in the blend. Blends which contain a minimum of 51% rye or bourbon may use the title "Rye (or Bourbon)— A Blended Whiskey." There are also on the market a number of blends of straight whiskies of varying ages. They contain no neutral spirits and as a result are higher in price.

RUM

Rum is a liquor that is obtained from the fermentation and subsequent distillation of any sugar cane product. It may be made from the fermented mash of juice crushed from the sugar cane plant, molasses, or "blackstrap." It is one of the most versatile of liquors in the number of uses to which it may be put and in the varieties made. In flavor rum may range from an almost characterless white rum to extremely strong flavored "robust" rums. The extreme variety in color, flavor, aroma, and bouquet results from the difference in the cane used, the climate and soil conditions, and the differences in methods of fermentation and distillation. Rum is made in most of the islands of the West Indies as well as on the Eastern seaboard of the United States (primarily New England and Philadelphia). In determining quality it is best to be guided by the name, trademark, and reputation of the maker. It is well to remember that color has nothing to do with the alcoholic content—which is specifically stated on the bottle. While there are no hard and fast rules, nevertheless one of the simplest ways of determining the type of rum to use is to keep in mind three major generalized classifications: white label, gold label, and heavy rum.

White label: Refers to light bodied rum that is light in color and has a delicate flavor and aroma. It usually has an alcoholic content of 86 proof. Use it in such drinks as Bacardi cocktails and daiquiris.

Gold label: Refers to a darker colored rum with a stronger rum flavor and a stronger aroma. It has about the same alcoholic content as white label. Use it in cooking and in such drinks as Cuba libre, rum collins, or rum Manhattans.

Heavy rum: Refers to a rum that is very dark in color with a pungent flavor and aroma. Alcoholic content may vary from 90 to 151 proof. Use it in such drinks as planters punch, rum swizzles, and rum milk punch.

BRANDY

Brandy is a distilled liquor that is made from fruit. Unless otherwise stated the term brandy applies to the liquor obtained from the distillation of grape wine and the subsequent aging of the distillate. The law requires that any brandies made from fruit other than grape must be referred to by the name of the fruit as apple brandy, apricot brandy, cherry brandy, and so forth. One of the most famous brandies is Cognac. To qualify as Cognac the brandy must be distilled from grapes grown in a prescribed region around the city of Cognac in France. Second in fame is Armagnac which is produced in another region in France. Brandies are often a blend of several distillations. They should not be bottled at less than 80 proof and are frequently allowed to age for many years. If a brandy is younger than 2 years a statement showing the age must appear on the bottle. Excellent brandies are made in the United States—most of them in California from wines which have proven themselves well qualified for the purpose. Applejack or apple brandy is a distinctive American product which is winning general acceptance throughout the world. It is a distillation of apple cider.

CORDIALS AND LIQUEURS

The terms cordials and liqueurs are interchangeable. There are an almost endless variety of them. Although methods of blending and aging may differ nevertheless they are essentially made by the addition of various flavorings and sweetening agents to grain alcohol or other alcoholic liquors (chiefly brandy) to achieve a desired taste, aroma, and color. The alcoholic content of cordials varies greatly. Most of them are sweet but there are some that have a dry after-taste although they seem to be sweet while one is drinking them. Certain cordials are standardized and very similar ones are produced by a number of manufacturers. Examples are apricot, blackberry, cherry, and peach cordials or non-fruit cordials like anisette, cacao, kummel, and sloe gin. Others have distinct flavors that are achieved only by the makers and cannot be duplicated, and in some cases have become quite famous. Examples are: Benedictine, Forbidden Fruit, Chartreuse, Cordon Rouge, and Grand Marnier. In general cordials should not be served before a meal in place of cocktails. They are usually very sweet and may destroy the appetite.

GENERAL WINE INFORMATION

In the home that maintains a kosher kitchen the problem of wine service is very simple because only kosher wines are served, and that immediately limits the number of available wines. Such wines should be properly labeled. A number of recipes for homemade wines are included in the Passover recipe section. There are only two colors in wines—red and white. White wines, therefore, may range in color from the palest straw to deep, dark brown. All red wine is dry, with the exception of port, and wine of port style, which is sweet. There are some exceptions, such as the red wines to which sugar has been added; and they will be so marked on the label. White wines vary in sweetness from very dry to very rich sweet wines. When used by the wine trade, the word "dry" means the opposite of sweet.

SERVING WINES

The do's and don'ts that have been enumerated by so-called connoisseurs who would have you memorize each and every rule before serving a single drop of wine are so numerous and complex that they are frightening to a hostess who would like to serve wine. The few simple suggestions given below are based on the assumption that one drinks and serves wine for enjoyment. They are based on the preferences of the vast majority of wine drinkers who do abide by certain preferences in order to get the maximum enjoyment from drinking wine.

1. According to the rules red still wines should always be served at room temperature. Despite this rule experience indicates that most Americans like their wines, whether red or white, slightly chilled. Most people like white wines slightly colder than red wines but this too is a matter of personal preference. Sparkling wines should always be well chilled. Champagne is, for example, at its best when served at a temperature of 35° to 40°F.
2. One set of wine glasses is enough for the average family despite the outmoded rules which may have had sound reasons for their origins in some cases. For example in the past before wine making became standardized some wines were actually dirty. Dark red glasses were traditionally used with those wines to hide

the dirt. Champagne is served in hollow stemmed glasses only because some people like to see bubbles rising to the surface. Manufacturers are producing an all-purpose glass that is tulip-shaped which seems to imprison the flavor of fine wines and in that way one may enjoy the fine odor as well as the taste.

3. It is quite proper to serve only one wine with a meal. For this purpose select a plain sound wine such as a medium dry sherry. One good wine is far simpler and more palatable than half a dozen of doubtful quality.

4. Red or white light wines may be served with almost all dishes. Avoid, however, serving dry wines with sweet dishes or foods that have sweet sauces and avoid serving red wines with shellfish. For some inexplicable reason shellfish seems to have a property that makes red wine taste unpleasantly metallic to some people. This, of course, presents no problem to the home that maintains a kosher kitchen because shellfish are not kosher.

5. Some of the customs that have entrenched themselves so that they are almost traditional include the service of white wines with hors d'oeuvres, fish, and white meats—and red wines with cheeses, salads, and dark meats—and the serving of white wines before red wines and dry wines before sweet wines.

To remove a cork: Hold the bottle with a thick napkin around the neck to avoid injury if the neck should break. Wipe the rim of the bottle before serving.

WINE IN COOKING

Many good cooks regard wine as a basic necessity in cooking very much like salt and pepper. When used in cooked dishes wine flavors will add background for the natural food flavors of dishes for the same reasons that wine has been served as a constant companion beverage for food for thousands of years. The addition of wine to a dish is often the difference between a savory, tasty dish or one that is flat tasting; however, like any seasoning, wine should be used discreetly so that the wine taste is not the primary one.

Any good wine is suitable for cooking. There is no such thing as a "cooking wine." The same care should be given to a choice of wine for your cooked dishes as you give to a choice of table wines. Wines that have turned sour should be used in salad dressings or tart sauces. Incidentally, it is well to remember that the alcoholic content of wine is lost when the wine is subjected to heat. The alcohol is driven off in the form of vapors by the heat and only the wine-borne flavors remain. A wine-cooked dish, therefore, cannot be regarded as alcoholic.

The choice of types of wine to use in cooked dishes very closely resembles the selections you make in serving table wines. Actually you should experiment with wine flavors to determine which you like best in your cooked dishes. Here, however, are some concrete suggestions. With soups try a sherry. For fish use any dry white wine. For meats use a dry red wine. For desserts use sweet wines such as sweet sherry or madeira. Brandy, rum, or liqueurs, too, are used with desserts. Appetizer wines such as vermouth or other flavored wines usually sold under brand names are rarely used in cooking because of the flavoring agents which have been added to them.

cocktails and short drinks

ALEXANDER COCKTAIL

1 ounce dry gin
¾ ounce creme de cacao

¾ ounce sweet cream

Shake well with cracked ice. Strain.

Brandy alexander: Substitute brandy for gin.

APPLEJACK COCKTAIL

1½ ounces applejack
    Juice of ½ lemon

½ ounce grenadine or 1 teaspoon
    sugar

Shake well with cracked ice. Strain.

BACARDI COCKTAIL

2 ounces Bacardi rum
    Juice of ½ lime

½ teaspoon sugar
3 dashes grenadine

Shake well with cracked ice. Strain.

BARBARY COAST COCKTAIL

¾ ounce dry gin
¾ ounce Scotch whiskey

¾ ounce creme de cacao
½ ounce sweet cream

Shake well with cracked ice. Strain.

BELMONT COCKTAIL

1½ ounces dry gin
¾ ounce grenadine

1 teaspoon sweet cream

Shake well with cracked ice. Strain.

BETWEEN-THE-SHEETS COCKTAIL

¾ ounce rum (Gold Label)
¾ ounce Cointreau

¾ ounce brandy
    Juice of ½ lemon

Shake well with cracked ice. Strain.

BLUE BLAZER

3 ounces Scotch whiskey

3 ounces boiling water

Use 2 large mugs with handles. Put the Scotch in 1 mug, the boiling water in the other. Light the Scotch with a match. While blazing, pour the ingredients 4 or 5 times from 1 mug to the other. If it is well done, it will look like a stream of liquid fire. Add 1 teaspoon fine grain sugar. Serve in a small tumbler with a piece of lemon peel.

BOMBAY COCKTAIL

2 ounces brandy
¼ ounce sweet vermouth
¼ ounce dry vermouth

3 dashes curacao
1 dash anisette

Shake with ice. Strain.

BRANDY COCKTAIL

Juice of ½ lime
2 ounces brandy

4 dashes curacao

Add 1 ice cube. Stir. Strain.

BRANDY BLAZER COCKTAIL

3 ounces brandy
1 lump sugar

1 piece of orange peel

Combine in a small thick glass. Light with match. Stir with long spoon. Strain into cocktail glass.

BRANDY CRUSTA COCKTAIL

Moisten the edge of a small wine glass with lemon and rub edge into powdered sugar to frost edge. Combine the following in a mixing glass.

1½ ounces brandy
½ ounce curacao
3 dashes maraschino liqueur

1 dash Angostura bitters
4 dashes lemon juice

Add cracked ice, stir, and strain into prepared glass. Serve with a slice of orange.

BRANDY FLIP

2 ounces brandy
1 teaspoon sugar

1 egg

Combine with crushed ice. Shake well. Strain. Top with grated nutmeg.

Variations: Substitute claret, port, rum, or sherry for brandy.

BRANDY VERMOUTH COCKTAIL

1½ ounces brandy
½ ounce sweet vermouth

1 dash Angostura bitters

Stir.

BRONX COCKTAIL

1 ounce dry gin
¾ ounce sweet vermouth

¾ ounce dry vermouth
½ ounce orange juice

Shake well with cracked ice. Strain.

BRONX COCKTAIL (Dry)

3 slices orange
1 sliver pineapple

1 ounce dry gin
1 ounce dry vermouth

Place fruit in mixing glass, muddle well, add cracked ice, gin, and vermouth. Shake well, strain, and serve. (If desired, the fruit may be transferred into the glass in which the drink is served.) Use large cocktail glass.

CAFE AU KIRSCH COCKTAIL

1 ounce kirsch
1 ounce Cognac

1 white of egg
1 ounce cold black coffee

Shake well with cracked ice. Strain. Serve in wine glass.

CAFE DE PARIS COCKTAIL

White of 1 egg
3 dashes anisette

1 teaspoon fresh cream
1½ ounces dry gin

Shake well with cracked ice. Strain.

CHAMPAGNE COCKTAIL

1 cube ice (optional)
Angostura bitters
1 lump sugar

1 slice orange
1 piece lemon peel

Serve in "saucer" champagne glass. Place lump of sugar in glass. Saturate it with bitters. Add ice if desired. Squeeze on top the piece of lemon peel. Fill with chilled champagne. Stir gently. Serve with orange slice.

CLOVER CLUB COCKTAIL

½ teaspoon fine grain sugar
4 dashes grenadine
2 ounces dry gin

White of 1 egg
Juice of ½ lime or lemon

Shake well with cracked ice. Strain. Serve in wine glass.

Clover leaf: Same as above with sprig of mint on top.

COBBLERS

Fill goblet with finely shaved ice. Add 1 teaspoon fine grain sugar. Add 3 ounces of burgundy, claret, sauterne, sherry, port, or Rhine wine, brandy, or whiskey. Stir well and garnish with slices of orange or slivers of pineapple, and a sprig of mint.

CREME DE MENTHE FRAPPE

Fill a cocktail glass with finely shaved ice. Add 2 ounces creme de menthe. Serve with straw.

DAIQUIRI

2 ounces rum (white label)
Juice of ½ lemon or lime

1 teaspoon fine grain sugar

Shake well with finely cracked ice. Strain.

FROZEN DAIQUIRI

2 ounces rum (white label)
Juice of ½ lemon or lime
1 teaspoon fine grain sugar

Dash of maraschino
8 to 10 ounces shaved ice

Shake very vigorously or mix in electric mixer for 1 minute. Serve unstrained with straw in a "saucer" type champagne glass.

DAISIES

1½ ounces dry gin   Juice of ½ lemon
  3 dashes grenadine

Stir into a goblet half filled with finely shaved ice. Add a squirt of carbonated water. Garnish with fruit and a sprig of mint.

Variations: Brandy, applejack, rum, or whiskey may be used instead of gin.

DUBONNET COCKTAIL

1½ ounces Dubonnet   1 twist of lemon peel
1½ ounces dry gin

Stir in chilled glass. For drier cocktail add more gin.

JACK ROSE COCKTAIL

  Juice of ½ lemon   ½ ounce grenadine
1½ ounces applejack

Shake well with cracked ice. Strain.

MANHATTAN

 2 ounces rye   2 dashes Angostura bitters
¾ ounce sweet vermouth

Pour whiskey, vermouth, and bitters over cracked ice in mixing glass. Stir well to blend and dilute slightly. Strain. Serve with cherry.

Dubonnet Manhattan: Use 1½ ounces Dubonnet, 1½ ounces rye or bourbon and a dash of Angostura bitters.

Rum or Scotch Manhattan: Use Scotch or rum (gold label) instead of rye.

MARTINI COCKTAIL (Dry)

2 ounces dry gin   ¾ ounce dry vermouth

Stir well with ice. Strain. Serve with olive or pearl onion in glass and a twist of lemon peel, if desired.

MARTINI COCKTAIL (Sweet)

 2 ounces dry gin   Dash of orange bitters
¾ ounce sweet vermouth   (optional)

Stir well with ice. Strain. Serve with a cherry.

MIST

2 ounces rye, bourbon, or   Crushed ice
  Scotch whiskey   Twist of lemon peel

Fill old-fashioned glass with crushed ice. Pour whiskey over it. Serve with twist of lemon peel.

OLD FASHIONED COCKTAIL

1 teaspoon fine grain sugar
2 twists of lemon peel
1 or 2 dashes Angostura bitters

2 or 2½ ounces bourbon or rye
Several ice cubes

Put in glass sugar, 1 twist of lemon peel, and bitters to taste; stir well. Add 1 ounce of whiskey. Allow to blend thoroughly. Add ice cubes. Add remaining whiskey and twist of lemon peel. Serve with a small bar spoon and a maraschino cherry. If desired, it may be served with a slice of orange and a sliver of pineapple.

Variations: Applejack, brandy, gin, rum, vermouth, etc., may also be used instead of whiskey.

ON THE ROCKS

2 or 3 ounces rye, bourbon or
   Scotch

Several ice cubes
Twist of lemon peel

Pour whiskey over ice cubes in an old-fashioned glass. Serve with twist of lemon peel.

ORANGE BLOSSOM COCKTAIL

2 ounces dry gin
¼ teaspoon sugar

¾ ounce orange juice

Stir well with cracked ice. Strain.

SIDE CAR COCKTAIL #1

Juice of ½ lemon
¾ ounce Cointreau

1¾ ounces brandy

Stir well in ice. Strain.

Side car cocktail #2: Use ¾ ounce each of Cognac, Cointreau, and lemon juice.

STINGER COCKTAIL

2 ounces brandy

¾ ounce white creme de menthe

Shake with cracked ice. Strain.

WARD EIGHT

Juice of ½ lemon
Juice of ½ orange

1 teaspoon grenadine
1½ ounces rye

Shake with ice. Serve in 8 to 10 ounce tumbler. Fill with carbonated water. Garnish with orange slice and cherry.

WHISKEY SOUR

2 ounces rye or bourbon
½ ounce lemon or lime juice

½ teaspoon sugar

Put all ingredients in shaker and shake vigorously. Strain into glass. Decorate with slice of orange and a cherry. If desired, add a squirt of carbonated water.

Variations: Applejack, brandy, gin, or rum may be substituted for rye or bourbon.

eggnogs

EGGNOG

1 egg	2 ounces brandy
1 tablespoon fine grain sugar	¾ glass milk

Shake well with cracked ice. Strain. Serve with nutmeg on top.

Variations: Substitute port, rum, sherry, or whiskey for brandy.

BREAKFAST EGGNOG

1½ ounces brandy	1 egg
½ ounce curacao	4 ounces milk

Shake well. Strain into highball glass. Serve with grating of nutmeg on top.

EGGNOG BALTIMORE

1 egg yolk	¼ ounce Madeira wine
A grating of nutmeg	¼ ounce rum
1 tablespoon sugar	Milk
½ ounce brandy	

Beat the egg yolk with nutmeg until creamy. Combine with other ingredients except milk in a shaker. Add a few large pieces of cracked ice. Shake well. Strain into a highball glass. Fill with chilled milk.

EGGNOG FOR A CROWD

10 eggs, separated	12 ounces rum
1¼ pounds fine grain sugar	1 gallon milk
1 quart brandy	

Beat egg yolks until light. Add sugar, brandy, and rum. Stir until sugar is dissolved. Add milk slowly, stirring continually. Beat whites of eggs to a stiff froth and add to top of mixture. Fill glasses, putting some egg white on top. Grate a little nutmeg over each serving. Makes about 1½ gallons.

long drinks

APPLEJACK COOLER

1 tablespoon fine grain sugar	1½ ounces applejack
Juice of ½ lemon or 1 lime	

Shake well with cracked ice. Strain into highball glass. Add ice cubes, if desired. Fill with soda.

APRICOT COOLER

Juice of ½ lemon
Juice of ½ lime

2 dashes grenadine
1 ounce apricot brandy

Shake well with cracked ice. Strain into highball glass. Add ice cubes, if desired. Fill with soda.

GIN COOLER

2 ounces dry gin

1 teaspoon fine grain sugar

Dissolve sugar in gin. Add to tumbler with cracked ice. Fill with soda water.

Variations: Substitute 2 ounces rum or whiskey, or 3 ounces wine for gin.

HIGHLAND COOLER

1½ ounces Scotch whiskey

3 dashes creme de menthe

Add with 2 cubes of ice in highball glass. Add soda. Stir and serve with a sprig of mint.

LONE TREE COOLER

Juice of 1 lemon
Juice of ¼ orange
1 ounce grenadine

1 ounce dry gin
½ ounce dry vermouth

Shake well with cracked ice. Strain into highball glass. Add ice cubes, if desired. Fill with soda.

MANHATTAN COOLER

Juice of ½ lemon or lime
½ tablespoon fine grain sugar

4 ounces claret
3 dashes rum

Stir well with cracked ice. Strain into a highball glass. Add ice cubes, if desired. Fill with soda. Garnish with fruit.

ORANGE BLOSSOM COOLER

Juice of ½ orange
1 teaspoon sugar

1½ ounces dry gin

Shake with cracked ice. Strain into Tom Collins glass. Add ice cubes, if desired. Fill glass with carbonated water. Garnish with fruit.

RED WINE COOLER

Dissolve 2 teaspoons fine grain sugar in water. Add 4 teaspoons strained orange juice. Pour over ice cubes in highball glass. Fill glass with red wine. Garnish with lemon slice.

WHITE WINE COOLER

Pour 1 tablespoon sugar syrup over ice cubes in highball glass. Add ⅓ cup charged water. Fill glass with white wine. Garnish with half slice of orange and a sprig of mint.

HIGHBALLS

All highballs should be served in 8-ounce highball glasses. To prepare any highball, place an ice cube in the glass, add 1½ ounces of the liquor desired, and fill up the glass with carbonated water or ginger ale. Serve with a small bar spoon in glass and a twist of lemon peel, if desired. The following liquors may be used in preparing highballs: Applejack, bitters, bourbon, Cognac, gin, rye, rum, Scotch whiskey, and cordials.

TOM COLLINS

1 tablespoon fine grain sugar
   Juice of 1 lemon or 2 limes

2 ounces dry gin

Shake well with cracked ice. Strain into a 10 to 14 ounce glass. Add ice cubes and fill with sparkling water. Stir and serve.

Variations: Applejack, bourbon, brandy, rum, rye, Scotch whiskey, or vodka may be substituted for gin.

CUBA LIBRE

2 ounces rum (gold label)

Juice and rind of ½ lime

Squeeze lime juice into highball glass. Add rum, the lime rind, and ice cubes. Fill with cola. Stir and serve.

GIN BUCK

Juice of ½ lime

2 ounces dry gin

Pour into glass. Add cube of ice and fill up with ginger ale. Serve in highball glass.

GIN FIZZ

Juice of ½ lemon
Juice of ½ lime

1 tablespoon fine grain sugar
1½ ounces dry gin

Shake well with cracked ice; strain into glass. Fill with sparkling water. Stir slightly. Serve in 8-ounce highball glass.

Brandy fizz: Use 1½ ounces brandy instead of gin.

Golden fizz: Make same as plain Gin Fizz, adding the yolk of an egg. Serve in 8-ounce highball glass.

Silver fizz: Make same as plain Gin Fizz, adding the white of an egg. Serve in 8-ounce highball glass.

GIN RICKEY

  1 cube ice
1½ ounces gin

Juice of ½ or whole lime
Carbonated water

Place cube of ice, juice, and gin in glass. Fill with carbonated water. Serve with small bar spoon. Serve in 8-ounce highball glass.

Variations: Other rickeys may be made in the same way by substituting the liquor desired in place of the gin. Use applejack, bourbon, brandy, cordials, rum, rye, Scotch whiskey, and sloe gin.

MILK PUNCH

2 ounces whiskey, brandy, or rum   1 teaspoon sugar
8 ounces milk

Shake with cracked ice. Strain. Serve with grating of nutmeg on top.

MINT JULEP

2 or 3 ounces bourbon
6 or 7 mint leaves
1 teaspoon sugar

Shaved ice
Several mint sprigs dusted with
    powdered sugar

Place mint leaves in bottom of mug or tall glass. Add bar syrup or sugar. Crush well with spoon or muddler and fill container with shaved ice. Pour 2 or 3 ounces bourbon over ice and stir until mug or glass begins to frost. Refill to top with ice. If time allows, place in refrigerator for 15 to 20 minutes. When ready to serve, remove from refrigerator and top with a little whiskey. Add sprigs of mint. Serve with straws.

PLANTER'S PUNCH

3 ounces rum (heavy)
  Juice of ½ lemon

Dash of grenadine

Fill 10-ounce glass with crushed ice. Add all ingredients and stir. Fill glass with carbonated water. Decorate with a maraschino cherry, a slice of orange, a sliver of pineapple, and a sprig of mint.

RUM PUNCH

  Juice of ½ lemon
½ ounce pure maple syrup

2 ounces rum (heavy)
2 dashes grenadine

Shake well with ice. Pour into a 10-ounce tumbler filled with crushed ice. Garnish with sliver of pineapple, slice of orange, and a cherry.

SLINGS

1½ ounces dry gin   3 dashes bitters

Serve in a highball glass with cracked ice and filled with carbonated water. Garnish with a twist of lemon and, if desired, a grating of nutmeg.

Variations: Brandy, rum, or whiskey may be substituted for gin.

punches

BRANDY PUNCH

2 quarts brandy
4 ounces grenadine
8 ounces curacao
1¼ pounds fine grain sugar

Juice of 16 lemons
Juice of 4 oranges
2 quarts carbonated water

Dissolve the sugar in the juices. Mix with other ingredients except carbonated water. Pour over a block of ice in punch bowl. Add and stir in the chilled carbonated water just before serving. Serves about 25.

CARDINAL PUNCH

4 ounces sweet vermouth
8 ounces rum
8 ounces brandy
2 quarts claret

1½ pounds sugar
8 ounces sparkling white wine
2 quarts sparkling water

Combine the vermouth, rum, brandy, and claret. Add sugar and stir to dissolve. Pour over block of ice in punch bowl. Add wine and sparkling water. Stir only to blend. Garnish with fruit.

CHAMPAGNE PUNCH

4 ounces brandy
4 ounces maraschino
4 ounces curacao

½ pound fine grain sugar
2 quarts champagne
1 quart sparkling mineral water

Stir the sugar with the brandy, maraschino, and curacao to dissolve sugar. Pour over a block of ice in a punch bowl. Add and gently stir in champagne and mineral water just before serving. Serves about 25.

CIDER PUNCH

1 quart cider
1 ounce brandy
1 ounce curacao

1 ounce maraschino
8 ounces carbonated water

Add ice cubes. Stir gently. Garnish each serving with fruit. Serves 10.

CLARET CUP

1 quart claret
1 ounce maraschino

2 ounces curacao
2 tablespoons fine grain sugar

Use a large glass pitcher. Combine all ingredients. Serve with lots of ice. Garnish with slices of orange, slivers of pineapple, and sprigs of fresh mint. Serves 8 to 10.

CLARET PUNCH

½ pound fine grain sugar
3 quarts claret
4 ounces curacao

2 quarts sparkling water
½ pint lemon juice

Mix well, pour into punch bowl, surround bowl with cracked ice. Cut up oranges and pineapple and add some cherries. Place in a separate bowl, and serve in the glasses with the punch.

RHINE WINE PUNCH

4 ounces brandy
4 ounces maraschino liqueur
3 quarts Rhine wine

1 quart sparkling water
½ pound fine grain sugar
2 tablespoons tea leaves

Mix the brandy and maraschino with sugar and stir to dissolve. Add wine and sparkling water. Pour over block of ice in punch bowl. Tie tea leaves in piece of cheesecloth and leave in mixture for 10 minutes. Garnish with slices of fruit.

hot drinks

HOT BUTTERED RUM

1½ ounces rum (gold label)
  1 teaspoon sugar
  1 teaspoon butter

Freshly boiling water
Grated nutmeg

Place the rum, sugar, and butter in a hot tumbler or mug. Fill with boiling water and stir well. Top with freshly grated nutmeg.

Variations: Early New England recipes usually called for at least 2 ounces of rum per serving with as much as 1 tablespoon butter and the addition of 3 or 4 cloves.

HOT RUM LEMONADE

1 teaspoon sugar (about)
  Juice of ½ lemon

1 ounce rum (white label)
Slice of lemon

Combine in hot tumbler or mug. Add freshly boiling water as desired and slice of lemon.

HOT WINE LEMONADE

1½ teaspoons sugar (about)
  Juice of 1 lemon

2 ounces red or white wine
Slice of lemon

Combine in hot tumbler or mug. Add freshly boiling water as desired and top with slice of lemon.

TOM AND JERRY

 1 egg, separated
¾ ounce Jamaica rum

1 tablespoon fine grain sugar
¾ ounce brandy or rye

Beat yolk and white of egg separately, then mix together. Add the spirits and fill with boiling water. Grate nutmeg on top.

WHISKEY TODDY

1 teaspoon sugar
2 cloves
  Slice of lemon

Piece of cinnamon stick
1½ ounces rye or bourbon

Combine in glass. Add 1½ ounces boiling water or cold water, as desired. With cold water, add an ice cube.

Variations: Applejack, brandy, or rum may be substituted for rye or bourbon.

BLACKBERRY WINE

For each gallon of blackberries use 1 gallon water and ½ teaspoon each of cinnamon, cloves, ginger, and mixed spice. Mash berries well. Add the boiling water and the spices. Allow to stand in cool room for 3 days. Strain and add 3 pounds lump sugar for each gallon of liquid. Stir until sugar is dissolved. Leave in cool place to ferment. When fermentation stops, strain and bottle wine. Rock candy may be added during fermentation. Do not add yeast. Hastening fermentation spoils the natural flavor.

ELDERBERRY WINE

Put berries in a large kettle. Add only enough water to berries to keep them from burning. Cook only a few minutes, or just long enough to scald thoroughly. Strain through a cheesecloth and add 8 cups sugar to 10 cups berry juice. Use only granulated white sugar. Set away in a cool place to ferment. Skim daily until clear. When bubbles cease to rise to top of liquid, the wine is ready to bottle. Do not add yeast. Hurrying the fermentation or adding other liquor spoils the natural flavor.

VISHNIK

Whole sour cherries
2 cups neutral grain spirits

4 pounds sugar

Fill 1 gallon jug more than half full of cherries. Add sugar and alcohol. Shake to blend ingredients. Cork the jug but do not seal it. Let stand for 1 month. Add more alcohol to fill jug and cork loosely. Let stand at least 3 months longer before using.

Variation: Blackberries or black raspberries may be substituted for the cherries. Prepare as above.

CHERRY CORDIAL

12 pounds large sweet cherries
5 pounds sugar

1 pint brandy
1 quart boiled water, chilled

Remove stems from cherries; wash and drain. Place in a crock; add sugar and brandy. Cover with a double thickness of muslin. Keep at room temperature, stirring every day for 4 or 5 days to completely dissolve sugar. Then cover tightly and keep at room temperature for 2 weeks, then stir in chilled boiled water. Cover and store in a cool place. The cordial can be bottled after 6 weeks. The cherries are drained and may be eaten as is or may be used for preserves.

yeast breads

Despite nostalgic memories of the warm fragrance of freshly-baked breads and rolls, the modern homemaker tends to avoid breadmaking. Modern methods, however, have lessened the hazards in making perfect breads, and baking has become fun. No phase of the culinary arts gives a greater sense of accomplishment for the small amount of effort involved. With modern refrigeration, dough may be placed in the refrigerator and baked as needed. Now, fine-grained, home-baked loaves may be yours at any time. The characteristics of good loaves are rounded tops and smooth, evenly browned crusts free from cracks. They should be light for their size and free of dark streaks or doughy lumps. Crumbs should feel moist and elastic to the touch and the texture should be porous. Understanding something about the ingredients that go into breads and knowing how to combine them are the secrets of good baking.

Ingredients: The essential ingredients for making yeast breads are flour, liquid, yeast, and salt. To give the flavor and texture most people like, small amounts of sugar and shortening are added. Fancy breads of various kinds contain eggs, fruits, nuts, spices, or other ingredients in varying amounts.

Flour: Flour is the chief ingredient of bread. Wheat flour is the most widely used. All-purpose flour, which is a blend of hard and soft wheat, is usually used for breadmaking in the home. This flour contains the quality and quantity of gluten necessary to supply strength and elasticity to the dough. Some other kinds of flour are graham, rye, soy, buckwheat, etc. The kind of flour to use is specifically stated in each recipe given here.

Liquid: Water, milk, or a combination of these is most commonly used in making yeast breads. Some cooks like to use water in which potatoes have been cooked. Buttermilk or diluted evaporated milk may also be used. Fresh milk or buttermilk is scalded and cooled to lukewarm before the yeast is added. Scalding stops the enzyme action which might otherwise cause some softening of the dough. It also improves the bread texture and flavor. Occasionally fruit or vegetable juice is used to make novelty breads. Dry milk may be used by combining ¼ cup of dry milk and 1 cup of water to take the place of 1 cup of liquid milk.

Yeast: Active dry or compressed yeast is the leavening agent that gives yeast bread its characteristic flavor and texture. Its leavening action works best at a temperature of 80° to 85°F.

Compressed yeast: This yeast is very perishable. It keeps satisfactorily for about a week if stored in a refrigerator at 45° to 50°F. Compressed yeast comes in 3/5-ounce, 1-ounce, and 2-ounce cakes.

Dry yeast: For those who bake at home, active dry yeast is fast replacing compressed yeast, long sold in foil-wrapped cakes. Dry yeast in air-tight, moisture-proof packages gives good results until the expiration date on the package and can be used in place of compressed yeast in any recipe. One package or 1 scant tablespoon equals 1 cake (3/5-ounce) of compressed yeast. Both take 5 to 10 minutes to soften. Soften dry yeast in warm water (105° to 115°F.) and compressed yeast in lukewarm water (85° to 95°F.).

No-dissolve dry yeast: No-dissolve and instant blend yeasts can be used according to manufacturer's general directions (blending undissolved yeast with flour) or can be used in the traditional way (dissolving yeast in warm water). A wide variety of no-dissolve yeast recipes is given in the Yeast Bread Supplement on page 578.

Salt: Salt gives flavor to bread and helps control fermentation. Too much salt slows up the rising. From 1 to 1½ teaspoons salt per cup of liquid or per pound of flour is the usual proportion.

Sugar: Sugar is quick food for the yeast, from which it manufactures leavening gas. Sugar also adds flavor and helps to give a nice golden color to the crust. If a dough does not contain enough sugar, the bread bakes without browning. Breads that contain much sugar may brown too quickly unless they are baked at moderate temperatures. One tablespoon of sugar per cup of liquid or per pound of flour is the amount most often used in plain bread. Sweet breads, fancy breads, and rolls contain much larger amounts. In some fancy recipes honey, molasses, or brown sugar may be substituted for granulated sugar.

Shortening: Shortening adds flavor, increases tenderness, improves keeping quality. Butter gives an excellent flavor but any bland fat may be used in addition to, or instead of, butter.

Other ingredients: Most rolls and fancy breads contain whole eggs or egg yolks because, when added to yeast roll dough, eggs give a delicate texture and somewhat flaky crust. Eggs give rich flavor and deep creamy color to the crumb. To obtain an open grain and somewhat thick but crisp crust, like some French rolls or hard rolls, egg white and water are used for liquid. In various kinds of fancy breads and rolls, fruits, nuts, spices, and other flavorful ingredients are added.

WHITE BREAD (Straight Dough Method)

4 cups liquid (scalded)
¼ cup sugar
4 teaspoons salt
2 tablespoons shortening

1 cake compressed yeast or
    1 package dry granular yeast
¼ cup lukewarm water
About 12 cups sifted all-purpose flour

Scald liquid. Combine sugar, salt, shortening, and liquid. Cool to lukewarm. Add yeast which has been softened in ¼ cup lukewarm water. Add flour gradually and mix thoroughly. When dough is stiff, turn out on lightly floured board and knead until smooth and satiny. Shape into smooth ball. Place in greased bowl. Cover and let rise in warm place (80° to 85°F.) until doubled in bulk (2 to 2½ hours). Punch down. Let rise again. When light, divide into 4 equal portions. Round up each portion into a smooth ball. Cover well and let rest 10 to 15 minutes. Mold into loaves. Place in greased bread pans. Let rise until doubled in bulk. Bake in hot oven (400° to 425°F.) 40 to 45 minutes. Yield: 4 1-pound loaves.

Date or raisin bread: Add 1 cup quartered dates or whole seedless raisins to white or whole wheat dough just before shaping into loaves.

Graham or whole-wheat bread: Substitute brown sugar or molasses for sugar and 6 to 8 cups of graham (or whole wheat) for equal amount white flour.

Nut bread: Add ½ cup each, raisins and chopped nuts (⅜ teaspoon cinnamon, if desired) when preparing dough.

Oatmeal bread: Use 6 cups of uncooked oatmeal for 6 cups of white flour.

Rye bread: Use half rye flour and half white flour. Add 2 tablespoons caraway seed during kneading process, if desired. Molasses may be substituted for sugar.

Soybean bread: Add ¾ cup of soybean flour just before adding white flour. Reduce white flour same amount.

Whole-wheat prune bread: Add 2 tablespoons grated orange rind to soft dough. Knead 1½ cups chopped, dried prunes into dough after first rising and shape into loaves.

WHITE BREAD (Sponge Method)

Use same ingredients in same proportions as for **straight dough method,** except that dry cake yeast is used and is softened in 2 cups of the lukewarm liquid instead of in lukewarm water 20 to 30 minutes. Add 4 cups flour, to softened yeast, to form a thick batter, beating until smooth. Cover and let rise in a warm place (78°F.) overnight, or until very bubbly and a little more than doubled in bulk. Stir down risen sponge. Scald remaining 2 cups liquid. Add salt, sugar, and shortening. Cool to lukewarm and add to sponge. Add remaining flour gradually, until dough is moderately stiff. Turn out on floured board and proceed as directed in straight dough method.

CHALLAH (Braided White Bread)

6 tablespoons shortening	2 cakes compressed yeast
1½ cups scalded water or milk	½ cup lukewarm water
2 tablespoons sugar	3 eggs
2 teaspoons salt	About 7 cups sifted all-purpose flour

Melt shortening in scalded water or milk (or potato water, if desired). Pour into a large mixing bowl. Add sugar and salt and let cool to lukewarm. Dissolve yeast in lukewarm water. Let stand a little while. Then mix in eggs, reserving 1 yolk for the tops of the breads. Add egg and yeast mixture to the liquid mixture. Mix well and stir in 4 cups of flour, then 3 cups of flour. Turn out on a floured board and knead until smooth and elastic, about 5 minutes. Place in a greased large bowl. Oil top of dough with a little melted shortening to keep it from drying. Cover with a cloth and let rise in a warm place until double in bulk, about 1 to 2 hours. Punch down. Divide into 3 parts. Divide each part into 3 more parts and braid into 3 loaves. Place each braided loaf in a loaf pan. Mix the egg yolk that was reserved with 1 tablespoon cold water, and with a pastry brush spread over the loaves. Sprinkle with poppy seeds, if desired, and set aside to rise again (about 1 hour). Bake in moderate oven (375°F.) about 45 minutes to an hour, or until the loaves sound hollow when tapped and are lightly browned. Yield: 3 loaves.

POPPY SEED ROLLS

Use ⅓ of the recipe for CHALLAH. Form into small rolls (about 15 to 20). Spread with egg yolk mixture. Sprinkle with poppy seeds. Set aside to rise for about 1 hour. Bake in moderate oven (375°F.) 25 minutes, or until nicely brown. Yield: 15 to 20 rolls.

VIENNESE CRESCENTS

Use part of the recipe for CHALLAH. On a floured board, roll out pieces of dough. Cut into 4-inch triangular pieces. Roll each into a cylindrical shape. Flatten slightly and turn a little to form crescents. Place on baking sheet. Brush with egg yolk and water, and let rise about 1 hour. Bake in moderate oven (375°F.) 20 minutes.

SEMMEL ROLLS

Follow the recipe for *VIENNESE CRESCENTS* and, when ready to shape, cut into small even pieces. Knead into rounds about 1 inch high and 3 inches wide. Set in shallow pan, about 2 inches apart, and let rise slightly. Make a deep crease through the center of each with a knife handle, dipped in flour. Brush each with egg yolk and water. Let rise about one hour. Bake as for *VIENNESE CRESCENTS.*

NO-KNEAD WHITE BREAD (Basic Recipe)

1½ cups scalded milk
½ cup shortening
¼ cup sugar
2 tablespoons salt
1½ cups water

3 cakes compressed yeast or
3 packages dry granular yeast
3 eggs
9 cups sifted all-purpose flour

Combine milk, shortening, sugar, and salt. Cool to lukewarm by adding 1½ cups water. Add yeast and mix well. Blend in eggs. Add flour slowly. Mix until dough is well blended. Place in large, greased bowl and cover if the dough is to be chilled. Shape into 3 loaves on well-floured board. Place in greased pans (9x4x3 inches) and cover. Let rise in warm place until doubled in bulk, about 2 hours for chilled dough and 1 hour for unchilled dough. Bake in moderate oven (375°F.) 1 hour. Yield: 3 loaves.

Cheese bread: Blend in 2 cups grated cheese when flour is added.

Cinnamon loaves: Roll ⅓ the dough into 16 x 8 inch rectangle. Sprinkle with ¼ cup sugar and 1 teaspoon cinnamon. Roll as for jelly roll, starting with 8-inch edge and sealing edges. Place in greased pan. Use remaining dough plain or make 2 more cinnamon loaves from it.

Nut bread: Blend in 1 cup chopped nuts before flour is added.

NO-KNEAD WHOLE-WHEAT BREAD

1 cup milk
⅓ cup shortening
½ cup brown sugar
4 teaspoons salt
1 cup water

2 cakes compressed or
2 packages dry granular yeast
2 eggs
3 cups unsifted whole-wheat flour
3 cups sifted all-purpose flour

Scald milk, combine with shortening, sugar, and salt. Cool to lukewarm with 1 cup water. Add yeast and mix well. Blend in eggs, whole-wheat flour. Add gradually all-purpose flour. Mix until well blended. Place dough in greased bowl. Cover and store in refrigerator, or cold place, 2 hours, or until needed. Shape into 2 loaves on well-floured board. Place in greased pans (9x4x3 inches) and cover. Let rise in warm place (80 to 85°F.) until double in bulk, about 2 hours. Bake in moderate oven (375°F.) 1 hour. Yield: 2 loaves.

SWEDISH LIMPE

2 cups water
½ cup brown sugar
2 teaspoons caraway seed
1 tablespoon shortening
1 teaspoon chopped orange peel or
    1 scant teaspoon anise seed

½ cake compressed yeast
3 cups sifted all-purpose flour
    (about)
1 teaspoon salt
About 2 cups rye flour

Boil together water, sugar, caraway seed, shortening and orange peel (or anise seed) for 3 minutes. Let mixture become lukewarm. Add yeast. Stir thoroughly, gradually adding sufficient white flour to make a soft dough. Place dough in a warm place and let rise for 1½ hours. Then add salt and enough rye flour to make a stiff dough. Let rise again for 2 hours. Knead slightly and shape into loaf. Put into greased loaf pan (9x5x3 inches). Let rise again for half an hour. Bake in moderate oven (350°F.) for 1 hour. Yield: 1 loaf.

SALLY LUNN (Yeast-raised)

1 cup milk
2 tablespoons sugar
2 teaspoons salt
4 tablespoons butter or
    4 tablespoons margarine

1 cake compressed yeast
½ cup lukewarm water
3 eggs, well beaten
4 cups sifted all-purpose flour

Scald milk, add sugar, salt, and butter or margarine. Cool until lukewarm. Dissolve yeast in lukewarm water and add to milk mixture. Add eggs and flour to make a batter. Beat well. Cover and set in warm place, free from draft. Let rise until doubled in bulk, about 2½ hours. Stir down and pour into well-greased shallow baking pan. Cover and let rise until doubled in bulk, about 1½ hours. Sprinkle granulated sugar over top and bake in hot oven (400°F.) about 30 minutes. To serve, break into pieces, using fork. Serve warm with marmalade or jelly. Yield: 1 large cake.

CHEESE BREAD

3 tablespoons sugar
1 tablespoon salt
2 cups lukewarm water
2 cakes compressed yeast

2 eggs, well beaten
4 cups (1 pound) grated American
    cheese
7 to 8 cups sifted all-purpose flour

Dissolve sugar and salt in lukewarm water. Crumble in yeast and stir until dissolved. Add well-beaten eggs, grated cheese, and flour to make an easily handled dough. Knead dough quickly and lightly until smooth and elastic. Divide dough into 3 equal portions. Shape into loaves and place in greased bread pans. Cover and let rise in warm place, free from draft, until doubled in bulk, about 1¾ hours. Bake in moderate oven (375°F.) for 45 minutes. Yield: 3 loaves.

HERB BREAD

2 cups milk
4 tablespoons sugar
1 tablespoon salt
1 cake compressed yeast
2 eggs, well beaten

1 teaspoon nutmeg
4 teaspoons leaf sage
4 teaspoons caraway seed
8 cups sifted all-purpose flour
4 tablespoons shortening

Scald milk. Add sugar and salt. Cool to lukewarm. Crumble in yeast and stir until dissolved. Add eggs, nutmeg, sage, caraway seed, and half the flour. Beat ûntil smooth. Add melted shortening and remaining flour, or enough to make easily handled dough. Knead dough quickly and lightly until smooth and elastic. Place dough in greased bowl. Cover and set in warm place, free from draft. Let rise until doubled in bulk, about 2 hours. When light, divide into 2 equal portions and shape into loaves. Place in greased bread pans. Cover and let rise until doubled in bulk, about 1 hour. Bake in hot oven (425°F.) for 15 minutes, then reduce to moderate (375°F.) and bake 35 minutes longer. Yield: 2 loaves.

SALT-RISING BREAD

1 cup scalded milk
2 tablespoons sugar
¼ cup white corn meal
1 teaspoon salt

1 cup lukewarm water
2 tablespoons melted shortening
About 5½ cups sifted all-purpose
flour

Add 1 tablespoon sugar, corn meal, and salt to scalded milk. Beat well and turn into a large container. Cover and set in a pan of hot water (165°F.). Let stand in a warm place until it ferments, about 6 to 7 hours. The mixture should be light, spongy, and bubbly. When it is full of bubbles, stir in lukewarm water, 1 table-spoon sugar, and 2 cups flour. Beat thoroughly. Return the container to the hot water bath. This time it should be slightly higher than lukewarm (about 115°F.). Let rise until the sponge is very light and full of bubbles. Gradually stir in just enough of the remaining flour to make a stiff dough which can be handled easily. Knead until smooth and satiny, about 10 minutes. Divide into 2 parts. Let stand covered about 10 minutes. Shape into 2 loaves. Place in well-greased loaf pans. Brush with melted shortening. Cover and let rise in a warm place until doubled in bulk. Bake in moderate oven (375°F.) 10 minutes, then reduce heat to 350°F. and bake 25 minutes longer. Yield: 2 loaves.

AMERICAN RYE BREAD

1 cup milk
2 teaspoons molasses
1 tablespoon salt
1 cake compressed yeast

¾ cup lukewarm water
4 cups rye flour
2 cups sifted all-purpose flour
1 tablespoon melted shortening

Scald milk, add molasses and salt. Cool to lukewarm. Dissolve yeast in lukewarm water and add to lukewarm milk. Mix and sift flours. Add half the flour and beat until smooth. Add melted shortening and remaining flour, or enough to make easily handled dough. Knead dough quickly and lightly until smooth, about 5 minutes. Place dough in greased bowl. Cover and set in warm place, free from draft. Let rise until doubled in bulk, about 2½ hours. When light, divide into 2 equal portions. Shape into long loaves. Place on shallow greased pans which have been sprinkled lightly with corn meal. Cover and let rise again until light, about 70 minutes. Brush with white of egg, diluted with 1 tablespoon water, to glaze. With sharp knife, lightly cut 3 strokes diagonally across top. Bake in moderate oven (375°F.) 35 minutes, then increase heat to 425°F. and bake about 15 minutes longer. One tablespoon caraway seed may be used if desired. Yield: 2 loaves.

NOTE: By adding 1½ tablespoons white vinegar to above, an acid flavor is obtained. Dilute vinegar with ¼ cup of the water and add to dough after part of flour has been mixed in.

GLUTEN BREAD

1 cup milk	1 cup lukewarm water
1 tablespoon sugar	4 cups gluten flour
1 teaspoon salt	1 tablespoon melted shortening
1 cake compressed yeast	

Scald milk. Add sugar and salt. Cool to lukewarm. Dissolve yeast in lukewarm water and add to lukewarm milk. Add half the flour and beat until smooth. Add melted shortening and remaining flour, or enough to make easily handled dough. Knead dough quickly and lightly until smooth and elastic. Place dough in greased bowl. Cover and set in warm place, free from draft. Let rise until doubled in bulk, about 1¾ hours. When light, divide into 2 equal portions and shape into loaves. Place in greased bread pans. Cover and let rise until doubled in bulk, about 1 hour. Bake in hot oven (400°F.) 45 minutes. Yield: 2 loaves.

SWEET PUMPERNICKEL BREAD

1½ cups cold water	1 tablespoon caraway seed
¾ cup corn meal	2 cups cooled mashed potato
1½ cups boiling water	1 cake compressed yeast
1½ tablespoons salt	¼ cup lukewarm water
1 tablespoon sugar	About 6 cups rye meal or rye flour
2 tablespoons shortening	About 2 cups whole-wheat flour

Stir cold water into corn meal. Add to boiling water and cook, stirring constantly until thick. Add salt, sugar, shortening, and caraway seed. Let stand until lukewarm. Add potato and the yeast which has been softened in the lukewarm water. Add rye meal or rye flour and enough whole-wheat flour to form a soft dough. Stir in at first with a spoon and then with the hand. Turn out on a lightly floured board. Knead until it is smooth and elastic and does not stick to board. Place in greased bowl. Grease surface and let stand in a warm place (85°F.) until double in bulk. Divide the dough into 3 portions and form into balls. Let rest a few minutes. Roll 1 ball at a time, about twice the length and twice the breadth of the loaf pans. Fold in both ends so they overlap at center. Press sides to seal and then fold in the pressed sides so they overlap at center. Roll the loaf under the hands until it fits the pan. Place in greased pan with seam-side of loaf underneath. Grease surface and let rise until double in bulk. Bake in moderate oven (375°F.) about 1 hour. Yield: 3 loaves.

Sour dough pumpernickel: Before shaping loaves, take out 1 cup of dough and place it in a jar. Cover and set aside to ferment. When baking fresh batch of bread, stir down the sour dough and substitute it for yeast in above recipe.

BOBKE

1 cake compressed yeast	½ cup butter
1 cup lukewarm milk	3 eggs
¾ cup sugar	½ cup raisins
¼ teaspoon salt	
3¾ cups sifted all-purpose flour	

Sift the flour. Dissolve the yeast in a small amount of the warm milk. Add 1 teaspoon sugar, the salt, 1 cup flour, and remaining milk. Beat well. Cover and set aside to rise in a warm place (85°F.). When light, cream the butter and remaining sugar. Add the eggs and yeast mixture and beat together thoroughly.

Add remaining flour and raisins. Mix until smooth. Cover and set aside to rise until doubled in bulk, about 1 hour. Turn into 2 well-greased pans (8 inches square). Fill ⅓ full. Brush tops with melted butter and, if desired, sprinkle with *STREUSEL TOPPING.* Let rise about 1 hour. Bake in moderate oven (375°F.) 45 minutes.

SPEEDY PAN ROLLS

1 cup lukewarm water
⅓ cup melted shortening
1 tablespoon sugar
2 teaspoons salt

2 cakes compressed yeast or
  2 packages dry granular yeast
1 egg
3½ cups sifted all-purpose flour

Combine water, shortening, sugar, and salt. Add yeast and mix well. Blend in egg and add flour. Mix until dough is well blended and soft. Roll out on well-floured board and fit into greased pan (12x8 inches). Cut dough into rectangles (1x4 inches) with knife that has been dipped in melted butter. Let rise in warm place (80 to 85°F.) until double in bulk, about 30 minutes. Bake in hot oven (400°F.) 20 minutes. Yield: 2 dozen rolls.

NO-KNEAD RICH DINNER ROLLS

½ cup milk
¼ cup shortening
1 tablespoon sugar
2 teaspoons salt
½ cup water

1 cake compressed or
  1 package dry granular yeast
1 egg
3 cups sifted all-purpose flour

Scald milk. Combine with shortening, sugar, and salt. Cool to lukewarm by adding water. Add yeast. Mix well. Blend in egg, and add slowly all-purpose flour. Mix until dough is well blended and soft. Place in greased bowl, and cover. Store in refrigerator at least 2 hours, or until needed. Shape chilled dough into about 18 rolls, using desired shapes. Let rise in warm place (80 to 85°F.) until light, about 1½ hours. Bake in hot oven (425°F.) 20 minutes. Yield: about 18 rolls.

REFRIGERATOR ROLLS

2 cakes compressed or
  2 packages granular yeast
¼ cup lukewarm water
1 cup milk or other liquid
1½ teaspoons salt

¼ cup sugar
½ cup shortening
About 5 cups sifted all-purpose
  flour
3 beaten eggs

Soften yeast in lukewarm water. Scald milk. Add salt, sugar, and shortening and cool to lukewarm. Add 2 cups flour and beat well. Add yeast and beaten eggs. Blend thoroughly. Add remaining flour to make a soft dough. Turn out on lightly floured board and knead until satiny. Place in lightly greased bowl. Cover and let rise in warm place (80 to 85°F.) until doubled in bulk. Punch down. Form into smooth ball. Grease the surface lightly. Cover and put into refrigerator. It may be kept several days. When ready for use remove dough from refrigerator and punch down. Shape at once in any desired form. Or, if preferred, let dough stand in warm room for an hour before shaping. Place in greased pans and let rise until doubled in bulk. Bake in hot oven (425°F.) 15 to 20 minutes. Yield: about 2½ dozen rolls.

PLAIN ROLL DOUGH (Basic Recipe)

1 cake compressed or
    1 package granular yeast
1 cup lukewarm water
1 cup milk or other liquid
6 tablespoons sugar

2 teaspoons salt
¼ cup shortening
About 6 cups sifted all-purpose
    flour
1 egg, beaten

Soften yeast in lukewarm water. Scald milk. Add sugar, salt, and shortening. Cool to lukewarm. Add 1 cup flour. Beat well. Add softened yeast and egg. Mix well. Add enough more flour to make a soft dough. Turn out on lightly floured board and knead until satiny, about 10 minutes. Place in greased bowl. Cover and let rise until doubled in bulk. Punch down. Cover and let rest 10 minutes. Shape into rolls and put into greased pans. Let rise again until doubled. Bake in hot oven (425°F.) 15 to 20 minutes. Yield: 3½ dozen small rolls.

Whole-wheat rolls: Substitute ½ whole-wheat flour, in above recipe, for an equal quantity of white flour.

REFRIGERATOR POTATO ROLLS (Basic Recipe)

1 cup milk, scalded
1 cup hot mashed potato
½ cup shortening
¼ cup sugar
2 teaspoons salt

1 cake compressed or
    1 package granular yeast
½ cup lukewarm water
2 eggs, beaten
5 to 6 cups sifted all-purpose flour

Combine milk, potato, shortening, sugar, and salt in a large bowl. Let stand until lukewarm. Soften yeast in lukewarm water and add with eggs. Add 1½ cups flour and beat well. Cover and let stand in warm place (85°F.) until full of bubbles, about 1 hour. Stir in enough flour (3½ to 4½ cups) to make a fairly stiff dough. Knead on a lightly floured board until smooth. Return to lightly greased bowl, and grease top of dough. Cover, and chill in refrigerator. About 1½ hours before serving time, shape desired number of rolls. Place on greased pans. Let rise until doubled in bulk, about 1 hour. Bake in hot oven (425°F.) 15 to 20 minutes. Yield: about 3 dozen rolls.

NOTE: Remaining dough may be kept in refrigerator several days. Punch down before placing in refrigerator.

Butterscotch rolls: Butter muffin tins. Add 1 teaspoon butter, 1 teaspoon brown sugar, and 1 tablespoon chopped nuts. Form dough into medium-sized balls. Place 1 ball in each tin. Allow to rise until double in bulk. Bake in hot oven (425°F.) 25 minutes. Turn out while hot.

Date and walnut rolls: Prepare recipe for REFRIGERATOR POTATO ROLLS, using half white flour and half whole-wheat flour. Substitute brown sugar for white. Add 1 cup chopped, pitted dates and ½ cup chopped nuts. Shape into rolls. Allow to rise until double in bulk. Bake in hot oven (425°F.) 20 minutes. Frost with CONFECTIONERS' SUGAR ICING.

Nut and prune rolls: To the recipe for REFRIGERATOR POTATO ROLLS add ½ cup chopped nuts, 1 cup prunes, diced, and 1 teaspoon baking powder. Shape into rolls. Allow to rise until doubled in bulk. Sprinkle with cinnamon-sugar mixture. Bake in hot oven (425°F.) 20 minutes.

HOW TO SHAPE DINNER ROLLS

Bowknots: Roll dough under hand to ½ inch thickness. Cut in pieces about 6 inches long. Tie in knots. Place on greased baking sheet.

Butterflies: Roll dough into rectangular sheet ¼ inch thick and 6 inches wide. Brush with melted butter. Roll up jelly-roll fashion. Cut into pieces 2 inches long. Press across center of each piece with knife handle or small rolling pin.

Cloverleaf rolls: Form dough into small balls. Dip each into melted butter and place 3 balls in each section of a greased muffin pan.

Crescents: Roll ball of dough into circular shape about ¼ inch thick. Cut as you would a pie. Brush with melted butter, and roll up, beginning at the wide end. Curve into crescents on greased baking sheet.

Fan tans: Roll dough into very thin rectangular sheet. Brush with melted butter. Cut in strips about 1 inch wide. Pile 6 or 7 strips together. Cut pieces 1½ inches long and place on end in greased muffin pans.

Pan rolls: Form dough into small balls about 1 inch in diameter. Place ½ inch apart in greased pans.

Parker house rolls: Shape each 1-ounce portion of dough into a ball. Let rest 10 minutes. Flatten, using either small rolling pin or palm of hand. Brush half of each roll with melted margarine or butter. Fold over on ungreased half, and press down edge. Place on greased baking sheet or into greased pans.

Rosettes: Follow directions for BOWKNOTS. After tying, bring one end through center and the other over the side.

Snails: Roll dough under hand to form long pieces ½ inch in diameter. Cut into 8-inch lengths. Twist each piece by rolling ends in opposite directions. Coil to form snail. Tuck end under edge of roll to hold it in place.

ORANGE-FILLED ROLLS

Prepare recipe for *PLAIN ROLL DOUGH.* When dough is light, roll out on floured board into rectangular sheet ¼ inch thick. Spread with cooked ORANGE FILLING and roll up as for jelly roll. Cut into 1-inch pieces. Place in greased muffin pans. Cover and set in warm place, free from draft until light, about ¾ hour. Bake in moderate oven (375°F.) about 25 to 30 minutes. Yield: 2 dozen.

ORANGE FILLING

3 tablespoons cornstarch
¾ cup sugar
½ cup cold water
2 teaspoons grated lemon rind

½ cup orange juice
2 tablespoons lemon juice
2 tablespoons grated orange rind

Mix cornstarch and sugar together. Add water to make smooth paste. Add fruit juices and rind. Bring to boil, stirring constantly, and cook until thick. Cool.

BRIOCHE

2 cakes compressed yeast
1 cup milk, scalded and cooled
¾ cup butter or
    ¾ cup margarine
½ cup sugar

1 teaspoon salt
4 egg yolks
3 eggs
4½ cups sifted all-purpose flour
½ teaspoon lemon extract

Dissolve yeast in lukewarm milk. Cream butter or margarine, sugar, and salt together. Add to yeast mixture. Add remaining ingredients and beat thoroughly about 10 minutes. Cover, and let rise in warm place, free from draft, until light, about 3 hours. Stir down. Cover well and chill in refrigerator over night. Divide into small pieces. Shape into balls and place in greased muffin pans. Make an indentation in center of each and brush with melted butter or margarine. Into this hollow, press a small ball of dough. Let rise until doubled in bulk, about 1 hour. Brush over with a mixture of 6 tablespoons sugar and 2 tablespoons milk. Bake in hot oven (400°F.) about 20 minutes. Yield: 20.

Brioche coffee rolls: Follow recipe for *BRIOCHE*. After thoroughly chilling, shape dough into strips about 24 inches long. Cover and let rise in warm place, free from draft, until light, about 30 minutes. Twist each end of these strips in opposite directions and shape into a coil. Place in greased pans. Cover and let rise again until light, about 45 minutes. Bake in hot oven (400°F.) about 15 minutes. Brush with *CONFECTIONERS' SUGAR ICING* when cool. Yield: 1½ dozen rolls.

English bath buns: Shape *BRIOCHE* dough into large round buns. Place about 2 inches apart on greased baking sheet. Cover and set in warm place, free from draft. Let rise until light, about 1½ hours. Before baking, press into the tops sliced blanched almonds, chopped citron, and chopped candied orange peel. Brush with 1 tablespoon water mixed with one egg white beaten. Bake in moderate oven (350°F.) about 40 to 45 minutes. Yield: 2 dozen buns.

BAGEL

1 cup milk, scalded	1 cake compressed yeast
¼ cup butter	1 egg, separated
1½ tablespoons sugar	3¾ cups sifted all-purpose flour
½ teaspoon salt	1 teaspoon cold water

Add butter, sugar, and salt to milk. When lukewarm, add yeast, well-beaten egg white, and flour. Knead. Let rise about 1 hour. Roll out in small pieces, width of finger and twice the length, tapering at ends. Shape into rings, pinching ends together well. Let stand on floured board only until they begin to rise, about 10 minutes. Drop bagel one at a time into a pan of very hot water (just under boiling point). Cook on one side, just under the boiling point. Turn and cook the other side. They must be light, keep their shape, and not break apart. Place on a baking sheet. Beat the egg yolk with 1 teaspoon cold water to brush bagels before baking. If desired, sprinkle bagel with coarse salt or poppy seed before baking. Bake in hot oven (400°F.) until brown and crisp. Yield: about 24.

BEATEN BATTER (Basic Recipe)

1 cake compressed or	½ cup shortening
1 package dry granular yeast	About 3¼ cups sifted all-purpose
¼ cup lukewarm water	flour
1 cup milk	2 eggs
¼ cup sugar	½ teaspoon vanilla (optional)
1 teaspoon salt	

Soften yeast in lukewarm water. Scald milk and add sugar, salt, and shortening. Cool to lukewarm. Add 1 cup flour and beat well. Add softened yeast, eggs, and vanilla extract. Beat well. Add remaining flour to make a thick batter. Beat thoroughly until smooth. Cover and let rise until doubled, about 1 hour. Use with different toppings to make coffee cakes and puff rolls. Yield: 2 coffee cakes 8x8 inches or 2 9-inch cakes, or about 2½ dozen 2-inch puffs.

APPLE COFFEE CAKE

½ recipe BEATEN BATTER
3 to 4 medium apples
2 tablespoons melted butter or
   2 tablespoons melted margarine

¼ cup sugar
1 teaspoon cinnamon

When BEATEN BATTER is light, stir down. Spread evenly in greased 9-inch layer pan. Peel and slice apples. Arrange apple slices on top of batter, overlapping them in 2 circles. Brush with melted butter or melted margarine. Mix sugar and cinnamon and sprinkle over apples. Let rise until doubled, about 45 minutes. Bake in moderate oven (375°F.) 30 minutes. Yield: 1 coffee cake.

CRUMBLE COFFEE CAKE

½ recipe BEATEN BATTER
3 tablespoons milk

CRUMBLE TOPPING

When BEATEN BATTER is light, stir down. Spread evenly in greased pan (8x8 inches), or 9-inch layer pan. Brush with milk and sprinkle with CRUMBLE TOPPING. Let rise until doubled, about 45 minutes. Bake in moderate oven (375°F.) 30 minutes. Yield: 1 coffee cake.

CRUMBLE TOPPING

½ cup sifted all-purpose flour
¼ cup dry breadcrumbs
2 tablespoons sugar

½ teaspoon cinnamon
2 tablespoons butter or
   2 tablespoons margarine

Mix flour, breadcrumbs, sugar, and cinnamon. Cut in or rub in butter or margarine until crumbly.

CRANBERRY SWIRL COFFEE CAKE

½ recipe BEATEN BATTER
½ cup sweetened cranberry sauce

¼ cup sugar
¼ teaspoon cinnamon

When BEATEN BATTER is light, stir down. Spread evenly in greased 9-inch layer pan. With a floured spoon make grooves in swirl design on top of batter. Fill grooves with cranberry sauce. Mix sugar and cinnamon. Sprinkle evenly over top. Let rise until doubled, about 45 minutes. Bake in moderate oven (375°F.) 30 minutes. Yield: 1 coffee cake.

TEA PUFFS

½ recipe BEATEN BATTER
½ cup sliced almonds

¼ cup sugar
½ teaspoon cinnamon

When BEATEN BATTER is light, stir down. Drop by spoonfuls into greased muffin pans. Mix almonds, sugar, and cinnamon. Sprinkle over muffins. Let rise until doubled, about 45 minutes. Bake in moderate oven (375°F.) 25 minutes. Yield: about 16 2-inch puffs.

KUCHEN DOUGH (Basic Recipe)
For Yeast-Raised Coffee Cakes

4½ cups sifted all-purpose flour
 1 cake compressed yeast
 ½ cup lukewarm milk
 ½ cup lukewarm water
 ½ cup plus 1½ teaspoons sugar
 ½ cup butter

1 teaspoon salt
1½ tablespoons lemon juice
 (optional)
1 teaspoon grated lemon rind
2 eggs, beaten
1 teaspoon vanilla (optional)

Sift ½ cup flour into a large, warmed mixing bowl. Crumble yeast over it. Mix milk and water. Make a hollow in flour. Pour in ½ of the milk and water. Add 1½ teaspoons sugar. Stir until well blended. Cover bowl and set in a warm place for 20 minutes to rise. Cream butter until soft. Gradually add remaining sugar, blending until creamy. Add salt, lemon juice, and rind, eggs, vanilla, and remaining milk and water. Sift part of flour into butter mixture. Knead the rest in with the hands. Add yeast mixture. Knead well on floured board, about 5 minutes. Wash and grease bowl. Replace dough. Cover and let it rise in a warm place until it has doubled (3 hours). Shape as desired. Use desired filling and topping. Let stand about an hour before baking. Bake in moderate oven (350°F.) 20 to 30 minutes. Brush with melted butter from time to time, if desired. Yield: 1 large or 2 medium coffee cakes.

Rich coffee kuchen: Substitute cream for milk and water.

COFFEE RINGS OR BUTTER KUCHEN

Roll out *KUCHEN DOUGH* in 2 rectangles ⅓ inch thick. Brush with melted butter. Sprinkle with sugar and cinnamon, raisins, and chopped nuts. Roll up like a jelly roll. Lift on to greased baking sheets or pans and curve into rings. Let rise about 2 hours. If desired, sprinkle with sugar and cinnamon and spread with melted butter before baking or while still warm. Bake in moderate oven (350°F.) 20 to 30 minutes, or until brown. Ice with *CONFECTIONERS' SUGAR ICING.* Sprinkle with chopped nuts. To turn these rings into fancy tea rings, cut with a pair of scissors at about 1¼-inch intervals from the outside in but not all the way through. Spread the cut edges apart or turn cut side up. Let rise, bake, and ice and sprinkle as above.

Apple ring: Add 3 or 4 diced apples to the cinnamon and sugar, raisins and **nuts** above.

DANISH PASTRY

4 cakes compressed yeast
1 tablespoon sugar
1 cup lukewarm water
1 cup milk, scalded and cooled
7 cups sifted all-purpose flour
6 tablespoons shortening

½ cup sugar
3 eggs
½ teaspoon salt
½ teaspoon vanilla extract
½ teaspoon lemon extract
1½ cups cold butter or margarine

Dissolve yeast and 1 tablespoon sugar in lukewarm water. Add milk, then add 3 cups flour and beat until smooth. Cream shortening and sugar together thoroughly. Beat eggs until light, reserving 1 egg white. Add salt and flavoring to creamed mixture and mix well. Add to yeast-egg-flour mixture and beat well. Add remaining 4 cups flour gradually to make a moderately stiff dough. Knead lightly on floured board. Place in greased bowl. Cover and let rise ¼ in bulk. Roll out on floured board into oblong piece ½ inch thick. Divide butter into 2 portions. Distribute ½ the butter, cut into small pieces, over center third of dough. Fold 1 side over to cover butter. Place remaining pieces of butter on top, then fold other third of dough to completely cover this layer of butter. Press edges down well. Turn dough ¼ way around and roll out again to ½ inch thick. Fold ¼ of the dough at each end into center, then fold again together. Chill in refrigerator about ½ hour. Roll out to ½ inch thick, fold in fourths and chill ½ hour. Roll out again. The dough is now ready to shape. Shape as desired into crescents, pinwheels, braided rings, figure eights, etc. Place on greased pans and let rise in warm place, free from draft, until light, about ¾ hour. Brush with one egg white mixed with 1 tablespoon cold water. Bake in very hot oven (500°F.) until a light brown, about 5 minutes. Reduce heat to 400°F. and bake until done, about 10 to 25 minutes, depending upon size. Yield: 4 to 6 dozen.

SWEET DOUGH (Basic Recipe)

2 cakes yeast
¼ cup lukewarm water
1 cup milk
¼ cup butter
½ cup sugar
2 teaspoons salt

2 eggs, beaten
About 5 cups sifted all-purpose
   flour
1 teaspoon grated lemon rind
   (optional)

Soften yeast in lukewarm water. Scald milk. Add butter, sugar, and salt. Cool to lukewarm. Add flour to make a thick batter. Add yeast, eggs, and lemon rind. Beat well. Add enough flour to make a soft dough. Turn out on lightly floured board and knead until satiny. Place in greased bowl. Cover and let rise until doubled in bulk. When light, punch down. Shape into tea rings, rolls, or coffee cakes. Let rise until doubled in bulk. Bake in moderate oven (375°F.) 25 to 30 minutes for coffee cakes, 20 to 25 minutes for rolls. Yield: 2 12-inch tea rings or about 3½ dozen rolls.

BUBBLE LOAF

½ recipe SWEET DOUGH   CARAMEL GLAZE

When dough is light, punch down. Let rest 10 minutes. Divide into pieces about the size of walnuts. Shape into balls. Place 1 layer of balls, ½ inch apart, on bottom of greased loaf pan (8½x4½ inches). Arrange second layer on top of first, placing over spaces in first layer. Arrange third layer of balls. Pour CARAMEL GLAZE over all. Let rise until doubled, about 1 hour. Bake in moderate oven (350°F.) 35 to 40 minutes. Let stand in pan 5 minutes before turning out. Yield: 1 bubble loaf.

CARAMEL GLAZE

¼ cup dark corn syrup
1 tablespoon melted butter or
   1 tablespoon melted margarine

½ teaspoon lemon extract
¼ teaspoon vanilla extract

Combine all ingredients. Mix thoroughly.

HONEY TWIST

⅓ recipe *SWEET DOUGH*   *HONEY TOPPING*

When dough is light, punch down. Let rest 10 minutes. Shape into long roll about 1 inch in diameter. Coil the roll loosely into greased 9-inch layer pan or 8x8-inch pan, beginning at outer edge and continuing to center. Brush with *HONEY TOPPING*. Let rise until doubled, about 1 hour. Bake in moderate oven (350°F.) 30 minutes. Yield: 1 honey twist.

HONEY TOPPING

¼ cup softened butter or   1 egg white
   ¼ cup softened margarine   2 tablespoons honey
⅔ cup confectioners' sugar

Combine all ingredients and mix until smooth.

FROSTED SNAILS

1 recipe *SWEET DOUGH*   Chopped nuts
   CONFECTIONERS' SUGAR
   ICING

When *SWEET DOUGH* is light, punch down. Let rest 10 minutes. Roll into long rolls a scant ½ inch thick. Cut into pieces 9 inches long. Coil each piece loosely to form snail, tucking end of strip under roll. Let rise until doubled, about 45 minutes. Bake in moderate oven (350°F.) 20 minutes. When slightly cool, frost with *CONFECTIONERS' SUGAR ICING* and sprinkle with chopped nuts. Yield: about 3 dozen snails.

BOHEMIAN BRAID

Use ½ recipe for *SWEET DOUGH* and when it is light, divide into 9 portions. Roll each portion into a long roll. Braid 4 rolls loosely and place on greased baking sheet. Then braid 3 portions and place on top of first braid. Twist last 2 portions together and place on top, tucking ends under. Cover and let rise until doubled in bulk. Bake in moderate oven (350° to 375°F.) 40 to 45 minutes. Brush with *CONFECTIONERS' SUGAR ICING* and sprinkle with chopped nuts. Yield: 1 large braided loaf.

STOLLEN

Use ½ recipe for *SWEET DOUGH* or for *KUCHEN DOUGH* and when it is light add ½ cup raisins and ½ cup blanched chopped almonds and knead them in. Divide dough in 2 equal portions and round them up. Cover and let rest 10 to 15 minutes. Flatten out each ball of dough into an oval sheet. Brush ½ of each sheet with melted butter. Fold unbuttered half over buttered half, like *PARKER HOUSE ROLLS*. Place on greased baking sheets. Let rise until doubled in bulk. Bake in moderate oven (350° to 375°F.) 25 to 30 minutes. Brush with *CONFECTIONERS' SUGAR ICING* and sprinkle with chopped nuts. Yield: 2 Stollen.

BUTTERSCOTCH PECAN ROLLS

Into each muffin cup put ½ teaspoon butter and 1 teaspoon brown sugar. Sprinkle with ½ teaspoon water. Arrange 3 or 4 pecan halves in each muffin cup. Use 1 recipe for *SWEET DOUGH* and when it is light punch down and let rest 10 minutes. Roll dough out to rectangular sheet ½ inch thick and 9 inches wide. Brush lightly with melted butter and sprinkle generously with brown sugar. Roll jelly-roll fashion, sealing edges. Cut into 1-inch slices. Place slices, cut side down, into prepared muffin pans. Cover and let rise until doubled in bulk. Bake in moderate oven (375°F.) 20 to 25 minutes. Let rolls stand in pans 1 minute before turning them out. Yield: about 3½ dozen rolls.

CINNAMON ROLLS

Use ½ recipe for *SWEET DOUGH* and when it is light roll out to long narrow sheet ¼ inch thick. Brush with ¼ cup melted butter. Mix 1 cup sugar and 1½ teaspoons cinnamon, and sprinkle over dough. If desired, ½ cup raisins may be added. Roll up jelly-roll fashion and seal edge. Cut into 1-inch slices and place cut side down into well-greased muffin pans, ring mold, or deep cake pan. Brush tops with milk, and sprinkle with cinnamon and sugar mixture. Let rise until doubled in bulk. Bake in moderate oven (375°F.) 25 minutes. Yield: 3½ dozen rolls.

SWEDISH TEA RING

Use ½ recipe for *SWEET DOUGH* and when it is light roll into a rectangular sheet about ½ inch thick. Brush with melted butter and cinnamon. Nuts or raisins may be added. Roll jelly-roll fashion and shape into a ring on a greased baking sheet. Cut with a scissors at 1-inch intervals, almost through the ring. Turn each slice slightly on its side. Cover and let rise until doubled. Bake in moderate oven (375°F.) 25 to 30 minutes. Frost while warm with *CONFECTIONERS' SUGAR ICING*. Sprinkle thickly with chopped nuts. Yield: 1 tea ring.

KUGELHOPF OR BUNDKUCHEN (High Coffee Cake)

3 cakes yeast	5 eggs
1 cup lukewarm milk or	1 teaspoon salt
1 cup lukewarm cream	½ teaspoon grated lemon rind
4 cups sifted all-purpose flour	1 cup seedless raisins
1 cup sweet butter	⅓ cup blanched almonds, slivered
¾ cup sugar	Confectioners' sugar

Dissolve yeast in warm milk or cream. Sift in 1 cup flour and blend well. Set in warm place. Let rise about 1½ hours. Cream butter until it is soft and fluffy. Sift in sugar and beat until light and creamy. Add eggs, one at a time, beating after each addition. Beat in yeast mixture. Sift in remaining flour and salt, and mix well. Add lemon rind, raisins, and ½ of almonds. Mix batter well, or knead until it is smooth and elastic. Grease a 9-inch tube pan and sprinkle in remaining almonds. Over this place the dough. Cover and set aside to rise for 1½ hours, or until it is very light and high. Bake in moderate oven (350°F.) about 1 hour. When cool, dust top with confectioners' sugar. Yield: 1 large cake.

COFFEE CAKE WREATH

Use recipe for *KUGELHOPF*. When dough has risen, cut it in half and roll each half into 3 long strips. Braid them and shape into wreaths. Place on greased baking sheets or into greased tube pans. Let rise ½ hour. Brush with melted butter. Bake in moderate oven (350°F.) 20 to 30 minutes. Cool. Frost with confectioners' icing, if desired.

Filled coffee cake wreath: Follow recipe for *KUGELHOPF*. Roll out dough on a greased surface to a thickness of ⅓ inch. Spread evenly with desired filling. Roll up like a jelly roll. Brush with butter. Bake as directed.

KOLACKY

1 cup milk, scalded
⅓ cup shortening
⅓ cup sugar
1 teaspoon salt
Grated rind of 1 lemon

1 cake compressed or
    1 package dry granular yeast
2 beaten eggs
3 cups sifted all-purpose flour

Combine milk, shortening, sugar, salt, and lemon rind. Cool to lukewarm. Soften yeast in this mixture. Add eggs and flour. Beat well. Cover with damp cloth. Let rise in warm place (80 to 85°F.) until double, about 2 hours. Beat and let rise again until almost double, about 45 minutes. Turn onto lightly floured board. Knead slightly. Cover and let rest 10 minutes. Roll to ½ inch thickness. Cut into 3-inch rounds. Place on greased baking sheet. Cover, and let rise until almost double. Make deep depression in the center of rounds. Fill centers, and bake in hot oven (400° F.) 15 minutes.

KOLACKY FILLINGS

Apple filling: Core, pare, and cut 4 to 5 large apples into small pieces. Add enough water to prevent burning. Cook gently until soft. Mash and season to taste with cinnamon, sugar, and melted butter. Chill.

Cheese filling: Mix ⅔ cup dry cottage cheese, 1 egg, 1 tablespoon sugar, 1 tablespoon butter, and nutmeg and salt to taste. Beat smooth.

Poppy seed filling: Boil ¼ cup ground poppy seed and ¼ cup milk until thick. Add 1 teaspoon cinnamon, 1 tablespoon sugar, and 1 tablespoon butter. Chill.

Prune filling: Stew ½ pound prunes until soft, remove pits, and chop fine. Add 1 tablespoon melted butter, ¼ teaspoon cinnamon, and sugar to taste. Chill.

VIENNESE COFFEE RING

2 cakes yeast
¼ cup lukewarm water
1 cup milk
½ cup sugar
1 teaspoon salt

¼ cup shortening
1 egg, beaten
About 3¼ cups sifted all-purpose
    flour

Soften yeast in lukewarm water. Scald milk. Add sugar, salt, and shortening. Cool to lukewarm. Add egg, 1 cup flour, and yeast. Beat thoroughly. Add remaining flour to make a stiff batter. Beat 3 minutes. Pour into greased spring-form pan.

Sprinkle with topping described below. Let rise until doubled in bulk. Bake in moderate oven (375°F.) 35 to 40 minutes. Yield: 1 coffee ring.

Topping: Mix ⅓ cup sugar, ¼ teaspoon cinnamon, and ¼ cup chopped nuts.

ICE BOX SCHNECKEN

1 cake yeast
¼ cup lukewarm milk
½ cup melted butter
2 tablespoons sugar
½ cup thick sour cream
2 eggs
¼ teaspoon salt

2 cups sifted all-purpose flour
Butter
4 tablespoons brown sugar
1 teaspoon cinamon
⅔ cup chopped nuts
⅔ cup chopped raisins

Soften yeast in lukewarm milk. Add melted butter, sugar, sour cream, eggs, salt, and flour. Mix thoroughly, and set in refrigerator overnight. Divide dough into 2 parts. Roll out on a lightly floured board very thin (about ¼ inch). Dot well with butter. Sprinkle with brown sugar, cinnamon, nuts, and raisins. Roll up as for jelly roll. Cut into ½-inch slices. Place in a greased pan cut side down. Let rise in a warm place until doubled in bulk, about 2 hours. Bake in moderate oven (350°F.) about 45 minutes, or until light brown. Cool. Schnecken should be stored in a tight container to prevent drying out. If they are more than a day old, sprinkle lightly with water, cover, and reheat in a moderate oven. Yield: about 24.

NO-KNEAD SWEET ROLLS

½ cup milk
3 tablespoons shortening
3 tablespoons sugar
2 teaspoons salt
½ cup water
1 cake compressed yeast or
   1 package dry granular yeast

1 egg
3 cups sifted all-purpose flour
Mixture of:
   2 tablespoons melted butter
   ¼ cup sugar
   1 teaspoon cinnamon

Scald milk, and combine with shortening, sugar, and salt. Cool to lukewarm with ½ cup water. Add yeast and mix well. Blend in egg. Add flour gradually. Mix until dough is well blended and soft. Roll out dough on well-floured board to form rectangle (18x12 inches). Spread with mixture listed above. Prepared prune, apricot, or date-nut fillings may be used. Roll as for jelly roll and cut into 1-inch slices. Place slices, cut side down, in greased pan (12x8x2 inches) or greased muffin pans. Let rise until light, about 1 hour. Bake in moderate oven (375°F.) 25 to 30 minutes. Yield: 18 medium rolls.

ROHLIKY

3½ cups sifted all-purpose flour
1 teaspoon salt
2 tablespoons sugar
1½ cups less 1 tablespoon milk
¼ cup melted shortening

1 package compressed yeast or
   1 package dry granular yeast
¼ cup lukewarm water
Caraway seed

Scald milk, then cool to lukewarm. Sift together flour and salt into a mixing bowl. Make a depression in flour and put into it sugar and milk. Add shortening. Add yeast dissolved in ¼ cup lukewarm water. Mix all together well, cover, and let rise until double in bulk. Remove dough from bowl to slightly floured board. Knead lightly. Let stand 15 minutes to "come back." Then roll into large circular piece ¼ inch thick. Cut into long, narrow pie-shaped wedges. Roll up each piece beginning at wide end of triangle. Curve ends to give crescent shape. Moisten tops slightly with water, and sprinkle with salt and caraway seed. Let rise until light. Bake in hot oven (400°F.) 15 to 20 minutes.

VIENNA ROLLS

1 cake compressed yeast or
   1 package dry granular yeast
1 cup lukewarm water
1 tablespoon sugar
1 teaspoon salt

2 tablespoons melted shortening
About 4 cups sifted all-purpose
   flour
2 egg whites, beaten

Soften yeast in ¼ cup water. To the remaining water add sugar, salt, and shortening. Add 1 cup flour, beating well. Add yeast and egg whites. Mix thoroughly. Add enough more flour to make a soft dough. Knead until smooth and satiny, 5 to 8 minutes. Shape into smooth ball and put into greased bowl. Grease surface lightly. Cover and let rise until doubled, about 1½ hours. Punch down. Let rise again until doubled, about 45 minutes. Knead down and divide into small portions for rolls. Let rest 10 minutes. Shape into buns or Vienna rolls. Place 2½ inches apart on greased baking sheet. Cover and let rise until doubled, about 45 minutes. Before baking, place large flat pan filled with boiling water on bottom of oven to give crustiness. Bake in hot oven (450°F.) 20 minutes. Yield: 2 dozen large rolls.

FRENCH COFFEE CAKE

4 cups sifted all-purpose flour
1¼ cups sugar
1 teaspoon salt
½ pound butter
1 cup warm milk
3 eggs, separated

1 cake compressed yeast or
   1 package dry granular yeast
¼ cup warm water
2 teaspoons cinnamon
1 cup chopped nuts

Sift together flour, ¼ cup sugar, and salt. Cut in butter until size of small peas. Add milk and well-beaten egg yolks, stirring until a soft dough is formed. Add yeast, dissolved in warm water for 10 minutes. Beat, and let stand in cool place overnight. Divide dough into 2 parts. Roll each half into a rectangle on a floured board to ¼ inch thickness. Spread stiffly beaten egg whites over dough. Sprinkle with a mixture of cinnamon, 1 cup sugar and nuts. Roll as for jelly roll. Place in a greased pan in warm place, and let rise until loaves double in bulk. Bake in moderate oven (350°F.) 45 minutes. Frost while warm with *CONFECTIONERS' SUGAR ICING.* Yield: 2 loaves.

HASTY CARAMEL COFFEE CAKE

½ cup scalded milk
5 tablespoons shortening
1 tablespoon sugar
2 teaspoons salt
½ cup water

1 cake compressed yeast or
   1 package dry granular yeast
1 egg
3 cups sifted all-purpose flour
½ cup brown sugar
¼ cup chopped nuts

Combine milk, 3 tablespoons shortening, sugar, and salt. Cool to lukewarm with ½ cup water. Add yeast, and mix well. Blend in egg, and add gradually 3 cups flour. Mix until dough is well blended and soft. Spread in greased 10-inch skillet or 9-inch square pan. Blend together brown sugar, chopped nuts, and 2 tablespoons shortening. Sprinkle over top of dough. Let rise in warm place (80 to 85°F.) until light, about 45 minutes. Bake in moderate oven (375°F.) 25 to 30 minutes.

FRENCH BREAKFAST RING

⅓ recipe for SWEET DOUGH
2 tablespoons melted butter or
  2 tablespoons melted margarine
½ cup brown sugar

1 teaspoon cinnamon
CONFECTIONERS' SUGAR ICING
¼ cup chopped nuts

When dough is light, punch down, and let rest 10 minutes. Pat or roll into a rectangular sheet about ½ inch thick and 8 inches wide. Brush with butter or margarine. Sprinkle with brown sugar and cinnamon. Roll up like jelly roll, sealing edge. Form into ring on greased baking sheet. With scissors cut through ring almost to center, in slices about 1 inch thick. Turn each slice slightly, lifting every other one to center of the ring. Brush lightly with melted butter or margarine. Let rise until doubled, about 1 hour. Bake in moderate oven (350°F.) 25 to 30 minutes. When cool, frost with CONFECTIONERS' SUGAR ICING and sprinkle with chopped nuts. Yield: 1 breakfast ring.

SOUR CREAM KOLATCHEN

1 cake compressed yeast or
  1 package granular yeast
3 tablespoons sugar
2 tablespoons lukewarm milk
⅓ cup shortening
5 egg yolks, well-beaten
  Grated rind of 1 lemon

1 cup thick sour cream
3 cups sifted all-purpose flour
½ teaspoon salt
1 teaspoon baking soda
  Raisins or cherries
1 egg white, well beaten

Soften yeast and 1 tablespoon sugar in lukewarm milk. Cream shortening and 2 tablespoons sugar. Add egg yolks, lemon rind, sour cream, and yeast mixture. Mix well. Add flour sifted with salt and soda and beat thoroughly. Drop from teaspoon on well-greased pans or fill greased muffin tins half full. Place a raisin or cherry on top of each cake. Brush with beaten egg white. Sprinkle with sugar and let rise in a warm place until light, about 2 hours. Bake in moderate oven (375°F.) 25 minutes. Yield: about 36.

STREUSEL (Crumb) COFFEE CAKE

1½ cakes compressed yeast
½ cup and 1 tablespoon sugar
1 cup milk, scalded and cooled
4½ cups sifted all-purpose flour

¼ cup melted butter or
  ¼ cup margarine
¼ teaspoon salt
2 eggs, beaten

Dissolve yeast and 1 tablespoon sugar in lukewarm milk. Add 1½ cups flour. Beat until smooth. Cover and let rise in warm place, free from draft, until light, about ¾ hour. Cream butter or margarine and add sugar and salt. Add to yeast mixture. Add well-beaten eggs and remaining flour. Knead lightly. Place in well-greased bowl, cover and let rise in warm place until light, about 2 hours. Roll ½ inch thick and place in 2 well-greased shallow pans (8½x11½x2 inches). Let rise again until light, about 1½ hours. Prick tops with fork. Brush with butter or melted margarine, and sprinkle with *STREUSEL*, or *CINNAMON*, topping. Let rise in warm place about ½ hour. Bake in hot oven (400°F.) 20 minutes. Yield: 2 cakes.

STREUSEL TOPPING

⅓ cup butter or
   ⅓ cup margarine
⅓ cup sugar
½ cup sifted all-purpose flour

1 cup dry cake or
   1 cup breadcrumbs, ground
1 teaspoon cinnamon

Cream butter or margarine. Add sugar gradually, mixing well. Add remaining ingredients and stir until well mixed and crumbly.

CINNAMON TOPPING

6 tablespoons butter or
   6 tablespoons margarine
¾ cup sugar

6 tablespoons sifted all-purpose flour
1½ teaspoons cinnamon
⅛ teaspoon salt

Cream butter or margarine, add sugar gradually, mixing well. Add remaining ingredients and stir until well mixed and crumbly.

HONEY COFFEE CAKE

Use recipe for *STREUSEL (CRUMB) COFFEE CAKE*. Spread *HONEY NUT TOPPING* on cakes before baking, instead of *STREUSEL TOPPING*.

HONEY NUT TOPPING

4 tablespoons butter or
   4 tablespoons margarine
4 tablespoons sugar

4 tablespoons sifted all-purpose flour
4 tablespoons honey
½ cup chopped nuts

Cream butter or margarine. Add sugar, mixing well. Add flour and honey and beat until well mixed. Add nuts.

QUICK SUGAR-CRUNCH COFFEE CAKE

½ package compressed or
   dry granular yeast
¼ cup lukewarm water
1 teaspoon sugar
½ cup vegetable shortening
½ cup sugar

1 egg
2 cups sifted all-purpose flour
2½ teaspoons double acting baking
   powder
½ teaspoon salt
¼ cup milk

Crumble and sprinkle yeast in lukewarm water in small bowl; add 1 teaspoon sugar and mix well. Let stand until yeast is thoroughly dissolved, 5 to 15 minutes. Combine shortening, ½ cup sugar and unbeaten egg; beat until smooth. Mix and sift flour, baking powder, and salt; add half to shortening mixture and beat well. Add yeast mixture, then milk, then remaining flour mixture, beating after each addition until smooth. Spread half of batter in greased, deep 9-inch round layer pan. Sprinkle half of *SUGAR-NUT FILLING* over top of batter. Cover with rest of batter. Sprinkle with remaining filling. Bake in moderate oven (350°F.) 40 to 50 minutes. Serve warm or cold.

Sugar-nut filling: Mix 1 cup firmly packed brown sugar, 3 tablespoons sifted flour, and 1 teaspoon cinnamon. Cut in 3 tablespoons butter or margarine. Add 1 cup chopped nuts and mix.

BABA AU RHUM

1 cake compressed yeast	½ cup butter or
½ cup scalded milk	½ cup margarine
2 cups sifted all-purpose flour	½ teaspoon salt
½ cup sugar	1 tablespoon grated lemon rind
	3 eggs, well beaten

Dissolve yeast in milk, which has been cooled to lukewarm. Add ½ cup flour and 1 tablespoon sugar. Beat until smooth. Cover and let rise in warm place (80° to 85°F.) until doubled in bulk, about 1 hour. Cream butter or margarine. Add remaining sugar gradually. Cream until light and fluffy. Add salt, lemon rind, and eggs and beat until smooth. Stir in the remaining flour. Add the yeast mixture. Beat 15 minutes by hand or 5 minutes by electric mixer. Pour in greased casserole dish or mold of 1½ to 2 quart capacity. Cover and let rise until doubled in bulk, about 1 hour. Bake in moderate oven (350°F.) 40 to 50 minutes. Remove from oven. Prick top with tines of sharp fork. Turn out of pan and place cake (inverted) in pie plate. Pour *BABA SAUCE* over top and sides, then brush with *APRICOT GLAZE*. Allow cake to stand until most of *BABA SAUCE* is absorbed before serving. Makes one 9-inch cake.

Apricot glaze: Soak ¼ pound apricots overnight in just enough water to cover. Press through sieve. Measure equal parts pulp and sugar. Boil together 5 minutes, stirring constantly.

Baba sauce: Boil 1 cup sugar and 1 cup strong clear tea 5 minutes. Cool. Add 2 teaspoons rum extract.

OLD-FASHIONED SPICY DOUGHNUTS

1¼ cups milk	1½ teaspoons cinnamon
¼ cup shortening	¼ teaspoon nutmeg
½ teaspoon salt	⅛ teaspoon mace
1 cake compressed yeast	¾ cup sugar
About 5 cups sifted all-purpose	3 eggs
flour	

Scald milk. Add shortening and salt and cool to lukewarm. Add crumbled yeast and 2½ cups flour. Beat until smooth. Cover and let rise until bubbly. Mix spices with sugar and add to sponge with beaten eggs. Mix well. Add remaining flour to make a dough that can be kneaded. Knead until smooth. Cover and let rise until doubled in bulk. Roll out ½ inch thick and cut with floured doughnut cutter. Let rise on board until doubled in bulk. Fry in deep fat (375°F.) 3 minutes, or until lightly browned, first on one side and then on the other. Drain on unglazed paper. Yield: about 3 dozen doughnuts.

POLISH DOUGHNUTS

1 cake compressed or
    1 package dry granular yeast
¼ cup lukewarm water
    About 7 cups sifted all purpose flour
1¾ cups lukewarm, scalded milk
  4 egg yolks
  1 whole egg

½ cup granulated sugar
½ teaspoon vanilla
Grated rind of ½ orange or
    grated rind of ½ lemon
¼ cup melted butter
1 teaspoon salt

Dissolve yeast in lukewarm water. When dissolved, add 2 cups flour and the luke-warm milk. Let stand in warm place about 30 minutes. Beat eggs, sugar, vanilla, grated rind, and salt until light. Add to the yeast-flour mixture. Add melted butter and 5 cups flour and mix into sponge mixture. Cover and allow to rise in warm place until double in bulk, about 1 hour. When light, turn onto floured board and pat with hands until dough is ½ inch thick. Cut with doughnut cutter. Cover and let rise on board until light. Fry in deep fat (370°F.) until golden brown. Yield: about 4½ dozen.

RAISED DOUGHNUTS (Basic Recipe)

1¼ cups scalded milk
  1 cake compressed yeast
¾ cup sugar
4½ cups sifted all-purpose flour

3 tablespoons butter
1 egg, well beaten
1½ teaspoons nutmeg
1 teaspoon salt

Cool milk to lukewarm. Add crumbled yeast and 1 tablespoon sugar. Stir until dissolved. Add 1½ cups of flour and beat well. Cover and let rise in a warm place about 1 hour. Cream butter until fluffy. Add sugar, and cream together until light. Add egg, nutmeg, and salt, and stir into yeast mixture. Add remaining 3 cups flour, knead lightly, and place in a greased bowl. Brush with salad oil, cover with towel, and let rise until double in bulk, about 1½ hours. Roll on a floured board to ½ inch thickness. Cut with floured doughnut cutter. Let rise until double in bulk, about 1 hour. Fry in deep hot fat (370°F.) until brown, turning once. Drain on absorbent paper. Yield: about 2½ dozen.

Bismarcks: Roll dough ½ inch thick. Cut rounds with a 3-inch cookie cutter. Fry as for raised doughnuts. When cool, cut a short slit in side of each to the center. Put a teaspoon of jelly in center. Close tightly. Roll in sugar.

Crullers: 1. Roll dough ½ inch thick. Cut into strips ¾ inches long. Shape into twists or figure 8's. Fry as for raised doughnuts. 2. Roll dough ¼ inch thick. Cut into 2-inch squares. Make four slits in each. Then lift by picking up alternate strips between fingers and thumb. Fry same way.

BOHEMIAN SISKY

1 cake compressed or
    1 package dry granular yeast
¼ cup lukewarm water
    About 4½ cups sifted all-purpose
    flour
1 tall can evaporated milk

1 teaspoon salt
3 tablespoons sugar
4 tablespoons softened butter
3 egg yolks
1 teaspoon vanilla

Dissolve yeast in lukewarm water. Add 2 cups flour to milk that has been scalded and cooled to lukewarm. Add salt, sugar, and butter. Mix in dissolved yeast, and stir well. Cover and allow to stand in warm place until light and spongy, about 1 hour. Add egg yolks, vanilla, and remainder of flour, mixing until thoroughly blended. Cover and let rise in warm place until doubled in bulk, about 2 hours. Roll out to ½ inch thickness on lightly floured board. Cut with doughnut cutter and let rise on board about 30 minutes. Fry in deep fat (370°F.) with raised side down first. Turn and fry until golden brown. Drain on absorbent paper. Sprinkle with sugar. Yield: about 4½ dozen.

SPICY ORANGE DOUGHNUTS (No-Dissolve Yeast Method)

3¾ to 4¾ cups unsifted all-purpose
   flour
1½ cups sugar
 1 teaspoon salt
 1 tablespoon grated orange peel
 2 packages active dry yeast
 1 cup potato water

¼ cup (½ stick) margarine
½ cup mashed potatoes (at room
   temperature)
 1 egg (at room temperature)
  Peanut oil
 2 teaspoons ground cinnamon

In a large bowl thoroughly mix 1½ cups flour, ½ cup sugar, salt, orange peel, and undissolved active dry yeast. Combine potato water and margarine in a saucepan. Heat over low heat until liquid is warm. (Margarine does not need to melt.) Gradually add to dry ingredients and beat 2 minutes at medium speed of electric mixer, scraping bowl occasionally. Add potatoes, egg, and ½ cup flour, or enough flour to make a thick batter. Beat at high speed 2 minutes, scraping bowl occasionally. Stir in enough additional flour to make a soft dough. Turn out onto lightly floured board; knead until smooth and elastic, about 8 to 10 minutes. Place in greased bowl, turning to grease top. Cover; let rise in warm place, free from draft, until doubled in bulk, about 1 hour. Punch dough down; turn out onto lightly floured board. Roll dough out to ½-inch thickness and cut with 3-inch doughnut cutter. Place doughnuts on greased baking sheets. Cover; let rise in warm place, free from draft, until doubled in bulk, about 30 minutes. Fry in deep hot (375°F.) peanut oil until golden brown on both sides. Drain on paper towels. Combine remaining 1 cup sugar and cinnamon. Dip doughnuts in cinnamon-sugar mixtures. Makes about 2 dozen doughnuts.

quick breads

Breads which are leavened with baking powder, baking soda, steam, or air rather than with yeast, are called "quick" breads. They include biscuits, muffins, coffee cakes, shallow loaves (such as corn breads), deep loaves (such as nut breads), spoon breads, popovers, griddle cakes, and waffles. Most quick breads are easily made in a relatively short time. Specific directions are given in the recipes for each type.

BANANA TEA BREAD (Basic Recipe)

1¾ cups sifted all-purpose flour
2 teaspoons baking powder
¼ teaspoon baking soda
½ teaspoon salt

⅓ cup shortening
⅔ cup sugar
2 eggs, well beaten
1 cup mashed ripe bananas

Mix and sift flour, baking powder, baking soda, and salt. Cream shortening well. Add sugar gradually and continue beating until light and fluffy. Add eggs, mixing well. Add flour mixture alternately with bananas, a little at a time, mixing after each addition until smooth. Turn into a well-greased bread pan (8½x4½x3 inches). Bake in moderate oven (350°F.) 1 hour, or until bread is done. Yield: 1 loaf.

Banana apricot bread: Add 1 cup chopped dried apricots to flour mixture. Before adding, soak apricots in warm water until soft. Drain, dry well, and chop.

Banana nut bread: Add ½ cup coarsely chopped nuts to flour mixture.

Banana prune bread: Add 1 cup chopped, pitted prunes to flour mixture. Before adding, soak prunes in warm water until soft. Drain, dry well, and chop.

Banana raisin bread: Add 1 cup seedless raisins to flour mixture.

NUT BREAD (Basic Recipe)

2 cups sifted all-purpose flour
3 teaspoons baking powder
¼ cup sugar
½ teaspoon salt

1 cup chopped nuts
1 egg, well beaten
1 cup milk

Sift dry ingredients together. Stir in nuts. Combine egg and milk. Pour milk mixture into dry ingredients and stir quickly to mix. Turn into greased loaf pan (8½x4½ inches). Bake in moderate oven (350°F.) 45 minutes. Yield: 1 loaf.

Candied orange peel bread: Substitute 1 cup chopped candied orange peel for nuts.

Date nut bread: Substitute brown sugar for white, and ½ cup chopped dates for ½ cup nuts.

Fruit nut bread: Substitute 1 cup chopped dried apricots, raisins, or currants for ½ cup nuts.

Orange nut bread: Substitute ½ cup orange marmalade for sugar. Use only ½ cup milk. Add 1 tablespoon grated orange rind.

Whole-wheat bread: Substitute 1 cup whole-wheat or graham flour for 1 cup white flour and ¼ cup firmly packed brown sugar for granulated sugar.

WHOLE-WHEAT NUT BREAD (Basic Recipe)

1½ cups sifted all-purpose flour
5 teaspoons baking powder
1 teaspoon salt
¾ cup sugar
1½ cups whole-wheat flour
1 cup chopped nuts
1 egg
1¼ cups milk
6 tablespoons melted shortening

Sift white flour, baking powder, salt, and sugar together. Add whole-wheat flour and nuts and mix well. Beat egg slightly. Add milk and melted shortening. Combine with dry ingredients, stirring only enough to blend. Place in a well-greased loaf pan. Bake until golden brown in moderate oven (350°F.) for 50 to 60 minutes. Remove from pan. Cool before slicing. Yield: 1 large or 2 small loaves.

Fruit bread: Substitute 1 cup chopped dates, raisins, prunes, or figs for nuts.

Honey nut bread: Use honey instead of sugar.

Orange nut bread: Substitute ½ cup chopped candied orange peel for ½ cup chopped nuts.

ORANGE BREAD

2 large oranges
½ cup sugar
⅓ cup boiling water
1 egg, well beaten
1 cup milk
3 cups sifted all-purpose flour
4 teaspoons baking powder
½ teaspoon salt

Peel oranges. Cut rind in narrow strips. Cover rind with hot water and boil until tender. Drain. Add sugar and ⅓ cup boiling water, and boil orange peel for 20 minutes, stirring constantly. Remove from fire and continue stirring until cool. Add egg and milk. Sift flour. Measure and sift with baking powder and salt. Add to orange mixture. Mix thoroughly. Pour into well-greased loaf pan and let stand 20 minutes. Bake in hot oven (425°F.) about 1 hour. Cool before slicing. Yield: 1 loaf.

BRAN BREAD

3 cups sifted all-purpose flour
1 teaspoon salt
¼ cup sugar
4 teaspoons baking powder
1 cup bran
2 eggs
1 cup milk
¼ cup melted shortening

Sift flour, salt, sugar, and baking powder together and add bran. Beat eggs. Stir in milk and melted shortening. Pour liquid into dry ingredients all at once and stir only until dry ingredients are mixed. If desired, add ½ cup chopped raisins. Pour into a well-greased bread pan. Bake in moderate oven (375°F.) 50 to 60 minutes. Will keep well if wrapped in wax paper when cool. Yield: 1 loaf.

OATMEAL BREAD

2 cups sifted all-purpose flour
1 teaspoon salt
⅓ cup sugar
1 teaspoon baking powder
1 teaspoon baking soda
2 cups ground quick-cooking
    rolled oats

½ cup molasses
2 tablespoons melted shortening
2 cups sour milk or
    1⅔ cups sweet milk with
    4 tablespoons vinegar added
1 cup raisins

Sift flour, salt, baking powder, baking soda, and sugar together. Grind quick-cooking oats, or crush with a rolling pin. Add to other dry ingredients. Add molasses, shortening, and milk. Mix thoroughly and add raisins. Pour into greased loaf pan. Let set 20 minutes, then bake 1 hour in moderate oven (350°F.). Yield: 1 loaf.

BRAN RAISIN BREAD

1 egg
1 cup sugar
¼ cup molasses
1 cup sour milk
2 tablespoons melted shortening
1 cup prepared bran

2 cups sifted all-purpose flour
3 teaspoons baking powder
1 teaspoon salt
½ teaspoon baking soda
½ cup raisins

Beat egg slightly. Add sugar, molasses, milk, shortening, and bran. Sift flour, baking soda, salt, and baking powder. Mix raisins with flour, and add to the first mixture. Beat well. Bake in a well-greased loaf tin in moderate oven (350°F.) for 1¼ hours. Cool before slicing. Yield: 1 large loaf.

BANANA BRAN NUT BREAD

¼ cup shortening
½ cup sugar
1 egg, well beaten
1 cup prepared bran
1½ cups sifted all-purpose flour
2 teaspoons baking powder

½ teaspoon salt
½ teaspoon baking soda
½ cup chopped nut meats
1½ cups mashed bananas
2 tablespoons water
1 teaspoon vanilla

Cream shortening and sugar together well. Add egg and bran. Sift flour with baking powder, salt, and baking soda. Mix nuts with flour, and add alternately with mashed bananas to which the water has been added. Stir in vanilla. Pour into greased loaf tin. Let stand 30 minutes, then bake in moderate oven (375°F.) 1 hour. Cool before slicing. Yield: 1 loaf.

ARKANSAS DATE BREAD

1 cup sifted all-purpose flour
½ teaspoon salt
1 teaspoon baking soda
1 cup whole wheat flour
1 cup prepared bran

1 cup dates
½ cup molasses
1¼ cups sour milk
1½ tablespoons melted fat
1 egg, slightly beaten

Sift white flour once. Measure and sift again with salt and baking soda. Add whole wheat flour and bran. Cut dates in small pieces and mix through dry ingredients, with the finger tips. Add the molasses, sour milk, and fat to the egg, and stir this mixture into dry ingredients. Pour into a well-greased loaf pan. Bake in moderate oven (350°F.) for 1½ hours. Cool before slicing. Yield: 1 loaf.

BRAZIL NUT BREAD

3 cups whole-wheat flour
1½ cups all-purpose flour
5 teaspoons baking powder
2 teaspoons baking soda
1½ teaspoons salt
1½ cups brown sugar
1½ cups sliced Brazil nuts
3 cups sour milk or
3 cups buttermilk

Mix dry ingredients together. Add Brazil nuts and mix well. Add milk and stir well. Pour into 2 greased loaf pans. Bake about 1 hour in slow oven (325°F.). Yield: 2 loaves.

SALLY LUNN

2 cups sifted all-purpose flour
3 teaspoons baking powder
½ teaspoon salt
3 tablespoons sugar
2 eggs, separated
½ cup milk
½ cup melted shortening

Mix and sift flour, baking powder, salt, and sugar. Combine beaten egg yolks and milk. Add to flour mixture, stirring only enough to moisten the dry ingredients. Add the shortening. Fold in stiffly beaten egg whites. Turn into a greased square pan (8x8x2 inches). Bake in moderate oven (350°F.) about 30 minutes. Cut into squares. Serve hot.

STEAMED BROWN BREAD

1 cup sifted all-purpose flour
1 teaspoon baking powder
1½ teaspoons baking soda
1 teaspoon salt
1 cup whole-wheat flour
1 cup yellow corn meal
1½ cups seedless raisins
2 cups buttermilk or sour milk
¾ cup baking molasses

Sift white flour with baking powder, baking soda, and salt. Add whole-wheat flour, corn meal, and raisins. Combine buttermilk or sour milk and molasses. Add dry ingredients and mix thoroughly. Fill 3 No. 2 cans ⅔ full. The cans should be well greased. Cover with waxed paper and tie firmly with string. Steam in deep-well cooker or large kettle containing 2 cups hot water. Turn to high until boiling, then down to low. Total steaming time: 3½ hours.

Fruit brown bread: Add 1½ cups chopped uncooked prunes or dates to batter in place of raisins.

BOSTON BROWN BREAD

⅓ cup sifted all-purpose flour
½ teaspoon salt
¾ teaspoon baking powder
½ teaspoon baking soda
⅓ cup whole-wheat flour
⅓ cup corn meal
⅓ cup seedless raisins
½ cup milk
¼ cup molasses

Mix and sift flour, salt, baking powder, and baking soda. Add whole-wheat flour, corn meal, and raisins. Add milk and molasses. Stir until batter is well mixed. The mixture will seem thin. Fill greased molds not more than ⅔ full. Two 1-pound baking powder cans or 1 1-pound coffee can will hold this recipe. Cover tightly. Place molds on rack in deep kettle. Pour boiling water into kettle until it reaches half the height of molds. Cover and steam on top of stove for 2 hours if small molds are used, 3 hours if a large mold, keeping water boiling the entire period. Remove molds from water. Take off lids and dry molds in slow oven (300°F.) 15 minutes.

CORN BREAD

1 cup sifted all-purpose flour	½ cup yellow corn meal
3 teaspoons baking powder	1 cup milk
½ teaspoon salt	1 egg, well beaten
½ cup sugar	1 tablespoon melted shortening

Mix and sift flour, baking powder, salt, and sugar. Stir in corn meal. Add milk to beaten egg and stir into first mixture. Add shortening and blend. Turn into shallow, greased 8-inch pan. Bake in hot oven (400°F.) about 20 minutes. Cut into 6 squares. Serve hot.

SOUTHERN SPOON BREAD

2½ cups scalded milk	1½ tablespoons melted butter
1 cup sifted white corn meal	4 eggs, separated
1 teaspoon salt	1 teaspoon baking powder

Add scalded milk to corn meal, stirring until smooth. Add salt. Cook over hot water, stirring constantly, until thick. Stir in melted butter. Cool slightly. Beat egg yolks and add to cooled corn meal mixture. Add baking powder and mix well. Fold in stiffly beaten egg whites. Turn into hot, buttered casserole. Bake in moderate oven (375°F.) until firm and brown on top. Serve from casserole. Serves 8 to 10.

JOHNNY CAKE

2 cups yellow corn meal	2 tablespoons sugar
½ cup sifted all-purpose flour	1 egg, well beaten
½ teaspoon salt	1 cup milk
2 teaspoons baking powder	2 tablespoons melted shortening

Mix and sift dry ingredients. Add well beaten egg, milk, and melted shortening. Pour into greased pan. 8 inches square. Bake in hot oven (425°F.) until golden brown (about 25 minutes). Yield: 1 loaf.

BAKING POWDER BISCUITS (Basic Recipe)

2 cups sifted all-purpose flour	4 tablespoons shortening
3 teaspoons baking powder	⅔ to ¾ cup milk or
1 teaspoon salt	⅔ to ¾ cup water

Sift together dry ingredients. Cut shortening into flour with 2 knives or pastry blender until consistency of coarse meal. Add liquid, mixing lightly with a fork until a ball forms that separates from the sides of bowl. Turn out on lightly floured board. Knead gently ½ minute. Roll or pat out dough ½ inch thick. Cut with floured biscuit cutter. Bake on ungreased baking sheet in hot oven (450°F.) 12 to 15 minutes. Serve immediately. Yield: 1½ dozen biscuits.

Biscuit teasers: Place preserves or seasoned chopped meat between 2 thin biscuits. Press edges together. Brush with shortening or milk and bake.

Bran biscuits: Substitute 1 cup bran for 1 cup white flour.

Cheese biscuits: Add ¼ cup grated cheese to dry ingredients.

Chive biscuits: Add ¼ cup freshly chopped chives to mixture of flour and shortening.

Cream biscuits: Use 1 scant cup medium cream instead of shortening and milk or water.

Drop biscuits: Increase liquid in basic recipe to 1 cup. Drop from teaspoon on lightly greased baking sheet or muffin pans.

Fried biscuits: Drop spoonfuls of dough into hot greased pan. Turn when brown.

Fruit biscuits: Add ½ cup chopped dates, figs, prunes, or raisins to mixture of flour and shortening.

Mint biscuits: Add ¼ cup freshly chopped mint to mixture of flour and shortening.

Nut biscuits: Add ½ cup chopped nuts to mixture of flour and shortening.

Orange biscuits: Add 1 tablespoon grated orange rind to mixture of flour and shortening.

Orange tea biscuits: Add 1 teaspoon grated orange rind to dry ingredients. When biscuits have been cut, press into the top of each a small cube of sugar which has been dipped in orange juice or other fruit juice.

Peanut biscuits: Substitute ½ cup peanut butter for shortening.

Rich shortcake biscuits: To basic recipe, add 1 egg and 2 tablespoons sugar. Increase shortening to 6 tablespoons.

Savory biscuits: Add 1 teaspoon poultry seasoning to dry ingredients.

Sour milk or buttermilk biscuits: Add ½ teaspoon baking soda, sifting it with flour. Use sour milk or buttermilk for liquid.

Whole-wheat biscuits: Substitute 1 cup whole-wheat flour for 1 cup white flour. Use ¾ teaspoon salt instead of 1 teaspoon salt.

BISCUIT PINWHEELS

Prepare dough for *BAKING POWDER BISCUITS*. Roll into an oblong about 12 inches long and ¼ inch thick. Spread with desired filling as directed in the following variations. Roll lengthwise as tightly as possible, jelly-roll fashion. Pinch edge to the roll. Cut into 1-inch slices and place cut side down in greased muffin pans. Bake in hot oven (400°F.) 18 to 20 minutes. Yield: about 12 pinwheels.

Butterscotch pinwheels: Spread dough with 2 tablespoons melted shortening and ½ cup brown sugar. Roll and cut as directed above. Cream together ⅓ cup butter and ½ cup brown sugar. Spread thickly in each muffin pan and place 2 or 3 pecan halves in bottom of each pan before adding pinwheels. Bake.

Cinnamon currant pinwheels: Spread dough with 2 tablespoons melted shortening and mixture of ½ cup sugar and 1¼ teaspoons cinnamon. Sprinkle with ½ cup currants. Roll, cut, and bake.

Honey or maple pinwheels: Brush rolled dough with melted fat. Sprinkle with brown sugar. If desired, add chopped nuts, dates, or raisins. Roll and cut as directed.

Place 1 tablespoon honey or maple syrup in bottom of each greased muffin pan. Press cut biscuit into each section.

Jam pinwheels: Spread dough with 2 tablespoons melted shortening and ½ cup jam or marmalade; roll, cut, and bake.

Peanut butter pinwheels: Spread dough with 2 tablespoons melted shortening and ½ cup peanut butter; roll, cut and bake.

TRICKS WITH BISCUITS

Banana curls: Roll dough for *BAKING POWDER BISCUITS* into rectangular shape about ¼ inch thick. Brush with 2 tablespoons melted butter or melted margarine. Slice 2 medium-sized ripe bananas evenly over the dough. Mix 3 tablespoons brown sugar and ½ teaspoon cinnamon together and sprinkle over bananas. Roll as for jelly roll and cut in 1-inch slices. Place cut side up in well-greased muffin pans and brush top with melted butter. Bake in hot oven (400°F.) 15 minutes. Yield: 18 curls.

Biscuit sticks: Roll or pat out dough for *BAKING POWDER BISCUITS* and cut into sticks ½ inch wide and 3 inches long. Brush with melted butter. Bake in hot oven (425°F.) and serve them stacked log-cabin fashion.

Cheese rosettes: To recipe for *BAKING POWDER BISCUITS* add ½ cup grated American cheese before adding liquid. Substitute water for milk. Chill slightly before using. Roll out on floured surface to ¼-inch thickness. Cut into ½-inch strips about 6 inches long. Tie in bowknot. After tying bring one end through center and other end over the side and turn under. Place on greased baking sheet, dust with paprika, and bake in hot oven (400°F.) 10 to 15 minutes.

Cheese squares: Roll or pat dough for *BAKING POWDER BISCUITS* ¼ inch thick. Sprinkle lightly with grated cheese. With a sharp knife, cut dough into squares. Bake in hot oven (425°F.).

Cherry delights: Cut dough for *BAKING POWDER BISCUITS* into small rounds. With a smaller cutter, remove centers from half the rounds. Brush with rich milk. Place the rings on top of the whole rounds. Place ½ teaspoon cherry preserves in the center of each and bake in hot oven (425°F.) 12 to 15 minutes.

Marmalade crescents: Prepare dough for *BAKING POWDER BISCUITS*. Roll out ½ inch thick. Brush with 2 tablespoons melted butter or other melted shortening. Spread with marmalade or jam. Cut into 3-inch squares, then cut each square diagonally in half to make triangles. Roll each triangle jelly-roll fashion, starting with the long edge of the triangle. Shape into a crescent. Place on greased baking sheet and bake in a hot oven (450°F.) 12 to 15 minutes. Yield: about 16 crescents.

Pineapple squares: Add 2 tablespoons sugar to recipe for *BAKING POWDER BISCUITS* and roll out into rectangular sheet. Cut into strips 3 inches wide and 6 inches long. Brush with melted butter. Place 1 teaspoon crushed pineapple on ½ of each strip and fold the other end of the strip over the fruit. Press edges together with a fork. Prick tops with fork. Bake in hot oven (425°F.) 20 minutes. Serve hot or cold with cream or with fruit sauce.

Salad rounds: Roll dough for *BAKING POWDER BISCUITS* into a rectangular sheet ¼ inch thick. Sprinkle with ½ cup chopped, stuffed olives and fold in half. Cut into rounds, using a 2-inch cutter. Brush with rich milk. Bake in hot oven (425°F.).

Spice rings: Roll or pat dough for *BAKING POWDER BISCUITS* to ½-inch thickness. Cut with small, floured doughnut cutter. Bake both rings and centers in hot oven (425°F.) for about 15 minutes. While hot, brush with melted butter and roll in sugar mixed with cinnamon.

SCOTCH SCONES

2 cups sifted all-purpose flour	4 tablespoons shortening
3 teaspoons baking powder	¼ cup currants (optional)
1 teaspoon salt	2 eggs
1 tablespoon sugar	½ cup milk

Sift together flour, baking powder, salt, and sugar. Cut in shortening. Add currants, if desired. Beat together 1 whole egg and 1 egg yolk, reserving 1 white for the tops. Add milk to beaten eggs, and add all to dry ingredients. Stir only enough to make dough hold together. Turn out on lightly floured board and knead ½ minute. Roll out in circular shape to ½ inch thickness. Cut into pie-shaped wedges. Brush tops with white of egg, and sprinkle with sugar. Bake in hot oven (425°F.) 12 to 15 minutes. Yield: 10 to 12 scones.

TOMATO JUICE BISCUITS

3 cups sifted all-purpose flour	⅓ teaspoon baking soda
¾ teaspoon salt	6 tablespoons fat
3 teaspoons baking powder	1¼ cups tomato juice

Mix and sift flour, salt, baking powder, and baking soda. Cut fat into sifted ingredients. Add tomato juice to make a soft dough. Place in well-greased muffin tins. Bake in hot oven (450°F.) about 18 minutes. Yield: 24 small biscuits.

QUICK LEMON ROLLS (with Prepared Mix)

1 package hot roll mix	½ cup sugar
¾ cup warm water or milk	2 tablespoons grated lemon rind
1 egg, beaten	2 teaspoons lemon juice

Place yeast from package of mix (in small envelope) in bowl. Add warm water (98° to 115°F.), and stir until dissolved. Add beaten egg and roll mix from package. Blend thoroughly. Grease top, cover with waxed paper, and let stand in a warm place (85° to 90°F.) until light and double in bulk, 45 to 60 minutes. Drop by spoonfuls into 2-inch muffin cups, filling them ½ full. Blend sugar, lemon rind, and juice and sprinkle over rolls. Let rise until double in bulk. Bake in moderate oven (375°F.) about 20 minutes. Yield: 24 small rolls.

BOHEMIAN FRUIT BUNS (with Prepared Mix)

1 package hot roll mix	12 pitted prunes or
1 cup warm water	12 cooked dried apricots
	⅓ cup chopped nuts

Place yeast from package of mix (in small envelope) in bowl and add warm water (98° to 115°F.). Stir until completely dissolved. Add mix from package and blend thoroughly. Grease top and cover with waxed paper. Let stand in warm place (85° to 90°F.) until light and double in bulk (45 to 60 minutes). Turn out and knead about 30 strokes on a floured board. Roll to ½ inch thickness and cut into rounds with a 2½-inch biscuit cutter. Place on greased baking sheet. Let rise as before until double in bulk (about 45 minutes). Press an indentation in center of each bun. Roll a prune or apricot in nuts and place in depression of each roll. Bake in moderate oven (350°F.) 20 minutes. Drip confectioners' frosting over warm buns. To make frosting, mix 1 cup sifted confectioners' sugar with 4 teaspoons water and ½ teaspoon vanilla. Yield: 12 buns.

PLAIN MUFFINS (Basic Recipe)

2 cups sifted all-purpose flour	1 egg, well beaten
3 teaspoons baking powder	1 cup milk
½ teaspoon salt	3 tablespoons melted shortening
2 tablespoons sugar	

Sift together dry ingredients. Combine egg, milk, and shortening. Add quickly to flour mixture, stirring only until just moistened. Do not beat. Drop batter gently by spoonfuls into greased muffin pans, filling ⅔ full. Bake in hot oven (425°F.) 20 to 25 minutes, or until golden brown. Yield: 1 dozen 2-inch muffins.

Apple muffins: Add ¼ teaspoon cinnamon and 2 tablespoons shortening. Fold 1 cup finely chopped apples into batter.

Berry muffins: Add 1 cup berries (blueberries, sweetened blackberries, sweetened strawberries) to dry ingredients.

Bran muffins: Substitute 1 cup all-bran for 1 cup white flour. Soak bran in milk 5 minutes before mixing.

Cheese muffins: Add ½ cup grated mild cheese to dry ingredients.

Cherry muffins: Add to muffin batter, ¾ cup drained, chopped cherries, fresh or canned.

Corn-meal muffins: Substitute 1 cup corn meal for 1 cup white flour.

Cranberry muffins: To sifted dry ingredients add ¾ cup chopped cranberries mixed with 3 tablespoons sugar.

Dried fruit muffins: Add ½ cup chopped pitted dates, figs, or raisins to dry ingredients.

Marmalade muffins: Put ½ teaspoon butter or margarine and 1 teaspoon marmalade into each muffin cup. Drop batter for *PLAIN MUFFINS* on top.

Nut muffins: Add ½ cup chopped nuts to dry ingredients.

Oatmeal muffins: Substitute 1 cup quick-cooking oats for 1 cup white flour.

Orange muffins: Add 1 tablespoon grated orange rind to dry ingredients. Substitute orange juice for milk.

Parsley muffins: Omit sugar. Add 2 tablespoons minced parsley, stirring it into sifted dry ingredients.

Rice muffins: To flour mixture add 1 cup cold cooked rice and 2 well beaten eggs.

Sour cream muffins: Use only 1 teaspoon baking powder. Add ½ teaspoon baking soda. Increase salt to ¾ teaspoon. Substitute 1¼ cups thick sour cream for milk and shortening.

Sour milk or buttermilk muffins: Reduce baking powder to 1 teaspoon. Add ½ teaspoon baking soda, sifting it with flour. Use sour milk or buttermilk instead of sweet milk.

Soya muffins: Substitute ½ cup soya flour for ½ cup white flour.

Sweet cream muffins: Increase salt to ¾ teaspoon. Substitute 1¼ cups heavy cream for milk and shortening.

Whole-wheat muffins: Substitute 1 cup whole-wheat flour for 1 cup white flour.

BUTTER CRUST MUFFINS

1 cup sifted all-purpose flour
½ teaspoon salt
3 teaspoons baking powder
1 tablespoon sugar
½ cup corn meal

1 cup milk
1 beaten egg
¼ cup peanut butter
1 tablespoon melted shortening

Mix and sift flour, salt, baking powder, and sugar. Stir in corn meal. Combine milk, egg, peanut butter, and melted shortening. Add to dry ingredients and mix only until flour is moistened. Fill greased muffin tins ⅔ full. Bake in hot oven (400°F.) about 20 minutes. Yield: 12 muffins.

CHOCOLATE DATE MUFFINS

2 cups sifted all-purpose flour
4 teaspoons baking powder
½ teaspoon salt
½ cup sugar
½ cup cocoa

½ cup dates, sliced
1 cup milk
1 egg, beaten
2 tablespoons melted shortening

Sift flour, baking powder, salt, sugar, and cocoa together. Mix the sliced, pitted dates through the flour with the finger tips. Stir in the milk, the egg, and the shortening. Fill greased muffin pans ⅔ full. Bake in a moderate oven (350°F.) 20 minutes. Yield: 12 medium or 24 small muffins.

CRUMB MUFFINS (Basic Recipe)

¼ cup shortening
¼ cup sugar
1 egg, beaten
1 cup sifted all-purpose flour

3 teaspoons baking powder
½ teaspoon salt
1 cup fine, dry crumbs
1 cup milk

Cream the shortening. Stir in sugar, and add egg. Sift flour, baking powder, and salt together. Add crumbs. Add to first mixture alternately with milk. Fill greased muffin pans ⅔ full. Bake in moderate oven (375°F.) 25 minutes. Yield: 1 dozen muffins.

Berry crumb muffins: Add 1 cup huckleberries.

Date crumb muffins: Add ¾ cup chopped, pitted dates.

ORANGE RAISIN MUFFINS

2 cups sifted all-purpose flour
¾ teaspoon baking soda
½ teaspoon salt
⅓ cup sugar
½ cup raisins
1 egg, well beaten

⅓ cup orange juice
½ teaspoon grated orange rind
⅔ cup sour milk or
    ⅔ cup buttermilk
⅓ cup shortening

Sift, then measure flour. Sift twice with baking soda, salt, and sugar. Add raisins. Combine well-beaten egg, orange juice, rind, sour milk or buttermilk and shortening. Turn wet ingredients into dry ingredients and mix only until dry ingredients are dampened. Fill greased muffin tins ⅔ full. Bake in hot oven (425°F.) 25 minutes. Yield: 12 muffins.

SPICE MUFFINS

2 cups all-purpose flour
1 teaspoon ginger
1 teaspoon nutmeg
1 teaspoon cinnamon
3 teaspoons baking powder

1 teaspoon salt
1 egg, well beaten
½ cup sugar
¼ cup melted shortening
1 cup milk

Sift flour. Measure, and sift flour with spices, baking powder, and salt. Combine egg, sugar, shortening, and milk. Add dry ingredients. Beat only until smooth. Fill greased muffin tins ⅔ full. Bake in hot oven (425°F.) 15 to 20 minutes. Yield: 12 muffins.

POPOVERS (Basic Recipe)

2 eggs, well beaten
1 cup milk
1 tablespoon melted shortening

1 cup sifted all-purpose flour
¼ teaspoon salt

Combine eggs, milk, and shortening. Add to flour which has been sifted with salt. Beat until batter is smooth. Pour batter into hot or cold greased muffin pan or custard cups until about half full. Bake in hot oven (450°F.) 10 minutes (until popovers pop), then reduce temperature to moderate oven (350°F.) and bake 20 to 30 minutes longer, until dry. Remove them at once from the pan. Puncture to let steam escape. Serve hot. Yield: 6 to 8 popovers.

Cheese popovers: Mix ½ cup grated cheese and a few grains cayenne with smooth batter.

Stuffed popovers: Split popovers. Fill with scrambled eggs, creamed fish, or creamed vegetables, etc.

Whole-wheat popovers: Substitute ½ cup whole-wheat flour for ½ cup white flour.

HAMANTASCHEN (Parve)

4 cups sifted all-purpose flour
3 teaspoons baking powder
¾ cup sugar
¼ teaspoon salt

4 eggs
⅓ cup vegetable oil
Grated rind of 1 lemon or
    orange

Mix and sift dry ingredients. Add eggs, oil, and grated rind. Mix well. Knead until smooth. Roll out on a floured board to ⅛-inch thickness. Cut into 4-inch rounds. Place a heaping teaspoonful of filling (see filling recipes that follow) in the center of each and bring the edges together to form a triangle, pinching together to close securely. Bake on a greased baking sheet in a moderate oven (375°F.) until browned, about 30 minutes.

Hamantaschen kuchen: Use the recipe for QUICK COFFEE CAKE or for YEAST COFFEE KUCHEN and roll out to ¼-inch thickness. Fill with desired filling.

Hamantaschen rolls: Use the recipe for REFRIGERATOR ROLLS and roll out to ¼-inch thickness. Fill with desired filling.

HAMANTASCHEN COOKIE DOUGH

2 cups sifted all-purpose flour
2 teaspoons baking powder
½ teaspoon salt
½ cup butter

1 cup sugar
1 egg
2 tablespoons milk
1 teaspoon vanilla extract

Mix and sift flour, baking powder, and salt. Cream together butter and sugar. Add egg. Add dry ingredients alternately with milk. Add vanilla. Roll out to ¼-inch thickness. Cut into 2-inch rounds. Fill (see filling recipes that follow), and draw up sides to form a triangle. Bake in a moderate oven (375°F.) until lightly browned, about 45 minutes.

HAMANTASCHEN POPPY SEED FILLING

2 cups poppy seed
1 cup water or 1 cup milk
¼ cup sugar

½ cup honey
⅛ teaspoon salt
1 egg, well beaten

Pour boiling water over poppy seed. Let stand until seeds have settled, and drain. Put through grinder, using finest blade, or pound in a mortar. Combine with liquid, sugar, honey, and salt. Cook over low flame until thick, stirring frequently. Allow to cool. Add egg. Mix well.

Variations of poppy seed filling: 1. Add ½ cup seedless raisins and ½ teaspoon grated lemon rind. Cook with other ingredients.
2. Add ¼ cup finely chopped almonds or ¼ cup finely chopped walnuts.
3. Add ½ cup grated apple and ¼ cup finely chopped nuts.

HAMANTASCHEN PRUNE FILLING

1 pound prunes
2 teaspoons lemon juice

Grated rind of 1 lemon

Soak the prunes several hours or overnight. Cook until soft. Drain, and remove pits. Chop fine. Add lemon juice and lemon rind.

QUICK COFFEE CAKE (Basic Recipe)

1½ cups sifted all-purpose flour
½ cup sugar
2 teaspoons baking powder
½ teaspoon salt

1 egg
⅔ cup milk
3 tablespoons melted shortening

Mix and sift flour, sugar, baking powder, and salt. Beat egg, add milk and shortening. Add to flour mixture, stirring only until flour is moistened. Pour into greased 9-inch square cake pan. Sprinkle with *STREUSEL TOPPING*. Bake in hot oven (425°F.) about 25 minutes. Yield: 1 coffee cake.

STREUSEL TOPPING

2 tablespoons butter or margarine	¼ cup dry breadcrumbs
2 tablespoons sugar	½ teaspoon cinnamon
¼ cup all-purpose flour	

Cream together butter and sugar. Add flour, crumbs, and cinnamon. Mix to consistency of coarse crumbs. Sprinkle over coffee cake batter.

Apple coffee cake: Cover dough with a layer of thinly sliced tart apples. Sprinkle with brown sugar and nutmeats. Beat 1 egg with ¼ cup cream or rich milk. Pour over top. Bake in hot oven (400°F.) about 40 minutes.

Currant coffee cake: Currants may be used in the same way as nuts, in nut coffee cake, or may be combined with them.

Dutch apple coffee cake: Spread dough in a shallow pan. Brush with melted butter. Cover with thinly sliced tart apples in parallel rows. Sprinkle generously with sugar and cinnamon. Bake in hot oven (400°F.) about 35 minutes.

Iced coffee cake: After baking, ice cake with *CONFECTIONERS' SUGAR ICING*, then sprinkle with minced candied fruit, chopped nuts, or combination of fruits and nuts.

Nut coffee cake: Glaze the top of the cake before baking with a mixture of slightly beaten egg white and water, or with a mixture of 3 tablespoons sugar and 1 tablespoon water. Sprinkle thickly with chopped nuts. Almonds are particularly good.

Prune or plum coffee cake: Arrange pitted canned plums or prunes over batter. Pour over a little of the juice. Sprinkle with cinnamon and sugar. Bake in hot oven (400°F.) about 30 minutes.

Upside-down cherry coffee cake: In a deep cake pan melt 2 tablespoons butter. Sprinkle 4 tablespoons sugar over bottom of pan. Cover with sour canned cherries (or other fruit) that have been well drained. Cover with coffee cake dough. Bake in hot oven (400°F.) about 20 minutes.

PEACH COFFEE CAKE

3 tablespoons butter	1½ cups sifted all-purpose flour
¼ cup sugar	½ teaspoon salt
1 egg	1¾ teaspoons baking powder
½ cup milk	Sliced peaches (canned or fresh)

Cream butter and sugar. Beat egg and add milk. Add flour which has been sifted with baking powder and salt. Spread dough in an oblong pan. Cover with sliced peaches, sprinkle with flour and sugar, and dot with butter. Bake in hot oven (400°F.) 25 minutes.

PRUNE COFFEE CAKE

Use recipe for peach coffee cake, omitting peaches. Prepare batter. Pour into shallow pan. Cut 12 cooked prunes in half. Arrange on top of batter, skin down. Cover the whole with the following mixture:

½ tablespoon sifted all-purpose flour
2 tablespoons softened butter
¼ cup sugar

½ teaspoon salt
½ teaspoon cinnamon

Bake in hot oven (400°F.) 25 minutes.

NUT SPICE COFFEE CAKE

1½ cups sifted all-purpose flour
⅔ cup sugar
2 teaspoons baking powder
½ teaspoon salt
½ teaspoon cloves
½ teaspoon nutmeg

1 teaspoon cinnamon
⅓ cup shortening
1 egg, beaten
2 tablespoons molasses
⅔ cup milk
½ cup chopped walnut meats

Sift together into a bowl the flour, sugar, baking powder, salt, and spices. Cut in shortening with fork or pastry blender until mixture is like coarse crumbs. Reserve ½ cup of this mixture for top of coffee cake. To rest of crumb mixture add beaten egg, molasses, and milk. Mix lightly. Pour into large well-greased baking dish. Sprinkle top with remaining ½ cup of crumb mixture and the chopped walnut meats. Bake in moderate oven (350°F.) about 45 minutes. Serves 8.

OPEN-FACED APPLE CAKE

2 cups sifted all-purpose flour
2½ teaspoons baking powder
1 teaspoon salt
6 tablespoons shortening

About ¾ cup milk
3 medium-sized apples
3 tablespoons sugar
¼ teaspoon cinnamon

Mix and sift flour, baking powder, and salt. Cut in 4 tablespoons shortening thoroughly. Add just enough milk to hold dry ingredients together. Turn into 2 lightly greased 8-inch layer-cake pans. Peel and slice apples thinly and arrange over dough. Dot with remaining fat. Sprinkle with sugar and cinnamon. Bake in moderate oven (375°F.) about 20 minutes. Serve with cream.

QUICK HONEY KUCHEN

¾ cup sifted all-purpose flour
2½ teaspoons baking powder
¼ teaspoon salt
½ cup milk
¼ cup honey

1 egg, well beaten
3 tablespoons melted fat
1½ cups wheat flakes or
    1½ cups bran flakes

Sift flour with baking powder and salt. Combine milk, honey, and egg, and add to flour mixture. Add fat, mixing only enough to combine. Fold in flakes. Pour into greased pan. Sprinkle topping over batter. Bake in hot oven (400°F.) until done (25 minutes). Yield: 1 square cake (8″x8″x2″).

Honey kuchen topping: Mix together ¼ cup brown sugar, ½ teaspoon cinnamon, ¼ teaspoon nutmeg, 2 tablespoons melted butter, and ½ cup wheat or bran flakes. Sprinkle over batter in pan.

POPPY SEED KUCHEN

1½ cups sifted all-purpose flour
4 tablespoons sugar
½ teaspoon baking powder
⅛ teaspoon salt
1 egg yolk, beaten
1 cup milk

½ pound poppy seeds
¼ cup butter
½ cup cream
1 tablespoon grated lemon rind or
   1 tablespoon grated
   orange rind

Mix and sift flour, 1 tablespoon sugar, baking powder, and salt. Blend milk with egg yolk. Add to flour mixture. Blend well and let stand ½ hour. Grind poppy seeds well. Add remaining ingredients and mix well. Roll dough out ½ inch thick on a floured board. Place in a cake pan. Cover with poppy seed mixture. Bake in moderate oven (350°F.) about 30 minutes.

QUICK KUGELHOPF (High Coffee Cake)

1 cup butter
1 cup sugar
5 eggs
4 cups sifted all-purpose flour
½ teaspoon salt
4 teaspoons baking powder
1 cup milk

1 cup seedless raisins
1 teaspoon grated lemon rind
1 teaspoon vanilla
½ cup nutmeats, chopped
   (optional)
Confectioners' sugar

Cream butter until soft and fluffy. Sift in sugar gradually and beat until creamy and light. Add 1 egg at a time, beating well after each addition. Sift flour with salt and baking powder. Add sifted mixture in 3 parts to butter mixture alternating with milk in thirds. Beat smooth after each addition. Add raisins, lemon rind, vanilla, and nuts (if desired). Mix well and pour into greased 7-inch tube pan. Bake in moderate oven (350°F.) about 1 hour. When cooled, dust with confectioners' sugar.

ANITA'S COFFEE CAKE

2 cups sifted all-purpose flour
3 teaspoons baking powder
½ teaspoon salt
⅓ cup shortening
1 egg, beaten
½ cup milk

⅓ cup sugar
2 teaspoons cinnamon
⅓ cup buttered breadcrumbs
2 apples, peeled, cored, and
   sliced thin

Mix and sift flour, baking powder, and salt together. Cut in shortening until well mixed. Add egg to milk and then to flour, stirring quickly to form a moist dough. Pat out to ½-inch thickness in shallow greased pan. Mix sugar and cinnamon together. Sprinkle half over dough. Arrange sliced apples in rows to cover dough. Top with breadcrumbs and the remaining cinnamon-sugar mixture. Bake in moderate oven (350°F.) until done (30 minutes).

INDIVIDUAL COFFEE RINGS

2 cups sifted all-purpose flour
3 teaspoons baking powder
½ teaspoon salt
2 tablespoons sugar

⅓ cup shortening
⅓ cup milk
1 egg, well beaten
2 tablespoons melted butter

Mix and sift flour, baking powder, salt, and sugar. Cut in shortening. Combine milk and egg. Add to flour mixture, stirring quickly to form stiff dough. Turn out on lightly floured board. Knead slightly. Roll to ⅓-inch thickness. Cut with large doughnut cutter. Brush with melted butter. Top each ring with *RING TOPPING*. Bake in hot oven (450°F.) until done, about 12 minutes. Yield: about 12 cakes.

RING TOPPING

⅓ cup flour
2 tablespoons sugar
  Dash of salt

½ teaspoon cinnamon
2 tablespoons fat

Combine dry ingredients. Cut in fat.

BANANA DUTCH COFFEE CAKE

1 cup sifted all-purpose flour
1¼ teaspoons baking powder
½ teaspoon salt
2 tablespoons sugar
¼ cup shortening
1 egg, well beaten

3 tablespoons milk
3 firm bananas
2 tablespoons melted butter
2 tablespoons sugar
¼ teaspoon cinnamon
1 teaspoon grated orange rind

Mix and sift flour, baking powder, salt, and sugar. Cut in shortening. Combine egg and milk. Add to flour mixture and stir until mixture is blended. Turn the stiff dough into a greased baking pan (8x10x2 inches), and spread evenly over bottom of pan. Peel bananas and cut into ½-inch diagonal pieces. Cover surface of dough with overlapping pieces of bananas. Brush bananas with butter. Mix together sugar, cinnamon, and orange rind and sprinkle over top of bananas. Bake in moderate oven (350°F.) about 35 minutes. Serves 6 to 8.

BLUEBERRY COFFEE CAKE

½ cup shortening
½ cup sugar
2 eggs
1¾ cups sifted all-purpose flour
3 teaspoons baking powder

½ teaspoon salt
1 cup milk
⅔ cup blueberries
¼ cup brown sugar, firmly packed
½ teaspoon cinnamon

Cream shortening. Add sugar and cream thoroughly. Beat eggs, and add. Mix and sift flour, baking powder, and salt. Add alternately with milk to creamed mixture. Fold in blueberries. Turn into a greased 8-inch square pan. Sprinkle with mixture of brown sugar and cinnamon. Bake in moderate oven (350°F.) 50 minutes. Serve hot.

QUICK APPLE STRUDEL

2 cups sifted all-purpose flour
3 teaspoons baking powder
½ teaspoon salt
2 tablespoons sugar
4 tablespoons shortening
⅔ to ¾ cup milk

3 cups chopped apple
½ cup sugar
1 teaspoon cinnamon
Confectioners' sugar
Vanilla
Chopped nuts

Mix and sift flour, baking powder, salt, and sugar. Cut in shortening. Add milk to make a soft dough. Turn out on floured board and knead gently. Roll out ¼ inch thick. Brush with melted butter or melted margarine. Cover with chopped apple. Sprinkle sugar and cinnamon over apple. Roll jelly-roll fashion and form into a semicircle on a greased baking sheet. Bake in hot oven (425°F.) 20 to 25 minutes. While warm, frost with white frosting made by beating confectioners' sugar with a little hot water until smooth, and flavor with vanilla extract. Sprinkle chopped nuts over frosting. Yield: 12 1-inch slices.

GRIDDLE CAKES, PANCAKES (Basic Recipe)

1 or 2 eggs, well beaten
Scant 1½ cups milk
2 tablespoons melted shortening
2 cups sifted all-purpose flour

3 teaspoons baking powder
½ teaspoon salt
1 tablespoon sugar

Combine egg, milk, and shortening. Add to sifted dry ingredients. Beat only until smooth. Pour by spoonfuls onto hot, lightly greased or ungreased griddle. Bake until bubbles on top burst. Turn and bake on other side. Yield: about 15 medium-sized cakes.

Apple pancakes: Add 1 cup finely chopped tart apple to batter.

Banana pancakes: Add 1 thinly sliced banana to batter.

Blueberry pancakes: Add 1 cup fresh, or drained canned blueberries to batter.

Buckwheat cakes: Substitute 1 cup buckwheat for 1 cup white flour.

Cherry or peach pancakes: Add to batter 1 cup drained, chopped cherries or peaches, fresh or canned. Serve hot with butter and a syrup of sugar and cherry juice or sugar and peach juice.

Chocolate pancakes: Increase sugar to ⅓ cup. Add 1 square melted, unsweetened chocolate to liquid ingredients. Serve as dessert with sweetened, flavored whipped cream.

Corn-meal pancakes: Substitute ¾ cup corn meal for ¾ cup white flour and 1 tablespoon dark molasses for 1 tablespoon sugar.

Crumb pancakes: Substitute 1 cup breadcrumbs for ½ cup flour.

Nut pancakes: Add ¾ cup chopped pecans to dry ingredients.

Pineapple pancakes: Add 1 cup drained, crushed pineapple to batter. Bake slowly on greased hot griddle.

Rice pancakes: Substitute 1 cup cooked rice for 1 cup flour. Reduce milk to 1 cup. Add rice to egg-milk mixture.

Sour milk pancakes: Substitute scant 2 cups sour milk or scant 2 cups buttermilk for sweet milk. Use only 2 teaspoons baking powder and add 1 teaspoon baking soda.

Soya pancakes: Substitute ⅓ cup soya flour for ⅓ cup white flour.

Whole-wheat pancakes: Substitute 1 cup whole-wheat flour for 1 cup white flour.

CHEESE BLINTZES (Basic Recipe)

BATTER	FILLING
1 cup sifted all-purpose flour	1½ pounds dry cottage cheese
1 teaspoon salt	1 or 2 egg yolks, beaten
4 eggs, well beaten	1 tablespoon melted butter
1 cup milk or	Salt, sugar, and cinnamon to taste
1 cup water	

Sift flour and salt. Mix eggs with liquid. Stir in flour. Mix until smooth to form thin batter. Pour onto a hot lightly greased 6-inch skillet enough batter to form very thin cake, tilting the pan from side to side so that batter spreads evenly. Cook over a low heat on one side only until the top of cake is dry and blistered. Turn out on clean cloth, cooked side up. Allow to cool. Repeat until all batter is used. Filling: Mix cheese with egg yolks and butter and with salt, sugar, and cinnamon to taste. Place a tablespoon of mixture in center of each cake. Fold edges over to form envelope. Blintzes may be prepared and filled in advance and kept in refrigerator until ready to fry. Just before serving, fry in butter until brown on both sides, or bake in a moderate oven. Serve hot with sour cream, or with sugar and cinnamon mixture. Yield: about 10 blintzes.

Apple blintzes: Mix 2 cups peeled and cored chopped apples, 1½ tablespoons ground almonds, 1 egg white, powdered sugar, and cinnamon to taste. Proceed as for cheese blintzes. Serve with sugar and cinnamon mixture.

Cherry blintzes: Mix 1 cup drained, pitted canned cherries, dash of cinnamon, 1 tablespoon flour, and sugar to taste. Proceed as for cheese blintzes. Serve with sour cream or with cinnamon and sugar.

Blueberry blintzes: Substitute blueberries for cherries.

Meat blintzes: Combine 2 cups finely ground or chopped lean, cooked meat, 1 egg, ½ teaspoon salt, ¼ teaspoon pepper, and 2 tablespoons soup stock. Mix thoroughly. Use as filling instead of cheese. Use water instead of milk in batter for blintzes.

Other variations for blintzes: Substitute chopped, seasoned leftover meat, kasha, poppy seed filling, or preserves for cheese filling.

SWEDISH PANCAKES

2 cups sifted all-purpose flour	3 eggs
½ teaspoon salt	4 cups milk
1 tablespoon sugar	

Mix and sift flour, salt, and sugar. Beat eggs well and combine with milk. Gradually add flour mixture, beating until smooth. Use a special Swedish griddle containing several small molds or bake quickly in a greased, heavy, hot frying pan, making one large pancake at a time. Spread with jam. Roll large cakes and dust with powdered sugar. Stack small cakes. Reheat and serve. Yield: 14 to 16 large cakes or 24 to 30 small cakes.

RUMANIAN PANCAKES

1 cup sifted all-purpose flour	1 tablespoon sugar
1 cup milk	Dash of cinnamon (optional)
1 egg, beaten	Canned cherries
¼ teaspoon salt	Powdered sugar

Add flour to milk and beat until well blended. Add egg, salt, sugar, and cinnamon. Mix thoroughly. Bake on a greased griddle until brown on one side. Turn and brown on other side. Spread cherries over pancakes while hot. Roll up and sprinkle with powdered sugar. Serve hot as dessert. Serves 4.

GERMAN PANCAKE

½ cup sifted all-purpose flour
½ teaspoon salt
3 eggs, well beaten

About ¾ cup milk
2 tablespoons butter

Add flour and salt to eggs. Add milk, beating constantly with a rotary beater. Spread bottom and sides of a cold 10-inch skillet with butter. Pour in all the batter, and place in preheated hot oven (425°F.) for a few minutes. Reduce heat to slow (325°F.). When pancake is puffed up, crisp, and brown at edges (about 10 minutes) remove to hot platter. Serve with powdered sugar and lemon juice or with preserves. Serves 4.

CRÊPES SUZETTE (French Pancakes)

BATTER

¾ cup sifted all-purpose flour
2 teaspoons sugar
½ teaspoon salt
¾ cup milk
3 eggs, slightly beaten

SAUCE

½ cup sweet butter
½ cup powdered sugar
1 orange, juice and grated rind
¼ cup curacao or brandy

Mix flour, sugar, and salt. Add milk alternately with eggs. Beat until smooth. Grease bottom of heavy frying pan when very hot. Cover bottom of pan with thin layer of batter and quickly tilt pan so that the pancake is evenly paper-thin. Brown on both sides. Successful making of crêpes depends upon the thinness of the batter. If made ahead of time, pancakes may be reheated in oven. Roll each and serve with following sauce.

Crêpe suzette sauce: Cream butter (do not melt). Add powdered sugar, grated rind and juice of orange, and curacao or brandy. Arrange pancakes in row on hot platter. Pour over some of the sauce, sprinkle with brandy, and light just before serving. Yield: 10 to 12 5-inch pancakes.

NORWEGIAN PANCAKES

Use same batter and fry as for CRÊPES SUZETTE, but do not roll. Pile several flat pancakes on serving plate. Spread jelly or butter and maple sugar between them and over the top. Serve hot in pie-shaped wedges.

RUSSIAN PANCAKES

Use same batter as for CRÊPES SUZETTE. Drop from tip of tablespoon on hot, well-greased griddle to form small, thin pancakes. Fry until brown on both sides, turning only once. Serve hot with sour cream or with caviar and sour cream.

GERMAN APPLE PANCAKES

1 cup sifted all-purpose flour
½ teaspoon baking powder
  Pinch of salt
1 cup milk

5 eggs
2 tablespoons melted butter
  Hot applesauce

Mix and sift dry ingredients. Stir in 1 cup milk. Add unbeaten eggs one at a time, beating each separately into batter. Add melted butter. Pour into hot greased skillet. Put on direct heat for 1 minute, then bake in hot oven (425°F.) until browned, puffed, and curled up at edges, 20 to 25 minutes. Sprinkle with powdered sugar and lemon juice if desired. Serve at once with hot applesauce. Serves 4 to 6.

QUICK BLINI (Russian Pancakes)

¾ cup sifted all-purpose flour
⅓ teaspoon baking powder
¼ teaspoon salt

½ cup milk
1 egg, slightly beaten
2 tablespoons sour cream

Sift flour, baking powder, and salt together. Add remaining ingredients. Stir well. Bake on greased griddle, making each pancake very small (about 1½ inches across) and very thin. Brown on both sides, turning only once. Serve with caviar, melted butter, or sour cream. Yield: about 30 pancakes.

YEAST BLINI (Russian Pancakes)

3 cups warm milk
1 cake compressed yeast
2 cups fine buckwheat flour
4 eggs, separated

½ teaspoon salt
1 tablespoon sugar
2 teaspoons melted butter

Pour 1½ cups warm milk over crumbled yeast. Stir to dissolve and add enough flour to make a thick sponge. Cover with a warm cloth. Set in a warm place (80 to 85°F.) for about 2½ hours. Beat egg yolks with salt and sugar and stir in remaining warm milk. Add butter and stir into the raised sponge. Mix in remaining flour and stiffly beaten egg whites. Cover again and let rise at least 20 minutes. Bake small pancakes (about 3 inches across and not more than ¼ inch thick) on a hot, greased griddle. Brown lightly on both sides, turning only once. Serve with caviar or with melted butter and sour cream. Yield: about 30 pancakes.

OLD-FASHIONED BUCKWHEAT CAKES

2¼ cups boiling water
½ cake compressed yeast
2 tablespoons lukewarm water
1½ cups buckwheat flour

1 teaspoon salt
4 teaspoons sugar
½ cup sifted all-purpose flour
¼ teaspoon baking soda

Boil 2 cups water, cool to lukewarm. While it is cooling, dissolve yeast in 2 tablespoons lukewarm water. Reserve baking soda and 3 teaspoons sugar to add next morning, then add remaining ingredients and dissolved yeast to the 2 cups lukewarm water. Cover and let stand in a fairly warm place 12 hours (over night). The next morning add the other ¼ cup water, cooled to lukewarm, with soda and 3 teaspoons sugar dissolved in it. Mix well and bake on griddle. One-half cup of batter may be reserved as "seed." Use "seed" in place of yeast after first day. "Seed" should be stored in cool place. Yield: about 12 pancakes.

WAFFLES (Basic Recipe)

2 cups sifted all-purpose flour
3 teaspoons baking powder
2 tablespoons sugar (optional)
1 teaspoon salt

3 eggs, separated
1¼ cups milk
4 tablespoons melted shortening

Sift dry ingredients. Beat egg yolks. Add milk and melted shortening. Beat thoroughly. Add to dry ingredients. Combine quickly. Gently fold in egg whites, beaten stiff but not dry. Bake 3 or 4 minutes in a hot waffle iron. Yield: 5 to 6 waffles.

Apple waffles: Just before baking, add 1 cup of ½-inch cubes of raw apples to batter. Serve with cinnamon-sugar mixture, and butter.

Blueberry waffles: Mix 1 cup blueberries with 2 tablespoons sugar, and add to batter just before baking. Serve with powdered sugar.

Cheese waffles: Add 1 cup grated American cheese to batter before folding in beaten egg whites.

Coconut waffles: Before closing grids, sprinkle coconut over each waffle or add 1 cup shredded coconut to batter.

Corn-meal waffles: Substitute ½ cup corn meal for ½ cup white flour.

Date or fig waffles: Add 1 cup chopped dates or dried figs to batter just before baking. Serve with powdered sugar.

Ginger waffles: Add 4 tablespoons molasses and 1½ teaspoons ginger. Omit 4 tablespoons milk.

Orange waffles: Add 2 teaspoons grated orange rind to the egg yolk and milk mixture. If desired, substitute ½ cup orange juice for ½ cup milk.

Pecan waffles: Add 1 cup chopped pecans to batter or sprinkle over batter of each waffle before closing iron.

Sour cream waffles: Use only 1 teaspoon baking powder. Add ½ teaspoon baking soda. Substitute 1¼ cups thick sour cream for milk and shortening.

Sour milk waffles: Substitute 1½ cups sour milk or 1½ cups buttermilk for sweet milk. Add ¾ teaspoon baking soda and use only 2¼ teaspoons baking powder.

Whole-wheat waffles: Substitute ½ cup whole-wheat flour for ½ cup white flour.

APPLE WAFFLES #2

2 cups sifted cake flour
3 teaspoons baking powder
¼ teaspoon salt
2 eggs, separated

1 cup milk
⅓ cup melted butter
½ cup grated raw apple
2 tablespoons sugar

Mix and sift flour, baking powder, and salt. Beat egg yolks. Add milk and stir until mixed. Add flour all at once and beat until smooth. Add butter and apple. Mix until smooth. Beat egg whites until frothy. Add sugar and beat until stiff. Fold into batter. Bake in hot waffle iron until brown and crisp. Yield: 6 to 7 waffles.

CHEESE WAFFLES #2

2 cups sifted all-purpose flour
3 teaspoons baking powder
½ teaspoon salt
1 cup milk

4 tablespoons grated cheddar cheese
3 egg yolks
1 tablespoon melted butter
3 egg whites, stiffly beaten

Mix and sift dry ingredients. Heat milk, add cheese, and allow it to melt. Cool. Add the egg yolks. Beat and add the dry ingredients. Add melted butter. Fold in egg whites. Bake in hot waffle iron until brown. Serve with butter and tart jelly. Cheese flavor is quite pronounced. Yield: 5 to 6 waffles.

CORN WAFFLES

1⅓ cups sifted all-purpose flour
¼ teaspoon salt
2 teaspoons baking powder

1 egg, well beaten
⅔ cup milk
1 cup canned corn

Mix and sift dry ingredients. Combine egg and milk and add to flour. Add corn. Bake on hot, greased waffle iron. Serve with butter and maple syrup or honey. Yield: 4 to 5 waffles.

GINGERBREAD WAFFLES

2 eggs
¼ cup sugar
½ cup molasses
1 cup sour milk
1½ cups sifted all-purpose flour

1 teaspoon ginger
¼ teaspoon salt
1 teaspoon baking soda
1 teaspoon baking powder
⅓ cup melted shortening

Beat eggs until light. Add sugar, molasses, sour milk, and remaining dry ingredients sifted together. Beat until smooth and add shortening. Cinnamon and clove may be added if desired. Bake in a hot waffle iron. Serve with whipped cream, ice cream, or cold applesauce. Yield: about 5 waffles.

SOUR CREAM WAFFLES #2

2 eggs, separated
2 cups sour cream
2 cups sifted all-purpose flour

1 tablespoon corn meal
1 teaspoon baking soda
½ teaspoon salt

Beat whites and yolks of eggs separately. Mix with the beaten yolks, the cream, flour, corn meal, baking soda, and salt. Finally fold in the egg whites. Bake at once on a hot iron. Yield: 6 waffles.

RICE WAFFLES

1 cup sifted all-purpose flour
½ teaspoon salt
2 teaspoons baking powder
1 tablespoon sugar
2 egg yolks

1 cup milk
1 cup cold cooked rice
4 tablespoons melted butter
2 egg whites, stiffly beaten

Sift dry ingredients. Add egg yolks beaten with the milk. Beat until smooth. Add rice and melted butter. Fold in stiffly beaten egg whites. Bake on hot waffle iron. Serve at once. Yield: 4 waffles.

SPONGE CAKE WAFFLES

1 cup cake flour
1 teaspoon baking powder
¼ teaspoon salt
3 eggs, well beaten

1 cup sugar
3 tablespoons melted butter
¼ cup cold water
1 teaspoon vanilla

Sift together the flour, baking powder, and salt. Combine well beaten eggs and sugar. Add sifted dry ingredients, melted butter, water and vanilla, beating until smooth. Bake in a hot waffle iron until delicately browned, about 2 minutes. May be served as a shortcake. Sprinkle with powdered sugar, and serve with berries and whipped cream or ice cream. Yield: 6 waffles.

SWEET POTATO WAFFLES

4 tablespoons shortening	Salt, cayenne, and nutmeg
1 tablespoon sugar	¾ cup sifted all-purpose flour
1 egg, separated	1 cup mashed sweet potatoes
1 cup milk	2 teaspoons baking powder

Cream shortening and sugar until smooth. Add well beaten egg yolk, milk and seasoning, continuing to beat until smooth. Beat in the flour, sweet potatoes, and baking powder. Fold in the stiffly beaten egg white. Bake in a heated waffle iron until golden brown. Serve sprinkled with sugar and cinnamon. Serves 5 to 6.

FRITTER COVER BATTER

1 egg, slightly beaten	1 tablespoon melted shortening
1 cup milk or	1 cup sifted all-purpose flour
1 cup water or	½ teaspoon sugar
1 cup fruit juice	¼ teaspoon salt

Combine egg, milk, water, or fruit juice and shortening. Add gradually to dry ingredients. Mix until smooth. Dip fruit into cover batter and fry in deep fat, heated to 365°–370°F. Remove when light brown on both sides. Drain on absorbent paper. This cover batter may be used for apple, banana, or pineapple slices or for orange sections. Serve fruit fritters sprinkled with confectioners' sugar. It may also be used for seafoods or meats, but omit sugar from batter. Serves 6.

Variation 1: For a thicker batter decrease milk to ⅔ cup and add 1 teaspoon baking powder to flour with sugar and salt. Use with berries or very juicy fruits.

Variation 2: Vary by adding ¼ teaspoon cinnamon, nutmeg, or grated rind of lemon or orange.

FRITTER BINDING BATTER

1¾ cups sifted all-purpose flour	2 eggs, slightly beaten
3 teaspoons baking powder	1 cup milk
1 tablespoon sugar	1 tablespoon melted shortening
½ teaspoon salt	

Sift dry ingredients. Omit sugar unless batter is to be used for fruit. Combine eggs, milk, and shortening. Mix liquid and dry ingredients and stir until smooth. Add 1 to 2 cups chopped vegetables, cooked or canned, or chopped fruit, well drained, or 1 to 2 cups drained corn. Drop from a tablespoon into deep hot fat (365° to 370°F.). Turn as soon as fritter comes to surface. Remove from fat when well browned on both sides. Drain on absorbent paper. Serves 6.

SWEDISH TIMBALE CASES

½ cup milk	¾ cup sifted all-purpose flour
2 egg yolks, beaten	½ teaspoon salt

Add milk to egg yolks. Gradually stir in flour sifted with salt. Mix well, cover, and set aside 1 hour. Heat deep fat to 370°F. and heat timbale iron in it for 2 to 3 minutes. Drain and dip into batter to within ¾ inch of top. Immediately return to hot fat and hold there until case is crisp and lightly browned. If batter slips off, the iron is too cold. If it sticks to iron, it is too hot. Yield: 24 timbale cases.

APPLE FRITTERS

2 large apples
¼ cup sugar
4 tablespoons lemon juice
1 cup sifted all-purpose flour
½ teaspoon salt
2 teaspoons baking powder
1 egg, separated
½ cup milk

Core and pare the apples. Cut in thin round slices. Sprinkle sugar and lemon juice over apples and let stand ½ hour. Mix and sift dry ingredients twice. Beat egg yolk and add milk. Combine dry ingredients with liquid and blend quickly. Fold in the stiffly beaten egg white. Dip apple slices in batter and fry in deep hot fat (360°F.). Drain on a paper. Serve hot with syrup. Serves 6.

BRANDIED APPLE FRITTERS

Peel and core 6 small, soft, sweet apples. Cut in thin rounds. Soak in a mixture of equal parts brandy, lemon juice, and sugar. Drain and dust with flour. Sauté in butter until light brown, turning carefully. Sprinkle with powdered sugar and cinnamon mixture. Serve very hot. Serves 6.

ARMENIAN CHEESE BOURAG

2 cups sifted all-purpose flour
¼ teaspoon salt
3 teaspoons baking powder
3 tablespoons butter
About ½ cup milk
½ pound grated sharp cheese
3 tablespoons minced parsley
¼ teaspoon salt

Sift together the flour, salt, and baking powder. Cut in the butter, and mix to a dough with milk. Roll out very thin on a floured board. Cut into 4-inch squares. Mix remaining ingredients together. Put squares together by pairs with 2 tablespoons of cheese mixture between. Press edges well together and fry until brown in deep hot fat (360° to 370°F.). Drain and serve. Serves 6.

BRANDIED BEET FRITTERS

4 egg yolks
2 tablespoons flour
3 tablespoons heavy cream
3 tablespoons brandy
Grated rind of ½ lemon
¼ teaspoon nutmeg
1 teaspoon sugar
2 finely chopped, cooked beets

Combine ingredients in order given. Stir until smooth and drop by spoonfuls on hot greased griddle. Bake like pancakes. Yield: about 14 small cakes.

CHEESE FRITTERS

1¼ cups sifted all-purpose flour
¼ teaspoon salt
2 teaspoons baking powder
⅔ cup milk
1 egg, well beaten
¾ cup grated American cheese

Mix and sift flour, salt, and baking powder. Mix together the milk and egg. Combine the two mixtures. Add grated cheese and beat 3 minutes vigorously, or until smooth. Drop by tablespoons into deep hot fat (360° to 370°F.). Fry until brown. Drain on paper. Serve hot. Serves 6.

COTTAGE CHEESE FRITTERS

1 cup cottage cheese	1 cup flour
1 egg, well beaten	2 teaspoons baking powder
¼ cup milk	½ teaspoon salt

Add cottage cheese to egg and beat until thoroughly blended. Stir in milk. Mix and sift flour, baking powder, and salt. Add to first mixture and stir in lightly. Drop by spoonfuls into deep, hot fat (375°F.). Fry until brown (2 to 4 minutes). Drain on absorbent paper. Yield: 10 to 12 fritters.

FANNIE'S FINGERS

2 eggs, separated	8 small peeled bananas
3 tablespoons melted butter	Flour
⅔ cup scalded milk	Pinch of salt
¼ cup anise liqueur	

Beat egg yolks and add 1 tablespoon butter. Put in top of double boiler over hot water. Add milk, stirring constantly. Cook until mixture coats silver spoon, about 5 minutes. Cool. Add 1 tablespoon liqueur and fold in stiffly beaten egg whites to which salt has been added. Slice bananas lengthwise. Marinate in remaining liqueur 1 hour. Dip in flour, then in egg mixture. Brown lightly in butter. Serve at once. Serves 8.

PINEAPPLE FRITTERS

4 slices pineapple	1 teaspoon melted butter
2½ tablespoons flour	⅓ cup fine, dry breadcrumbs
½ teaspoon salt	2 tablespoons shortening
1 egg, well beaten	½ lemon

Drain and dry pineapple. Dip in seasoned flour, then in egg mixed with melted butter, then in crumbs. Sauté each slice in hot shortening (360°F.) until brown on both sides. Serve with a dash of lemon juice. Serves 4.

HUSH PUPPIES

2 cups corn meal	1 teaspoon salt
1 tablespoon flour	3 tablespoons finely chopped onion
1 teaspoon baking powder	1 egg, well beaten
½ teaspoon baking soda	1 cup buttermilk

Mix and sift dry ingredients. Add onion, well beaten egg, and buttermilk. Drop by the spoonful into hot fat. Fry until golden brown. Drain on absorbent paper. It is believed that originally they were fried in the same fat in which fish was being fried. Serves 6 to 8.

GRIMSLICH

3 cups bread cubes
2 eggs, separated
½ cup sugar

¼ cup raisins or
   ¼ cup chopped figs
1 teaspoon cinnamon
¼ cup ground, blanched almonds

Soak bread cubes in water for a few minutes. Press out as much water as possible. Add egg yolks, sugar, raisins or figs, cinnamon, and almonds. Blend well. Fold in stiffly beaten egg whites. Drop by tablespoonfuls into hot vegetable oil in skillet. Brown on both sides. Drain on absorbent paper. Serve with stewed fruit. Serves 6.

BAKING POWDER DOUGHNUTS (Basic Recipe)

2 eggs, well beaten
1 cup sugar
2 tablespoons softened shortening
3½ cups sifted all-purpose flour
4 teaspoons baking powder

½ teaspoon salt
¼ teaspoon nutmeg
¼ teaspoon cinnamon
¾ cup milk

Combine eggs, sugar, and shortening. Beat well. Mix and sift flour, baking powder, salt, nutmeg, and cinnamon. Stir in alternately with milk to egg mixture. Chill dough 2 hours. Roll ⅓-inch thick on a floured board. Cut with doughnut cutter. Fry a few at a time in deep hot fat (370°F.), turning once. Drain on absorbent paper. Yield: 2 dozen.

Buttermilk or sour milk doughnuts: Substitute buttermilk or sour milk for sweet milk. Use only 2 teaspoons baking powder. Add 1 teaspoon baking soda.

To sugar doughnuts: When cool, place one at a time in a paper bag with confectioners' sugar and shake well.

To glaze doughnuts: Gradually add ⅓ cup boiling water to 1 cup confectioners' sugar and mix well. Dip warm doughnuts into glaze.

POTATO DOUGHNUTS

4½ cups sifted all-purpose flour
4 teaspoons baking powder
1 teaspoon salt
1 teaspoon baking soda
1 teaspoon nutmeg

2 eggs, well beaten
1 cup sugar
2 tablespoons salad oil
1 cup mashed potato
1 cup sour milk

Mix and sift flour, baking powder, salt, baking soda and nutmeg. Beat eggs and sugar until light. Add oil, potato, and milk, beating until smooth. Stir in flour mixture. Chill thoroughly. Roll on a floured board to ½-inch thickness. Cut with doughnut cutter. Fry in deep hot fat (370°F.). Drain on absorbent paper. Yield: about 3 dozen.

MOLASSES DOUGHNUTS

½ cup molasses
½ cup granulated sugar
2 eggs
1½ tablespoons melted butter
5 cups sifted all-purpose flour

1 teaspoon soda
1 teaspoon salt
½ teaspoon ginger or
   1 teaspoon nutmeg
1 cup thick sour milk

Beat molasses, sugar, and eggs until smooth. Add butter. Mix and sift 2 cups flour with the soda, salt, and ginger or nutmeg. Add alternately with the sour milk to the first mixture. Add sifted flour to make dough that can be handled easily. Chill in refrigerator. Roll dough a little at a time. Shape with small doughnut cutter. Fry in deep hot fat (370°F.). Drain on absorbent paper. Yield: about 4 dozen.

FRENCH TOAST (Basic Recipe)

2 eggs
Dash of salt
1 tablespoon sugar

⅔ cup milk
6 slices white bread

Beat eggs slightly. Add salt, sugar, and milk. Dip bread into milk mixture. Cook on hot, well-greased griddle or skillet. Brown on one side. Turn and brown on other side, or fry in deep hot fat 1 to 2 minutes, or until browned. Serve with syrup, preserves, or cinnamon and sugar mixture.

French toast fingers: Cut slices of bread into fingers about 1 inch wide. Prepare as FRENCH TOAST. Serve with confectioners' sugar or tart jelly.

Hawaiian French toast: Substitute ⅔ cup pineapple juice for milk. Serve toast on half slices of heated pineapple.

Honey French toast: Add ¼ cup honey to milk mixture of FRENCH TOAST.

Orange French toast: Substitute ⅔ cup orange juice and 1 teaspoon grated orange rind for milk. Serve with honey.

TEA TOASTS

Cut bread very thin. If desired, remove crusts, cut slices into halves or strips. Spread hot toast with butter, then with desired mixture. Place under broiler long enough to melt sugar, about 2 minutes.

Cinnamon toast: Use 1½ teaspoons cinnamon and 2 tablespoons brown sugar.

Honey cinnamon toast: Use mixture of honey and cinnamon to taste.

Honey toast: Use strained honey.

Maple toast: Use maple sugar.

Orange toast: Use mixture of ½ tablespoon grated orange rind, 2 tablespoons orange juice, and ¼ cup sugar.

Vanilla baked toast: Cut slices of bread into thirds. Combine ½ cup milk, 1 tablespoon sugar, and ½ teaspoon vanilla. Brush surface of bread. Toast in slow oven (300°F.) until crisp, dry, and golden.

Melba toast: Cut stale bread into ¼-inch slices. Bake in slow oven (300°F.) until brown and dry, 15 to 20 minutes.

Toast strips: Cut slices ⅓ inch thick. Remove crusts. Spread butter on both sides. Cut slices in ½-inch strips. Lightly brown under broiler.

Milk toast: Place hot buttered toast in cereal bowl. Serve with scalded milk seasoned with salt and pepper. Allow about ½ cup per slice.

Cream toast: Serve hot buttered toast with thin white sauce made of cream or serve with scalded cream. Allow ½ cup per slice.

Toast points: Remove crusts from ½-inch slices. Toast. While hot, cut into 4 triangles. Use as a garnish.

Toast cups: Trim crusts from ¼-inch slices of fresh bread. Brush with melted butter. Press each slice into custard cup so that bread forms a cup. Bake in moderate oven until crisp and brown, 15 to 20 minutes.

Croustades: Cut slices of bread 3 inches thick. Remove crusts and cut slices into rounds or squares. Hollow out centers, leaving ¼-inch wall around sides and bottom. Brush top and sides with melted butter. Brown in moderate oven (350°F.) 15 to 20 minutes. Serve hot, filled with creamed mixtures.

Croutons: Cut bread in ½-inch slices. Remove crusts. Spread both sides lightly with butter. Cut slices into ⅓-inch strips, then into cubes. Toast lightly in oven. Serve with soups.

BREAD CRUMBS

Buttered brown crumbs: Fry crumbs gently in melted butter, or brown buttered crumbs in moderate oven, stirring often.

Buttered crumbs: Add 2 tablespoons melted butter to ½ cup fine sifted crumbs. Mix. Sprinkle over scalloped and baked foods before baking.

Fine bread crumbs: Use stale bread, or dry out sliced bread in a very slow oven (300°F.). Crush and roll into fine crumbs. Sift and roll coarse crumbs again.

Soft moist crumbs: Use day old but soft bread. Remove crusts. Crumble with fingers. Grate into coarse crumbs, or tear out with a fork. To measure, pack lightly into cup.

CHEESE CROUTONS

¼ pound American cheese, grated
¼ cup shortening
½ cup sifted all-purpose flour
Few grains cayenne

Combine grated cheese with shortening. Blend in flour and cayenne. Chill until firm. Break off bits of dough and roll into tiny balls about the size of large peas. Bake in a hot oven (450°F.) 5 minutes. Serve with soup.

GARLIC BREAD

Slice a long loaf of Vienna, Italian, or French bread to about a half inch from the bottom so that the loaf remains intact at the bottom. Melt ¼ cup butter. Add 1 clove garlic cut into several pieces. Let stand for 15 minutes. Spread cut surface of slices with garlic butter. Place in a moderate oven (375°F.) until heated through, 12 minutes. Before baking, sprinkle bread with grated cheese, if desired.

PIZZA

Prepare *WHITE YEAST BREAD DOUGH* or dough for *BAKING POWDER BISCUITS*. Roll thin to fit circular pans. Brush with olive oil, and spread with tomato paste or thinly sliced fresh tomatoes. Sprinkle with salt, pepper and grated cheese. Sprinkle with thyme or mixed dried herbs. Bake at once in moderate oven (375°F.) about 30 minutes. Serve warm. Sliced onions may be added with tomato paste.

QUICK CHEESE PIZZA

6 English muffins	12 thin slices of cheese
3 ripe tomatoes or	Olive oil
1¼ cups drained stewed tomatoes	Salt and pepper
24 anchovy filets	

Break apart muffins. Toast until slightly crisp. Thinly slice tomatoes. Place 1 slice of tomato or 2 tablespoons stewed tomatoes on each muffin half. Add 2 anchovy filets. Add another layer of tomato or stewed tomatoes. Top with slice of cheese. Sprinkle with olive oil, salt, and pepper. Broil until cheese melts. Serves 4–6.

ONE BOWL PIZZA (No-Dissolve Yeast Method)

2½ to 3 cups unsifted all-purpose flour	1 package active dry yeast
1½ teaspoons sugar	1 cup very hot tap water
2 teaspoons salt	2 tablespoons peanut oil

In a large bowl thoroughly mix 1 cup flour, sugar, salt, and undissolved active dry yeast. Gradually add very hot tap water and peanut oil to dry ingredients and beat 1 minute at low speed of electric mixer, scraping bowl occasionally. Stir in enough additional flour to make a soft dough. Turn out onto lightly floured board; knead until smooth and elastic, about 8 to 10 minutes. Place in greased bowl, turning to grease top. Cover; let rise in warm place, free from draft, until doubled in bulk, about 45 minutes. Punch dough down and divide in half. Press each piece of dough into a greased 12-inch pizza pan, forming a standing rim of dough. Fill with filling (below) and bake as directed. Makes 2 pizzas.

TOMATO SAUCE—CHEESE PIZZA FILLING

1 6-ounce can (2/3 cup) tomato paste	½ pound Mozzarella cheese, sliced
½ cup water	about ⅛ inch thick
1 teaspoon salt	4 tablespoons olive or salad oil
1 teaspoon crushed oregano	4 tablespoons grated Parmesan cheese
Dash of pepper	

Mix together the tomato paste, water, salt, oregano, and pepper. On each circle of dough arrange half of the Mozzarella cheese. Spread evenly half of the tomato mixture; sprinkle evenly 2 tablespoons oil and 2 tablespoons grated Parmesan cheese. Bake in moderate oven (375°F.) until done, 30 to 35 minutes. Cut in slices and serve. Makes filling for 2 12-inch round pans.

MUSHROOM-ONION PIZZA FILLING

1 cup chopped onions	1 can (3-ounce) sliced mushrooms,
1 teaspoon salt	drained
1 teaspoon oregano leaves	1 cup shredded Mozzarella cheese
¼ cup peanut oil	1 tablespoon peanut oil
	Paprika

Cook onions, salt, and oregano in ¼ cup peanut oil until onions are tender. Spread over surface of 1 pizza crust. Top with mushrooms and cheese. Drizzle with 1 tablespoon peanut oil and sprinkle with paprika. Bake in moderate oven (350°F.) about 30 to 35 minutes, or until done. Cut into slices and serve. Makes enough for 1 12-inch pizza.

cakes

Many a homemaker has won an enviable reputation as a born cook because of her ability to bake fluffy, delicate cakes. Success in making cakes need not depend on a knack for baking or good luck. If you know the few simple, basic rules for making cakes and always follow them, you should never have a failure, nor ever need to say that you had poor luck with a cake. Baking a cake is fun if you are sure of success every time. Success is due to an understanding of the underlying principles of cakemaking.

Cakes may be divided into two basic types: those made with shortening (fat or oil) and those made without shortening, the angel or sponge cakes. Although the two are very different in the way they are mixed and in their appearance and texture, nevertheless many of the same rules of cakemaking apply to both.

Ingredients: The finished cake can be only as good as the ingredients that go into making it. Cake flour, made from soft wheat, has a tender gluten and is best for cakes made with shortening and for angel and sponge cakes. The recipes in this section specify the kind of flour to be used. Where the type of flour is not specified, all-purpose flour is meant. Although we do not recommend the substitution of flours, all-purpose flour may be used instead of cake flour in some of the recipes, with some loss in the fineness of the cake's texture. If an all-purpose flour is substituted for cake flour, use 2 tablespoons less per cup of all-purpose flour. Only fine-grain granulated sugar is satisfactory for cakes. When brown sugar is specified, all lumps should be crushed by rolling, and it is best to sift the sugar after crushing it. To measure brown sugar, pack firmly in cup. Unless otherwise specified, any of the bland vegetable fats may be used for shortening. However, butter or margarine does give a more desirable flavor. Use medium-sized eggs of good quality. They increase more in volume on beating if they are at room temperature. In fact, all ingredients should be at room temperature. Except where specifically indicated, a compromise amount of baking powder has been used to assure satisfactory results with any brand.

Methods of mixing cakes: Cakes may be mixed by various methods. This section contains recipes for cakes that are mixed by the standard or conventional method, by the muffin or quick method, and by the newer "all-in-one" method, in which all of the ingredients but the eggs and part of the milk are added at one time and mixed or beaten by machine a definite number of strokes or length of time. In addition, recipes are listed for the popular chiffon cakes with vegetable oil used as the shortening and for torten, which are essentially cakelike desserts.

TROUBLE CHART

Although you think you have followed directions very carefully for mixing and baking your cake, the cake may not turn out as expected. This is not a matter of chance but is caused by something you did or failed to do during mixing or baking. Study the following chart, note the sections that name any faults of your cake, and try to determine where you have slipped.

Cake is coarse-grained:
1. Insufficient creaming of fat and sugar.
2. Oil used instead of a hard fat (in conventional or quick-mix cakes).
3. All-purpose flour used.
4. Too much baking powder or baking soda.
5. Oven not hot enough.

Cake is heavy:
1. Too much mixing.
2. Too much fat or liquid.
3. Not enough sugar, baking powder, or baking soda.
4. Baking temperature not right.

Cake has soggy layer at bottom:
1. Ingredients not thoroughly mixed.
2. Fat too soft.
3. Too little baking powder or baking soda.
4. Too much liquid.
5. Lower part of oven not hot enough.
6. Egg whites not beaten sufficiently (in chiffon cakes).

Cake is not sufficiently risen:
1. Not enough baking powder or baking soda.
2. Pan too large for amount of batter.
3. Baking temperature wrong.

Cake falls:
1. Too much sugar, fat, liquid, baking powder, or baking soda.
2. Too little flour.
3. Too short a baking period.
4. Oven not hot enough.
5. Cake pans jarred during baking before cake was firm enough to hold shape.

Cake is dry and crumbly:
1. Too much flour, baking powder, or baking soda.
2. Too little fat, sugar, or liquid.
3. Cornstarch used with an all-purpose flour.
4. Cocoa substituted for chocolate without adding more fat.
5. Egg whites overbeaten (in conventional cakes).
6. Cake overbaked or baked too long in too slow an oven.

Cake has a tough crust:
1. Not enough fat or sugar.
2. Too much flour.
3. Baked in floured pan.
4. Baked too long.
5. Oven too hot.

Top of cake is cracked or rounded too much:
(*Top of a standard loaf cake should be slightly cracked*).
1. Too much flour.
2. Not enough liquid.
3. Batter overmixed after addition of flour.
4. Oven too hot at beginning of baking.

Cake ran over pan:
1. Too much batter for size of pan.
2. Oven not hot enough.
3. Too much baking powder or baking soda.
4. Too much sugar.

Color of crust is uneven:
1. Ingredients not well blended.
2. Oven temperature uneven.
3. Oven too crowded.
4. Cake placed too close to edge of oven.

Cake is higher on one side than other:
1. Oven grate not level.
2. Oven temperature uneven (crust forms sooner in the hotter part of the oven, so the side of the cake on the hot side of the oven will not rise as much as on the other).
3. Batter spread unevenly in pan.
4. Dented pan used.

Cake is burned:
1. Oven heats unevenly.
2. Oven too full for good circulation of heat.
3. Oven too hot.
4. Cake placed too near side of oven.
5. Oven too hot for kind of baking pan used.

Crust is too light in color:
1. Oven not hot enough, especially at last period.
2. Not enough sugar, fat, baking powder, or baking soda.
3. Not enough batter to fill pan properly.
4. Baking temperature too low for type of baking pan used.

Cake has a sticky crust:
1. Too much sugar.
2. Not baked long enough.
3. Not cooled properly.

Crust is soggy or doughy:
1. Cake allowed to steam while cooling.
2. Insufficient baking period.
3. Cake baked too slowly.

Cake sticks to pan, or crust comes off in balls:
1. Pan not properly greased.
2. Too much sugar.
3. Cake left in pan too long.

Cake falls apart while being taken from pan:
1. Too much fat, sugar, baking powder, or baking soda.
2. Insufficient baking time.
3. Baked in too slow an oven.
4. Carelessly removed from pan.
5. Removed from pan before cooled.

Cake is tough:
1. Too little fat or sugar.
2. Too much flour.
3. Batter overmixed (in a plain cake).
4. Oven too hot.
5. Cake baked too long.

STEPS IN MAKING A CAKE WITH SHORTENING

1. Read the complete recipe and directions carefully.
2. Assemble all ingredients you will need. Have them at room temperature.
3. Be sure the oven will be heated by the time your cake is ready to bake.
4. Assemble all utensils needed.
5. Prepare pans for baking. (The batter should be put in pans as soon as mixed.)
6. Measure ingredients accurately with standard measuring cups and spoons.
7. Mix ingredients according to directions of the specific recipe.
8. Because the cake will rise in baking, the pans should not be filled more than ⅔ full. Spread the batter evenly in the pan. For layers and cupcakes be sure the batter is divided evenly among the pans. The following guide will be helpful in determining the size of pans for any recipes: A cake with shortening containing 2 cups flour may be baked in (a) 2 layer-cake pans 9 inches in diameter or 8 inches square, (b) 1 loaf pan 4x8 inches, (c) 12 average muffin cups, (d) 1 sheet pan 8 to 9 inches square and 2 inches deep.
9. Place pans in preheated oven, as near the center of the oven as possible and away from the sides. Be sure the pans are well separated from each other and that there is plenty of space around each for complete circulation of heat. Check to see that the oven temperature is accurate and correctly set.
10. Test the cake at about the end of the baking time given in the recipe to see if it is done. Your cake is done: (a) when the center surface springs back on being touched lightly; (b) when an inserted toothpick or metal cake tester comes out clean.
11. Upon removing a cake from the oven, place the pan on a wire rack. Let it stand and cool 5 to 10 minutes. Loosen cake from edges of pan. Place rack over top of cake and invert quickly. Leave cake on rack. If cake is placed on a board or plate, the bottom becomes soggy. If waxed paper was used in the bottom of the pan, remove it from the cake immediately.
12. Cool cake before frosting. If cakes are frosted while still warm, they absorb too much frosting and become soggy. To frost, brush off loose crumbs and place bottom sides together with filling or frosting. Cover sides first, then the top, spreading frosting to edges with a light swirling motion.

TWO- OR THREE-EGG BUTTER CAKE (Basic Recipe)

½ cup shortening	4 teaspoons baking powder
1½ cups sugar	¼ to ½ teaspoon salt
2 large eggs or	1 cup milk
3 medium eggs	¼ to 1 teaspoon vanilla to taste
3 cups sifted cake flour	

Cream together shortening and sugar. Add eggs, 1 at a time, beating after each. Sift together flour, baking powder, and salt. Add alternately with milk to creamed mixture. Add vanilla. Pour into lightly greased pans. For a 2-layer cake, bake in moderate oven (375°F.) 25 minutes. For a loaf cake, bake in slow oven (325°F.)

40 to 45 minutes. Cool in pans for 5 to 10 minutes. Remove from pans and cool on wire rack.

Banana cake: Add crushed bananas to cake filling. Ice with BANANA FROSTING.

Chocolate cake: Use ⅜ cup shortening instead of ½ cup, and 2⅞ cups flour instead of 3 cups. Melt 2 ounces unsweetened chocolate, over warm (not boiling) water, and add with vanilla.

Cocoa cake: Reduce flour to 2½ cups. Add 5 tablespoons cocoa. Sift cocoa with dry ingredients.

Coconut cake: Add ½ cup shredded coconut to batter. Ice with COCONUT FROSTING.

Marble layer cake: Divide batter into 2 parts and add 1 square melted chocolate to one part. Put by spoonfuls into 2 greased layer pans, alternating light and dark mixtures. Decorate with CHOCOLATE FROSTING.

Mocha coffee: Use ½ cup strong coffee and ½ cup water, instead of milk.

Nut cake: Add ½ cup nutmeats broken in pieces to batter.

Orange coconut cake: Flavor with 1 tablespoon orange rind instead of vanilla. Substitute orange juice for milk. Mix in ½ cup grated coconut with the liquid. Cover cake with ORANGE FROSTING and shredded coconut.

Spice cake: Reduce cake flour to 2¾ cups and add 1 teaspoon cinnamon, ½ teaspoon cloves, and ½ teaspoon allspice or nutmeg.

White cake: Use 4 to 6 egg whites, instead of 2 to 3 whole eggs.

Yellow cake: Use 4 to 6 egg yolks, instead of 2 to 3 whole eggs, and add extra teaspoon of baking powder. (1½ teaspoons grated orange rind may be used instead of vanilla.)

ONE-EGG BUTTER CAKE (Basic Recipe)

2 cups sifted cake flour	1 cup sugar
¼ teaspoon salt	1 egg
2½ teaspoons baking powder	1 teaspoon vanilla
⅓ cup shortening	⅔ cup milk

Sift together flour, salt, and baking powder. Cream shortening until soft and smooth, and gradually add sugar, beating until light and fluffy. Beat in egg and vanilla. Add dry ingredients alternately with milk. Turn into greased pan and bake. In single square pan: moderate oven (350°F.) 50 minutes. In 2 layer pans: moderate oven (375°F.) 25 minutes. In cupcake pans: moderate oven (375°F.) 25 minutes. Cool layers 5 to 10 minutes in pan before removing and cooling on wire rack. Remove cupcakes from pans at once and cool on wire rack. Yield: 2 8-inch layers, 1 8-inch square cake, or 1½ dozen cupcakes.

Boston cream pie: Bake in 2 layers. Spread CREAM FILLING between layers. Sift powdered sugar over top.

Caramel cake: Add 4 tablespoons caramel flavoring with the liquid.

Chocolate cake: Add 1 square melted chocolate to creamed shortening.

Raisin cake: Prepare batter. At the last, add ½ cup raisins which have been dredged with 2 tablespoons cake flour.

Short cake: Bake in shallow pan. Cut in rounds. Split each round in 2 parts. Spread fruit between each part and on top. Serve with whipped cream. Garnish with fruit.

Spice cake: Reduce cake flour to 1⅞ cups and add 1 teaspoon cinnamon, ¼ teaspoon cloves, and ¼ teaspoon allspice or nutmeg.

Washington pie: Bake in 2 layers. Spread jam or jelly between layers. Sift powdered sugar over top.

White cake: Use 2 egg whites in place of whole egg. Fold in stiffly beaten whites last.

Yellow cake: Use 2 egg yolks in place of whole egg, and 1 teaspoon grated orange rind for the flavoring.

ONE-BOWL FEATHER CAKE

1¾ cups sifted all-purpose flour
  3 teaspoons baking powder
  1 teaspoon salt
⅓ cup melted shortening

1 cup sugar
¾ cup milk
1 teaspoon vanilla
1 egg

Sift together flour, baking powder, and salt. Combine shortening, sugar, milk, vanilla, and unbeaten egg. Add to dry ingredients. Beat well for about 3 minutes. Turn into 2 8-inch greased layer pans. Bake in moderate oven (350°F.) 25 minutes. Cover with BUTTERSCOTCH FROSTING.

VELVET BUTTER CAKE (Basic Recipe)

2 cups sifted cake flour
3 teaspoons baking powder
½ teaspoon salt
⅔ cup butter or other shortening

1 cup sugar
3 eggs, separated
⅔ cup milk
1 teaspoon flavoring

Sift together three times flour, baking powder, and salt. Cream butter until soft and gradually add sugar, creaming until light and fluffy. Mix in well-beaten egg yolks. Add dry ingredients alternately with milk, stirring vigorously after each addition. Continue stirring for 2 minutes or about 300 strokes. Fold in the stiffly beaten egg whites and flavoring. Turn into lightly greased baking pans and place in center of preheated oven. Bake in 2 9-inch layer pans in moderate oven (375°F.) 25 to 30 minutes, or in loaf pan (8x8x2 inches) in moderate oven (350°F.) 40 to 60 minutes. Remove from oven, loosen edges with knife, and turn out, inverted, on cake rack. Cool and ice. If cake fails to come out immediately spread a cold damp cloth over bottom of pan for a moment or two.

White velvet cake: Omit egg yolks. Add ½ cup shortening.

Banana nut cake: Bake in 2 layers. Cool and fill with BANANA NUT FILLING.

Coconut velvet cake: With stiffly beaten egg whites and flavoring fold in ½ cup shredded coconut and 2 additional tablespoons milk. Ice with BOILED FROSTING. Cover with coconut or with chocolate sprinkles.

Gold cake: Omit egg whites. Substitute ½ cup butter and ¾ cup milk for butter and milk stated. Use ½ teaspoon orange extract flavoring.

Lady Baltimore cake: Bake WHITE VELVET CAKE above in 2 9-inch layers. Fill with LADY BALTIMORE FILLING. Ice with BOILED FROSTING.

Marble cake: Divide batter in two parts. To one part, add 1½ ounces of melted, unsweetened chocolate, stirring it in well. Put the 2 batters into a greased loaf baking pan by alternate tablespoonfuls. Pass a spatula through the batter to blend slightly.

Spice cake: Sift ¾ teaspoon each of cloves, cinnamon, and nutmeg with the flour. Substitute brown sugar, packed firmly, for white sugar. Ice with *CARAMEL FROSTING.*

Velvet raisin cake: At the last add ⅔ cup seedless raisins dredged with a little of the flour. Ice with *CARAMEL FROSTING.*

CINNAMON BUTTER CAKE

1½ cups cake flour
2 teaspoons baking powder
¼ teaspoon salt
⅓ cup butter

⅔ cup sugar
2 eggs, well beaten
½ cup milk
½ teaspoon vanilla

Sift flour, measure, and sift 3 times with baking powder and salt. Cream butter until soft, and gradually blend in sugar. Add eggs and beat until smooth and fluffy. Add dry ingredients and milk alternately, beating after each addition, beginning and ending with flour. Add vanilla. Bake in a well-buttered 8-inch square cake pan in moderate oven (350°F.) until golden brown, or 30 minutes. Cool on cake rack. Spread top and sides with *CINNAMON BUTTER FROSTING.*

4-EGG BUTTER CAKE (Basic Recipe)

3 cups sifted cake flour
4 teaspoons baking powder
¼ to ½ teaspoon salt
1 cup shortening

2 cups sugar
4 eggs
1 cup milk
½ to 1 teaspoon vanilla

Sift together flour, baking powder, and salt. Cream shortening until soft and smooth. Gradually add sugar, creaming until light and fluffy. Add eggs, one at a time, beating after each addition. Add dry ingredients alternately with milk. Add vanilla. Turn into lightly greased pans. For layer cake, bake in moderate oven (375°F.) 25 minutes. For a loaf cake, bake in slow oven (325°F.) 40 to 45 minutes. Cool in pans 5 to 10 minutes. Remove from pans and cool on wire rack.

Chocolate cake: In *4-EGG BUTTER CAKE* recipe, use ⅞ cup shortening instead of 1 cup, and 2⅞ cups flour instead of 3 cups, and 2 ounces melted unsweetened chocolate added with the vanilla.

Cupcakes: Pour into lightly greased cupcake pans, ⅔ full. Bake in moderate oven (375°F.) 20 to 25 minutes. Remove from pans and cool on wire rack. Yield: 24 cupcakes.

PRALINE CAKE

3 cups sifted all-purpose flour
3 teaspoons baking powder
1 teaspoon salt
½ cup shortening

1 cup sugar
2 eggs
¾ cup milk
1 teaspoon vanilla

Mix and sift flour, baking powder, and salt. Cream shortening and sugar together. Add eggs one at a time and beat thoroughly after each addition. Add dry ingredients alternately with milk and vanilla to creamed mixture. Mix after each addition. Turn into 2 greased, paper-lined 8-inch square pans. Bake in moderate oven (375°F.) 20 to 25 minutes. Let cool several minutes in pans. Remove and frost with *PRALINE FROSTING*.

GRAHAM CRACKER CAKE

½ cup butter
1 cup sugar
3 eggs, separated
1 pound graham crackers, crushed fine

2 teaspoons baking powder
1 teaspoon vanilla
¾ cup milk
1 cup chopped nutmeats

Cream butter and sugar. Add egg yolks and beat thoroughly. Combine graham crackers and baking powder. Add vanilla, milk, and nutmeats. Mix thoroughly. Fold in stiffly beaten egg whites. Pour into well-greased shallow pan. Bake in moderate oven (375°F.) about 30 minutes. Serve with whipped cream.

COCONUT FLUFF CAKE

2¼ cups sifted cake flour
4½ teaspoons double-acting baking powder
1½ teaspoons salt
1¾ cups sugar

¾ cup vegetable shortening
1⅛ cups milk
1 teaspoon vanilla
1 teaspoon almond extract
⅔ cup egg whites, unbeaten

Mix and sift flour, baking powder, salt, and sugar. Add shortening and milk. Beat for 2 minutes until batter is well blended and glossy. If electric mixer is used, beat at low to medium speed for same period of time. Add 1 teaspoon vanilla, almond extract, and egg whites. Beat 2 minutes. Pour into 2 lightly greased, floured, 8-inch square layer-cake pans or 9-inch round layer cake pans. Bake in moderate oven (350°F.) 35 to 40 minutes. Frost with *FLUFFY WHITE FROSTING*. Cover with coconut.

Loaf cake: Turn batter into lightly greased, floured loaf pan. Bake in moderate oven (350°F.) 40 to 45 minutes.

SNOW WHITE CAKE

4 cups sifted cake flour
5 teaspoons double-acting baking powder
1½ teaspoons salt
2¼ cups sugar

¾ cup vegetable shortening
1½ cups milk
¾ cup egg whites, unbeaten
1½ teaspoons vanilla

Sift together flour, baking powder, salt, and sugar. Add shortening and 1 cup milk. Beat for 2 minutes until batter is well blended and glossy. If electric mixer is used, beat at low to medium speed for same period of time. Add ½ cup milk, egg whites, and vanilla. Beat 2 minutes. Pour into 3 lightly greased, floured, 9-inch layer-cake pans. Bake in moderate oven (350°F.) 30 to 35 minutes. Frost with *FUDGE FROSTING*.

ONE-BOWL WHITE LAYER CAKE (Basic Recipe)

2 cups sifted cake flour
1⅓ cups granulated sugar
1 teaspoon salt
½ cup shortening

1 cup milk
1 teaspoon vanilla
3½ teaspoons baking powder
4 egg whites, unbeaten

Sift flour, sugar, and salt into mixing bowl or bowl of electric mixer. Add shortening, which is at room temperature, ⅔ of milk to which vanilla has been added. Beat 150 strokes, scraping bowl and spoon frequently. (Or beat 2 minutes on #2 speed of electric mixer.) Add baking powder and beat a few seconds. Add egg whites and remaining milk. Beat 300 strokes. (Or 2 minutes on #2 speed of electric mixer.) Scrape sides of bowl and spoon frequently during beating process. Bake in 2 well-greased, floured 9-inch layer tins in moderate oven (350°F.) 30 minutes.

Cupcakes: Fill pans ½ full. Bake in moderate oven (350°F.) 15 to 18 minutes.

One-bowl chocolate cake: Omit ¼ cup of flour. Add ½ cup cocoa to dry ingredients before sifting.

One-bowl orange cake: Spread ORANGE CONFECTIONERS' FROSTING between layers and on top.

One-bowl spice cake: Omit vanilla. Add and sift with flour 1 teaspoon nutmeg, ½ teaspoon cinnamon, and ¼ teaspoon cloves.

Quick coconut berry cake: Spread a tart berry jelly between layers and on top. Sprinkle with shredded coconut.

LEMON FLUFF CAKE

2 cups sifted cake flour	1 cup sugar
2½ teaspoons baking powder	2 teaspoons grated lemon rind
½ teaspoon salt	¾ cup milk
½ cup shortening	3 egg whites

Sift together flour, baking powder, and salt. Cream shortening. Add sugar gradually, creaming until light and fluffy. Add grated lemon rind. Add dry ingredients alternately with milk, stirring after each addition until smooth. Beat egg whites until stiff. Fold into mixture until well blended. Turn into 2 greased 8-inch layer pans. Bake in moderate oven (375°F.) 25 to 30 minutes. Cool in pans 5 to 10 minutes. Remove from pans. Cool on wire rack. Spread LEMON FILLING between layers. Sprinkle top with confectioners' sugar.

JEFF'S BIRTHDAY CAKE

2½ cups sifted cake flour	½ cup vegetable shortening
3¼ teaspoons double-acting baking powder	1 cup milk
1 teaspoon salt	½ cup egg whites, unbeaten
1½ cups sugar	1 teaspoon vanilla

Mix and sift flour, baking powder, salt, and sugar. Add shortening and ⅔ cup milk. Beat for 2 minutes until batter is well blended and glossy. If electric mixer is used, beat at low to medium speed for same period of time. Add ⅓ cup milk, egg whites, and vanilla. Beat for 2 minutes. Pour into 2 lightly greased, floured 8-inch layer-cake pans. Bake in moderate oven (350°F.) 35 to 40 minutes. Frost with PEPPERMINT CANDY FROSTING.

Loaf cake: Pour batter into lightly greased, floured loaf pan. Bake in moderate oven (350°F.) 40 minutes.

PINEAPPLE LAYER CAKE

2 cups sifted cake flour	1 cup less 2 tablespoons canned
1½ cups sugar	pineapple juice
3½ teaspoons double-acting	1 teaspoon vanilla
baking powder	3 egg whites, unbeaten
1 teaspoon salt	PINEAPPLE FILLING #2
1 teaspoon grated lemon rind	1 cup whipping cream, whipped
½ cup vegetable shortening	

Mix and sift flour, 1¼ cups sugar, baking powder, and salt. Add lemon rind, shortening, pineapple juice, and vanilla. Beat all together 200 strokes (2 minutes by hand or with mixer at low speed). Scrape bowl and spoon or beater. Add egg whites and beat 200 strokes (2 minutes by hand or with mixer at low speed). Turn into 2 square greased pans (8x8x2 inches). Bake in moderate oven (350°F.) 25 to 30 minutes. Chill layers and split in half. Sweeten whipped cream with ¼ cup sugar. Spread *PINEAPPLE FILLING* and sweetened whipped cream between layers. Cover top with whipped cream. Garnish corners with bits of pineapple. Chill cake several hours in refrigerator before serving, and keep in refrigerator until used up.

GOLDEN CAKE

½ cup vegetable shortening	1 cup milk
2½ cups sifted cake flour	1 teaspoon vanilla
1½ cups sugar	4 egg whites, unbeaten, or
4 teaspoons double-acting	2 whole eggs
baking powder	
1 teaspoon salt	

Place shortening in bowl. Mix and sift flour, sugar, baking powder, and salt. Add to shortening. Add ⅔ cup milk and the vanilla. Beat all together for 2 minutes with medium speed of electric mixer or 300 strokes by hand (150 strokes per minute). With rubber scraper keep batter scraped from sides and bottom of mixing bowl throughout the mixing. Scrape bowl and beaters thoroughly. Add whole eggs or egg whites and ⅓ cup milk. Beat again for 2 minutes. Scrape bowl and beaters. Turn into 2 9-inch round pans each of which has been fitted with two circles of heavy waxed paper. Bake in moderate oven (375°F.) about 25 minutes. Cool on rack 5 minutes. Use end of knife to loosen sides of cake from pan. Turn out on rack to cool. Frost with *GOLDEN CREAM FROSTING*. Top with pecans.

CHOCOLATE CAKE (Basic Recipe)

2 cups sifted cake flour	1 cup sugar
3 teaspoons baking powder	2 eggs, separated
¼ teaspoon salt	3 ounces (squares)
½ teaspoon baking soda	melted chocolate
½ cup butter or	1¼ cups milk
½ cup other shortening	1 teaspoon vanilla

Sift flour once before measuring, then 3 times with baking powder, salt, and baking soda. Cream butter until soft and smooth. Gradually add sugar, creaming until light and fluffy. Add beaten egg yolks. Then add melted chocolate. Add milk alternately with dry ingredients, beating until smooth after each addition.

Continue beating for 2 minutes (about 300 strokes). Fold in flavoring and stiffly beaten egg whites. Turn into lightly greased pans and bake.

For layers: Bake in 2 9-inch pans, in moderate oven (375°F.) 30 minutes.

For loaf: Bake in pan (8x8x2 inches) in moderate oven (350°F.) 50 to 60 minutes. Turn out on cake rack to cool. Ice with CHOCOLATE FROSTING.

Chocolate almond cake: Prepare BASIC CHOCOLATE LAYERS. Prepare CHOCOLATE SEVEN MINUTE FROSTING. Add chopped almonds to ⅓ of frosting. Spread between layers. Decorate top with almonds.

Chocolate cream cake: Prepare CHOCOLATE LAYERS. Spread CREAM FILLING between layers. Spread BOILED FROSTING on top and sides of cake.

Chocolate maple cake: Bake chocolate layers. Spread MAPLE WALNUT FROSTING between layers and on top of cake. Decorate with walnut halves.

Chocolate marshmallow cake: Bake cake in a loaf pan (8x8x2 inches). While still warm, place over the top, marshmallows cut in half and rinsed in cold water. Let cool. Cover with CHOCOLATE BUTTER FROSTING.

OLD FASHIONED CHOCOLATE CAKE

2½ cups sifted cake flour
4 teaspoons double-acting
  baking powder
1 teaspoon salt
1½ cups sugar

¾ cup vegetable shortening
1 cup milk
3 eggs, unbeaten
1 teaspoon vanilla

Sift together flour, baking powder, salt, and sugar. Add shortening and ⅔ cup milk. Beat for 2 minutes until batter is well blended and glossy. If electric mixer is used, beat at low to medium speed for same period of time. Then add ⅓ cup milk, eggs, and vanilla and beat for 2 minutes. Pour into 2 lightly greased, floured, 8-inch square or 9-inch round layer cake pans. Bake in moderate oven (350°F.) 35 to 40 minutes. Frost with CHOCOLATE FROSTING.

FEATHER DEVIL'S FOOD CAKE

½ cup shortening
1 cup white sugar
1 cup light brown sugar
2 eggs, beaten
3 squares chocolate
½ cup hot water

2½ cups sifted cake flour
½ teaspoon baking soda
2 teaspoons baking powder
1 teaspoon salt
⅔ cup milk
1 teaspoon vanilla

Cream shortening until soft and smooth. Gradually add sugar, beating until light and fluffy. Beat in eggs. Melt chocolate in water in top of double boiler, stirring until thick and smooth. Cool slightly. Add to fat-sugar-egg mixture and mix well. Sift together flour, baking soda, baking powder and salt three times. Add alternately with milk and vanilla, beating well after each addition. Turn into 2 greased 9-inch layer pans. Bake in moderate oven (350°F.) 30 to 35 minutes. Put layers together and cover cake with SEVEN MINUTE FROSTING. Garnish with chopped nuts or chocolate shot.

FUDGE CAKE

3 squares (3 ounces)
  melted chocolate
¼ cup boiling water
2 cups sifted cake flour
1 teaspoon baking soda
1 teaspoon salt

1¼ cups sugar
⅓ cup melted vegetable shortening
1 cup sour cream
2 eggs, unbeaten
1 teaspoon vanilla

Melt chocolate in water, stirring until well blended and thick. Sift together flour, baking soda, salt, and sugar. Add shortening and sour cream. Beat for 2 minutes, or until batter is well blended and glossy. If electric mixer is used, beat at low to medium speed for same period of time. Add cooled chocolate mixture, eggs, and vanilla. Beat for 2 minutes. Pour into 2 lightly greased, floured, 8-inch layer cake pans. Bake in moderate oven (350°F.) for 35 to 40 minutes. Note: Sweet cream may be substituted for sour cream but add 1 tablespoon lemon juice. Frost with *CREAMY CHOCOLATE FROSTING.*

CHOCOLATE MOCHA CAKE

2 cups sifted cake flour
½ teaspoon double-acting
  baking powder
1 teaspoon baking soda
1 teaspoon salt
1 teaspoon cinnamon
½ cup cocoa

1½ cups sugar
½ cup vegetable shortening
⅔ cup buttermilk or
  ⅔ cup sour milk
½ cup cooled, strong coffee
2 eggs, unbeaten
1 teaspoon vanilla

Sift together flour, baking powder, baking soda, salt, cinnamon, cocoa, and sugar. Add shortening, ⅓ cup buttermilk or ⅓ cup sour milk, and coffee. Beat all together for 2 minutes until batter is well blended and glossy. If electric mixer is used, beat at low to medium speed for same period of time. Add another ⅓ cup buttermilk or ⅓ cup sour milk, eggs, and vanilla and beat again for 2 minutes. Pour into 2 lightly greased, floured 8-inch layer cake pans. Bake in moderate oven (350°F.) 30 to 35 minutes. Frost with *MOCHA FROSTING.* Decorate cake with chocolate shavings.

Cupcakes: Fill lightly greased muffin pans ⅓ to ½ full. Bake in moderate oven (375°F.) 20 minutes. Yield: 18 cupcakes.

Loaf cake: Pour batter into lightly greased, floured loaf pan (10x10x2 inches or 13x9x2 inches). Bake in moderate oven (350°F.) 40 to 45 minutes.

BASIC DEVIL'S FOOD CAKE

¾ cup cocoa
¾ cup brown sugar
1¼ cups milk
½ cup shortening
1 cup granulated sugar
3 eggs

1¼ teaspoons vanilla
2 cups sifted cake flour
1 teaspoon baking powder
1 teaspoon salt
¾ teaspoon baking soda

Mix cocoa with brown sugar. Scald milk over medium heat, add gradually to brown sugar mixture. Beat until smooth. Cool. Cream shortening. Add granulated sugar gradually, creaming together until light and fluffy. Add eggs 1 at a time, beating after each addition. Add vanilla. Sift together flour, baking powder, salt, and baking soda. Add alternately with cocoa mixture to fat-sugar-egg mixture, mixing until smooth. Pour into greased layer pans. Bake in moderate oven (350°F.) 25 to 30 minutes. Cool in pans 5 to 10 minutes. Remove from pans and cool on wire rack. Frost with CARAMEL FROSTING. Sprinkle with chopped nuts.

CHOCOLATE ICICLE CAKE

1¾ cups sifted cake flour
3 teaspoons double-acting
   baking powder
1 teaspoon salt
1¼ cups sugar
½ cup cocoa
⅔ cup vegetable shortening
1 cup milk
2 eggs, unbeaten
1 teaspoon vanilla

Sift together flour, baking powder, salt, sugar, and cocoa. Add shortening and ⅔ cup milk. Beat for 2 minutes until batter is well blended and glossy. If electric mixer is used, beat at low to medium speed for same period of time. Add ⅓ cup milk, eggs, and vanilla. Beat 2 minutes. Pour into 2 lightly greased, floured, 8-inch layer-cake pans. Bake in moderate oven (350°F.) 30 to 35 minutes. Frost cooled layers with FLUFFY COOKED FROSTING. Decorate edges with melted chocolate, letting the chocolate run down the sides to form "icicles."

CHOCOLATE MARASCHINO CAKE

½ cup shortening
1 cup sugar
1 square (1 ounce)
   melted chocolate
1 egg, beaten
1¾ cups sifted cake flour
1 teaspoon baking soda
½ teaspoon salt
1 cup liquid (use juice from
   3-ounce bottle of Maraschino
   cherries plus buttermilk or
   sour milk to make 1 cup)
Maraschino cherries from
   3-ounce bottle, cut in
   small pieces
½ cup chopped nuts

Cream shortening. Gradually add sugar, and cream until light and fluffy. Add melted chocolate and egg. Blend well. Mix and sift flour, baking soda, and salt, and add alternately with liquid. Stir in cherries and nuts. Turn into a greased loaf baking pan (8x8x2 inches). Bake in moderate oven (350°F.) 30 to 35 minutes. Frost with 7-MINUTE FROSTING.

HONEY CHOCOLATE CAKE

3 squares melted unsweetened
   chocolate
⅔ cup honey
1¾ cups sifted cake flour
1 teaspoon baking soda
¾ teaspoon salt
½ cup butter or
   ½ cup other shortening
½ cup sugar
1 teaspoon vanilla extract
2 eggs, unbeaten
⅔ cup water

Blend chocolate and honey. Sift flour once, measure, add baking soda and salt, and sift together 3 times. Cream butter until soft. Add sugar gradually, creaming until light and fluffy. Add chocolate-honey mixture and vanilla. Mix well. Add eggs, 1 at a time, beating thoroughly after each addition. Add flour, alternately with water, a small amount at a time, beating after each addition until smooth. Bake in 2 greased 8-inch layer pans in moderate oven (350°F.) 30 to 35 minutes. Spread with *CHOCOLATE FROSTING*.

RED DEVIL'S FOOD CAKE

½ cup shortening
1½ cups sugar
½ cup cocoa
2 eggs
2 cups sifted cake flour

½ cup milk
2 teaspoons baking soda
1 cup boiling water
1 teaspoon vanilla

Line bottoms of 2 8-inch cake pans with waxed paper. Cream shortening and add sugar and cocoa. Cream thoroughly and then add eggs and beat well. Add flour alternately with milk in which baking soda has been dissolved. Add boiling water and vanilla. Turn into cake pans. Bake in moderate oven (350°F.) 30 minutes. Frost as desired.

APPLESAUCE CAKE

½ cup shortening
1 cup brown sugar
2 eggs, well beaten or
    4 egg yolks, well beaten
2 cups sifted cake flour
½ teaspoon salt
1 teaspoon cinnamon

½ teaspoon cloves
½ teaspoon nutmeg
1 teaspoon baking soda
¾ cup chopped dates
1 cup chopped nuts
1 cup cold applesauce

Cream shortening. Add sugar gradually, and cream together until smooth and fluffy. Mix in eggs or egg yolks. Sift flour with salt, spices, and baking soda. Add dates and nuts, blend with flour. Add flour mixture alternately with applesauce to shortening sugar-egg mixture and mix until smooth. Pour into greased pans. Bake in moderate oven (350°F.) 30 to 35 minutes for layer pans, and 45 to 50 minutes for loaf pan. Cool in pans 5 to 10 minutes, then remove and cool on wire rack. Ice with *BROWN SUGAR FROSTING*; decorate with walnut halves.

CARAMEL CAKE

2¼ cups sifted cake flour
3 teaspoons baking powder
1 teaspoon salt
½ cup shortening

1¼ cups sugar
3 eggs, separated
¼ cup caramel syrup
¾ cup cold water

Sift flour, baking powder, and salt 3 times. Cream shortening. Gradually add sugar, beating until soft and smooth. Mix in well-beaten egg yolks. Combine caramel syrup and water. Add alternately with dry ingredients. Beat 2 minutes and fold in egg whites, beaten until stiff but not dry. Turn into 2 greased 8-inch layer pans. Bake in moderate oven (350°F.) 30 to 35 minutes. Spread *CARAMEL BOILED FROSTING* between layers and on top.

Caramel syrup: Melt 2 cups sugar in a heavy frying pan, stirring constantly. Add ¾ cup hot water. Cook until lumps which will form upon addition of water have been dissolved and until mixture is a heavy syrup. Cool and measure.

HONEY ORANGE CAKE

½ cup shortening
½ cup sugar
½ cup honey
1 egg
2 cups all-purpose flour
2 teaspoons baking powder

¼ teaspoon baking soda
¼ teaspoon salt
½ cup finely-shredded orange peel
¼ cup orange juice
1 teaspoon grated lemon rind or
   1 teaspoon lemon flavoring

Cream shortening. Add sugar gradually, creaming until light and fluffy. Add honey, beating until smooth. Beat in egg. Sift together dry ingredients three times. Add orange peel. Combine orange juice and lemon rind or flavoring. Add dry ingredients alternately with orange juice to creamed mixture beginning and ending with flour mixture. Spread in well-greased square cake pan. The mixture is quite thick. Bake in moderate oven (350°F.) about 45 to 60 minutes. Let stand 7 or 8 minutes before removing cake from pan. Serve plain, iced, or with hot fruit sauce, warm or cold. Yield: 16 2-inch squares.

Honey orange sauce: Blend ½ cup orange juice with ⅓ cup honey. Pour over the warm or cold cake or serve separately.

BANANA SPICE CAKE

2 cups sifted cake flour
2½ teaspoons double-acting
   baking powder
1 teaspoon salt
1 teaspoon cinnamon
1 teaspoon allspice
½ teaspoon cloves
½ teaspoon nutmeg

¾ cup sugar
½ cup firmly packed brown sugar
½ cup melted vegetable
   shortening
¾ cup milk
2 eggs, unbeaten
1 teaspoon vanilla

Sift together flour, baking powder, salt, cinnamon, allspice, cloves, nutmeg, and sugar. Add brown sugar, shortening, and ½ cup milk. Beat for 2 minutes until batter is well blended and glossy. If electric mixer is used, beat at low to medium speed for same period of time. Then add ¼ cup milk, eggs, and vanilla and beat for 2 minutes. Pour into 2 lightly greased, floured, 8-inch layer-cake pans. Bake in moderate oven (350°F.) for 30 to 35 minutes. Frost with *BANANA FROSTING*.

BANANA LAYER CAKE

1¾ cups sifted cake flour
1 teaspoon baking powder
¼ teaspoon salt
⅓ cup shortening
⅓ cup granulated sugar
½ cup brown sugar

2 eggs, well beaten
1 teaspoon vanilla
1 teaspoon baking soda
4 tablespoons milk
1 cup mashed bananas

Sift flour with baking powder and salt. Cream shortening until soft and smooth. Gradually add granulated sugar and brown sugar, beating until fluffy. Beat in eggs and vanilla. Dissolve baking soda in milk. Add with bananas to creamed mixture. Add dry ingredients, beating until smooth. Turn into 2 greased 8-inch layer pans. Bake in moderate oven (350°F.) 30 to 35 minutes. Cool 5 to 10 minutes in pans. Remove from pans and cool on wire rack. Spread *LEMON FILLING* between layers. Cover top and sides with whipped cream. Decorate with border of fluted sliced bananas on top. To flute, draw lines with fork down sides of bananas, then slice.

GOLD BUTTER CAKE

2 cups sifted cake flour	5 egg yolks
3 teaspoons baking powder	1 whole egg, beaten
½ teaspoon salt	⅔ cup milk
½ cup butter	1 teaspoon vanilla
1 cup sugar	

Sift together flour, baking powder, and salt 3 times. Cream butter and sugar until light and fluffy. Mix in egg yolks and egg. Add dry ingredients alternately with milk and vanilla, beating only until smooth after each addition. Turn into greased 9-inch square pan. Bake in moderate oven (350°F.) about 45 minutes. Spread top with CHOCOLATE FROSTING and frost sides with BUTTER-SCOTCH NUT FROSTING.

Apricot gold butter cake: Prepare half the recipe for GOLD BUTTER CAKE. Line well-greased shallow pan with 1 cup drained, cooked, sweetened dried apricots. Pour batter over apricots. Bake in moderate oven (350°F.) about 35 minutes. Serve hot with apricot sauce.

MAPLE CREAM CAKE

⅓ cup butter	1 teaspoon baking soda
1 cup sugar	2½ tablespoons cocoa
2 eggs	1 cup sour milk
1¾ cups sifted cake flour	1 teaspoon vanilla
1 teaspoon baking powder	

Cream butter and sugar until light and fluffy. Add eggs and mix well. Mix and sift dry ingredients and add alternately with milk and vanilla, beating smooth after each addition. Pour into 3 greased and floured 8-inch layer pans. Bake in moderate oven (375°F.) 25 minutes. Turn out on cake racks to cool. Fill with MAPLE CREAM FILLING. Frost with CHOCOLATE FROSTING.

BURNT SUGAR CAKE

2 cups sifted cake flour	2 eggs, well beaten
3 teaspoons baking powder	⅓ cup BURNT SUGAR
½ teaspoon salt	1 teaspoon vanilla
1 cup less 1 tablespoon sugar	⅔ cup milk
½ cup shortening	

Sift together flour, baking powder, and salt. Melt ⅓ cup sugar in heavy pan over low heat, stirring until liquid becomes golden brown. Cream shortening. Gradually add sugar, creaming until light and fluffy. Add eggs, burnt sugar, and vanilla. Add dry ingredients alternately with milk. Turn into 2 greased 8-inch layer pans. Bake in moderate oven (375°F.) 25 to 30 minutes. Cool in pans 5 to 10 minutes. Remove from pans and cool on wire rack. Frost with a white frosting flavored with BURNT SUGAR.

HOT MILK CAKE

2 eggs, unbeaten
1 cup sugar
1 cup sifted cake flour
1 teaspoon baking powder
⅛ teaspoon salt
1 tablespoon shortening
½ cup hot milk

Beat eggs light and thick. Slowly add sugar, and beat until very light and thick. Sift flour, baking powder and salt. Fold into egg and sugar mixture all at one time. Melt shortening in hot milk and add all at once. The addition of flour and milk should take only about 60 seconds. Turn into well-greased and floured cake pan with center tube. Bake in moderate oven (350°F.) 30 minutes. Cool. Split crosswise. Spread with *LEMON FILLING.*

PRUNE CAKE

3 cups sifted all-purpose flour
1¼ teaspoons baking soda
1 teaspoon salt
1½ teaspoons nutmeg
1 teaspoon allspice
1½ teaspoons cinnamon
¾ teaspoon cloves
¾ cup shortening
1½ cups sugar
3 eggs
1½ cups sour milk or
   1½ cups buttermilk
1½ cups cut up, cooked,
   pitted prunes

Sift together dry ingredients three times. Cream shortening and sugar until light and fluffy. Beat in eggs, one at a time. Add dry ingredients alternately with sour milk or buttermilk, beating until smooth after each addition. Add prunes and blend well. Turn into large, greased tube pan. Bake in moderate oven (350°F.) 1½ hours, or until done. Cool. Spread with *SEVEN MINUTE FROSTING.* Decorate with grated orange rind.

WHOLE-WHEAT NUT CAKE

1 cup sifted all-purpose flour
2 teaspoons baking powder
¼ teaspoon salt
½ teaspoon cinnamon
½ teaspoon nutmeg
¼ teaspoon allspice
½ cup whole-wheat flour
¾ cup chopped nuts
¼ cup butter
¾ cup sugar
2 eggs, beaten
½ teaspoon vanilla
⅔ cup milk

Sift together all-purpose flour, baking powder, salt, cinnamon, nutmeg, and allspice. Blend in whole-wheat flour and chopped nuts. Cream butter. Add sugar gradually. Add eggs and vanilla and blend well. Add sifted dry ingredients alternately with milk, beating until smooth after each addition. Turn into well-greased loaf pan. Bake in moderate oven (350°F.) 40 to 50 minutes. Remove from pan and cool on cake rack. Cover with *ORANGE CREAM CHEESE ICING.*

SOUR CREAM SPICE CAKE

¼ cup shortening
1 cup brown sugar
1 egg
¾ cup thick sour cream
1¾ cups sifted cake flour
¼ teaspoon baking soda
2 teaspoons baking powder
⅛ teaspoon salt
¼ teaspoon cloves
2 teaspoons cinnamon

Cream shortening. Add sugar gradually. Add egg and beat well. Add sour cream. Sift flour with baking soda, baking powder, salt, cloves, and cinnamon. Add 2 tablespoons of the dry ingredients to the creamed mixture. Beat thoroughly. Add dry ingredients to the first mixture, beating well. Pour into a well-greased and floured pan (8x12x2 inches). Bake in moderate oven (350°F.) 30 minutes.

Frosted spice cake: Spread CONFECTIONERS' SUGAR ICING on top and sides.

POUND CAKE

1¼ cups butter
½ teaspoon mace
  Grated rind of ½ lemon
1½ cups sugar

6 eggs, separated
3 cups sifted cake flour
¼ to ½ teaspoon salt

Cream butter until soft. Add mace and lemon rind, then gradually add sugar, beating until mixture is light and fluffy. Slowly add well-beaten egg yolks. Fold in stiffly beaten egg whites. Add flour and salt, beating until batter is smooth. Turn into a tube pan which has been lined with waxed paper. Bake in slow oven (300° to 325°F.) 1 to 1¼ hours.

ORANGE LOAF CAKE (One-Bowl Method)

2 cups sifted cake flour
1¼ cups sugar
1½ teaspoons double-acting
  baking powder
1 teaspoon salt

½ cup vegetable shortening
½ cup orange juice
1 tablespoon grated orange rind
½ to ⅔ cup eggs, unbeaten

Mix and sift flour, sugar, baking powder, and salt into mixing bowl. Add shortening and orange juice and orange rind. Beat 2 minutes at low speed, or 300 strokes by hand. Add eggs and again beat 2 minutes at low speed, or 300 strokes by hand. Turn into greased loaf baking pan (5x9¼x2¾ inches). Bake in slow oven (325°F.) 1½ hours.

FUDGE NUT LOAF CAKE

½ cup shortening
2 cups sugar
1¼ teaspoons salt
2 teaspoons vanilla
2 eggs

4 squares (4 ounces) chocolate
2 cups sifted cake flour
2 teaspoons baking powder
1½ cups milk
1 cup chopped nutmeats

Cream shortening. Add sugar, salt, and vanilla. Cream until fluffy. Add eggs, one at a time, beating well after each addition. Melt chocolate and add to creamed mixture. Beat until well combined. Mix and sift flour and baking powder. Add alternately with milk, adding flour first and last. Add nutmeats, and mix until thoroughly blended. Grease bottom of cake pan (13x9x1½ inches). Dust lightly with flour. Turn batter into pan. Bake in moderate oven (350°F.) 40 minutes. Cool and frost with CHOCOLATE NUT FROSTING.

Layers: Bake in 2 8-inch layer pans in moderate oven (375°F.) 25 to 30 minutes. Cool and spread a custard filling between layers. Frost as above.

HURRY-UP LOAF CAKE

2¼ cups cake flour
2¼ teaspoons baking powder
½ teaspoon salt
1 cup sugar

⅓ cup softened shortening
1 cup milk
1 teaspoon vanilla

Sift flour once. Measure. Add baking powder, salt, and sugar and sift together 3 times. Add shortening, milk, and vanilla. Mix only enough to dampen all flour, then beat vigorously about 1 minute. Turn into greased, lined loaf pan (8x8x2 inches). Bake in moderate oven (375°F.) until done, about 40 minutes.

PARTY CUPCAKES

2 cups sifted all-purpose flour
3 teaspoons baking powder
¼ teaspoon salt
½ cup butter

1 cup sugar
2 eggs
¾ cup milk
1 teaspoon vanilla

Sift together flour, baking powder, and salt. Cream butter and sugar until soft and creamy. Add eggs. Beat until light and fluffy. Add dry ingredients alternately with milk, mixing thoroughly. Add vanilla. Divide batter into 3 parts. Leave ⅓ of batter plain. Fill muffin pans ⅔ full. Bake in moderate oven (375°F.) 20 to 30 minutes. Frost with chocolate frosting and chocolate shots when cool.

Fruit cup cakes: To ⅓ of batter add ⅓ cup raisins, ⅓ cup citron, and ⅓ cup coconut. Bake. Frost with *BUTTER FROSTING.* Garnish with fruits.

Spice nut cakes: To ⅓ of batter add ⅓ cup grated nuts and ¼ teaspoon each of cinnamon and cloves. Serve plain or frosted.

CHOCOLATE CHIP CUPCAKES

⅓ cup vegetable shortening
¾ cup sugar
2 eggs
1 teaspoon vanilla
2¼ cups sifted cake flour

3 teaspoons double-acting
    baking powder
1 teaspoon salt
⅔ cup milk
1 package chocolate chips

Cream shortening. Add sugar gradually, creaming continually. Beat in 1 egg at a time and add vanilla. Mix and sift flour, baking powder, and salt. Add to first mixture alternately with milk. Place half of batter in greased muffin pans. Sprinkle with half of chocolate chips. Add remaining batter and sprinkle with remaining chocolate chips. Bake in moderate oven (375°F.) 20 to 25 minutes. Yield: 18 cupcakes.

THRIFTY FRUIT CAKE

2 cups sugar
2 cups boiling water
2 tablespoons butter
1 pound raisins
1 teaspoon baking soda
3 cups sifted cake flour

1 teaspoon salt
1 teaspoon nutmeg
1 teaspoon cinnamon
½ teaspoon cloves
1 cup chopped nutmeats
⅓ pound citron, cut fine

Boil together the sugar, water, butter, and raisins until sugar is dissolved. Let stand until cold. Then add baking soda to mixture. Sift together cake flour, salt, nutmeg, cinnamon, and cloves. Add to cold mixture. Then add chopped nutmeats and citron. Line tube pan with greased wax paper. Pour in batter. Bake in slow oven (325°F.) 1 to 1½ hours.

DARK FRUIT CAKE

¼ pound citron, cut fine
1 pound chopped raisins
1 pound currants
4 cups sifted cake flour
½ pound butter
1 cup sugar
5 egg yolks, beaten
½ cup cider
½ cup tart jelly

½ cup sour cream
1 cup molasses
2 teaspoons baking powder
½ teaspoon baking soda
1 teaspoon salt
1 teaspoon cinnamon
1 teaspoon nutmeg
2 cups chopped nuts
5 egg whites, beaten

Combine citron, raisins, and currants and rub in 2 cups of flour, so that fruit is separated into small pieces. Cream butter. Add sugar, egg yolks, cider, jelly, sour cream, and molasses. Sift twice remaining 2 cups flour, baking powder, baking soda, salt, cinnamon, and nutmeg. Stir into liquid mixture. Add floured fruit, and nuts. Fold in well-beaten egg whites. Bake in tube pan lined with greased paper in very slow oven (250° to 275°F.) about 3 hours. This cake will weigh 5 to 6 pounds.

ORANGE FRUIT CAKE

2½ cups sifted cake flour
1½ teaspoons baking soda
½ teaspoon salt
1 teaspoon cinnamon
½ teaspoon cloves
¼ teaspoon allspice
½ cup finely cut citron
½ cup finely cut candied pineapple
½ cup quartered candied cherries

½ cup broken nutmeats
½ cup shortening
2 cups sugar
2 eggs, well beaten
1 tablespoon grated orange rind
3½ tablespoons vinegar and enough
　　sour cream to make 1 cup
¾ cup orange juice

Sift flour, baking soda, salt, cinnamon, cloves, and allspice together. Add cut fruit and nuts and mix well. Cream shortening. Add 1 cup sugar gradually and cream until fluffy. Add eggs and grated orange rind. Beat well. Add vinegar and sour cream alternately with the flour mixture to the creamed ingredients. Mix until thoroughly blended. Pour into well-greased 9-inch tube pan. Bake in moderate oven (350°F.) 1 hour. After cake is removed from oven, and while it is still hot, pour over it 1 cup sugar mixed with orange juice. Let cake cool before removing from pan.

FRUIT CAKE WITH WHOLE NUTS

4 eggs, separated
1 cup sugar
¼ cup wine
1 cup sifted all-purpose flour
1 teaspoon baking powder
⅛ teaspoon salt

1 cup chopped candied pineapple
1 pound whole pitted dates
½ pound whole candied cherries
½ pound walnut halves
½ pound pecan halves
½ pound whole Brazil nuts

Beat egg yolks. Add sugar, and cream together thoroughly. Add wine, and mix well. Add flour sifted with baking powder and salt. Fold in stiffly beaten egg whites. Add chopped pineapple, dates, cherries, and nuts to batter. Mix well. Grease 2 pans (4½x9x5 inches). Line with waxed paper and grease again. Carefully add cake mixture with a spoon. Bake in slow oven (325°F.) about 1½ hours. Cool thoroughly. Remove paper and store in an airtight container.

WHITE FRUIT CAKE

4 cups sifted cake flour	1 pound finely cut citron
2 teaspoons baking powder	1 pound finely chopped almonds
⅓ teaspoon salt	1 cup butter
½ teaspoon baking soda	1½ cups sugar
½ pound each candied lemon peel,	1½ tablespoons lemon juice
orange peel, and cherries, chopped	10 egg whites, beaten stiff
1 pound chopped raisins	

Sift flour 3 times with baking powder, salt, and baking soda. Combine candied lemon peel, orange peel, cherries, raisins, citron, and nuts. Dredge with 1 cup of flour mixture. Cream butter and sugar until fluffy. Add flour slowly. When well mixed, stir in floured fruits and nuts and lemon juice. Fold in egg whites. Pour in tube pans or into small loaf pans lined with heavy oiled paper. Bake in very slow oven (250°F.) 2½ hours, then raise heat to 300°F., and bake 20 minutes longer.

SUPER SPONGE CAKE (Basic Recipe)

1 cup sifted cake flour	2 tablespoons lemon juice
5 eggs, separated	1 teaspoon grated lemon rind
1 cup sugar	½ teaspoon salt

Sift flour three times. Using a rotary beater, beat egg yolks until thick and lemon-colored. Gradually add half the sugar, beating thoroughly, and then the lemon juice and grated lemon rind. Beat until thick. Beat egg whites and salt until stiff enough to form peaks but not dry. Fold in remaining sugar, then the yolk mixture. Fold in flour gently. Turn at once into ungreased tube pan. Powdered sugar sifted over top makes a delicate crust. Bake in preheated slow oven (325°F.) 50 to 60 minutes or until done. Remove from oven and invert pan 1 hour, or until cake is cool.

Cocoa sponge cake: Replace ¼ cup flour with ¼ cup cocoa. Replace 1 tablespoon lemon juice with 1 tablespoon water. Sift cocoa with flour.

Jelly roll: Omit 2 eggs from recipe. Add ¼ cup water and 1 teaspoon baking powder. Line bottom of flat rectangular pan with greased paper. Spread cake evenly in thin layer. Bake in moderate oven (350°F.) about 15 minutes. While hot turn onto cloth sprinkled with powdered sugar and remove greased paper. Trim edges. Spread with soft jelly and roll up.

Orange sponge cake: Add grated rind and juice of ½ orange. Grate rind before cutting orange. Omit 1 tablespoon lemon juice.

Pineapple meringue sponge: Bake sponge in layers. Spread crushed pineapple between layers and on top. Top with meringue. Place in slow oven with door ajar, until meringue is delicate brown in color.

Sponge layer cake: Bake in layer pans in moderate oven (350°F.) about 30 minutes. Spread jam or jelly between layers. Sprinkle powdered sugar on top.

ECONOMICAL SPONGE CAKE (Basic Recipe)

1½ cups sifted cake flour
1 teaspoon baking powder
⅛ teaspoon salt
3 eggs

1 cup sugar
⅓ cup water
1 teaspoon vanilla or
    lemon extract

Sift flour with baking powder and salt. Beat eggs with rotary beater until very light and frothy. Gradually add sugar, beating until thick and light colored. Then add water and vanilla or lemon extract. Fold in dry ingredients, blending well. Turn into ungreased tube pan or two 8-inch layer pans. Bake in moderate oven (350°F.) 25 to 35 minutes. Invert pan 1 hour, or until cold, before removing cake.

Orange sponge cake: Substitute orange juice for water and 1 tablespoon grated orange rind for other flavoring.

Sponge cupcakes: Fill cupcake pans ⅔ full. Bake in moderate oven (350°F.) about 15 minutes. Top with LEMON FROSTING, ORANGE FROSTING, or PINE-APPLE FROSTING.

HOT MILK SPONGE CAKE

1¼ cups sifted cake flour
2 teaspoons baking powder
¼ teaspoon salt
2 eggs

1 cup sugar
1 tablespoon lemon juice or
    1 teaspoon vanilla
½ cup hot milk

Sift together 3 times flour, baking powder, and salt. Beat the eggs until very thick and light, about 10 minutes. Gradually add sugar, beating constantly. Add flavoring. Fold in dry ingredients, a small amount at a time. Add milk, mixing quickly until batter is smooth. Turn into an ungreased 9-inch tube pan. Bake in moderate oven (350°F.) 35 to 45 minutes. Remove from oven. Invert pan on rack until cold before removing cake.

SPICED SPONGE CAKE

2 cups sifted cake flour
2 teaspoons baking powder
¼ teaspoon salt
½ teaspoon allspice
½ teaspoon cloves
½ teaspoon nutmeg

4 egg yolks
1 cup sugar
1 teaspoon vanilla
½ teaspoon almond extract
1 cup boiling water
4 egg whites, stiffly beaten

Sift together twice flour, baking powder, salt, allspice, cloves, and nutmeg. Beat egg yolks with rotary beater until thick and lemon-colored. Gradually add sugar and continue beating until thick and light-colored. Add vanilla and almond extract. Add boiling water slowly and continue beating for 3 minutes until light and foamy. Gradually beat in dry ingredients with rotary beater until flour is thoroughly blended. Fold in egg whites. Bake in 10-inch ungreased tube pan in moderate oven (350°F.) 45 minutes. Invert pan and cool 1 hour. Serve plain or cover with COFFEE WALNUT FROSTING.

CINDERELLA SPONGE CAKE

1 cup sifted cake flour
½ teaspoon salt
2 tablespoons lemon juice
1½ teaspoons grated lemon rind

1 tablespoon water
⅓ cup egg yolks
1 cup sugar
¾ cup egg whites

Sift together flour and salt twice. Combine lemon juice, lemon rind, water, and egg yolks and beat with rotary beater until very thick. Gradually add cup sugar, a tablespoon at a time, beating thoroughly after each addition. Sift dry ingredients into egg mixture gradually, folding in carefully. Beat egg whites until stiff, but not dry, and fold into batter, handling gently. Turn into ungreased 9-inch tube pan. Bake in slow oven (325°F.) 60 to 70 minutes. Cool in inverted pan about 1 hour. Serve unfrosted, or cut across into 2 layers and fill with *LEMON FILLING* and frost with *MERINGUE*.

ANGEL FOOD CAKE (Basic Recipe)

1¼ cups sifted cake flour
1¾ cups sugar
½ teaspoon salt
1½ cups egg whites
 (11 to 13 eggs)

1¼ teaspoons cream of tartar
1 teaspoon vanilla
1 teaspoon almond extract

Sift and measure flour. Sift together 5 times flour, sugar, and salt. Beat egg whites with a rotary beater until foamy, add cream of tartar, continue beating until stiff but not dry. Whites should be glossy and moist, and should cling to bottom and sides of bowl. Using a whisk type beater, blend in flavoring and fold in dry ingredients. Do not stir. Turn into 10-inch ungreased tube pan. Bake in slow oven (325°F.) 1 to 1¼ hours. Invert pan on rack until cake is cold or about 1 hour.

Smaller angel food cake: Use 1 cup flour, 1¼ cups sugar, ¼ teaspoon salt, 1 teaspoon cream of tartar, 1 cup egg whites, 1 teaspoon vanilla, ½ teaspoon almond extract. Bake in 9-inch tube pan.

Chocolate angel food: Substitute ¼ cup cocoa for ¼ cup flour. Sift cocoa with 1 cup of sugar. Omit almond extract.

Maraschino angel food: Drain and cut up ½ cup maraschino cherries. Pour ¼ of batter into pan. Sprinkle cherries over batter. Add another ¼ of batter. Continue alternating batter and fruit until all used.

Marble angel food: Add 2 tablespoons chocolate syrup to half the batter. Omit almond extract. Alternate layers of white and chocolate batters in pan.

Orange angel food: Fold in 1 tablespoon grated orange rind. Substitute 1 teaspoon orange extract for almond extract. Cover with *ORANGE FROSTING*.

Peppermint angel food: Use 1 teaspoon peppermint extract or a few drops peppermint oil as flavoring. Add few drops red or green coloring.

Pineapple angel food: Dice ½ cup pineapple. Follow method for *MARASCHINO ANGEL FOOD* above.

Spice angel food: Sift 1 teaspoon cinnamon, ¼ teaspoon nutmeg, ¼ teaspoon allspice with flour.

Tutti-frutti angel food: Tint batter to a pink color with vegetable coloring. Fold in 1 cup finely chopped candied fruits.

Yellow and white angel food: Prepare *ANGEL FOOD CAKE*, omitting flavoring. Divide batter into 2 parts. Into one part fold in 4 well-beaten egg yolks, 2 tablespoons flour, and 1 teaspoon lemon extract. Into the second part fold in 1 teaspoon vanilla. Drop by spoonfuls into pan, alternating white and yellow batter.
Loosen from sides and center with knife and remove from pan.

ANGEL FOOD SWIRL CAKE

¾ cup plus 2 tablespoons sifted
  cake flour
1½ cups sifted sugar
1¼ cups egg whites
¼ teaspoon salt

1¼ teaspoons cream of tartar
1 teaspoon vanilla
¼ teaspoon almond extract
3 tablespoons cocoa

Sift together 2 times ¾ cup flour and ½ cup sugar. Beat egg whites with salt until foamy. Sprinkle 1¼ teaspoons cream of tartar over egg whites and continue beating until stiff, but not dry. Fold in ¾ cup additional sugar, a small amount at a time. Add vanilla and almond extract. Sift in dry ingredients gradually, folding in carefully. Divide batter in half. Sift together 2 tablespoons cake flour and 2 tablespoons sugar. Add to one half of batter. Sift together 2 tablespoons sugar and 3 tablespoons cocoa and fold into remaining half of batter. Into an ungreased 9-inch tube pan, place alternate spoonfuls of light and dark batters. Bake 60 minutes in slow oven (325°F.). Invert pan until cake is cold, or about 1 hour.

JELLY ROLL #2

1 cup sifted cake flour
2 teaspoons baking powder
¼ teaspoon salt
3 eggs
¼ cup cold water

1 cup sugar
1 teaspoon vanilla
Confectioners' sugar
1 glass jelly
Cherries and nuts for garnish

Sift flour, baking powder, and salt. Beat eggs until thick and lemon colored. Add cold water and sugar, beating well. Gradually fold in sifted ingredients. Add vanilla. Turn into well-greased sheet cake pan (10x15 inches) lined with greased brown or waxed paper. Bake in hot oven (425°F.) 12 to 15 minutes. Place tea towel on table, cover with waxed paper, sprinkle with confectioners' sugar. Turn hot cake onto waxed paper. Spread with jelly. Hold paper and towel firmly with thumb and first finger. Lift and roll. Cool. Unwrap. Garnish with cherries and nuts. Serves 6.

Chocolate roll: In *JELLY ROLL* recipe, replace ¼ cup of the flour with ¼ cup of cocoa before sifting. Fill with cream filling, or with whipped cream if cooled before rolling.

PEPPERMINT ROLL

½ cup confectioners' sugar
3 tablespoons cocoa
⅛ teaspoon salt
5 eggs, separated

¾ cup heavy cream
½ cup crushed peppermint stick
  candy

Mix and sift sugar, cocoa, salt and add to well-beaten egg yolks. Mix well and fold in egg whites, stiffly beaten. Turn onto a greased sheet pan (15½x10½ inches) lined with greased and floured heavy waxed paper. Bake in moderate oven (350°F.) 20 to 25 minutes. Turn onto a cloth sprinkled with confectioners' sugar. Let cool slightly. Spread with whipped cream into which peppermint candy has been folded. Roll and wrap in waxed paper. Chill in refrigerator.

DAFFODIL CAKE

¾ cup plus 2 tablespoons sifted
    cake flour
1 cup plus 2 tablespoons sifted sugar
¾ cup egg whites
¼ teaspoon salt

¾ teaspoon cream of tartar
¼ teaspoon orange extract
3 egg yolks
¼ teaspoon vanilla

Sift ¾ cup flour and ½ cup sugar together twice. Beat egg whites with salt until foamy. Sprinkle cream of tartar over egg whites and continue beating until stiff, but not dry. Fold in ½ cup additional sugar, a small amount at a time. Sift in dry ingredients gradually, folding in carefully. Divide batter in half. Combine 2 tablespoons sugar, 2 tablespoons cake flour, orange extract, and egg yolks, beaten until thick and lemon colored. Fold into ½ of batter. Blend ¼ teaspoon vanilla into remaining ½ of batter. Place by spoonfuls yellow and white batters alternately into ungreased 9-inch tube pan. Bake in slow oven (325°F.) 60 minutes. Invert pan until cake is cold, or about 1 hour.

GOLD CAKE

3 cups sifted cake flour
2 teaspoons baking powder
10 egg yolks
1 teaspoon vanilla or
    1 teaspoon lemon extract

¼ teaspoon salt
2 cups sugar
1 cup cold water

Sift flour with baking powder. Beat egg yolks until thick and very light. Add flavoring and salt. Gradually beat in sugar. Add flour alternately with water, beating after each addition until smooth. Turn batter into ungreased 10-inch tube pan. Bake until golden brown in moderate oven (350°F.) 50 to 60 minutes. Invert pan on cake rack 1 hour, or until cold, before removing from pan. This cake uses up leftover Angel Food egg yolks. Serve as shortcake with fruits or with dessert sauces.

DELUXE PETITS FOURS

2 cups sifted cake flour
2½ teaspoons baking powder
½ teaspoon salt
1¼ cups sugar

1 cup heavy cream
½ cup egg whites, unbeaten
1 teaspoon vanilla

Sift together flour, baking powder, salt, and sugar. Whip heavy cream until stiff and add sifted dry ingredients, egg whites, and vanilla. Beat for 2 minutes, or until batter is well blended and glossy. If electric mixer is used, beat at low to medium speed for same period of time. Pour into lightly greased shallow pan lined with waxed paper. Bake in moderate oven (350°F.) 20 to 25 minutes. Turn out on cake rack while warm and remove waxed paper. Cool. Cut with fancy cutters or sharp knife into small squares, diamonds, triangles or any desired shape. Frost with PETIT FOUR FROSTING and ornamental frosting. Decorate with colored sugar, candied fruits, and nuts. Yield: sheet cake (15x10 inches).

HUNGARIAN APPLESAUCE CAKE

2 cups sifted cake flour	Grated rind of 1 lemon
1 teaspoon baking powder	1 egg, well beaten
½ teaspoon salt	1½ cups thick applesauce
½ cup butter	1 teaspoon baking soda
1 cup sugar	½ cup seedless raisins
1 teaspoon cinnamon	½ cup chopped nuts

Mix and sift flour, baking powder, and salt. Cream together butter, sugar, cinnamon, and lemon rind until soft and smooth. Add egg and beat until fluffy. Add applesauce, baking soda, raisins, and nuts. Add dry ingredients and mix well. Turn into well-greased and floured cake pan. Bake in moderate oven (350°F.) 1½ hours.

NORWEGIAN APPLE CAKE

2 cups toasted crumbs	Butter
½ teaspoon nutmeg	1 cup heavy cream, whipped
2 cups applesauce	Jelly

Combine crumbs and nutmeg. Arrange alternate layers of crumbs and applesauce in a buttered pudding dish. Dot each layer with butter and top with crumbs. Press down well. Bake in slow oven (325°F.) 45 minutes. Cool, turn out, and spread with whipped cream and dot with jelly. Serves 6.

BLITZKUCHEN

1⅛ cups sifted cake flour	1 egg white diluted with
1 teaspoon baking powder	1 tablespoon water
½ cup butter	¼ teaspoon salt
1 cup sugar	¾ cup sugar
4 eggs, separated	2 tablespoons cinnamon
1 teaspoon grated lemon rind	½ cup chopped nuts
3 tablespoons milk	

Mix and sift flour and baking powder. Cream butter until soft and smooth. Gradually add sugar, beating until light and fluffy. Add well-beaten egg yolks and lemon rind. Gradually add flour, beating well. Add milk and beat again. Beat egg whites with salt until stiff, but not dry. Gently fold into batter. Pour into 2 greased pans (8x12 inches) and spread with diluted egg white. Sprinkle liberally with combination of sugar, cinnamon, and nuts. Bake in moderate oven (375°F.) 20 minutes. Serve either hot or cold.

LEMON CHIFFON CAKE (Basic Recipe)

2¼ cups sifted cake flour	¾ cup cold water
1½ cups sugar	2 teaspoons vanilla
3 teaspoons baking powder	Grated rind of 1 lemon (optional)
1 teaspoon salt	1 cup egg whites (7 or 8)
½ cup salad oil	½ teaspoon cream of tartar
5 egg yolks, unbeaten	

Mix and sift flour, sugar, baking powder, and salt. Add oil, egg yolks, water, vanilla, and (if desired) lemon rind. Beat with a spoon until smooth. Whip egg whites with cream of tartar until very stiff peaks are formed. Gently fold cake mixture into egg whites until well blended. Do not stir. Pour into ungreased 10-inch tube pan (4 inches deep) immediately. Bake in slow oven (325°F.) 55 minutes, then at 350°F. 10 to 15 minutes, or until top springs back when lightly touched. Invert pan on rack until cold. To remove from pan, loosen from sides and tube with spatula.

Banana chiffon cake: Reduce water to ⅓ cup. Use only 1 teaspoon vanilla or lemon rind. Add 1 cup sieved very ripe bananas (2 to 3 bananas) to egg yolk mixture. Bake in slow oven (325°F.) 65 to 70 minutes.

Hawaiian chiffon cake: Substitute ¾ cup canned unsweetened pineapple juice for vanilla and lemon rind. Fold in 1 cup shredded coconut with egg whites. Bake in slow oven (325°F.) 65 to 70 minutes.

Orange chiffon cake: Omit vanilla and lemon rind. Add grated rind of 2 oranges (about 3 tablespoons) to egg yolk mixture. Baking time same as for *LEMON CHIFFON CAKE.*

Walnut chiffon cake: Omit lemon rind. After egg mixture has been folded into egg whites, sprinkle over top of batter, gently folding in with a few strokes 1 cup very finely chopped walnuts. Baking time same as for *LEMON CHIFFON CAKE.*

PECAN CHIFFON CAKE

1 cup sifted cake flour	½ teaspoon vanilla
½ cup firmly packed brown sugar	½ teaspoon almond flavoring
¾ teaspoon salt	½ cup egg whites
1½ teaspoons baking powder	¼ teaspoon cream of tartar
¼ cup salad oil	¼ cup granulated sugar
3 egg yolks	½ cup finely chopped pecans
6 tablespoons water	

Mix and sift into a mixing bowl the flour, brown sugar, salt, and baking powder. Make a hollow in center and add salad oil. Add in order, egg yolks, water, vanilla, and almond flavoring. Beat with a spoon until smooth. Put egg whites into a large mixing bowl. Add cream of tartar. Beat with rotary or electric beater until whites form soft peaks. Add granulated sugar gradually, beating after each addition. Beat until meringue is just stiff enough not to slide when bowl is inverted. Pour egg yolk mixture over meringue. Gently fold yolks and pecans into meringue until well blended. Turn into ungreased loaf pan (5x10x3 inches). Bake in a slow oven (325°F.) 50 minutes. Frost with *BUTTER FROSTING.*

BREADCRUMB CAKE

3 eggs	¼ teaspoon cinnamon
1 cup sugar	¼ teaspoon almond extract
2 cups crumbs, from very dry oven-toasted bread	¼ teaspoon salt
	1 teaspoon vanilla

Beat eggs, add sugar, and stir in other ingredients. Spread mixture evenly into shallow greased pan. Bake in slow oven (300°F.) about 30 minutes. Cake has a texture and flavor similar to macaroons.

AUSTRIAN FILBERT CAKE

8 eggs, separated   1¾ cups filberts, ground
1¼ cups sugar   ½ teaspoon finely ground coffee

Beat together egg yolks and sugar until thick and creamy. Add filberts and coffee and gently fold in stiffly beaten egg whites. Bake in a well-buttered pan in a moderate oven (350°F.) 1 hour. Sift a little powdered sugar over the top, if desired. Serves 12.

GINGERBREAD (Basic Recipe)

2 cups sifted all-purpose flour   ¼ cup shortening
1 teaspoon ground ginger   ¼ cup sugar
¾ teaspoon baking soda   1 egg
¾ teaspoon cinnamon   ¾ cup molasses
¼ teaspoon ground cloves   ¾ cup milk
1 teaspoon salt

Sift together dry ingredients. Cream shortening. Gradually add sugar, beating until light and fluffy. Add egg and beat well. Stir molasses into the milk. Add dry ingredients alternately with molasses mixture, beating thoroughly. Turn into greased layer or loaf pans or in muffin pans. Bake in moderate oven (350°F.) 30 to 40 minutes for layers, 35 to 45 minutes for loaf, and 20 to 25 minutes for cupcakes. Yield: 2 8-inch layers or 1 large loaf or 1½ dozen cupcakes.

Ginger nut or raisin cake: Stir in one cup of nuts or raisins.

Ginger orange cake: Replace milk with orange juice and add 1 tablespoon grated orange rind to creamed shortening and sugar.

Gingerbread Washington pie: Prepare the recipe for GINGERBREAD and bake in well-greased pie plate. When cool, split in two. Make half the recipe of CORN-STARCH PUDDING. Cool. Spread between layers. Sprinkle top layer with powdered sugar.

Gingerbread upside-down cake: Melt 2 tablespoons butter in 9-inch-square cake pan. Add ¼ cup molasses. Arrange 1 cup sliced fruit in decorative pattern in the pan. Pour 1 recipe of GINGERBREAD over fruit. Bake in moderate oven (350°F.) 45 minutes to 1 hour. Turn out upside-down.

LEKACH (Traditional Honey Cake)

3½ cups sifted cake flour   ½ cup raisins
1½ teaspoons baking powder   ½ cup chopped nuts
1 teaspoon baking soda   ¼ cup chopped citron
1 cup sugar   ½ teaspoon allspice
6 eggs, well beaten   ½ teaspoon cinnamon
1 cup honey   ½ teaspoon ground cloves
2 tablespoons vegetable oil   2 tablespoons brandy

Mix and sift flour, baking powder, and baking soda. Add sugar gradually to eggs and beat until light. Stir in honey and oil. Add raisins, nuts, citron, allspice, cinnamon, cloves, and brandy. Mix in flour, beating vigorously. Pour into cake pan lined with greased paper. Bake in slow oven (300°F.) 1 hour. Invert pan until cake is cold.

Variation: For more economical cake, substitute 4 eggs plus ½ cup hot coffee or hot tea for 6 eggs, and dilute honey with hot liquid before combining.

HONEY CAKE

Scant 3 cups sifted cake flour
2 teaspoons baking powder
½ teaspoon salt
1 cup butter
1 cup strained honey

4 eggs, well beaten
1 tablespoon lemon juice
1 teaspoon grated lemon rind
1 cup cut citron
¾ cup chopped nuts

Mix and sift flour, baking powder, and salt. Cream butter with honey. Blend in eggs, lemon juice, and lemon rind. Add dry ingredients. Blend smoothly. Mix in citron and nuts. Pour into large loaf pan lined with greased paper. Bake in moderate oven (350°F.) 1 hour.

FRENCH ORANGE FIG CAKE

1½ cups sifted cake flour
2 teaspoons baking powder
½ teaspoon salt
⅓ cup butter

1 cup sugar
1 egg plus 1 egg yolk
1 teaspoon orange juice
½ cup milk

Mix and sift flour, baking powder, and salt. Cream butter. Add sugar gradually, beating until very fluffy. Add beaten eggs combined with orange juice. Add dry ingredients alternately with milk. Start and end with flour. Beat until well blended. Pour into 2 greased and floured cake pans. Bake in moderate oven (350°F.) 25 minutes. Remove and cool. Put together with *FIG FILLING*. Frost with *ORANGE FROSTING*.

DUTCH PLUM CAKE

2 cups sifted all-purpose flour
4 teaspoons baking powder
½ teaspoon salt
1 tablespoon sugar
⅓ cup butter
1 egg, beaten

⅔ cup milk
Plums, stoned and quartered
Sugar
Cinnamon
Cream

Mix and sift flour, baking powder, salt, and sugar. Cut in butter. Add beaten egg and enough milk to make a soft dough. Spread dough in a greased baking dish with the fingers. Cover with layer of plums. Sprinkle with sugar and cinnamon. Dot with bits of butter. Bake in hot oven (400°F.) 30 minutes. Serve with cream.

HUNGARIAN PLUM CAKE

½ cup butter
1 cup sugar
2 eggs
1 cup sifted all-purpose flour
1 teaspoon baking powder

½ teaspoon salt
2 teaspoons cinnamon
½ teaspoon lemon extract
10 fresh or canned plum halves

Cream butter, add ½ cup sugar, and cream until light and fluffy. Add eggs one at a time and beat well. Add flour which has been sifted with baking powder, salt, and 1 teaspoon cinnamon. Add lemon extract. Pour into a well-greased pan (11x6x2 inches). Press the plum halves into batter. Sprinkle mixture of ½ cup sugar and 1 teaspoon cinnamon over top. Bake in hot oven (400°F.) 30 minutes. Serves 5 to 6.

Hungarian apple cake: Substitute 3 sliced tart apples for plums.

Hungarian peach cake: Substitute 10 halves of fresh or canned peaches for plums.

POPPY SEED CAKE

2 cups sifted cake flour
3 teaspoons baking powder
½ teaspoon salt
⅔ cup poppy seed
1 cup milk

⅔ cup butter
1½ cups sugar
1 teaspoon vanilla
4 egg whites
Custard filling

Mix and sift flour, baking powder, and salt. Soak poppy seed in ¾ cup milk 2 hours or more. Cream butter and sugar until soft and smooth. Add poppy seed mixture, and cream again until light and fluffy. Stir in ¼ cup milk with vanilla. Add sifted dry ingredients alternately with remaining milk in 3 parts. Beat well after each addition. Beat egg whites until stiff, but not dry. Fold gently into batter. Bake in 2 well-greased 9-inch layer cake pans in moderate oven (375°F.) 20 minutes. Cool and spread custard filling between layers. Serve with chocolate sauce.

CHEESE CAKE #1 (Basic Recipe)

1 package zwieback
½ cup melted butter
3 tablespoons powdered sugar
3 eggs, separated
1 cup granulated sugar
Grated rind and juice of 1 lemon

½ teaspoon salt
½ teaspoon grated nutmeg
1 cup heavy cream, whipped stiff
1 teaspoon vanilla (optional)
½ cup all-purpose flour, sifted twice
1 pound cottage cheese, sieved

Crush zwieback with a rolling pin. Combine crumbs with butter and powdered sugar. Press half of mixture in bottom and around sides of a well-greased, deep, round baking pan or spring form. Beat egg yolks until light. Gradually add granulated sugar, beating thoroughly. Add grated rind and juice of lemon, salt, nutmeg, vanilla-flavored whipped cream and flour. Mix thoroughly with the cheese and rub though a sieve to insure absolute smoothness. Fold in stiffly beaten egg whites. Pour carefully on top of zwieback mixture. Spread remaining crumb mixture over the top. Bake in slow oven (275°F.) until firm, 1 hour, or until set. Turn off heat. Let stand in oven 1 hour, or until cooled. Remove rim of spring form, and place with tin bottom on serving plate.

Apricot cheese cake: Arrange layer of strained, cooked dried apricots on zwieback crust. Cover with cheese mixture.

Pineapple cheese cake: Arrange a layer of well-drained crushed pineapple on zwieback crust. Cover with cheese mixture.

Prune cheese cake: Place a layer of strained, cooked prunes on zwieback crust. Cover with cheese mixture.

Strawberry cheese cake: Place a layer of well-drained, mashed strawberries, which have been cooked for 5 minutes in a little sugar syrup, on zwieback crust. Cover with cheese mixture.

CHEESE CAKE #2

1 package (5¾ ounces) zwieback	¼ cup sifted all-purpose flour
1¼ cups sugar	1½ pounds dry cottage cheese
½ teaspoon cinnamon	1 teaspoon vanilla
½ cup melted butter	1 tablespoon grated lemon rind
3 eggs, separated	1 cup whipping cream

Crush zwieback. Add ¼ cup sugar, cinnamon, and melted butter. Mix thoroughly and line bottom and sides of an 8-inch spring form pan. Chill while making filling. Beat egg yolks until thick and lemon colored. Blend 1 cup sugar and the flour together. Add to beaten yolks, mixing thoroughly. Rub cottage cheese through a sieve and add to yolk mixture, beating well. Stir in vanilla and lemon rind. Whip cream until stiff. Lightly fold cream into cheese mixture, and fold in stiffly beaten egg whites. Turn cheese mixture into crumb-lined spring form pan. Bake in a slow oven (300°F.) for 1¼ hours. Cool thoroughly on cake rack before removing sides of pan. Serve with sugared grapes. Serves 8.

CHEESE TORTE

2 cups breadcrumbs	1½ teaspoons lemon juice
1½ cups sugar	1½ teaspoons grated lemon rind
1 teaspoon cinnamon	1 cup cream
½ cup melted butter	3 cups cottage cheese
4 eggs	4 tablespoons flour
⅛ teaspoon salt	¼ cup chopped nutmeats

Combine crumbs with ½ cup sugar, cinnamon, and butter. Set aside ¾ cup crumb mixture for topping. Press remaining mixture into 9-inch pan, lining bottom and sides. Beat eggs with remaining sugar until light. Add salt, lemon juice, lemon rind, cream, cheese, and flour. Beat thoroughly until well blended. Turn into lined pan, sprinkle with remaining crumbs and nutmeats. Bake in moderate oven (350°F.) about 1 hour, or until center is set. Turn off or reduce heat. Open oven door and let stand in oven 1 hour, or until cooled. Serves 10 to 12.

CHIFFON CHEESECAKE

½ pound cottage cheese	3 eggs, separated
2 tablespoons flour	⅓ cup sugar
3 tablespoons butter	½ cup heavy cream
Dash of salt	1 teaspoon lemon juice

Rub cheese through coarse sieve. Blend in flour, soft butter, and salt. Add egg yolks one at a time and beat until well blended. Add half the sugar, heavy cream, and lemon juice. Beat egg whites until stiff, then beat in remaining sugar. Fold into cheese mixture. Turn into a crumb-lined spring form (5 inches wide, 2 inches deep). Bake in slow oven (275°F.) 1½ hours, or until firm. This cheesecake will shrink and fall in the center on cooling. Serve when perfectly cold.

HUNGARIAN CHEESECAKE

RICH PIECRUST or
HUNGARIAN MUERBE TEIG
1 cup dry cottage cheese
1 cup thick sour cream
⅓ cup sugar
½ teaspoon salt

3 eggs, well beaten
1 teaspoon grated lemon rind
1 egg white, slightly beaten
1 cup crushed canned pineapple
½ cup seedless raisins, whole or chopped

Line a spring form or a large pie plate with the piecrust dough or *HUNGARIAN MUERBE TEIG*. Rub cheese through a sieve and measure. Add sour cream, sugar, salt, eggs, and grated lemon rind, beating well. Brush dough with egg white, sprinkle evenly with crushed pineapple and raisins. Pour mixture into spring form or pie tin. Bake in a hot oven (450°F.) 10 minutes, reduce the heat to moderate (350°F.), and bake 20 minutes longer, or until browned. Serve cold.

Hungarian muerbe teig: Cream 4 tablespoons butter. Beat in 2 egg yolks, ⅛ teaspoon salt, and 2 tablespoons lemon juice. Combine with a mixture of 1½ cups sifted all-purpose flour and 1 teaspoon baking powder. Work to a smooth dough with 2 to 3 tablespoons cold water. Pat out ¼ inch thick and press into pie plate or spring form with the fingers.

HONEY CHEESE PIE

9 ounces cream cheese
½ cup strained honey
3 eggs, slightly beaten
¼ teaspoon salt

1½ cups milk
Juice and grated rind of ½ lemon
½ recipe *PLAIN PASTRY*
Nutmeg

Cream the cheese until soft. Combine honey, eggs, salt, and milk. Add gradually to cheese, mixing until blended. Add lemon juice and rind. Pour filling into pastry-lined 9-inch pie pan. Sprinkle with nutmeg. Bake in hot oven (450°F.) 10 minutes, reduce temperature to slow (325°F.), and bake ½ hour longer, or until knife inserted in center of filling comes out clean. Cool.

GERMAN CHEESE CAKE

RICH PIECRUST or
MUERBE TEIG
¾ cup butter
1 cup sugar

3 eggs
2 cups dry cottage cheese
1 tablespoon cornstarch
Grated rind of 1 lemon

Roll out dough and line a spring form. Cream butter, add the sugar and cream thoroughly. Beat in eggs, one at a time. Rub the cottage cheese through a sieve and add to mixture, with the cornstarch and lemon rind. Beat until well blended. Turn into the lined spring form. Bake in a hot oven (450°F.) 10 minutes. Reduce heat to moderate (350°F.) and bake 20 to 30 minutes longer, or until lightly browned. Serve cold. A large pie plate may be used instead of the spring form.

PINEAPPLE CHEESE CAKE #2

1½ cups zwieback crumbs
⅔ cup sugar
3 tablespoons melted butter
1 cup well drained crushed pineapple
2 tablespoons flour
¼ teaspoon salt

2 packages (3 ounces each) cream cheese
½ teaspoon vanilla extract
3 egg yolks
⅔ cup light cream
3 egg whites
½ cup whipping cream

Mix together zwieback crumbs, ⅓ cup sugar, and melted butter. Pat crumb mixture into a 10-inch pie pan. Spread crushed pineapple on top of crumb mixture. Add flour, ⅓ cup sugar, and salt to softened cream cheese. Beat until thoroughly blended. Add vanilla extract, egg yolks, and ⅔ cup light cream to cheese mixture. Beat until smooth and creamy. Beat egg whites until fluffy and fold into cheese mixture. Pour over pineapple in pie pan. Bake in slow oven (325°F.) about 1 hour. To serve, garnish cake with whipped cream.

HOLLYWOOD CHEESE CAKE

18 rolled zwieback or
   1½ cups zwieback crumbs
3 tablespoons butter
2 tablespoons sugar
1 pound cream cheese
½ cup sugar
⅛ teaspoon cinnamon

½ teaspoon vanilla
1 teaspoon grated lemon rind
1 tablespoon lemon juice
2 eggs, separated
1 cup thick sour cream
1 tablespoon sugar
1 teaspoon vanilla

Blend the zwieback crumbs with the butter and 2 tablespoons sugar. Press onto the bottom of a 9-inch spring pan. Bake in a slow oven (300°F.) for 5 minutes. Cool. Blend cream cheese, softened at room temperature, with the ½ cup sugar, cinnamon, ½ teaspoon vanilla, lemon rind, and lemon juice. Add the egg yolks, one at a time, mixing well after each yolk is added. Fold in stiffly beaten egg whites and pour the mixture on top of the crumbs. Bake in a slow oven (300°F.) 45 minutes. Blend the sour cream with the 1 tablespoon sugar and 1 teaspoon vanilla. Spread this mixture over the top of cake. Return to oven for an additional 10 minutes. Cool before removing from pan. Do not invert.

LEMON CHEESE CAKE

¼ cup butter
¾ cup sugar
¼ teaspoon salt
4 eggs, separated
2 cups creamed cottage cheese, sieved

½ cup cream
Grated rind of ½ lemon
1 teaspoon lemon juice
¾ cup sifted cake flour
3 tablespoons fine, dry breadcrumbs

Cream butter, sugar, and salt until light and fluffy. Add egg yolks, one at a time, beating well after each addition. Mix cottage cheese with cream and mix into first mixture with the lemon rind and juice. Add flour and blend thoroughly. Beat egg whites until stiff, but not dry, and fold in. Butter a square cake pan (8x8x2 inches). Sprinkle with crumbs and pour in the cheese mixture. Bake in slow oven (325°F.) about 1½ hours.

UPSIDE-DOWN CAKE (Basic Recipe)

   FOR CAKE BATTER:
1 cup sifted cake flour
1½ teaspoons baking powder
¼ teaspoon salt
¼ cup shortening
½ cup sugar
1 egg

¼ cup milk
1 teaspoon vanilla
   FOR BOTTOM OF PAN:
2 tablespoons butter
½ cup brown sugar
1 teaspoon grated lemon rind
1½ cups fruit

Mix and sift flour, baking powder, and salt. Cream shortening and sugar. Add egg and beat well. Add flour mixture alternately with milk to creamed mixture. Add vanilla. Melt butter in a round 9-inch cake pan. Sprinkle brown sugar evenly over butter. Add lemon rind. Arrange fruit in cake pan. Pour batter over this. Bake in moderate oven (375°F.) 30 minutes. Turn out at once. Serves 5.

Note: Pineapple slices, sliced fresh or canned peaches, fresh, stewed, dried, or canned apricots or plums, fresh or canned cherries may be used. To use cherries, replace lemon rind with ½ teaspoon cinnamon and simmer mixture in pan for 10 minutes and cool.

BANANA UPSIDE-DOWN CAKE

2 tablespoons butter
½ cup firmly packed brown sugar
3 medium bananas, cut in quarters
½ cup raisins
   Walnut halves
¼ cup shortening
⅔ cup sugar

2 eggs, beaten
1 teaspoon vanilla
1½ cups sifted cake flour
2 teaspoons baking powder
½ teaspoon salt
⅓ cup milk

Melt butter. Add brown sugar, and stir until well blended. Pat into the bottom of a square 8-inch baking pan. Arrange bananas, raisins, and nuts over this and pat down gently. Cream shortening. Add sugar gradually and cream thoroughly. Add eggs and beat well. Add vanilla. Mix and sift flour, baking powder, and salt. Add flour mixture alternately with milk to creamed mixture, stirring and blending after each addition. Beat slightly to make smooth. Pour batter carefully over bananas. Bake in moderate oven (350°F.) until done, about 55 minutes. Turn out upside down.

CHOCOLATE UPSIDE-DOWN CAKE

1 cup sifted all-purpose flour
2 teaspoons baking powder
½ teaspoon salt
¾ cup sugar
6 tablespoons cocoa
2 tablespoons shortening

½ cup milk
1 teaspoon vanilla
⅓ cup chopped nuts
¾ cup firmly packed brown sugar
1¾ cups hot water

Mix and sift flour, baking powder, salt, sugar, and 2 tablespoons cocoa. Cut in shortening until mixture resembles coarse crumbs. Stir in milk and vanilla, and add nuts. Pour into a greased 9-inch layer-cake pan. Mix brown sugar and remaining cocoa and sprinkle over batter. Pour water carefully over surface of batter. This water forms a sauce when cake is baked. Bake in moderate oven (350°F.) 40 minutes.

PEACH UPSIDE-DOWN CAKE

4 tablespoons melted butter
¾ cup firmly packed brown sugar
6 canned peach halves
¼ cup shortening
¾ cup sugar
1 egg

1 teaspoon lemon juice
2 teaspoons grated lemon rind
1½ cups sifted cake flour
2 teaspoons baking powder
½ teaspoon salt
½ cup milk

Mix butter and brown sugar together and pat into bottom of square 8-inch cake pan. Arrange peach halves over this, cut side down. Cream shortening and sugar together. Add egg, lemon juice and rind. Beat until fluffy. Mix and sift flour, baking powder, and salt. Add to creamed mixture alternately with milk. Pour batter over peaches carefully. Bake in moderate oven (375°F.) 45 minutes. Turn out upside-down. Serve plain or with whipped cream.

ALMOND CAKE (Mandeltorte)

9 egg yolks
9 tablespoons sifted flour
¾ pound very finely ground
    unblanched almonds
1 to 1½ cups sugar

Grated rind of 1 lemon
9 egg whites stiffly beaten
1 cup heavy cream, whipped
About ¼ cup sugar
Powdered sugar

Beat egg yolks until thick and lemon colored. (Old German recipes usually call for 30 minutes of beating.) Blend in flour. Mix well. Add almonds, sugar to taste, and lemon rind. Mix thoroughly. Fold in egg whites. Turn into ungreased 9-inch tube pan. Bake in slow oven (325°F.) 1 hour. When cold, cut into 2 layers. Spread bottom layer with whipped cream which has been sweetened with sugar. (A thick, rich custard may be used instead of the whipped cream.) Cover with top layer and sprinkle with sifted powdered sugar. This cake improves and takes on the consistency of a macaroon if allowed to stand for 2 to 3 days.

APPLE TORTE

Apples
⅔ to 1 cup sugar
Cinnamon
1 cup brown sugar

1 cup sifted all-purpose flour
⅓ cup melted butter
Chopped pecans
Whipping cream

Peel and slice cooking apples. Place in greased pan, 2 inches deep, almost filling with apples. Sprinkle with about ¾ cup sugar, depending on tartness of apples, and cinnamon to taste. Prepare topping by combining brown sugar, flour, and butter to form a crumbly mixture. Place this mixture on top of apples, pressing down to form crust. Sprinkle top with pecans. Bake in moderate oven (375°F.) 30 to 45 minutes, or until apples are tender and crust is firm. Serve hot or cold with whipped cream.

APPLESAUCE TORTE

2 cups crushed graham crackers
2 tablespoons melted butter
½ teaspoon cinnamon
3 eggs, separated

¾ cup evaporated milk
Grated rind and juice of ½ lemon
2 cups sweetened applesauce

Mix cracker crumbs with melted butter and cinnamon. Line bottom and sides of a spring form with mixture, reserving ¾ cup to sprinkle over top. Beat egg yolks very light. Add milk, lemon juice, grated rind, and applesauce. Mix thoroughly. Fold in stiffly beaten egg whites. Pour into lined form. Cover with remaining crumbs. Bake in moderate oven (350°F.) 50 to 60 minutes. Turn off heat and let cool in oven another hour.

BLITZ TORTE

1⅓ cups sifted cake flour
1⅓ teaspoons baking powder
⅛ teaspoon salt
½ cup shortening
1½ cups sugar
4 eggs, separated

5 tablespoons milk or
   5 tablespoons cream
1 teaspoon vanilla
½ teaspoon cinnamon
½ cup shredded blanched almonds

Mix and sift flour, baking powder, and salt 3 times. Cream shortening. Gradually beat in ½ cup sugar. Add egg yolks, one at a time, beating after each addition until the mixture is light and fluffy. Alternately add dry ingredients with milk, starting and ending with flour and beating after each addition until smooth. Add vanilla. Spread batter in two 9-inch greased pans. Beat egg whites until stiff. Gradually beat in 1 cup sugar and cinnamon. Spread in equal amounts on top of each layer. Sprinkle thickly with almonds. Bake in slow oven (325°F.) 25 minutes. Increase heat to (350°F.) and bake 30 minutes longer. Remove cake from pans. Cool. Put layers together with crushed sweetened fruit and whipped cream.

BREAD TORTE

6 eggs, separated
1¼ cups sugar
1⅙ cups breadcrumbs
½ teaspoon baking powder
½ teaspoon cinnamon
⅛ pound citron, cut fine
1 cup ground, unblanched almonds

Rind and juice of 1 lemon
¼ teaspoon salt
½ cup sherry wine
3 tablespoons water
2 whole cloves
1 stick cinnamon

Beat egg yolks until light. Sift in 1 cup sugar and beat until creamy. Combine breadcrumbs, baking powder, cinnamon, citron, almonds, lemon rind, and lemon juice. Add to creamed mixture and mix well. Beat egg whites with salt until stiff, but not dry. Gently fold into batter. Bake in spring form in moderate oven (350°F.) about 1 hour. Combine wine, water, cloves, cinnamon stick, and ¼ cup sugar. Heat, but do not boil. Strain and pour slowly over cake immediately upon removing from oven. Let stand until cake is cool and all liquid is absorbed. Remove from pan. Spread with *CREAMY CHOCOLATE FROSTING.*

CARROT TORTE

5 eggs, separated
1 cup sugar
⅜ cup matzo meal
⅛ cup matzo cake meal
½ teaspoon baking powder

1 cup raw carrots, grated
2 cups blanched almonds, chopped
1 teaspoon cinnamon
¼ teaspoon salt

Beat egg yolks until light. Sift in sugar and continue beating until thick and lemon colored. Sift together matzo meal, matzo cake meal, and baking powder. Stir into the egg yolk mixture and add carrots, cinnamon, and almonds. Stir well. Beat egg whites with salt until stiff but not dry. Lightly fold into the mixture. Pour into spring form. Bake in slow oven (300°F.) 1¼ hours. Serve plain, or with a wine sauce.

CHOCOLATE NUT TORTE

1 recipe for *PLAIN PASTRY*
5 eggs, separated
½ cup sugar

¼ cup blanched almonds, toasted
   and shredded
Pinch of salt
⅔ cup cocoa

Line a pie plate with *PLAIN PASTRY*. Beat egg yolks until light. Gradually beat in the sugar, alternately with almonds, and mix thoroughly. Beat egg whites with salt until stiff. Gradually beat the cocoa into egg whites, about 3 tablespoons at a time, beating well after each addition. Fold one mixture into the other, blending well. Spread evenly over the unbaked shell. Bake in moderate oven (350°F.) until crust is done and top browned, about 30 minutes. Serve cool.

CRUMB LAYER TORTE

10 eggs, separated
2 cups sugar
1 pound ground walnuts
1 cup sieved white breadcrumbs

1½ tablespoons grated orange rind
Jam
1 cup heavy cream, whipped with
   ¼ teaspoon salt

Beat egg yolks until thick and lemon colored. Gradually beat in the sugar, walnuts, breadcrumbs, and orange rind. Gently fold in the stiffly beaten egg whites. Pour into 3 buttered 9-inch layer-cake pans. Bake in moderate oven (350°F.) 30 to 40 minutes. Remove from pans and cool. Put layers together with jam. Cover top and sides with whipped cream.

DATE AND NUT TORTE

2 eggs
2 tablespoons flour
1 teaspoon baking powder
¼ teaspoon salt

¾ cup sugar
1 cup chopped dates
1 cup chopped nuts
½ teaspoon vanilla

Beat eggs until very light. Sift flour. Add baking powder, salt, and sugar and sift again. Add to beaten eggs. Add dates, nuts, and vanilla and blend well. Spread evenly in well-greased pan (8x8 inches). Bake in slow oven (325°F.) 40 to 50 minutes. Serve warm, topped with whipped cream.

DOBOS TORTE

BATTER:
¾ cup sifted cake flour
¼ teaspoon salt
6 eggs, separated
1 cup sugar
1 teaspoon vanilla

FILLING:
½ cup sugar
4 large eggs
4 squares bittersweet chocolate
2 tablespoons boiling water
⅞ cup butter
1 teaspoon vanilla

Mix and sift flour and salt 4 times. Beat egg yolks until light and lemon colored. Gradually beat in sugar, and with last addition add vanilla. Gradually add flour. Beat well. Beat egg whites until stiff, but not dry, and fold in lightly. Grease 4 8-inch cake pans and pour in a thin layer of batter, spreading evenly. Reserve half the batter for remaining 4 layers. Bake in moderate oven (375°F.) 5 to 8 minutes. Remove cake at once from pans. Grease and refill pans with remaining batter. Set layers aside to cool.

Filling: Combine in top of double boiler sugar and eggs. Cook over boiling water, beating constantly until mixture begins to thicken. Cool slightly. Cut chocolate into small pieces. Dissolve in boiling water and keep warm until needed. Cream butter until light. Add melted chocolate and vanilla. Combine with egg mixture. Spread filling between layers. Place toothpicks through top layers to hold layers in place until filling sets. Spread with *CARAMEL GLAZE.*

Caramel glaze: Melt and brown in a skillet 3 tablespoons powdered sugar and pour over the cake. Spread with a hot knife. Let cake stand in cool place 24 hours before serving.

HOLIDAY TORTE

1 cup sugar
1 cup crushed graham crackers
  (12 crackers)
1 teaspoon baking powder
½ cup finely chopped nuts
3 egg whites, beaten stiff
Whipped cream

Fold sugar, cracker crumbs, baking powder, and chopped nuts into the beaten egg whites. Spread in a greased 9-inch pie pan. Bake in moderate oven (350°F.) 30 minutes. Cool. Serve with whipped cream.

LINZER TORTE

1¼ cups sifted cake flour
1 tablespoon sifted cocoa
½ teaspoon cinnamon
¼ teaspoon ground cloves
¼ teaspoon salt
1 cup butter
1 cup sugar
2 eggs
1 teaspoon grated lemon rind
1 cup ground, unblanched almonds
Jam or preserves

Sift flour. Mix with cocoa, cinnamon, cloves, and salt and sift together 3 times. Cream butter. Gradually sift in sugar, beating until light and fluffy. Add eggs 1 at a time, beating after each addition. Add lemon rind. Add dry ingredients and nuts and mix thoroughly. Continue stirring for about 30 minutes. If the dough is very soft, chill it. Roll out between wax paper to thickness of about ⅛ inch. Line bottom and sides of a baking pan. Cover generously with jam or preserves. Roll and cut remaining dough into strips and make a lattice over top. Bake in hot oven (400°F.) about 1 hour. Fill in the hollows with additional jam or preserves before serving.

PERSIAN TORTE

1 cup sifted cake flour
1 teaspoon baking powder
12 eggs, separated
1½ cups sugar
½ pound grated sweet chocolate

Mix flour and baking powder and sift together 3 times. Beat egg yolks until thick and lemon colored. Add sugar gradually and continue beating 15 minutes. Add grated chocolate and flour mixture to egg yolk mixture. Beat egg whites until a point of egg white will stand upright when whip is pulled out. Fold into egg yolk mixture. Pour batter into 3 greased 9-inch layer-cake pans. Bake in moderate oven (350°F.) 40 minutes. Invert pans ½ hour to cool. Remove cakes from pans. Cool thoroughly. Spread black walnut frosting or whipped cream between layers, on top, and on sides.

VIENNESE SACHER TORTE

½ cup sweet butter
½ cup plus 2 tablespoons
   confectioners' sugar
4 ounces melted sweet chocolate
6 eggs, separated
1 tablespoon grated lemon rind

1 teaspoon cinnamon
½ teaspoon cloves
1 cup plus 2 tablespoons very
   fine toasted white breadcrumbs
⅛ teaspoon salt
Apricot jam

Cream butter until soft and creamy. Gradually add sugar and continue beating until well blended. Beat in chocolate and egg yolks, one at a time, beating well after each addition. Stir in lemon rind, cinnamon, cloves, and breadcrumbs. Mix well. Beat egg whites with salt until stiff, but not dry. Fold lightly into batter. Bake in 2 greased 8-inch cake pans in a slow oven (325°F.) 25 minutes. Remove from pans and cool. Spread apricot jam between layers. Frost with CHOCOLATE FROSTING.

GERMAN SAND TORTE

1 cup sifted all-purpose flour
2 teaspoons baking powder
1 cup sifted cornstarch
½ teaspoon salt
1 cup butter

1 cup sifted sugar
6 eggs, separated
1 tablespoon lemon juice
Grated rind of 1 lemon
2 tablespoons brandy

Mix and sift together flour, baking powder, cornstarch, and salt. Cream butter until soft. Gradually add sifted sugar, beating until light and fluffy. Add beaten egg yolks with lemon juice, lemon rind, and brandy. Mix in sifted dry ingredients and blend well. Beat egg whites until stiff but not dry. Fold into batter. Bake in a greased 9-inch tube pan in moderate oven (350°F.) 45 minutes.

SCHAUM TORTE

6 egg whites
½ teaspoon baking powder
⅛ teaspoon salt
2 teaspoons vanilla
2 teaspoons vinegar

2 teaspoons water
2 cups sifted sugar
Sweetened berries or
   other fruit
1 cup heavy cream, whipped

Combine egg whites, baking powder, and salt and beat until stiff. Combine vanilla, vinegar, and water. Mix well. Slowly add sifted sugar ½ teaspoon at a time to beaten egg whites, alternating with a few drops of the liquid, beating constantly. After all ingredients have been added, continue to beat for several minutes. (Or, if using an electric beater, combine all ingredients except the sugar. Beat at a high speed until the mixture is stiff, then add sugar 1 teaspoonful at a time and continue beating.) Bake in 2 10-inch spring forms, well greased with butter and lightly dusted with flour. Bake in slow oven (275°F.) 1½ hours. Fill layers with sweetened berries or fruit. Top with whipped cream which has been flavored with ½ teaspoon vanilla.

DANISH ALMOND SCHAUM TORTE

6 egg whites	8 drops almond essence
2 cups sugar	1 tablespoon vinegar
1 to 1½ teaspoons vanilla	1 cup heavy cream, whipped

Beat egg whites until stiff, but not dry. Gradually beat in 6 tablespoons sugar, 2 tablespoons at a time. Add vanilla, almond essence, and vinegar. Fold in remaining sugar. Pour into a buttered and lightly floured round baking pan. Bake in a very slow oven at 250°F. until torte has risen and set. Then increase oven heat to 300°F. and continue baking until lightly browned. Total baking time 1 hour or longer. Fill with whipped cream. Cut in wedges and serve topped with ice cream if desired.

VIENNESE SCHAUM TORTE OLYMPUS

4 eggs, separated	½ teaspoon vanilla
½ teaspoon salt	2 cups whipping cream
1 cup sugar	Raspberries, strawberries, or currants
¼ cup plus 1 tablespoon lime juice	Rum

Beat egg whites with ¼ teaspoon salt until stiff but not dry. Slowly beat in sugar, not more than 1 tablespoon at a time. Alternate this with a few drops of mixture of 1 tablespoon lime juice and the vanilla. Pour into a greased 12-inch pie tin. Bake in slow oven (275–300°F.) 1 hour. Allow to cool in oven with the door open. Combine slightly beaten egg yolks with ¼ cup lime juice and remaining salt in top of a double boiler. Blend well and cook over boiling water until thickened. Cool and fold in 1 cup whipped cream. Spread thick over cooled meringue pastry. Cover and place in refrigerator for a few hours. Whip remaining cream and spread over the filling. Garnish with berries soaked in good grade of rum.

STRAWBERRY CREAM TORTE

¼ cup shortening	¾ cup sifted cake flour
¼ cup sugar	¼ teaspoon salt
½ teaspoon vanilla extract	1 teaspoon baking powder
2 egg yolks	¼ cup milk

Cream shortening until fluffy. Gradually beat in ¼ cup sugar. Beat in vanilla extract and egg yolks. Sift flour, salt, and baking powder together and add alternately with milk to egg mixture. Pour batter into a well-greased 8-inch square cake pan. Top with a meringue made of:

3 egg whites	½ cup sugar
⅛ teaspoon cream of tartar	

Method: Beat egg whites until stiff. Add cream of tartar. Beat in sugar gradually. Spread on cake batter. Bake in slow oven (250°F.) 25 minutes. Increase heat to moderate (350°F.) and bake 20 minutes longer. Remove from oven and cool. Top with 1 cup of heavy cream, whipped until stiff, then mixed with 1 cup sliced strawberries. Garnish with whole berries.

RUSSIAN STRAWBERRY TORTE

2 cups sifted all-purpose flour	1 cup strawberry jam
½ teaspoon salt	2 cups whipped cream
1 cup butter	⅛ teaspoon almond extract

Sift together flour and salt. Cut in the butter with 2 knives or pastry blender until the mixture looks like fine barley. Add enough cold water to hold dough together. Roll out on lightly floured board. Fold 4 times and roll out again. Separate dough into three parts and roll out into 3 rounds. Prick each with a fork several times. Bake in a hot oven (400°F.) until brown, about 30 to 45 minutes. Spread 1 round with jam and cover with whipped cream flavored with almond extract. Cover with another baked round, spread with jam and whipped cream, and top with third round. Spread with jam and a thick layer of whipped cream.

WALNUT TORTE

8 eggs, separated
1 cup sugar
1 cup sifted cake flour
½ teaspoon cream of tartar

⅛ teaspoon salt
1 teaspoon vanilla extract
⅔ cup ground walnut meats

Beat egg yolks with a rotary beater until thick and lemon colored. Add sugar gradually and continue beating. Add flour by sifting a small amount at a time over mixture and folding until well blended. Beat egg whites until foamy. Sift cream of tartar and salt over them and beat until a point of egg white will stand upright when whip is pulled out. Add extract. Fold egg-white mixture into egg-yolk mixture. Fold in walnut meats. Turn batter into a 10-inch tube pan which has been rinsed with cold water. Bake in a slow oven (325°F.) 1 hour and 25 minutes. Invert pan 1 hour before removing torte. When cold, frost with *CARAMEL FROSTING* or whipped cream to which walnuts have been added.

ZWIEBACK APPLE TORTE

8 peeled, sliced apples
1½ cups sugar
2 tablespoons butter
½ cup water
1⅔ cups evaporated milk
4 eggs
1 teaspoon cinnamon

1½ teaspoons vanilla
½ teaspoon salt
   Grated rind of ½ lemon
18 pieces of zwieback
⅓ cup sugar
⅓ cup butter

Cook apples slowly in saucepan with 1 cup sugar, 2 tablespoons butter, and water until tender. Combine milk, eggs, cinnamon, and ½ cup sugar. Add to apples. Cook slowly, stirring constantly, until thickened. Add vanilla, salt, and lemon rind. Crush zwieback fine and mix with remaining ingredients. Spread and press half the zwieback mixture on bottom and sides of a well-buttered 9-inch spring form. Pour in apple mixture. Cover with remaining crumbs. Bake in slow oven (325°F.) 45 minutes. Cool and chill. Garnish with whipped cream and cherries. Serves 10 to 12.

cake frostings and fillings

There are two types of frostings, cooked and uncooked. Each type of frosting should be smooth and creamy and thick enough to spread easily without losing its shape. There are also two types of fillings, starchy and fruit. Fillings are generally used between the layers of a cake which is to be frosted. Sometimes they are used as a sauce over cake which is to be served warm. Nuts may be combined with the fruit fillings. To give variety to frostings the use of food coloring, which comes in liquid, paste, or powder form, is suggested. To apply a complicated decorating design, use a pastry tube and bag. First, outline the design on the frosted cake with a sharp-pointed knife, then apply the decorative design.

BOILED FROSTING (Basic Recipe)

1½ cups granulated sugar	3 tablespoons corn syrup
Dash of salt	2 egg whites
½ cup water	½ teaspoon vanilla

Cook sugar, salt, water, and corn syrup to the soft ball stage (239°F.). Remove mixture from flame. Beat egg whites quickly with a rotary beater. Pour hot syrup slowly in a fine stream over egg whites, beating constantly. Add vanilla and continue beating until frosting stands up in peaks. Quickly spread on cake. On a rainy or humid day, boil syrup to higher temperature. If frosting hardens before spreading, beat in a few drops of hot water. Yield: frosting for top and sides of 2 9-inch layer cakes or 24 cupcakes.

Apricot frosting: Fold ½ cup cooked apricot pulp into beaten frosting.

Brown sugar frosting: Substitute brown sugar for white. Omit corn syrup and cook to 250°F. instead of 239°F.

Chocolate frosting: Add ¼ cup cocoa or 2 squares (2 ounces) melted chocolate to sugar, and cook with sugar and water.

Coconut frosting: Sprinkle plain, tinted, or toasted shredded coconut over frosting.

Coffee walnut frosting: Substitute coffee for water. Omit vanilla. Add ½ cup chopped walnuts to beaten frosting.

Colored frosting: Tint frosting with vegetable coloring as desired. Flavor as desired.

Fruit frosting: Fold chopped candied cherries, chopped candied pineapple, or other chopped candied fruit into beaten frosting.

Ginger frosting: Use ¼ cup brown sugar and 1 cup granulated sugar. Fold in ½ cup finely chopped, drained preserved ginger just before spreading.

Lady Baltimore frosting or filling: Chop and fold ¼ cup each of dried figs, pitted dates, seedless raisins, walnuts, and blanched almonds into beaten frosting. If desired, substitute almond extract for vanilla.

Lemon frosting: Fold into frosting 2 tablespoons lemon juice and 1 teaspoon lemon rind just before spreading.

Lord Baltimore frosting or filling: Fold ½ cup toasted coconut, ¼ cup chopped candied cherries or chopped maraschino cherries, ¼ cup chopped, toasted, blanched almonds or chopped pecans into beaten frosting.

Marshmallow frosting: Cut marshmallows into quarters. Arrange on top of cake. Spread frosting over them, or fold in half-melted marshmallows just before spreading.

Molasses frosting: Substitute 3 tablespoons molasses for corn syrup.

Nut frosting: Sprinkle whole or chopped nuts over frosting.

Peppermint frosting: Flavor with a few drops of peppermint instead of vanilla.

Strawberry frosting: Fold ½ cup crushed strawberries into beaten frosting.

SEVEN MINUTE FROSTING (Basic Recipe)

2 egg whites, unbeaten	⅓ cup cold water
1½ cups granulated sugar	1 tablespoon light corn syrup
⅛ teaspoon salt	1 teaspoon vanilla

Place egg whites, sugar, salt, water, and corn syrup in top of double boiler. Place over boiling water and beat constantly with a large double egg beater or electric beater at high speed until frosting will stand in peaks, about 7 minutes. Remove from heat, beat in vanilla. Quickly spread on cake. Yield: frosting for top and sides of 2 9-inch layer cakes or 2 dozen cupcakes.

Chocolate frosting: Stir into beaten frosting 2 squares melted chocolate.

Coconut frosting: Sprinkle plain, tinted, or toasted coconut over frosting while still soft.

Coffee frosting: Omit vanilla. Substitute coffee for water.

Colored frosting: Tint frosting as desired. Flavor as desired.

Fruit frosting: Fold ½ cup chopped candied cherries, chopped candied pineapple, or other candied fruit into beaten frosting.

Lemon frosting: Substitute 2 tablespoons lemon juice and grated rind of 1 lemon for 2 tablespoons water, the corn syrup, and vanilla.

Marshmallow frosting: Fold in 1 dozen quartered marshmallows with flavoring.

Orange frosting: Substitute 3 tablespoons orange juice and grated rind of 1 orange for 3 tablespoons water, the corn syrup, and vanilla.

Peppermint candy frosting: Fold ¼ cup crushed hard peppermint candy into beaten frosting. Garnish sides of cake with additional ¼ cup of crushed hard peppermint candy.

Sea foam frosting: Omit corn syrup. Substitute 1½ cups brown sugar for granulated sugar.

BANANA BUTTER FROSTING

½ cup mashed ripe banana	¼ cup butter
½ teaspoon lemon juice	3½ cups sifted confectioners' sugar

Mix together banana and lemon juice. Beat butter until creamy. Add sugar and banana alternately, a small amount at a time, beating until frosting is light and fluffy. Makes enough frosting for top and sides of 2 9-inch layers.

BURNT SUGAR

Heat and stir 1 cup sugar over medium flame until it foams up dark orange in color. Remove from heat. Slowly add 1 cup hot water. Return to flame and boil until sugar is dissolved. Keep and use as needed for flavoring icings and whipped cream.

BUTTER FROSTING (Basic Recipe)

¼ cup butter
2 cups sifted confectioners' sugar
⅛ teaspoon salt

3 tablespoons cream
1 teaspoon vanilla

Cream butter until soft. Slowly stir in 1 cup sugar and the salt. Add additional sugar alternately with cream, beating thoroughly after each addition until creamy and smooth. Beat in vanilla. Additional cream may be added to give frosting spreading consistency. Yield: frosting to cover top and sides of 2 8-inch layer cakes or 2 dozen cupcakes.

Almond frosting: Omit vanilla. Add 1 teaspoon almond flavoring.

Apricot frosting: Omit cream. Add ¼ cup cooked apricot pulp and 1 teaspoon lemon juice.

Chocolate frosting: Melt 2 squares unsweetened chocolate over hot water. Blend with 2 tablespoons boiling water. Add vanilla reduced to ½ teaspoon and salt. Substitute 2 tablespoons milk for cream.

Cinnamon frosting: Substitute cinnamon for vanilla.

Coffee frosting: Substitute strong coffee for cream.

Lemon frosting: Substitute lemon juice and 1 egg yolk for the cream and vanilla. Add 1½ teaspoons grated lemon rind.

Maple walnut frosting: Substitute maple flavoring for vanilla. Add ½ cup chopped walnuts with the last of the sugar.

Mint frosting: Color frosting green. Substitute mint flavoring for vanilla. Or melt peppermint candy and add to frosting for flavor and color.

Mocha frosting: Substitute coffee for cream. Add 1½ tablespoons cocoa with the creamed butter.

Orange frosting: Substitute 1 egg yolk and 2 tablespoons orange juice for the cream. Substitute grated orange rind for vanilla.

Pineapple frosting: Omit cream. Add about ¼ cup drained crushed pineapple. Use lemon juice for flavoring.

Pistachio frosting: Color frosting pale green. Add a few drops almond extract.

Strawberry frosting: Omit liquid. Add about ¼ cup crushed strawberries. Use lemon juice for flavoring. Decorate with whole strawberries.

BUTTERSCOTCH FROSTING

1 cup light brown sugar
1/3 cup white sugar
1/3 cup hot water

1 egg white, beaten
1/2 teaspoon vanilla
Few grains salt

Mix together brown sugar, white sugar, and water over low flame until thoroughly dissolved. Bring to a boil and cook until syrup spins a long thread. Pour syrup slowly over egg white, beating constantly. Add vanilla and salt. If desired, 1/3 cup chopped nutmeats may be added.

CARAMEL FROSTING

1½ cups firmly packed brown sugar
1 cup top milk or light cream
2 tablespoons butter

1/2 teaspoon vanilla
1/8 teaspoon salt

Combine sugar and milk and bring to boil, stirring constantly. Stirring occasionally, boil to soft ball stage (236°F.). Remove from heat and add butter, vanilla, and salt. Cool to lukewarm and beat until of spreading consistency. Yield: frosting for top and sides of 2 8-inch layers or 24 cupcakes.

EASY CHOCOLATE FROSTING

3 tablespoons butter
2 ounces chocolate
2¾ cups confectioners' sugar

1 teaspoon vanilla
1/3 cup hot milk

Combine butter and chocolate in top of double boiler. Cook over boiling water until chocolate is melted. Combine sifted confectioners' sugar with vanilla and hot milk and blend well. Add melted chocolate and beat until smooth and thick.

CREAMY CHOCOLATE FROSTING

1 cup brown sugar
3 ounces chocolate
1/4 teaspoon salt
1/3 cup evaporated milk or
    1/3 cup cream

3 tablespoons butter
1 teaspoon vanilla
Confectioners' sugar

Combine brown sugar, chocolate, salt, and milk or cream in a saucepan. Bring to the boiling point. Cook on medium flame until slightly thickened, about 5 minutes. Remove from fire. Add butter and vanilla. Cool slightly. Add enough sifted confectioners' sugar for proper consistency to spread. Beat until smooth. Spread between layers and on top and sides of cake. Cover with coconut, if desired.

CHOCOLATE MOCHA FROSTING

1/4 cup butter
1/4 cup strong coffee
2 cups confectioners' sugar

1/4 cup cocoa
1/2 teaspoon salt
1 teaspoon vanilla

Have butter and liquid at room temperature. Sift together sugar, cocoa, and salt. Combine all ingredients and beat until smooth and fluffy. Spread on cake. Yield: enough frosting for 2 9-inch layers.

SUPREME CHOCOLATE NUT FROSTING

½ cup butter
1 egg
2 squares chocolate
1⅓ cups confectioners' sugar

⅛ teaspoon salt
1 teaspoon vanilla
1 cup chopped nuts

Cream butter until soft and creamy. Beat in egg. Melt chocolate and add to butter-egg mixture. Add confectioners' sugar, salt, and vanilla. Beat until smooth and creamy. Stir in chopped nuts. Yield: frosting for 1 large loaf cake or 24 cupcakes.

CHOCOLATE FUDGE FROSTING #1

4 cups sugar
2 cups water
½ teaspoon salt
4 squares (4 ounces) unsweetened
　chocolate

4 tablespoons light corn syrup
4 tablespoons butter
2 teaspoons vanilla

Combine sugar, water, salt, chocolate, and syrup in a saucepan. Heat slowly over low heat until sugar is dissolved. Cook at low temperature to soft ball stage (234°F.). Remove from heat. Add butter and cool to lukewarm (110°F.). Add vanilla and beat until thick and creamy. Makes enough frosting for top and sides of 3 layers (8 inches).

CHOCOLATE FUDGE FROSTING #2

3 cups granulated sugar
3 squares (3 ounces) chocolate
1½ tablespoons butter
⅛ teaspoon cream of tartar

¼ teaspoon salt
⅔ cup milk
2 teaspoons vanilla

Combine all ingredients except vanilla and cook without stirring until a small amount of syrup dropped into cold water forms a soft ball (238°F.). Cool slightly, add vanilla, and beat vigorously until the mixture thickens. Use as filling and frosting for chocolate or fudge cakes.

COCONUT MOROCCO FROSTING

2 egg whites, unbeaten
1½ cups firmly packed brown sugar
　Dash of salt
5 tablespoons water

1 square unsweetened chocolate,
　melted and cooled
1 teaspoon vanilla
1½ cups moist, sweetened coconut

Combine egg whites, sugar, salt, and water in top of double boiler, beating with rotary egg beater until thoroughly mixed. Place over rapidly boiling water. Beat constantly with rotary egg beater and cook 7 minutes, or until frosting will stand in peaks. Remove from boiling water. Fold in chocolate and vanilla. Do not beat mixture. Spread on cake. Sprinkle with coconut while frosting is still soft.

PLAIN CONFECTIONERS' FROSTING

Add enough top milk or cream to 2 cups confectioners' sugar to make of spreading consistency. Add dash of salt and 1 teaspoon vanilla extract.

CONFECTIONERS' ICING FOR COOKIES

1 tablespoon butter or vegetable
  shortening
½ teaspoon vanilla
Few grains salt

About 1 cup confectioners'
  sugar, sifted
2 tablespoons milk

Soften shortening. Add vanilla and salt. Work in sugar and milk alternately, beating until smooth.

CREAM CHEESE ICING (Basic Recipe)

1 package cream cheese
1 tablespoon milk

1½ cups sifted confectioners' sugar
1 teaspoon vanilla

Soften cheese with milk. Gradually add confectioners' sugar and vanilla. Beat until creamy.

Cream cheese chocolate icing: Increase milk to 3 tablespoons, and confectioners' sugar to 2½ cups. Add 2 squares melted unsweetened chocolate and ⅛ teaspoon salt. Omit vanilla.

Orange cream cheese icing: Substitute 2 tablespoons orange juice and 1 teaspoon grated orange rind for milk and vanilla.

DIVINITY FROSTING

2½ cups sugar
½ cup light corn syrup
½ cup water

2 egg whites
¼ teaspoon salt
1½ teaspoons flavoring

Heat, without boiling, sugar, syrup, and water in saucepan until sugar is dissolved, stirring constantly. Uncover and boil rapidly until syrup spins a thread (242°F.). Let cool slightly. Beat egg whites with salt until stiff but still glossy. Pour syrup over egg whites, beating constantly. Add flavoring and continue beating until mixture is thick enough to hold shape when cold. Spread on cake. If frosting becomes too thick, soften with a few drops of hot water.

Divinity nut frosting: Fold ½ cup chopped nuts into beaten frosting.

FLUFFY COOKED FROSTING

1¼ cups sugar
¼ teaspoon cream of tartar
½ cup water

3 egg whites
½ cup confectioners' sugar
½ teaspoon vanilla extract

Combine 1 cup sugar, the cream of tartar and the water and stir over low flame until thoroughly dissolved. Bring to a boil and cook to the medium-hard ball stage (250°F.). Beat egg whites until stiff but not dry. Fold in remaining ¼ cup sugar, a tablespoon at a time, beating after each addition. Slowly pour syrup into egg whites, beating constantly. Beat in sifted confectioners' sugar and the vanilla. Yield: frosting to cover top and sides of 2 9-inch layers.

FLUFFY UNCOOKED FROSTING

2 egg whites
1 tablespoon vinegar
1 teaspoon lemon juice
Few grains salt

2 teaspoons cornstarch
About 2½ cups sifted confectioners'
  sugar

Beat egg whites until stiff. Add vinegar, lemon juice, salt, and cornstarch. Continue beating. Gradually add sugar until of consistency to spread. Use to frost sponge cakes.

FONDANT FROSTING

The fondant used for frosting cakes is exactly the same as the remelted fondant in which candies are dipped. Cakes which are to be dipped into fondant frosting must be brushed over with white of egg, slightly beaten with 1 tablespoon confectioners' sugar, several hours before they are to be frosted.

GOLDEN CREAM FROSTING

¼ cup shortening
¼ cup butter
½ teaspoon salt
1 teaspoon vanilla

1 egg yolk
1¾ to 2 cups sifted confectioners'
    sugar
1 tablespoon milk

Cream shortening and butter until soft and fluffy. Beat in salt, vanilla, and egg yolk. Add sugar alternately with milk, beating constantly. Yield: frosting for top and sides of 2 9-inch layers.

HONEY ALMOND FROSTING

2 egg whites, unbeaten
¼ cup honey

1 cup toasted, chopped almonds

Combine egg whites and honey in top of double boiler, beating with rotary egg beater until thoroughly mixed. Place over rapidly boiling water, beating constantly with rotary egg beater, and cook 7 minutes, or until frosting will stand up in peaks. Remove from boiling water. Add ½ of nuts. Spread on cake, sprinkling remaining nuts over top of cake while frosting is still soft. Yield: frosting to cover tops and sides of 2 8- or 9-inch layers.

EASY FLUFFY HONEY FROSTING

1 egg white
  Dash of salt

½ cup honey

Beat egg white with salt until stiff enough to hold up in peaks, but not dry. Pour honey in fine stream over egg white, beating constantly until frosting holds its shape. (Beat about 2½ minutes with electric mixer, or about 4 minutes by hand.) Yield: frosting to cover tops of 2 8-inch layers.

LEMON CONFECTIONERS' FROSTING (Basic Recipe)

1 egg yolk
1½ tablespoons lemon juice
1 tablespoon grated orange rind

⅛ teaspoon salt
2 cups confectioners' sugar

Combine egg yolk, lemon juice, orange rind, and salt. Beat until smooth. Gradually mix in sugar and beat until of spreading consistency. Yield: frosting for 2 layers or 20 cupcakes.

Lime confectioners' frosting: Substitute lime for lemon juice and ¼ teaspoon grated lemon for orange rind. Tint lightly with green coloring.

Orange confectioners' frosting: Substitute 2 tablespoons orange juice for lemon juice and omit grated orange rind.

MOCHA CHOCOLATE FROSTING (Uncooked)

6 tablespoons cocoa	1 teaspoon vanilla
6 tablespoons hot fresh coffee	3 cups confectioners' sugar
6 tablespoons butter	

Mix cocoa and coffee. Add butter and vanilla and beat until smooth. Add confectioners' sugar and beat until of spreading consistency.

MOLASSES MOCHA FROSTING (Basic Recipe)

2 cups sifted confectioners' sugar	1 tablespoon cold coffee
¼ cup butter	1 tablespoon molasses
1 egg white, unbeaten	1 teaspoon vanilla

Add 1 cup sugar gradually to butter and egg white. Mix well. Add remaining sugar alternately with coffee, molasses, and vanilla. Beat well. Spread on tops and sides of 2 8-inch layers or on tops of 2 9-inch layers.

Molasses chocolate frosting: Add 3 tablespoons cocoa or 1 square melted chocolate.

Molasses orange frosting: Omit coffee and vanilla. Add 2 tablespoons orange juice, 1 teaspoon grated orange rind, and ½ teaspoon grated lemon rind.

ORNAMENTAL FROSTING

Cream 2 tablespoons butter. Blend in 2 cups sifted confectioners' sugar, mixing well. Add ½ teaspoon vanilla and 2 to 4 tablespoons hot cream, a little at a time, until frosting is of right consistency to press through a cone made from heavy brown paper. Divide into 3 or more parts and tint each a different pastel color by adding vegetable coloring, a drop at a time. Decorate cakes by pressing frosting through paper cones.

PENUCHE FROSTING

2 cups brown sugar	⅔ cup cream
1 tablespoon butter	¼ teaspoon salt

Combine all ingredients. Stir over low heat until sugar is dissolved. Boil until a small amount of syrup forms a soft ball when dropped into cold water (238°F.). Cool, beat, and spread while still slightly warm. One cup chopped nutmeats may be added.

PETITS FOURS FROSTING

Combine 2 cups sugar, 1 cup water, and ⅛ teaspoon cream of tartar. Cook over direct heat to 226°F., or a thin syrup. Stir only until sugar is dissolved. Remove from heat. Pour into top of double boiler and cool to somewhat above lukewarm (110°F.). Gradually add 1 to 2 cups sifted confectioners' sugar until frosting is of proper consistency to pour. Place a few cakes in rows on a wire rack over a cookie sheet, allowing considerable space between cakes. Pour frosting over cakes, covering tops and sides and allowing frosting to drip onto cookie sheet. Keep over hot water when not pouring. If it becomes too thick, add a few drops hot water.

If too thin, add a little more sifted confectioners' sugar. Scrape frosting from cookie sheet, reheat, and use for other cakes. Repeat the process until cakes are completely coated. Decorate with ORNAMENTAL FROSTING, colored sugar, candied fruit, or nuts.

PRALINE FROSTING

1 cup firmly packed light brown sugar	2 tablespoons butter
½ cup granulated sugar	¾ cup chopped pecans
¼ cup corn syrup	1 teaspoon vanilla
½ cup top milk or	
½ cup light cream	

Combine sugars, syrup, and milk or cream in saucepan and cook to soft ball stage (236°F.). Remove from heat. Add butter but do not stir. When cool beat until spreading consistency is reached. Add nuts and vanilla. Yield: frosting for top and sides of 2 9-inch layers.

SPICY RAISIN FROSTING

1¾ cups confectioners' sugar	½ teaspoon nutmeg
1 tablespoon cocoa	½ cup sweetened condensed milk
½ teaspoon cinnamon	½ teaspoon vanilla
½ teaspoon cloves	½ cup raisins

Combine ingredients in order given. Use to frost spice cakes.

TUTTI-FRUTTI FROSTING

2 egg whites	¾ cup toasted, chopped, blanched
1½ cups sugar	almonds
¼ cup maraschino cherry juice	¼ cup macaroon crumbs
1 tablespoon lemon juice	⅛ teaspoon grated orange rind
	20 cut up maraschino cherries

Combine egg whites, sugar, and fruit juice. Cook over boiling water, beating constantly until icing will stand in peaks. Fold in remaining ingredients and spread over cake.

APPLE CAKE FILLING

¾ cup sugar	1 tablespoon water
1 tablespoon flour	1 egg, beaten
3 tablespoons lemon juice	1 cup grated apple

Combine all ingredients. Cook over very low heat until thick, 8 to 10 minutes. Cool. Spread between layers. Frost cake with 7-MINUTE FROSTING.

Pineapple coconut filling: Substitute 1 cup drained crushed pineapple for the grated apple, and add ½ cup freshly grated coconut.

APRICOT CAKE FILLING

½ pound dried apricots	½ cup crushed pineapple
½ cup sugar	1 cup chopped nuts

Wash apricots and place in a saucepan. Barely cover with water. Add sugar. Cover. Simmer over low heat about 30 minutes. Strain. Add well-drained crushed pineapple, then add nuts. Cool. Spread between layers.

CARAMEL CAKE FILLING

½ cup brown sugar	½ teaspoon baking soda
2 cups sugar	½ cup butter
1 cup buttermilk	1 tablespoon vanilla

Combine sugars, buttermilk, baking soda, and butter. Cook until syrup forms a soft ball when a small amount is dropped into cold water (238°F.). Cool. Add vanilla. Beat until creamy. Spread over cake.

CREAM FILLING (Basic Recipe)

¾ cup sugar	2 cups scalded milk
5 tablespoons flour	2 eggs, slightly beaten
¼ teaspoon salt	1 teaspoon vanilla

Combine dry ingredients. Slowly stir in milk. Cook in double boiler over boiling water for 15 minutes, or until thick. Add a little of the hot mixture to eggs. Stir in remaining hot mixture. Cook over simmering water for 3 minutes. Cool and add vanilla. For a richer filling, add 2 tablespoons butter to hot cooked custard. Yield: filling for 4 large layers or 24 large cream puffs or 24 eclairs.

Banana filling: Substitute 1 teaspoon lemon juice for vanilla. Add medium-sized mashed banana to filling.

Butterscotch filling: Substitute ¾ cup brown sugar for granulated sugar. Add 2 tablespoons butter to cooked filling.

Chocolate filling: Increase sugar to 1 cup. Add 2 squares unsweetened chocolate to milk before cooking. Beat until smooth.

Coconut filling: Add 1 cup shredded coconut to filling.

Coffee filling: Substitute ½ cup strong fresh coffee for ½ cup milk. Proceed as directed.

Creamy custard filling: Fold ½ cup whipped heavy cream into chilled filling.

Pineapple filling #1: Substitute lemon juice for vanilla. Add ½ cup crushed, drained pineapple to filling.

DATE CAKE FILLING

1 pound chopped, pitted dates	⅓ cup sugar
1 tablespoon lemon juice	⅛ teaspoon salt
½ cup water	1 cup finely chopped nuts

Combine all ingredients except nuts and bring to boiling point, stirring constantly until thick. Add nuts and cool. Spread between layers.

FIG CAKE FILLING

⅓ cup sugar	¼ pound chopped figs
2 tablespoons cornstarch	2 tablespoons lemon juice
½ cup boiling water	1 tablespoon grated lemon rind

Mix together sugar and cornstarch in a saucepan and add water. Cook until thick and smooth. Add figs, lemon juice, and rind. Cool. Spread between layers.

FRUIT CAKE FILLING AND ICING

2 cups sugar
6 tablespoons cornstarch
1 cup drained, crushed pineapple
1 cup chopped maraschino cherries
1 cup liquid (pineapple juice
   plus water)

2 tablespoons butter
Juice of 2 lemons
1 cup chopped nuts
1 4-ounce can coconut
¼ cup brandy or rum (optional)

Combine sugar, cornstarch, pineapple, cherries, liquid, and butter in a saucepan. Stir until well blended. Cook over low heat until very thick, stirring frequently. Remove from heat, add lemon juice, nuts, coconut, and liquor. Blend well. Cool. Spread between layers and on top and sides of cake.

GOLDEN CREAM FILLING

1½ tablespoons plain gelatin
 4 tablespoons water
 8 egg yolks
⅛ teaspoon salt

1 cup confectioners' sugar
4 tablespoons strong fresh coffee
1 pint whipping cream, whipped

Soften gelatin in water. Beat egg yolks with salt until thick. Beat sugar in gradually. Dissolve softened gelatin in hot coffee. Add to egg-sugar mixture. Let stand until partially set. Fold in whipped cream. Yield: filling and topping for 2 9-inch layers.

LEMON FILLING (Basic Recipe)

¾ cup sugar
5 tablespoons flour
⅛ teaspoon salt
⅔ cup water

1 egg, slightly beaten
1 tablespoon butter
1 teaspoon lemon rind
⅓ cup lemon juice

Combine sugar, flour, and salt in top of double boiler. Add water and blend thoroughly. Cook over boiling water until thickened, stirring constantly. Cover and cook additional 10 minutes, stirring occasionally. Stir in a little of the hot mixture into slightly beaten egg. Slowly stir into the remaining hot mixture. Cook over simmering water for 2 minutes, stirring constantly. Cool slightly. Add butter and lemon rind. Chill and add lemon juice. Yield: filling for 2 9-inch layers.

Lemon cream filling: Fold ½ cup whipped, heavy cream into chilled *LEMON FILLING.*

Orange filling: Proceed as for *LEMON FILLING.* Decrease sugar to ½ cup, water to ½ cup, lemon juice to 1 tablespoon, lemon rind to ½ teaspoon. Add 1 tablespoon orange rind. When chilled, add ½ cup orange juice.

Orange coconut filling: Add ½ cup shredded coconut to *ORANGE FILLING.*

Orange cream filling: When filling is chilled fold in ½ cup whipped heavy cream and ½ cup plain or toasted shredded coconut.

Orange date filling: Add ½ cup chopped dates to *ORANGE FILLING.*

MAPLE CREAM FILLING

4 egg yolks
¾ cup confectioners' sugar
¾ cup milk

½ cup butter
2 teaspoons maple flavoring

Beat egg yolks until thick and lemon-colored. Add sugar and milk and cook in double boiler, stirring constantly, until thick, about 10 minutes. Cool. Cream butter until fluffy. Add thoroughly cold custard and maple flavoring. Beat with rotary beater until smooth. Yield: frosting for 3-layer 8-inch cake.

PINEAPPLE FILLING #2

¾ cup sugar
2½ tablespoons cornstarch
⅛ teaspoon salt
    Grated rind of 1 lemon
¼ cup lemon juice

3 egg yolks, beaten slightly
½ cup canned pineapple juice
2 tablespoons butter

Mix sugar, cornstarch, and salt in top of double boiler. Add lemon rind and lemon juice and mix well. Add egg yolks, pineapple juice, and butter and blend. Place over boiling water. Cook until thick and smooth, stirring constantly (about 15 minutes). Yield: filling for 2 8-inch layers.

SOUR CREAM FILLING

2 eggs
⅔ cup sugar
1 cup sour cream

Pinch of salt
½ teaspoon vanilla

Beat eggs until thick. Gradually add sugar, beating constantly. Add sour cream and salt. Cook over boiling water until thickened, stirring constantly (about 15 minutes). Cool. Add vanilla. Yield: filling for 2 9-inch layers.

WHIPPED CREAM FILLING (Basic Recipe)

½ teaspoon plain gelatin
1 tablespoon cold water
3 tablespoons confectioners' sugar

¼ teaspoon vanilla
½ cup heavy cream

Soften gelatin in cold water. Place over boiling water. Stir until dissolved. Mix with sugar, vanilla, and cream. Whip until stiff. Chill thoroughly before spreading. Yield: filling for 2 9-inch layers.

Applesauce filling: Omit vanilla. Decrease cream to ⅓ cup. Before chilling, fold in ½ cup chilled, thick applesauce and ½ teaspoon cinnamon.

Chocolate filling: Increase sugar to 4 tablespoons. Mix with 2 tablespoons cocoa before adding cream.

Coffee filling: Substitute coffee for water.

Pineapple filling: Omit vanilla. Decrease cream to ⅓ cup. Before chilling, fold in ½ cup drained, crushed pineapple.

candies

Candies are usually classified into two general types, cream candies and hard candies. Each type has many variations. The two types are determined by the thickness of the syrup or the extent to which the sugar is caramelized in the candymaking process. The syrup becomes thick as it boils. The creamy candies, such as fondant and fudge, form crystals, which must be very small in order to avoid a coarse, grainy texture. Note that these candies are stirred only until the sugar is dissolved. The hard candies, such as butterscotch and caramels, are non-crystalline. It's important to pour and cool hard candies quickly.

Utensils: The saucepans used in making candies should be flat-bottomed and should have straight sides and smooth inner surfaces. Use deep, rather than narrow, saucepans and be sure they are large enough to allow candy to boil without danger of boiling over. The pans should be sufficiently heavy to minimize scorching. Before starting to make candy, assemble all ingredients and utensils so that they will be handy. A heavy spoon with a wooden handle is preferable for stirring and beating. The wooden handle does not heat readily. Bowls should be smooth.

Prevention of crystal formation: Sugar crystals that form on the sides of the pan are removed by wiping with a damp cloth wrapped around a fork. Do this several times during cooking because, if permitted to remain, they will start crystal formation as the candy is beaten or poured from the pan. Do not scrape the saucepan as candy is being poured. Scraping starts crystal formation.

Beating: Creamed candies should be cooled, without stirring, to lukewarm before beating. If they are not cooled before they are beaten, large crystals will form. If large crystals do form, a little water may be added and the candy cooked again to the correct stage.

TEMPERATURE AND CANDY TESTS

It is necessary to use a candy thermometer to insure uniformity and consistency in results. The bulb should be entirely immersed in mixture without touching the pan. With practice, however, the following cold water tests will give satisfactory results.

Soft ball: (236°–238°F.) When dropped into cold water, syrup will form soft ball which quickly loses its shape on removal. When using brown sugar, or on rainy or damp days, boil to higher temperature.

Firm ball: (244°–250°F.) Syrup will form a firm but plastic ball in cold water which can be easily handled in the water and becomes soft on removal. Use for caramels.

Hard ball: (250°–258°F.) Syrup forms firm ball in cold water but is plastic and can easily be handled in cold water. Use higher temperature on rainy or damp days. Use for divinity, nougat, popcorn balls.

Very hard ball: (258°–266°F.) Syrup loses most of plastic quality in cold water. Ball will roll on buttered plate. Use for taffy.

Light crack: (290°–300°F.) Syrup will form brittle threads in cold water. Spiral softens when removed from water. Use for butterscotch.

Hard crack: (300°–310°F.) Syrup forms brittle threads in cold water which remain brittle on removal. Use for brittle candy.

CANDIED GRAPEFRUIT PEEL

Peel fruit, keeping peel in large pieces. Wash and trim out most of white from inside. Cut into strips or triangles. Cover with cold water. Boil 5 minutes. Drain. Cover again with cold water. Boil 5 minutes. Drain. Repeat twice, or until peel is tender. Weigh drained peel. Weigh an equal amount of honey and sugar, using half of each. Add ⅓ cup water for each cup honey and sugar. Add peel. Simmer until peel is glazed, about 20 minutes. Drain. Roll in granulated sugar.

Orange or lemon peel: Simmer peel until tender without changing water, 20 to 30 minutes. Proceed as above.

Chocolate citrus peel: Dip candied peel in melted sweet chocolate.

SPICED NUTS

¼ cup sugar
2 teaspoons cinnamon
⅛ teaspoon nutmeg
⅛ teaspoon cloves

1 cup nuts (almonds, pecans, English walnuts, Brazil nuts, etc.)
1 slightly beaten egg white

Mix sugar and spices in a small bowl. Add nutmeats to egg white, a few at a time, in order to coat them well. Drop into the bowl of sugar and spices. When well coated, place on buttered baking sheet and brown in slow oven (300°F.) for 30 minutes.

GLACE NUTS

1 cup sugar
⅛ teaspoon cream of tartar

½ cup water

Combine ingredients and heat to boiling. Stir until sugar is dissolved. Wipe all grains of sugar from sides of saucepan with a damp cloth. Boil without stirring to the light crack stage (290°F.). Remove sugar crystals around edge of pan with wet cloth. Remove saucepan from fire. Set in pan of cold water to stop boiling immediately. Remove from cold water and set in pan of hot water. Using a fork, dip each nut into syrup, drain, and place on waxed paper. If syrup becomes too thick, reheat over hot water.

TOASTED NUTS

Brown the prepared nuts in a little melted butter over a low flame, shaking the pan to brown evenly, or spread out in a shallow pan and place in a very slow oven (250°F.) until lightly browned, about 15 minutes.

SALTED NUTS

Shell and blanch nuts, if necessary. Wash and dry thoroughly. Melt ½ teaspoon butter in a shallow pan. Add 1 layer of shelled nuts. Place in moderate oven (350°F.) about 10 minutes. Stir and turn nuts frequently. Pour onto absorbent paper to drain off any excess butter. Sprinkle with salt, to taste. About 1½ to 2 teaspoons salt per pound nuts is the usual amount.

FRENCH FRIED NUTS

Fry shelled dry nuts in deep hot fat (370°F.) until lightly browned, 4 to 5 minutes. Drain on absorbent paper. Sprinkle with salt.

MARZIPAN

2 egg whites
1 cup almond paste

½ teaspoon lemon extract or
½ teaspoon vanilla extract
1 cup confectioners' sugar

Beat egg whites. Mix with almond paste. Add flavoring and enough sugar to make mixture stiff enough to handle. Allow to stand overnight. Divide, color, and flavor to imitate fruit or vegetable, such as pears, apples, etc. Mold into shapes. It may also be cut into small pieces and dipped into chocolate or other coating, or used as the center of candied cherries, dates, or prunes. Commercial almond paste may be used. To prepare 1 cup almond paste blanch and pound 2⅔ cups shelled almonds into fine consistency.

CHOCOLATE FUDGE (Basic Recipe)

2 squares unsweetened chocolate
⅔ cup milk
2 cups sugar

⅛ teaspoon salt
2 tablespoons butter
1 teaspoon vanilla extract

Break chocolate into small pieces. Add to milk in saucepan. Cook over low heat, stirring constantly until mixture is smooth. Add sugar and salt and stir until sugar is dissolved and mixture boils. Cook slowly, without stirring, until a small quantity dropped into cold water forms a soft ball (236°F.). Remove from heat. Add butter and vanilla without stirring. Cool to lukewarm (110°F.). Beat until fairly thick. Pour at once into greased pan. Cool. Cut into squares. Yield: about 1¼ pounds.

Brown sugar fudge: Substitute 1 cup firmly packed brown sugar for 1 cup granulated sugar.

Coconut fudge: Add ½ cup chopped, shredded coconut just before pouring into greased pan.

Creamy chocolate fudge: Add 2 tablespoons light corn syrup with sugar.

Fruit fudge: Stir ½ cup chopped dates, figs, candied fruit, dried fruit, or raisins into fudge just before pouring into pan.

Fudge nut and fruit balls: Add chopped nuts and chopped cherries, dates, or figs to beaten fudge and mix until just blended. Mold into even-sized balls with hands. Roll each in finely ground nuts.

Marshmallow fudge: Cut 12 marshmallows into small pieces. Add to fudge just before pouring into pan.

Mocha fudge: Decrease milk to ⅓ cup. Add ⅔ cup fresh strong coffee.

Nut fudge: Add ½ cup broken nutmeats just before pouring into pan.

Peanut butter fudge: Substitute ¼ cup peanut butter for butter and add when beating fudge after it has cooled to lukewarm (110°F.).

Penuche: Substitute brown sugar for white and water for milk.

Sour cream fudge: Substitute sour cream for milk. Omit butter and cook to slightly higher temperature (238°F.).

Vanilla fudge: Omit chocolate from recipe for *CHOCOLATE FUDGE* and increase vanilla to 1½ teaspoons.

SOUR CREAM PENUCHE

3 cups light brown sugar
½ cup granulated sugar
1½ cups thick sour cream

1 tablespoon butter
½ cup broken nutmeats

Combine sugar, sour cream, and butter and cook to soft ball stage (236°F.). Cool to lukewarm and beat until mixture loses its gloss. Add nuts just before end of beating period. Pour into buttered pan. Cut when hardened.

HONEY PENUCHE

2 cups brown sugar
¼ teaspoon salt
⅔ cup white sugar
1 cup milk

¼ cup honey
3 tablespoons butter
½ cup chopped nuts

Combine all ingredients except butter and nuts. Cook over low flame to 240°F. Stir just enough to prevent sticking. Remove from fire, add butter. Cool to lukewarm. Do not stir. When cooled, beat until candy begins to thicken. Add nuts and turn into greased shallow pan. When firm, cut into squares. Yield: about 24 squares.

ENGLISH TOFFEE

½ pound brown sugar
½ pound butter

½ pound milk chocolate
½ pound almond meats, salted slightly

Cook sugar and butter very slowly over an asbestos pad, stirring constantly, to prevent separating. Cook to hard-crack stage (310°F.), when mixture becomes brittle and crunchy in cold water. Add some whole nuts when taken from the fire. Have a buttered pan ready sprinkled with browned and ground nuts and a layer of melted chocolate. Pour the toffee onto this foundation. After it has cooled a little, add another layer of melted chocolate and ground nuts. If the toffee separates, add 2 cups of white sugar, 2 cups brown sugar, ¼ teaspoon baking soda, and 1½ cups milk and make up into creamy penuche.

COOKED FONDANT (Basic Recipe)

2 cups sugar
¾ cup boiling water
⅛ teaspoon cream of tartar

⅛ teaspoon salt
½ teaspoon vanilla

Place sugar, water, cream of tartar, and salt in saucepan over hot fire. Stir constantly until, but not after, sugar has dissolved. Do not splash syrup. Remove spoon. Do not use it again after syrup boils. Remove sugar crystals around edge of pan with wet cloth. Let syrup boil until it reaches 238°F., or until it forms soft ball in cold water. Be sure bulb of thermometer is down in syrup yet does not touch bottom of pan. Add vanilla without stirring. Pour syrup in a thin sheet onto chilled platter to cool quickly. Do not scrape out saucepan. When syrup is cool, work it with flat wooden spoon until it creams. When it forms a soft creamy mass, work it with palms of hands in same way as bread dough until it is smooth. Place fondant in an earthenware or glass dish. Cover with damp cloth. After 24 hours fondant is ready to mold. It will keep for months in a cold place if covered with moist cloth or stored in tightly covered jar.

Brown sugar: Substitute 1 cup firmly packed brown sugar for 1 cup granulated sugar.

Cherry or nut balls: Form ripened fondant into tiny balls. Press each between two halves of cherries or nutmeats, or roll each in chopped coconut, chopped nutmeats, cocoa, or chopped semi-sweet chocolate.

Chocolate: Knead 2 squares (2 ounces) melted unsweetened chocolate and ½ teaspoon vanilla into 1 cup ripened fondant.

Coffee: Substitute strong fresh coffee for water.

Loaves: Add fruit and nuts to fondant. Pack into loaf pan. Let stand until firm. Cut into slices.

Mints: Melt ripened fondant slowly over hot water. Color and flavor. Drop from teaspoon onto waxed paper.

Nut creams: Knead fondant, and flavor with almond extract or coffee extract. Knead into it a mixture of chopped nuts or moist coconut. Shape into balls, squares, or patties which may be dipped in melted dipping chocolate.

Stuffed fruits: Prepare dates, figs, or prunes. Stuff with fondant.

Tutti-frutti: Knead fondant. Add cherry extract or almond extract. Knead chopped mixture of raisins, dates, figs, candied cherries, citron, orange peel, or other candied fruit into ripened fondant. Shape into a flat cake. Cut after it stands 1 hour.

Wintergreen creams: Melt portion of fondant in top part of double boiler until soft enough to drop from a spoon. Add a tiny bit of red vegetable coloring to tint delicate pink and 1 to 2 drops oil of wintergreen flavoring, stirring enough to blend. If fondant is too thick add few drops of hot water. If too thin, let stand 5 to 10 minutes to thicken. Drop from a teaspoon on waxed paper or lightly buttered flat surface.

CHOCOLATE BONBONS

Melt very slowly in top part of double boiler a good quality of specially prepared dipping chocolate, sweetened or unsweetened. Do not heat water under chocolate above 120°F. (slightly more than lukewarm), since overheating spoils chocolate for dipping. Stir constantly while melting to keep constant temperature. When melted, beat thoroughly. Keep heat very low while dipping. To dip centers, use a fork or confectioners' dipper. Drop a center into chocolate. Cover completely with chocolate. Remove with dipping fork. Drop onto waxed paper. The room in which dipping is done should be cool, so that chocolate may harden quickly. Fruit, nuts, mints, plain fondant, and other candies may be dipped in chocolate. One pound dipping chocolate will cover 70 to 80 assorted centers.

UNCOOKED FONDANT (Basic Recipe)

1 egg white	¾ teaspoon vanilla
½ tablespoon water	2¾ cups confectioners' sugar

Combine egg white, water, and vanilla in a bowl. Beat until well blended. Add sugar gradually until mixture is very stiff. Knead with hands until smooth. Wrap in waxed paper. Store in refrigerator to use as desired.

Cherry fondant balls: Color fondant pink. Form into balls. Press a maraschino cherry into each.

Chocolate fondant: Add 2 squares (2 ounces) melted, unsweetened chocolate to fondant. Blend thoroughly.

Chocolate nut cubes: Combine fondant and chopped pecans. Cut into tiny cubes and dip in melted chocolate.

Chocolate peppermints: Add a few drops of essence of peppermint to fondant. Mix it thoroughly. Melt 2 squares unsweetened chocolate in top of double boiler. Form small balls of fondant. Press into round, flat patties. Dip in melted chocolate. Place on waxed paper to dry.

Coconut or chocolate fondant balls: Form fondant balls. Roll in shredded coconut or chocolate.

Fondant nougats: Add chopped dates, nuts, figs, and maraschino cherries to fondant. Spread on waxed paper. Cut into squares. Dip each square in powdered sugar.

Nut brown patties: Make small balls of fondant. Roll in dry cocoa. Press flat with half a nut on each.

Pistachio fondant balls: Color fondant green. Form into small balls. Press flat with a pistachio nut.

Strawberry fondant: Coat ripe, unhulled strawberries with fondant, leaving stems uncoated. Roll in powdered sugar. Store in refrigerator until ready to serve.

UNCOOKED BUTTER FONDANT

Add 2 teaspoons butter to 3 tablespoons boiling water. Add sifted confectioners' sugar a little at a time until the mixture is pliable and may be molded by hand. Use as other fondants.

VANILLA CARAMELS (Basic Recipe)

2 cups sugar	½ cup butter
1⁄16 teaspoon salt	1 tall can evaporated milk
2 cups corn syrup	1 teaspoon vanilla extract

Combine sugar, salt, and syrup in saucepan. Cook over low heat until sugar is completely dissolved. Bring to boil. Cook until a little syrup dropped from teaspoon into cold water forms firm ball (244°F.). Add butter and milk a little at a time so that mixture does not stop boiling. Continue cooking to 242°F. Remove from heat. Add vanilla, stirring only to blend. Pour into buttered pan. Mark into squares. Cut when cold. Yield: about 72 pieces.

Chocolate: Cook 4 squares unsweetened chocolate with sugar, salt, and syrup.

Coconut: Add 1 cup toasted, shredded coconut after removing from heat.

Coffee: Substitute 1 teaspoon coffee extract for vanilla extract.

Fruit: Add 1 cup diced figs, dates, or raisins before pouring into buttered pan.

Honey: Substitute 2 cups honey for corn syrup. Decrease butter to ¼ cup. Cook to firm ball stage (244°F.).

Nut: Add 1 to 1½ cups chopped nutmeats before pouring into pan.

DIVINITY (Basic Recipe)

2 cups sugar	2 egg whites
1 cup water	1½ cups chopped walnuts
¼ cup corn syrup	1 teaspoon vanilla
⅛ teaspoon salt	

Heat sugar, water, corn syrup, and salt, stirring constantly until sugar has dissolved. Continue to cook without stirring until syrup when dropped in cold water forms a hard ball (250°F.). Beat egg whites. Pour syrup slowly into them and continue to beat until candy is stiff enough to hold its shape. Add nuts and vanilla. Drop by spoonfuls onto waxed paper, or turn into buttered pan and cut in 1-inch squares when firm. Pack in a tin box. Keep covered because it dries out quickly.

Brazil nut divinity: Use Brazil nuts instead of walnuts.

Brown sugar divinity or sea foam: Substitute 1 cup firmly packed brown sugar for 1 cup granulated sugar.

Cherry divinity: Color delicate pink with vegetable coloring. Add ½ cup chopped candied cherries.

Chocolate divinity: After syrup and egg whites have been combined, add 2 squares melted unsweetened chocolate.

Coconut divinity: Add ½ cup toasted, shredded coconut.

Fruit divinity: Chopped dates, figs, or other dried or candied fruit may be added.

Maple divinity: Decrease water to ¼ cup. Add ¾ cup maple syrup.

Neapolitan divinity: Divide candy into 3 parts. Color 1 part with strawberry or cherry coloring. Add 1 square melted unsweetened chocolate to second part. Spread white, or third, part in bottom of buttered pan. Add pink part, then chocolate part. Press together. Let harden before cutting into squares.

Orange divinity: Add 3 tablespoons coarsely grated orange rind with vanilla and nuts.

PEANUT BRITTLE

1 cup sugar	⅛ teaspoon salt
½ cup chopped roasted peanuts	

Melt sugar in a heavy skillet over low heat, stirring constantly until sugar is golden brown. Remove from stove. Add nuts and salt, and stir just enough to mix. Pour onto a buttered pan in a thin sheet. When cold, break in pieces.

ALMOND BRITTLE

3 cups corn flakes
½ cup seedless raisins
½ cup coarsely chopped almonds,
blanched
1 cup sugar

½ teaspoon butter
⅛ cup vinegar
¼ cup water
¼ teaspoon salt

Combine corn flakes, raisins, and almonds in large pan and warm in oven. Boil remaining ingredients to hard crack stage (300°F.). Pour slowly over corn flake-almond mixture, blending lightly but thoroughly. Spread in pan lined with waxed paper. When cool, break or cut in pieces. Yield: 1 pound.

NUT BRITTLE

1½ cups shelled peanuts
¼ teaspoon salt
1 cup sugar
½ cup light corn syrup

½ cup water
1½ tablespoons butter
½ teaspoon lemon extract

Sprinkle nuts with salt and warm in oven. Put sugar, corn syrup, and water in pan. Stir until it boils. Wash down sides with wet pastry brush and cook to 295°F., or until mixture is very brittle when tried in cold water. Add butter, lemon extract and nuts, and pour into a shallow greased pan. As soon as it can be handled, turn the mass over and pull and stretch it out as thin as possible. Break into irregular pieces.

CRACK TAFFY

1¼ cups molasses
1 tablespoon vinegar
¾ cup sugar

⅛ teaspoon salt
⅛ teaspoon baking soda
1 tablespoon butter

Blend molasses, vinegar, and sugar. Boil carefully to very hard ball stage (270°F.). Remove from the fire. Add remaining ingredients, stirring until well mixed. Pour into greased tins. Let stand until cool. Crack with a mallet or hammer.

WALNUT TAFFY

Boil 2 cups sugar and 1 cup light corn syrup together to very hard ball stage (266°F.). Pour onto greased platter. Sprinkle with ½ cup chopped walnuts. When cool enough to handle pull until cold, light, and firm, mixing in nuts. Stretch out into long rope and cut into serving pieces.

SALT WATER TAFFY

Mix 1 cup sugar, 3 tablespoons cornstarch, and few grains salt. Add ½ cup water and ⅔ cup honey. Cook to very hard ball stage (266°F.). Pour into greased pan. Cool. Pull until porous. Cut in 1-inch pieces.

RAISIN PEANUT CLUSTERS

Wash 2½ cups seedless raisins and dry thoroughly on a towel. Melt ½ pound sweet or dipping chocolate over warm water and cool to lukewarm. Add raisins, 1 cup shelled, roasted peanuts, and ¼ teaspoon salt. Mix well. Drop from teaspoon on waxed paper or shape in paper candy cups. Yield: about 50 small clusters.

WALNUT CLUSTERS

Break up ½ pound sweet cooking chocolate and melt over hot water, stirring constantly. Stir in 1½ cups broken walnut meats. Drop by tablespoons on waxed paper. Chill. Yield: 24 clusters.

HONEY NOUGAT

½ cup honey	2 egg whites, stiffly beaten
2 cups sugar	⅛ teaspoon salt
¼ cup water	¾ cup chopped nutmeats

Combine honey, sugar, and water. Cook to hard ball stage (258°F.). Beat eggs with salt until stiff. Add syrup gradually, beating constantly until it stands up in peaks. Spread in greased shallow square pan. Top with nutmeats. Cool and cut in rectangular pieces. Yield: about 24 pieces.

BUTTERSCOTCH (Basic Recipe)

2 cups brown sugar	¼ teaspoon salt
¼ cup light corn syrup	⅓ cup butter
1 cup water	¼ teaspoon vanilla

Place sugar, corn syrup, water, and salt in saucepan. Cook over low flame, stirring until sugar dissolves. Continue cooking without stirring until mixture reaches temperature of 290°F. Add butter, remove from heat, and add vanilla. Pour into a buttered shallow pan. Cool slightly. Mark into squares. When cold, break into pieces. Yield: about 1⅛ pounds.

Butterscotch lollypops: Cook sugar mixture to 290°F. Stir in butter and vanilla quickly. Pour into greased lollypop molds, or drop from end of teaspoon onto greased flat pan. Place stick in each pop.

Lemon butterscotch: Substitute a few drops oil of lemon for vanilla.

LOLLYPOPS (Basic Recipe)

2 cups sugar	½ teaspoon oil of lemon
⅔ cup light corn syrup	Few drops yellow coloring
1 cup water	

Place sugar, corn syrup, and water in saucepan. Cook over low flame, stirring until sugar dissolves. Continue cooking, without stirring, to hard crack stage (310°F.). Wrap wet cloth around a fork. While cooking, wipe crystals from sides of pan with wet cloth. Grease lollypop molds or flat surface. When temperature of 310°F. is reached, add oil of lemon and coloring, stirring both in quickly. Pour immediately into greased molds, or drop from end of spoon onto flat greased surface. Press end of stick into each pop as soon as each is dropped from spoon. Loosen lollypops as soon as they are firm and before they are cold.

Variations of lollypops: Vary flavoring and coloring by using oil of lime and green coloring, oil of peppermint and pink coloring, and oil of cinnamon and red coloring. To form faces, use Life Savers or raisins for eyes, pieces of prune for mouth, and coconut for hair. Have all decorations ready to add while lollypops are hot.

MOLASSES POPCORN BALLS (Basic Recipe)

1 tablespoon butter	½ teaspoon salt
1 cup sugar	4 quarts popped corn
1 cup molasses	

Melt butter. Add sugar, molasses, and salt. Boil on medium heat until very hard ball stage (260°F.). Pour over corn. Stir corn thoroughly while pouring syrup over it. Butter hands lightly. Shape into balls. Yield: 12 to 14.

Cereal popcorn balls: Substitute 3 cups puffed cereal for similar amount of popcorn and mix before adding syrup.

Colored popcorn balls: Omit molasses. Use 1½ cups light corn syrup and add any desired vegetable coloring and 1 teaspoon vanilla.

Nut caramel corn: Add ½ cup nuts to popcorn before adding syrup. Cool slightly. Shape into balls.

Popcorn chop suey: Substitute 1 cup shelled roasted peanuts and 1 cup shredded coconut for similar amount of popcorn. Mix before adding syrup.

Raisin popcorn balls: Add ½ cup raisins to popcorn before adding syrup.

TURKISH PASTE

3 tablespoons gelatin	3 tablespoons lemon juice
½ cup cold water	Green coloring
½ cup hot water	Mint flavoring
1 pound sugar	1 cup finely chopped nuts
¼ teaspoon salt	

Soften gelatin in cold water for 5 minutes. Bring hot water and sugar to boiling point. Add salt and gelatin. Stir until gelatin has dissolved. Simmer 20 minutes. Remove from fire and when cool add lemon juice, coloring, and mint flavoring. Stir in nuts. Let mixture stand until it begins to thicken. Stir again before pouring into a pan that has been rinsed with cold water. Have the layer of paste about 1 inch thick. Let stand overnight in cool place. Moisten sharp knife in boiling water. Cut candy in cubes. Roll in powdered sugar.

STUFFED FIGS

½ pound dried, whole figs	Grated rind of 1 lemon
½ cup orange juice	Chopped pecan nutmeats
1 tablespoon sugar	

Clip stem end from figs. Cover with orange juice. Add sugar and lemon rind. Bring to boil. Let simmer, covered, until fruit is tender. Drain well. When cool, insert a knife in stem end and work back and forth to open a pocket. Fill with chopped pecan meats. Allow a whole half pecan meat to emerge from the opening. Pat fruit into original shape and roll in fine granulated sugar or confectioners' sugar. Let dry overnight before storing. Yield: about 1 pound.

PARISIAN SWEETS

½ pound figs	½ pound nutmeats
½ pound dried apricots or	Confectioners' sugar
½ pound seedless raisins	

Wash and pick over fruits. Combine with nutmeats. Grind through a meat chopper, using medium knife. Roll out about ½ inch thick on a board sprinkled with confectioners' sugar. Cut into small pieces or make balls and roll them in confectioners' sugar. Store in a tin box or a tight jar.

PRALINES

4 cups sugar	2 cups cream
1 teaspoon salt	3 cups pecan nutmeats

Make a syrup with 3 cups of sugar, salt, and cream. Melt other cup of sugar slowly in a heavy skillet. Stir constantly until caramelized. Add all of syrup at once, stirring constantly and rapidly. Boil mixture without stirring to temperature of 238°F., or to soft ball stage. Pour into a flat pan. Cool. Beat until it begins to be creamy. Add nuts. Drop by spoonfuls onto waxed paper to form flat, round cakes. Yield: about 40 pralines.

TAFFY APPLES

Boil together 1 cup white sugar, 1 cup brown sugar, ½ cup vinegar, and ½ cup water. Cook until small amount dropped in cold water cracks between fingers (290°F.). Dip apples on sticks in syrup. Cool.

CEREAL PUFF BALLS

1 cup sugar	1 tablespoon butter
½ cup corn syrup	¼ teaspoon baking soda
3 tablespoons water	Puffed cereal

Dissolve sugar and corn syrup with water over very low heat. Boil to very hard ball stage (258°F.). Remove from fire. Stir in butter and baking soda. Pour while still hot over puffed cereal and as soon as possible form into tiny balls. Or it may be packed into a buttered loaf pan and cooled and sliced.

FRUIT SQUARES

1 cup raisins	¼ cup candied cherries
1 cup pitted dates	1 cup chopped walnuts
⅓ cup dried figs	2 to 3 tablespoons orange juice
½ cup dried apricots	Confectioners' sugar
½ cup candied orange peel	

Grind together fruits and nuts. Mix in enough orange juice to hold together. Press into 8x8x2-inch pan. Chill overnight. Cut and sift sugar over top. Makes 24 pieces.

cookies

Most cookies are easily prepared and they keep for a relatively long time—longer than most other desserts. Specific directions are given with each recipe so that perfect cookies can be made every time. Here, however, are some general rules that apply to all cooky making. Preheat oven to temperature given in the recipe about 15 minutes before you want to bake the cookies. Prepare the baking sheets and pans in advance by greasing them, unless otherwise stated, with any mild-flavored unsalted shortening. Use a pastry brush or soft paper. Only doughs containing a high proportion of shortening are baked on ungreased sheets or pans. When making drop cookies, allow at least 2 inches between cookies. They spread considerably.

Ingredients: Any mild-flavored fat is acceptable for cookies; however, part butter—preferably half—will improve flavor unless the recipe specifically calls for another shortening. The flour may be cake flour, whole-wheat, or all-purpose. Many recipes name a specific flour to be used. Where just "flour" is called for, that means all-purpose flour. When substituting cake flour for all-purpose flour, add 2 more tablespoons of cake flour for each cup called for in the recipe.

Shaping: For easy handling, chill the dough, if necessary. For rolled cookies, shape the dough into medium-sized balls, roll out, and cut with cutters dipped in flour. Shake off excess flour each time. Save the scraps from each rolling, re-chill, and roll out again. The recipes in this section give directions for dropped, molded, sliced, pressed and rolled cookies, and bar cookies. Whichever method is followed, remember that all cookies should be uniform in size and thickness so that they will bake evenly. To obtain a glaze over the cookies, brush with egg white or beaten egg yolk before baking.

Decorations: For decorating cookies the following materials may be used: nuts, chocolate bits or shavings, shredded coconut, candied bits of fruit such as pineapple, cherries, citron, colored candies and sugars, dots of marmalade and jellies. For putting cookies together fruit fillings, softened marshmallows, and frosting may be used.

How to tell when cookies are done: Crisp cookies; when delicately browned. Drop cookies; when touched lightly with finger, spring back in shape. Bar cookies; still moist when done, follow time given in recipe. Overbaking makes cookies hard and dry. Watch timing carefully and test when minimum time is reached. Better yet, bake and test 1 cooky before placing panful in oven.

COOLING AND STORING COOKIES

Remove cookies from baking sheet with a spatula. Place them in a single layer on a wire cake rack. When cool, transfer to a metal container lined on the bottom with waxed paper.

To keep cookies crisp: Use a can with a loose cover. The cookies will remain dry and crisp except in very humid weather, and may then be dried out in the oven.

To keep soft and chewy: Use an air-tight container. A slice of apple will help keep them moist, soft, and mellow. Change the fruit frequently to insure freshness.

POPPY SEED COOKIES

1 cup poppy seed
½ cup scalded milk
½ cup butter
½ cup sugar
2 ounces (squares) melted chocolate
¼ cup currants (optional)

1½ cups sifted all-purpose flour
1 teaspoon baking powder
⅛ teaspoon salt
½ teaspoon cinnamon
¼ teaspoon ground cloves
¼ cup raisins (optional)

Soak poppy seed in hot milk for ½ hour. Cream butter and sugar. Add remaining ingredients and mix thoroughly. Drop by teaspoonfuls on greased baking sheets. Bake in moderate oven (350°F.) 20 minutes. Yield: about 30.

HONEY POPPY SEED COOKIES

2 cups flour, sifted
1 tablespoon sugar
4 eggs, slightly beaten

2 tablespoons vegetable oil
1 pound honey (1 cup)
¼ pound poppy seed

Mix together flour, sugar, eggs, and vegetable oil. Knead until smooth, about 5 minutes. Roll out ¼ inch thick on a lightly floured board. Cut into 2-inch squares. Fold over into triangles and prick tops with a fork. Bake on a greased cooky sheet in moderate oven (350°F.) until lightly browned, about 15 minutes. Drop cookies into boiling honey, stirring constantly. After 3 minutes add poppy seed. Stir constantly and cook until a rich brown. Sprinkle with 2 tablespoons cold water, stir well, and remove from heat. Place on a greased platter. Separate cookies with wet hands. Chill. Yield: about 4 dozen.

MANDELBRODT (Komishbrodt)

2¾ cups sifted all-purpose
flour (about)
4 teaspoons baking powder
½ teaspoon salt
3 eggs
1 cup sugar (scant)

6 tablespoons vegetable oil
Grated rind of 1 lemon
½ teaspoon vanilla or almond extract
⅓ cup coarsely chopped, blanched
almonds

Mix and sift flour, baking powder, and salt. Beat eggs and sugar together until light. Add remaining ingredients in order given and blend well. The dough should be soft. With floured hands form 2 long loaves about 3 inches wide and ¾ inch high on a well floured board. Bake in long narrow pans or on greased cooky sheets in moderate oven (350°F.) until lightly browned, 40 to 50 minutes. While still warm cut into ½-inch slices and return to oven to toast until browned, or brown quickly under broiler flame. Yield: about 30 to 40.

Chocolate filled mandelbrodt: Mix and add 3 teaspoons cocoa and 1 teaspoon sugar to ¼ of the dough. Form into a ½-inch roll and wrap rolled and flattened white dough around it. Shape into 2 rolls and bake.

DROP KICHLACH

3 eggs
½ cup vegetable oil

1 tablespoon sugar
⅞ cup sifted all-purpose flour

Beat eggs together with oil, sugar, and flour for about 20 minutes. Drop by teaspoonfuls onto a greased cooky sheet, allowing 2 inches between cookies for spreading. Bake in a slow oven (300°F.) 15 to 20 minutes. Yield: about 24.

MOHN KICHLACH

About 1¼ cups sifted all-purpose
   flour
2 tablespoons sugar
¼ teaspoon salt

3 eggs
½ cup vegetable oil
¼ cup poppy seed

Mix and sift dry ingredients. Make a well in center and add eggs, oil, and poppy seed, gradually beating with a fork until blended into a smooth mixture. Drop by teaspoonfuls on greased baking sheets, allowing 2 inches between cookies for spreading. Bake in slow oven (325°F.) about 20 minutes. Yield: about 40 cookies.

EIER KICHLACH

2 cups sifted all-purpose flour,
   scant
¾ teaspoon baking powder

¾ teaspoon salt
3 eggs, beaten

Mix and sift flour, baking powder, and salt. Add eggs and knead well, about 5 minutes. Roll out on floured board about ¼ inch thick and sprinkle with sugar. Prick all over with a fork. Cut into diamonds or rectangles about 3 inches long. Bake on lightly floured cooky sheets in moderate oven (350°F.), or until lightly browned, about ½ hour. Yield: about 50 cookies.

PARVE SUGAR COOKIES (Basic Recipe)

4 cups sifted all-purpose flour
2 teaspoons baking powder
½ teaspoon salt
2 eggs
¾ cup vegetable oil

¼ cup warm water
1 cup sugar
Grated rind of 1 lemon
2 teaspoons lemon juice
1 teaspoon vanilla

Mix and sift flour, baking powder, and salt. Combine and mix thoroughly with remaining ingredients and knead until smooth (about 5 minutes). Roll out on floured board about ⅛ inch thick. Sprinkle with cinnamon and sugar. Run rolling pin over sheet again. Cut with cooky cutters. Bake on greased cooky sheets in moderate oven (350°F.) until light brown, 20 minutes. Yield: about 6 dozen.

Variations: Substitute flavorings, or sprinkle cookies with colored sugar; add shredded coconut, melted chocolate, or finely chopped nuts.

TEIGLACH

SYRUP
1 cup honey
1 cup sugar
2 teaspoons ginger
DOUGH
About 2 cups sifted all-purpose
   flour

¼ teaspoon ginger
¼ teaspoon salt
3 eggs, well beaten
2 tablespoons oil
Chopped nutmeats (optional)
Raisins (optional)

Mix and sift flour, ¼ teaspoon ginger, and salt. Gradually add flour mixture to eggs, oil, and, if desired, nuts and raisins, making a soft dough just stiff enough to handle. Divide dough into several parts. Roll each into a long rope about ½ inch in diameter and cut into ½-inch pieces. Bring honey, sugar, and 2 teaspoons ginger to a rolling boil in a deep kettle. Drop pieces of dough in a few at a time to prevent lowering of temperature. Cover and simmer ½ hour, shaking pan occasionally to prevent sticking. When top layer has browned, turn gently with a wooden spoon to bring bottom ones to top. Cook until all are golden brown and sound hollow when stirred. To test, break one open and if inside is crisp and dry, remove from heat. Add 2 tablespoons boiling water. Remove teiglach to large platter with perforated spoon, placing them so that they do not touch each other. If desired, roll in sugar and chopped nuts. Cool and store like other cookies.

Variation: To serve teiglach in syrup, add ½ cup boiling water and stir just before turning off heat. Let cool slightly and pour into jars while still warm. Do not cover until cooled.

ROLLED SUGAR COOKIES (Basic Recipe)

2 cups sifted all-purpose flour	1 cup sugar
1½ teaspoons baking powder	1 egg, well beaten
½ teaspoon salt	1 teaspoon vanilla
½ cup butter or other fat	1 tablespoon milk or cream

Sift together 1½ cups flour, baking powder, and salt. Cream fat; add sugar gradually and cream until light and fluffy. Add egg, vanilla, and milk. Add sifted dry ingredients, then gradually add remaining flour until dough is stiff enough to handle. Chill at least 1 hour. Roll ⅛ inch thick on lightly floured board and shape with floured cookie cutters. Place on ungreased cookie sheets. Sprinkle with plain or tinted sugar. Bake in moderate oven (375°F.) 8 to 10 minutes. Yield: 50 to 60 small cookies.

Dropped sugar cookies: Use only 1½ cups flour and 1 teaspoon baking powder. Drop by teaspoonfuls 2 to 3 inches apart on greased cookie sheets. For flat cookies, press with knife or fork dipped in cold water or flatten with floured bottom of glass. If mixture is too firm shape into small balls and flatten as above. Bake in moderate oven (375°F.) 8 to 10 minutes.

Almond rolled cookies: Add ⅓ cup chopped, blanched almonds and grated rind of ½ lemon, to flour mixture. Sift with dry ingredients ½ teaspoon each of cinnamon, clove and nutmeg.

Butterscotch rolled cookies: Substitute 1 cup firmly packed brown sugar for granulated sugar.

Candied fruit rolled cookies: Add ¼ cup chopped candied cherries, pineapple, orange, lemon, or grapefruit peel to flour mixture. Cookies may also be garnished with bits of fruit before baking.

Caraway seed rolled cookies: Add 2 tablespoons caraway seed.

Chocolate rolled cookies: Add 2 ounces melted unsweetened chocolate with beaten egg. 1 cup finely chopped nuts may be added to sifted dry ingredients.

Coconut orange rolled cookies: Omit vanilla and add 1¼ teaspoons grated orange rind. Add 1 cup shredded coconut to flour mixture.

Coconut rolled cookies: Add ½ cup shredded coconut to flour mixture, or sprinkle coconut over cookies before baking.

Crisp rolled sugar cookies: Roll dough ¼ inch thick. Cover with sugar before baking.

Date nut rolled cookies: Add ¼ cup each chopped dates and nuts to flour mixture.

Fruit rolled cookies: Add ½ cup of chopped apricots, prunes, dates, figs, or raisins to flour mixture.

Ginger rolled cookies: Add ¼ cup candied ginger, cut fine.

Lemon rolled cookies: Substitute 1 teaspoon lemon extract and 2 teaspoons grated lemon rind for vanilla.

Maple sugar rolled cookies: Substitute finely crushed maple sugar for white sugar.

Molasses rolled cookies: Substitute ¼ cup brown sugar and ¼ cup molasses for white sugar. Omit milk. Add 1 teaspoon ginger and ½ teaspoon baking soda.

Nut rolled cookies: Add ½ cup chopped nutmeats to flour mixture.

Orange rolled cookies: Substitute orange juice for milk. Add grated rind of ½ orange. Use 2 egg yolks instead of whole egg.

Peanut butter rolled cookies: Use ½ cup peanut butter and ½ cup brown sugar instead of butter and sugar. Add 1 tablespoon milk or cream.

Pinwheel cookies #1: Divide dough into 2 equal parts. Blend 1 ounce melted chocolate into one part. Roll each part to ⅛ inch thickness on separate pieces of floured waxed paper. Then place white dough on top of chocolate dough, remove waxed paper. Roll up as for a jelly roll. Wrap firmly in waxed paper. Chill. Slice and bake in hot oven (400°F.) about 8 minutes.

Raisin rolled cookies: Add ½ cup raisins to fat and sugar-egg mixture.

Sand tarts: Roll chilled dough ¼ inch thick and cut in desired shapes. Brush with egg white and sprinkle with mixture of 4 tablespoons sugar and 1 teaspoon cinnamon. Decorate with blanched almond halves and candied fruits.

Sour cream rolled cookies: Reduce baking powder to ½ teaspoon. Add ¼ teaspoon nutmeg and ¼ teaspoon baking soda. Sift with flour. Substitute ½ teaspoon lemon extract for vanilla. Use ⅓ cup sour cream instead of 1 tablespoon milk.

Spice rolled cookies: Omit vanilla. Sift with dry ingredients ¼ teaspoon each allspice, cinnamon, and cloves.

SNICKERDOODLES

2¾ cups sifted all-purpose flour	1 cup soft shortening
2 teaspoons cream of tartar	1½ cups sugar
1 teaspoon baking soda	2 eggs
½ teaspoon salt	

Sift together flour, tartar, baking soda, and salt. Cream shortening, gradually beat in sugar and eggs and stir in dry ingredients. Chill dough. Roll into balls the size of small walnuts. Roll in mixture of 2 tablespoons sugar and 2 teaspoons cinnamon. Place about 2 inches apart on ungreased baking sheet. Bake in hot oven (400°F.) until lightly browned, but still soft, about 8 to 10 minutes. (These cookies puff up at first, then flatten out with crinkled tops.) Yield: about 5 dozen 2-inch cookies.

SPRINGERLE

3½ cups sifted all-purpose flour
3 teaspoons baking powder
½ teaspoon salt

4 eggs, separated
3¾ cups sugar
Grated rind of 1 lemon

Sift together flour, baking powder, and salt. Beat egg yolks until very light, sifting in 1 cup sugar while beating. In a separate bowl, beat egg whites until stiff and fold in 1 cup sugar. Combine the 2 mixtures. Beat in remaining sugar and continue beating until bubbles rise. Slowly stir in dry ingredients with grated lemon rind. Add more flour if necessary to make a stiff dough. Chill several hours. Roll out with wooden springerle rolling pin. Cut around the pictures. Bake on greased cooky sheets in slow oven (300°F.) 30 to 40 minutes. Remove from pans when cool. Store in covered container. Yield: about 50 cookies.

HONEY LEBKUCHEN

4 cups sifted cake flour
¼ teaspoon baking soda
¾ teaspoon cinnamon
⅛ teaspoon nutmeg
⅛ teaspoon cloves
⅔ cup honey
½ cup brown sugar, firmly packed

2 tablespoons water
1 egg, slightly beaten
¾ cup shredded candied orange peel
¾ cup shredded candied citron
1 cup almonds, blanched and
    shredded

Sift flour once and measure. Add soda and spices, and sift together 3 times. Combine honey, sugar, and water and boil 5 minutes. Cool. Add flour, egg, fruits, and nuts. Press dough into a cake and wrap in waxed paper. Store in refrigerator 2 or 3 days to ripen. Roll ¼ inch thick on lightly floured board. Cut in 1x3 inch strips. Bake on greased baking sheet in moderate oven (350°F.) 15 minutes. When cool, spread with *TRANSPARENT GLAZE*. Store at least 1 day before serving. Yield: about 5 dozen strips.

NOTE: These cookies are characteristically hard and chewy. They develop a better flavor upon storage. Store 2 weeks or longer for best flavor.

Transparent glaze: Combine 2 cups sifted confectioners' sugar and 3 tablespoons boiling water. Add 1 teaspoon vanilla. Beat thoroughly. Spread on cookies while glaze is still warm.

LEBKUCHEN

1½ cups sifted cake flour
1½ teaspoons baking powder
½ teaspoon salt
1 teaspoon cinnamon
1 teaspoon allspice
1 cup finely chopped nuts

1 cup finely chopped citron
2 tablespoons shortening
2 cups brown sugar
4 eggs, well-beaten
3 tablespoons confectioners' sugar
Milk

Mix and sift dry ingredients. Add nuts and citron. Cream shortening thoroughly, blend in brown sugar and add eggs. Add flour-nut mixture. Spread in greased square pan. Bake in moderate oven (350°F.) 30 minutes. While still warm, spread with icing made by mixing confectioners' sugar and milk to thin paste. Cut into squares or strips. Yield: 3 dozen squares.

PFEFFERNUESSE

4 cups sifted all-purpose flour
1 teaspoon baking soda
½ teaspoon salt
1 tablespoon cinnamon
1 teaspoon cloves
1 teaspoon nutmeg
¼ teaspoon black pepper
1 tablespoon crushed cardamom
    seed

1 teaspoon anise seed
¼ pound candied orange peel
½ pound citron
2 tablespoons butter
2½ cups powdered sugar
5 eggs, separated
1½ teaspoons grated lemon rind
    About ¼ cup milk or water
1 cup confectioners' sugar

Mix and sift flour, soda, salt and spices. Stir in seed, then ground orange peel and citron. Mix together butter and sugar; add well-beaten egg yolks and lemon rind and beat thoroughly. Gradually stir in flour-fruit mixture and fold in stiffly beaten egg whites. Chill 1 hour. Shape in small balls the size of walnuts. Place on cloth and let stand, uncovered, overnight at room temperature. In the morning brush balls with thin confectioners' icing made by gradually stirring milk into confectioners' sugar. Place on ungreased baking sheet and bake in moderate oven (350°F.) 15 to 20 minutes. Yield: about 7½ dozen.

VIENNESE CRESCENTS

4 cups sifted all-purpose flour
1½ cups butter
¼ teaspoon salt

Powdered sugar
1 cup unblanched almonds,
    ground fine

Work flour, butter, salt, and 4 tablespoons powdered sugar into a soft dough. When blended, add almonds and mix well. Chill dough in refrigerator at least 2 hours. On a slightly floured board, shape chilled dough into little finger-thick rolls. Cut into pieces 2 inches long and shape into crescents. Bake on slightly floured cookie sheet in moderate oven (350°F.) 10 to 15 minutes, but do not let them color. Roll carefully in confectioners' sugar while still hot.

HUNGARIAN BUTTER COOKIES

1½ cups butter
1 cup sugar
2 eggs, separated

1 tablespoon rum
4 cups all-purpose flour
½ cup chopped nuts

Cream butter, gradually add sugar, creaming until fluffy. Beat in egg yolks and rum. Work in flour to a smooth dough. Roll out to ⅛ inch thickness. Shape with cooky cutter.

Topping: Beat 2 egg whites very stiff. Drop ½ teaspoon egg white on each cooky. Sprinkle a few chopped nuts on top. Bake in moderate oven (350°F.) about 10 minutes or until golden brown.

POPPY SEED WAFERS

1 cup sifted cake flour
1 cup sifted whole-wheat flour
½ teaspoon salt
1 tablespoon sugar

4 tablespoons shortening
Ice water
Poppy seed

Sift cake flour into a bowl. Stir in whole-wheat flour, salt, and sugar. Cut in shortening with a pastry blender or 2 knives and add enough ice water for dough to hold together when pressed lightly. Roll out paper-thin on a floured board. Sprinkle with poppy seed and cut with a knife or pastry wheel into 1-inch squares. Transfer with a spatula to a greased baking sheet. Bake in hot oven (425°F.) until brown, 3 or 4 minutes. Cool and store in a covered container.

Variations: Caraway seed, celery seed or sesame seed may be substituted for the poppy seed. Yield: about 5 dozen.

MORAVIAN SPICE COOKIES

½ cup brown sugar, firmly packed
¾ teaspoon baking soda
½ teaspoon salt
¾ teaspoon ginger
¾ teaspoon ground cloves

¾ teaspoon cinnamon
¼ teaspoon each nutmeg and allspice
1 cup molasses
½ cup softened butter
4½ cups sifted all-purpose flour

Sift together brown sugar, baking soda, salt, and spices. Heat but do not boil molasses. Add softened butter and blend well. Cool slightly. Add brown sugar mixture and beat thoroughly. Blend in flour with hands. Keep dough in refrigerator until ready to use. It will keep for weeks. For baking, break off small pieces of dough. Roll paper-thin and cut into fancy shapes or rounds. Place on slightly buttered baking sheet. Bake in moderate oven (375°F.) 6 to 8 minutes. Yield: about 5 dozen cookies.

CREAM CHEESE KOLACKY

2 cakes (6 ounces) cream cheese
½ pound butter

2 cups sifted all-purpose flour

Cream together butter and cheese. Gradually stir in flour. Chill thoroughly 1 to 2 hours, or until ready to bake. Roll out very thin. Cut out with rim of small size glass, preferably wine glass. Place on ungreased cooky sheet and press center of each. Spread filling in center. Bake in moderate oven (350°F.) about 10 minutes, or until slightly browned. Let cool and sprinkle with powdered sugar. Filling may be apricot and prune butter, cheese mixture, or thick preserves.

RUSSIAN RYE HONEY CAKES

1 cup honey
½ cup sifted rye flour

½ cup sifted cake flour

Heat honey in saucepan until hot and thin. Mix the 2 flours and heat in another pan, shaking constantly and being careful it does not change color. Remove honey from heat and gradually beat in the flour. Continue beating with a large spoon until dough comes off the spoon easily. Shape as desired or roll out and cut with cutters. Bake in moderate oven (350°F.) on greased baking sheets until well browned, about 10 to 15 minutes. Will keep indefinitely. Yield: about 50 cookies.

NORWEGIAN ALMOND STICKS (Mandelstaenger)

3½ cups sifted all-purpose flour
½ teaspoon baking powder
3 eggs, well beaten
1 cup sugar

1 cup butter, melted
1 egg white, unbeaten
¼ cup chopped almonds

Sift together flour and baking powder. Beat together eggs and sugar and blend in melted butter. Gradually stir in flour and mix well. Roll out thin on lightly floured board and cut into narrow finger-length strips. Place on greased and lightly floured cooky sheet. Brush with unbeaten egg white and dot with chopped almonds. Bake in moderate oven (350°F.) 8 to 10 minutes. Yield: 50 to 70 cookies.

PEANUT BUTTER COOKIES

3 cups sifted all-purpose flour
1 teaspoon baking soda
½ teaspoon salt
1 cup butter or other shortening
1 cup granulated sugar

1 cup brown sugar
2 eggs, well beaten
1 cup peanut butter
1 teaspoon vanilla

Sift flour with soda and salt. Cream butter, gradually add sugar, and blend well. Add eggs, peanut butter, and vanilla. Add dry ingredients, mixing thoroughly. Roll into balls the size of a walnut. Place on a baking pan. Press with fork to about ¼ inch thickness. Bake in a moderate oven (350°F.) 12 to 15 minutes, until golden brown. Yield: about 120 cookies.

ITALIAN ANISE COOKIES

2 cups sifted all-purpose flour
½ teaspoon baking powder
⅛ teaspoon salt

1 teaspoon anise seed (rolled fine)
3 eggs
1 cup sugar

Sift flour with baking powder, salt, and anise seed. Beat eggs until thick and lemon colored and add sugar gradually. Add dry ingredients and mix thoroughly. Drop from teaspoon on greased baking sheet. Bake in moderate oven (350°F.) 8 to 10 minutes.

GREEK ALMOND COOKIES

3 cups (¾ pound) almonds, blanched
    and ground

3 egg whites, stiffly beaten
2 cups confectioners' sugar

Mix nuts with sugar and add stiffly beaten egg whites. Squeeze dough through press in various shapes. Bake on greased baking sheet in slow oven (300°F.) 30 minutes. Yield: about 50 cookies.

CITRON COOKIES

2 cups sifted cake flour
1 teaspoon cream of tartar
½ teaspoon baking soda
½ teaspoon salt
½ cup butter
1 cup sugar

2 eggs, separated
Candied citron
Candied cherries
¼ teaspoon each vanilla and
    almond extract

Sift together flour, cream of tartar, baking soda, and salt. Cream butter and sugar until light and fluffy and beat in egg yolks 1 at a time, beating well after each addition. Gradually stir in dry ingredients and mix well. Fold in stiffly beaten egg whites flavored with vanilla and almond. Add enough flour to make dough soft enough to roll out easily. Roll out on floured board to ⅛ inch thickness. Cut with floured cooky cutters. Arrange cherries and candied citron (cut into small pieces and strips) in flower designs on cookies. Place on greased cooky sheet. Bake in hot oven (400°F.) 8 to 10 minutes. Store between layers of waxed paper in airtight container.

GINGER SNAPS

2 cups sifted all-purpose flour	½ teaspoon cinnamon
¼ cup sugar	½ cup dry breadcrumbs
1 teaspoon baking soda	½ cup molasses
½ teaspoon salt	½ cup melted shortening
3 teaspoons ginger	2 tablespoons ice water

Sift together flour, sugar, baking soda, salt, ginger, and cinnamon. Add crumbs, molasses, shortening, and water. Mix thoroughly. Roll ⅛ inch thick on lightly floured board or canvas. Shape with cooky cutter. Bake on ungreased baking sheet in moderate oven (375°F.) 10 minutes.

Refrigerator ginger snaps: Dough may be shaped in roll, wrapped in waxed paper and stored in refrigerator. Cut chilled roll in ⅛-inch slices and bake as above. Yield: about 7 dozen 2-inch cookies.

RUSSIAN ALMOND COOKIES (Lepeshki)

2 cups sifted cake flour	½ teaspoon almond extract
½ teaspoon salt	¼ teaspoon vanilla
1 cup butter	24 almonds, split in half
½ cup powdered sugar	

Sift flour and salt twice. Cream butter, gradually add sugar, beating well. Add flavoring. Gradually stir in flour, mixing well. Chill and roll into balls the size of a walnut. Flatten, and place on a greased baking sheet. Press half an almond on top of each cookie. Bake in a slow oven (300°F.) until browned, 18 to 20 minutes. Yield: about 48 cookies.

PEANUT CRUNCH COOKIES

1 cup shortening	1 teaspoon baking powder
1 cup granulated sugar	1 teaspoon baking soda
1 cup brown sugar, firmly packed	½ teaspoon salt
2 eggs	½ cup chopped peanuts (if plain
1 cup peanut butter, plain or	peanut butter is used)
crunchy	1 tablespoon water
3 cups sifted all-purpose flour	1 teaspoon vanilla

Cream shortening with sugar. Add eggs and beat in peanut butter. Add sifted dry ingredients and fold in peanuts, if used, water, and vanilla. Roll dough into small balls. Place on greased cooky sheets and press at right angles with tines of fork dipped in water. Bake in moderate oven (350°F.) 15 minutes. Yield: about 4 dozen.

FILLED COOKIES

Method #1: Prepare recipes for ROLLED SUGAR COOKIES and desired filling. Bake the sugar cookies. When cool spread filling on half the cookies and cover with remaining cookies to make "sandwiches."

Method #2: Prepare recipes for *ROLLED SUGAR COOKIES* and desired filling. Roll out dough ⅛ inch thick. Shape with cooky cutter. Place 1 teaspoon filling on half the cookies. Cover with remaining rounds, pressing edges together with fork. Bake on ungreased baking sheet in moderate oven (375°F.) 10 to 15 minutes. Yield: about 2 dozen (2½-inch) filled cookies.

Method #3: Prepare recipe for *ROLLED SUGAR COOKIES.* Roll out and cut into squares. Fill and fold over diagonally to make triangles with filling in pocket thus formed. Bake in moderate oven (375°F.) 8 to 10 minutes.

Method #4: Proceed as in #3 and fold squares or roll into cornucopias, with filling peeking out at wide end of horn. Twist pointed end of horn to give curled effect. Bake in moderate oven (375°F.) 8 to 10 minutes.

DATE RAISIN COOKY FILLING

½ cup raisins, chopped
1 cup chopped dates
½ cup sugar
2 teaspoons grated lemon rind

1 tablespoon cornstarch
¼ cup cold water
1 tablespoon lemon juice
½ cup nuts, chopped

Combine raisins, dates, sugar, and lemon rind in a saucepan. Dissolve cornstarch in water and add to fruit mixture. Cook over low flame, stirring constantly until thickened. Blend in lemon juice and nuts. Use in **Method #2—FILLED COOKIES.**

FIG COOKY FILLING

1 cup ground figs
¼ cup orange juice
2 teaspoons grated orange rind
¼ cup water

⅛ teaspoon salt
¼ cup sugar
¼ cup chopped nuts

Mix together all ingredients except nuts. Cook until mixture thickens, about 5 minutes, stirring constantly. Cool and add nuts.

PRUNE COOKY FILLING

1 cup chopped cooked prunes
¼ cup sugar
2 teaspoons grated orange rind

½ cup nuts (optional)
¼ teaspoon salt
¼ teaspoon vanilla extract

Mix all ingredients, stirring until sugar is dissolved.

REFRIGERATOR COOKIES (Basic Recipe)

½ cup shortening
½ cup brown sugar
¾ cup granulated sugar
1 egg
1 teaspoon vanilla

½ cup chopped nutmeats
2 cups sifted all-purpose flour
2 teaspoons baking powder
½ teaspoon salt

Cream shortening. Add sugars and cream together thoroughly. Add egg and beat well. Add vanilla and nutmeats. Mix and sift flour, baking powder, and salt. Add to creamed mixture and mix well. Shape into rolls about 1½ inches in diameter. Wrap each in waxed paper. Chill in refrigerator several hours or overnight. Cut chilled rolls in ⅛-inch slices. Place on greased cooky sheet. Bake in hot oven (425°F.) 8 to 10 minutes. Yield: 4 dozen cookies.

Almond refrigerator cookies: Substitute ½ cup finely ground blanched almonds for chopped nutmeats.

Checkerboard cookies: Divide dough into 2 equal parts. Add 1 square (ounce) cooled, melted chocolate to 1 part. Leave other part plain. Line a freezing tray with waxed paper. Pack half the chocolate dough into bottom and cover with uniform layer of plain dough. Add another layer of chocolate and top with final layer of plain dough. Cover with waxed paper and chill several hours. Turn the layered loaf out on waxed paper. Slice with thin sharp knife into ¼ inch slices. Place 4 slices together so that, when viewed from the end, each chocolate strip lies above a plain strip. Slice thinly across checkerboard pattern. Bake as directed.

Chocolate refrigerator cookies: Add 2 ounces (squares) melted chocolate or 4 tablespoons cocoa to fat-sugar-egg mixture.

Coconut orange refrigerator cookies: Omit vanilla and add 2 tablespoons grated orange rind to coconut cookies.

Coconut refrigerator cookies: Substitute ½ cup coconut for nutmeats.

Fruit refrigerator cookies: Substitute ½ cup currants, raisins, or any mixture of dried fruits, cut into small pieces, for nutmeats.

Ginger refrigerator cookies: Substitute 2 tablespoons molasses for 2 tablespoons sugar and add ¼ cup finely chopped candied ginger or 1 tablespoon ginger.

Peanut butter refrigerator cookies: Substitute ½ cup peanut butter for ½ cup shortening.

Pinwheel cookies: Divide dough into 2 equal parts. Add 1 square (ounce) cooled melted chocolate to 1 part. Leave other part plain. Roll each part ⅛ inch thick and place one sheet on top of the other. Roll up as for jelly roll. Wrap firmly in waxed paper and chill. Slice and bake.

Spice refrigerator cookies: Add and sift with dry ingredients 1 to 2 teaspoons mixed spices (cinnamon, ginger, and nutmeg).

BUTTERSCOTCH COOKIES (Basic Recipe)

4 cups sifted all-purpose flour	2 cups brown sugar, firmly packed
1 teaspoon baking soda	2 eggs
1 teaspoon cream of tartar	1 teaspoon vanilla
½ teaspoon salt	1 cup chopped nuts
1 cup butter or other fat	

Sift together flour, baking soda, cream of tartar, and salt. Cream butter or other fat and sugar until light and fluffy. Add eggs and vanilla, beating well. Add dry ingredients and nuts and mix thoroughly. Shape into rolls. Wrap each in waxed paper, or press into cooky molds. Chill until very firm. Slice thin and bake on ungreased baking sheet in hot oven (400°F.) 8 to 10 minutes. Yield: about 6 dozen 2-inch cookies.

Butterscotch coconut cookies: Omit chopped nuts and add 2 cups shredded coconut to fat-sugar-egg mixture.

Butterscotch date cookies: Omit nuts and add 2 cups of finely chopped dates to sifted dry ingredients.

Chocolate nut cookies: Add 3 squares melted, unsweetened chocolate to fat-sugar-egg mixture.

Coconut orange cookies: Substitute 1 cup granulated sugar for 1 cup brown sugar. Add 3 cups shredded coconut to sifted dry ingredients. Omit vanilla and flavor with 2 tablespoons grated orange rind and ¾ teaspoon lemon extract.

Filled butterscotch cookies: Prepare dough and shape into rolls. Chill and cut into thin slices. Put filling between two, pressing together with fork. Bake in moderate oven (375°F.) 10 to 12 minutes.

Raisin cooky filling: Mix together 2 cups ground raisins, ½ cup brown sugar, ⅛ teaspoon salt, and 2 tablespoons cornstarch. Add 1 cup water gradually, mixing well. Cook until thickened, stirring constantly. Cool before using.

THREE-IN-ONE COOKIES

2 cups sifted all-purpose flour	1 tablespoon milk
1 teaspoon baking powder	½ teaspoon vanilla extract
½ teaspoon salt	1 square chocolate, melted
½ cup shortening	1 tablespoon orange juice
1 cup sugar	1 tablespoon grated orange rind
1 egg	

Sift together flour, baking powder, and salt. Cream shortening and sugar until light and fluffy. Add egg, milk, and vanilla; stir in dry ingredients. Mix thoroughly. Divide dough into thirds. To one-third add melted chocolate, mixing it in thoroughly. To another third add orange juice and rind, mixing well. Leave remaining third plain. Shape each third into a roll. Wrap in waxed paper. Chill until very firm. Slice thin and bake on greased cooky sheets in hot oven (400°F.) 10 minutes. Yield: about 5 dozen small cookies.

DANISH DANDIES

8 egg yolks	½ teaspoon salt
1 cup shortening (use at least ½ butter)	½ teaspoon vanilla extract
	½ teaspoon lemon extract
¾ cup sugar	1¾ to 2 cups sifted all-purpose flour

Hard-cook egg yolks. Press through sieve. Cream shortening and sugar until light and fluffy. Add salt, flavoring extracts, and egg yolks. Mix well. Add flour to make moderately stiff dough. Shape into rolls and wrap in waxed paper or press into cooky molds. Chill. Slice ⅛ inch thick. Bake on ungreased baking sheets in hot oven (400°F.) 8 to 10 minutes.

NOTE: Dough may be formed into balls an inch in diameter. Press with fork, or with bottom of tumbler. Yield: about 8½ dozen cookies.

Spritz cookies: Force dough through cooky press into various shapes.

BROWN SUGAR DROPS (Basic Recipe)

3½ cups sifted all-purpose flour	2 cups brown sugar
1 teaspoon baking soda	2 eggs
1 teaspoon salt	½ cup sour milk or buttermilk
1 cup soft shortening	

Sift together flour, baking soda, and salt. Cream shortening, gradually beat in sugar and eggs. Stir in sour milk or buttermilk. Gradually stir in flour and beat thoroughly. Chill at least 1 hour. Drop rounded teaspoonfuls about 2 inches apart on lightly greased baking sheet. Bake in hot oven (400°F.) until set (when touched lightly with finger almost no imprint remains), about 8 to 10 minutes. Yield: about 6 dozen 2½-inch cookies.

Coconut drops: Add 1 cup moist shredded coconut to batter.

Fruit drop cookies: Add 1½ cups broken pecans, 2 cups candied cherries, cut in halves, and 2 cups cut-up dates to batter. Decorate each cooky with a pecan half. Make cookies slightly smaller.

Nut drops: Add 1 cup cut-up nutmeats to batter.

Salted peanut drop cookies: Follow recipe for *BROWN SUGAR DROPS*, using 2 instead of 3½ cups flour and adding 2 cups rolled oats and 1 cup wheat flakes cereal. Add 1 cup coarsely chopped salted peanuts (without husks). Bake until brown, 12 to 14 minutes.

COCONUT MACAROONS (Basic Recipe)

2 tablespoons sifted cake flour	2 egg whites
½ cup sugar	½ teaspoon vanilla
¼ teaspoon salt	2 cups shredded coconut

Mix and sift flour, salt, and sugar. Beat egg whites until stiff and peaky but not dry. Fold in whites. Add vanilla and fold in coconut. Drop by teaspoonfuls onto lightly greased paper-covered baking sheet. Allow space for spreading and rising. Bake in moderate oven (350°F.) about 20 minutes, or until golden brown and dry on surface. Yield: about 20 2-inch macaroons.

Cake crumb macaroons: Substitute ¾ cup cake crumbs for 1 cup coconut.

Caramel nut macaroons: Substitute ½ cup brown sugar and 1 cup chopped nuts for white sugar and coconut.

Cherry coconut macaroons: Add ½ cup chopped candied cherries.

Chocolate chip macaroons: Substitute ½ cup chocolate chips for 1 cup coconut.

Condensed milk macaroons: Omit sugar and egg whites. Mix coconut, flour, salt, and vanilla with sweetened condensed milk.

Corn flake macaroons: Substitute 2 cups corn flakes for coconut.

Orange macaroons: Add 1 tablespoon grated orange rind with egg whites. Sprinkle grated orange rind over macaroons when done.

Popcorn macaroons: Substitute 2 cups popcorn for coconut.

Rice macaroons: Substitute puffed rice for coconut and add ¼ cup chopped nutmeats.

MOLASSES COOKIES (Basic Recipe)

2 cups sifted all-purpose flour	½ cup shortening
1½ teaspoons baking powder	¼ cup sugar
½ teaspoon salt	1 egg
¼ teaspoon baking soda	¼ cup milk
1 teaspoon ground ginger	¾ cup molasses
1 teaspoon cinnamon	

Mix and sift together flour, baking powder, salt, baking soda, ginger, and cinnamon. Cream shortening and gradually add sugar, creaming well; add egg. Mix milk and molasses. Add dry ingredients alternately with liquid, beating until smooth after each addition. Drop from teaspoon on lightly greased baking sheet. Bake in mod erate oven (350°F.) about 12 minutes. Yield: 4 dozen cookies.

Coconut gems: Add 1 cup coconut and 1 tablespoon milk.

Oatmeal molasses cookies: Use only 1 cup white flour and add 1½ cups rolled oats.

Raisin molasses cookies: Add ½ cup nuts and raisins to any of the variations.

Whole-wheat molasses cookies: Replace ½ the white flour with whole-wheat flour.

CHOCOLATE CHIP COOKIES

1 cup shortening
¾ cup brown sugar, firmly packed
¾ cup granulated sugar
2 eggs, well beaten
1 cup chopped nuts

½ pound sweet or semi-sweet chocolate, cut in small pieces
1 teaspoon vanilla
2½ cups sifted all-purpose flour
2 teaspoons baking powder
¼ teaspoon salt

Cream fat and sugars together until light. Add eggs and blend. Add nuts, chocolate, and vanilla. Sift flour, baking powder, and salt together and add. Mix thoroughly. Drop onto cooky sheets. Bake in slow oven (325°F.) about 20 minutes. Yield: about 4 dozen.

OATMEAL COOKIES (Basic Recipe)

1 cup sifted all-purpose flour
1 teaspoon baking powder
½ teaspoon salt
¾ cup shortening
1 cup brown sugar

2 eggs
1 teaspoon vanilla
⅓ cup milk
3 cups rolled oats

Sift together flour, baking powder, and salt into bowl. Cut in shortening, add sugar, eggs, vanilla, and about half the milk. Beat until smooth, about 2 minutes. Fold in remaining milk and the rolled oats. Drop from a teaspoon onto greased baking sheet. Bake in moderate oven (375°F.) 12 to 15 minutes. Yield: 4 dozen cookies.

Chocolate chip oatmeal cookies: Add 1 7-ounce package chocolate chips to batter.

Coconut oatmeal cookies: Add 1 cup coconut to batter.

Date oatmeal cookies: Add 1 cup chopped dates to batter.

Nut oatmeal cookies: Add 1 cup chopped nuts to batter.

Raisin spice oatmeal cookies: Sift 1 teaspoon cinnamon and ¼ teaspoon nutmeg with dry ingredients. Omit vanilla. Add 1 cup raisins to batter.

COFFEE AND SPICE DROPS (Basic Recipe)

1 cup soft shortening
2 cups brown sugar
2 eggs
½ cup cold coffee
3½ cups sifted all-purpose flour

1 teaspoon soda
1 teaspoon salt
1 teaspoon nutmeg
1 teaspoon cinnamon

Cream shortening, gradually beat in sugar and eggs and beat thoroughly. Stir in cold coffee. Sift together flour, soda, salt, nutmeg, and cinnamon and stir in. Chill at least 1 hour. Drop rounded teaspoonfuls about 2 inches apart on lightly greased baking sheet. Bake in hot oven (400°F.) until set (when touched lightly with finger, almost no imprint remains), about 8 to 10 minutes. Yield: about 6 dozen 2½-inch cookies.

Applesauce drop cookies: Include 1 teaspoon cloves with other spices. Add 2 cups well drained thick applesauce, 1 cup cut-up raisins, and ½ cup coarsely chopped nuts to batter. Bake 9 to 12 minutes.

Hermits: Add 2½ cups halved seeded raisins and 1¼ cups broken nuts to batter. Be careful not to overbake.

Mincemeat drop cookies: Add 2 cups well drained mincemeat to batter.

Spiced prune drops: Include ¼ teaspoon cloves with other spices. Add 2 cups cut-up cooked prunes (pitted and well drained), and 1 cup broken nuts to batter.

OLD-FASHIONED SOUR CREAM DROPS (Basic Recipe)

2¾ cups sifted all-purpose flour	1½ cups sugar
½ teaspoon baking soda	2 eggs
½ teaspoon baking powder	1 cup thick sour cream
½ teaspoon salt	1 teaspoon vanilla
½ cup soft shortening	

Sift together flour, baking soda, baking powder, and salt. Cream shortening. Gradually beat in sugar and eggs. Stir in sour cream and vanilla. Gradually stir in dry ingredients. Chill at least 1 hour. Drop rounded teaspoonfuls about 2 inches apart on lightly greased baking sheet. Bake until delicately browned, in hot (425°F.) oven (when touched lightly with finger, almost no imprint remains), about 8 to 10 minutes. Yield: about 5 dozen 2½-inch cookies.

Chocolate cream drops: Add 2 squares melted unsweetened chocolate (2 ounces) to fat-sugar-egg mixture. Add 1 cup cut-up nuts to batter. Frost cooled cookies with chocolate icing.

Coconut cream drops: Add 1 cup moist shredded coconut to batter.

Fruit and nut drops: Add and sift with dry ingredients 1 teaspoon cinnamon, ½ teaspoon cloves, and ¼ teaspoon nutmeg. Add 1 cup cut-up dates or raisins and 1 cup cut-up nuts to batter. The spices may be omitted if desired.

SUGAR JUMBLES (Basic Recipe)

1⅛ cups sifted all-purpose flour	½ cup sugar
¼ teaspoon soda	1 egg
½ teaspoon salt	1 teaspoon vanilla
1 cup soft shortening (part butter)	

Sift together flour, soda, and salt. Mix shortening, sugar, egg, and vanilla together thoroughly. Stir in dry ingredients. Drop rounded teaspoonfuls about 2 inches apart on lightly greased baking sheet. Bake in moderate oven (375°F.) until delicately browned (cookies should still be soft), about 8 to 10 minutes. Cool slightly, then remove from baking sheet. Yield: about 3 dozen 2-inch cookies.

Chocolate chip jumbles: Substitute ¾ cup (half white and half brown) sugar for ½ cup granulated sugar. Add ½ cup chopped nuts and 1 package (7 ounces) chocolate chips.

Orange chocolate chip jumbles: Add 1 teaspoon grated orange rind to the shortening mixture of above.

Coconut jumbles: Add 1 cup moist shredded coconut to batter.

Glazed orange jumbles: Add 1½ teaspoons grated orange rind and 1 cup chopped nuts to batter. Bake. While hot, dip tops of cookies in an orange glaze made as follows: Heat together ⅓ cup sugar, 3 tablespoons orange juice, and 1 teaspoon grated orange rind.

Nut jumbles: Add 2 cups nutmeats to batter.

3-in-1 jumbles: Divide dough of basic recipe into 3 parts. Add ½ square melted unsweetened chocolate to 1 part. Drop ½ cup whole nutmeats into batter, coating each nut well. Add ½ cup moist shredded coconut to second part. Leave third part plain and drop 14 nut-stuffed dates into batter. Coat each date well. Each coated date and nut makes a cooky.

QUICK MAPLE NUT DROPS

⅔ cup maple syrup
1 can (1⅓ cups) sweetened
   condensed milk

2 cups crushed graham cracker crumbs
1 teaspoon vanilla
1 cup chopped nuts

Cook maple syrup and condensed milk in heavy pan until thickened, about 3 minutes. Be careful not to scorch. Cool slightly and add remaining ingredients. Drop from teaspoon onto greased baking sheet. Bake in moderate oven (350°F.) 15 minutes. Remove from pan at once. Cookies will be hard if overbaked. Store in jar to soften.

NOTE: Be sure to use sweetened condensed milk. Same results will not be obtained with evaporated milk. Yield: about 36 small cookies.

PECAN PRALINE COOKIES

1 cup brown sugar, firmly packed
½ cup shortening
1 egg, slightly beaten

½ teaspoon vanilla
1 cup sifted all-purpose flour
½ cup broken pecans

Cream shortening and sugar until light. Add slightly beaten egg and vanilla. Add flour and mix well. Fold in nuts. Drop mixture onto ungreased baking sheet, leaving plenty of room between cookies to allow for spreading. Bake in slow oven (300°F.) until lightly browned. Yield: about 24 cookies.

CHOCOLATE MOUNDS

2 cups sifted all-purpose flour
2 teaspoons baking powder
½ teaspoon baking soda
1 teaspoon salt
½ cup cocoa

½ cup shortening
1 cup sugar
2 eggs
½ teaspoon vanilla extract
1 cup buttermilk or sour milk

Sift together flour, baking powder, baking soda, salt, and cocoa. Cream together shortening and sugar until light and fluffy. Add eggs and vanilla extract, beating well. Add dry ingredients alternately with buttermilk or sour milk. Drop by teaspoonfuls on ungreased baking sheet. Bake in moderate oven (350°F.) 12 to 15 minutes. While still warm, brush with confectioners' sugar icing. Yield: 4 dozen cookies.

SPICED FIG BALLS

½ cup dried figs (packed in cup)
½ cup shortening
½ cup molasses
¼ cup sugar
¼ teaspoon ginger
1 egg, beaten
1 teaspoon vanilla

½ teaspoon lemon extract
1 teaspoon baking soda
½ teaspoon cinnamon
¼ teaspoon nutmeg
¼ teaspoon salt
2⅞ cups sifted flour (3 cups, less 2 tablespoons)

Cover figs with boiling water and let stand 10 minutes. Drain, clip off stems, and cut fine with scissors (if moist figs are used softening may be eliminated). Combine shortening, molasses, and sugar. Heat to boiling. Cool to lukewarm and add ginger, beaten egg, vanilla, and lemon extract. Add sifted baking soda, spices, salt, and flour. Stir in chopped figs. Drop by teaspoonfuls onto greased baking sheet. Bake in moderate oven (375°F.) 12 minutes. Yield: 3 dozen.

ORANGE HONEYS

3 cups sifted all-purpose flour
3 teaspoons baking powder
½ teaspoon salt
½ cup shortening
½ cup sugar
1 egg

1 teaspoon vanilla extract
1 cup honey
¼ cup chopped nuts
¼ cup chopped candied orange peel
¼ cup chopped candied lemon peel

Sift together flour, baking powder, and salt. Cream together shortening and sugar until light and fluffy. Add egg and vanilla, beating well. Blend in honey. Add dry ingredients, nuts, orange and lemon peels, mixing thoroughly. Drop by teaspoonfuls on greased baking sheet. Bake in moderate oven (375°F.) 10 minutes. Yield: about 7½ dozen cookies.

COFFEE DROPS

3½ cups sifted all-purpose flour
1 teaspoon baking powder
1 teaspoon baking soda
1 teaspoon cinnamon
1 teaspoon nutmeg
¼ teaspoon salt

1 cup shortening
2 cups brown sugar, firmly packed
2 eggs
¾ cup cold coffee
1 cup raisins
½ cup chopped nuts

Sift together flour, baking powder, baking soda, cinnamon, nutmeg, and salt. Cream together shortening and sugar and add eggs, beating well. Add dry ingredients alternately with coffee, mixing well. Stir in raisins and nuts. Drop from teaspoon on greased baking sheet, about 2 inches apart. Bake in hot oven (400°F.) 10 minutes. Yield: about 5 dozen cookies.

MONKEY FACES

2½ cups sifted all-purpose flour
1 teaspoon baking soda
½ teaspoon salt
½ teaspoon ginger
½ teaspoon cinnamon
½ cup shortening

1 cup brown sugar, firmly packed
1 teaspoon vinegar
½ cup buttermilk or
  ½ cup sour milk
½ cup molasses
Raisins or currants for faces

Sift together flour, baking soda, salt, ginger, and cinnamon. Cream together shortening and sugar until light and fluffy. Add vinegar and blend well. Combine buttermilk or sour milk with molasses. Add dry ingredients alternately with milk. Drop by teaspoonfuls on ungreased baking sheet. Make faces with currants or raisins. Bake in moderate oven (350°F.) 10 to 15 minutes. Yield: about 6 dozen cookies.

PEANUT DROP COOKIES

2 cups sifted all-purpose flour
2 teaspoons baking powder
½ teaspoon salt
½ cup shortening
1 cup sugar

2 eggs
½ teaspoon vanilla extract
¼ cup milk
1½ cups chopped peanuts

Sift together flour, baking powder, and salt. Cream together shortening and sugar until light and fluffy. Add eggs and vanilla. Mix well. Add dry ingredients alternately with milk, beating after each addition. Stir in peanuts. Drop by teaspoonfuls on ungreased baking sheets. Bake in hot oven (400°F.) 10 minutes. Yield: about 4 dozen cookies.

BROWNIES (Basic Recipe)

¾ cup sifted all-purpose flour
½ teaspoon baking powder
½ teaspoon salt
2 squares (2 ounces) unsweetened
  chocolate

⅓ cup shortening
1 cup sugar
2 eggs
½ cup broken nuts

Sift together flour, baking powder, and salt. Melt chocolate with shortening over hot water and beat in sugar and eggs. Add dry ingredients and mix thoroughly. Stir in nuts. Spread in well-greased square pan (8x8x2 inches). Bake in moderate oven (350°F.) until top has dull crust, about 30 to 35 minutes. When done a slight imprint will be left when top is touched lightly with finger. Cool and cut squares before removing from pan. Yield: 16 2-inch squares.

Chocolate frosted brownies: Prepare BROWNIES and frost with CHOCOLATE FROSTING before cutting into squares.

Tea brownies: Follow basic recipe, chopping nuts finely. Spread batter in 2 well-greased oblong pans (9x13x2 inches). Sprinkle with ¾ cup blanched and finely sliced green pistachio nuts. Bake 7 to 8 minutes. Cut immediately into squares or diamonds. Remove from pan while warm.

MOLASSES BROWNIES

⅔ cup butter
⅔ cup confectioners' sugar
⅔ cup molasses
1 teaspoon vanilla

1 egg
1¾ cups sifted all-purpose flour
⅛ teaspoon baking soda
1 cup chopped nutmeats

Cream butter and sugar until fluffy. Stir in molasses and vanilla. Beat in egg. Add flour which has been sifted with baking soda. Mix well and stir in nuts. Spread batter in 2 well-greased and slightly floured 9-inch square pans. If desired, sprinkle top with chopped nuts or place a pecan half in the center of each brownie. Bake in moderate oven (350°F.) 25 minutes. Yield: about 6 dozen.

CHEWY CHOCOLATE BROWNIES

2 eggs, well beaten
1¼ cups brown sugar, firmly packed
1 teaspoon vanilla

2 squares melted chocolate
½ cup sifted all-purpose flour
1 cup broken pecans

Add sugar, vanilla, and melted chocolate to beaten eggs. Add flour and ½ the nuts. Spread ½ inch thick in buttered square pan. Sprinkle remainder of nuts over batter. Bake in slow oven (325°F.) 20 to 25 minutes. Cut into squares while warm. Roll in confectioners' sugar, if desired. Yield: 16 bars.

PRUNE SQUARES

1 cup whole dried prunes
3 eggs
1 cup sugar
1 cup sifted all-purpose flour

1 teaspoon baking powder
⅛ teaspoon salt
¾ cup chopped nuts

Wash prunes and soak 3 to 4 hours. Drain and cut into fine pieces. Beat eggs and add sugar gradually. Add sifted dry ingredients and mix well. Stir in prunes and nuts. Turn into shallow greased pan. Bake in moderate oven (350°F.) ½ hour. Cut into squares. Frost or dust with confectioners' sugar. Yield: 12 squares.

APPLE SLICES

4 cups sifted all-purpose flour
½ teaspoon salt
2 cups sugar

1 cup butter
5 cups sliced tart apples
1 teaspoon cinnamon

Combine flour, salt, and sugar and cut in butter until crumbly. Reserve ½ cup and lightly press half of the remainder into bottom of greased pan (about 9x12 inches). Place in moderate oven (375°F.). Bake 10 minutes. Remove from oven and spread with apple slices which have been mixed with the reserved ½ cup crumbs and cinnamon. Top with remaining crumbs and return to oven. Continue baking at 375°F. until lightly browned (about 30 minutes). Yield: about 24.

ALMOND JAM BARS

1½ cups sifted all-purpose flour
½ cup sugar
½ teaspoon baking powder
½ teaspoon salt
½ teaspoon cinnamon
¼ teaspoon cloves

½ cup shortening
½ teaspoon almond extract
¼ teaspoon vanilla
1 egg, beaten
¼ cup milk
¾ cup jam

Sift together flour, sugar, baking powder, salt, cinnamon, and cloves. Cream together shortening and flavoring. Cut or rub shortening into flour mixture. Combine egg and milk and add to flour mixture. Mix until well blended. Spread about ⅓ of the mixture into greased pan (7x11 inches). Cover evenly with jam. Spread remaining mixture over jam. Bake in hot oven (400°F.) 25 to 30 minutes. When cool, cut into bars. Yield: 28 bars, 1x2½ inches.

DATE NUT BARS

3 eggs
3 tablespoons water
1 cup sugar
1 cup sifted all-purpose flour
1 teaspoon baking powder
½ teaspoon salt
2 cups chopped pitted dates
1 cup chopped nutmeats
½ cup sifted confectioners' sugar

Beat eggs until light. Add water and mix in sugar. Sift flour, baking powder, and salt together. Mix chopped dates and nuts with flour and combine with egg mixture. Mix well. Spread batter ½ inch thick in greased pan. Bake in hot oven (400°F.) about 20 minutes. Cool and cut into bars. Roll bars in confectioners' sugar just before serving. Yield: about 36.

PEANUT BUTTER DATE BARS

½ cup sifted cake flour
1¼ teaspoons baking powder
¼ teaspoon salt
½ teaspoon nutmeg
½ teaspoon cinnamon
¼ teaspoon allspice
¼ cup butter
½ cup peanut butter
1 cup sugar
2 eggs, well beaten
⅔ cup finely cut dates
½ teaspoon vanilla

Sift flour with baking powder, salt, and spices. Cream butter and peanut butter thoroughly. Add sugar gradually to beaten eggs and beat until light and deep yellow. Stir into creamed mixture. Add flour mixture and beat until blended. Add dates and vanilla. Turn into shallow greased, waxed paper-lined pan. Bake in moderate oven (350°F.) 45 minutes. Turn out on rack. Remove paper. Cool and cut into bars or squares. Yield: about 24 bars.

TOFFEE SQUARES

1 cup butter
1 cup brown sugar, firmly packed
2 cups sifted all-purpose flour
1 egg yolk
1 teaspoon vanilla
1 8-ounce bar milk chocolate
1 cup chopped nutmeats

Cream butter. Add brown sugar and cream until light and fluffy. Add beaten egg yolk, vanilla, and sifted flour. Spread thinly on cookie sheet. Bake in moderate oven (350°F.) 15 to 20 minutes. Melt chocolate and spread over top while warm. Sprinkle with nuts. Cut into squares while warm. Yield: 24 bars.

COCONUT PINEAPPLE SQUARES

1 tablespoon butter
1 tablespoon sugar
1 cup sifted all-purpose flour
3 teaspoons baking powder
1 teaspoon salt
3 eggs, well beaten
1 cup drained, crushed pineapple
1 cup sugar
1 tablespoon melted butter
2 cups shredded coconut

Cream butter and 1 tablespoon sugar. Sift flour, baking powder, and salt together. Add to creamed mixture and mix until crumbly. Add half the eggs and mix thoroughly. Spread in 8-inch square pan. Cover with pineapple. Mix 1 cup sugar, melted butter, and coconut; add remaining eggs and blend well. Spread over top of pineapple. Bake in moderate oven (350°F.) 30 to 35 minutes. Cut into squares. Yield: 24 bars.

FROSTED COFFEE BARS

1½ cups sifted all-purpose flour	1 cup brown sugar
½ teaspoon baking powder	1 egg
½ teaspoon baking soda	½ cup hot coffee
½ teaspoon salt	½ cup raisins
½ teaspoon cinnamon	¼ cup chopped nuts
¼ cup shortening	COFFEE ICING

Sift together flour, baking powder, baking soda, salt, and cinnamon. Cream together shortening and sugar. Add egg and beat well. Add coffee and gradually stir in dry ingredients. Add raisins and nuts and beat thoroughly. Spread in greased pan (11x16 inches). Bake in moderate oven (350°F.) 15 to 20 minutes. While still warm frost with COFFEE ICING. Cool and cut into bars. Yield: 28 bars.

FRUIT SPICE BARS

1 cup sifted all-purpose flour	½ cup molasses
¼ teaspoon baking soda	2 eggs, beaten
½ teaspoon salt	¼ teaspoon vanilla extract
½ teaspoon ginger	1 cup raisins
¼ cup shortening	¼ cup chopped nuts
¼ cup brown sugar	

Sift together flour, baking soda, salt, and ginger. Cream together shortening and sugar until light and fluffy. Add molasses, eggs, and vanilla and mix well. Gradually stir in dry ingredients, beating after each addition. Fold in raisins and nuts. Spread batter in shallow greased pan (7x11 inches). Bake in moderate oven (350°F.) 30 minutes. Cut into bars. Yield: 21 bars, 1x3¾ inches.

PECAN SPICE BARS

3 egg yolks	1 teaspoon cinnamon
1 cup dark brown sugar, firmly packed	½ teaspoon cloves
⅔ cup sifted all-purpose flour	1 teaspoon vanilla
1 teaspoon baking powder	3 egg whites, beaten stiff
⅛ teaspoon salt	½ cup broken pecans

Beat egg yolks until thick and lemon colored. Add sugar and beat well. Sift flour with baking powder, salt, and spices, and add to mixture. Stir well. Fold in vanilla, stiffly beaten egg whites, and nuts. Pour into greased, waxed paper-lined square pan. Bake in moderate oven (350°F.) 25 minutes. Cool for 5 minutes, cut into thin bars, and roll in spicy sugar (⅓ cup confectioners' sugar mixed with ¼ teaspoon cloves). Yield: 16 bars.

FROSTED SPICE BARS

1½ cups sifted all-purpose flour
1 teaspoon baking powder
1 teaspoon cinnamon
½ teaspoon nutmeg
½ teaspoon allspice
¼ teaspoon cloves
¼ teaspoon salt
¾ cup shortening

½ cup sugar
¼ cup molasses
2 eggs
1 cup raisins
½ cup chopped nuts
⅓ cup milk
1 teaspoon vanilla

Sift flour with baking powder, spices, and salt. Cream shortening and add sugar and molasses, mixing thoroughly. Beat in eggs, 1 at a time. Add raisins and nuts to flour mixture and add alternately with milk. Add vanilla. Beat well, and spread evenly in well-greased pan. Bake in moderate oven (350°F.) 20 to 25 minutes. Yield: about 1½ dozen.

CHOCOLATE INDIANS

¾ cup sifted all-purpose flour
½ teaspoon baking powder
½ teaspoon salt
2 squares unsweetened chocolate
⅓ cup shortening

1 cup sugar
2 eggs, well beaten
1 teaspoon vanilla
¾ cup chopped walnuts or pecans

Sift together flour, baking powder, and salt twice. Melt chocolate and shortening in top of double boiler over boiling water. Gradually add sugar to beaten eggs, beating well between additions. Add melted chocolate and blend well. Gradually stir in flour, mixing thoroughly. Add vanilla and nuts. Bake in greased baking pan (about 8x8 inches) in moderate oven (350°F.) about 25 minutes, or until brown and slightly shrunk from side of pan. Remove from oven. Cut into squares in the pan while still warm. Yield: 18 to 24 bars.

COCONUT PEANUT BUTTER STICKS

1 cup sifted all-purpose flour
1 teaspoon baking powder
¼ teaspoon salt
¼ cup shortening
½ cup peanut butter

1 cup sugar
2 eggs, well beaten
1 cup shredded coconut
½ teaspoon vanilla

Sift flour, baking powder, and salt several times. Cream shortening, beat in peanut butter. Gradually beat in sugar until the texture is spongy. Add eggs. Stir in dry ingredients, coconut, and vanilla. Spread in paper-lined, greased 8x12-inch pan. Bake in moderate oven (350°F.) until done, about 25 minutes. Cut into strips while still warm and roll in confectioners' sugar. Yield: about 36.

BANANA BARS

2 cups sifted all-purpose flour
2 teaspoons baking powder
½ teaspoon salt
¼ cup shortening
1 cup sugar
2 eggs

1 cup mashed bananas (3 medium)
½ teaspoon lemon extract
½ teaspoon vanilla
½ cup chopped nuts
CONFECTIONERS' SUGAR
ICING

Sift together flour, baking powder, and salt. Cream together shortening and sugar; add eggs, beating well. Add dry ingredients alternately with mashed bananas. Add flavoring extracts and nuts and beat thoroughly. Spread batter in greased pan (8x13 inches). Bake in moderate oven (350°F.) 30 minutes. While still warm, frost with thin CONFECTIONERS' SUGAR ICING. When cool, cut into bars or squares.

Banana drop cookies: Drop dough by teaspoonfuls on greased baking sheets and bake in moderate oven (350°F.) 12 to 15 minutes. Yield: 32 bars, 1x4 inches, or about 4 dozen cookies.

NUT CAKES

1 cup sifted all-purpose flour	4 eggs
1 teaspoon baking powder	1 teaspoon vanilla extract
½ teaspoon salt	2 teaspoons cinnamon
¾ cup shortening	½ cup chopped nuts
1 cup sugar	

Sift together flour, baking powder, and salt. Cream together shortening and sugar until light and fluffy. Add eggs, one at a time, beating well after each addition. Add vanilla extract. Add dry ingredients and beat thoroughly. Spread in shallow greased pan (11x16 inches). Sprinkle cinnamon and nuts over top of batter. Bake in moderate oven (375°F.) 25 minutes. Cut into bars or squares. Yield: 55 bars, 1x3¼ inches.

SCOTCH TEAS

½ cup butter	½ teaspoon salt
1 cup brown sugar, firmly packed	1 teaspoon baking powder
2 cups rolled oats	

Melt butter and stir in sugar. When well blended add rolled oats, salt, and baking powder, mixed together. Spread in greased 8-inch square pan. Bake in moderate oven (350°F.) 30 minutes. Cool about 5 minutes and cut into squares. Remove from pan as soon as cookies are cool enough to hold together, and before entirely cooled. Yield: 12 cookies.

PIRATE BLOCKS

2 eggs	½ teaspoon salt
1 cup brown sugar, firmly packed	½ cup chopped pitted dates or
14 graham crackers	raisins
1½ teaspoons baking powder	½ cup chopped nutmeats

Beat eggs and sugar together until light and fluffy. Roll graham crackers into fine crumbs. Mix with baking powder and salt and add to egg mixture. Add dates and nuts. Spread in greased 8-inch square pan. Bake in slow oven (300°F.) 25 minutes. Cut in squares while warm. Sprinkle with confectioners' sugar, if desired. Yield: about 16.

OATMEAL DATE BARS

½ cup sifted all-purpose flour	½ cup rolled oats
½ cup sugar	16 dates, pitted and chopped
½ teaspoon salt	¼ cup milk
1 teaspoon baking powder	2 eggs, separated

Sift dry ingredients together and stir in rolled oats. Add chopped dates. Add milk to beaten egg yolks and stir into dry ingredients. Fold in stiffly beaten egg whites carefully. Turn into lightly greased and floured 8-inch square pan. Bake in moderate oven (375°F.) 25 minutes. Dust with confectioners' sugar while warm and cut into bars. Yield: 12 bars.

RAISIN BARS

1 cup raisins	1 cup sugar
1½ cups sifted all-purpose flour	1 tablespoon hot water
2 teaspoons baking powder	1 teaspoon vanilla
½ teaspoon salt	½ cup chopped nuts
2 eggs	

Pour boiling water over raisins and let stand 10 minutes. Drain. Sift together flour, baking powder, and salt. Beat eggs, adding sugar gradually. Add hot water and vanilla and mix well. Add dry ingredients, beating thoroughly. Fold in raisins and nuts. Spread in paper-lined pan (7x11 inches). Bake in moderate oven (375°F.) 30 minutes. Cut into bars. Yield: 21 bars, 1x3¾ inches.

SCOTCH SHORTBREAD (Basic Recipe)

1 cup soft butter	2½ cups sifted all-purpose flour
¾ cup sugar	

Cream butter and add sugar gradually, blending thoroughly. Add flour slowly. Mix thoroughly to a smooth dough. Chill. Roll out about ½ inch thick. Shape with a cooky cutter, or cut into fancy shapes (small leaves, ovals, squares, etc.). Flute edges if desired by pinching between fingers as for pie crust. Place on ungreased baking sheet. Bake in slow oven (300°F.) about 20 to 25 minutes or until golden brown. Yield: about 2 dozen 1x1½-inch cookies.

Butterscotch shortbread: Substitute 1 cup firmly packed brown sugar for granulated.

Graham shortbread: Substitute 1 cup graham flour for white.

Honey shortbread: Use only ½ cup sugar and add 4 tablespoons honey.

Shortbread cookies: Roll dough to ¼ inch thickness. Cut into desired shapes. Prick all over with fork. Bake about 20 minutes.

MERINGUES OR KISSES (Basic Recipe)

4 egg whites	1 cup fine granulated sugar
¼ teaspoon salt	1 teaspoon vanilla

Beat egg whites and salt until stiff and dry. Beat in sugar gradually, sprinkling in 2 tablespoonfuls at a time. Add vanilla and continue beating until mixture holds its shape. Shape in mounds with a spoon, pastry bag, or tube on greased cooky sheets covered with lightly greased heavy paper. Bake in very slow oven (250°F.) 50 to 60 minutes. Remove from paper while still warm. If desired, shape in pairs. Yield: about 30 large or 60 small meringues.

Coconut kisses: Fold in 1 cup shredded coconut before shaping.

Creole kisses: Before shaping, fold in 1 cup finely pounded nut brittle.

Date and walnut meringues: Fold 1 cup each chopped dates and nuts into meringue mixture. Shape.

Maple nut kisses: Substitute 1 cup finely grated maple sugar for white sugar. Fold 1 cup ground nuts into meringue mixture.

Meringue shells: Shape in 3-inch mounds. Bake 1 to 1¼ hours. Remove from oven. Scoop out soft center with a spoon and place in oven to dry. To serve, fill center with ice cream or sweetened fruit, and top with whipped cream or dessert sauce.

Mushroom meringues: Shape with pastry bag or tube into rounds the size of mushroom caps. Sprinkle with cocoa or chocolate. Shape stems like mushroom stems. Bake, remove from paper, and place caps on stems.

Nut meringue shells: Fold in 1 cup chopped nutmeats (almonds, cashews, English walnuts, pecans, or pistachio nuts) before shaping into 3-inch mounds.

Pecan kisses: Substitute 1 cup firmly packed brown sugar for white. Fold 1 cup chopped nutmeats into meringue mixture.

HUNGARIAN CREAM CHEESE KIPFEL

1 cup butter	½ pound nuts, chopped
1 cup (½ pound) cream cheese	4 tablespoons sugar
2 cups sifted all-purpose flour	Grated rind of 1 lemon
½ teaspoon salt	Dash of cinnamon

Combine quickly with hands the butter, cheese, flour, and salt. Place in refrigerator over night. Roll out ⅛ inch thick on floured board. Cut into 2-inch squares. Mix together nuts, sugar, lemon rind, and cinnamon. Place a small amount on each square, fold over, and seal edges. Bake in moderate oven (375°F.) 10 to 15 minutes. Sprinkle with powdered sugar. Yield: about 80 cookies.

Variation: Kipfel may also be filled with jam or stewed dried fruit.

BERLINKRANZ

4 hard-cooked egg yolks	1 pound butter
2 cups confectioners' sugar	6 cups sifted all-purpose flour
4 raw egg yolks	Egg white
½ teaspoon almond extract	Crushed loaf sugar
½ teaspoon vanilla	

Mash hard-cooked egg yolks and work in confectioners' sugar. Add raw yolks, slightly beaten, the flavoring, and then butter and flour. Chill dough. Mold bits of dough into strips 4 to 5 inches long and twice as thick as a lead pencil. Form into rings with ends crossed. Dip into slightly beaten egg white. Sprinkle with the crushed loaf sugar. Bake in moderate oven (375°F.) until delicately browned, 8 to 10 minutes. Yield: about 8 dozen cookies.

FRIED BOHEMIAN TWISTS

2 cups sifted all-purpose flour	2 egg yolks
1 tablespoon sugar	1 whole egg
1 teaspoon butter	2 tablespoons cream
½ teaspoon salt	Confectioners' sugar

Combine flour, sugar, butter, and salt. Add 2 egg yolks, 1 at a time, and blend until smooth. Add whole egg and mix well. Add cream gradually. Knead on a slightly floured board until dough does not cling to the board or hands. Roll to paper thinness. Cut into 4x6-inch oblongs with a pastry wheel. Make several slashes in each lengthwise without cutting edges. Lift with a fork and poke a corner or two through the gashes. Twist and drop into hot fat (370°F.). Fry until golden brown, turning once. Drain on absorbent paper. Sprinkle with confectioners' sugar. Yield: 12 twists.

ALMOND PASTE MACAROONS

1 pound *ALMOND PASTE*	4 tablespoons sifted cake flour
2 cups sugar	⅔ cup sifted confectioners' sugar
¼ teaspoon salt	⅔ cup egg whites, unbeaten

Soften *ALMOND PASTE* with hands and work in sugar, salt, flour, confectioners' sugar, and egg whites. Drop by teaspoonfuls 2 inches apart on ungreased wrapping paper placed on baking sheet. Pat tops lightly with fingers dipped in cold water. Bake in slow oven (325°F.) until set and delicately browned, about 18 to 20 minutes. Remove from paper. Yield: about 5 dozen 2-inch macaroons.

ALMOND PASTE

Grind 2 cups blanched almonds, thoroughly dried (not toasted), through finest knife of food grinder. Then grind twice again. Mix in 1½ cups sifted confectioners' sugar. Blend in ¼ cup egg whites, unbeaten, and 2 teaspoons almond extract. Mold into ball. Place in tightly covered container in refrigerator for at least 4 days to age. Yield: 1 pound.

CARROT COOKIES

1 egg, slightly beaten	Dash of salt
½ cup shortening	1 cup quick cooking oats
⅛ teaspoon baking soda	1 cup chopped nuts
½ cup honey	½ cup seedless raisins
1 cup sifted all-purpose flour	½ cup grated raw carrot
1 teaspoon baking powder	1 teaspoon vanilla

Combine egg with shortening and cream slightly. Stir baking soda into honey and add to shortening-egg mixture. Mix and sift flour, baking powder, and salt; stir into first mixture. Combine and mix oats, nuts, raisins, and carrot; combine both mixtures until well blended, then stir in vanilla. Drop from teaspoon onto greased baking sheet, flattening each with tines of a fork. Bake in moderate oven (350°F.) about 12 minutes, or until lightly browned. Makes about 48.

desserts

An almost endless variety of desserts are offered in the many sections of this book. Choosing the right dessert is as much of an art as preparing it. Included here are the famous desserts of many lands as well as the desserts every family depends on from day to day. Well cooked and attractively served, the plain ones, too, can be exciting. Always choose a dessert that suits your menu. If the meal has been light choose a rich dessert, or select a light one for a heavy meal. Plan to make your choice of desserts an essential part of your food planning pattern. They can go a long way in rounding out the needs for essential nutrients—especially for the children.

BAKED CUSTARD (Basic Recipe)

⅓ cup sugar
¼ teaspoon salt
4 eggs, slightly beaten

3 cups milk, scalded
½ teaspoon vanilla
Few grains nutmeg

Add sugar and salt to eggs. Beat until thoroughly mixed. Add milk to egg mixture, stirring constantly. Add vanilla. Strain into buttered custard cups and sprinkle lightly with nutmeg. Set molds in baking pan. Pour enough hot water into pan to reach level of custard. Bake in slow oven (325°F.) until firm, 25 to 35 minutes, or until silver knife put into center comes out clean. Chill. Serves 6 to 8.

Large mold: Use 6 eggs, bake 1 to 1½ hours. Use silver knife test.

Bread pudding: Substitute 1 cup breadcrumbs for 2 of the eggs. Add raisins, candied peel, or other chopped fruit. Mix and bake.

Caramel custard: Add ½ cup caramelized sugar syrup to milk, or pour 1 to 1½ table-spoons caramel syrup into each cup before pouring in custard mixture. Bake. Un-mold to serve.

Chocolate custard: Add 2 squares unsweetened chocolate to milk before scalding. Beat with rotary beater until blended.

Coconut custard: Add ¾ cup shredded coconut to custard mixture.

Date or nut custard: Mix 1 cup either chopped dates or nuts with custard before baking.

Fruit custard: Place pieces of soft or soaked dried apricots or other fruit in bottom of molds before pouring in custard.

Gingerbread custard: Use 1½ cups crumbled gingerbread. Place 3 tablespoons in each buttered cup before pouring in custard.

Golden custard: Use 8 egg yolks. Omit whites.

Honey custard: Substitute ½ cup honey for sugar. Omit vanilla and nutmeg. Add dash of cinnamon.

Maple custard: Pour 1 to 1½ tablespoons maple syrup into each cup. Pour in custard mixture carefully so that syrup is not disturbed. Bake. Unmold to serve. Or substitute 4 tablespoons maple syrup or sugar for white sugar in recipe.

Marshmallow custard: Put 2 cut up marshmallows into bottom of each cup. Sprinkle with shredded coconut before pouring in custard.

Rice custard: Add 1 cup cooked rice to strained custard and grated rind of ½ lemon.

Silver custard: Substitute 2 egg whites for each whole egg.

SOFT CUSTARD (Basic Recipe)

3 to 4 eggs, slightly beaten, or
    4 to 6 egg yolks
3 tablespoons sugar

⅛ teaspoon salt
2 cups milk, scalded
1 teaspoon vanilla

Combine beaten eggs, sugar, and salt. Slowly stir in scalded milk, stirring constantly. Strain, then cook over simmering water 5 minutes or until mixture thickens and coats back of spoon. Add flavoring, strain at once, and chill. Serve as sauce or dessert. Serves 4 to 6.

Almond custard: Top each portion with chopped toasted almonds before serving.

Chocolate custard: Melt 2 squares unsweetened chocolate. Blend with scalded milk before adding to eggs. Add 1 tablespoon sugar.

Coconut custard: Pour soft custard into baking dish. Beat 3 egg whites until stiff. Fold in ⅓ cup sugar and ½ cup coconut. Spread over custard. Brown delicately in slow oven (300°F.). Chill.

Coffee custard: Substitute 1 cup strong coffee for 1 cup milk.

Cornstarch pudding: Substitute 3 tablespoons cornstarch for eggs.

Custard whip: Fold ½ cup whipped cream into cool custard.

Floating island: Prepare soft custard with 4 egg yolks. Pour into sherbet glasses and chill. Beat 2 egg whites, sweeten, and drop by spoonfuls on top of each serving. Garnish with a bit of jelly or cherry on top of egg white.

Fruit custard: Add any desired fresh or dried fruit to cup before pouring in custard.

Fruit delight: Prepare soft custard. Slice fruit (peaches, oranges, strawberries, or bananas) into a bowl. Pour over the custard, or alternate layers of fruit and stale sponge cake. Chill and serve with whipped cream.

Macaroon pudding: Pour soft custard over macaroon or cooky crumbs. Chill.

Orange custard: Substitute 1 tablespoon grated orange rind for vanilla. Put orange sections in bottom of each cup before pouring in custard. Or add ¼ cup chopped candied orange peel to cool custard.

Spanish custard cream: Substitute 1 tablespoon plain gelatin for 2 eggs. Soak gelatin in ¼ cup cold milk. While gelatin is soaking, prepare soft custard with balance of milk. When soft custard is done, pour it slowly over soaked gelatin. Stir until dissolved. Chill.

Tapioca custard: Substitute 3 tablespoons tapioca for 2 of the eggs. Cook tapioca in milk until transparent, 5 to 10 minutes. Then add to egg yolk mixture. Proceed as for soft custard.

Tipsey custard pudding: Substitute sherry for vanilla. Pour over pieces of stale sponge cake. Chill.

Yellow custard: Substitute 4 egg yolks for eggs. Serve plain or with fruit, or use for *FLOATING ISLAND*.

DIET CUP CUSTARD

3 half grain tablets saccharine, crushed	½ teaspoon vanilla
2 cups milk	Pinch of salt
	3 eggs, slightly beaten

Dissolve saccharine in little milk. Add with vanilla and salt to the eggs and stir. Add remaining milk. Pour into 4 buttered custard cups. Set in pan of hot water. Bake in a moderate oven (350°F.) until firm in center. Each portion gives about 100 calories. Serves 4.

BLANC MANGE (Cornstarch Pudding) (Basic Recipe)

3 to 4 tablespoons cornstarch	¼ cup cold milk
¼ cup sugar	1¾ cups scalded milk
⅛ teaspoon salt	1 teaspoon vanilla

Mix cornstarch, sugar and salt with cold milk. Add scalded milk to cornstarch mixture, slowly. Cook in top of double boiler over simmering water until smooth and thickened throughout, about 10 minutes. Cover and cook 10 to 15 minutes, stirring 2 or 3 times. Cool slightly. Add vanilla. Mix thoroughly. Pour into molds and chill. Serve plain or with fruit, nuts, and whipped cream, or sauce. Serves 6.

Butterscotch blanc mange: Substitute ½ cup firmly packed brown sugar for granulated. Add 2 tablespoons butter to mixture before cooling.

Caramel blanc mange: Add ¼ cup caramelized sugar syrup to milk after scalding.

Chocolate blanc mange: Add 2 ounces bitter chocolate to scalded milk. Beat until chocolate and milk are smooth. Add 2 extra tablespoons sugar to cold milk mixture. Or add 3 to 4 tablespoons cocoa and 2 extra tablespoons cornstarch. Mix with cold milk mixture.

Chocolate cream blanc mange: Fold ½ cup whipped cream or 2 beaten egg whites into chocolate pudding.

Coconut blanc mange: Add ½ cup shredded coconut before molding.

Coffee blanc mange: Substitute 1 cup strong coffee for 1 cup milk.

Creamy blanc mange: Add 2 egg whites, beaten stiff with vanilla.

Fluffy blanc mange: When pudding is cooked, stir a small amount of hot mixture into 2 slightly beaten egg yolks. Stir into remaining hot mixture and cook 2 minutes, stirring constantly. Cool slightly. Fold in 2 egg whites, beaten stiff, but not dry. Cool.

Fruit blanc mange: Add ½ cup crushed pineapple or other chopped or crushed fruits or berries before molding, or fill bottom of mold with fruits and pour pudding over fruit.

Layered blanc mange: Use artificial coloring; add to part of pudding before molding. Mold in layers, alternating colors.

Molded blanc mange: Increase cornstarch to 4 tablespoons. Flour may be substituted for cornstarch (5 to 7 tablespoons).

Nut blanc mange: Add ½ cup broken nutmeats to pudding.

BLACKBERRY FLUMMERY

2 cups blackberry juice, from canned or cooked fresh blackberries	3 tablespoons cornstarch ¼ teaspoon salt
½ cup sugar (if juice is unsweetened)	2 tablespoons lemon juice

Heat blackberry juice in a double boiler. Mix and sift sugar, cornstarch, and salt. Add to juice and stir until mixture thickens. Cover and cook 15 to 20 minutes. Remove from heat and add lemon juice. Beat well. Pour into serving dish. Chill. Serve with plain or whipped cream. Serves 6.

NORWEGIAN PRUNE PUDDING

½ pound prunes	1 stick cinnamon (1 inch)
2 cups cold water	1⅓ cups boiling water
1 cup sugar	⅓ cup cornstarch
Dash of salt	1 tablespoon lemon juice

Wash and soak prunes in cold water 1 hour. Boil until soft in same water. Drain and reserve juice. Pit the prunes. Crack pits, remove meats, and add to prunes. Combine prunes and juice. Add sugar, salt, cinnamon stick, and boiling water. Simmer 10 minutes. Mix cornstarch with enough cold water to give pouring consistency. Add to prune mixture and cook 5 minutes, stirring constantly. Remove stick of cinnamon. Add lemon juice. Turn into a mold. Chill thoroughly. Serve with cream. Serves 6.

APPLE MERINGUE PUDDING (Basic Recipe)

⅓ cup cornstarch	1 tablespoon orange rind or
1 cup sugar	1 teaspoon lemon rind
¾ teaspoon salt	24 small vanilla wafers
3 cups milk, scalded	2 cups canned pie apples
3 eggs, separated	

Mix cornstarch, ⅔ cup sugar and ½ teaspoon salt in top of double boiler and slowly pour over scalded milk. Cook over boiling water, stirring almost constantly until mixture thickens. Cover. Cook 15 minutes, stirring occasionally. Pour hot mixture very slowly over beaten egg yolks, stirring constantly. Return to double boiler and cook 2 to 3 minutes. Cool and add flavoring. Arrange alternate layers of vanilla wafers, apple slices, and cooled mixture in 1½-quart baking dish, ending with pudding. Beat egg whites with ¼ teaspoon salt until foamy; add ⅓ cup sugar gradually, beating until it stands up in soft peaks. Pile lightly on pudding. Bake in moderate oven (350°F.) until delicately browned, 15 minutes. Chill before serving. Serves 6.

Banana meringue pudding: Substitute 3 large ripe sliced bananas for apples and 1½ teaspoons vanilla for rind.

Chocolate meringue pudding: Add 2 squares unsweetened chocolate to milk before scalding. Use only 2 eggs; decrease sugar in meringue to ¼ cup. Omit rind; add 1½ teaspoons vanilla.

Citrus fruit meringue pudding: Substitute 1½ cups drained orange or sweetened grapefruit segments for apples.

Coconut meringue pudding: Substitute 1 cup shredded coconut for apples. Sprinkle ¼ cup coconut over meringue before baking. Omit rind; add 1½ teaspoons vanilla.

Peach meringue pudding: Substitute 2 cups fresh or drained canned sliced peaches for apples.

Pineapple meringue pudding: Substitute 2 cups drained, canned diced or crushed pineapple for apples.

TAPIOCA CREAM (Basic Recipe)

⅓ cup quick-cooking tapioca
⅓ cup sugar
⅛ teaspoon salt

2 eggs, separated
4 cups milk, scalded
1 teaspoon vanilla

Combine tapioca, sugar, salt, and egg yolks in top of double boiler. Add milk slowly and mix thoroughly. Cook until tapioca is transparent, stirring often. Remove from heat. Fold into stiffly beaten egg whites. Add vanilla. Serve warm or cold with cream. Serves 6.

Butterscotch tapioca: Substitute light brown sugar for white. Add 2 tablespoons butter to cooked mixture before folding in egg whites. When done, fold in ½ cup chopped nutmeats.

Chocolate tapioca: Add 2 squares unsweetened chocolate to milk. Heat and beat with rotary beater until blended. Increase sugar to ⅔ cup. Proceed as in basic recipe.

Coconut tapioca: Add ½ cup shredded coconut to milk. Instead of folding in egg whites, pour mixture into buttered baking dish. Fold ½ cup sugar into stiffly beaten egg whites. Pile on top. Bake in slow oven (300°F.) 15 minutes.

Date, apricot or prune tapioca: Add ½ cup chopped dates, prunes, or steamed apricots to mixture before folding in egg whites.

Fresh berry tapioca: Fold 2 cups crushed blueberries, raspberries, or strawberries into partially cooked tapioca. Chill.

Fruit tapioca: Arrange slices of fruit, canned or fresh in sherbet glasses, before pouring in mixture. Chill.

Honey tapioca: Substitute ⅓ cup honey for sugar.

Jelly tapioca parfait: Arrange *TAPIOCA CREAM PUDDING* in alternate layers with a berry jelly in parfait glasses. Use just enough jelly to cover cream. Serve with whipped cream.

Nut tapioca: Add ½ cup chopped nuts to mixture before pouring into molds.

Tapioca gelatin parfait: Prepare colored gelatin. Fill half of each parfait glass with gelatin. Fill rest of glass with tapioca. Garnish with cubes of gelatin.

BREAD PUDDING (Basic Recipe)

2 eggs, beaten
About ¼ cup sugar
½ teaspoon salt
1 teaspoon vanilla

¼ teaspoon nutmeg
4 cups scalded milk
2 cups bread cubes
¼ cup soft butter

Combine eggs, sugar, salt and flavoring. Add scalded milk and mix well. Add bread and pour into buttered baking dish. Set baking dish in pan of hot water. Bake in moderate oven (350°F.) 45 to 50 minutes, or until a knife inserted in center comes out clean. Serve warm or cold with cream, plain or whipped, hard sauce or lemon sauce. Cake, gingerbread, or breadcrumbs may be substituted for bread cubes. Serves 6.

Individual bread puddings: Pour mixture into 6 buttered individual baking cups. Bake as directed 35 to 45 minutes, or until knife inserted in center comes out clean.

Banana bread pudding: Slice 1 or 2 bananas over top before baking.

Butterscotch bread pudding: Substitute ½ cup firmly packed brown sugar for granulated. Melt butter with sugar in a skillet, stirring until evenly brown. Slowly add to milk. Cook until blended. Proceed as directed.

Caramel bread pudding: Use ½ cup sugar. Caramelize sugar and dissolve in milk before pouring over crumbs.

Chocolate bread pudding: Melt 2 squares unsweetened chocolate in milk. Beat until blended.

Coconut bread pudding: Add ½ cup moist shredded coconut just before pouring into baking pan. Sprinkle top with extra coconut if desired.

Fruit bread pudding: Add ½ cup chopped raisins, dates, or figs just before pouring mixture into baking pan.

Honey bread pudding: Substitute ¾ cup strained honey for sugar and ¾ teaspoon lemon extract for vanilla.

Marmalade bread pudding: Add ½ cup orange marmalade to mixture.

Marshmallow bread pudding: Cover top of baked pudding with marshmallows: Return to oven until melted and slightly browned.

Mocha bread pudding: Substitute 2 cups light cream and 2 cups fresh coffee for milk.

Nut bread pudding: Add ½ cup chopped nutmeats to chocolate or butterscotch bread pudding.

BROWN BETTY (Basic Recipe)

⅓ cup melted butter
2 cups soft breadcrumbs
3 cups sliced apples
½ cup sugar
Cinnamon or nutmeg, to taste

⅓ cup chopped nuts (optional)
Grated rind of 1 lemon
2 tablespoons lemon juice
½ cup water

Mix butter with breadcrumbs. Arrange in a buttered baking dish, first a layer of crumbs, then a layer of apples. Sprinkle apples with some of the sugar, spice, and chopped nuts. Repeat until fruit and crumbs are used, topping dish with crumbs.

Combine lemon rind, juice, and water. Pour over top of dish. Bake in moderate oven (350°F.) 45 minutes. If crumbs get too brown before time is up, cover dish. Serve with cream, lemon, or hard sauce. Serves 6.

Apricot or prune betty: Substitute 2½ cups stewed apricots or prunes for apples. Use fruit juice in place of lemon juice and water.

Banana betty: Substitute sliced bananas for apples.

Blueberry betty: Substitute 2½ cups blueberries or other berries for apples. **Sugar** may be reduced to ¼ cup.

Cherry betty: Substitute 3 cups stoned cherries for apples.

Corn flake betty: Substitute corn flakes for breadcrumbs. Bake in shallow dish.

Peach betty: Substitute sliced peaches for apples.

Pineapple betty: Substitute 3 cups diced, canned pineapple for apples. Reduce sugar to ¼ cup.

Rhubarb betty: Substitute 2½ cups stewed rhubarb for apples. Omit water.

COTTAGE PUDDING (Basic Recipe)

¼ cup shortening	¼ teaspoon salt
¾ cup sugar	2 teaspoons baking powder
1 egg	Dash of nutmeg
2 cups sifted all-purpose flour	1 cup milk

Cream shortening and sugar. Add egg and beat until light and frothy. Sift together flour, salt, baking powder, and nutmeg. Add alternately with milk to creamed shortening and sugar, beating after each addition. Bake in greased baking pan about 35 minutes in moderate oven (350°F.). Serve warm with butterscotch, chocolate or lemon sauce, or with sweetened fresh or canned fruits. Serves 6.

Individual puddings: Bake in muffin pans in hot oven (400°F.) 20 to 25 minutes.

Berry pudding: Add 1 cup blueberrries to batter. Serve with hard sauce. Other drained, canned, or fresh fruits may be used the same way.

Chocolate chip pudding: Add 1 cup chocolate bits to pudding.

Fruit topped pudding: Place any desired fruits in bottom of baking pan before adding batter. Invert to serve.

OLD FASHIONED RICE PUDDING (Basic Recipe)

¾ cup uncooked rice	½ teaspoon salt
1½ quarts milk	¼ teaspoon nutmeg
¾ cup sugar	¾ cup seedless raisins

Wash rice. Add milk, sugar, nutmeg, and salt. Place in a buttered 2½-quart baking dish. Bake in moderate oven (325°F.) 2½ hours, stirring twice during first hour. Stir brown crust into pudding several times during the remainder of baking. Add raisins ½ hour before pudding is done. Then allow crust to form again on pudding. Serve warm or cold with cream, if desired. To reduce baking time, cook rice 10 to 15 minutes in the milk in double boiler before baking. Serves 6 to 8.

Apricot rice pudding: Substitute well-drained, soaked apricots for raisins. Cut apricots in strips.

Brown rice pudding: Substitute ¾ cup brown rice for white. Bake same way.

Brown sugar rice pudding: Substitute ¾ cup firmly packed brown sugar for white. Omit raisins. Serve cold.

Chocolate rice pudding: Mix ¼ cup cocoa with rice and sugar mixture. Serve with sweetened whipped cream.

Date rice pudding: Substitute ¾ cup chopped, pitted dates for raisins.

Honey rice pudding: Substitute ½ cup honey for sugar.

Molasses rice pudding: Substitute ½ cup molasses for sugar and ½ teaspoon cinnamon for nutmeg. Add 1½ tablespoons butter at last stirring.

Prune rice pudding: Substitute ¾ cup well-drained, pitted, soaked prunes for raisins. Cut prunes in strips.

RICE KUGEL

1 cup rice	4 eggs
1 teaspoon salt	½ teaspoon cinnamon
4 cups boiling water	1 teaspoon grated lemon rind
¼ cup butter or chicken fat	½ cup seedless raisins
½ cup confectioners' sugar	¼ cup chopped nuts

Cook rice in boiling salted water until tender, about 30 minutes; drain. Cream fat and sugar. Beat in eggs, 1 at a time. Add cinnamon, lemon rind, raisins, and chopped nuts. Mix well. Add cooked rice. Bake in a greased casserole in moderate oven (350°F.) until brown, about 1 hour. Serve hot or cold. Serves 6.

VANILLA SOUFFLE (Basic Recipe)

4 tablespoons butter	3 eggs, separated
5 tablespoons flour	5 tablespoons sugar
¼ teaspoon salt	1 teaspoon vanilla
1 cup milk	1 teaspoon almond extract

Melt butter in top part of double boiler. Blend in flour and salt. Slowly add milk. Heat to boiling, stirring constantly. Remove from heat. Cool. Beat egg yolks until thick and lemon colored; add sugar and pour over first mixture. Add flavorings; stir in stiffly beaten egg whites. Pour into greased baking dish. Set into pan of hot water. Bake in moderate oven (325°F.) until firm, 50 to 60 minutes. Serve at once, plain or with whipped cream or vanilla sauce. Serves 6.

Butterscotch nut soufflé: Use ⅔ cup firmly packed brown sugar instead of granulated sugar. Add 1 tablespoon butter. Fold in cup finely chopped nutmeats (pecans or walnuts) with the beaten egg yolks.

Chocolate soufflé: Use only 4 tablespoons flour; stir in 2 squares melted chocolate into hot milk mixture.

Fruit soufflé: Place 2 cups canned, drained fruit cut into pieces (apricots, peaches, or pineapple) on bottom of baking dish. Pour soufflé over fruit. Bake as directed.

Lemon soufflé: Use only ⅔ cup milk. Add ⅓ cup lemon juice when thickened. Omit vanilla and almond. Add 1 teaspoon grated lemon rind.

Macaroon soufflé: Omit butter, flour, and sugar. Break 12 macaroons into the milk and proceed as in *VANILLA SOUFFLÉ.*

Mocha soufflé: Use ⅔ cup strong hot coffee and ⅓ cup cream instead of milk.

Orange soufflé: Substitute 1 cup orange juice for milk. Omit vanilla and almond. Add 1 tablespoon each of lemon juice and grated orange rind.

Pineapple soufflé: Substitute 1 cup pineapple juice for milk. Omit vanilla and almond. Add 1 tablespoon lemon juice and ½ teaspoon grated lemon rind. Fold in ½ cup drained crushed pineapple with beaten egg yolks.

PRUNE SOUFFLE (Basic Recipe)

4 tablespoons sugar	2 teaspoons lemon juice
1 cup prune pulp	5 egg whites

Combine sugar and prune pulp and heat until sugar has dissolved. Add lemon juice. Beat egg whites until frothy. Fold in. Turn into a baking dish and bake in moderate oven (350°F.) about 40 minutes. When done, sprinkle with powdered sugar. Serve at once from baking dish with cream. Serves 4.

Apple soufflé: Substitute 1 cup thick apple sauce for prune pulp.

Apricot soufflé: Substitute 1 cup apricot pulp for prune pulp. Add ¼ teaspoon almond extract with lemon juice.

Cherry soufflé: Substitute sweet cherry pulp for prunes and cherry brandy for lemon juice.

Peach soufflé: Substitute 1 cup peach pulp for prune pulp. Add ¼ teaspoon almond extract with lemon juice.

VANILLA FONDUE (Basic Recipe)

1 cup milk, scalded	¼ teaspoon salt
⅓ cup sugar	3 eggs, separated
1 cup soft bread cubes	1 teaspoon vanilla
1 tablespoon butter	

Scald milk in top of double boiler. Add sugar, stirring until melted. Add bread cubes, butter, and salt. Cool and add well-beaten egg yolks and vanilla. Fold in stiffly beaten egg whites. Turn into baking dish, greased on bottom only. Set in pan of hot water. Bake in moderate oven (350°F.) until knife inserted in center comes out clean, 50 to 60 minutes. Serve at once. Serves 4 to 6.

Chocolate fondue: Melt and add 2 squares chocolate to milk. Beat until well blended. Use only ½ teaspoon vanilla.

Date fondue: Increase sugar to ½ cup. Add 1 cup finely cut, pitted dates just before folding in egg whites. Use only ½ teaspoon vanilla.

Vanilla fruit fondue: Add 1 cup well drained fruit just before folding in egg whites.

BAKED PEACH PUDDING (Basic Recipe)

2 cups milk
2 cups soft breadcrumbs
¼ teaspoon salt
⅔ cup sugar
2 eggs, beaten

2 tablespoons butter
¼ teaspoon nutmeg
2 cups sliced peaches, fresh or
   canned

Scald milk and pour over breadcrumbs. Cool. Add salt, sugar, eggs, and nutmeg. Mix. Fold in peaches. Turn into buttered casserole. Bake in moderate oven (350°F.) 1¼ hours. Cover with meringue or serve with cream. Serves 6.

Baked apple pudding: Use 2 cups peeled sliced apples in place of peaches.

Baked blueberry pudding: Use 2 cups blueberries or other berries to replace peaches.

Baked cherry pudding: Use 2 cups pitted, halved cherries to replace peaches.

Baked plum pudding: Use 2 cups sliced pitted plums to replace peaches.

TIPSY PUDDING (Basic Recipe)

2 stale sponge layers
½ cup sherry
3 cups milk
⅓ cup sugar
¼ teaspoon salt
2 eggs

1 teaspoon vanilla
2 tablespoons chopped candied
   cherries
2 tablespoons slivered, toasted
   almonds

Break cake into about 12 pieces and arrange in serving bowl. Pour sherry over cake and chill several hours or overnight. Scald milk in top of double boiler. Mix together sugar, salt, and eggs. Add scalded milk very slowly, stirring constantly. Return to double boiler. Cook over boiling water until mixture thickens slightly and will coat back of spoon, about 5 minutes. Cool. Add vanilla. Chill. Pour ¾ of custard over cake. Chill several hours before serving. Pour remaining custard over pudding when ready to serve. Garnish with cherries and almonds. Serves 6.

Individual tipsy puddings: Use 6 small squares of cake. Place in individual dishes. Pour an equal amount of sherry over each. Proceed as directed.

Ladyfinger tipsy pudding: Use 24 ladyfingers instead of sponge cake. Split ladyfingers. Spread 12 with jelly. Sandwich together and put 2 in bottom of each dessert cup. Stand 4 halves up around inside edge. Pour sherry and custard over each.

Layered tipsy pudding: Instead of breaking cake into pieces, split cake layers. Spread with jam. Put together and place in large bowl. Pour sherry over cake and proceed as directed.

INDIAN PUDDING (Basic Recipe)

⅓ cup yellow corn meal
½ teaspoon salt
4½ cups milk

½ cup molasses
½ teaspoon ginger
½ teaspoon cinnamon

Combine corn meal, salt, and ½ cup milk. Scald 4 cups milk in top of double boiler. Add moistened corn meal, stirring constantly. Cook 20 minutes, or until thickened. Add molasses, ginger, and cinnamon. Pour into a greased baking dish.

Bake in moderate oven (300°F.) for 2 hours. Serve warm with vanilla ice cream, or chill and serve with cream. Serves 6.

Apple Indian pudding: Pare and slice 2 apples. Add to thickened mixture. Add sugar to taste.

Date or fig Indian pudding: Add ½ cup pitted, chopped dates or chopped figs to thickened mixture.

DATE AND NUT PUDDING (Basic Recipe)

¾ cup sifted flour
1½ teaspoons baking powder
½ teaspoon salt
1½ cups chopped, pitted dates

¾ cup almonds, walnuts, or pecans
3 eggs
¾ cup sugar

Mix and sift flour, baking powder, and salt. Add dates and nuts. Beat eggs until light. Add sugar and mix well. Add to dry ingredients. Turn into greased, deep 9-inch pie pan. Bake in slow oven (325°F.) 35 to 40 minutes. Cut into wedges while warm. Tear into pieces and serve in dessert glasses topped with whipped cream or desired sauce. Serves 6.

Apricot nut pudding: Substitute well drained, soaked, dried apricots for the dates. Cut apricots in strips.

Prune and nut pudding: Substitute well drained, soaked, dried prunes for dates. Pit prunes and cut in strips.

APPLE SCHALET

2 tablespoons sugar
4 tablespoons shortening
1 egg, slightly beaten
1 cup sifted all-purpose flour
⅛ teaspoon salt

3 tablespoons cold water
6 medium-size apples
½ cup seedless raisins
1 tablespoon sugar
½ teaspoon cinnamon

Cream 2 tablespoons sugar and shortening. Add egg and mix well. Sift flour and salt. Add to creamed mixture with the water. On a floured board roll dough out in several layers to fit a well greased casserole. Combine remaining ingredients. Alternate layers of dough and filling, starting and ending with dough. Bake in slow oven (325°F.) until brown, about 1½ hours. Serves 6 to 8.

CARROT PUDDING

½ cup shortening
½ cup brown sugar
1 egg
1 cup grated raw carrots
½ teaspoon soda
1 teaspoon baking powder
½ teaspoon salt

½ cup seedless raisins
½ cup currants
2 teaspoons grated lemon rind
1¼ cups sifted all-purpose flour
½ teaspoon cinnamon
½ teaspoon nutmeg
1 tablespoon water

Cream shortening and brown sugar. Add egg and mix well. Add carrots and remaining ingredients. Mix thoroughly and pour into a greased casserole. Bake in moderate oven (350°F.) until browned, about 1 hour. Serves 6 to 8.

APPLE CRUMBLE PUDDING

Apples
½ cup granulated sugar
Cinnamon
1 cup brown sugar

1 cup flour
⅓ cup butter, melted
Chopped pecans
Whipping cream (optional)

Peel and slice cooking apples and place in greased baking dish 2 inches deep or in a very deep pie pan, almost filling dish with apples. Sprinkle with the ½ cup or more granulated sugar, depending on tartness of apples, and cinnamon to taste. Prepare topping by combining brown sugar, flour, and butter to form a crumbly mixture. Place mixture on apples, pressing down to form a crust. Sprinkle top with chopped pecans. Bake in moderate oven (375°F.) 30 to 45 minutes, or until apples are tender and crust is firm. Serve with plain cream or sweetened whipped cream.

RUSSIAN CHEESE PUDDING

3 eggs, separated
1 cup sugar
¼ cup butter, melted
2 cups cottage cheese, dry
Yolks of 4 hard-cooked eggs

½ teaspoon vanilla
Dash of salt
3 tablespoons flour
½ cup raisins

Mix raw egg yolks and sugar thoroughly. Add butter and beat well. Put cheese and hard-cooked egg yolks through a fine sieve. Add to creamed mixture with vanilla, salt, flour, and raisins. Mix well. Fold in stiffly beaten egg whites. Bake in a greased casserole in a slow oven (300°F.) 35 to 40 minutes. Serves 6 to 8.

RHUBARB PUDDING

4 cups rhubarb, cut in pieces
2 tablespoons orange juice
½ cup sugar
¼ teaspoon cinnamon
1 tablespoon butter
¼ cup melted shortening

⅓ cup firmly packed brown sugar
⅔ cup flour
⅛ teaspoon salt
¼ teaspoon baking soda
⅔ cup rolled oats

Arrange rhubarb in shallow, greased pan. Sprinkle with orange juice, sugar, and cinnamon. Dot with butter. Melt shortening and brown sugar together. Sift flour, salt, and baking soda, and mix with oats. Blend with sugar mixture, crumbling well. Spread over rhubarb. Bake in moderate oven (375°F.) 40 minutes. Serve warm or cold with light cream. Serves 6.

STEAMED PUDDINGS—BASIC DIRECTIONS

Pudding mixtures may be prepared in special pudding molds, or small cylindrical tins with tight covers such as baking powder cans. Molds may be tightly covered with parchment paper, aluminum foil, or several layers of heavy waxed paper, letting it extend at least an inch over the edge and tied in place. The mold and cover should be thoroughly greased. Mold should be only ⅔ full.

If a steamer is not available, place a trivet or wire rack in a large covered kettle or roasting pan. Place the covered molds on the trivet or rack. Add water to just below the top of trivet. Cover, let water boil slowly to form steam. Water should be boiling in kettle or steamer when food is ready for cooking. Keep water boiling, constantly refilling with boiling water as needed. When done, remove molds and let stand a few minutes, or set in cold water for a few seconds before unmolding.

If desired, the batter may be poured directly into the upper part of a double boiler and cooked over boiling water. The water should not touch the upper part. The sides and cover of double boiler insert should be well greased.

STEAMED VANILLA PUDDING (Basic Recipe)

⅓ cup shortening
1 cup sugar
1 teaspoon vanilla
1½ cups sifted cake flour

1½ teaspoons baking powder
⅛ teaspoon salt
½ cup milk
3 egg whites

Cream shortening, add ⅔ cup sugar and vanilla. Cream until light and fluffy. Mix and sift dry ingredients. Add in thirds to shortening, alternating with milk, mixing well after each addition. Beat egg whites until stiff but not dry. Gradually add remaining sugar, beating continuously. Carefully fold into batter. Fill individual greased molds ¾ full. Steam until done, about ½ hour. Serve with fruit sauce. Serves 6 to 8.

Almond pudding: Substitute almond extract for vanilla.

Chocolate pudding: Melt and cool 2 squares unsweetened chocolate. Add with sugar-egg mixture.

Raisin nut pudding: Add ½ cup each seedless raisins and nuts with sugar-egg mixture.

Raisin pudding: Add 1 cup seedless raisins with sugar-egg mixture.

STEAMED APRICOT PUDDING

½ pound dried apricots
1½ cups sifted cake flour
2 teaspoons baking powder
¼ teaspoon salt

¼ cup butter or other fat
½ cup sugar
2 eggs
½ cup milk

Wash apricots, chop fine, and mix with 2 tablespoons of flour. Sift remaining flour with baking powder and salt. Cream the fat. Add sugar and well-beaten eggs. Add alternately with milk to sifted dry ingredients. Stir in apricots. Pour into a greased mold, cover, and steam 2 hours. Serve hot with hard sauce.

PLUM PUDDING

2 cups sifted flour
2 teaspoons baking powder
½ teaspoon salt
2 teaspoons cinnamon
½ teaspoon nutmeg
½ teaspoon allspice
1 pound raisins
½ pound currants

½ pound finely sliced citron
Orange or lemon peel
½ pound beef suet
½ cup brown sugar
2 eggs
½ teaspoon almond extract
¾ cup liquid (coffee, fruit juice, sherry, or combined)

Sift together dry ingredients. Add fruit. Grind or finely chop suet. Cream well, adding sugar gradually. Add eggs and beat well. Add flavoring to liquid. Alternately add dry and liquid ingredients to suet-sugar mixture. Fill a greased mold ⅔ full. Cover tightly. Steam 4 to 6 hours, depending on size of mold.

STEAMED CARROT PUDDING

1 cup ground raw carrots
1 cup ground raw apples
1 cup seedless raisins
½ cup brown sugar
½ cup molasses
1 cup ground suet
½ teaspoon baking soda

1 teaspoon baking powder
1 cup sifted flour
½ cup breadcrumbs
½ teaspoon nutmeg
½ teaspoon cloves
½ teaspoon cinnamon

Combine all ingredients, pour into greased mold. Steam 2½ hours. Serve hot with lemon sauce. Serves 10.

STEAMED CHOCOLATE PUDDING

1 tablespoon butter
¾ cup sugar
1 egg yolk, beaten
½ cup water
1½ cups flour

3 teaspoons baking powder
1 square melted unsweetened
    chocolate
1 egg white, beaten stiff

Cream butter with sugar. Add beaten egg yolk and water. Add sifted flour and baking powder. Add melted chocolate and fold in stiffly beaten egg white. Butter top section of a 1-quart double boiler. Pour in pudding mixture. Steam about 2 hours. Serves 6.

Steamed chocolate nut pudding: Add ½ cup chopped walnuts to above.

HUNGARIAN PLUM PUDDING

2 cups stale breadcrumbs
1 cup scalded milk
½ cup sugar
2 eggs, separated
1¼ cups seedless raisins
1¼ cups currants
¼ cup finely cut citron

¼ cup grape juice
½ teaspoon nutmeg
1 teaspoon cinnamon
¼ teaspoon each cloves and mace
1½ teaspoons salt
½ cup butter, melted

Soak breadcrumbs in milk and let cool. Combine sugar, beaten egg yolks, raisins, currants, and citron. Add milk mixture and butter. Mix well. Add remaining ingredients and fold in stiffly beaten egg whites. Pour into buttered mold. Cover and steam 5 hours. Serve hot with hard sauce. Serves 6.

STEAMED APPLE PUDDING

6 apples
¼ cup sugar
¼ teaspoon cinnamon
¼ cup water
1 cup sifted flour

2½ teaspoons baking powder
½ teaspoon salt
1 tablespoon shortening
About ⅓ cup milk

Wash, pare, and quarter apples. Cut into slices about ¼ inch thick. Add sugar, cinnamon, and water. Cover and cook over low heat until tender. Stir carefully if necessary. Mix and sift flour, baking powder, and salt. Cut in shortening. Add milk, mixing quickly to make a soft dough. Pat out to fit the size of pan in which the apples are cooking. Place dough over apples. Cover pan and put in steamer. Steam pudding about 1 hour. Turn out onto a large plate, apple side up. Serve warm with lemon sauce. Serves 6.

gelatins

LEMON GELATIN (Basic Recipe)

2 tablespoons plain gelatin	⅛ teaspoon salt
½ cup cold water	¾ cup lemon juice
2½ cups boiling water	1 teaspoon grated lemon rind
¾ cup sugar	

Soak gelatin in cold water 5 minutes. Add hot water, sugar, and salt. Stir until dissolved. Add fruit juice and grated rind. Pour into mold and chill until firm. Serve with plain or whipped cream, custard sauce, or fruits. Serves 6 to 8.

Fruit Bavarian cream: When gelatin begins to set, beat until foamy. Fold in 1 cup heavy cream which has been whipped and sweetened. Add desired fruit pulp. Mold and chill.

Fruit gelatin: Substitute canned fruit juices for water. If juices are sweet, they may replace sugar as well as the liquid and flavoring. Add fruit when gelatin starts to set. NOTE: Gelatin will not jell with fresh pineapple. Always bring fresh pineapple to a boil, or use canned pineapple. Fresh pineapple contains an enzyme (bromelin) which prevents gelatin from becoming stiff.

Gelatin squares: Cut firm gelatin into cubes. Pile one or more colors in each cup or serve with cubed fruit.

Grape gelatin: Substitute 1 teaspoon orange rind for lemon rind. Reduce sugar to ½ cup and reduce lemon juice to 1 tablespoon. Substitute 1½ cups grape juice for 1½ cups water.

Lemon snow or sponge pudding: When gelatin begins to set, beat with rotary beater until foamy. Beat 2 to 3 egg whites until stiff and beat into gelatin foam. Mold and chill.

Molded fruit salads: Use lemon gelatin to mold fruits, vegetables, fish, or meat. Tomato juice, chicken, or meat stock may be substituted for liquid; seasonings may be varied. For specific recipes see salad section.

Orange gelatin: Substitute 1½ cups orange juice for 1 cup water. Reduce lemon juice to ¼ cup. Substitute orange rind for lemon rind.

Prune jelly: Substitute 1½ cups prune juice for 1½ cups liquid. Add ½ cup each of raisins, cooked chopped prunes, and chopped nutmeats. Mold and chill.

Riced gelatin: Chill gelatin until very firm. Force through potato ricer. Pile into serving dishes. Combine several colors per serving.

Whipped gelatin: When gelatin is soft and quivery, beat with a rotary beater until light and fluffy. Mold or pile into serving dishes.

BAVARIAN CREAM (Basic Recipe)

1 tablespoon plain gelatin	¼ teaspoon salt
¼ cup cold water	1 cup milk
2 egg yolks	1 cup cream, whipped
½ cup sugar	½ teaspoon vanilla

Soften gelatin in cold water. Beat egg yolks with sugar and salt. Add to milk and cook in double boiler until thick. Add gelatin. Stir until dissolved. Cool. When mixture begins to thicken, fold in whipped cream and vanilla. Turn into dampened mold and chill. Unmold and serve with fruit sauce. Serves 6.

Butterscotch Bavarian cream: Omit white sugar. Cook ¾ cup brown sugar with 2 tablespoons butter for a few seconds, then add to hot mixture.

Maple Bavarian cream: Substitute shaved maple sugar for white sugar. Add ½ cup chopped pecans or walnuts.

STRAWBERRY BAVARIAN CREAM (Basic Recipe)

1 tablespoon plain gelatin	⅛ teaspoon salt
2 tablespoons cold water	1 tablespoon lemon juice
1½ cups crushed strawberries	1 cup heavy cream, whipped
About ½ cup sugar	

Soften gelatin in cold water 5 minutes. Heat over hot water, stirring until dissolved. Remove from heat. Add berries, sugar, salt, and lemon juice. Mix well. Cool until slightly thickened. Fold in whipped cream. Turn into mold and chill. Bottom of mold may be garnished with whole berries. Unmold and serve plain, or with additional whole berries and whipped cream. Serves 6.

Apricot Bavarian cream: Substitute diced apricots for strawberries.

Banana berry Bavarian cream: Substitute ¾ cup of mashed ripe banana for ¾ cup crushed berries.

Charlotte russe: Line parfait glasses with lady fingers, thin strips of angel food or sponge cake, or macaroons. Fill with any *BAVARIAN CREAM* mixture; garnish with pieces of fruit. Chill.

Macaroon Bavarian cream: Add ¾ cup crushed macaroons with whipped cream.

Nut Bavarian cream: Add ¾ cup chopped nutmeats with whipped cream.

Peach Bavarian cream: Substitute diced peaches for strawberries.

Raspberry Bavarian cream: Substitute crushed raspberries for strawberries.

MARMALADE BAVARIAN

1 package orange gelatin	½ cup heavy cream
1¾ cups hot water	⅓ cup orange marmalade
¼ teaspoon salt	

Dissolve gelatin in hot water. Add salt. Chill until cold and syrupy. Fold in cream, whipped only until thick and shiny, but not stiff. Fold in marmalade. Chill until slightly thickened. Turn into mold. Chill until firm. Unmold. Garnish with whipped cream and additional orange marmalade. Serves 6.

BANANA BAVARIAN CREAM

1 package lemon gelatin	⅔ cup sugar
1 pint warm water	½ cup heavy cream
¼ teaspoon salt	5 bananas

Dissolve gelatin in warm water. Add salt and sugar. Chill until cold and syrupy. Fold in cream, whipped only until thick and shiny, but not stiff. Crush bananas to pulp with silver fork and fold at once into mixture. Chill until slightly thickened. Turn into mold. Chill until firm. Unmold. Serve with tart fruit sauce. Serves 8.

ORANGE BAVARIAN CREAM (Basic Recipe)

2 tablespoons plain gelatin	1½ cups orange juice and pulp
½ cup cold water	¼ teaspoon salt
½ cup boiling water	3 egg whites
1 cup sugar	2 cups cream, whipped
4 to 5 tablespoons lemon juice	

Soak gelatin in cold water 5 minutes. Add boiling water and sugar and stir until dissolved. Add lemon and orange juice and pulp. Chill until partially set and beat until foamy. Add salt to egg whites and beat until stiff. Fold into gelatin. Fold in whipped cream and turn into a wet mold. Chill until firm. Unmold on platter and garnish with orange sections. Serves 8 to 10.

Variations: Substitute other fresh fruits or cooked dried fruits for orange juice and pulp. Use drained juice instead of orange juice. Reduce sugar in accordance with sweetness of cooked fruit.

Orange charlotte russe: Line mold with split lady fingers and fill with mixture.

SPANISH CREAM (Basic Recipe)

1 tablespoon plain gelatin	½ cup sugar
¼ cup cold water	⅛ teaspoon salt
2 cups scalded milk	1 teaspoon vanilla
3 eggs, separated	

Soften gelatin in cold water 5 minutes. Add milk. Combine egg yolks, sugar, salt, and gelatin mixture in top of double boiler. Cook over hot water 5 minutes, stirring constantly until sugar is dissolved. Cool until slightly thickened. Add vanilla. Fold in stiffly beaten egg whites. Turn into molds. Chill until firm. Unmold and serve with chocolate sauce, whipped cream, or fruit. Serves 6.

Chocolate Spanish cream: Melt 2 squares unsweetened chocolate in milk. Beat with rotary beater until blended.

Coffee Spanish cream: Increase sugar to ⅔ cup. Substitute 1½ cups fresh hot coffee for 1½ cups milk.

Macaroon Spanish cream: Fold ¾ cup crushed macaroons into egg whites.

Mocha Spanish cream: Increase sugar to ⅔ cup. Decrease milk to ½ cup. Add 1½ cups fresh hot coffee with 2 squares unsweetened chocolate dissolved in it.

Orange Spanish cream: Omit vanilla and water. Add ½ teaspoon each grated lemon and orange rind and 1 tablespoon lemon juice. Reduce scalded milk to 1½ cups. Soften gelatin in ½ cup orange juice.

LALLA ROOKH CREAM

3 eggs, separated
½ cup sugar
½ cup cream
1 tablespoon plain gelatin

2 tablespoons milk
1 tablespoon rum
1 cup cream, whipped

Beat yolks and add sugar and cream. Cook over hot water, stirring constantly, until mixture coats spoon. Soften gelatin in 2 tablespoons milk; add to mixture and stir until dissolved. Remove from heat. Cool, add rum, stiffly beaten egg whites, and whipped cream. Turn into mold. Chill until mixture holds its shape. Serve, garnished with maraschino cherries and cherry juice. Serves 4.

SHERRY GELATIN

2 tablespoons plain gelatin
¼ cup cold water
1¼ cups boiling water
¾ cup sugar

¼ teaspoon salt
¼ cup orange juice
2 tablespoons lemon juice
1 cup sherry

Soften gelatin in cold water. Add boiling water, sugar, and salt. Stir until dissolved. Add orange and lemon juices and sherry. Mix well. Turn into molds and chill. Serves 6.

GINGERBREAD GELATIN BETTY

1 package orange gelatin
1 cup boiling water
½ cup cold water

1⅓ cups sweetened apple sauce
1 tablespoon lemon juice
Dash of salt
1 cup gingerbread crumbs

Pour boiling water over gelatin and stir until dissolved. Add cold water, apple sauce, lemon juice, and salt. Let cool until partly thickened, then stir in gingerbread crumbs. Turn into mold. Chill until firm. Serve topped with whipped cream. Serves 6.

Chocolate cake betty: Use chocolate cake crumbs instead of gingerbread.

CHERRY GELATIN SOUFFLE

1 tablespoon plain gelatin
4 tablespoons cold water
3 eggs, separated
1 teaspoon grated lemon rind
2 tablespoons lemon juice

⅔ cup sugar
¼ teaspoon salt
⅔ cup canned, drained cherries
½ cup heavy cream, whipped

Soften gelatin in water 5 minutes. Beat egg yolks slightly and add lemon rind, lemon juice, sugar, and salt. Cook over boiling water in top of double boiler, stirring constantly, until mixture thickens. Add gelatin and stir until dissolved. Add cherries. Cool. When it begins to stiffen, fold in whipped cream and beaten egg whites. Turn into mold and chill. Unmold when firm and garnish with slices of pineapple and peaches. Serves 8.

Banana soufflé: Omit cherries. Use 1 cup mashed bananas mixed with ¼ cup pineapple juice. Line mold with thin slices of sponge cake.

Pineapple soufflé: Decrease sugar to ½ cup. Use canned crushed pineapple instead of cherries.

CHOCOLATE SPONGE (Basic Recipe)

1½ tablespoons plain gelatin   ¼ teaspoon salt
¼ cup cold water   ¼ cup boiling water
1½ squares chocolate   3 eggs, separated
⅓ cup sugar   1 teaspoon vanilla

Soak gelatin in cold water 5 minutes. Melt chocolate in top of double boiler. Add sugar, salt, and boiling water. Bring to boil. Remove from heat, add gelatin, and stir until dissolved. Slowly add to slightly beaten egg yolks. Chill until mixture begins to thicken. Fold in stiffly beaten egg whites and vanilla. Turn into dampened mold and chill. Serve with whipped cream. Serves 6.

Chocolate charlotte: Line mold with lady fingers or sponge cake before pouring in gelatin mixture.

Macaroon chocolate sponge: Add ¾ cup crushed macaroons.

Nut chocolate sponge: Add ¾ cup chopped nutmeats.

MOLDED JELLY ROLL

1 box raspberry gelatin   1½ cups cream, whipped
1 cup boiling water   1 jelly roll with red jelly
1 cup raspberry juice   1 cup heavy cream, whipped
2½ cups canned drained raspberries   Fresh raspberries

Dissolve gelatin in boiling water. Add berry juice. Set aside to thicken. Fold canned berries into whipped cream and add to gelatin mixture. Line a spring-form pan with ½ inch thick slices of jelly roll. Pour in gelatin mixture and chill 5 hours in refrigerator. Turn out on platter; garnish with whipped cream and fresh raspberries. Serves 10 to 12.

Variations: Use strawberries, blackberries, blueberries, etc., instead of raspberries.

SUGAR HONEY PEACH TORTE

1 cup finely crushed graham crackers   2 teaspoons plain gelatin
¼ cup and 1 tablespoon granulated   2 tablespoons lemon juice
    sugar   ¼ teaspoon grated lemon rind
4 tablespoons melted butter   ½ cup whipping cream, whipped
¾ cup syrup from canned cling peaches   1½ cups canned cling peach slices
⅛ teaspoon salt

Blend crumbs, 1 tablespoon sugar, and butter. Pat into bottom and halfway up sides of loaf pan (about 7½x3½x3 inches). Chill. Heat syrup, ¼ cup sugar, and salt together. Soften gelatin in lemon juice and dissolve in hot syrup. Blend in rind. Cool until mixture reaches consistency of unbeaten egg white. Fold in whipped cream and well drained peach slices. Pour into crumb-lined pan. Chill thoroughly. Cut into slices to serve. Serves 6.

FRUIT REFRIGERATOR CAKE

1 pint raspberries or strawberries   1 pint heavy cream
10 tablespoons sugar   2½ dozen lady fingers
1 tablespoon plain gelatin   3 large ripe bananas, sliced
4 tablespoons cold water

Pick over berries. Wash and drain. Add 4 tablespoons sugar and chill until ready to use. Soften gelatin in cold water. Place over boiling water to dissolve. Whip cream, beating in 4 tablespoons sugar gradually. Add gelatin and beat to smooth consistency. Spread layer of whipped cream mixture over mold lined with lady fingers. Over this spread half the sugared berries. Add another layer of lady fingers, then a layer of bananas, sprinkled with 2 tablespoons sugar. Add another layer of cream and finally a layer of lady fingers. Chill overnight.

desserts—miscellaneous

BASIC SPECIAL SHORTCAKE

2 cups sifted all-purpose flour	⅓ cup shortening
4 teaspoons baking powder	¾ cup milk
½ teaspoon salt	Butter
1 tablespoon sugar	Fruit

Mix and sift dry ingredients and work in the shortening with the fingers or a knife. Gradually add enough milk to form a soft dough, mixing with a knife. Toss dough onto floured board. Pat or roll to ½ inch thickness. Bake in sheet for large shortcake or cut with biscuit cutter. Bake in very hot oven (450°F.) 12 to 15 minutes. When done, split into 2 parts. Spread with butter and cover bottom halves with sweetened fruit. Top with other halves and cover with fruit. Serve hot with cream, if desired. Serves 6 to 8.

Peach or strawberry shortcake: Follow above recipe.

Special strawberry shortcake: Use *BASIC SPECIAL SHORTCAKE* recipe, reducing shortening to 4 tablespoons and adding 2 eggs, 1 cup orange juice, and ¼ teaspoon lemon extract.

FRUIT COBBLER (Basic Recipe)

1 cup sugar, if unsweetened fresh or canned fruit is used, or ¼ cup sugar, if sweetened canned fruit is used	Cinnamon
4 tablespoons all-purpose flour	2 cups canned fruit and ¾ cup juice or 3 cups diced fruit, either fresh or canned

Mix sugar, flour, and cinnamon. Add juice and mix with fruit. Pour into greased casserole. Arrange biscuits on top. Bake in hot oven (400°F.) 20 minutes. Serves 6.

To make biscuits use: 2 cups sifted all-purpose flour, 4 teaspoons baking powder, 2 tablespoons sugar, ½ teaspoon salt, ½ cup shortening, 1 egg, and ½ cup milk.

Method: Mix and sift flour, baking powder, sugar, and salt. Cut in shortening. Add milk to beaten egg and add to flour mixture to make a soft dough. Pat or roll out on floured board. Cut into desired shapes. Arrange over fruit and bake.

APPLE ROLY-POLY (Basic Recipe)

BISCUIT OR SHORTCAKE DOUGH
4 tablespoons butter
3 tablespoons sugar
½ teaspoon cinnamon

3 or 4 tart apples, chopped
½ cup brown sugar
1 tablespoon lemon juice
½ cup water

Prepare recipe for biscuit or shortcake dough and pat dough into a rectangle about ½ inch thick. Brush with soft butter; sprinkle with sugar and cinnamon mixture. Spread chopped apples over this. Roll like jelly roll. Cut into 1½-inch crosswise slices. Place slices cut side up in a buttered baking dish about 2 inches deep, leaving space between. Make a syrup of brown sugar, lemon juice, and water. Pour over biscuits. Bake in hot oven (400°F.) 30 to 40 minutes. Serve warm, with whipped or plain cream. Serves 6.

Blackberry roly-poly: Substitute 2 cups blackberries for apples.

Blueberry roly-poly: Substitute 2 cups blueberries for apples.

Fruit dumplings: Follow *ROLY-POLY* recipe, patting dough to ¼-inch thickness. Cut into individual servings (squares or triangles). Fill with fruit, moisten edges with milk, pinch together. Bake in the syrup.

Peach roly-poly: Substitute 2 cups diced peaches for apples.

DEEP DISH PLUM DESSERT (Basic Recipe)

3 cups unsweetened chopped plums
¾ cup light corn syrup
¼ teaspoon cinnamon

¼ teaspoon nutmeg
2 tablespoons shortening

Wash, pit, and chop plums. Add corn syrup and spices. Pour into a shallow greased baking dish. Dot plums with 2 tablespoons of shortening. Cover with crust. Serves 6.

To make crust, use: 1½ cups sifted all-purpose flour, 2 teaspoons baking powder, 2 tablespoons sugar, ½ teaspoon salt, 6 tablespoons shortening, and ½ cup milk.

Method: Sift flour with baking powder, sugar, and salt. Cut in shortening. Add milk to make a soft dough. Roll out ½ inch thick. Make several slashes in dough for steam to escape. Place over fruit to fit dish. Sprinkle with 2 tablespoons sugar. Bake in hot oven (400°F.) 45 minutes. Serve warm. Serves 8.

Variations: Apples, blackberries, cranberries, huckleberries, cherries, or peaches may be substituted for plums. Amount of syrup will vary according to fruit used. Sugar and fruit juice may be used instead of corn syrup.

BAKED FRUIT DUMPLINGS

Roll *BISCUIT DOUGH* ¼ inch thick. Cut into 4-inch squares. Use 6 small apples, apricots, or peaches. Place whole fruit, pared and cored or pitted, in center of each square. Sprinkle 1 tablespoon sugar and cinnamon or nutmeg mixture over fruit in each dumpling. Dot with butter. Bring corners up over fruit. Pinch edges together. Prick with fork. Bake in moderate oven (350°F.) 30 minutes. Serve with dessert sauce. One recipe for biscuit dough makes 6 dumplings. The amount of sugar and cinnamon or nutmeg mixture may be varied depending upon individual taste or sweetness of fruit.

STEAMED BERRY DUMPLINGS

Stew enough blueberries, loganberries, or blackberries to make 1 quart. Sweeten to taste with sugar. If desired, use canned berries, heated to boiling point. Roll *BISCUIT DOUGH* to ½ inch thickness. Cut into small biscuits. Drop into boiling berries. Cover and cook 12 to 15 minutes. Serve hot with berry sauce poured over dumplings.

Steamed apple dumplings: Use thin applesauce instead of berries. Proceed as directed for *STEAMED BERRY DUMPLINGS*.

HUNGARIAN PLUM DUMPLINGS

1½ pounds boiled potatoes	12 to 15 freestone plums
2 eggs, slightly beaten	1 teaspoon cinnamon
1 teaspoon salt	½ cup sugar
About 2 cups sifted all-purpose flour	1 cup breadcrumbs
	About ¼ cup butter

Cook potatoes in jackets. Peel and mash. Add eggs and salt. Mix well. Sift in enough flour to make a smooth dough. Roll out to ½ inch thickness on a floured board and cut into 3-inch squares. Pit the plums; fill cavities with cinnamon and sugar. Place a plum on each square. Fold dough around plums to form balls. Cook 10 minutes, covered in boiling salted water. Drain well. Roll dumplings in breadcrumbs which have been browned in butter. Serve hot. Serves 6 to 8.

Variations: Apricots filled with cinnamon and sugar, or sliced and sugared apples, may be substituted for plums.

APPLE PAN DOWDY

Grated rind of ½ lemon	¼ teaspoon salt
2 cups sliced apples	¼ cup milk
¼ cup molasses or	¼ cup melted shortening
¼ cup brown sugar	½ cup sugar
1 cup sifted cake flour	1 egg
1 teaspoon baking powder	

Add grated rind to apples. Place apples in a layer in bottom of a greased baking pan and cover with molasses or brown sugar. Make a batter with remaining ingredients. Pour batter over apples. Bake in moderate oven (350°F.) about 35 minutes. Loosen cake from sides of pan with a spatula. Invert on a large serving plate. Serve with hard sauce or cream. Serves 4 or 5.

APPLE CRISP (Basic Recipe)

4 cups sliced apples, tightly packed	1 cup sugar
½ teaspoon cinnamon	¾ cup sifted all-purpose flour
½ cup water	¼ teaspoon salt
1 teaspoon grated lemon rind	½ cup butter

Arrange apples in shallow, greased casserole. Sprinkle with cinnamon. Add water and lemon rind. Work together sugar, flour, salt, and butter until crumbly. Spread over top. Bake, uncovered, in a moderate oven (350°F.) until apples are tender and top is browned. Serve warm plain or with cream. Serves 6.

Dried prune or dried apricot crisp: Soak 3 cups dried fruit 1 hour or more and substitute for apples.

Peach or pear crisp: Substitute 4 cups sliced peaches or pears for apples.

NOTE: If desired, ¾ cup firmly packed brown sugar may be substituted in basic recipe and all variations. Crushed corn flakes may be used instead of flour.

OLD-FASHIONED APPLE CRISP

6 medium cooking apples
1½ cups moist breadcrumbs
¾ cup sugar
1½ teaspoons cinnamon

1½ tablespoons butter
2 tablespoons grated orange rind
⅓ cup water

Pare, core, and slice apples and place ½ in casserole. Combine breadcrumbs, sugar, and cinnamon and sprinkle ½ over apples. Dot with ½ the butter. Repeat with remaining apples, crumbs, and butter. Sprinkle with orange rind and add water. Cover and bake in moderate oven (375°F.) 45 minutes. Serves 6.

GERMAN APFEL KRAPFEN

¾ pound apples, cored and diced
½ cup sugar
¼ cup white wine or lemon juice
2 ounces candied orange or lemon rind, shredded fine

¾ cup raisins, seeded
1 teaspoon cinnamon
Rich *PIE CRUST DOUGH*

Combine apples, sugar, and wine or lemon juice in a saucepan. Simmer gently until it forms a pulp. Continue cooking gently until thick and dry. Gradually add orange rind, raisins, and cinnamon. Mix well. Roll dough out ⅛ inch thick and cut into 4-inch squares. Fill squares with mixture. Lay another square over the top. Wet edges and pinch together gently all around. Glaze top or not as desired. Bake in a hot oven (450°F.) 10 minutes, then reduce heat to 350°F. and bake 30 minutes longer, or until browned. Three tablespoons apricot jam may be substituted for the candied rind.

BLUEBERRY GRUNT

1⅓ cups blueberries
1½ cups water
⅔ cup sugar
¼ teaspoon salt

1¾ teaspoons baking powder
1⅓ cups sifted all-purpose flour
1 tablespoon shortening
⅓ cup milk or more

Pick over and wash blueberries. Put in a well greased 2-quart casserole. Add water and sugar and put into a hot oven (400°F.). Mix and sift salt, baking powder, and flour. Cut shortening into flour mixture with a knife. Gradually add milk to make a soft dough, handling the mixture as little as possible. When the blueberries have been in the oven about 5 minutes. drop in spoonfuls of the dough. Cover and continue baking about 25 minutes. Serves 5 to 6.

CRANBERRY GRUNT

2 cups cranberries
1 cup chopped apples
½ cup water
⅓ cup and 2 tablespoons sugar
¼ cup and 2 tablespoons butter
¼ teaspoon powdered cloves

½ teaspoon nutmeg
1½ cups sifted flour
3 teaspoons baking powder
¼ teaspoon salt
⅓ cup milk

Simmer cranberries and apples in water about 10 minutes. Blend ⅓ cup sugar, 2 tablespoons butter, and spices with cranberries and apple. Pour 1¾ cups of mixture into a baking dish which has been brushed with butter. To make dough for pinwheels, sift flour, 2 tablespoons sugar, baking powder, and salt. Cut in ¼ cup butter with pastry blender or 2 knives. Add milk, stirring until flour is just moistened. Place on floured board, roll ½ inch thick. Brush with melted butter. Spread remaining cranberry-apple mixture, drained. Roll as for jelly roll. Cut into 1-inch slices. Arrange slices, cut side down, over cranberry mixture. Bake in a hot oven (425°F.) about 20 minutes, or until crust is nicely browned. Serve warm, or chilled with whipped cream. Serves 6.

HESTERLISTE (Snowballs)

1 teaspoon butter
¼ teaspoon salt
1 tablespoon sugar
1 egg
1 tablespoon heavy cream

1 teaspoon brandy (optional)
About 1 cup flour
About ¼ cup confectioners' sugar
1 teaspoon cinnamon

Mix butter, salt, and sugar with the egg. Add cream, brandy, and enough flour to make a stiff dough. Break dough into pieces about the size of a walnut. Roll each piece out separately on a floured board just as thin as possible without tearing (the thinner the better). Make 3 lengthwise slashes in the center of each piece of rolled-out dough and run fork in and out of slashes. Lower into deep, hot fat (not more than a few at a time), and fry until light brown on both sides, turning only once. Remove from fat. Sprinkle with confectioners' sugar and cinnamon. Yield: 12 to 14.

AUF LAUF

1 cup milk
½ cup sifted all-purpose flour

3 eggs, separated
Dash of salt

Bring milk to boiling point and stir flour in quickly. Cook until thick, stirring constantly. Remove from heat and beat in egg yolks, 1 at a time. Beat egg whites with salt until stiff. Fold into batter. Bake in a well-greased casserole in hot oven (425°F.) until brown, about 20 minutes. Serve hot with jelly or preserves. Serves 4 to 6.

desserts—refrigerator

ALMOND REFRIGERATOR CAKE

⅔ cup butter
2 cups powdered sugar
4 eggs, separated
1 teaspoon orange extract

¼ teaspoon almond extract
½ cup shredded almonds
Lady fingers
18 macaroons

Cream butter and sugar. Add egg yolks, beating well. Add flavorings and almonds. Fold in stiffly beaten egg whites. Line mold with lady fingers. Add layer of filling, then a layer of macaroon crumbs. Repeat until 3 layers of filling are used. Cover with macaroons and chill at least 24 hours before serving. Serves 6.

ANGEL FOOD CHOCOLATE TORTE

1 large *ANGEL FOOD CAKE*
1 cup sweet butter
2½ cups confectioners' sugar
1½ teaspoon vanilla
2 squares (2 ounces) melted
   chocolate

6 tablespoons cocoa
⅛ teaspoon salt
2 cups whipping cream
½ cup salted pistachio nuts,
   chopped

Slice cake into 3 layers. Cream butter well. Beat 2 cups confectioners' sugar into the butter and cream well. Add 1 teaspoon vanilla and melted chocolate. Mix well and spread between layers. Mix and sift ½ cup confectioners' sugar, cocoa, and salt. Add to the cream and chill 2 hours or more. Add ½ teaspoon vanilla to cream and whip until stiff. Spread on tops and sides of cake. Sprinkle chopped nuts around sides of cake. Chill thoroughly (2 hours or more) before serving. Serves 12 to 16.

REFRIGERATOR CHEESE CAKE

2 eggs
¼ cup milk
¾ pound cottage cheese
6 tablespoons sugar
2 tablespoons flour
¼ teaspoon salt
½ teaspoon grated lemon rind

¾ teaspoon lemon juice
⅔ cup cream, whipped
½ package zwieback, rolled fine
¼ cup sugar
¼ teaspoon cinnamon
⅛ teaspoon salt
2 tablespoons butter, melted

Beat eggs. Add milk and cottage cheese. Combine 6 tablespoons sugar, flour, ¼ teaspoon salt, and lemon rind. Add to cheese mixture and cook in top of double boiler until thick, about 10 minutes, stirring occasionally. Remove from fire. Add lemon juice. Cool and fold in whipped cream. Combine zwieback crumbs, ¼ cup sugar, cinnamon, ⅛ teaspoon salt, and butter. Line a loaf pan with waxed paper. Arrange cheese and crumb mixtures in alternate layers. Chill in refrigerator about 5 hours, or over night. Serves 6 to 8.

CHOCOLATE TORTE

2 squares bitter chocolate
½ cup sugar
¼ cup milk
4 egg yolks, beaten
1 cup butter

1 cup confectioners' sugar
4 egg whites, stiffly beaten
¼ teaspoon salt
Lady fingers or sponge cake

Melt chocolate over hot water in top of double boiler. Combine ½ cup sugar, milk, and beaten egg yolks. Add to chocolate and cook until thick and smooth. Cool. Cream butter until very soft. Add confectioners' sugar and cream thoroughly. Add chocolate mixture and mix well. Fold in stiffly beaten egg whites to which salt has been added. Pour into straight-sided cake or torte pan that has been lined with lady fingers. Chill in refrigerator several hours. Serve with whipped cream to which crushed peppermint candy has been added. Serves 6.

CHOCOLATE REFRIGERATOR CAKE

4 squares unsweetened chocolate
½ cup sugar
  Dash of salt
¼ cup hot water

4 eggs, separated
1 teaspoon vanilla
1 cup heavy cream, whipped
2 dozen lady fingers

Melt chocolate over hot water. Add sugar, salt, and water, stirring until sugar is dissolved and mixture is blended. Remove from boiling water. Add egg yolks, 1 at a time, beating thoroughly after each addition. Place over boiling water and cook 2 minutes, stirring constantly. Remove from heat. Add vanilla and fold in beaten egg whites. Chill. Fold in whipped cream. Line bottom and sides of a waxed paper-lined mold with lady fingers. Turn chocolate mixture into mold. Place remaining lady fingers on top. Chill over night in refrigerator.

CRANBERRY REFRIGERATOR CAKE

1 egg white
2 cups cranberry sauce
½ cup chopped nutmeats

SPONGE CAKE
½ cup heavy cream, whipped
  and sweetened

Beat egg white until stiff. Combine with cranberry sauce and fold in chopped nutmeats. Slice layers of *SPONGE CAKE* to fit a loaf pan. Alternate layers of cake and sauce until pan is full, finishing with a layer of cake. Place weight on top. Let stand in refrigerator 8 hours. Unmold. Garnish with whipped cream. Cut in slices to serve.

GINGERSNAP REFRIGERATOR CAKE

½ cup soft butter
1 cup confectioners' sugar
2 eggs
1 teaspoon vanilla
1 cup pineapple, cut fine

3 bananas, cut fine
½ cup chopped almonds
¾ cup heavy cream, whipped
½ pound ginger snaps, crushed fine

Cream butter and sugar. Beat in eggs and vanilla. Whip mixture until creamy. Combine fruit, nuts, and whipped cream. Fold in 1 tablespoon confectioners' sugar. Cover bottom of a deep pan with crumbs. Pour creamed mixture over this, and sprinkle with crumb mixture. Add layer of whipped cream mixture. Sprinkle remaining crumbs on top. Chill in refrigerator over night.

MAPLE REFRIGERATOR CAKE (Cooked)

⅔ cup maple syrup
1⅓ cups sweetened condensed milk

½ cup heavy cream, whipped
24 vanilla wafers

Blend syrup and milk and bring slowly to boil in heavy saucepan. Cook gently until thickened, about 4 minutes. Cool and fold in whipped cream. Pour into a waxed paper-lined pan in a thin layer. Cover with layer of wafers. Repeat until all of maple mixture is used. Finish with layer of wafers. Chill in refrigerator 6 hours. Turn out on small platter. Remove waxed paper.

MARSHMALLOW REFRIGERATOR CAKE

2 cups marshmallows, quartered
¾ cup heavy cream
2 cups stale cake crumbs
3 tablespoons chopped nuts

3 tablespoons chopped Maraschino cherries
¼ cup chopped dates

Soak marshmallows in cream ½ hour. Add remaining ingredients. Press mixture into a mold. Let stand in refrigerator over night.

ORANGE REFRIGERATOR CAKE

5 tablespoons lemon juice
½ cup orange juice
1 teaspoon orange rind
⅓ teaspoon grated lemon rind
¼ teaspoon vanilla

3 tablespoons chopped, blanched almonds
1¼ cups sweetened condensed milk
Lady fingers or *SPONGE CAKE*

Combine fruit juices, grated rind, vanilla, almonds, and condensed milk. Line mold with waxed paper. Put layer of lady fingers in bottom. Cover with fruit mixture and another layer of lady fingers, repeating until mixture is used, and topping with lady fingers. Chill over night. Slice to serve.

PEACH REFRIGERATOR CAKE

1⅓ cups sweetened condensed milk
¼ cup lemon juice
1 cup sliced peaches

2 stiffly beaten egg whites
2 dozen chocolate wafers

Blend milk and lemon juice thoroughly. Add sliced peaches. Fold in egg whites. Line pan with waxed paper. Cover with fruit mixture, topping with layer of chocolate wafers. Repeat until fruit mixture is all used, topping with layer of wafers. Chill in refrigerator 6 to 8 hours. Unmold. Remove waxed paper.

PINEAPPLE REFRIGERATOR CAKE

1 cup butter
2¾ cups confectioners' sugar
4 eggs, separated
1 teaspoon lemon extract

30 to 35 lady fingers
1½ cups grated pineapple
1 cup candied cherries
2 cups heavy cream, whipped

Cream butter until soft. Add sugar and cream until fluffy. Beat yolks until lemon colored. Then beat into butter and sugar mixture. Fold in flavoring and stiffly beaten egg whites. Line deep pan with split lady fingers. Cover with ⅓ of mixture. Spread with ½ fruit. Over this spread ½ the whipped cream. Add layer of lady fingers. Repeat, topping with creamed mixture. Chill in refrigerator at least 12 hours.

VANILLA REFRIGERATOR CAKE

Arrange a layer of vanilla wafers in bottom of a loaf pan. Spread slightly sweetened whipped cream over wafers to a depth of about ¼ inch. Then place another layer of wafers and whipped cream, repeating until pan is ¾ full and ending with wafers. Chill in refrigerator over night. Serve with chocolate syrup.

QUICK GINGER ROLL

1 cup whipping cream   18 thin gingersnaps
1 teaspoon almond extract

Whip cream very stiff. Add flavoring and spread on wafers. Pile on top of each other as spread. Lay roll on side on serving dish. Cover top and sides with remaining cream. Chill at least 3 hours. Slice diagonally for serving.

Quick chocolate roll: Use chocolate wafers instead of gingersnaps.

VANILLA REFRIGERATOR PUDDING (Basic Recipe)

¾ cup sweet butter   About 1 teaspoon vanilla
1½ cups powdered sugar   *SPONGE CAKE* or
  6 eggs, separated   *LADY FINGERS*

Cream butter until light and fluffy. Add sugar. Cream well. Add egg yolks, one at a time. Add vanilla or other flavoring. Fold in stiffly beaten egg whites. Line mold with lady fingers or strips of cake. Cover with mixture. Chill in refrigerator 24 hours. Serves 6.

Chocolate: Melt 1½ squares chocolate. Add slowly to first mixture.

Fruit: Add ¼ cup each well-drained crushed pineapple and chopped maraschino cherries to mixture before folding in egg whites.

Lemon: Omit vanilla. Add juice and rind of 1 lemon to first mixture.

Macaroon: Add ¾ cup finely crushed, sifted macaroon crumbs to mixture before folding in egg whites.

desserts—frozen

FROZEN DESSERTS—DEFINITIONS

Frozen desserts are divided basically into three groups (1) ice creams, (2) ices and sherbets, (3) mousses and parfaits. These have bases of either a cream, plain or whipped, or custard, fruit juice or water.

Frappé: The same mixtures as ices or sherbets, frozen only to a mushy consistency

French ice cream: Made with egg yolks or thickening; has a rich custard base.

Ice cream: Made of cream, sweetened and flavored, with or without a custard base or other thickening.

Mousse: Whipped cream, flavored, sweetened and frozen without stirring; made with or without added thickening of gelatin or other material.

Parfait: Whipped cream, flavored, sweetened with sugar, syrup, enriched with egg whites or yolks; frozen without stirring.

Philadelphia ice cream: Made without thickening; light cream, sweetened and flavored.

Sherbet: Ices made of fruit juices, sweetened and combined with water, milk or cream; frozen until firm.

Water ice: Made of fruit juice, sweetened and extended with water. Added gelatin gives ice a velvety texture.

DIRECTIONS FOR FREEZING ICE CREAM

Crank freezer ice cream: Scald can and dasher with boiling water. Drain and cool. Pour cool ice cream mixture into can. Fill only ⅔ full, allowing for expansion. Place can in freezer, adjust dasher and cover. Pack finely crushed ice and ice cream salt (coarse salt) around can, using about 8 parts ice to 1 part salt for ice cream; 6 to 1 for sherbets. Turn dasher slowly (about 40 turns per minute) until ice partially melts and forms a brine (about 5 minutes). Then turn rapidly and constantly (about 100 turns per minute) until crank turns hard. Remove ice from around top of can. Take off lid and remove dasher. Cork opening in lid. Replace lid. Drain off salty water and add enough ice and salt (in proportions of 3 to 1) to refill freezer, heaping it over top of can. Let ice cream ripen 3 to 4 hours.

Mechanical refrigerator ice cream: Refrigerators vary greatly; therefore follow directions for freezing ice cream that come with your refrigerator. If not available, follow these instructions. Set control to coldest setting at least 30 minutes before mixture is ready. Keep at this temperature throughout. For smooth texture in refrigerator ice cream, freeze to consistency of mush. Empty into chilled bowl and beat with rotary beater until smooth and fluffy but not melted. Return quickly to cold tray. Freeze firm. When egg whites are to be folded in last, reserve 2 tablespoons sugar for each egg white. Beat egg whites until foamy, then gradually add sugar while beating until mixture forms peaks. Fold in before final freezing.

CUSTARD ICE CREAM (Basic Recipe)

2 cups milk
1 tablespoon flour
¾ cup sugar
¼ teaspoon salt

2 egg yolks, slightly beaten
2 cups heavy cream
1 tablespoon vanilla

Scald 1½ cups milk. Mix flour, sugar, and salt. Add remaining cold milk. Add scalded milk slowly. Cook over hot water 7 minutes, stirring constantly. Stir hot mixture slowly into egg yolks. Cook and stir 2 minutes longer. Cool. Add cream and vanilla. Freeze. Yield: 1½ quarts.

PHILADELPHIA ICE CREAM (Basic Recipe)

1 quart light cream
1 cup sugar

Dash of salt
2 teaspoons vanilla

Scald cream. Add sugar and stir until dissolved. Add salt and vanilla. Cool and freeze. Yield: 1½ quarts.

GELATIN ICE CREAM (Basic Recipe)

1 tablespoon plain gelatin	⅛ teaspoon salt
2 tablespoons cold water	2 cups light cream
2 cups milk	2 teaspoons vanilla
¾ cup sugar	

Soften gelatin in cold water. Scald milk and add gelatin, sugar and salt. Stir until dissolved. Cool. Add cream and vanilla. Freeze. Yield: 1½ quarts.

FRENCH ICE CREAM (Basic Recipe)

½ cup sugar	2 cups scalded milk
⅛ teaspoon salt	2 cups heavy cream
5 egg yolks, slightly beaten	2 teaspoons vanilla

Mix sugar, salt, and egg yolks. Add scalded milk slowly, mixing well. Cook over hot water until mixture coats spoon (5 to 8 minutes). Cool, strain, and add cream and vanilla. Freeze. Yield: 1½ quarts.

ICE CREAM VARIATIONS
(Use Custard, Gelatin, French, or Philadelphia Recipes)

Bisque: Substitute 2 tablespoons sherry for vanilla. Add ¾ cup chopped nutmeats just before freezing.

Burnt almond: Add 1 cup finely chopped, blanched, and toasted almonds to caramel ice cream mixture.

Butter crunch: Add ¾ pound finely crushed butter crunch to mixture just before freezing.

Caramel: Add ¼ cup caramel flavoring with cream and vanilla.

Chocolate: Melt 2 squares unsweetened chocolate. Add ¼ cup hot water and blend thoroughly. Add to hot mixture.

Coffee: Scald ⅓ cup ground coffee with milk or cream. Strain before adding other ingredients. Omit vanilla.

Grape-nut: Add 1 cup grape-nuts. Use only 1 teaspoon vanilla. Add ½ teaspoon almond extract.

Macaroon: Add 1 cup crushed macaroons just before freezing. Reduce sugar to ½ cup.

Maple: Substitute maple syrup or maple sugar for white sugar. If desired, stir in 1 cup chopped nutmeats when partially frozen.

Mint: Substitute mint flavoring for vanilla; add green coloring.

Peach: Use only 1 teaspoon vanilla; add ½ teaspoon almond extract. Just before freezing, add 2 cups crushed peaches, sweetened with ½ cup sugar.

Peanut brittle: Add ¾ cup finely crushed peanut brittle to mixture just before freezing.

Peppermint: Add ¾ cup finely crushed peppermint stick candy to mixture just before freezing.

Pineapple: Substitute 1 tablespoon lemon juice for vanilla. Add 2 cups well drained, crushed pineapple just before freezing.

Pistachio: Add 1 teaspoon almond extract and green coloring. Add ¾ cup chopped pistachio nuts.

Strawberry or raspberry: Combine 2 cups mashed berries with ½ cup sugar; add just before freezing.

Tutti-frutti: Use only ½ teaspoon vanilla. Combine and add 4 teaspoons maraschino cherry juice, ½ cup chopped maraschino cherries, ½ cup drained crushed pine-apple, and ½ cup chopped nutmeats just before freezing.

REFRIGERATOR ICE CREAM (Cooked Base)

⅔ cup sugar
1½ tablespoons cornstarch
1½ cups top milk
2 eggs, separated

2½ teaspoons vanilla
¼ teaspoon salt
1 cup cream, whipped

Combine sugar and cornstarch in top of double boiler. Gradually stir in milk. Cook over boiling water, stirring constantly, until mixture thickens. Cover and cook 10 minutes. Stir a little of hot mixture into beaten egg yolks. Add yolks to remaining hot mixture. Cook over hot, not boiling, water, stirring constantly for 3 minutes. Cool. Add vanilla and salt. Fold beaten egg whites into cooled custard. Pour into refrigerator tray and freeze until firm throughout. Remove to chilled bowl. Quickly beat with rotary beater until smooth. Fold in whipped cream. Return to cold tray. Freeze. Yield: 6 to 8 servings.

Banana: Add 1 cup sieved ripe bananas and 1 teaspoon lemon juice to chilled mix-ture before folding in whipped cream.

Chocolate: Add 1½ squares melted chocolate to milk and egg mixture. Blend well.

Coffee: Substitute ½ cup strong coffee for ½ cup milk.

Frozen pudding: Combine and add with the whipped cream, ½ teaspoon grated orange rind, ½ cup mixed chopped candied fruit, ¼ cup chopped maraschino cherries, and 3 tablespoons maraschino cherry juice.

Mint: Reduce vanilla to 1 teaspoon. Add oil of peppermint to taste (few drops) and green coloring.

Peach: Add 1¼ cups mashed peaches to chilled mixture just before folding in whipped cream.

Peanut brittle: Add 1 cup crushed peanut brittle before final freezing.

Raspberry or strawberry: Add 1¼ cups crushed berries to chilled mixture just before folding in whipped cream.

REFRIGERATOR ICE CREAM (Uncooked Base)

2 teaspoons gelatin
½ cup cold water
1¾ cups evaporated milk

½ cup sugar
2 teaspoons vanilla
1½ cups heavy cream, whipped

Soften gelatin in cold water. Dissolve in hot milk. Add sugar and vanilla. Cool. Turn into freezing tray and chill until slightly thickened. Fold in whipped cream. Return to tray and freeze to mushlike consistency. Turn into chilled bowl and beat until smooth, but not melted. Return to cold tray and freeze. Yield: 1 quart.

Banana: Add 1 cup ripe mashed bananas and 1 teaspoon lemon juice with whipped cream.

Cherry: Add 1¼ cups chopped pitted cherries to chilled mixture just before folding in whipped cream.

Chocolate: Melt 2 squares chocolate in milk; beat with rotary beater until blended. Increase sugar to ¾ cup. Use only 1 teaspoon vanilla.

Ginger: Add 2 tablespoons ginger syrup with vanilla. Add 3 tablespoons chopped preserved ginger with whipped cream.

Nut brittle: Grind or crush ¼ pound nut brittle and fold in before final freezing.

Orange pecan: Substitute orange juice for milk and increase cream to 2 cups. Fold in 1 cup broken pecan meats before final freezing.

Pistachio: Use only 1 teaspoon vanilla. Add ½ teaspoon almond extract. Add green coloring. Add ½ cup chopped pistachio nuts with whipped cream.

Strawberry: Add 1 cup mashed sweetened berries to cool gelatin-milk mixture before chilling. Use only 1 teaspoon vanilla.

BUTTERSCOTCH ICE CREAM (Refrigerator)

3 tablespoons flour	1¼ cups scalded milk
⅔ cup firmly packed brown sugar	2 teaspoons desired flavoring
¼ teaspoon salt	1 tall can evaporated milk, chilled

Mix flour, sugar, and salt. Stir to smooth paste with some milk. Add to remaining milk in top of double boiler. Cook until thickened, stirring constantly. Cover and cook 10 minutes. Add flavoring and cool. Pour into refrigerator tray, freeze until firm. Whip evaporated milk until it is thick and will hold shape. Fold in pudding mixture and beat with rotary beater until well blended. Pour again into refrigerator tray. Freeze. Yield: 1 quart.

LOGANBERRY ICE CREAM (Refrigerator)

½ cup loganberries	1 tablespoon lemon juice
⅔ cup sweetened condensed milk	1 cup heavy cream, whipped
½ cup water	

Wash and pick over berries. Force through sieve. Mix pulp, milk, water, and lemon juice. Chill. Fold in whipped cream. Turn into freezing tray and freeze 2 to 4 hours or until firm. Stir well twice during freezing. Yield: 1 quart.

Red raspberry ice cream: Substitute red raspberries for loganberries.

Strawberry ice cream: Substitute strawberries for loganberries.

RED PLUM ICE CREAM (Refrigerator)

8 red plums	1 teaspoon gelatin
¾ cup sugar	2 tablespoons cold water
1½ cups water	2 tablespoons lemon juice
2 tablespoons corn syrup	1 cup heavy cream, whipped

Cook plums with sugar and water 15 minutes, or until soft. Remove stones and force pulp through sieve. Add corn syrup and gelatin softened in water. Stir over heat until dissolved. Cool. Add lemon juice and fold in cream. Turn into freezing tray. Freeze 2 to 4 hours or until frozen to desired consistency, stirring once during freezing. Serves 6.

LEMON ICE (Basic Recipe) Crank Freezer Method

1 quart water	¼ teaspoon salt
1¼ to 1½ cups sugar	1 egg white
1 cup strained lemon juice	

Boil water and sugar together 2 minutes, then put aside. When cold, add lemon juice, salt, and unbeaten egg white. Freeze with a mixture of 1 part salt to 4 to 6 parts ice. Turn crank slowly until ice is firm. Remove dasher and pack freezer with more ice and salt. Let ice stand 1 hour or more to ripen.

Berry ice: Make syrup of 1 cup sugar and 2 cups water. Mash 1 quart berries and press through sieve. Add to syrup. Cool and freeze. Raspberries, blackberries, or strawberries may be used.

Cherry ice: Make syrup of 1 cup sugar and 2 cups water. Grind 1 quart pitted cherries and press through sieve. Add to syrup. Cool and freeze.

Grape ice: Make syrup of 1 cup sugar and 2 cups water. Add 2 cups grape juice, ¼ cup orange juice, and 4 tablespoons lemon juice. Cool, strain, and freeze.

Lime ice: Substitute lime juice for lemon juice. Add green coloring.

Mint ice: To lemon ice, add ¼ teaspoon mint flavoring and 2 tablespoons finely minced mint leaves.

Orange ice: Make syrup of 1 cup sugar and 2 cups water. Add 2 cups orange juice and 4 tablespoons lemon juice. Cool, strain, and freeze.

ICES (Basic Recipe) Mechanical Refrigerator Method

⅔ cup sugar	1½ teaspoons gelatin
Pinch of salt	3 tablespoons water
1½ cups water	Fruit juice, as desired

Boil sugar, salt, and water 5 minutes. Soak gelatin in 3 tablespoons water. Dissolve in hot syrup. Cool and add fruit juices (see variations below). Freeze in freezing tray to a mush-like consistency. Remove to a chilled bowl; break into small pieces. Beat with rotary beater until fluffy (1 to 2 minutes). Return to freezing tray and freeze until firm.

Berry ice: Use 2 cups red raspberries or strawberries crushed and sieved and 1 tablespoon lemon juice.

Cherry ice: Use 2 cups ground cherries and juice, 1 tablespoon lemon juice, and few grains nutmeg. Omit ½ cup water.

Cranberry ice: Use 2 cups cooked strained cranberries.

Lemon or lime ice: Use ⅓ cup of lemon or lime juice.

Mint ice: To lemon ice add ¼ teaspoon peppermint flavoring and 2 tablespoons finely minced mint leaves.

Orange ice: Add 1 tablespoon grated orange rind to hot syrup and cool. Use 1½ cups orange juice and 2 tablespoons lemon juice.

ORANGE SHERBET (Basic Recipe) Crank Freezer Method

2 cups milk and 1 cup cream or 3 cups rich milk	1½ cups orange juice
1¼ cups sugar	2 tablespoons lemon juice
	¼ teaspoon salt

Heat 1 cup milk. Add sugar and stir until dissolved. Add other ingredients. Use freezing mixture of 1 part salt to 4 to 6 parts ice. Turn crank freezer slowly. After freezing, remove dasher. Pack freezer with more ice and salt. Let sherbet stand an hour or more to ripen. Yield: about 3 pints.

Lemon sherbet: Omit orange juice. Use 1 cup lemon juice and ½ cup water.

Pineapple sherbet: Substitute 1 cup drained crushed pineapple for ½ cup orange juice.

BASIC SHERBET RECIPE—Mechanical Refrigerator Method

2 teaspoons gelatin	Pinch of salt
2¼ cups cold water	Fruit and juice as desired
1 cup sugar	2 egg whites

Soak gelatin in ¼ cup cold water. Cook sugar and 2 cups water together 2 to 3 minutes. Add soaked gelatin and dissolve thoroughly. Add salt and fruit juice. Freeze in freezing tray to mush-like consistency. Remove mixture to a chilled bowl and break into small pieces. Add unbeaten egg whites and beat until fluffy (1 minute). Turn into cold trays and freeze until firm. Serves 6.

Apricot sherbet: Use 2 cups apricot pulp and 2 tablespoons lemon juice.

Lemon or lime sherbet: Use ½ cup of lemon or lime juice and rind of ½ lemon.

Orange sherbet: Omit 1 cup of water. Use 1½ cups orange juice, rind of ½ orange, and ¼ cup lemon juice.

Peach and cherry sherbet: Use 1½ cups peach pulp, 2 tablespoons orange juice, and ¼ cup maraschino cherries, diced fine.

Pineapple sherbet: Use 1 cup crushed pineapple and 1 tablespoon lemon juice.

Raspberry sherbet: Use 1½ cups crushed fresh or canned raspberries and 2 tablespoons lemon juice.

ORANGE CREAM SHERBET (Refrigerator Method)

¾ cup granulated sugar	1 tablespoon lemon juice
¾ cup water	½ cup coffee cream
Grated rind of 1 orange	2 egg whites
1½ cups orange juice	Few grains salt

Cook sugar and water together slowly 10 minutes. Add grated rind, cooking 2 minutes longer. Strain. Add syrup to fruit juices. Cool. Pour into freezing tray. Freeze until firm. Remove to a chilled bowl and beat quickly until light. Add coffee cream. Fold in stiffly beaten egg whites to which the salt has been added. Turn into tray and freeze. If mixture separates, stir occasionally. Serves 6 to 8.

PEACH MILK SHERBET

1½ cups mashed or sieved ripe peaches	1 cup heavy cream or 1 tall can evaporated milk, whipped
½ cup sugar	2 tablespoons lemon juice

Mix peaches and sugar. Stir until sugar is dissolved. Mix whipped cream or milk with lemon juice and fold in sweetened peaches. Pour into freezing trays and freeze quickly. Makes about 3 pints.

NOTE: This must be eaten when first frozen. Texture becomes unsatisfactory in a short time.

VANILLA PARFAIT (Basic Recipe)

1 cup sugar
¾ cup water
2 egg whites

¼ teaspoon salt
1 tablespoon vanilla
1½ cups heavy cream

Boil sugar and water to 230°F. or until it forms a thread. Beat egg whites until frothy. Add salt and beat until stiff but not dry. Slowly pour hot syrup over egg whites, beating constantly. Continue beating until mixture is cool and holds shape. Add vanilla and fold in whipped cream. Turn into chilled trays and freeze until firm. Serve with additional whipped cream, fruits, and nuts. Serves 8.

Banana parfait: Fold in 1 cup mashed ripe banana with whipped cream. Omit vanilla. Add 1 teaspoon lemon juice.

Chocolate parfait: Add 2 squares unsweetened shaved chocolate to hot syrup. Beat with rotary beater until blended before adding other ingredients.

Coffee parfait: Substitute ¾ cup of strong coffee for water.

Maple parfait: Substitute 1 cup hot maple syrup for sugar syrup.

Maraschino cherry parfait: Substitute ¼ cup maraschino cherry juice for equal amount of water in making syrup. Add ⅓ cup or more diced maraschino cherries with whipped cream.

Pineapple parfait: Add 1 cup crushed well drained pineapple and 1½ tablespoons lemon juice with whipped cream. Omit vanilla.

Strawberry or raspberry parfait: Add 2 cups crushed berries and 1¼ tablespoons lemon juice with whipped cream. Omit vanilla.

Toasted coconut parfait: Add ½ cup toasted shredded coconut with whipped cream.

GOLDEN PARFAIT (Basic Recipe)

½ cup sugar
¼ cup water
4 egg yolks

Few grains salt
1½ teaspoons vanilla
1½ cups whipping cream

Boil sugar and water together. Pour slowly over well-beaten egg yolks. Cook until mixture coats spoon. Cool. Add salt and vanilla. Fold in whipped cream. Turn into chilled tray. Freeze until firm. Serve with additional whipped cream, if desired.

Butterscotch parfait: Substitute ⅔ cup brown sugar for white and add 2 tablespoons butter.

Maple nut parfait: Substitute ½ cup maple syrup for sugar and water. Heat syrup over low heat and proceed as directed. Add ½ cup chopped nuts.

VANILLA MOUSSE (Basic Recipe)

1 teaspoon gelatin
1 cup light cream or rich milk
6 tablespoons sugar
¹⁄₁₆ teaspoon salt

1 cup heavy cream
½ teaspoon vanilla
2 egg whites

Soak gelatin until soft in little cream or milk. Heat remainder and pour over gelatin. Add sugar and salt, stir until dissolved. Chill. Whip heavy cream. When gelatin mixture has thickened slightly, beat to incorporate air. Add vanilla. Fold in whipped cream and well-beaten egg whites. Freeze until firm. Yield: about 1 quart.

Apple sauce mousse: Omit vanilla. Add 2 cups cinnamon-flavored apple sauce and 2 tablespoons lemon juice with the cream.

Banana mousse: Add 1 cup mashed ripe banana and 2 teaspoons lemon juice with whipped cream.

Burnt almond mousse: Melt 8 teaspoons sugar carefully and stir in ½ cup ground almonds. Heat until almonds are browned. Add to milk or light cream. Add ¼ teaspoon almond extract. Omit vanilla.

Chocolate mousse: Add 2 squares unsweetened chocolate to milk or light cream. Add ½ cup sugar. Heat in top of double boiler, beating with rotary beater until blended.

Coffee mousse: Substitute ½ cup strong coffee for ½ cup light cream.

Maple mousse: Substitute ⅓ cup maple syrup for sugar.

Peach mousse: Add 2 cups peach pulp and ¼ cup sugar. Omit vanilla. Add ¼ teaspoon almond extract.

Peanut brittle mousse: Substitute ¼ pound finely ground peanut brittle candy for sugar.

Peppermint mousse: Substitute ¼ pound crushed peppermint stick candy for sugar. Add green coloring.

Strawberry or raspberry mousse: Add 1 to 2 cups crushed berries and 1 to 2 tablespoons lemon juice with whipped cream. Omit vanilla.

APRICOT MOUSSE

1 cup dried apricots (⅓ pound)	1 tall can evaporated milk
1 cup hot water	(1⅔ cups), chilled
½ cup sugar	3 tablespoons lemon juice
¼ cup orange juice (optional)	

Wash apricots in cold water. Pour the hot water over them and cook slowly in a covered pan until tender. Press through a coarse sieve. Mix apricot pulp, sugar, and orange juice and stir until sugar is dissolved. Chill. Whip milk very stiff. Fold in lemon juice, then fruit mixture. Pour at once into cold freezing trays. Freeze until firm. Yield: 3 pints.

Prune mousse: Wash 1 cup prunes in cold water. Pour 1 cup cold water over them and soak for 2 hours. Simmer slowly in same water in a covered pan until tender. Press through a coarse sieve. Substitute prunes for apricots in *APRICOT MOUSSE* and decrease sugar to ¼ cup.

CRANBERRY MOUSSE

1 can cranberry sauce (1½ cups)	1 cup evaporated milk, chilled
¼ cup orange juice	2 tablespoons lemon juice

Mash cranberry sauce. Add orange juice. Whip milk very stiff. Fold in lemon juice and cranberry mixture. Pour at once into cold freezing trays. Freeze until firm. Yield: 1 quart.

NOTE: Fresh cranberries can be used. Cook 2½ cups cranberries with 1¼ cups water slowly until tender. Press through a coarse sieve. Add 1¼ cups sugar and boil 10 minutes. Chill, then proceed as above.

GOLDEN MOUSSE

1 cup mashed ripe bananas
2 tablespoons orange juice
¼ cup shredded coconut
3 tablespoons brown sugar

Few grains salt
⅛ teaspoon grated orange rind
1 cup heavy cream, whipped

Combine all ingredients. Fold in stiffly whipped cream. Turn into freezing tray. Freeze rapidly, without stirring, until firm. Serves 6 to 8.

PEACH MOUSSE #2

1½ cups mashed peaches
    (4 to 5 medium-sized)
½ cup sugar

1 tall can evaporated milk
    (1⅔ cups), chilled
2 tablespoons lemon juice

Select ripe, fine-flavored peaches. Peel and stone. Mash with fork or potato masher. Add sugar and stir occasionally until it is dissolved. Whip milk very stiff. Fold in lemon juice, then peaches. Pour at once into cold freezing trays. Freeze until firm. Yield: 3 pints.

Banana mousse: Use mashed bananas in place of peaches in PEACH MOUSSE recipe. Increase lemon juice to 3 tablespoons. Add 1 teaspoon grated lemon rind.

Pineapple mousse: Substitute an equal quantity of canned crushed pineapple for peaches in PEACH MOUSSE.

PISTACHIO MOUSSE

Whip 1 cup cream until it is just fluffy and will hold its shape, but not until stiff. Carefully fold in 1 tablespoon powdered sugar, 1 teaspoon vanilla, 1 teaspoon almond extract, a few drops of green coloring, and ½ cup chopped pistachio nuts. Pour into chilled tray. Freeze until firm. Yield: 1 pint.

STRAWBERRY MOUSSE

2 cups strawberries
¾ cup sugar
¼ cup water
½ teaspoon cream of tartar

Few grains salt
2 egg whites, beaten stiff
½ pint heavy cream, whipped

Wash and hull berries. Mash and force through a coarse sieve. Combine sugar, water, cream of tartar, and salt in saucepan and cook to thread stage (230° to 235°F.). Pour hot syrup onto beaten whites, beating constantly until mixture will hold a point. Fold in strawberry pulp and whipped cream. Turn into refrigerator tray and freeze at least 1 hour.

Variations: Use raspberries or blackberries in place of strawberries. Strain blackberry pulp through a fine sieve to eliminate seeds.

VANILLA MARLOW

30 marshmallows
¾ cup milk or water

2 teaspoons vanilla
1½ cups heavy cream, whipped

Melt marshmallows in hot milk or water. Cool. Add flavoring. Chill. When mixture begins to thicken, combine with whipped cream. Pour into tray and freeze without stirring.

Banana marlow: Omit vanilla. Add 1 cup mashed ripe banana and 1 tablespoon lemon juice to hot milk.

Chocolate marlow: Add 2 squares melted chocolate to hot milk.

Peach marlow: Add 2 cups peach pulp and 1 tablespoon lemon juice to hot milk. Substitute 1 teaspoon almond extract for vanilla.

BISCUIT TORTONI

1 cup milk
3 eggs, separated
¾ cup sugar
⅛ teaspoon salt

¾ cup crumbled macaroons
2 teaspoons vanilla
¼ cup maraschino cherries, chopped
1 cup cream, whipped

Scald milk. Add gradually to beaten egg yolks which have been mixed with sugar. Cook in top of double boiler for 5 minutes, stirring constantly. Cool. Fold in stiffly beaten egg whites beaten with salt. Add crumbled macaroons, vanilla, and chopped cherries. Fold in whipped cream; freeze in refrigerator tray, or in individual cups. Sprinkle crumbled macaroons over the top. Serves 6.

Variation: Use sherry instead of vanilla flavoring.

BAKED ALASKA

1 to 1½ inch *SPONGE CAKE*
1 quart ice cream

4 egg whites
½ cup confectioners' sugar

Cover a bread board with heavy wrapping paper. Arrange cake on paper and ice cream on cake. Have cake extend ½ inch beyond edge of cream. Beat egg whites until stiff. Gradually add sugar and continue beating until stiff. Spread meringue over entire surface of ice cream and cake edge. Sprinkle generously with confectioners' sugar (about ¼ cup). Place in hot oven (450°F.) until lightly browned, 3 to 5 minutes. The board, paper, cake, and meringue are poor conductors of heat and prevent ice cream from melting. Serves 6 to 8.

Individual baked alaska: Cut individual rounds or squares of sponge cake. Cover and bake as above.

Fruit alaska: Cover cake with a layer of fresh or stewed fruit. Arrange ice cream on top. Cover with meringue. Bake as above.

Rum alaska: Place 2 half egg shells open side up in top of meringue before baking. Bake; fill shells with rum. Set aflame and serve.

With nuts: Sprinkle chopped nutmeats over meringue.

FROZEN FRUIT PUDDING

¼ cup milk
¼ cup sugar
⅛ teaspoon salt
½ teaspoon grated orange rind

½ teaspoon vanilla
5 teaspoons maraschino cherry juice
½ cup mixed cut fruit
1 cup cream, whipped

Combine ingredients and slowly fold into whipped cream. Pour into chilled tray. Freeze to desired consistency. For the fruit use raisins, cherries, pineapple, and citron. Serves 6.

GRAHAM CRACKER PUDDING (Basic Recipe)

2 cups graham cracker crumbs
10 marshmallows, quartered
1 cup walnuts, chopped
½ cup confectioners' sugar

1 teaspoon vanilla
1 cup shredded coconut
½ cup cream
½ cup cream, whipped

Mix crumbs, marshmallows, walnuts, sugar, vanilla, coconut, and cream. Pack into refrigerator tray lined with wax paper. Freeze until firm. To serve, slice with knife dipped in hot water. Top with whipped cream. Serves 8 to 10.

Macaroon crumb pudding: Substitute 2 cups macaroon crumbs for graham crackers.

Pineapple crumb pudding: Substitute ½ cup crushed pineapple for coconut and ½ cup pineapple juice for ½ cup cream.

Prune crumb pudding: Substitute 1 cup cooked prune pulp for ½ cup cream.

Vanilla or chocolate crumb pudding: Substitute 2 cups vanilla or chocolate crumbs for graham crackers.

FROZEN VANILLA CUSTARD

1 egg, separated
¼ cup sugar
½ teaspoon vanilla extract

1 small can evaporated milk
   (⅔ cup), chilled

Beat egg yolk. Add sugar and vanilla. Beat until sugar is dissolved. Beat egg white stiff. Fold into yolk mixture. Whip milk very stiff. Fold in egg mixture lightly. Pour at once into cold freezing tray. Freeze until firm. Yield: 1 pint.

Chocolate chip: Fold in 2 squares semi-sweet chocolate, shaved or grated, after combining egg and sugar mixture with whipped milk.

Cocoa: Omit sugar. Use in its place a syrup made by blending ¼ cup sugar, ¼ cup cocoa, and ½ cup water and boiling until thick. Chill syrup, then add to the beaten egg yolk.

Lemon: Omit vanilla. Fold 3 tablespoons lemon juice and ½ teaspoon grated lemon rind into whipped milk before adding egg and sugar mixture.

Peanut brittle: Fold ⅔ cup crushed peanut brittle into egg and sugar mixture, then add to whipped milk.

eggs and cheese

COOKING HINTS

One general rule applies to all egg and cheese cookery. They should always be cooked at low or moderate temperatures. Too high temperatures and prolonged cooking make cheese tough and stringy and toughen whites of eggs. When cooking eggs, water should be kept below boiling point. Fat should be kept below point at which it smokes and the egg sputters. For baked dishes oven heat should be moderate and the baking dish containing the food should be set in a pan of hot water. Always remove eggs from refrigerator in ample time to have them at room temperature before cooking. If whites and yolks are to be separated, do this immediately upon taking them from refrigerator.

EGGS COOKED IN THE SHELL

Cover eggs completely with cold water and bring gradually to simmering (just below boiling). Do not let the water boil.

Coddled eggs: Bring water to boiling. Put eggs in carefully and take the pan off the stove at once. Cover pan to hold steam and let the eggs cook in the hot water 5 to 8 minutes.

Hard-cooked eggs: Simmer 25 to 30 minutes. Serve hot in shell or plunge eggs into cold water and remove shell.

Soft-cooked eggs: Simmer 3 to 5 minutes. Break hot into cup for serving.

SCRAMBLED EGGS (Basic Recipe)

5 eggs
½ cup milk or cream
½ teaspoon salt
⅛ teaspoon pepper
2 tablespoons butter

Beat eggs, milk, and seasoning slightly. Melt butter in skillet or top of double boiler. Pour in eggs and cook until soft and creamy, stirring and scraping mixture from bottom and sides of pan occasionally. Serve at once on warm dish. Garnish with parsley and dash of paprika. Serves 4.

Cheese scramble: Place scrambled eggs on toast. Cover with grated cheese and brown in oven.

Cream cheese rabbit: Use ⅔ cup milk. When almost done crumble and stir in 1 small package (3 ounces) cream cheese. Serve on toast.

Fish scramble: Add ½ cup cooked, flaked fish.

Green pepper scramble: Remove seeds and membranes from 2 medium green peppers. Parboil 5 minutes. Chop fine. Add when eggs begin to thicken.

Mushroom scramble: Drain and chop canned mushrooms. Add to egg mixture before cooking. If fresh mushrooms are used, chop and sauté in fat before adding egg mixture.

Savory scrambled eggs: Add 1 tablespoon chopped parsley, ½ teaspoon grated onion, and ½ tablespoon chopped chives.

Scrambled eggs with cottage cheese: Reduce milk to ¼ cup. Add ½ to ¾ cup cottage cheese and 1 tablespoon chopped chives or parsley when eggs are almost done.

Scrambled eggs with sour cream: Substitute sour cream for milk. Add chopped young onions, if desired.

Scrambled eggs with toast cubes: Sauté 1 cup toast cubes until golden brown before adding egg mixture.

Spinach scramble: Add ½ cup well-drained, finely chopped cooked spinach.

Tomato scramble: Add ½ cup cooked tomatoes.

Vegetable scramble: Add ½ cup chopped cooked vegetables.

POACHED EGGS (Basic Recipe)

Fill heavy shallow pan ⅔ full of water to which ⅛ teaspoon salt has been added. Bring to boiling point. Break eggs into a saucer and slip into gently boiling, salted water. Bring to simmering, remove from heat and cover. Let stand about 5 minutes, or until eggs are as firm as you want them. Remove eggs carefully with a skimmer or perforated spoon and serve on toast. Add salt and pepper to taste. Egg poachers may be used to help keep the shape of the egg. One tablespoon of vinegar may be added to each quart of water to help set the white of egg.

Poached eggs and corned beef hash: Serve poached eggs on cakes of corned beef hash. Garnish with parsley.

Poached eggs au gratin: Arrange poached eggs in shallow, buttered baking dish. Pour over medium white sauce. Sprinkle with grated cheese. Brown in slow oven (325°F.).

Poached eggs in cheese sauce: Pour 2 cups cheese sauce into shallow pan. Poach eggs in sauce. Serve on buttered toast.

Poached eggs in milk: Substitute milk for water in poaching eggs. Pour milk over toast.

Poached eggs on creamed toast: Pour hot white sauce over toast. Place poached egg on each slice. Sprinkle with chopped parsley.

Poached egg oriental: Mix cooked rice with white sauce. Season with grated onion and minced celery. Top each serving with poached egg.

Spinach and eggs: Serve poached eggs on bed of well-seasoned cooked spinach. Top with cheese sauce.

FRIED EGGS

Break each egg into small dish and slip into frying pan containing melted fat. Cook over low heat until the whites are firm. To cook tops, baste hot fat over eggs, or cover tightly with a lid. To cook on both sides flip eggs over when white is partially firm and cook until set. Sprinkle with salt and pepper and serve at once.

BAKED (Shirred) EGGS

Place 1 tablespoon cream in each buttered ramekin or custard cup. Break an egg into each, season with salt and pepper. Place cups on baking sheet and bake in slow oven (325°F.) until eggs are firm (15 to 20 minutes).

Baked eggs in noodle cups: Make nest of seasoned cooked noodles in each cup. Break an egg in each and bake until set.

Baked eggs in potato cups: Make nest of seasoned mashed potatoes. Break egg in each and bake. For additional flavoring add finely chopped chives.

Baked eggs in rice cups: Line cups with cooked rice. Break an egg into each. Bake in slow oven (325°F.) until eggs are set, 15 to 20 minutes. Serve with hot cheese sauce.

Baked eggs in toast cups: Cut crust from slices of bread and gently press bread into greased cups. The four corners will extend up to the tops of the custard cups, forming a cup. Break an egg into each cup. Season with salt and pepper. Dot with butter or add 1 tablespoon cream for each egg. Bake for 15 minutes in moderate oven (350°F.).

Baked eggs in tomatoes: Cut a slice from stem end of each tomato. Remove enough pulp so that an egg may be placed in each. Season with salt and pepper. Cover with buttered breadcrumbs. Arrange in pan or cups. Bake in slow oven (325°F.) until crumbs are brown and eggs are set, about 25 minutes.

Baked eggs with cheese: Sprinkle grated cheese over each egg or mix grated cheese with bread crumbs and sprinkle over eggs.

Baked eggs with crumbs: Dot eggs with butter. Sprinkle with seasoned fine, dry breadcrumbs. Bake until eggs are set and crumbs lightly browned.

Eggs florentine: Place 3 or 4 tablespoons chopped, cooked spinach in each cup. Season with salt and pepper. Dot with butter. Drop an egg in each and sprinkle with fine breadcrumbs. Bake 10 minutes in slow oven (325°F.), then sprinkle with grated cheese and bake additional 10 minutes.

CREAMED EGGS (Basic Recipe)

Blend ¼ cup flour thoroughly with ¼ cup melted fat. Gradually add 2 cups milk. Cook over hot water, stirring constantly, until thick. Quarter 6 hard-cooked eggs, add to sauce, season with salt and pepper, and heat. Serve on hot toast. Optional: 2 teaspoons of Worcestershire sauce or grated onion may be added. Serves 4.

Creamed eggs with tomatoes: Sauté or broil 1-inch-thick slices of tomatoes. Arrange tomato slices on toast. Cover with creamed eggs.

Curried eggs: Season sauce with curry.

Eggs à la king: Add ½ to 1 cup sliced cooked mushrooms, ½ cup cooked peas, and 1 pimiento (canned) sliced in thin strips to creamed mixture. Heat thoroughly. Broil thick slices of tomato for 5 minutes. Place one slice on each serving of buttered hot toast, and pour over creamed mixture.

Eggs goldenrod: Separate whites and yolks. Chop or slice whites and add to sauce. Press yolks through sieve and sprinkle over each serving. Sprinkle with paprika.

PUFFY OMELET (Basic Recipe)

4 eggs, separated
½ teaspoon salt
Pinch of pepper

4 tablespoons milk
1 tablespoon butter

Beat yolks until thick. Add salt, pepper, and milk. Beat egg whites until they form peaks. Fold whites into yolks. Pour into well buttered hot skillet, spreading mixture evenly and cooking slowly until omelet puffs up and is firm on the bottom. Bake in moderate oven (350°F.) until top is slightly dry, about 5 minutes, and springs back when pressed lightly with finger tip. Cut about halfway through omelet at the center; fold over with a spatula. Serve immediately on hot platter. Serves 2 or 3.

Cheese omelet: Add 2 tablespoons grated cheese to egg yolk mixture.

Jelly omelet: Spread jelly on omelet before folding.

Onion omelet: Sauté minced onion in butter. Fold in before cooking.

Parsley omelet: Add 2 tablespoons minced parsley when folding in egg whites.

Potato omelet: Add ½ cup seasoned mashed potatoes to egg yolk mixture.

Puffy omelet with sauce: Pour cheese, tomato, or mushroom sauce over omelet after folding.

Rice omelet: Add ⅓ cup cooked rice and ½ teaspoon tomato ketchup to egg yolk mixture.

Tomato omelet: Cover half of omelet with slices of broiled or grilled tomato before folding, or serve omelet with hot tomato sauce.

FRENCH OMELET (Basic Recipe)

6 eggs
⅓ cup milk
¾ teaspoon salt

⅛ teaspoon of pepper
2 tablespoons butter

Beat eggs until whites and yolks are well mixed. Add milk, salt, and pepper. Melt butter in skillet. Pour in mixture and place over moderate heat. While cooking, lift edges and tip skillet so uncooked mixture flows under cooked portion. When bottom is browned fold over. Serves 3 to 4.

Cheese omelet: Sprinkle with ¼ cup grated American cheese before folding.

Crouton omelet: Sauté 1 cup small bread cubes in butter. Add to mixture.

Mushroom omelet: Sauté ½ to 1 cup chopped mushrooms in butter for 3 or 4 minutes. Add egg mixture and cook as directed.

Noodle omelet: Boil and drain 3 ounces noodles. Fry in fat until golden brown. Add 4 eggs lightly beaten and seasoned with salt and pepper. Turn into a hot greased frying pan and cook slowly until set and browned on the bottom. Fold onto a hot platter.

Rum omelet: Omit milk and decrease salt to ⅛ teaspoon. Add 2 tablespoons of water, 2 teaspoons powdered sugar, and 2 tablespoons rum to beaten eggs. Cook as directed. After turning omelet onto hot platter pour 3 to 4 tablespoons rum around it. Ignite rum and serve at once. Sprinkle omelet with additional sugar if desired.

Savory omelet: Add to egg mixture 3 tablespoons minced parsley and ¼ teaspoon each of minced fresh or dried thyme or 2 tablespoons finely chopped chives.

Sweet omelet: Omit pepper. Add 1½ tablespoons confectioners' sugar and ½ teaspoon vanilla. Serve, sprinkled with confectioners' sugar.

Vegetable omelet: Sauté 2 tablespoons minced onion in butter. Add ½ to 1 cup canned or cooked peas, lima beans, or mixture of vegetables. Season to taste and heat. Pour over omelet before folding or add to white sauce and pour over folded omelet.

ITALIAN OMELET

6 tablespoons olive oil	¼ teaspoon salt
2 tablespoons butter	Dash pepper
2 cups sliced or chopped zucchini	1 tablespoon grated parmesan-type
4 eggs	cheese
3 tablespoons chopped parsley	

Heat 2 tablespoons of the oil and 1 tablespoon of the butter in a frying pan. Add zucchini and cook slowly, stirring often, until vegetable is limp and lightly browned, or about 5 minutes. Cool thoroughly. Beat eggs until fluffy. Add parsley, salt, pepper, cheese, and cooled zucchini. Heat remaining oil and butter in a clean pan. Add egg-zucchini mixture and cook over a moderately high flame, lifting mixture around edge, until only center remains uncooked. Place under a very low broiler flame and cook until center is firm. Turn out on a platter and cut into pie-shaped wedges to serve. Serves 2.

SMOKED SALMON (Lox) AND EGGS ON TOAST

Thin slices of smoked salmon	Poached or fried eggs
Buttered toast	

Dip the salmon into boiling water. Drain and place on toast. Cover with poached or fried eggs.

DEVILED EGGS

6 hard-cooked eggs, shelled	¾ teaspoon prepared mustard
1 tablespoon cream or mayonnaise	½ teaspoon Worcestershire sauce
1½ teaspoons vinegar	(optional)
Dash of pepper	¼ teaspoon salt

Cut eggs in halves lengthwise. Remove yolk, force through sieve. Add seasonings and beat until smooth and fluffy. Fill egg whites with mixture. Garnish tops with dash of paprika, chopped parsley, or chopped chives.

Hot deviled eggs: If desired, substitute cream or evaporated milk for mayonnaise. To serve, heat eggs in top of double boiler and serve with hot cheese or tomato sauce. Serve on buttered hot toast or arrange around boiled rice ring.

Savory deviled eggs: Season to taste with additional seasonings such as onion juice, sardine, cheese, anchovies, pickles, olives, or chives.

POACHED EGGS À LA REINE

Place circular pieces of toast in baking dish. Cover with sliced fresh mushrooms sautéed in butter and moistened with cream. Poach eggs and arrange on mushrooms. Pour over this a medium white sauce to which Parmesan cheese has been added. Sprinkle with grated cheese. Brown in moderate oven (375°F.).

ESCALLOPED EGGS AND CHEESE

4½ tablespoons melted butter
1½ tablespoons flour
1 cup milk
¼ teaspoon salt
⅛ teaspoon paprika

⅛ teaspoon pepper
1 cup breadcrumbs
6 hard-cooked eggs, sliced
½ cup grated sharp cheese
1 teaspoon Worcestershire sauce

Prepare white sauce of 1½ tablespoons butter, flour, milk, and seasonings. Arrange in greased casserole in layers: half the crumbs, eggs, cheese, and sauce. Top with remaining crumbs mixed with 3 tablespoons butter. Bake in a moderate oven (375°F.) until sauce is bubbly and delicately browned, about 40 minutes. Serve plain, or with tomato sauce. Serves 6.

CHEESE FONDUE (Basic Recipe)

1 cup milk, scalded
1 cup soft bread cubes
1 tablespoon butter
½ teaspoon salt

⅛ teaspoon pepper
1¼ cups grated American cheese
3 eggs, separated

Scald milk over hot water; add bread cubes, butter, and seasonings. Add cheese and stir over low heat until melted. Stir portion of cheese mixture into well beaten yolks. Add remaining cheese mixture. Cool slightly. Fold in egg whites beaten stiff but not dry. Pour into baking dish with bottom only greased. Set in pan of hot water. Bake in moderate oven (350°F.) until knife inserted in center comes out clean, 50 to 60 minutes. Serve at once. Serves 6.

Fish fondue: Substitute 1 cup finely flaked cooked or canned fish for cheese. Add just before folding in egg whites.

Vegetable fondue: Substitute 1 cup finely chopped or ground cooked or canned vegetables for cheese. Add just before folding in egg whites.

EGG AND COTTAGE CHEESE SOUFFLE

4 eggs, separated
1 cup cottage cheese
1 cup thin cream

About 1 teaspoon salt
¼ teaspoon pepper

Beat yolks slightly. Mix with cottage cheese, cream, and seasonings. Fold in stiffly beaten egg whites. Pour into greased baking dish. Set in pan of hot water. Bake in moderate oven (350°F.) until set and top is slightly browned, or until knife inserted in center comes out clean. Serve at once. Serves 4.

CHEESE SOUFFLE (Basic Recipe)

¼ cup butter
¼ cup flour
1 cup milk
1 cup grated sharp American cheese

½ teaspoon salt
½ teaspoon mustard (optional)
Few grains pepper
4 eggs, separated

Melt butter. Stir in flour. Gradually add milk and cook about 5 minutes, stirring constantly until mixture thickens. Add cheese and seasonings. Stir until melted. Add some of hot sauce slowly to beaten yolks, mixing thoroughly. Add egg mixture to remainder of sauce. Cut and fold in stiffly beaten egg whites. Pour into greased casserole and set in shallow pan of hot water. Bake in a slow oven (325°F.) until set and a light golden brown, 30 to 40 minutes. Serves 6.

Chive cheese soufflé: Add ½ teaspoon finely chopped chives and 1 teaspoon finely chopped parsley with the stiffly beaten egg whites.

Coffee soufflé: Follow recipe for *FRENCH SOUFFLE*, substituting ¾ cup strong coffee and ¼ cup sweet cream for milk. Double quantity of sugar.

Egg soufflé: Omit cheese. Proceed as directed.

Fish soufflé: Substitute 1 cup cooked flaked fish for cheese.

French soufflé: Omit cheese and seasonings. Add ¼ cup sugar. Serve as dessert.

Mushroom cheese soufflé: Sauté ½ cup finely chopped mushrooms in butter for a few minutes. Add with stiffly beaten egg whites.

Tomato cheese soufflé: Substitute 1 cup tomato juice for milk.

Vegetable soufflé: Substitute 1 cup finely chopped or ground vegetables for cheese.

TOP-OF-THE-RANGE SOUFFLE

1½ cups milk	¼ teaspoon pepper
2 tablespoons butter	6 eggs, beaten
¾ teaspoon salt	Chopped parsley

Heat milk and butter in top of double boiler. Add seasonings to eggs and beat until very light. Add hot milk to eggs and beat thoroughly. Return to top of double boiler and cook for 30 minutes over simmering water. Do not stir. Serve hot with mushroom sauce. Garnish with parsley. Serves 6.

EGGPLANT SOUFFLE

2 tablespoons butter	¾ cup soft crumbs
2 tablespoons flour	2 eggs, separated
1 cup tomato juice	1 teaspoon grated onion
2 cups mashed cooked eggplant	Salt and pepper
1 cup cottage cheese	

Melt butter and blend in flour. Gradually add tomato juice, stirring until thick and smooth. Add eggplant, cheese, crumbs, beaten egg yolks, and onion. Season to taste with salt and pepper. Fold in stiffly beaten egg whites. Turn into greased casserole and bake in moderate oven (350°F.) 45 minutes, or until set. Serves 6.

CHEESE CRUMB SOUFFLE (Basic Recipe)

1 cup milk, scalded	½ teaspoon salt
1¼ cups fine, soft breadcrumbs	¼ teaspoon paprika (optional)
1½ cups grated sharp American cheese	½ teaspoon baking powder
	4 eggs, separated

Pour scalded milk over crumbs and cheese. Add seasoning and baking powder. Pour part of mixture into beaten egg yolks. Add egg mixture to remainder of sauce. Fold in stiffly beaten egg whites. Turn into individual baking dishes. Bake in moderate oven (350°F.) until delicately browned and firm to touch, about 30 minutes. Serve at once. Serves 6.

Salmon soufflé: Substitute 1½ cups finely flaked canned salmon for cheese. Add ¼ cup minced green pepper. 2 teaspoons lemon juice, and ½ teaspoon onion juice.

WELSH RABBIT (Basic Recipe)

2 tablespoons butter	1 cup milk or cream
2 tablespoons flour	½ teaspoon dry mustard
½ teaspoon salt	1 cup grated cheese
Few grains cayenne	4 slices of toast

Prepare white sauce by melting butter, blending in flour, salt, and cayenne, and gradually adding milk. Cook over hot water, stirring constantly until thick. Add mustard and cheese, stirring until cheese is melted and mixture smooth. Serve hot on toast. Serves 4.

Baked rabbit: Pour rabbit over toast. Bake in slow oven (325°F.) until golden brown, about 15 minutes.

English monkey: Substitute ½ cup stale breadcrumbs for flour in sauce. Add 1 slightly beaten egg to sauce.

Olive rabbit: Add ½ cup sliced stuffed olives to sauce.

Onion rabbit: Sprinkle grated or minced onion over rabbit.

Rum tum tiddy: Add 1 teaspoon Worcestershire sauce and 1 slightly beaten egg to tomato rabbit.

Sardine rabbit: Arrange 3 or 4 sardines on each slice of buttered toast. Place under hot broiler 2 to 3 minutes. Pour over rabbit sauce. Serve at once.

Tomato rabbit: Substitute 1 cup condensed tomato soup for milk. If desired, add 1 tablespoon each minced onion and green pepper.

Tuna rabbit: Add ½ cup flaked tuna fish to sauce.

QUICK MOCK WELSH RABBIT

Measure ¾ cup grated American cheese in a cup. Pour boiling water over it to fill cup. Let stand for 10 minutes in a warm place. Drain water off carefully. Pour the remaining creamy mass over hot toast. Season and serve at once.

RICE AND NUT RABBIT

Mix together 1 tablespoon flour and 2 tablespoons water in top of double boiler over boiling water. Stir in 1¼ cups milk and ½ cup grated cheese, stirring until cheese is melted and mixture smooth. Add ½ cup each cooked rice and chopped nuts and ½ teaspoon salt. Heat thoroughly. Serve on toast.

CHEESE CHARLOTTE

1¾ cups milk	½ cup evaporated milk or cream
6 slices white bread, fresh or stale	Salt, pepper, nutmeg, to taste
3 eggs, separated	½ pound Swiss cheese, grated

Scald milk. Dip 4 slices bread, cut in half, in milk and line baking dish. Cut other 2 slices bread into small cubes and soak in milk. Let stand. Beat egg yolks. Add evaporated milk, soaked bread and milk, and seasoning. Stir in cheese. Fold in stiffly beaten egg whites. Pour mixture into well-greased baking dish. Bake in moderate oven (350°F.) 25 to 35 minutes, or until inserted knife comes out dry. Serves 4.

EGG PANCAKE

2 eggs	⅓ cup sifted all-purpose flour
½ teaspoon salt	½ cup milk
1 tablespoon sugar	1 teaspoon cooking fat

Beat eggs, salt, and sugar together. Add flour and milk to eggs. Beat until smooth. Heat fat in a deep skillet (10 to 12 inch) until drop of water in skillet sizzles. Pour in all of batter. Cook two minutes. Place in very hot oven (450°F.) and bake 15 minutes or until surface is brown. Let stand in pan until ready to serve. Dot with butter and sweetened fruit or marmalade, syrup, or honey. Roll or fold from opposite sides to center, making three layers. Turn out on warm platter. Sprinkle with confectioners' sugar. Serves 2.

Apple egg pancake: Add 1 layer of thinly sliced apple just before placing it in oven.

EGG FOO YONG

1 cup coarsely chopped cooked turkey or chicken	1 tablespoon finely chopped green pepper or parsley
2 tablespoons cooking fat	6 eggs, slightly beaten
1 can bean sprouts, drained	1 teaspoon salt
½ cup chopped onion	Fat for frying
½ cup chopped celery	

Brown chicken lightly in 2 tablespoons fat. Add bean sprouts, onion, celery, and green pepper. Cover and cook a few minutes until onion is transparent. Cool slightly. Spoon chicken-vegetable mixture into beaten eggs, straining out liquid in bottom of pan. Add salt. Mix thoroughly. Pour ¼ cup mixture into hot fat, about ½ inch thickness. Cook until brown on both sides, turning once. Drain. Serve hot with sauce. Yield: 12 cakes.

To make sauce: Combine the juice from the cooked vegetables in above recipe with 1 cup juice from canned bean sprouts. Set aside ¼ cup of the liquid. Heat remainder to boiling. Blend 1 tablespoon cornstarch, 1 teaspoon sugar, and the ¼ cup reserved liquid. Add to boiling juice. Cook, stirring constantly until thickened. Add 2 tablespoons soy sauce.

NUT AND CHEESE LOAF

1 tablespoon chopped onion	1 cup dry breadcrumbs
1 tablespoon butter	¾ cup boiling water
1 cup grated cheese	1 egg, beaten
1 cup chopped walnut meats	Salt and pepper, to taste

Cook onion in butter for a few minutes. Mix cheese, nutmeats, breadcrumbs, and water. Add melted butter, onion, and egg. Bake in a small pan in moderate oven (350°F.) about 30 minutes. Serve with tomato sauce.

SWEDISH CHEESE CUSTARD

2 cups milk
2 eggs, well beaten
Salt

1 cup grated cheese
Dash of paprika

Add milk to beaten eggs and mix well. Add salt, paprika, and grated cheese. Mix thoroughly. Pour into a well-oiled mold. Cover with paper and place in a pan of hot water. Bake in moderate oven (350°F.) until set. Chill, unmold, and serve over lettuce with any desired dressing. Serves 6.

TOMATO CHEESE BAKE

6 slices buttered bread
½ pound American cheese
2 eggs
1 cup cooked tomatoes

1 cup tomato juice
½ teaspoon salt
⅛ teaspoon pepper
1 tablespoon minced onion

Cut bread and cheese into cubes. Arrange in alternate layers in a buttered baking dish. Beat eggs slightly. Add tomatoes, tomato juice, and seasonings. Pour over bread and cheese. Bake in moderate oven (375°F.) 45 to 50 minutes. Serves 6.

CHEESE DREAM PIE

3 tablespoons butter
1 teaspoon ground sage
12 slices bread
½ pound sliced American cheese

3 cups milk
1½ teaspoons salt
⅛ teaspoon cayenne
3 eggs

Blend butter and sage. Trim crusts from bread. Spread 6 slices with butter mixture, top with slices of cheese and slices of bread. Cut each into three triangles. Arrange in 2 layers in a deep 9-inch pie dish or shallow casserole. Add milk and seasonings to slightly beaten eggs and pour over cheese sandwiches. Bake in moderate oven (350°F.) about 45 minutes. Serves 6 to 8.

KAISERSCHMARRN (Emperor's Omelette)

4 eggs, separated
2½ tablespoons sugar
⅞ cup milk
1 cup flour, sifted
⅛ teaspoon salt

3 tablespoons butter
Powdered sugar
Vanilla bean
3 tablespoons seedless raisins

Combine egg yolks with sugar, milk, flour, and salt, and mix thoroughly until smooth. Carefully fold in stiffly beaten egg whites. Melt 1 tablespoon butter in large pan. Pour in enough mixture to cover pan about ¼ inch in depth. Cook gently and allow to puff. Turn and brown lightly on other side. Do not cook too long or it will become dry. With 2 forks tear into small pieces about the size of a quarter. Put torn schmarrn onto a plate sprinkled with powdered sugar in which a bit of vanilla bean has been kept and leave until 3 more omelettes are prepared in the same manner and torn. Melt 1 tablespoon butter in a skillet. Add torn omelettes and raisins. Sprinkle with powdered sugar. Stir in the skillet for about 5 minutes or until thoroughly heated. Serve on warm plate with a tart fruit compote (sour cherries, cranberries, or stewed prunes). Serves 4.

CHEESE CASSEROLE

6 slices bread
½ pound American cheese, thinly sliced
2 eggs
1 cup milk

½ teaspoon salt
Few grains pepper
Butter

Place 2 slices of bread in a greased baking dish. Cover with half the cheese. Repeat, finishing with slices of bread. Beat eggs and add milk, salt, and pepper. Pour into baking dish. Dot with bits of butter. Bake in slow oven (325°F.) 30 minutes. Serves 4 to 6.

CHEESE CROQUETTES

1 pound American cheese
½ teaspoon dry mustard
6 drops Tabasco sauce
¼ teaspoon salt
2 teaspoons Worcestershire sauce

1 tablespoon flour
4 egg whites
1 tablespoon water
Dry breadcrumbs

Grind cheese in food chopper, then mash to paste with fork. Add seasoning and flour. Fold in 3 stiffly beaten egg whites. Form into firm balls about ½ inch in diameter. Chill in refrigerator. Just before cooking, roll in breadcrumbs, then in remaining egg white, beaten and mixed with water, then roll again in crumbs. Fry in deep hot fat (375°F.) until golden brown. Drain on absorbent paper. Insert toothpicks and serve hot. Yield: about 32.

EGG AND CHEESE TIMBALES

1½ tablespoons cooking fat
1 tablespoon flour
1½ cups milk
⅓ pound sharp cheese, chopped
½ teaspoon salt

⅛ teaspoon pepper
1½ teaspoons Worcestershire sauce
½ teaspoon mustard, scant
1½ teaspoons chopped pimiento
3 eggs

Melt fat. Add flour and blend well. Add milk and cook over low heat, stirring constantly until thickened. Add cheese and stir until blended. Remove from heat and add seasonings and pimiento. Pour slowly into beaten eggs, stirring constantly. Pour into well-greased custard cups. Set cups in pan of hot water and bake in slow oven (325°F.) until firm, about 45 minutes, or until knife inserted in center comes out clean. Unmold to serve. Chopped pickle relish, chili sauce, or whole cranberry sauce are good accompaniments. Serves 4.

CHEESE PATTIES

3 tablespoons butter
1 tablespoon chopped green pepper
1 tablespoon chopped onion
3 cups cooked rice
1½ cups grated American cheese

1 tablespoon chopped pimiento
1 egg, beaten
¾ teaspoon salt
Dash black pepper
Fine dry breadcrumbs

Melt butter in top part of double boiler. Add green pepper and onion. Simmer over direct heat for 5 minutes. Blend in rice, add cheese and pimiento, and heat over hot water until cheese is melted, stirring constantly. Fold in beaten egg, salt, and pepper. Cool. Shape into 12 patties of uniform size. Dip in breadcrumbs. Pan-fry patties in butter until golden brown. Serve with creamed vegetable. Serves 6.

EGG AND SPINACH CASSEROLE

2 cups cooked spinach
3 tablespoons butter
1 small onion, chopped
¼ cup flour
1 cup milk
½ cup spinach liquor

1 teaspoon salt
Dash of pepper
½ teaspoon prepared horseradish
½ teaspoon prepared mustard
6 hard-cooked eggs

Drain spinach and chop fine. Melt butter in top of double boiler over boiling water. Add onion and cook until tender. Stir in flour until well blended. Add milk and spinach liquor and cook, stirring constantly until mixture thickens. Season with salt and pepper. Add horseradish and mustard. Fold in chopped spinach and reheat. Pour into greased casserole. Top with stuffed eggs made as follows: Cut hard-cooked eggs in halves lengthwise. Remove yolks and mash with 2 tablespoons minced onion, ¼ teaspoon prepared mustard, 3 tablespoons salad dressing, ¼ teaspoon salt, and a dash of pepper. Refill whites with mixture. Place stuffed eggs on top of creamed spinach. Cover and bake in moderate oven (375°F.) 15 minutes. Serves 6.

CHEESE CUTLETS

⅔ cup grated cheese
2 cups mashed potatoes
4 tablespoons minced pimiento

1 cup cooked navy or lima beans,
  ground
1 teaspoon salt

Combine all ingredients. Shape into cutlets about ½ inch thick. Sauté in a small amount of hot fat. Serve with horseradish sauce. Serves 6.

KOCH KAESE (Cooked Cottage Cheese)

4 cups dry cottage cheese
2 tablespoons butter
½ teaspoon salt

⅛ teaspoon paprika (optional)
1 cup milk
2 teaspoons caraway seed

Place cheese in a bowl in a warm place and stir once daily for 3 or 4 days. Cheese will ferment and become waxy throughout. Melt butter in top of double boiler. Add cheese, salt, and paprika. Cook and stir over low heat until hot. Add milk and caraway seed. Cook 10 minutes, stirring constantly. Pour into a bowl and chill thoroughly. Serve with rye bread and beer.

BLENDER WELSH RABBIT

1½ cups milk
1 egg
1 teaspoon Worcestershire sauce
1 teaspoon salt

¼ teaspoon dry mustard
½ teaspoon paprika
1 tablespoon cornstarch
½ pound diced sharp Cheddar cheese

Heat milk. Put all ingredients except milk in container in order given. Add hot milk gradually and blend thoroughly, about 1 minute. Heat in double boiler over hot water until thick, about 5 minutes. Serve over hot toast. Serves 4.

fish

Modern refrigeration and rapid transportation make it possible for inlanders as well as those living on the shore to enjoy the great variety of fish all the year round. Fish is frequently less costly than meat and, like meat, it is a primary source of protein and the essential vitamins and minerals. Fish dishes, very often, are time-savers for the busy homemaker, inasmuch as the cooking time for most fish is short. Fish, then, should always be kept in mind as an alternate, not a substitute, for meat in the daily menu. The flavor of fish is delicate. When properly cooked and skillfully combined with other foods it soon becomes a favorite dish several times a week.

FISH COOKERY

How to cook fish depends on their fat content. Best for baking and broiling are fat fish such as salmon, shad, mackerel, lake trout, and whitefish. Lean fish such as cod, flounder, haddock, pike, rosefish, sea bass, striped bass, perch, and carp are preferred for cooking in water because they are firmer after cooking. But they may be baked or broiled if basted with melted fat. Both fat and lean fish are suitable for frying. Most important point in fish cookery—don't overcook. Cook just until fishes can be easily flaked.

To cook frozen fish: Cook without thawing or thaw in a cold place, and cook exactly as fresh fish. Frozen fish should be "hard frozen" when bought. Never refreeze fish after it thaws.

How to select fish: Fresh fish is highly perishable and must be handled with care and kept as cold as possible from the time it is caught until it is cooked. The inexperienced homemaker should select a reliable dealer who is supplied daily, and on whose guidance she may depend. In a good market the fish is packed in ice at all times or, if frozen, stored in a freezer. Fresh fish has a characteristic fresh odor which will be pleasant and is best described as "fresh," which the homemaker soon learns to detect. When fresh, fish has a firm and elastic flesh that leaves no impress to the touch of the fingers, red gills, bright and bulging eyes, and closely adhering scales.

How to buy fish: The same fish may have a variety of names in markets from different parts of the country. In localities close to supply sources there is frequently available local fish that is not generally known. Fish may be purchased either dressed or drawn. Dressed fish have the scales, head, fins, tail, and entrails removed; drawn fish have only the scales and entrails removed. When buying a fish to bake whole ask the dealer to remove the fine fin bones within the flesh as well as the blood line.

How much fish to buy: When bought whole with skin, bones, head, and tail in place, one pound will serve two. One pound of steaks will serve 3. One pound of fillets will serve 4.

To keep fish: Wrap fish closely in waxed paper if it's to be stored in the refrigerator with other food or place in a glass dish and cover closely. If it's not to be used for a day or two, clean it before wrapping.

Canned fish: In using canned fish, the more attractive higher grades are better for salads or serving plain. For such dishes as casseroles or fish cakes, lower grades will do. They are just as nutritious and flavorful as top quality. The oil or salty liquid from canned fish adds flavor and food value to sea food dishes. Use the oil, for instance, as fat in the white sauce in making creamed tuna fish. Brine may be part of the liquid in jellied fish salad.

FISH PREPARATION HINTS

The cleaning of fish is usually taken care of at the market. However, occasionally the homemaker will be faced with the problem of preparing a fish just as it's taken from the water.

To remove fish scales: Hold fish by the tail. Scrape a blunt-edged knife over the fish from tail to head. Hold knife at a slant to prevent scales from flying.

To skin fish: Cut out the fins, preferably with a kitchen scissors. Cut away a narrow strip of skin along the entire length of back. Cut and loosen skin at the gills and pull skin off toward tail, following closely with a knife to avoid tearing the flesh. Skin the other side the same way.

To dress fish: Make a slit in the stomach of the fish. Remove entrails and any clotted blood. Remove head and tail unless fish is very small, when they may be left on. Wash thoroughly under cold water. Wipe with a dry cloth.

To bone fish: Use a very sharp pointed knife. Begin at the tail end and slip the knife between the flesh and the backbone and cut the entire length of each side of fish. Keep knife as close as possible to backbone. On larger fish do not cut all the way through back but keep the two sides together for stuffing. Smaller fish are cut into separate fillets.

To remove fish odor from hands and utensils: Rub the hands and utensils with salt and wash with cold water. Always pour the water in which fish has been washed down the drain at once. Pour in some salt and flush the drain with cold water.

BAKED STUFFED WHOLE FISH

Use fish weighing 3 to 5 pounds. Head and tail may be removed. Fish may be boned. Have fish slit and cleaned. Rub inside with salt. Stuff with any desired stuffing. Fasten edges together. Place on parchment paper in shallow baking pan. Brush with melted butter. Sprinkle with salt. Bake in hot oven (400°F.), allowing 10 minutes per pound, adding 5 minutes additional to total baking time for each pound over 5 pounds. Serve on hot platter with sauce.

BAKED FISH FILLETS OR STEAKS

Use fillets or steaks ½ to 1 inch thick. Use bass, haddock, halibut, perch, pickerel, pike, trout, salmon, tuna, or flounder. Dip in well-salted milk, using 1 tablespoon salt to each cup milk. Then roll fish in finely sifted breadcrumbs. Place in a greased baking pan, using 1 tablespoon butter to each pound of fish. Dot with butter. Bake according to method #1 or #2. Serve hot with sauce.

Method #1: Bake in hot oven (400°F.) in uncovered pan for 15 to 25 minutes, basting once if fish is lean.

Method #2: Bake in very hot oven (500°F.) in uncovered pan for 10 to 12 minutes, depending upon thickness of fish.

Baked fillets in milk: Omit milk and breadcrumbs. Brush fillets on all sides with melted butter. Sprinkle with salt and pepper. Place in baking pan and cover with milk. Bake uncovered, 15 to 25 minutes, in a moderate oven (350°–375°F.).

Baked fish with tomato sauce: Omit milk and crumbs. Sprinkle fish with salt and pepper. Cover with tomato sauce and bake according to Method #1.

BAKED STUFFED FILLETS

Place large fillet in greased baking dish. Season with salt, pepper, and lemon juice. Cover with desired stuffing. Place second fillet over stuffing. Brush with melted butter, or cover with buttered crumbs. Bake, uncovered, in moderate oven (350°F.) 30 to 40 minutes. Baste with melted butter.

BAKED STUFFED FISH STEAKS

Wipe steaks with damp cloth. Sprinkle with salt and pepper. Brush with melted butter. Place 1 steak in baking dish. Spread with any desired stuffing. Put second steak on top. Top with sliced onion, sliced green pepper, and canned tomatoes or sliced fresh tomatoes. Spoon 2 tablespoons melted butter over vegetable. Bake in hot oven (400°F.) 45 to 50 minutes. Serve with sauce.

BROILED FISH

Small fish are split and broiled whole. Cut fillets and steaks into serving size portions. Sprinkle both sides with salt and pepper. Place fish on preheated greased broiler pan about 2 inches from heat, skin side up, unless skin has been removed. Broil until slightly browned, 5 to 8 minutes. Baste with melted fat. Turn carefully. Brush other side with fat. Cook 5 to 8 minutes, or until fish flakes easily when tested with fork. Remove carefully to hot platter. Serve plain, or with lemon butter.

PLANKED FISH

Use whole fish, fillets, or steaks as in other baked fish recipes. Dry fish thoroughly and season both sides with salt and pepper. Brush with oil or melted butter. Bake skin side down on a well-oiled plank or oven-proof platter in a hot oven (400°F.) 20 to 30 minutes. If fish is lean, baste frequently. When done, remove from oven. Edge plank with mashed or Duchess potatoes. Brown under broiler. Garnish with lemon wedges and parsley. Arrange other vegetables on plank. Serve from plank.

POACHED OR "BOILED" FISH

Use lean fish, whole, large slices, fillets, or steaks. Wrap or tie fish in cheesecloth. Cover with hot water. Add 1 tablespoon lemon juice or vinegar for each quart of water, ¼ cup diced celery, a parsley sprig, a few slices of onion, and a bay leaf. Simmer (do not boil), allowing 6 to 10 minutes per pound for whole fish, 10 to 20 minutes per pound for large slices, fillets, or steaks. Drain. Remove cheesecloth and serve hot with sauce, or use the cooked fis'. in baked, creamed, or escalloped dishes. Use liquid to prepare soups or sauces.

STEAMED FISH

Clean and wash fish. Sprinkle with salt and pepper. Place one layer deep on a rack in a steamer over boiling water. Steam 20 to 40 minutes, or until flesh flakes easily from bone with a fork. Serve in the same manner as POACHED FISH or chill and use in salads.

PAN-FRIED FISH

Dip fish in mixture of milk and egg. Roll in seasoned crumbs, corn meal, or flour. Heat cooking fat or salad oil (enough to be ⅛ inch deep) in skillet. When hot but not smoking fry fish at moderate heat. Brown one side, turn carefully, and brown other side. Total time about 10 minutes, depending upon thickness of fish. Drain on absorbent paper. Serve hot.

DEEP-FRIED FISH

Leave very small fish whole. Cut fillets and steaks into serving pieces. Roll in seasoned flour. Dip in mixture of slightly beaten egg and water, allowing 2 tablespoons cold water for each egg. Roll in dry breadcrumbs or cracker meal. Arrange a few pieces in frying basket just to cover bottom. Do not overlap pieces. Fry in hot deep fat (370°F.) until golden brown. Drain on absorbent paper. Serve hot.

OVEN FRIED FILLETS

2 pounds fish fillets
1 teaspoon salt
1 tablespoon paprika
¼ teaspoon pepper

1 cup milk
1 cup breadcrumbs
4 tablespoons butter or other fat

Cut fillets into serving pieces. Season with salt, pepper, and paprika. (If frozen fillets are used, let them thaw before cutting.) Dip the fish in milk and roll in crumbs. Place in a well-greased baking pan. Pour melted fat over fish. Place pan on shelf near the top of a very hot oven (500°F.) and bake 10 to 12 minutes, or until fish flakes easily when tested with a fork. Serve immediately on a hot platter, plain or with a sauce. Serves 6.

COURT BOUILLON

¼ cup each chopped celery, carrot,
  onion, parsley root, turnip
2 tablespoons butter
6 cups water
2 teaspoons salt

2 tablespoons vinegar
6 peppercorns
4 cloves
2 bay leaves
3 pounds fish

Sauté chopped vegetables 2 minutes in melted butter. Add all other ingredients except fish. Cover and boil 15 minutes. Cool slightly and add the fish tied in cheesecloth. Simmer until fish is done, about 30 minutes. Gently remove fish to a hot platter. Strain liquid. Serve either as a soup or make a sauce of it, using 1 cup liquid and 1 tablespoon flour mixed with a little cold water. Simmer gently for 5 minutes or until thick and smooth.

POACHED SALMON STEAKS

Place fish steaks on a heatproof plate or pie pan. Place plate or pan on a large square of cheesecloth. Bring corners of cheesecloth up over plate and tie securely. Put about a half inch of water in the bottom of a large frying pan or kettle. Use one big enough to hold plate or pie pan. Add ½ teaspoon salt and 1 teaspoon pickling spices to water. Bring water to a boil, then turn down heat so that water simmers. Place plate of fish steaks in simmering water. Cover and let simmer 10 minutes. Remove steaks and drain. Serve hot, garnished with big onion slices, curls of green pepper, chili sauce, and limes or lemons. To prepare limes or lemons, slice each in half. Scoop out a section of each half. Fill scooped out part with chili sauce.

HADDOCK FILLETS AMANDINE

Preheat broiling compartment and pan (350°F.) for 10 minutes. Wipe 2 pounds haddock fillets with damp cloth. (Fillets of ocean perch, cod, sole, or flounder may also be used.) Place fillets, skin side down, on preheated broiling pan. Brush with melted fat. Season with salt and pepper, and place 2 inches from source of heat. Broil 10 to 20 minutes, or until fish flakes easily when tested with fork. Serve with *ALMOND SAUCE.*

Almond sauce: Blanch ½ cup almonds by dropping them into boiling water, draining as soon as the skins loosen (takes 1 to 2 minutes) and then plunging in cold water. Drain again. On removing the skins, dry nuts thoroughly on a towel. Slice lengthwise, brown 2 tablespoons butter in a heavy skillet, add slivered almonds, and toast gently. Spread over broiled fillets before serving.

FISH STEAK GENEVOISE

Broil fish steaks (halibut, cod, or pollock) 5 to 7 minutes on each side or until done. Fish will flake easily when touched with a fork. Serve with *GENEVOISE SAUCE.*

GENEVOISE SAUCE

1 tablespoon butter	½ cup dry red wine
1 onion, sliced	½ cup water or fish stock
1 carrot, sliced	1 tablespoon butter
1 sprig of parsley	½ tablespoon flour

Melt butter, add onion and carrot. Cover pan and simmer a few minutes or until vegetables are soft. Add parsley, wine, and water or stock. Cook slowly until reduced to about ¾ cup. Add butter creamed with the flour and bring back to boiling point. Season to taste and pour over the fish.

BARBECUED BUTTERFISH

Any small fish such as butterfish, flounder, porgies, or sea trout may be used. Have fish cleaned and drawn. Do not have heads and tails removed. Sprinkle with garlic salt and pepper. Place a square of butter on each fish. Place on preheated broiler. Broil 5 to 8 minutes.

COLD SALMON STEAKS

Put about ¼ inch of water in the bottom of a large frying pan or kettle. Sprinkle salmon steaks with salt and pepper. Wrap each steak in a sheet of aluminum foil and place in pan with water. Cover and let simmer about 10 minutes. Remove wrapped steaks and dry on paper towel. Chill in foil in refrigerator. Serve with an egg slice and a spicy mayonnaise or egg sauce.

"BOILED" FISH WITH EGG SAUCE

4 cups hot water	1 small parsley root, diced
¼ cup butter	1 tablespoon salt
¼ sliced lemon	3 pounds whole fish
1 onion	2 egg yolks
10 or 12 peppercorns	1 tablespoon cold water
1 diced celery stalk	2 tablespoons finely ground almonds

Put hot water in large kettle. Add butter, lemon, onion, peppercorns, celery stalk, parsley root, and salt. Bring to boil and cook slowly 5 minutes. Add whole fish, wrapped in cheesecloth. Simmer until done, about 30 minutes. Remove fish and strain liquid. Beat egg yolks with cold water until light. Add almonds. Pour strained liquid slowly over this mixture. Bring to boiling point, stirring constantly, but do not boil. Pour sauce over fish. Chill and serve cold. Serves 6.

"BOILED" FISH WITH TOMATO SAUCE

3 pounds fish, whole or sliced	4 cups water
2 large sliced onions	2 tablespoons butter
3 diced carrots	1 cup strained canned tomatoes
1 celery root, diced	1 cup sweet cream
1 parsley root, diced	1 tablespoon flour

Salt fish well, inside and out. Chill in refrigerator for several hours. Add onion, carrots, celery root, and parsley root to water in a large kettle. Simmer slowly 10 minutes. Add fish (wrapped in cheesecloth), butter, tomatoes, and, if needed, hot water to cover. Simmer 30 minutes. Remove fish to platter, keeping hot. Strain liquid and reserve 2 cupfuls. Add sweet cream blended with flour to the 2 cups hot liquid and simmer until thick and smooth, about 5 minutes. Pour over hot fish and serve immediately. Serves 6.

FRENCH ROLLED FISH FILLETS

1 tablespoon butter	4 peeled, quartered small tomatoes
2 tablespoons minced onion	¼ pound mushrooms, sliced
1½ teaspoons salt	½ cup dry wine
Speck pepper	½ cup cold water
1½ pounds fish fillets	

Grease a large frying pan with butter. Strew onions over it. Roll each fillet like a jelly roll, place in frying pan, seam side down. Sprinkle salt and pepper over fillets. Arrange tomatoes around and place mushrooms over top. Pour over wine and water. Cover and simmer 10 minutes, or until fish is tender. Remove fish to hot platter, keeping warm while preparing sauce. To prepare sauce cook liquid left in frying pan until about 1 cupful remains. Cream 3 tablespoons softened butter. Add 3 tablespoons flour. Add to the liquid and simmer until thickened. Sprinkle fish with parsley. Pour sauce over fish. Broil until browned over top. If desired, small cooked potato balls may be placed around fish before pouring over sauce and broiling. Serves 4.

WHITEFISH CASSEROLE

2 carrots, diced
½ cup green beans, diced
1 onion, minced
2 large potatoes, cubed
½ cup diced celery

Salt and pepper, to taste
1 pound whitefish, sliced
1 can condensed tomato soup
½ cup sour cream

Grease casserole. Place mixed vegetables on the bottom and top with slices of fish. Season with salt and pepper. Combine tomato soup and sour cream. Pour over the top. Dot with butter. Bake in a moderate oven (350°F.) until mixture is heated through, fish is flaky and lightly browned, about 1 hour. Baste with the sauce while baking. Serves 4.

GEFILTE FISH (Basic Recipe)

3 pounds fish (use pike and
    carp or pike and whitefish)
Salt as required
2 large onions, sliced
2 eggs
¼ cup matzo meal or breadcrumbs

1 teaspoon salt
About ⅛ teaspoon pepper
About 2 tablespoons cold water
1 stalk celery, diced
1 large carrot, sliced
Cold water to cover
Chopped parsley

Sliced: Cut fish into 2-inch slices. Carefully remove flesh and bones without breaking skins. (If desired, bones may be left attached to each cut of skin.) Salt the skins and bones and place in a covered bowl in refrigerator while preparing filling. Put the flesh and 1 onion through a food chopper, then place in a wooden chopping bowl and chop until smooth. Add eggs, matzo meal or breadcrumbs, 1 teaspoon salt, pepper to taste, and enough cold water to make a light soft mixture. Blend thoroughly. Wet hands with cold water. Form oval cakes of mixture and fit them into skins. Place head bones and any other bones in the bottom of a deep heavy kettle. Add remaining onion, celery, carrot, and cold water to cover. Cover kettle and bring to a quick boil. Remove cover. Reduce heat and cook at a very slow boil 1½ to 2 hours. The liquid should be reduced by half. Allow to cool slightly before removing fish to a platter carefully so as to retain shape. Serve warm or thoroughly chilled, garnished with sliced, cooked carrot and chopped parsley. If served cold, use the jellied sauce as a garnish. Serve with prepared horseradish. Serves 6.

Variations: Two slices of white bread may be substituted for matzo meal or breadcrumbs. Soak the bread in cold water and squeeze out. If bread is used it may not be necessary to moisten the chopped fish mixture with cold water. If desired, one raw carrot may be grated and added to fish mixture.

Balls: Shape the prepared fish mixture into balls. Place the skin and bones in the bottom of kettle before adding vegetables and fish balls. Cook as in basic recipe.

Whole: Do not section the fish. Fillet the fish, being careful not to break skin and to leave head and tail intact. Prepare filling as in basic recipe. Fill the whole skins with this mixture, shaping to look natural. Use a deep, oval pot and place the fish on a trivet over the vegetables in the pot. Cover with cold water and bring slowly to boiling point. Cook at a slow boil for 1½ to 2 hours.

Baked gefilte fish: Prepare as in basic recipe. If stuffed whole, place in well greased baking pan. Sprinkle with breadcrumbs. Dot with butter. Bake in hot oven

(425°F.) until done, about 1 hour. If desired, shape into small patties, roll in fine crumbs and bake in moderate oven (375°F.) 12 to 15 minutes.

Fried gefilte fish: Form the prepared mixture into small patties. Roll in fine crumbs and fry until done.

MARINATED FISH (Pickled or Jellied Fish)

5 pounds pike, pickerel, or	18 allspice
whitefish	20 peppercorns
2 cups vinegar	1 teaspoon sugar
2 cups cold water	5 onions, sliced
1 teaspoon salt	½ lemon, sliced
5 bay leaves	

Cut fish in 2-inch slices. Salt well and chill in refrigerator for several hours. When ready rinse off salt. Boil together vinegar, water, salt, spices, sugar, and 1 sliced onion for 20 minutes. Add lemon slices and cook 5 minutes more. Remove lemon. Add fish slices and simmer gently until done. Place in a large crock in alternate layers with raw sliced onions. Pour the hot liquid over all. Keeps for several weeks if kept in refrigerator. Liquid forms a jelly.

SCHARFE FISH

3 pounds pike or lake trout	½ teaspoon peppercorns
Salt	1 lemon, sliced
1 celery root, diced	2 tablespoons butter
1 parsley root, diced	2 tablespoons ground almonds
1 large onion, sliced	2 egg yolks
1 carrot, diced	Parsley sprigs

Clean fish. Sprinkle well with salt, inside and out. Slice into 2-inch slices and place in refrigerator for several hours or over night. Line a large pot with the celery root, parsley root, onion, and carrot. Add peppercorns, lemon, butter, and almonds. Place fish on top of this and add hot water to cover. Simmer until fish is done, about 30 minutes. Remove fish. Strain liquid and reserve 1 cup. Use this to make a sauce by gradually adding it to the egg yolks beaten with 1 tablespoon cold water. Pour over fish and serve, garnished with carrots and parsley. Serves 6.

"BOILED" FISH WITH CREAM SAUCE

1 celery root, diced	1 cup cream
1 sprig parsley, minced	1 tablespoon butter
1 sliced onion	1 tablespoon flour
3 pounds fish, whole	1 tablespoon cold milk
Water to cover	Salt, to taste
1 teaspoon salt	Pepper, to taste
1 tablespoon vinegar	

Line the bottom of a large pot with celery root, sprig parsley, and sliced onion. Place whole fish over this. Add water to cover, 1 teaspoon salt, and vinegar. Bring to boil and simmer until fish is done, about ½ hour. Remove fish, keeping hot. Scald cream and butter. Blend flour with cold milk and add to hot cream. Cook about 5 minutes, or until smooth and thick, stirring constantly. Season with salt and pepper and pour over hot fish. Serves 6.

FISH FILLETS POACHED IN WINE

Arrange flounder or haddock fillets in shallow casserole. Sprinkle with salt. Cover with dry white wine to same depth as the fillets. Cover and bake in a moderate oven (350°F.)about 20 minutes. Place fillets on platter, keeping hot. Strain liquid and use in preparing sauce. For each cup of liquid, melt 2 tablespoons butter, blend in 2 tablespoons flour, and slowly add hot fish liquid. Bring to boil. Season to taste with salt and cayenne. Pour over fish and serve.

HUNGARIAN STEWED FISH

3 pounds fish	1 cup red wine
1½ cups chopped mushrooms	Parsley
2 carrots, sliced	4 cloves
2 onions, chopped	Salt and pepper, to taste
1½ cups water	1½ tablespoons capers

Use carp, whitefish, trout, or other lean fish. Place the fish, cut into strips, in a pan. Add mushrooms, carrots, onions, water, wine, parsley, cloves, salt, and pepper. Simmer gently 1 hour. Add capers and serve on hot toast. Serves 6.

WHITEFISH IN WINE SAUCE

Clean and dry 3 pounds whitefish. Cut into serving slices. Place in a casserole and half cover with any white wine. Dot with ¼ cup butter. Cover with lemon slices with rind and seeds removed. Cover casserole, slowly bring to a boil and simmer until tender, about 15 minutes. Serves 6 to 8.

SWEET AND SOUR FISH

3 pounds pike, carp or whitefish	1½ cups raisins
½ cup brown sugar	2 tablespoons sherry wine
Juice of 1 lemon	Salt, to taste
1 onion, diced	Several sprigs parsley
1 stick cinnamon	1 lemon, sliced

Clean fish and sprinkle with salt. Place in refrigerator for several hours. Slice fish in serving portions and cover with boiling water. Simmer gently until tender. Remove fish to a platter. Using 1 cup of the fish liquid, make a sauce by adding sugar, lemon juice, onion, cinnamon, raisins and wine. Simmer until mixture is thick, about 10 minutes. Strain and pour over fish. Chill and serve cold. Garnish with parsley sprigs and sliced lemon. Serves 6.

FILLETS BAKED IN MUSHROOM SAUCE

1 cup fresh mushrooms	2 cups milk
¼ cup butter	1 pound fillets
3 tablespoons flour	½ teaspoon salt
½ teaspoon salt	½ cup buttered breadcrumbs
Dash cayenne	

Wash and slice mushrooms. Cook gently in butter 5 minutes. Add flour and seasoning, mixing to smooth paste. Add milk gradually, stirring constantly, and cook until thickened. Cut fillets into individual servings. Place in baking dish and sprinkle with salt. Cover with mushroom sauce. Sprinkle over with crumbs. Bake in moderate oven (375°F.) ½ hour. Serves 4.

FRESH SALMON WITH HORSERADISH SAUCE

3 pounds fresh salmon
Salt, to taste
¼ cup melted butter
2 tablespoons minced parsley

¾ cup grated horseradish
2 cups whipping cream
1 tablespoon lemon juice

Clean, bone, and salt fish. Chill in refrigerator for several hours. Place in a large kettle. Add boiling salted water to cover and cook until done, 30 minutes. Remove carefully to a hot platter and pour over melted butter and minced parsley. Serve hot with *HORSERADISH SAUCE.*

Horseradish sauce: Fold horseradish into stiffly beaten cream. Add salt and lemon juice, to taste. Serve in separate bowl. The fish is served hot and the sauce cold. Serves 6.

FISH PAPRIKASH

3 large onions, sliced
1½ tablespoons cooking fat
1½ teaspoons paprika

1 cup cold water
Salt and pepper, to taste
3 pounds pike, carp, or bass

Fry onions gently in fat until golden brown. Add paprika. Mix well and add water. Season with salt and pepper. Add fish fillets, cut into serving slices. Bring to boil, then simmer gently about 45 minutes, shaking the pan occasionally to prevent sticking. Add more water, if necessary. Gently remove fish to a platter. Strain sauce and pour over fish. Serves 6.

PAN-BAKED OCEAN PERCH WITH PICKLED ONIONS

Place two 1-pound packages of ocean perch in a glass baking dish. Add salt and pepper, to taste. Melt ¼ pound butter (¼ cup) and mix in 2¼ cups cracker meal. Cover the fillets with the butter-crumb mixture. Sprinkle with chopped parsley, if desired. Bake 30 minutes in a moderate oven (350°F.), or until fish is tender and crumbs browned. Serve with pickled onions and beets, if desired. Serves 6.

Variations: Haddock or flounder fillets may be substituted for ocean perch.

STRIPED BASS CREOLE

Clean a 4-pound striped bass, rub with oil or fat, and season with salt and pepper. Place fish in a greased baking pan. Add ½ cup tomato juice and sprinkle 1 tablespoon finely chopped onion over the fish. Place in a moderate oven (350°F.) and bake about 30 minutes, basting occasionally. Remove from oven. Pour 1 cup *CREOLE SAUCE* over fish. Sprinkle top with breadcrumbs and dot with butter. Place in oven until browned. Serves 5.

Creole sauce for bass: Simmer together 1½ cups canned tomatoes, 1 green pepper, thinly sliced, and ½ cup mushrooms, thinly sliced, about 10 minutes. In a separate saucepan, melt 1 tablespoon butter and gradually add 1 tablespoon flour, cooking and stirring over low heat until well blended. Stir 1 cup fish stock or hot water into the blended flour and fat. When thoroughly mixed, add to the first mixture and cook 2 minutes longer.

BROILED FISH FILLETS WITH PUFFY SAUCE

Preheat broiling compartment and pan under full heat (550°F.) for 10 minutes. Wipe fillets with a damp paper towel. Place fillets skin side down on preheated broiling pan. Place pan 2 inches from source of heat. Broil about 5 minutes. Take from oven and spread with *PUFFY SAUCE.*

PUFFY SAUCE

½ cup mayonnaise
 Dash cayenne pepper
1 tablespoon chopped parsley

2 tablespoons chopped sour pickle
1 egg white, beaten stiff, but
 not dry

Combine ingredients. Spread evenly over top of fish. Broil 3 to 5 minutes, or until sauce has puffed and is golden brown. Serve immediately. Makes enough sauce for 6 fillets.

SPINACH STUFFED FILLETS

1 pound spinach or kale
1 onion, chopped
1 tablespoon butter
 Salt and pepper, to taste

1½ pounds fish fillets
1 egg, beaten
¼ cup breadcrumbs

Wash spinach thoroughly. Cook spinach and onion together with only water that clings to leaves. When tender, drain and chop. Add butter and seasoning, to taste. Cool. Meanwhile cut fillets into 2-inch strips. Add egg and crumbs to cooled spinach. Spread the mixture on each fillet. Roll and fasten with toothpicks. Place, cut side up, in greased baking dish. Bake in a hot oven (400°F.) for 20 minutes. Serves 6.

ROLLED STUFFED FILLETS

4 fillets
¼ teaspoon salt

⅛ teaspoon pepper
2 tablespoons melted butter

Cut skinned fillets into serving-size portions. Season with salt and pepper. Place a tablespoon of favorite stuffing on each fillet and roll fish around it. Fasten with toothpick. Place rolls on well-greased baking pan and brush top of each with melted butter. Bake in moderate oven (350°F.) about 25 minutes. Remove toothpicks and garnish with parsley. Serve immediately plain or with favorite fish sauce. Serves 4.

CURRIED FISH

1½ to 2 pounds dressed fish
 2 tablespoons cooking fat
 1 tablespoon green pepper,
  chopped
 1 small onion, chopped
 ¼ cup celery, chopped

2 tablespoons flour
1 cup liquid from simmered fish
¼ to 1 teaspoon curry powder
 Salt, to taste
2 to 3 cups cooked rice
3 tablespoons parsley, chopped

Simmer fish about 10 minutes in a small quantity of water in a shallow pan. Drain and save liquid. Melt fat. Cook green pepper, onion, and celery in fat a few minutes. Stir in flour, then add fish liquid with milk or water to bring the quantity to 1 cup. Cook until thickened, stirring constantly. Add curry powder and salt, to taste. Remove skin and bones from cooked fish. Arrange on a hot platter with a border of rice. Pour sauce over fish and sprinkle with chopped parsley. Serves 6.

STUFFED FISH WITH SOUR CREAM

¼ pound sliced fresh mushrooms
2 onions, chopped fine
3 tablespoons butter
1 teaspoon paprika

2 cups sour cream
¾ cup breadcrumbs
3 pounds lean fish
Salt

Lightly sauté mushrooms and onions in butter. Sprinkle with paprika. Add 1 cup sour cream and simmer until tender. Add breadcrumbs and mix well. Stuff fish with mixture. Place fish on cloth or parchment paper in bottom of roasting pan. Season with salt. Bake in hot oven (400°F.) 20 minutes, or until done. Baste often with butter and remaining cream. Serves 6.

FILLETS IN WINE, PORTUGUESE STYLE

Crush or chop 3 cloves garlic. Add 1 teaspoon salt, ¼ teaspoon red pepper, 1 cup wine vinegar, and 1½ cups water. Pour over 2 pounds fish fillets and leave over night. Drain from liquid, fry in deep fat, or sauté until delicately browned. Serves 6.

FISH ESCALLOPED WITH PEPPERS

1 pound halibut
2 cups medium white sauce
1 green pepper, chopped fine

2 slices white bread, crumbled
2 tablespoons ketchup
Worcestershire sauce to taste

Simmer halibut in salted water 10 minutes. Pour off water. Shred the fish, then add 2 cups medium white sauce. Add shredded or chopped green pepper, crumbled bread, and ketchup. Let heat to boiling. Add Worcestershire sauce, if desired. Pour into casserole or ramekins. Cover top with breadcrumbs. Dot with butter. Brown in hot oven (425°F.) about 15 minutes.

ONION FILLET OF SOLE

2 cups chopped onions
2 cups medium white sauce
1 pound fillet of sole
Milk

Crumbs
¼ cup grated American cheese
Paprika

Cook onions in rapidly boiling salted water until tender. Drain. Season and mix with 1 cup white sauce. Turn into greased casserole. Wipe fish, dip in milk, roll and fasten with toothpicks. Roll in crumbs and put in casserole on top of onions. Add remaining white sauce and sprinkle with cheese and paprika. Bake in moderate oven (375°F.) 25 minutes. Serves 4.

FLOUNDER WITH SMOKED SALMON

4 fillets of flounder
Flour
Salt and pepper, to taste

4 tablespoons melted butter
Juice of 1 lemon
Smoked salmon slices

Dredge fillets lightly with flour. Season with salt and pepper. Sauté in hot butter until lightly browned. Transfer to a flat glass baking dish. To drippings in pan, add the lemon juice. Garnish fillets with strips of smoked salmon. Pour lemon sauce over all and heat briefly under broiler flame. Serves 4.

PLANKED FISH WITH BROWN BUTTER SAUCE

4 whiting or 4 small or 2 large porgies
Salt and paprika, to taste
Salad oil, butter, or margarine
2 to 3 cups mashed potatoes

1 clove garlic
2 tablespoons lemon juice
2 tablespoons minced parsley

Have fish cleaned and weighed at market. Place plank in oven and preheat for 10 minutes or while preparing fish. Grease well before adding fish. Dip fish in cold salted water and dry surface. Place on center of hot plank. Sprinkle with paprika and brush with fat. Bake in preheated oven, allowing about 1½ minutes for every ounce. When fish is almost tender, remove from oven. Garnish with mashed potatoes. Return to oven and bake until potatoes are lightly browned. While fish is baking, prepare sauce. Melt ⅓ cup butter, add garlic, and cook until butter is browned. Remove garlic. Add lemon juice, parsley, and ⅛ teaspoon salt. Pour over fish when done. Serves 4.

fish—cooked or canned

CREAMED FISH (Basic Recipe)

Combine 1½ cups flaked fish, cooked or canned, and 1½ cups medium WHITE SAUCE. Heat over hot water. Season to taste with salt and pepper. Serve on toast, crisp crackers, or corn bread. Tomato or creole sauce may be substituted for WHITE SAUCE.

Creamed fish in noodle ring: Prepare NOODLE RING. Place on hot serving plate. Place creamed fish in center. Garnish.

Creamed fish with eggs: Use 1 cup flaked fish and 2 or 3 hard-cooked eggs, sliced.

Creamed fish with vegetables: Increase white sauce to 2 cups and add 1½ cups diced cooked vegetables.

Fish au gratin: Place creamed fish in greased baking dish and cover with ½ cup buttered crumbs mixed with ¼ cup of grated cheese. Bake in moderately hot oven (400°F.) until sauce is bubbly and the top is well browned, 20 to 30 minutes.

SCALLOPED FISH (Basic Recipe)

2 cups flaked, cooked fish
2 teaspoons grated onion
1 teaspoon lemon juice

1½ cups medium white sauce
1 cup buttered crumbs

Arrange fish in a greased casserole or individual ramekins. Sprinkle with onion and lemon juice. Add white sauce. Cover with buttered crumbs. Bake in a moderate oven (375°F.) until crumbs are brown, 20 to 25 minutes. Serves 6.

Scalloped fish and eggs: Increase medium WHITE SAUCE to 2 cups. Arrange fish, 3 sliced hard-cooked eggs, and sauce in alternate layers in casserole, sprinkling each layer with onion and lemon juice.

Scalloped fish mushroom casserole: Substitute canned cream of mushroom soup for the WHITE SAUCE. If necessary, dilute soup with a little milk.

Scalloped fish with potato border: Substitute mashed potatoes for buttered crumbs.

SALMON OR TUNA LOAF

1 pound (#1 can) salmon or tuna	1 tablespoon minced parsley
2 cups soft breadcrumbs	Dash of cayenne pepper
½ cup milk	2 tablespoons melted butter
1 egg, well beaten	1 tablespoon lemon juice
1 teaspoon salt	

Flake fish and add remaining ingredients. Mix well. Pack into greased baking pan. Set in pan of hot water and bake in moderate oven (375°F.) about 40 minutes, or until loaf becomes firm. Serve hot with medium white sauce, egg sauce, or tomato sauce. Serves 6.

Salmon or tuna cakes: Drop mixture on hot greased griddle. Flatten and brown on both sides. Serve with white sauce, egg, or tomato sauce.

CREOLE FISH PIE

⅓ cup sliced onions	¼ teaspoon salt
¼ cup green pepper strips	1⅔ cups canned tomatoes
1 tablespoon butter or margarine	1 can (7 ounces) tuna fish
1 tablespoon flour	Buttered crumbs

Sauté onions and green pepper in butter until soft, about 10 minutes. Stir in flour and salt. Add tomatoes and cook 10 minutes, stirring constantly. Drain fish, break into large pieces and place in greased shallow casserole. Cover with tomato mixture. Sprinkle with corn flake crumbs or buttered breadcrumbs. Garnish top with cooked onion rings and pepper strips. Bake in a moderate oven (350°F.) 15 to 20 minutes, or until lightly browned. Serves 4.

FISH PATTIES

1½ cups flaked, cooked, or canned fish	1½ cups mashed potatoes
½ teaspoon salt	1 tablespoon minced onion
1 egg	⅛ teaspoon pepper
	Flour and fat

Combine all ingredients except flour and fat. Shape mixture into patties and roll in flour. Brown in fat. Serves 4.

Fish potato puffs: In FISH PATTIES recipe, add 2 egg yolks instead of a whole egg to the mixture of fish and potato. Add seasonings and fold in stiffly beaten egg whites. Put mixture into greased custard cups and bake in a moderate oven (350°F.) 30 minutes. Serves 4.

FISH CROQUETTES

3 cups cooked flaked fish	1 tablespoon minced onion
5 tablespoons butter	1 tablespoon minced parsley
5 tablespoons flour	1 teaspoon vinegar
¾ teaspoon salt	1 cup fine dry breadcrumbs
⅛ teaspoon pepper	1 egg, slightly beaten
1½ cups milk	2 tablespoons cold water

Mash fish with fork. Melt butter in saucepan and blend in flour, salt, and pepper. Add milk slowly and cook until very thick, stirring constantly. Add onion, parsley, vinegar, and fish. Mix well. Chill several hours. Shape into croquettes (about 12). Roll in crumbs and dip in egg mixed with water. Roll again in crumbs. Chill at least 1 hour. Fry in hot deep fat (375°F.) until golden brown, 2 to 3 minutes. Drain on absorbent paper. Serve with creamy egg sauce or creole sauce. Serves 6.

SWEET AND SOUR CANNED SALMON

1 tall can salmon	1 teaspoon salt
3 onions, sliced	½ cup vinegar
2 tablespoons flour	¼ cup raisins
3 tablespoons sugar	2 egg yolks

Remove skin and bones from salmon. Drain and save liquid. Simmer onions in uncovered pan with enough water to cover until tender, about 20 minutes. Drain and place over salmon on a platter. Save 1 cup of liquid. Mix flour, sugar, and salt in saucepan. Add onion liquid, vinegar, and raisins. Heat to boiling point and simmer about 5 minutes. Pour hot liquid slowly into beaten egg yolks, stirring constantly to prevent curdling. Simmer gently until smooth and thickened, about 5 minutes. Pour immediately over salmon and onions. Serve hot or cold. Serves 4.

FISH NEWBURG

2 cups flaked, cooked fish	Dash of cayenne
3 tablespoons butter	¾ cup light cream
1½ tablespoons flour	⅓ cup milk
1 teaspoon salt	3 tablespoons sherry
½ teaspoon paprika	2 egg yolks
¼ teaspoon nutmeg	Hot toast

Use haddock, cod, flounder, sole, or whitefish. Separate cooked fish into large flakes. Melt butter and blend in flour and seasonings. Add cream and milk slowly. Cook until thickened, stirring constantly. Add fish, and heat through. Mix sherry and egg yolks. Add to fish mixture and cook 2 or 3 minutes longer. Serve at once on hot toast. Garnish with minced parsley. Serves 4 to 6.

FISH PIE

3 cups mashed potatoes	3 tablespoons minced parsley
2 cups flaked, cooked fish	½ to ¾ cup grated cheese
1½ cups WHITE SAUCE	

Line bottom and sides of a buttered baking dish with mashed potatoes. Place in alternate layers the flaked fish, WHITE SAUCE thoroughly mixed with parsley, and cheese. Repeat, finishing with the cheese. Bake in hot oven (425°F.) 20 minutes, or until firm and lightly browned. Serves 6.

KEDGEREE

1 pound cooked fish
2 cups hot cooked rice
4 hard-cooked eggs
⅛ teaspoon pepper

3 tablespoons minced parsley
½ cup light cream
1 tablespoon butter
1 teaspoon salt

Use cod fillets, pickerel, pike, sole, flounder, or haddock. Flake fish and place in top part of double boiler with remaining ingredients. Heat thoroughly over boiling water. Pinch of curry powder may be added, if desired. Serves 4.

FISH TIMBALES

2 tablespoons butter
2 tablespoons flour
1 cup milk
2 eggs, slightly beaten
2 cups flaked, cooked or
    canned fish

1 tablespoon lemon juice
1 tablespoon chopped parsley
1 teaspoon minced onion
Salt to taste

Prepare sauce of butter, flour, and milk. Add beaten eggs, fish, and seasonings. Pour mixture into greased custard cups and bake in pan of hot water in moderate oven (350°F.) 30 minutes. Turn timbales onto a hot platter and garnish with lemon slices. Serve at once. Any fish that can be separated from bones easily may be used. Serves 6.

SALMON SOUFFLE

3 tablespoons butter
3 tablespoons flour
⅛ teaspoon pepper
1 cup milk
1 cup flaked, canned salmon

2 tablespoons lemon juice
1 teaspoon Worcestershire sauce
Dash of Tabasco sauce
3 eggs, separated

Heat butter, blend in flour and pepper. Add milk and cook, stirring until thickened. Add salmon, lemon juice, Worcestershire, and Tabasco. Beat egg yolks slightly. Add, stirring, to mixture. Stir over very low heat until thickened again. Beat egg whites until stiff but not dry. Fold into salmon mixture. Pour into a glass 10-inch pie pan. Bake in moderate oven (350°F.) until lightly browned and firm in the center. Serve immediately with tomato sauce. Serves 4.

TOASTED SALMON FILLETS

Break 2 cups (1 tall can) canned salmon into large pieces. Roll in mayonnaise or tartar sauce, then in breadcrumbs. Place on buttered baking sheet. Bake in hot oven (450°F.) 10 to 15 minutes. Serves 6.

SALMON-RICE BALL CASSEROLE

1 tall can salmon
1 cup cooked rice
2 eggs, slightly beaten
1 tablespoon minced onion

1 teaspoon salt
½ cup breadcrumbs
1 can condensed mushroom soup

Combine all ingredients except mushroom soup. Mix well. Shape into balls. Dilute mushroom soup with 1 can water and pour into casserole. Arrange salmon balls in sauce. Bake in moderate oven (350°F.) 30 minutes. Serves 6.

SALMON BASKET

1 loaf bread
1 cup milk
1 tall can salmon

1 tablespoon butter
1 teaspoon finely chopped onion
Salt and pepper

Cut crusts off loaf of bread. Hollow out the inside. Add 1 cup of crumbs to milk; cook over a low burner until smooth. Remove from flame; add flaked salmon, butter, and seasonings. Fill loaf with the mixture and brush the outside with melted butter. Bake in a hot oven (425°F.) until golden brown. Serves 6.

SALMON CROQUETTES

1 tall can salmon
Salt and pepper to taste
2 beaten eggs

½ cup buttermilk
½ cup flour
¼ teaspoon baking soda

Mix salmon, seasonings, and eggs. Add milk and flour sifted with baking soda. Mix well. Drop batter from a spoon into deep, hot fat (375°F.). Fry until golden brown, turning once. Drain on absorbent paper and serve. Serves 6 to 8.

TUNA AND NOODLES AU GRATIN

3 tablespoons butter
2 tablespoons flour
1½ cups milk
1 teaspoon salt
¼ teaspoon pepper

½ teaspoon paprika
½ pound American cheese, grated
1 4-ounce can sliced mushrooms
1 7½-ounce can tuna
1 4-ounce package noodles, cooked

Make a white sauce of butter, flour, milk, and seasoning. Add cheese and stir until smooth. Place mushrooms, flaked tuna, and noodles in greased baking dish in order named, with part of cheese sauce over each layer. Garnish with a few button mushrooms. Bake in a hot oven (400°F.) 20 minutes, or until golden brown. Serves 4 to 6.

HALIBUT MOLDED CASSEROLE

1 pound halibut
2 eggs
½ cup milk

½ cup cracker meal
1 tablespoon butter
Salt and pepper, to taste

Put halibut through the food chopper. Beat eggs and add milk, cracker meal, and melted butter. Combine with halibut. Add salt and pepper, to taste. Pour into a greased mold. Bake in pan of hot water in moderate oven (350°F.) about 25 minutes. Unmold onto a large platter. Surround with potato balls. Serve with HOLLANDAISE SAUCE. Serves 4.

EGGS AND TUNA FISH CASSEROLE

1½ cups canned tuna fish, flaked
6 hard-cooked eggs, chopped
1 green pepper, chopped

2 cups medium WHITE SAUCE
Salt and pepper, to taste
Buttered crumbs

Combine fish, eggs, and green pepper, which may be parboiled for 5 minutes if preferred. Add to white sauce. Season to taste. Pour into greased baking dish. Top with crumbs. Bake in moderate oven (375°F.) 20 minutes, or until crumbs are brown. Serves 8.

SALMON AND POTATOES EN CASSEROLE

4 tablespoons butter or margarine	¼ teaspoon pepper
2 tablespoons cornstarch	1 tablespoon minced green pepper
2½ cups milk	4 cups thinly sliced raw potatoes
1 medium onion, minced	1 1-pound can salmon, flaked
1 teaspoon salt	1 cup crushed potato chips

Melt butter or margarine and blend in cornstarch. Add milk, onion, salt, pepper, and green pepper. Cook, stirring until thickened. Place alternate layers of potatoes, salmon with liquid from can, and sauce in a greased casserole. Cover and bake in moderate oven (350°F.) about 20 minutes. Remove cover. Sprinkle with potato chips and bake until potatoes are tender, about 25 minutes. Serves 6.

fish—salt

FINNAN HADDIE (Smoked Haddock)

Baked finnan haddie: Cut into serving pieces. Place in greased baking dish. Add 1½ cups milk for 1½ pounds fish. Dot with butter and sprinkle with paprika. Bake in slow oven (325°F.) 25 to 30 minutes.

Broiled finnan haddie: Broil in a greased broiler until browned on both sides. Remove to pan and cover with hot water. Let stand 10 minutes. Drain. Brush with butter.

Creamed finnan haddie: Cover with cold water and bring slowly to boil. Let stand over hot water 20 minutes. Drain and separate into large flakes. For each cup fish add 1 tablespoon butter, 2 hard-cooked eggs, sliced thin, and ½ cup cream. Heat and serve. If desired, sprinkle with grated cheese and place under broiler to brown.

Poached finnan haddie: Cover fish with milk or water and bring slowly to boil. Simmer 10 to 15 minutes over low heat. Serve with butter sauce.

Steamed finnan haddie: Steam over boiling water until tender, 15 to 20 minutes. Each piece should be exposed to steam. Do not pile on top of each other. Serve with butter sauce.

CODFISH BALLS (Basic Recipe)

2 cups flaked salt codfish	¼ cup milk
3½ cups diced, pared raw potatoes	⅛ teaspoon pepper
2 eggs, slightly beaten	Dash celery salt
2 tablespoons butter	Paprika

Shred fish into small flakes and place in sauce pan. Cover with cold water. Heat slowly to boiling point. Drain. Repeat, using fresh water if fish is hard and salty. Combine with potatoes and cook, covered, in about 2 cups boiling water, until potatoes are tender. Drain well and mash thoroughly. Add remaining ingredients. Beat with spoon until light and fluffy. Chill. Shape into balls or drop by spoonfuls into deep hot fat (375°F.). Fry until browned. Drain on absorbent paper. Serve with tomato sauce, ketchup, egg sauce, or chili sauce. Serves 6.

Codfish hash: Spread mixture evenly in a large, hot, well-greased skillet. Cook slowly until a brown crust forms on bottom. Fold like an omelet.

Codfish patties: Shape into patties. Brown on both sides in hot fat.

Curried codfish balls: Add 1 teaspoon curry powder to mixture.

LOX (Smoked Salmon) AND POTATO CASSEROLE

4 potatoes, thinly sliced	1 egg
1 onion, minced	2 cups milk
¼ pound smoked salmon	Salt and pepper, to taste

Place a layer of potatoes in a buttered casserole. Sprinkle with onion and smoked salmon. Repeat procedure until ingredients are used. Beat egg and milk together with salt and pepper. Pour over potatoes. Add milk, if necessary, to cover. Bake in a slow oven (300°F.) 1 hour, or until browned. Serves 4.

SALT MACKEREL AND KIPPERS

Baked salt mackerel: Soak 8 to 12 hours in cold water. Drain. Dry and dredge with flour. Place in greased baking dish. Add ½ cup milk per 2 pounds fish. Sprinkle with paprika. Bake in moderate oven (350°F.) about 25 minutes.

Broiled salt mackerel: Soak salt mackerel 8 to 12 hours to remove excess salt. Drain and wipe dry. Place skin side down on greased broiler rack. Brush with melted butter. Broil 10 to 12 minutes, basting frequently. Serve with butter and lemon wedges or any fish sauce. Allow about ⅓ pound per serving.

Broiled kippers: Place dry kippers in pan and cover with cold water. Heat to boiling. Drain and dry. Broil 8 to 10 minutes. Baste with butter. Canned kippers need only to be drained of oil and broiled about 5 minutes.

Sautéed kippers: Soak smoked kippers in boiling water to cover 10 minutes. Drain. Sauté in hot oil or butter in skillet about 5 minutes, turning once. Serve with butter sauce.

PICKLED HERRING #1

3 milt herring	1½ cups white wine vinegar
⅔ to 1 cup onion, sliced	½ cup boiling water
1 small bay leaf	½ cup thick sour cream
3 to 4 peppercorns	

Wash herring and soak over night. Drain and remove entrails and scales, reserving milt. Remove backbone and, if desired, small bones. Head and tail may be removed or not, as desired. Leave whole or cut in large pieces. Arrange herring and onions in layers in a jar or crock. Combine remaining ingredients and pour over herring. Cover and let stand in cool place for 2 to 3 days. Will keep a week or more in refrigerator.

HERRING IN WINE SAUCE

Clean herring. Remove fins, tail, and head. Leave skin on. Cut into 1-inch pieces. Prepare marinade of equal parts vinegar, wine, and brown sugar. Add well mashed milt and a bay leaf for each herring. Place herring in glass jar and cover with marinade. Let stand several hours before serving.

BAKED HERRING

3 herrings
6 medium onions, sliced

Butter
Sweet cream

Soak herring in cold water several hours, changing water occasionally. Pour boiling water over onions, bring to a boil, and drain. Skin, bone, and cut herring into serving pieces. Place slices in buttered casserole, cover with sliced onions, and dot with butter. Bake in a moderate oven (350°F.) 20 minutes, or until onions are lightly browned. Add a little sweet cream and bake 10 minutes longer. Serve with baked potatoes. Serves 6 to 8.

BAKED HERRING WITH PAPRIKA SAUCE

4 to 6 herring fillets
  Salt and pepper, to taste
1 onion, sliced

1 teaspoon paprika
1 cup evaporated milk
2 tablespoons fat

Season fillets. Place in baking dish and top with onion slices. Blend paprika with milk and pour over fish. Dot with fat. Bake in moderate oven (350°F.) 40 minutes. Serve at once, garnished with parsley. Serves 6.

HERRING AND POTATO CASSEROLE

2 large herrings
6 medium-size cooked potatoes
2 medium-size onions

¼ cup soft breadcrumbs
2 tablespoons butter

Soak herring over night in cold water. Drain, clean, and fillet. Cut into 1-inch pieces. Place herring, potatoes, and onions in alternate layers in greased casserole, beginning and ending with potatoes. Sprinkle with breadcrumbs and dot with butter. Bake in hot oven (425°F.) 25 to 30 minutes. Serves 6.

PICKLED HERRING #2

6 matjes herring
6 milts from herring
6 large onions, sliced

1 cup vinegar
¼ cup mixed pickling spices
½ lemon, sliced

Soak herring in water over night. Clean and skin. Bone, if desired. Thoroughly pound the milt on a wooden board. Slice herring into 1-inch slices or leave whole. Place in jar in alternate layers with onion and lemon slices. Pour over vinegar mixed with spices and milt. Cover and keep in cool place three days. Will keep a week or longer. Serve cold.

Pickled herring with sour cream: In above recipe add ½ pint sour cream at the last.

HERRING FORSHMAK

2 herrings
1 slice white bread
1 cup milk
1 onion, chopped

2 eggs, beaten
1 large apple, grated
Mashed potatoes
Breadcrumbs

Soak herring in cold water for several hours. Clean, remove all bones and chop very fine. Soak bread in milk. Brown onion in butter and add to herring. Place mixture in a greased casserole and cover with well-beaten eggs, bread which has been removed from the milk, grated apple, and a layer of mashed potatoes over all. Top with breadcrumbs. Bake in a moderate oven (350°F.) 30 minutes. Serves 6 to 8.

CREAMED SALT CODFISH

2 cups shredded codfish
4 tablespoons butter
4 tablespoons flour

2 cups milk
⅛ teaspoon pepper

Cover codfish with water. Heat slowly to boiling point. Repeat once or twice if fish is hard and very salty. Drain well. Heat butter. Add codfish and cook over low heat about 2 minutes. Blend in flour. Slowly add milk. Cook until thickened, stirring constantly. Add pepper. Serve on toast or baked potatoes. Serves 6.

CODFISH CASSEROLE

2 cups shredded codfish
1⅔ cups milk
2 beaten eggs
½ cup grated cheese
1 tablespoon chopped onion

1 tablespoon chopped green
   pepper (optional)
1 cup dry breadcrumbs
2 tablespoons melted butter

Let cold water run over fish for 15 minutes. Cover with cold water. Heat slowly to boiling, but do not boil. Drain. Repeat process once more. Combine fish and remaining ingredients except buttered crumbs. Pour into greased 1½ quart casserole. Top with buttered crumbs. Place in pan of hot water. Bake in moderate oven (350°F.) 40 minutes. Serve with egg sauce. Serves 5.

CODFISH VEGETABLE PIE

2 cups cooked codfish
4 tablespoons butter
2 tablespoons onion (optional)
6 tablespoons flour
¼ teaspoon pepper

3 cups milk
1 cup cooked peas
1 cup cooked celery
1 cup cooked carrots
3½ cups mashed potatoes

Shred cod, pulling it apart with forks or shears. If salt cod is used, freshen by covering with cold water and heating to boiling point. Drain, cover with cold water, and repeat process until codfish tastes fresh, about 4 times. If fresh cod is used, simmer fish in water until tender. Melt butter in top of double boiler. Add onion and cook over direct heat 5 minutes but do not brown. Blend in flour and pepper. Add milk and cook over hot water until thick, stirring occasionally. Add diced cooked vegetables and codfish. Pour into a 1½-quart casserole. Top with border of mashed potato. Brown in a hot oven (400°F.) for 15 to 20 minutes. Serves 6.

FINNAN HADDIE RABBIT

In double boiler, heat ½ pound old English cheese, cut small, with 1 cup heavy cream and 1 cup flaked finnan haddie. When well blended, stir in 1 beaten egg and serve on toast. Serves 6.

fruits

For a light dessert to top off a heavy meal, fresh fruit, raw or cooked, is most welcome. Fruits are not only high in essential nutrients but they also have a general appeal and are simple to prepare. All fruits should be washed carefully before using, because the sprays used on fruit trees may be harmful. Many fruits darken when peeled. This is harmless but detracts from the appearance, and can be avoided if the fruit is dipped immediately into citrus or pineapple juice.

For economy in low cost meals, use dried fruits as often as possible. They are one of the magic fruits of the kitchen. A clever cook can prepare tempting, tasty desserts. Weight for weight, dried fruits outshine the fresh fruit in minerals and most other food values.

APPLE SAUCE (Basic Recipe)

Wash, pare, and core 8 cooking apples. Add about ½ cup water and ⅛ teaspoon salt. Cook in covered pot until soft. Add about ½ cup sugar while hot. Simmer just long enough to melt sugar. Amount of sugar and water varies with sweetness and juiciness of apples. For additional flavoring, add with sugar, nutmeg, cinnamon, grated lemon rind or juice, or a combination of spices. Serves 8.

Honey apple sauce: Substitute ½ cup honey for sugar. Add 1 to 2 teaspoons grated lemon rind.

Minted apple sauce: Add ¼ cup chopped mint with sugar.

Orange apple sauce: Add 2 to 3 teaspoons grated orange rind with sugar.

Rosy cinnamon apple sauce: Cook ⅓ cup red cinnamon candies with apples.

Spiced apple sauce: Substitute ⅓ cup firmly packed brown sugar for granulated sugar. Add ¼ teaspoon cinnamon and 1 teaspoon grated lemon rind.

Strained apple sauce: Do not pare apples. Remove any bruised spots. Cut into quarters and cook until soft. Force through a coarse sieve. Add sugar and flavoring. Simmer to dissolve sugar.

APRICOT, GRAPE, PEACH OR PEAR SAUCE

Follow method for *APPLE SAUCE*, using one fruit or combinations for tasty variations.

BAKED APPLE SAUCE

6 to 8 tart apples	⅔ cup water
Cinnamon, to taste, or	¾ cup sugar
2 thin slices lemon	

Wash apples (do not peel), remove bruised spots, and cut in quarters. Place in a baking dish. Add cinnamon or lemon and water. Cover; bake in moderate oven

(375°F.) until tender, 20 to 30 minutes. Put through a strainer. Add sugar and mix. Serve hot or cold. Serves 6 to 8.

Creamed apple sauce: Substitute ⅔ cup light cream for water. Add ½ teaspoon cinnamon and ¼ teaspoon nutmeg with sugar.

Honey apple sauce: Substitute honey for sugar. Add 1 tablespoon grated lemon rind.

Maple apple sauce: Substitute 1 cup maple syrup for sugar and water.

Orange apple sauce: Add 2 tablespoons grated orange rind while cooking.

BAKED APPLES (Basic Recipe)

Wash baking apples. Core ⅔ of the way down from top of apples. Do not break through blossom end of skins. Put in baking dish. Fill each cavity with sugar, cinnamon, and nutmeg. Allow ¼ teaspoon cinnamon or nutmeg to 8 apples. If nutmeg is used, add to each apple a few drops of lemon juice and a few gratings of lemon rind. Cover dish with boiling water ¼ inch in depth. Cover and bake in a moderate oven (375°F.) about 40 minutes, or until apples are soft. Remove cover, bake 10 minutes longer. If baked uncovered, baste occasionally with syrup in pan. Remove apples. Boil syrup until thick and pour over apples. Serve hot or cold with cream.

Apple rings: Cut apples crosswise in rings and place in casserole. Add sugar, water, and lemon juice. Bake until tender.

Cranberries in baked stuffed apples: Fill the cavity in the center of the apple with cranberry sauce or jelly. Add sugar to water in pan if filling is not sufficiently sweet. Bake.

Honey baked apples: Substitute ½ cup honey for sugar.

Maple or brown sugar baked apples: Substitute maple or brown sugar for granulated.

Marshmallow baked apples: Stuff cavities with any suggested stuffings. When baked, top with marshmallow and return to oven to brown, about 5 minutes.

Rosy cinnamon apples: Add red cinnamon candies to water before baking.

Stuffed baked apples: Before baking, stuff cavities with mincemeat, chopped dates and nuts, sliced bananas, or bananas and cranberries combined, marmalade, jelly, crushed pineapple, etc.

Old-fashioned baked apples: Peel apples, cut in halves, and remove cores. Place cut side up in baking pan. Fill cavities with mixture of raisins and brown sugar. Sprinkle with few drops of lemon juice. Dot with butter. Cover bottom of pan with boiling water. Bake in moderate oven (375°F.) until soft, about 25 minutes.

Baked apples in cream: Peel and core 12 medium sized sour apples. Roll in 3 tablespoons melted butter, then in sugar and cinnamon, and lastly in buttered breadcrumbs. Place apples in a shallow baking dish. Fill centers with sugar and cinnamon. Add bits of butter. Bake in 400°F. oven. When apples have baked about 20 minutes, add ½ cup cream. Continue baking until well done. Serves 6.

Praline apples: Bake apples as in Basic Recipe, adding only the sugar and cinnamon. Cool them and place in sherbet or dessert dishes. Place ⅔ cup granulated sugar and ½ cup blanched and shredded almonds in a saucepan over a medium flame. Heat until sugar is caramelized golden brown. Spoon quickly over apples. Cool. Serve with whipped cream.

BAKED PEACHES OR PEARS

Bake in same way as *BAKED APPLES*. Molasses may be substituted for sugar with pears. Lemon juice may be added to increase tartness.

APPLE COMPOTE (Basic Recipe)

1½ pounds cooking apples	Few grains salt
1½ cups water	Slice of lemon (optional)
¾ cup sugar	Candied orange peel (optional)

Wash, pare, and quarter ripe apples. Drop into cold water to prevent discoloration. Bring to a boil sugar, salt, lemon, and orange peel. Drop apple quarters, a few sections at a time, into syrup. Cover and simmer gently until fruit is transparent and tender, turning apples when half done. Serve hot or cold. If fruit is very hard, precook before adding to syrup. Serves 6.

Apple raisin compote: Add ¾ cup seedless raisins. Cook with apples.

Apple slices: Cut crosswise into circles. Add to syrup and simmer until tender.

Cinnamon apple rings: Cut apples in rings. Add ½ cup red cinnamon candies to sugar and water.

Glazed apples: Core apples. Cook whole, unpeeled, in colored syrup. Score the skin in small squares before cooking to keep fruit from bursting.

Minted apples: Color syrup pale green. When apples are done, flavor syrup with oil of peppermint.

PEACH OR PEAR COMPOTE

Prepare like *APPLE COMPOTE*. Stick a clove in each fruit before cooking.

BAKED DRIED FRUIT COMPOTE

Combine several varieties of dried fruit (pears, prunes, etc.). Wash in warm water. Drain. Place in a baking dish and barely cover with water. For each pound of fruit add ½ cup sugar or ⅔ cup honey and 3 slices of orange or lemon. Cover and bake in slow oven (325°F.) 1½ hours. Chill and serve topped with custard, sprinkled with shredded coconut or lemon rind.

FRIED APPLES

Wash, quarter, and core firm apples. Slice in medium thin pieces. Sauté in small amount of hot fat until brown. If tart, sprinkle with a little brown sugar or honey while cooking.

Apple fritters: Pare and core apples. Cut into medium thin slices or wedges. Cover with fritter batter and fry.

Broiled apple rings: Core and slice firm apples about ½ inch thick. Arrange in pan. Sprinkle with brown sugar and butter if tart. Bake in broiling oven until brown and tender.

APRICOT WHIP

⅔ cup (scant) dried apricots
¼ cup sugar

⅔ cup evaporated milk, chilled
1⅓ tablespoons lemon juice

Wash apricots. Cover with 1 cup water and soak several hours or overnight. Simmer gently until tender in same water. Press through a coarse sieve. Yield is approximately ⅔ cup pulp. Dissolve sugar in hot pulp. Chill mixture. Whip chilled evaporated milk until stiff. Add lemon juice and continue whipping until blended. Fold in cold apricot whip. Serves 6.

Variations: Any fruit pulp from stewed dried fruit, well drained canned fruit, fresh fruit, or berries or a combination of fruit pulps or apple sauce may be used for this whip. The amount of sugar used will vary with the sweetness of the fruit.

Frozen apricot whip: Prepare as above. Freeze in a refrigerator tray or a mold packed in ice and salt.

ROSY APPLE COMPOTE

6 tart apples
2 cups sugar
2 cups water

Red coloring or
    Red cinnamon candies
⅛ teaspoon salt

Select tart, firm apples that will hold shape when cooked. Wash, pare, and core. In a pan large enough to hold all the apples, make a syrup of the sugar and water. Add red coloring or red candies and salt. Put in apples. Cover. Simmer until apples are tender when pierced with a toothpick. Drain and place at once on plates for serving. Fill centers with tart jelly, and on top add a spoonful of hard sauce, grated coconut, or chopped nuts. Or serve apples cold with whipped cream. The syrup may be used in fruit drinks, or for cooking more apples.

Rosy apple slices: Follow directions for ROSY APPLE COMPOTE, cutting peeled and cored apples into ¾-inch-thick slices. When slices are tender, remove from pan and boil syrup until thick. Serve slices with thick syrup.

CARAMEL FRIED APPLES

3 cups apples
2 tablespoons butter

½ cup sugar
½ cup water

Pare apples and cut into good-sized pieces. Let butter become hot in pan. Put in apples, sugar, and, lastly, water. Let cook without stirring until apples are soft and sugar and butter become a golden brown on bottom of pan.

AMBROSIA CUP #1

2 cups strawberries
1 cup diced pineapple

1 cup sugar
½ cup shredded coconut

Wash and drain berries. Remove hulls and cut in halves. Add pineapple and sugar. Mix thoroughly. Chill. Garnish each serving with shredded coconut. Serves 6.

AMBROSIA CUP #2

1 large grapefruit
2 oranges
1½ cups canned pineapple cubes,
    drained

Shredded moist coconut
½ cup sugar

Pare grapefruit and cut out segments by cutting close to membrane. Peel orange and cut up into segments. Alternate layers of grapefruit, orange, pineapple, and shredded coconut in a bowl. Sprinkle with ½ cup sugar. Chill thoroughly. Serve in cups, garnished with maraschino cherries. Serves 6.

AVOCADO APRICOT WHIP

1½ cups cooked, sweetened dried apricots

1 cup whipping cream
1 cup diced avocado

Sieve apricots. Whip cream until thick, but not stiff, and whip apricots into cream gradually. Add avocado and mix lightly. Chill. Serves 6. This may be varied with any fruit in season instead of apricots.

FRUIT FILLED AVOCADO

2 medium-size avocados
   Salt, to taste
2 cups grapefruit sections

1½ dozen stuffed olives
French dressing

Prepare halves of avocados. Scoop out flesh, leaving a thin layer to hold shells in form. Cut portion removed into cubes and sprinkle with salt. Cut grapefruit sections into cubes. Cut olives into rounds. Toss fruit together lightly and refill shells. Add dressing and chill. Serves 4.

AVOCADO À LA KING

2 pimientos, cut into strips
1 cup medium WHITE SAUCE

1½ cups mushrooms
2 cups cubed avocado

Add pimiento strips to WHITE SAUCE with mushrooms and heat thoroughly. Add cubed avocado just before serving to avoid actual cooking. Serve in croustades or patty shells, or over toast points, or with rice, spaghetti, or noodle rings.

BAKED BANANAS (Basic Recipe)

6 firm bananas
2 tablespoons melted butter

⅛ teaspoon salt
2 tablespoons lemon juice

Select ripe bananas, skin, scrape off the stringy fibers, and, if desired, split in half lengthwise. Place in buttered baking pan. Brush with melted butter; sprinkle with salt and lemon juice. Bake in moderate oven (375°F.) until tender, about 15 to 20 minutes. Serve hot or cold.

Banana newburg: Sprinkle FRIED BANANAS with brown sugar while cooking. Add a little sherry and let them simmer a few minutes.

Bananas with sherry or rum: Pour a little sherry or rum over bananas while baking.

Broiled bananas: Prepare as for baking. Place in shallow pan and broil until tender, 6 to 8 minutes.

Fried bananas: Cut bananas in half lengthwise. Sauté in butter until lightly browned. Serve hot. For dessert: Sprinkle with brown sugar while frying.

Fried banana scallops: Cut peeled ripe bananas into 1-inch lengths. Dip in slightly beaten salted egg, then in crumbs (use cornflakes, breadcrumbs, or cracker crumbs). Fry in hot deep fat (375°F.) until golden brown, 1½ to 2 minutes. Drain on absorbent paper. Serve hot.

Fried bananas with rum: Pour some rum into the pan when *FRIED BANANAS* are done. Light it. Baste bananas with flaming syrup. Serve immediately.

Glazed baked bananas: Sprinkle brown or white sugar over bananas 5 minutes before removing from oven.

Honey baked bananas: Sprinkle honey over bananas with the butter and lemon juice.

With cranberries: Pour 1¼ cups hot cranberry sauce over bananas. Bake until tender.

ARMENIAN APRICOT COMPOTE

1 pound apricots	Sugar
¼ pound prunes	Almonds, blanched and peeled
¼ pound seedless raisins	

Soak together apricots and prunes overnight in cold water to cover. In the morning, add raisins and additional water to cover if necessary. Simmer until tender, 20 to 30 minutes, and add sugar to taste. Serve cold. Garnish each serving with 6 or 7 almonds. Serves 8 to 10.

BAKED FRESH FRUIT COMPOTE

Combine several varieties of fresh fruits in a baking dish. Add syrup made of 1 part water to 1 part sugar. Cover and bake in a moderate oven (350°F.) until tender, 15 to 20 minutes.

FRUIT SNOW

1 cup fruit, dried or sliced	1 teaspoon lemon juice
Sugar to taste	2 egg whites

Use soft fresh fruit or any stewed fruit (apples, prunes, bananas, peaches, or apricots). If very juicy fruits are used, the juice should be drained thoroughly before rubbing through a sieve. Sour, raw apples may be grated. Sweeten fruit pulp to taste and add lemon juice. Beat egg whites until stiff, then beat in sweetened fruit pulp and continue beating until the mixture is very fluffy. Pile lightly in individual serving dishes and chill thoroughly. Serve with cream or soft custard. Garnish with jelly. Serves 4 to 6.

DANISH CHESTNUTS IN RUM

Steam or roast 1 pound chestnuts until soft. Remove shells and arrange on a flat silver dish. Sprinkle thickly with 1¼ cups powdered sugar. Pour ½ cup heated rum over all. Set fire to rum just before serving. When flames die down, serve 2 or 3 to each person with hot, strong, black coffee.

BANANA PRUNE COMPOTE

¾ cup sugar	2 cups cooked drained prunes
1 cup water	2 bananas, sliced
1 tablespoon lemon juice	2 tablespoons tart jelly
Pinch of salt	

Combine sugar, water, lemon juice, and salt. Boil 5 minutes. Chill. Arrange fruits in serving glasses. Cover with syrup. Garnish with tart jelly. Serves 6.

BANANA FRITTERS

3 bananas
1 tablespoon sugar
2 tablespoons lemon juice

1 teaspoon orange juice
2 teaspoons grated orange rind
FRITTER COVER BATTER

Peel and quarter bananas. Sprinkle with sugar, lemon and orange juice, and orange rind. Cover and let stand ½ hour. Dip in *FRITTER COVER BATTER*. Fry in deep fat (365°F.) until brown on all sides. Drain on absorbent paper. Sprinkle with powdered sugar. Serve with desired sauce. Serves 6.

GLAZED FRIED BANANAS

Peel 6 firm bananas. Brush with lemon juice. Roll in sugar. Fry bananas slowly in butter until tender and golden brown, turning them to brown evenly. Serve hot. Serves 6.

SERVING FRESH BERRIES

Pick over berries. Wash in colander. Hull or remove stems. Sprinkle with powdered sugar. If fruit is too tart, let stand 1 to 2 hours. A sprinkling of lemon juice will neutralize excess tartness.

STEWED BERRIES

1 quart berries
½ to 1 cup boiling water

½ to 1 cup sugar
Lemon juice to taste

Wash, drain berries. Place in sauce pan. Add ½ cup of water. Cover and cook until tender, 5 to 10 minutes, adding more water as required. Add sugar when almost done, and lemon juice to taste.

STEWED SOUR CHERRIES

Wash cherries and remove stems. Add a small amount of boiling water and simmer until nearly tender. Add sugar to taste and cook a few minutes longer.

STEWED FRESH FRUIT

For 2½ pounds fruit, such as apples, peaches, pears, plums, apricots, ½ cup sugar is usually adequate. Amount of sugar added may vary depending upon sweetness of fruit. Cook fruit in covered pan. Bring to quick boil, reduce heat to gentle simmer, and continue cooking until fruit is tender. Add sugar or sweetening last 5 minutes of cooking. A dash of salt added just before removing from fire brings out natural sweetness of fruit. Serves 5.

CRANBERRY SAUCE (Basic Recipe)

1 pound (4 cups) cranberries
1½ cups sugar

2 cups water

Wash, pick over, and drain cranberries. Put berries, sugar, and water in saucepan. Bring slowly to boiling point. Cover and cook slowly about 10 minutes, or until skins burst. Skim and cool. Yield: about 4 cups.

Baked cranberry sauce: Wash and pick over berries. Place in a baking dish. Add 1¾ cups sugar and 1 cup water for each quart of berries. Cover and bake in slow oven (325°F.) 30 minutes, or until berries are tender.

Cranberry apple sauce: Combine 2 cups each of cranberries and sliced, pared apples, ¾ cup water, and 1 cup sugar. Cover and cook slowly until tender, about 20 minutes. Cool slightly. Beat until fluffy.

Glazed cranberries: Prepare as in basic recipe. Do not drain thoroughly. Measure and mix equal parts sugar and berries in the top of double boiler. Cook over hot water until sugar forms thick syrup, about 1 hour, and berries are glazed. Stir carefully a few times at the start.

Molded cranberry sauce: Increase sugar to 2 cups. Cook until a thin syrup is formed, about 20 minutes. Pour into mold; chill.

CRANBERRY STRAWBERRY COMPOTE

Cook 1 pound cranberries, in water to cover, in covered pot about 5 minutes. Add 1 cup sugar and 2 cups strawberries. Cook 5 to 8 minutes. Serve cold.

STEWED DRIED FIGS

Wash 1 cup figs. Remove stems. Cover with water. Cover and simmer until tender, 20 to 25 minutes. Add ¼ cup sugar and simmer 10 minutes.

FRUIT WHIP (Basic Recipe)

1 cup sieved, canned fruit pulp	Sugar
Pinch of salt	1 egg white

Combine fruit pulp and salt. Sweeten to taste. Add egg white. Beat until stiff enough to hold shape. Chill. Pile lightly in serving cups. Serves 6.

BUFFET FRESH FRUIT DESSERT

1 cup sugar	6 cups prepared assorted fruits:
1 cup water	pitted cherries, melon balls, sliced
1 pound plums	peaches, and sliced ripe pears
1 pound peaches, pitted	1 ANGEL or SPONGE CAKE
4 sprigs mint	

Boil together sugar and water, plums, peaches, and mint until fruit is tender. Strain and chill about 6 hours. Arrange prepared fruits on large platter. Garnish attractively with more mint leaves. To serve, place whole cake which has been cut, the platter of fruit, and the dish of sauce on the buffet table. Serve fruit over cake and top all with sauce. Serves 8.

FRUIT CREAM

1 cup pinapple juice	1 cup whipping cream, stiffly
½ cup orange juice	whipped
24 marshmallows, diced	Vanilla wafers

Heat fruit juices to boiling point. Add marshmallows and stir until dissolved. Chill until partially set. Fold in stiffly whipped cream. Line shallow pan with vanilla wafers. Cover with cream mixture. Add layer of vanilla wafers. Cover with remaining cream mixture. Chill in refrigerator overnight. Serves 6 to 8.

HOT FRUIT COMPOTE

Combine a variety of canned or cooked fruits. Heat with a small amount of juice. Flavor with brandy, sherry, or rum.

BLACK AND GOLD COMPOTE

1 cup purée from cooked dried
    apricots
½ cup apricot juice
½ cup granulated sugar
2 tablespoons plain gelatin

3 tablespoons cold water
2 cups cooked dried prunes
1 cup diced pineapple
1½ cups pineapple juice
    Few drops lemon juice

Combine apricot purée, apricot juice, and sugar. Heat to boiling and remove from fire. Soften gelatin in cold water. Add to hot purée and stir until gelatin dissolves. Pour into shallow pan. Chill in refrigerator until firm. Cut into cubes. Pit prunes and cut into fair-sized pieces. Arrange in stemmed glasses with apricot cubes and pineapple. Combine pineapple and lemon juices and pour over fruits. Serves 6.

CRYSTALLIZED GRAPES

Select perfect red or purple grapes. Wash and drain well. Cut into small clusters. For each pound of grapes use ½ cup water and 1 cup sugar. Combine water and sugar and boil 5 minutes. Dip each cluster of grapes separately into hot syrup. Let excess syrup drain off. Sprinkle grapes at once with granulated sugar. Place on cake rack to harden and place rack in refrigerator.

FROSTED GRAPES

Select perfect red or purple grapes. Wash and dry well. Cut into small clusters. Beat egg white until slightly frothy. Sprinkle it over the grapes. Dust with granulated sugar. Let dry.

BROILED GRAPEFRUIT

Prepare grapefruit halves by loosening fruit sections. Sprinkle each with sugar. Set in pan and place under broiler so that rack is 4 inches under flame. Cook with broiler door open until outer skin begins to brown and fruit is heated through. Serve hot as appetizer or dessert. If desired, sprinkle with brown sugar and wine before broiling.

BROILED HONEYED GRAPEFRUIT

Remove seeds from halves of grapefruit. Core and loosen sections. Spread with honey and sprinkle with cinnamon and mace. Dot with butter. Brown under moderate flame of broiler unit. Serve at once.

BAKED GRAPEFRUIT

2 cups crushed corn flakes
½ cup brown sugar, firmly packed
½ teaspoon cinnamon

¼ cup melted butter
2 grapefruit, halved and cored

Combine corn flakes, sugar, cinnamon, and butter. Fill and top the halves of grapefruit in which the sections have been loosened. Bake in hot oven (400°F.) about 10 to 12 minutes. Serve at once. Serves 4.

MELON BALL BASKET

1 honeydew melon	½ cup sweet wine (marsala,
1 cantaloupe, halved and seeded	muscatel, or port)

Make a basket by cutting wedges from both sides of upper half of honeydew melon, leaving a ¾-inch strip between wedges for a handle. Be sure handle is not cut but remains attached to lower half of melon. Remove seeds carefully. With a melon ball cutter form balls from the meat of the lower half of melon, hollowing out entire lower half, and from the cut-out wedges. Cut balls from halves of cantaloupe. Trim some of the meat from inside the melon handle with a knife. Return the balls to basket, arranging them to show contrasts in color between honeydew and cantaloupe balls. Pour wine over balls. Chill thoroughly. Serves 6.

ORANGE FRITTERS

Peel oranges and separate into sections. Remove seeds making as small openings as possible. Dip sections in *FRITTER COVER BATTER*. Fry in deep hot fat.

BROILED PEACHES

Drain peaches well. Place hollow-side-up in shallow pan. Place a dot of butter in each. Sprinkle lightly with salt. Broil under moderate flame until light brown. Serve hot as a garnish.

PEACHES WITH BRANDIED CREAM

½ cup heavy cream	3 tablespoons powdered sugar
1 tablespoon brandy flavoring	Few grains mace
Few grains salt	8 fresh peaches

Whip cream slightly. Add flavoring, salt, 1 tablespoon sugar, and mace. Whip until cream is thickened. Peel and slice peaches. Add remaining sugar and mix well. Arrange in serving dishes and top with cream. Serves 4.

PEARS IN WINE SAUCE

6 uniform-size green winter pears	2 teaspoons lemon juice
1 teaspoon grated lemon rind	4 cloves
Concord grape wine	1 2-inch stick cinnamon, broken
Water	1 cup sugar

Peel pears. Place in saucepan and cover with equal amounts of wine and water. Add remaining ingredients. Cover and simmer until tender. Chill. Serve in sauce. Serves 6.

STEWED DRIED PEARS

Wash 1 cup dried pears. Remove remaining parts of core. Cover with water. Cover and simmer until tender, about 40 minutes. Add ⅓ cup sugar and simmer 5 minutes.

Steamed dried pears: Add ¼ cup sugar and ⅓ cup water to 1 cup dried pears and steam until tender.

STUFFED PEARS

¼ cup whipping cream
¼ cup chopped nutmeats
½ tablespoon sugar

¼ teaspoon vanilla
6 halves canned pears

Combine stiffly whipped cream, nuts, sugar, and vanilla. Pile lightly into hollows of pear halves placed in chilled sherbet cups. Serves 6.

BAKED PEAR MACAROON

½ cup melted butter
½ cup brown sugar, firmly packed
2 cups coarse dry breadcrumbs

⅓ cup strained honey
1 teaspoon cinnamon
4 medium-size fresh pears

Combine butter, sugar, crumbs, honey, and cinnamon. Peel pears and coat outside of each pear with this mixture. Set pears upright in greased pan. Bake in moderate oven (375°F.) until tender, about 30 minutes. Serve with cream. Serves 4.

Baked peach macaroon: Substitute fresh peaches for pears.

FRESH PINEAPPLE

Wash pineapple. Cut off leafy end and a slice from stem end. Stand pineapple upright and cut off skin in strips from top to bottom. Remove eyes with pointed knife or special pineapple knife. Prepare as below. Sprinkle with sugar and chill. Sugar will dissolve as it stands.

Shredded: Cut very thin slices. Shred with a fork.

Slices: Cut into thin serving slices. Cut out round core.

Spears: Cut prepared pineapple into wedges with core removed. Cut into strips.

Wedges or cubes: Cut slices into wedges or cubes after core is removed.

Broiled pineapple: Drain slices well. Brush with melted butter. Sprinkle with sugar. Broil under moderate heat until lightly browned.

Pineapple ambrosia: Cut prepared pineapple into slices or cubes. Add 1 cup each of orange and grapefruit sections and ½ cup shredded coconut. Chill 1 hour or more before serving.

Pineapple compote: Cube or shred 1 medium-size pineapple. Make syrup by combining 2 cups sugar and 1 cup water and stirring over low heat until sugar dissolves. Bring to boil and cook 5 minutes. Add pineapple. Cover and cook 10 minutes. Chill.

Sauteed pineapple slices: Drain pineapple well. Dip slices in flour. Sauté in hot fat, turning to brown on both sides.

TOASTED PINEAPPLE MERINGUES

6 slices pineapple
2 egg whites, beaten stiff

¼ cup confectioners' sugar

Drain pineapple thoroughly and place in a shallow, buttered baking pan. Beat egg whites until stiff. Whip in confectioners' sugar and pile lightly on slices. Brown delicately in a slow oven (325°F.). Serve with a fruit sauce made by boiling 1 cup of pineapple juice with ⅓ cup sugar and ¼ cup lemon juice until thickened. Serves 6.

GLAZED PINEAPPLE RINGS

Drain pineapple slices and place on broiling rack. Beat cranberry sauce until smooth and spreadable. Add just a little of pineapple juice to make it spread more readily, if necessary. Spread each pineapple slice with sauce. Place in preheated broiler under moderate flame. Broil until heated through and glazed, about 10 to 15 minutes. Serve with poultry.

PLUM COMPOTE

6 large firm plums
1½ cups boiling water

About ¾ cup sugar

Place washed fruit in saucepan and cover with the boiling water. Cover and simmer 10 minutes. Add sugar to taste and stir until dissolved. Cover and cook 10 minutes longer.

STEWED PRUNES (Basic Recipe)

½ pound dried prunes
3 cups hot water

1 to 2 tablespoons sugar
Slice of orange or lemon

Wash prunes and soak in hot water 1 to 2 hours. Simmer in same water until tender. Add sugar and lemon or orange slice last 5 minutes of cooking. If syrup is very thin, remove prunes and boil down syrup. Serve hot or cold.

Prunes and apricots: Use ¼ pound each of dried prunes and dried apricots. Double the amount of sugar.

Prunes and peaches or pears: Use ¼ pound each of dried prunes and dried peaches or pears. Increase sugar slightly.

Prune pudding: To 1½ cups pitted prune pulp and juice add a mixture of ¼ cup cornstarch, ¼ teaspoon cinnamon, and ¼ cup cold water. Cook until clear and thick, stirring constantly. Chill.

Prune whip: Add 1 tablespoon sugar and few grains salt to 1 cup strained prune pulp. Cut and fold pulp into 2 stiffly beaten egg whites. Add 1 tablespoon lemon juice. Serve cold or bake in slow oven (300°F.) about 20 minutes.

Stuffed prunes: Remove stones and stuff cavities with cottage cheese or cream cheese. Top with chopped nuts.

SPICED PRUNES

1 pound dried prunes
1 quart water
⅛ teaspoon salt
1 cup sugar

8 whole allspice
8 whole cloves
3 small pieces stick cinnamon
¼ cup vinegar

Wash large prunes and soak over night in water to cover. Add sugar and spices tied in a cheesecloth bag and simmer 15 to 20 minutes. Add vinegar and cook about 10 minutes longer, or until the syrup is fairly thick. Serves 6.

PRUNES IN WINE SAUCE

1 pound large prunes
1 cup Concord grape wine
  Water
2 thin slices of lemon

1 bay leaf
¼ teaspoon cinnamon
3 cloves
½ tablespoon cornstarch

Wash prunes. Place in a saucepan and add wine and enough water to cover. Add lemon slices, bay leaf, cinnamon, and cloves. Cover and let stand over night. Next day, dissolve the cornstarch in a little of the juice and add to prunes. Cover and simmer until tender, 20 to 30 minutes. Chill and serve in the sauce. Serves 6.

BAKED QUINCES

6 quinces
3 tablespoons sugar
12 orange slices (¼ inch thick)

¼ cup macaroon crumbs
2 tablespoons butter

Select ripe fruit. Wash, pare, and remove cores. Place cut side up in greased baking pan. Place skins and cores in saucepan. Add sugar and orange slices. Cover with boiling water and boil 20 minutes. Strain. Pour 2 tablespoons of this liquid over each half of quince. Cover and bake in moderate oven (350°F.) until tender and red, about 2 to 2½ hours. Sprinkle with crumbs and dot with butter. Bake, uncovered, in hot oven (425°F.) until brown, about 5 minutes. Serves 6.

STEWED RHUBARB (Basic Recipe)

Cut off leaves and stem ends. Wash 2 pounds rhubarb. Peel only if stalks are tough. Cut into 1-inch pieces. Add ½ cup hot water. Simmer, covered, 10 minutes. Add ¾ cup sugar and simmer 5 minutes longer, or until tender. The amount of sugar necessary may vary with the tartness of the rhubarb. Add dash of cinnamon, if desired. Serves 6 to 8.

Steamed rhubarb: Cook in top of double boiler until tender, about ½ hour.

Baked rhubarb: Arrange alternate layers of diced rhubarb and sugar in baking dish. Sprinkle top with sugar. Bake in slow oven (300°F.) until rhubarb is deep red in color, about 1 hour.

Rhubarb whip: Whip 1 pint of heavy cream until stiff. Sweeten. Fold into 1 cup stewed rhubarb. Place each serving in a sherbet glass which has been lined with lady fingers or pineapple spears. Chill.

Rhubarb with berries: Mix equal amounts of diced rhubarb and fresh berries. Add sugar to taste. Let stand 1 hour or more. Heat slowly until sugar dissolves. Simmer without stirring until rhubarb is tender.

Rhubarb with pineapple: Mix equal parts diced rhubarb and diced fresh pineapple. Sweeten to taste. Let stand 1 hour or more. Heat slowly until sugar dissolves. Simmer until rhubarb is tender.

RHUBARB DESSERT OMELET

2 egg yolks
¼ cup confectioners' sugar
½ teaspoon grated lemon rind
4 egg whites

⅛ teaspoon salt
½ tablespoon butter
1½ cups fresh rhubarb sauce

Beat yolks and add sugar and lemon rind. Beat egg whites with salt until stiff but not dry. Fold in first mixture. Melt butter in heavy skillet. Pour in egg mixture and cook until puffy. Spread fruit sauce over top and roll. Sprinkle with confectioners' sugar. Cut and serve at once. Serves 4.

STRAWBERRIES WITH SOUR CREAM

Cut strawberries in halves. Sprinkle with sugar and let stand 30 minutes. Serve with thick sour cream and powdered sugar, if desired.

STRAWBERRY WHIP

⅔ cup crushed chilled strawberries
½ cup confectioners' sugar

1 egg white, stiffly beaten
1 tablespoon lemon juice (optional)

Combine ingredients in a bowl. Beat until stiff enough to hold shape. Serves 6.

Apple whip: Substitute grated raw apples for strawberries.

OLD-FASHIONED GLAZED FRUITS

1 tablespoon lemon juice
¼ cup molasses
1 tablespoon butter

4 servings canned or cooked
  peaches, pears, apricots, or
  pineapple

Combine lemon juice and molasses. Bring slowly to boil and boil 3 minutes, stirring constantly. Arrange fruit in well-greased baking dish. Pour molasses mixture over fruit. Dot with butter. Place in broiler or bake in moderate oven (375°F.) about 10 minutes, basting occasionally. Serves 4.

GLAZED FRESH FRUIT

Use uncooked fruit. Arrange fruit in well-greased baking casserole. Mix lemon juice and molasses together (do not precook) and pour over fruit. Dot with butter. Bake in moderate oven (350°F.) about 45 minutes, basting occasionally so that fruit will be evenly glazed.

DRIED FRUIT TZIMMES

2 pounds mixed dried fruits
  (apricots, peaches, pears,
  prunes, raisins)
½ cup white or brown rice

¼ cup honey
½ teaspoon salt
Dash of cinnamon
2 cups boiling water

Wash fruit and drain. Combine with remaining ingredients. Heat to boiling. Simmer slowly about 20 minutes or until rice is tender and liquid is almost completely absorbed. Shake pot occasionally to prevent sticking, adding a little boiling water if necessary. Serve hot or cold. Or turn into a shallow casserole, dot with butter, and brown slightly under broiler flame. Serves 4 to 6.

macaroni, noodles and spaghetti

These three are the best known of more than 150 shapes of wheat pastes that help balance the family budget and intrigue children and gourmets too. The quality depends almost entirely upon the wheat used. The pastes made from durum wheat break with a clean sharp edge and keep their shape during cooking. Noodles are made of a similar dough but have eggs or egg yolks added. Spinach noodles are a fine green in color. For homemade noodle recipes and variations, see the *SOUP ACCESSORIES* section.

Homemakers should use more of this wheat paste family because it is easy to use, quick to cook, and its bland flavor blends well with meats, soups, cheese, eggs, fish, and vegetables. When combined with protein foods, and accompanied by a green salad, they make a well-rounded meal. There is an endless, to-be-explored intrigue in the variety of shapes that seem to taste special because they look so different.

HOW TO BOIL MACARONI, NOODLES, AND SPAGHETTI

For each ½ pound of macaroni, noodles, or spaghetti use 3 quarts of fresh cold water and 2 tablespoons salt. Have salted water boiling rapidly. Gradually drop the macaroni, noodles, or spaghetti into water so that water does not stop boiling. To cook unbroken spaghetti, dip ends into the boiling water, and, when ends are soft, gradually coil the rest into the water. Boil uncovered until tender, 9 to 12 minutes, stirring occasionally. Do not overcook. Drain in colander and rinse with hot water. Serve hot at once. Spaghetti with *TOMATO SAUCE* or any of its variations and grated Parmesan cheese; macaroni with any desired sauce; noodles with butter, salt, and pepper, or any desired sauce; or use boiled macaroni, noodles, or spaghetti in other recipes.

BAKED MACARONI AND CHEESE (Basic Recipe)

2 teaspoons grated onion
½ pound grated cheese
2 cups medium *WHITE SAUCE*

1 package (8 ounces) macaroni
½ cup buttered crumbs
Paprika

Add onion and half the grated cheese to *WHITE SAUCE*. Blend well. Cook macaroni, drain, and rinse. Place in alternate layers with sauce in buttered casserole. Sprinkle with crumbs, remaining cheese, and paprika. Bake uncovered in moderate oven (375°F.) about 25 minutes, or until crumbs are browned. Serves 6 to 8.

MACARONI VARIATIONS

Spaghetti: Substitute spaghetti for macaroni in basic recipe or Macaroni Variations.

Macaroni with tomato sauce: Omit onion and paprika. Substitute tomato sauce for *WHITE SAUCE*.

Italian macaroni: Add sautéed minced onion and garlic to tomato sauce. Pour on macaroni and sprinkle Parmesan cheese on top.

Spanish macaroni: Add ¼ cup chopped green pepper which has been fried until soft in 1 tablespoon oil, and 1 tablespoon each of minced onion, celery, and pimiento to tomato sauce.

Macaroni and hard cooked eggs: Alternate layers of macaroni and slices of hard cooked egg. Cover with medium WHITE SAUCE and bake.

Quick macaroni or spaghetti casserole: Combine 2 cups cooked spaghetti or macaroni with 1½ cups condensed tomato soup or purée and ½ cup grated cheese. Mix well and pour into greased casserole. Sprinkle with ½ cup buttered crumbs. Bake in moderate oven (350°F.) until browned, about 30 minutes.

Macaroni salmon casserole: Cook ½ pound macaroni. Drain, rinse, and drain again. Add 1 cup medium WHITE SAUCE, 1 pound can salmon, 1 small green pepper, chopped fine, ½ teaspoon salt, ⅛ teaspoon pepper, asparagus tips, and ¾ cup grated American cheese. Place in greased casserole and sprinkle ¼ cup cheese over top. Bake in moderate oven for 35 minutes. Serves 6.

CREAMY MACARONI PATTIES

4 tablespoons shortening	1 tablespoon chopped parsley
5 tablespoons flour	1 teaspoon scraped onion
1 cup milk	Fine dry breadcrumbs
1 teaspoon salt	1 egg
½ pound grated cheese	1 tablespoon water
1½ cups cooked macaroni	4 tablespoons cooking fat

Melt shortening. Blend in flour. Add milk and salt. Stir until smooth and thickened. Remove from heat. Add grated cheese and stir until cheese is melted. Add macaroni, cut into small pieces, parsley, and onion. Turn into well-greased pan. Chill until firm. Cut into patties. Dip in fine crumbs, then in beaten egg which has been diluted with water, then again in crumbs. Fry in hot fat until brown. Serve with tomato sauce. Serves 5.

Macaroni croquettes: Prepare above recipe. Shape into croquettes when chilled. Fry in deep fat (375°F.) until browned. Drain on absorbent paper. Serve with cheese sauce.

MACARONI MOUSSE

1 cup uncooked macaroni	1 tablespoon chopped parsley
1½ cups scalded milk	1 tablespoon chopped onion
1 cup soft breadcrumbs	1 teaspoon salt
¼ cup butter	½ pound grated American cheese
1 pimiento, chopped fine	3 eggs, separated

Cook, drain, and rinse macaroni. Pour scalded milk over breadcrumbs. Add melted butter, pimiento, parsley, onions, salt, grated cheese, and beaten egg yolks. Add macaroni cut in small pieces. Fold in stiffly beaten egg whites. Turn into buttered baking dish. Set in pan of hot water and bake in moderate oven (325°F.) 40 minutes. Cover for first half of baking period. Serve with mushroom sauce, garnished with pimiento and parsley. Serves 6.

MACARONI AND ASPARAGUS CASSEROLE

3 cups cooked macaroni
2 tablespoons cooking fat
3 tablespoons flour
1 teaspoon salt
1/16 teaspoon pepper

2 cups milk
2 dozen cooked or canned
   asparagus tips
1 cup grated Parmesan cheese
1/4 cup fine dry breadcrumbs

Cook and drain macaroni. Prepare white sauce of fat, flour, salt, pepper, and milk. In greased 1½-quart casserole place ½ of macaroni and ½ of asparagus. Sprinkle with ½ the cheese. Cover with ½ of WHITE SAUCE. Add rest of macaroni, asparagus, and cheese. Cover with rest of sauce. Cover with breadcrumbs. Bake in moderate oven (350°F.) about 30 minutes. Serves 4 to 6.

MACARONI NUT CASSEROLE

2 cups elbow macaroni
2 teaspoons salt
2 quarts boiling water
1 cup grated American cheese
1 cup chopped walnuts

2 cups canned tomatoes
1 teaspoon salt
1/4 teaspoon pepper
1/2 tablespoon minced onion

Drop macaroni into rapidly boiling salted water and boil 9 minutes. Drain in strainer and pour cold water over it to separate pieces. Put ⅓ in bottom of greased 1½-quart casserole. Sprinkle ½ cup cheese over top, then ½ cup nuts. Repeat layers, using ½ of remaining macaroni and rest of cheese and nuts. Top with macaroni. Season tomatoes with salt, pepper, and onion. Pour over macaroni mixture in casserole and cover. Bake in moderate oven (350°F.) until cheese is melted, 30 minutes. Serves 4 to 6.

BROAD NOODLE PUDDING (Basic Recipe)

8 ounces broad noodles
3 tablespoons cooking fat
3 eggs, separated
1 teaspoon cinnamon

1/4 teaspoon nutmeg
3/4 cup chopped seedless raisins
1/2 cup sugar
1/8 teaspoon salt

Boil, drain, and rinse noodles. Add fat, well beaten egg yolks and remaining ingredients, lastly folding in stiffly beaten egg whites. Mix well and pour into a greased casserole. Bake in moderate oven (350°F.) about 45 minutes, or until browned. Serves 4 to 6.

With almonds: Reduce raisins to ½ cup. Add ¼ cup chopped almonds.

With apples and nuts: Use only ¼ cup raisins. Add ⅔ cup sliced, peeled apple and ¼ cup chopped nuts.

With breadcrumbs: Sprinkle with 3 tablespoons buttered or dry breadcrumbs before baking.

With cracklings (grieben): Omit nutmeg. Use only ¼ teaspoon cinnamon. Substitute ¾ cup chopped cracklings for raisins. Use chicken fat for the fat.

With prunes or apricots: Substitute chopped dried prunes or apricots for raisins. Add 1 tablespoon lemon juice and ¼ teaspoon grated lemon rind.

BAKED NOODLE RING

8 ounces egg noodles
2 eggs, beaten
½ cup milk
½ tablespoon melted butter

½ teaspoon salt
Dash of white pepper
1 tablespoon tomato ketchup
½ cup grated cheese

Boil, drain, and rinse noodles. Combine noodles, eggs, milk, butter, seasonings, and cheese. Mix well. Pour into well-buttered ring mold. Set in pan of hot water. Bake in moderate oven (350°F.) until firm, about 45 minutes. Unmold on a platter. Fill center with creamed fish, eggs, or vegetables. Garnish with quartered tomatoes and parsley or a border of cooked peas around outside of ring. Serves 6.

Buttered noodle ring: Boil ½ pound noodles. Rinse with hot water and drain. Add ¼ cup butter and stir well. Pack in a ring mold. Unmold on platter. Fill center and garnish as above. Serves 6.

SOUR CREAM NOODLE RING

4 ounces broad noodles
1 cup sour cream
1 egg, slightly beaten
1 cup cottage cheese

½ teaspoon salt
Dash of pepper
¼ cup melted butter

Cook, drain, and rinse noodles. Combine with remaining ingredients and turn into buttered ring mold. Bake in slow oven (300°F.) about 1½ hours. Unmold and fill center with creamed mushrooms, or fish, as desired.

NOODLE AND COTTAGE CHEESE CASSEROLE

8 ounces noodles
1 pound dry cottage cheese
2 eggs, beaten
1 tablespoon sugar (optional)

¼ cup butter
½ cup sour cream
1 teaspoon salt
⅛ teaspoon white pepper

Cook, drain, and rinse noodles. Combine with remaining ingredients and mix well. Pour into greased casserole and bake in moderate oven (375°F.) 45 minutes. Serves 6.

CHEESE AND NOODLE BAKE

1 cup grated cheese
3 cups cooked noodles
1 cup tomato juice

2 tablespoons grated onion
1 tablespoon parsley
Salt and pepper

Arrange alternate layers of cheese and noodles in buttered casserole. Combine tomato juice, onion, and parsley. Add salt and pepper to taste and pour over noodles. Sprinkle with cheese. Bake in moderate oven (350°F.) 30 minutes. Serves 6.

POPPY SEED NOODLES

8 ounces broad noodles
3 tablespoons poppy seeds
½ cup blanched toasted almonds, chopped
1 tablespoon melted butter

1 teaspoon lemon juice
½ teaspoon salt
⅛ teaspoon white pepper
Sprig parsley, minced

Boil, drain, and rinse noodles. Blend poppy seeds and almonds with butter. Add remaining ingredients. Mix lightly with hot noodles. Serves 6.

SCALLOPED NOODLES AND TUNA FISH

8 ounces noodles	¾ teaspoon salt
4 tablespoons butter	Few grains of pepper
3 tablespoons flour	1½ cups flaked tuna fish
2 cups milk	½ cup soft breadcrumbs

Cook noodles about 10 minutes. Drain. Melt 3 tablespoons butter in double-boiler. Add flour and mix well. Add milk gradually and cook, stirring constantly until thickened. Add salt and pepper. Combine sauce, noodles, and tuna fish. Add more salt if desired. Pour into a buttered baking dish. Sprinkle with crumbs mixed with 1 tablespoon melted butter. Bake in moderate oven (375°F.) 20 to 25 minutes. Serves 6.

SPINACH NOODLES

¼ cup spinach, cooked, drained, and puréed	¼ teaspoon salt
	2 cups sifted flour
1 egg, beaten	

Combine spinach, egg, and salt. Stir flour in gradually. Knead until smooth. Place dough in a covered dish for ½ hour. Roll into paper-thin sheets. Spread out on cloths to dry. Before they are too dry to handle fold over into a roll and cut into very thin shreds. Toss apart and permit them to dry thoroughly. Store in a glass jar until ready to use.

NOODLE CHILI

1 pound ground beef	2 cups canned kidney beans
12 scallions or	½ teaspoon sugar
1 large bermuda onion	½ teaspoon salt
½ can tomatoes (No. 2 can)	½ teaspoon chili powder
2 cups cooked noodles	

Brown beef quickly in 1 tablespoon hot fat in heavy skillet. Add scallions whole or large onion sliced crosswise ¼ of an inch thick. Add tomatoes, peeled and chopped, if fresh ones are used. Add beans and noodles with 1 cup of water in which they were boiled, then sugar, salt, and chili powder. Cover closely and simmer for 1 hour. Serves 6.

NOODLE AND APPLE CASSEROLE

1 package (8 ounces) broad noodles	¼ cup sugar
3 tablespoons melted butter	½ teaspoon cinnamon
½ teaspoon salt	3 cups sliced apples

Cook, drain, and rinse noodles. Mix well with butter, salt, sugar, and cinnamon. Peel, core, and slice apples. Place alternate layers of noodle mixture and apples in a greased casserole, starting and ending with noodles. Dot with 2 tablespoons butter. Bake in slow oven (325°F.) until apples are tender, about 45 minutes. Serves 6 to 8.

NOODLE AND PRUNE CASSEROLE

8 ounces broad noodles	1 cup prune liquid
2 cups stewed, pitted prunes	1 teaspoon cinnamon
¼ cup butter or chicken fat	¼ cup breadcrumbs

Boil and drain noodles. Place alternate layers of noodles and prunes in a greased casserole, starting and ending with noodles. Melt butter or chicken fat in prune liquid, add cinnamon and pour over noodles. If the prunes were stewed unsweetened, add about ¼ cup sugar to liquid. Sprinkle with breadcrumbs. Bake in moderate oven (350°F.) until crumbs are browned, about 20 minutes. Serves 6 to 8.

BUTTERED NOODLES

Boil 1 package (8 ounces) noodles in 3 quarts boiling salted water until tender. Drain in a colander and rinse with hot water. Add 3 tablespoons butter, salt, and pepper, to taste. Stir gently. Serve as soon as butter melts. Serves 4 to 6.

FRIED NOODLES

Boil fine noodles. Drain, rinse with cold water and drain again. Spread in thin layer and chill. Fry in deep hot fat (390°F.) until brown, about 1 minute. Drain on absorbent paper. Sprinkle with salt.

NOODLES WITH CRUMBS

Boil and drain 1 package (8 ounces) noodles. Season with salt and pepper. Brown ¾ cup seasoned buttered crumbs and sprinkle over noodles. Serves 4 to 6.

SPAGHETTI WITH SAUCE

Prepare *TOMATO-MEAT SAUCE, TOMATO-WINE SAUCE* or *SPAGHETTI SAUCE*. Cook spaghetti, drain, and rinse. Place on hot platter. Pour over hot sauce.

BAKED SPAGHETTI WITH SAUCE

Combine desired sauce with cooked spaghetti. Turn mixture into greased casserole and top with buttered crumbs. Bake in moderate oven (350°F.) 30 minutes, then sprinkle grated cheese over top. Bake until cheese is melted and lightly browned, 5 minutes.

CHEESE SPAGHETTI MOLDS

4 ounces spaghetti	Dash cayenne
2 eggs, slightly beaten	1 tablespoon grated onion
1 cup milk	2 tablespoons chopped parsley
1 cup cottage cheese	2 tablespoons minced green pepper
1 teaspoon salt	or pimiento

Cook spaghetti in 1 quart boiling salted water until tender. Drain and rinse with cold water. Mix remaining ingredients thoroughly, add spaghetti, and pour into 5 well-greased custard cups. Set cups in a pan of hot water. Bake in moderate oven (350°F.) until mixture is firm and a knife inserted in the center comes out clean, or about 30 minutes. Serve with creamed vegetables. Serves 5.

SPAGHETTI OLIVE MUSHROOM CASSEROLE

1 package spaghetti	1 onion
2 cups tomatoes	2 tablespoons butter
1 teaspoon salt	½ cup stuffed olives
½ pound mushroom caps	1 cup grated cheese

Boil the spaghetti. Cook tomatoes and salt until thickened, 15 minutes. Fry sliced mushrooms and chopped onion in butter. Add olives, sliced, and tomatoes. In a baking dish put layers of spaghetti and vegetables with the spaghetti on the top and bottom. Cover with cheese. Bake in moderate oven (375°F.) 20 minutes, or until brown. Serves 6.

BAKED MEAT BALLS WITH SPAGHETTI

1 pound ground beef
¼ cup soft breadcrumbs
1 egg
1 teaspoon salt
2 tablespoons cooking fat or salad oil

1 onion, sliced
½ green pepper, sliced
4 ounces spaghetti, cooked
1½ cups canned tomatoes

Combine ground beef, breadcrumbs, egg, and salt. Mix well. Shape into balls. Brown in melted fat. Place in casserole. Brown onion and green pepper slightly in meat drippings. Meanwhile cook spaghetti in boiling salted water. Drain. Rinse with hot water. Place in casserole. Add browned onion and green pepper. Combine tomatoes with meat drippings in frying pan and pour over spaghetti and meat balls in casserole. Season to taste. Cover and bake 1 hour in moderate oven (350°F.). Serves 4.

SPAGHETTI TIMBALES

3 tablespoons minced onion
4 tablespoons green pepper, minced
4 tablespoons fat or butter
3 tablespoons flour
   Salt and pepper

2 cups milk
1 cup grated American cheese
2 eggs, well beaten
2 cups cooked spaghetti

Sauté onion and green pepper in fat until tender. Add flour and seasoning. Stir until well blended. Add milk gradually, stirring constantly to prevent lumping. Bring to boiling point and cook 2 minutes. Remove sauce from stove and add cheese. Stir until melted. Add eggs and spaghetti. Pour mixture into well-greased individual baking dishes. Set dishes into pan of hot water. Bake in moderate oven (350°F.) until firm, about 1 hour. Turn out timbales from dishes. Serve hot with cheese sauce, garnished with pimiento. Serves 6.

MACARONI BAKED WITH SOUR CREAM

6 ounces macaroni
3 tablespoons melted butter or margarine

1 cup sour cream
½ cup grated cheese

Cook macaroni in boiling salted water. Drain and toss with melted butter. Turn into greased baking dish. Make a well in center. Pour in sour cream. Sprinkle grated cheese over all. Bake in hot oven (400°F.) until top is brown. Serves 4.

rice and other cereals

Several varieties of rice are available. However, the primary concern of the home-maker should be to see that the rice she buys is enriched.

White: White rice is sold as polished (coated) and unpolished (uncoated) rice. Polished rice is the least desirable; however, the snowy whiteness of polished rice is popular. In the process of preparing the inner portion of the grain, which is what you get when you buy white rice, essential food values are removed. The enriching process replaces some of them. White rice is often covered with a harmless talc or glucose to increase eye appeal. It washes off easily.

Converted rice: This is white rice which retains most of the original vitamins because of the manufacturing process followed in processing it.

Brown rice: This is preferable to white rice because it is a whole grain rice, retains the essential food values. It has a pleasing nutty flavor. It is, however, more perishable than white rice and requires greater care in packing and storing.

Wild rice: This is not a real rice but is actually the seed of a marsh grass. It has a distinctive flavor but it is quite expensive and often hard to obtain.

To wash rice: Place rice in strainer or colander. Run cold water over it into a bowl until the water in the bowl is completely clear.

BOILED RICE

Wash rice thoroughly in cold water. For each cup of rice use 2 quarts boiling water and 2 teaspoons salt. Add rice gradually to rapidly boiling salted water. Boil until tender, 25 to 30 minutes, lifting occasionally with fork to prevent from sticking. Do not stir. Turn into colander and rinse with hot water. To keep hot, cover colander with cloth and place over hot water. One cup uncooked rice makes 3 or more cups cooked rice.

Brown rice: Cook as above but allow 40 to 50 minutes.

Boiled wild rice: Cook as for *BOILED RICE* but allow more time, about 35 to 40 minutes. Serve plain or mixed with sliced mushrooms and finely chopped onions which have been sautéed in butter.

STEAMED RICE

Wash rice in cold water. For each cup rice allow 2 cups boiling water and 1 teaspoon salt. Add boiling salted water to rice in top part of double boiler. Cover. Cook until water is absorbed, 12 to 15 minutes. Continue cooking over boiling water until tender, 15 to 20 minutes. Uncover last 5 minutes of cooking for rice to dry and fluff.

STEEPED WILD RICE

Wash rice thoroughly in cold water. Drain. Cover 1 cup rice with 1 quart boiling water. Let stand about 40 minutes. Drain and cover again with boiling water. Let stand 20 minutes. Repeat this twice again using fresh boiling water each time. Last time, add 2 teaspoons salt and then drain thoroughly. Serve with 1 tablespoon melted butter and season to taste.

RICE VARIATIONS

Baked rice: Fill a greased casserole with 3 to 4 cups cooked rice. Beat 2 eggs lightly with 1½ to 2 cups milk and pour over rice. Season with salt and pepper. Dot with butter and sprinkle with paprika. Bake in a moderate oven (350°F.) until browned.

Pimiento rice: To 2 cups hot cooked rice, add ¾ to 1 cup grated cheese and 2 chopped pimientos.

Rice and cheese: Serve cooked rice with cheese sauce or add ¾ to 1 cup grated cheese to hot cooked rice.

Rice cooked in milk: Cook as for *STEAMED RICE*, substituting scalded salted milk for water.

Rice custard pudding: To 1 cup rice cooked in milk, add 3 eggs beaten with ½ cup sugar and 1 teaspoon vanilla or lemon extract for the last 5 minutes of cooking.

Rice with dessert sauces: Serve hot or cold cooked rice with butterscotch or chocolate sauce.

Rice with mushroom almond sauce: Combine 1 cup *BROWN SAUCE*, ¼ cup sliced sautéed mushrooms, and ¼ cup sliced toasted almonds. Serve hot over 2 cups hot cooked rice. Serves 4 to 6.

Rice timbales: Pack cooked rice in buttered molds. Let stand in hot water about 10 minutes. Unmold, garnish with a mushroom cap, and serve with cheese sauce.

Spanish rice #1: Brown 1 cup rice in 3 tablespoons fat before boiling. Cook rice in 4 cups tomato juice instead of water. Sauté ¼ cup minced onion and add with celery, green pepper, and pimiento, all chopped. Turn into greased casserole and bake until brown in moderate oven (350°F.) 30 minutes. Serves 6.

Yellow rice: Cook rice in milk and add ½ cup cream and 1 egg for last 5 minutes of cooking.

RICE RING

Combine 2 cups cooked rice with 2 tablespoons melted fat and 1 teaspoon salt. Turn into greased ring mold. Place mold in pan of hot water. Bake in moderate oven (350°F.) 25 minutes. Unmold on platter and fill center with creamed fish, meat, vegetable, as desired. Sprinkle with paprika. Garnish outside of ring with border of cooked peas.

Brown rice ring: Substitute steamed brown rice in above recipe.

RICE CROQUETTES (Basic Recipe)

3 tablespoons butter	1½ cups cooked rice
3 tablespoons flour	Fine dry breadcrumbs
½ teaspoon salt	1 egg, slightly beaten
1 cup milk	

Melt butter and blend in flour and salt. Add milk and cook until thickened, stirring constantly. Add rice. Mix and spread on shallow plate to cool. Shape into 6 croquettes. Roll in crumbs, then in beaten egg and again in crumbs. Fry in deep hot fat (375°F.) until brown. Drain on absorbent paper.

Cheese rice croquettes: Mix grated cheese with a few drops onion juice. If necessary, moisten with a little milk. Shape into small balls. Coat with thick layer of rice mixture. Proceed as in basic recipe.

Cranberry rice croquettes: Cut chilled cranberry sauce into cubes. Coat with chilled rice mixture. Proceed as in basic recipe.

Pimiento rice croquettes: Add 2 tablespoons chopped pimiento to rice mixture.

Rice croquettes with jelly: Make a depression in the top of each croquette when shaping them, or form into balls, then into nests. Proceed as in basic recipe. To serve, place a spoonful of tart red jelly in each.

Savory rice croquettes: Add ¼ teaspoon paprika and 1 tablespoon ketchup to rice mixture.

Sweet rice croquettes: Add 2 tablespoons powdered sugar and grated rind of ½ lemon before cooling mixture.

Tomato rice croquettes: Substitute tomato juice for milk. Cook 1 tablespoon grated onion with flour.

SPANISH RICE #2

½ cup chopped onions	3 cups cooked rice
½ cup chopped green pepper	½ teaspoon chili powder
3 tablespoons cooking fat or salad oil	1 teaspoon salt
2½ cups canned tomatoes	⅛ teaspoon pepper

Cook onions and pepper in hot fat until browned. Add tomatoes, rice, and remaining ingredients, mixing thoroughly. Cook in skillet about 30 minutes, or turn into casserole and bake in moderate oven (350°F.) 30 minutes. Before baking cover with crumbs and dot with fat. Serves 6.

Spanish rice with beef: Sauté 1 cup ground meat with pepper and onions. Add remaining ingredients as for *SPANISH RICE*.

CURRIED RICE

1 cup uncooked rice	3 cups boiling water or meat stock
2 tablespoons cooking fat or salad oil	1 to 2 tablespoons curry powder
1 tablespoon chopped onion	2 teaspoons salt

Wash rice. Drain. Heat fat in frying pan. Add rice and onion and stir until rice is golden brown. Add boiling water or stock and seasonings. Cover and cook slowly until tender, about 30 minutes.

TURKISH RICE

3 tablespoons butter or other fat	⅔ cup diced celery
1 onion, chopped	1 pound rice, washed thoroughly
1 green pepper, chopped	1½ teaspoons salt
1 clove garlic, finely minced (optional)	2 cups canned tomatoes
½ pound fresh mushrooms	2 cups water
	2 tablespoons chopped parsley

Melt butter in saucepan; add onion, green pepper, garlic, sliced mushrooms, and celery. Brown over low heat, then add washed rice, salt, tomatoes, and water. Stir to blend. Pour mixture into large buttered casserole. Cover and bake until rice has absorbed liquid and is tender. Uncover, stir to blend ingredients, then top with crumbs. Dot with fat and grated cheese if desired. Brown uncovered in moderate oven (375°F.). Garnish with chopped parsley. Serves 6 to 8.

Turkish rice with meat or chicken: Use salad oil instead of butter and add about 2 cups diced cooked meat or chicken to the sautéed vegetables. Add remaining ingredients as for *TURKISH RICE.*

BAKED RICE WITH CHEESE

Combine 3 cups cooked rice with 2 cups *CHEESE SAUCE.* Turn into baking dish or individual baking cups. Bake in hot oven (400°F.) about 15 minutes.

ALMOND RICE LOAF

Cook 1 cup rice in boiling water until tender. Drain. Sauté ½ cup almonds in butter. Sprinkle bottom of well-greased small loaf pan with part of almonds. Mix remaining almonds with rice. Turn into pan. Set aside in warm place until serving time. Unmold on platter. Serve with creamed or curried eggs.

ITALIAN RICE (Risotto)

Sauté ½ cup washed, uncooked rice in 2½ tablespoons butter until delicately browned, about 3 minutes. Add 1 cup canned tomatoes and 1 cup vegetable stock. Season to taste with salt, pepper, and onion salt. Add ¼ cup grated cheese. Simmer until all liquid is absorbed by rice, about 25 minutes. Serves 4.

GREEN RICE CASSEROLE

2 cups cooked rice	1 egg, beaten
½ cup grated sharp cheese	2 tablespoons minced onion
1 cup milk	½ cup minced parsley

Combine and mix all ingredients. Add salt to taste. Turn into greased casserole. Bake in slow oven (325°F.) 30 minutes. Serve with creamed seafoods.

RICE AND CHEESE LOAF

2 cups uncooked rice	2 eggs
1 clove garlic	¾ teaspoon salt
½ pound American cheese, grated	¼ cup finely cut parsley
1⅔ cups evaporated milk	1 tablespoon grated onion

Boil rice until tender in salted water to which garlic has been added. Remove garlic. Drain and rinse rice. Melt cheese in milk over boiling water. Beat eggs. Add salt, parsley, onion, rice, and melted cheese. Pour into buttered loaf pans. Bake in moderate oven (350°F.) 1 hour. Serves 8.

HONEY, RICE, AND DATE PUDDING

2 eggs, beaten light	⅓ to ½ cup honey
1 cup milk	2 cups cooked rice
½ cup chopped dates or raisins	

Mix beaten eggs and milk. Arrange alternate layers of rice, dates or raisins in a greased baking dish. Drizzle honey over each layer. Repeat until all rice and fruit is used. Pour egg-milk mixture over all. Bake in moderate oven for 45 minutes. Serves 6.

STUFFED RICE BALLS (Russian Style)

¼ pound dried mushrooms or
    ½ pound fresh mushrooms
1 cup rice
1 onion, minced

1 tablespoon flour
4 tablespoons ketchup
Dry breadcrumbs
Lemon juice

Boil mushrooms in salted water until tender. Drain and chop, saving the stock. Boil rice in mushroom stock and water. Brown onion in vegetable oil. Combine mushrooms, onion, flour, and 1 tablespoon ketchup. Shape into small balls and use as filling for larger balls of rice. Roll in breadcrumbs and fry in vegetable oil. Mix remaining ketchup with lemon juice and use as dressing for fried rice balls. Serve very hot. Serves 4 to 6.

FRIED RICE BALLS

Wash 1 cup rice. Cook in double boiler in 1 cup boiling water until rice completely absorbs water. Add 2 cups scalded milk and 1½ teaspoons salt. Cook until rice is soft. Spread on shallow pan until cold. Shape into 1-inch balls. Fry in deep hot fat (375°F.) until delicately brown.

RICE PATTIES

Combine cold cooked rice with beaten egg, allowing 1 egg for every 2 cups of rice. Form small cakes and cook on both sides in fat in skillet. Serve with fish or meat, or as dessert topped with syrup.

BEEF AND RICE IN CABBAGE CASSEROLE

Wash ½ cup uncooked rice. Mix with 1 cup raw ground beef, 1 tablespoon chopped onion, salt and pepper to taste. Cook 1 medium head cabbage in boiling salted water until leaves are pliable. Remove leaves whole from head. Wrap a leaf around 1 rounding tablespoon of meat mixture. Arrange in a greased casserole. Cover with tomato sauce. Cover and bake in moderate oven (350°F.) for 1 hour. Serves 6.

ITALIAN BAKED RICE

4 cups cooked rice
2 teaspoons salt
1½ cups tomato juice

½ cup chopped pimiento
¾ cup grated cheese
⅛ teaspoon pepper
Breadcrumbs

Combine ingredients and turn into a buttered casserole. Cover top with crumbs. Dot with butter. Bake in moderate oven (350°F.) 30 minutes. Serve in casserole. Serves 6.

RICE BAKED WITH TOMATOES AND CHEESE

1 cup uncooked rice
2 cups canned or fresh sliced tomatoes
¾ cup grated cheese

⅓ cup chopped pimientos
Salt and pepper, to taste

Boil rice until tender. Drain. Combine with remaining ingredients. Bake in greased baking dish 30 minutes in moderate oven (350°F.). Serve hot.

HOW TO COOK CEREALS

Quick-cooking oats: To 3 cups rapidly boiling salted water, gradually add 1½ cups quick-cooking oats. Stirring constantly, cook 2½ minutes or longer if desired.

Quick-cooking wheat cereal: To 2½ cups rapidly boiling salted water, gradually add ½ cup quick-cooking wheat cereal. Stir constantly until thickened. Cook slowly 5 minutes.

Rolled oats: To 3 cups rapidly boiling salted water, gradually add 1½ cups rolled oats. Stirring constantly, cook 5 minutes or longer, if desired.

Wheat cereal: To 3 cups rapidly boiling salted water, gradually add ½ cup wheat cereal. Stir constantly until thickened. Cook slowly 15 minutes.

Cereal cooked in milk: Substitute scalded milk for water in the recipe. Add cereal to scalded milk. Cook, covered, over hot water until thickened and done.

Cereal cooked with fruit: Follow recipes given above, adding ¼ cup chopped dried apricots, pitted dates, figs, pitted prunes, raisins, or nutmeats a few minutes before cooking is completed.

TEMPTING WAYS TO SERVE COOKED CEREALS

Add dried fruits such as raisins, dates, and prunes.

Cook cereal with milk or use part milk instead of water.

Combine 2 or more cereals and cook together.

Serve cereals with honey, molasses, brown sugar, or maple syrup instead of white sugar.

Slice cold leftover cereal and fry. Serve with butter and syrup.

Mix leftover cereal with ground cooked meat, fish, or vegetables. Chill. Slice and fry.

Use leftover cereal as part of stuffing for fish, meats, and poultry.

Use leftover cereal as a stuffing for baked apples. Fill cored centers. Top with brown sugar and bake.

Add sweetening and desired flavorings to leftover cereal. Turn into custard cups. Chill and serve with dessert sauces.

POLENTA

4 cups water
1 teaspoon salt

1 cup yellow corn meal
¾ cup grated Parmesan cheese

Using top of double boiler over direct flame bring 3 cups water and salt to brisk boil. Combine corn meal and 1 cup water and gradually add to boiling water. Cook, stirring constantly, until thick, about 5 minutes. Place over boiling water. Cover and cook 30 minutes. Add ½ cup grated cheese. Turn into greased casserole and sprinkle top with remaining cheese. Bake in moderate oven (350°F.) until browned. Serve with tomato sauce. Serves 4.

KASHE (Buckwheat Groats)

1 cup buckwheat groats
½ teaspoon salt
½ teaspoon paprika

1 egg
1 cup boiling water
1 tablespoon cooking fat

Mix thoroughly the groats, salt, paprika, and egg. Bake in greased casserole in moderate oven (350°F.) until brown. Stir in water and fat. Cover and return to oven for 20 minutes. Serves 4 to 5.

Top of the stove method: Mix 1 cup groats and 1 egg in a frying pan and place on fire. Stir constantly until the kernels are separated and dry. Turn into a preheated kettle. Add 2 cups boiling water, 1 teaspoon salt, and 2 tablespoons fat. Cover tightly. Cook on a medium flame ½ hour. Add additional boiling water, if necessary. Serves 4 to 5.

ITALIAN GNOCCHI

½ cup farina
1 tablespoon butter
½ teaspoon salt
2 cups hot milk
1 beaten egg
½ pound sharp cheese, grated
¼ cup chopped onions

¼ cup chopped green pepper
2 tablespoons fat
2 cups tomatoes, canned
1 teaspoon salt
⅛ teaspoon pepper
Pinch of cayenne

Stir farina, butter, and salt into hot milk and cook in top of double boiler 15 minutes. Add egg and cheese. Reserve ½ cup grated cheese. Pour into shallow, greased pan. Chill, then cut into 12 squares and place in large flat baking dish. Brown chopped onion and green pepper in hot fat. Add other ingredients and cook 10 minutes. Pour sauce over farina squares. Sprinkle with remaining cheese. Bake in slow oven (325°F.) until cheese is melted, about 15 minutes. Serves 4.

FRIED HOMINY GRITS

1 cup hominy grits
3 cups water

1½ teaspoons salt
3 tablespoons corn meal

Gradually stir hominy grits into rapidly boiling salted water. Cook about 1 hour over hot water, stirring occasionally. Turn into a greased 1-quart loaf pan. Chill until firm. Cut into ½-inch slices and dip in corn meal. Sauté hominy slices in hot fat until browned on both sides. Serve hot with syrup or honey. Serves 6.

HOMINY GRITS MUSH

¾ cup hominy grits
3½ cups boiling water

1¼ teaspoons salt

Slowly add hominy grits to boiling salted water, stirring constantly. Cook 45 minutes over a low flame. Serves 5.

HALF AND HALF FRIED MUSH

½ cup corn meal
½ cup soybean grits

3 cups boiling water
1 teaspoon salt

Mix corn meal and grits. Gradually add to boiling salted water, stirring constantly to prevent lumping. Cover and simmer 20 minutes. Turn into a loaf pan which has been rinsed with cold water. Cover with waxed paper. When cold, unmold and cut in ½-inch slices. Fry in very hot fat until golden brown. Serves 5.

GRITS AU GRATIN

¾ cup grits
3 cups boiling water
1 teaspoon salt
½ pound sharp cheese, grated

1 cup milk
½ cup buttered breadcrumbs
¼ teaspoon paprika

Slowly stir grits into boiling, salted water in top of double boiler over direct flame. Cover, place over boiling water and continue cooking 45 minutes, stirring occasionally. Alternate layers of cooked grits and grated cheese in greased baking dish. Add milk and sprinkle with breadcrumbs and paprika. Bake in slow oven (325°F.) 30 minutes. Serves 6.

YELLOW CORN MEAL MUSH

Using top of double boiler over direct flame, add 1 teaspoon salt to 2½ cups briskly boiling water. Combine ½ cup yellow corn meal and ½ cup water. Slowly add to boiling water. Cook, stirring constantly, until thick, about 5 minutes. Place over boiling water. Cover and cook ½ hour longer, stirring occasionally. Serves 4 to 6.

WHITE CORN MEAL MUSH

Using top of double boiler over direct flame, add 1 teaspoon salt to 3 cups briskly boiling water. Gradually add ½ cup white corn meal. Cook, stirring constantly, until thick, about 10 minutes. Place over boiling water. Cover and cook ½ hour longer, stirring occasionally. Serves 4 to 6.

FRIED MUSH

Turn cooked cereal into a greased mold. Cover to prevent crust from forming. Chill until firm. Cut into ½-inch-thick slices. Dip in flour or corn meal. Sauté in butter or salad oil, browning on both sides. Cook slowly, if desired dry and crisp. Serve with maple or corn syrup or molasses.

meats

KOSHER MEATS

The rules of kashruth provide that animals used for food be quadrupeds that chew the cud and have cloven hooves such as sheep, goats, deer, and cattle. Only the forequarters of these quadrupeds are permitted. Beef, veal, and lamb are the favorites in the Jewish kitchen. The meat is sectioned in a number of cuts from the neck to and including seven ribs. The manner in which the meat is sectioned may vary in different parts of the country. The same general sections may be referred to by different names in various localities. There are a number of cuts in the forequarter that may be used for steaks. In the recipe sections that follow a number of suggestions are included for tenderizing meats and for preparing delicious steaks from the kosher cuts.

Below are listed the major cut sections and their general uses.

BEEF

Brisket of beef: Use in potted or stewed dishes and in soup, or bone and use for corned beef.

Chuck: Use for soups, stews, braised dishes, or boned and rolled for pot roast.

Chuck steaks: Use for braised, potted, or stewed dishes.

Neck of beef: Use unboned for soups and stews, or bone and use for ground meat, or boned and rolled and used in braised dishes.

Plate or navel: Use for boiled beef, in stews, or bone and roll for roasts.

Ribs: Use for standing or rolled rib roasts and steaks.

Shank: Use for pot roast, stews, soups, or for ground meat.

Short ribs: Use for soups, stews, or in braised dishes.

Shoulder of beef: Use boned or unboned for pot roast and roasts. Slice thin for steaks or to be stuffed and rolled as in meat birds.

LAMB

Breast of lamb: Use unboned with a pocket for dressing, roasted, or potted, or cut up and use in stews.

Neck of lamb: Use in stews.

Rack of 7 ribs with part of upper section: Use for crown roast with dressing.

Shank: Use for soups or bone for ground meat, or use unboned for pot roast or braised dishes.

Shoulder chops: Broil or fry.

Shoulder of lamb: Use for pot roast or roast, boned or unboned, or cut up and use in stews.

312

VEAL

Breast of veal: Use unboned with a pocket for dressing, roasted, or potted, or cut up for stews.

Rib or shoulder chops: Pan fry.

Shank: Bone for ground meat or use unboned for pot roast or braised dishes.

Shoulder: Slice for veal cutlets or steaks, or use boned or unboned for pot roast or roast.

beef

The different cuts of beef vary in tenderness. It is necessary, therefore, to determine the cooking method to be followed and to select the cuts of meat best suited to that method. For cooking by dry heat—roasting, broiling, and pan-broiling—select tender cuts with small amounts of connective tissue. For cooking by moist heat—braising, stewing, and soup-making—select the less tender cuts. The less tender cuts are more economical and are equal in food value to the tender cuts. All cuts of meat may be made equally tender and tasty through the selection of the proper cooking method. Other means for making meat tender are grinding, pounding, and marinating. Grinding cuts up the connective tissue and the meat may then be cooked like any other tender meat. Pounding tenderizes by cutting through the connective tissue. Marinating, which is accomplished by letting the meat stand in an oil-acid mixture like French dressing, softens the connective tissue.

BROILED STEAK

Have tender steak cut at least 1 inch thick. Trim off excess fat. Preheat broiler. Place steak on rack. Insert broiler pan and rack so that top surface of 1-inch steak will be 2 inches from heat and 2-inch steak will be 3 inches from heat. If this distance must be less, temperature should be reduced accordingly so that moderate broiling temperature is maintained. It is sometimes advisable to leave door open to maintain moderate temperature. When one side is nicely browned, season with salt and pepper, turn, and finish cooking on second side. Steaks cut 1 inch thick require 15 to 20 minutes for broiling. 2-inch steaks require 30 to 35 minutes.

BROILED STEAK—SEARING METHOD

Preheat broiler until very hot (450–500°F.). Place steak under flame so that top of steak is 2 to 3 inches from source of heat. Sear or brown on each side, turning only once, allowing 5 minutes for each. Leave door open. Reduce heat to slow (300°F.) or place steak 6 to 7 inches from source of heat and finish cooking. When half done, season top side, turn, and finish cooking. Season other side and serve. Allow the same time as for even temperature method, including searing in total time. The searing method produces a steak with surface nicely browned while interior may be rare or medium.

PLANKED STEAK

Broil steak, cutting time for top side by 5 minutes. Place less done side up on a greased broiling plank. Season. With pastry tube arrange border of mashed potatoes around edge of plank. Place one or more cooked vegetables between steak and potatoes. Brush all with melted cooking fat. Place in broiler 3 inches from flame and brown potatoes. Garnish with parsley, watercress, tomato wedges or slices.

PAN-BROILED STEAK

Use tender steak ¾ to 1 inch thick. Trim off excess fat. Heat heavy skillet moderately and grease very lightly. Place steak in it. Brown quickly on both sides. Reduce heat. Cook slowly until done, pouring off fat as it accumulates. To test, cut near bone. Season with salt and pepper and serve.

CHUCK STEAK WITH ONIONS

2 pounds chuck steak
5 or 6 onions, sliced
  Cooking fat or salad oil

2 teaspoons salt
½ teaspoon pepper

Brown steak quickly on both sides in hot frying pan. Reduce heat. Cook 30 minutes, turning frequently. Add onions. Cover and cook slowly until tender. Uncover. Brown slightly, if desired. Season with salt and pepper. Serve with onions surrounding meat. Serves 6.

PEPPER CHUCK STEAK

¼ cup melted cooking fat or salad oil
3 pounds beef chuck, in 2 cuts
6 green peppers, seeded
  Salt and pepper, to taste
3 large onions, sliced thin
2½ cups canned tomatoes

1 cup tomato sauce
½ cup beef stock or water
2 bay leaves
2 sprigs green celery leaves
1 sprig thyme
8 sprigs fresh parsley

Brown beef well on both sides in hot fat. Place 1 steak in baking pan. Cover steak with 3 green peppers, cut in strips. Season with salt and pepper. Over this place other steak and cover with remaining green peppers cut in strips and mixed with onions. Combine tomatoes and sauce and pour over all. Season with salt and pepper. Pour beef stock or water over this. Add a bouquet garni made up of bay leaves, celery leaves, thyme, and parsley tied with thread. Bring to boil. Cover and bake in moderate oven (350°F.) 2 to 2½ hours. Baste several times with gravy. Remove bouquet garni. Serve steak on hot platter. Serves 6.

STANDING RIBS OF BEEF

Select a 2 or 3 rib roast (4 to 5 pounds). Have the chine bone removed to make carving easier. Season with salt and pepper. Insert a meat thermometer so that the bulb reaches the center of the largest muscle. Be careful that bulb does not rest on fat or bone. Place fat side up on a rack in an open roasting pan. Do not add water. Do not cover. Roast in slow oven (300°F.) to desired degree of doneness. Allow 18 to 20 minutes per pound for cooking a rare roast, 22 to 25 minutes per pound for a medium, and 27 to 30 minutes per pound for a well-done roast. Thermometer will read 140° for rare, 160° for medium, and 170° for well-done.

ROLLED RIB ROAST

Select a 3-rib boned and rolled roast. Season with salt and pepper. Place roast, fat side up, on rack in pan. Insert meat thermometer in thickest part of meat. If roast hasn't a generous fat covering, place suet over top. Proceed as for *STAND-ING RIBS OF BEEF*, increasing roasting time 10 minutes per pound.

BEEF POT ROAST (Basic Recipe)

2 onions, sliced
2 tablespoons cooking fat or salad oil
3 to 5 pounds beef
Flour

Salt and pepper
1 cup boiling water or stock
2 bay leaves (optional)

Brown onions in hot fat. Sprinkle meat with flour; brown on all sides; season with salt and pepper. Add water or stock and bay leaves. Cover tightly; simmer slowly until meat is tender, about 3 hours. Add more water or stock if necessary. Serves 6 to 8.

Pot roast with chili sauce: Add 2 cups chili sauce when meat has been simmering 1½ hours. Continue cooking another 1½ hours.

Pot roast with olives: Before browning, cut slits in meat and insert stuffed olives. Continue as in basic recipe.

Pot roast with potatoes: Boil peeled potatoes for 15 minutes. Drain and add to pot roast during last 45 minutes of cooking.

Pot roast with tomato juice: Substitute tomato juice or stewed tomatoes for water.

Pot roast with vegetables: Add whole carrots, onions, and potatoes during last 45 minutes of cooking time.

Oven pot roast: After seasoning meat, lay pieces of suet over the top. Put meat on rack in roasting pan. Cover closely and cook until tender in moderate oven (375°F.) about 1½ to 2½ hours. About 35 minutes before meat is done, place six peeled medium potatoes in pan around meat. Turn potatoes in drippings and sprinkle with salt. Cover and cook until meat and potatoes are tender. Before serving remove lid to allow potatoes to brown.

BAVARIAN POT ROAST

Season 4 pounds chuck roast with salt and pepper. Dredge in flour and brown in hot fat. Add 1 bay leaf, 4 tablespoons red wine, and 3 tablespoons water. Roast in slow oven (300°F.) until done, 1½ to 2 hours. Serve with boiled potatoes, browned with meat. Serves 8.

SWISS STEAK (Basic Recipe)

2 pounds beef, 1 inch thick
Salt and pepper, to taste

⅓ cup flour
2 cups cooked or canned tomatoes

Season meat with salt and pepper. Sprinkle with flour. Pounding helps make meat tender. Cut meat into serving pieces and brown in fat. Add tomatoes or juice. Cover and simmer gently until tender, 2 to 2½ hours. Serves 6.

Spanish steak: Follow recipe for *SWISS STEAK*, using 1½ pounds of meat. Brown ¾ cup chopped onion and 1½ cups chopped green pepper in fat. Cook 1½ cups macaroni in boiling salted water. Mix macaroni, onions, and pepper with tomato sauce. Serve over meat. Serves 6.

Swiss steak with brown gravy: Use water instead of tomatoes. When done, remove meat. Add water if needed to make 2 cups total liquid, and, if necessary, thicken with flour blended with cold water.

Swiss steak with onion gravy: Add 2½ cups thinly sliced onions to SWISS STEAK WITH BROWN GRAVY during last ½ hour of cooking.

Veal swiss steak: Veal may be substituted for beef.

SAUERBRATEN

4 pounds beef	2 tablespoons sugar
Cider vinegar	3 bay leaves
1 teaspoon salt	8 whole cloves
¼ teaspoon pepper	1 large onion, sliced
1 slice lemon	1 teaspoon peppercorns

Put meat in crock. Cover with vinegar and other ingredients. Let stand 2 days. Remove meat from vinegar solution and drain. Reserve ½ cup of liquid to add to gravy. Dredge meat in flour. Brown on both sides in fat in heavy skillet. Add 1 cup seasoned liquid. Cover closely and simmer until tender, about 2 hours. Lift meat onto serving platter. Put 2 tablespoons flour in skillet. Stir well. Add 1½ cups water and ½ cup vinegar. Boil together for few minutes. Serve with meat. Serves 6 to 8.

BRAISED SHORT RIBS OF BEEF

4 pounds short ribs	1 cup boiling water
Flour	1 cup cooked or canned tomatoes
2 teaspoons salt	1 clove garlic
Dash of pepper	6 medium potatoes
2 tablespoons salad oil or	12 small onions
melted fat	6 medium carrots

Dredge short ribs in flour seasoned with salt and pepper. Brown on all sides in hot oil or fat. Place in heavy kettle and add water, tomatoes, and garlic. Cover and simmer over low heat 1½ hours. Add pared vegetables. Cook until vegetables and meat are tender, ½ to 1 hour. Arrange meat and vegetables on platter. Thicken gravy with 1½ tablespoons flour and 2 tablespoons water for each cup of liquid. Serve over meat. Serves 6.

MEAT BIRDS

1½ to 2 pounds beef, cut	Flour
¼ to ½ inch thick	2 tablespoons cooking fat or salad oil
1½ to 2 cups bread dressing	1 cup tomato juice or meat stock
Salt and pepper	

Cut meat into pieces about 3x5 inches. Pound to any desired thinness. Put mound of dressing in center of each piece; roll and fasten with toothpicks or tie with cord. Sprinkle with salt and pepper, roll in flour, and brown on all sides in hot fat. Add about ½ cup liquid. Cover tightly and simmer until tender, about 1 hour. Add liquid in small quantities as required. Remove toothpicks or cord before serving. Gravy may be thickened. Serves 6.

Variations: Lamb or veal may be substituted for beef.

Meat bird casserole: Prepare birds as above. Brush with 2 tablespoons fat and place in greased casserole. Bake in slow oven (325°F.), basting occasionally with fat and hot water. Remove cover for last 10 minutes to brown birds.

BEEF, LAMB, or VEAL STEW (Basic Recipe)

Veal or lamb breast, veal, lamb, or beef shoulder or chuck meat are all good for stew. Cut 1 to 2 pounds meat into large cubes. Sprinkle with salt, pepper, and flour. Brown in hot fat and add 1 sliced onion. Add water to cover. Cover and cook slowly 1 to 1½ hours. Then add turnips, carrots, and chopped green peppers, if desired. Cook until meat and vegetables are tender. The stew should have plenty of gravy, very slightly thickened. Season to taste with salt and pepper. Serve with dumplings. If dumplings are omitted, add 4 small potatoes with other vegetables.

Meat stew en casserole: Prepare as above. Cook in casserole in moderately slow oven. Top with unbaked biscuits or pastry for last 20 to 30 minutes of cooking.

Meat stew with noodles or rice: Omit vegetables. Serve meat with noodles or rice cooked in meat stock.

To thicken stews: Use 1 to 1½ tablespoons flour for each cup liquid. Blend flour with an equal amount of cold liquid to make a smooth paste. Pour into slowly cooking stew, stirring constantly until thickened throughout. Cook slowly an additional 5 minutes. Season to taste.

HUNGARIAN GOULASH

3 pounds chuck of beef
Hot melted cooking fat
3 pints stock
2 cloves garlic
1 bay leaf

1 teaspoon salt
Few grains cayenne
6 medium sized potatoes, cut
   same size as beef
1 tablespoon paprika

Cut meat into 1 to 1½-inch pieces. Brown quickly in hot fat. Add stock, garlic, bay leaf, salt and cayenne; simmer very slowly 2½ hours. Add potatoes, simmer 35 to 40 minutes longer, and add paprika. Thicken sauce (3 to 4 cups) by gradually adding 3 tablespoons melted fat blended with 3 tablespoons flour. Stir until well blended and smooth. Serves 6 to 8.

MEAT PIE

3 tablespoons chopped onion
2 tablespoons chopped green pepper
½ cup diced celery
1 cup diced cooked meat
4 tablespoons cooking fat

4 tablespoons flour
2 cups meat stock
½ cup diced cooked carrots
½ recipe BAKING POWDER
   BISCUITS

Slowly brown onion, pepper, celery, and cooked meat in hot fat, stirring constantly. Add flour slowly, stirring constantly until brown. Add remaining ingredients. Heat thoroughly. Pour into shallow, well-greased baking dish. Cover with biscuit dough. Bake in hot oven (450°F.) about 15 minutes, or until crust is browned. Serves 6.

Shepherd's pie: Prepare ingredients as for meat pie. Pour into shallow greased baking dish. Cover with layer of well seasoned mashed potatoes. Dot with fat. Bake in hot oven (400°F.) until well browned. Serves 6.

PICKLING BRINE FOR CORNED BEEF

2 cups coarse salt
4 quarts water (about)
1 teaspoon saltpeter
¼ cup sugar

1 tablespoon mixed whole spices
1 teaspoon paprika
15 bay leaves
4 to 5 cloves garlic

Dissolve salt in water. Combine with remaining ingredients except garlic and boil for 5 minutes. Cool. Place beef in a stoneware crock. Add 4 to 5 cloves of sliced garlic and pour over the brine. Cover with a large heavy plate and weight it down with a tightly sealed jar filled with water to keep the meat well under the solution. Keep in a cool place, turning once a week. Leave in brine 3 weeks. This amount will pickle 10 pounds of beef or tongue.

To cook corned beef: Wash well to remove brine. Place in a large kettle and cover with boiling water. Simmer until tender, about 3 hours.

NEW ENGLAND BOILED DINNER

4 pounds corned beef
6 whole small carrots
6 turnips, diced

6 whole small potatoes, peeled
1 head cabbage, cut in wedges
6 whole small onions

Cover beef with cold water. Bring to boiling. Simmer slowly 40 to 50 minutes per pound, 3½ hours. Add carrots, turnips, potatoes, and onions 45 minutes before beef is done. Add cabbage for last 15 minutes. Serves 6 to 8.

Boiled short ribs: Use beef short ribs instead of corned beef. Simmer until almost tender. Add vegetables and salt and pepper to taste.

Corned beef hash: Combine equal parts chopped cooked corned beef and chopped boiled potatoes. Shape into patties and brown in hot fat.

Thrifty corned beef hash: Chop all leftovers from NEW ENGLAND BOILED DINNER. Form into patties and brown in hot fat.

BRISKET OF BEEF WITH SAUERKRAUT

2 pounds brisket of beef
1 large onion, sliced
1 bay leaf
Salt, to taste

2 cups sauerkraut
1 potato, grated
1 apple, sliced
½ tablespoon caraway seed

Place meat in large pot with cold water to cover. Bring to boil and skim. Add onions, bay leaf, and salt, to taste. Simmer until tender, about 2 hours. In another pot place sauerkraut, potato, and apple. Add 2 cups water and simmer 1½ hours. Remove meat with ¼ of its liquid. Add to sauerkraut. Sprinkle with caraway seed and simmer 15 minutes longer. Serves 6.

SWEET-SOUR BEEF WITH CABBAGE

1 small head cabbage, shredded
1 onion, chopped
2 tablespoons cooking fat or salad oil
Salt and pepper, to taste

2 pounds brisket of beef
4 large tomatoes, sliced
Juice of 1 lemon
About 2 tablespoons brown sugar

Brown cabbage and onion in hot fat. Season with salt and pepper. Cook meat in water to cover 1 hour. Add cabbage and tomatoes; simmer until meat is tender, about 1½ hours. Add lemon juice and sugar to flavor sweet and sour. If sauce is too watery, add a sprinkling of flour. Let cook until smooth. Serves 6.

CARROT TZIMMES

2½ to 3 pounds brisket of beef
6 carrots, sliced
6 medium sweet potatoes, cut
  in small pieces
1 small onion (optional)

2 tablespoons chicken fat or
  vegetable shortening
2 tablespoons flour
Salt and pepper, to taste
½ to ¾ cup brown sugar

Season meat and let stand several hours. Simmer in water to cover until tender, about 2½ hours. Add vegetables for last half hour. Melt fat in pan. Add flour and stir until smooth. Gradually add 2 cups of meat gravy, stirring constantly until thick and smooth. Add 1 teaspoon salt, ½ teaspoon pepper and brown sugar. Pour gravy over meat in a roasting pan. Bake in moderate oven (350°F.) until nicely browned, about ½ hour. Serves 6.

SWEET POTATO AND PRUNE TZIMMES

1½ pounds prunes
2 pounds brisket of beef
Salt and pepper, to taste

6 medium sized sweet potatoes
½ cup sugar
1½ tablespoons lemon juice

Soak prunes several hours or over night in cold water to just cover. Combine prunes, water, and meat in a heavy pot. Season with salt and pepper. Bring to a boil and simmer over very low heat until meat is almost tender, about 1½ hours. Remove meat and prunes from gravy. Add pared and sliced sweet potatoes. Place meat and prunes on top of potatoes and sprinkle with sugar and lemon juice. Cover and bake in moderate oven (350°F.) until potatoes are tender and meat browned, about 40 minutes. Serve hot. Serves 6.

BRISKET OF BEEF WITH BEANS #1

2 cups dried lima or navy beans
2 pounds brisket of beef
1 large onion, sliced
2 teaspoons mustard

1 tablespoon molasses
¾ cup brown sugar
¾ cup boiling water
1 teaspoon salt

Soak beans in cold water over night. Drain and cover with fresh water. Simmer until beans are almost tender. Drain again. Place brisket, beans, and onion in casserole. Mix and add other ingredients. Add more boiling water, if necessary, to just cover beans. Cover closely. Bake in slow oven (275°F.) until meat is tender, 5 hours. Serves 6.

BRISKET OF BEEF WITH BEANS #2

2 cups navy beans
2 pounds brisket of beef

Salt and pepper, to taste
1 large onion, sliced

Soak beans in cold water over night. Slowly heat beans to boiling point in same water. Season meat and let stand about 1 hour. Add to beans with onions. Cover and simmer until beans and meat are tender, about 2½ hours. Add more water if necessary. Serves 6.

Brisket of beef with vegetables and beans: Follow directions in Brisket of Beef with Beans #2, using only 1 cup beans. During last hour of cooking add 1 cup stewed tomatoes, 1 cup whole kernel corn, and ½ cup diced celery.

BRISKET WITH CABBAGE AND SWEET POTATOES

2 pounds beef brisket	1 onion
Water	6 sweet potatoes
Salt and pepper, to taste	1 medium head cabbage

Cover meat with water. Add seasoning and onion. Cover and simmer slowly until tender, allowing 1 hour per pound of meat. Add pared sweet potatoes ½ hour before meat is done. Add quartered cabbage last 15 minutes. When tender, remove meat and vegetables to platter. Prepare a gravy of 2 cups of the liquid. Thicken with a paste of 2 to 3 tablespoons flour and cold water. Cook until smooth. Serves 6.

BRISKET WITH PRUNES AND SWEET POTATOES

2 pounds brisket of beef	6 medium sweet potatoes
1 pound prunes, washed	½ cup sugar
Boiling water	Sour salt (citric acid)

Simmer meat and prunes, just covered with water, about 1 hour. Cut potatoes in eighths. Place in casserole and cover with meat and prunes. Add sugar and a piece of sour salt. Cover and bake in moderate oven (350°F.) until browned. Add boiling water, if necessary. Serves 6.

SWEET AND SOUR BRISKET OF BEEF

2 pounds brisket of beef	2 tablespoons sugar
1 onion, sliced	⅔ cup boiling water
Juice of 1 lemon	Salt and pepper, to taste
1 bay leaf	Piece of dill

Place meat in kettle and add remaining ingredients. Cover tightly and simmer until tender, about 2½ hours. Taste and add more sugar and lemon juice, if necessary, to flavor sweet and sour. Serves 6.

SWEET AND SOUR POT ROAST

4 pounds beef	2 tablespoons vinegar or
2 large onions, sliced	Juice of 1 lemon
1 clove garlic, minced	1 tablespoon brown sugar
½ cup stock or water	Salt
2 bay leaves	3 tablespoons ketchup
6 potatoes, quartered	½ cup raisins

Brown meat on all sides in hot fat in heavy kettle. Add and brown onions and garlic. Add vegetable stock or water and bay leaves. Cover and simmer 1 hour. Add more hot stock if necessary to prevent burning. Add potatoes, vinegar, and brown sugar. Cover and simmer another hour. Add salt, ketchup, and raisins. Cover and cook ½ hour longer. Serve hot. Serves 8 to 10.

Variation: Omit potatoes and serve roast with noodles or brown rice.

ESSIC FLEISCH

2 pounds brisket of beef
6 medium-size onions, sliced
⅛ teaspoon salt
Dash each of pepper and thyme
1 bay leaf

Boiling water
1 cup honey
1 slice stale rye bread
Juice of 1 lemon

Place meat in a heavy pot and add onions, salt, pepper, thyme, and bay leaf. Add boiling water and simmer until meat is tender, about 2½ hours. Add more boiling water as needed. When meat is almost done add the honey. Stir often while cooking and watch carefully so that it doesn't burn. Soak the bread in a little water, mash it and when it's soft add to meat. Stir well. Add 2 additional cups boiling water and the lemon juice. Cook until meat browns well. Add salt and pepper, to taste. Serves 6.

DUTCH POT ROAST OF CHUCK WITH VEGETABLES

5 pound beef chuck, boned and rolled
Salt and pepper
Flour
3 tablespoons cooking fat or salad oil
1 cup boiling water
1 cup carrots, sliced
1 cup onions, minced

1 cup celery, diced
1 cup turnips, diced
¼ clove garlic, minced
2 tablespoons parsley, minced
2 cups stock
½ cup red wine or grape juice

Wipe meat with damp cloth. Season with salt and pepper. Roll in flour until thickly covered. Melt fat in heavy kettle and brown meat all over. Add boiling water and cover tightly. Simmer 4 hours, turning 3 times during cooking and adding water as necessary to maintain level. Add remaining ingredients. Cover and simmer until vegetables are tender, about ½ hour. Remove meat to hot platter and mask with vegetables. Strain gravy and return it to kettle. Reduce to 2 cups by rapid boiling and stir in a smooth paste of 1 to 2 tablespoons each of shortening and flour, depending on thickness of reduced liquid. Serve gravy in separate dish. Serves 10.

NORWEGIAN BEEF BIRDS

1½ to 2 pounds beef,
    cut ¼ to ½ inch thick
1½ teaspoons salt
½ teaspoon pepper
¼ teaspoon ginger
¼ teaspoon cloves

⅓ pound ground beef
¼ pound marrow
4 sprigs of parsley, minced
3 cups hot stock or water
Flour
5 tablespoons cooking fat

Have meat sliced ¼ to ½ inch thick. Pound until thin and cut into pieces 3x5 inches. Sprinkle each with seasoning. Place 1 tablespoon ground meat, a little marrow, and a little minced parsley on each. Roll up and tie with string dipped in hot water. Roll in flour and brown on all sides in hot fat. Add hot stock or water. Cover and simmer ½ hour. Uncover pan and cook ½ hour longer. Lift out birds and remove strings. Boil gravy a few minutes longer and serve with meat. Serves 6.

JELLIED MEAT LOAF

1 tablespoon plain gelatin
¼ cup cold water
¾ cup boiling water
¼ cup vinegar
½ teaspoon salt
¼ cup diced celery
1 chopped pimiento

½ chopped green pepper
2 tablespoons finely minced onion
½ cup mayonnaise or boiled dressing
2 hard-cooked eggs, sliced
2 cups finely diced cooked meat

Soak gelatin in cold water, then dissolve in boiling water. Add vinegar and salt. Cool. When mixture begins to thicken, mix in all other ingredients except eggs. Rinse mold in cold water and arrange egg slices on bottom and sides. Pour in meat mixture. Chill until very firm. Serve on a bed of shredded lettuce. Serves 6.

ENGLISH BEEF STEW

1½ pounds shin of beef
4 tablespoons flour
½ teaspoon salt
¼ teaspoon pepper

4 onions, sliced thin
1 tablespoon cooking fat or salad oil
4 small carrots, diced
1 cup boiling water

Have beef cut low down through shin bone. Remove meat from bone and cut into 2-inch square pieces. Roll meat in flour seasoned with salt and pepper. Fry onions in hot fat until golden brown and place in large casserole or bean pot. Brown beef on all sides in same fat and add to onions. Add boiling water to pan in which beef was browned. Simmer a few minutes. Add carrots and boiling hot gravy to meat and onions. Cover closely and place in very slow oven (250°F.) 4 to 5 hours. Serves 4 to 5.

SOUTHERN BEEF STEW

2 pounds chuck beef
6 medium onions
6 medium potatoes
3 small carrots
1 teaspoon salt and pepper

2 tablespoons flour
6 tablespoons ketchup
1 tablespoon Worcestershire sauce
4 tablespoons soy sauce
8 stuffed olives

Cut meat in 2-inch pieces and place in large kettle. Cover with water and cook slowly 1½ hours. Add vegetables and cook until all are tender, about 45 minutes. Thicken with flour blended with a little water. Add ketchup, Worcestershire sauce, soy sauce, and olives, cut in small pieces. If soy sauce is added, use salt sparingly until soy sauce has been mixed into stew. Soy sauce contains salt. Serves 5.

RAGOUT OF BEEF

2 pounds lean beef
Salt and pepper, to taste
Flour
3 tablespoons fat
1 onion, chopped

1 green pepper, chopped
1 cup chopped celery and leaves
2 tablespoons chopped parsley
Paprika

Cut beef in 1-inch cubes. Sprinkle with salt and pepper and roll in flour. Brown well in hot fat, and while browning add onion, green pepper, celery, and parsley.

Sprinkle with paprika. Add water to cover. Simmer until meat is tender, 2½ to 3 hours. Thicken with 1 to 2 tablespoons flour blended with same amount of water. Add several spoonfuls of stew and stir mixture into stew. Cook 5 minutes longer. Season to taste with salt and pepper. Ketchup, chili sauce, or grated fresh horse-radish may be added, if desired. Serves 6.

BAKED BEEF STEW

Prepare same as *BAKED LAMB STEW*, using 4 cups canned tomatoes plus enough water to cover beef. Add 1 small bay leaf and 4 cloves. Other vegetables may also be added. Bake at slow heat (300°F.) for 3 hours.

BEEF MACARONI GOULASH

2 pounds lean beef	1 teaspoon salt
¼ cup chopped green pepper	½ teaspoon pepper
⅓ cup chopped onion	2 cups canned tomatoes
1 clove garlic, minced fine	2 cups cooked elbow macaroni

Cut meat in 1 to 1½-inch cubes. Place in heavy saucepan with green pepper, onion, garlic, salt, pepper, and boiling water to just cover. Simmer for 1 hour. Add tomatoes. Continue simmering until meat is tender, about 1 hour more. Add cooked macaroni. Heat thoroughly and serve at once. Serves 6.

BEEF MIROTON

2 onions, finely chopped	Pinch of thyme
3 tablespoons cooking fat	1½ cups sliced, cooked potatoes
1 tablespoon flour	¾ pound cooked beef
1½ to 2 cups stock	2 gherkins, sliced
1 tablespoon vinegar	1 teaspoon minced parsley
Salt and pepper, to taste	⅓ cup breadcrumbs

Cook onions in hot fat until golden brown. Stir in flour and add liquid slowly. When well combined, add vinegar. Boil 8 to 10 minutes. Pour some of the sauce in bottom of greased casserole. Add slices of beef. Season with salt, pepper, and thyme. Put potatoes in border around the beef. Pour in remaining sauce. Arrange sliced gherkins and minced parsley over top. Sprinkle with crumbs. Dot with fat. Brown in moderate oven (375°F.) 20 to 25 minutes. Serves 6.

BOILED. FRANKFURTERS

Cover frankfurters with boiling water. Simmer gently 6 to 8 minutes.

BROILED FRANKFURTERS

Cover frankfurters with boiling water. Let stand 6 to 8 minutes. Split lengthwise and brush with cooking fat or salad oil. Place skin side down on broiler rack about 2 inches from flame. Broil until brown.

SAUTEED FRANKFURTERS

Cover frankfurters with boiling water. Let stand 6 to 8 minutes. Split lengthwise and sauté in a little cooking fat or salad oil. Turn to brown both sides.

SAVORY FRANKFURTERS

8 frankfurters	2 tablespoons vinegar
1 tablespoon flour	2 teaspoons sugar
¾ cup water	1 teaspoon prepared mustard
½ cup ketchup	

Cut frankfurters in halves lengthwise. Place in skillet. Blend flour with 2 tablespoons water. Add remaining water, ketchup, vinegar, sugar, and mustard. Cook, stirring constantly, until thickened. Pour over frankfurters. Cover and simmer 25 minutes. Serves 4.

ground meats

MEAT LOAF (Basic Recipe)

1 pound ground meat, beef, veal, or lamb	½ cup stock
1 cup soft breadcrumbs	1 egg, slightly beaten
1 tablespoon minced onion	1 teaspoon salt
	⅛ teaspoon pepper
	1 tablespoon cooking fat

Mix all ingredients except fat. Place in a greased loaf pan and dot top with fat. Bake in moderate oven (350°F.) until done, 30 to 40 minutes. Serves 6.

1. Add grated carrot, chopped green pepper, pimiento, or sautéed mushrooms to mixture.

2. Cover meat loaf with ketchup or seasoned canned tomatoes before baking.

3. Substitute cooked oatmeal for breadcrumbs.

4. Bake loaf in layers, alternating with mashed seasoned potatoes or other cooked mashed vegetables.

5. Press half the mixture into loaf pan. Arrange 3 or 4 whole hard-cooked eggs (shells removed) in a lengthwise row in center of loaf. Pack remaining mixture on top of eggs. The rings of eggs will show when loaf is sliced.

6. **Carrot meat loaf:** Use only ¾ cup breadcrumbs. Add 2 cups mashed cooked carrots. Increase cooking time to 1 hour. Serves 8.

7. **Patties:** Add chopped green pepper and pimiento to mixture. Press in muffin tins and bake.

GROUND BEEF IN CABBAGE LEAVES #1

10 to 12 large cabbage leaves	½ cup raisins
1 pound ground beef	1 onion, sliced thin
½ cup cooked rice	Juice of 1 lemon
1 egg	About ¼ cup brown sugar
1 teaspoon salt	2 cups canned tomatoes
⅛ teaspoon pepper	1 cup water

Use large, whole, outside leaves of cabbage. Place in boiling water for 5 minutes to soften. Combine meat, rice, egg, salt, pepper, and half the raisins. Put a generous amount on each leaf. Fold in sides. Roll up and fasten with toothpicks. Shred the heart of cabbage. Line bottom of pot with shredded cabbage. Put stuffed cabbage on top, close together. Add remaining shredded cabbage, onion, raisins, lemon juice, sugar, tomatoes, and water. Simmer gently 2½ to 3 hours. Serves 6.

GROUND BEEF IN CABBAGE LEAVES #2

10 to 12 large cabbage leaves
1½ pounds ground beef
1 clove garlic, minced (optional)
4 tablespoons minced onion
3 tablespoons minced parsley

1 teaspoon salt
Dash of pepper
¾ cup boiling stock or tomato juice
Cooking fat

Use large, whole outside leaves of cabbage. Place in boiling water for 5 minutes to soften. Drain and dry on towel. Cut off hard ribs of leaves until as thin as leaf. Combine beef, garlic, onion, parsley, salt, and pepper and mix well. Put a generous amount on each leaf. Fold in sides, roll up, and fasten with toothpicks. Place close together in a greased casserole. Dot each with ¼ teaspoon fat. Pour stock or tomato juice over all. Bake in moderate oven (350°F.) until very tender, about 1 hour. Serves 6.

SWEET AND SOUR STUFFED PEPPERS

6 green peppers
1 pound ground beef
½ cup cooked rice or
    ½ cup dry breadcrumbs
1 onion, grated

1 carrot, grated
½ teaspoon salt
⅛ teaspoon pepper
2 eggs

Combine all ingredients and mix well. Stuff PREPARED PEPPERS (See Index) even with top. Place in casserole and add water to just cover. Cover and bake in moderate oven (350°F.) 40 minutes. Uncover. Add sweet and sour sauce. Increase heat to 400°F. Bake 10 minutes longer. Serves 6.

SWEET AND SOUR SAUCE

1 cup tomato purée
½ cup water
3 tablespoons lemon juice

3 tablespoons brown sugar
⅛ teaspoon paprika
½ cup raisins (optional)

Combine all ingredients in saucepan and cook over moderate heat 10 to 25 minutes.

SWEET AND SOUR MEAT BALLS

1 tablespoon dry breadcrumbs
2 cups hot water
1 onion, chopped
1 egg, beaten
1 pound ground beef
1 teaspoon salt

⅛ teaspoon pepper
¼ cup seedless raisins
1 lemon, sliced, seeds removed
About ¼ cup sugar
1 tablespoon cooking fat
1 tablespoon flour

Moisten crumbs with ½ cup hot water. Add onion, egg, meat, salt, and pepper; mix well. Form into small balls. Place in heavy pot and add remaining water, raisins, lemon, and sugar to taste for sweet and sour. Bring to boil. Cover and simmer until done, about 45 minutes. To thicken sauce, add paste of hot fat blended with flour and cook 5 minutes longer, stirring until smooth. Serve with broad noodles. Serves 6.

MEAT CROQUETTES

1 cup chopped cooked meat	1 tablespoon parsley, minced
½ cup soft crumbs	1 tablespoon lemon juice
½ cup thick WHITE SAUCE	Salt and pepper, to taste
1 tablespoon minced onion	1 egg, slightly beaten
1 egg	Dry, sifted, grated crumbs

Combine meat, soft crumbs, sauce , seasonings, parsley, onion, and 1 egg; mix well and chill. Shape into croquettes. Roll in dry crumbs; dip in egg and roll again in crumbs. Fry in deep hot fat (380°F.) until brown. Drain on absorbent paper. Serve with tomato sauce. Serves 4.

Nut and meat croquettes: Substitute ½ cup diced, cooked meat and ½ cup chopped nuts for chopped cooked meat.

CARNATZLACH (Rumanian Broiled Hamburgers)

1½ pounds ground beef	2 eggs, slightly beaten
1 onion, grated	1 teaspoon salt
1 carrot, grated	⅛ teaspoon pepper
1 clove garlic, minced	3 tablespoons flour
2 teaspoons poultry seasoning	¼ teaspoon paprika

Combine all ingredients except flour and paprika. Mix well. Form into rolls ¾ inch in diameter, 2 to 3 inches long, tapering at each end. Roll in flour seasoned with paprika. Broil under moderate heat, turning to brown all sides. Serves 6.

GROUND BEEF WITH NOODLES

2 pounds ground beef	1 cup diced onions
3 tablespoons cooking fat	1½ cups noodles
4 cups soup stock	Salt and pepper, to taste
2 cups diced celery	

Sauté meat in hot fat until brown. Add stock and simmer 30 minutes. Add celery and onion. Cook until vegetables are tender. Cook noodles in boiling salted water and drain. Place in a well-greased ring mold. Keep hot. To serve, unmold noodles and fill center with meat mixture. Serves 6.

CHILI CON CARNE

2 pounds ground beef	¼ cup chopped suet
1 teaspoon salt	2 tablespoons chili powder
2 tablespoons flour	2 cups canned tomatoes
¼ cup chopped onion	4 cups water
1 clove garlic, minced	2½ cups canned red kidney beans

Sprinkle meat with salt. Dredge with flour. Sauté onion and garlic in heated suet until browned. Add meat, then chili powder, tomatoes, and water. Cover and simmer 45 minutes. Add canned or cooked kidney beans and simmer 15 minutes. Serves 6.

Lima bean chili con carne: Use canned lima beans in place of kidney beans.

MEAT PATTIES

1 pound ground beef
¼ cup breadcrumbs
1 egg (optional)

1 teaspoon salt
½ teaspoon pepper
½ cup stock

Mix all ingredients thoroughly but do not pack. Shape into patties, 1 inch thick and 2 inches in diameter. Bake in hot oven (450°F.) in shallow pan about 5 inches from top of oven for 8 to 10 minutes. Serves 4 to 5.

Broiled meat patties: Place on broiler pan so meat is about 5 inches from heat. Broil on one side, turn and broil on second side. Total time about 18 minutes.

LAMB AND EGGPLANT CASSEROLE (Syrian Style)

1 medium eggplant
1 pound raw ground lamb
½ cup chopped onion
1 bay leaf

3 tablespoons minced parsley
1 teaspoon salt
¼ teaspoon paprika
1 cup canned tomatoes, chopped

Pare and chop eggplant until fine and combine with remaining ingredients. Pour into greased casserole. Cover and bake in moderate oven (350°F.) 45 minutes. Remove cover to brown top. Serves 4 to 6.

GREEK MUSACA (Beef and Eggplant)

1 large eggplant
  Salt and pepper
  Cooking fat or salad oil

2 large onions, minced
1 pound ground beef
2 cups canned tomatoes

Peel the eggplant and cut into ½-inch thick slices. Sprinkle each slice with salt and let stand 1 hour. Drain and brown eggplant in hot fat. Sauté onions in fat until transparent. Add beef, seasoned with salt and pepper to taste. Cook together until slightly brown. Place alternate layers of meat mixture and eggplant in greased casserole. Pour tomatoes over this and dot generously with fat. Bake in slow oven (325°F.) 1 hour. Serve hot. Serves 6.

CAUCASIAN DOLMA

4 green peppers
4 large fresh tomatoes
4 medium cucumbers
1 pound ground lamb

⅔ cup rice
1 onion, minced
3 tablespoons parsley, chopped
  Salt and pepper, to taste

Remove seeds from peppers. Scoop out centers of tomatoes and cucumbers to form cups. Mix meat, rice, tomato centers, onion, and parsley. Season to taste with salt and pepper. Stuff vegetable shells with this mixture. Place in a pan with just enough water to barely cover. Cover and bring to boil. Simmer for 1 hour. Serves 6.

TURKISH ONION DOLMAS

6 large onions, peeled
1 cup chopped mutton or lamb
1 cup boiled rice
2 tablespoons hot cooking fat or salad oil
1 small onion, grated

1 teaspoon minced parsley
½ cup pine nuts
  Salt, pepper, and paprika
  Hot broth
2 tablespoons tomato ketchup

Cut each onion lengthwise on one side. Place in boiling water to cover. Cook until tender enough to loosen leaves without taking from stem and drain. Mix mutton or lamb with rice, hot fat, grated onion, parsley, pine nuts, and salt and pepper, to taste. Moisten with broth. Slip some of this mixture between the outer leaves of the parboiled onions. Remove hearts and fill space with the onion and meat mixture. Place stuffed onions close together in a casserole. Sprinkle with salt, pepper, and paprika, to taste, and ketchup. Pour in enough stock to cover bottom of casserole only. Bake in moderate oven (350°F.) until tender. Serves 6.

STUFFED MEAT ROLL

Mix 1 slightly beaten egg with 1 pound of ground beef. On waxed paper, press out into sheet ½ inch thick. Spread with a mixture of 1 cup fine breadcrumbs, 1½ tablespoons minced onion, ¼ cup stock, salt and pepper to taste, and ¼ teaspoon sage. Roll up like a jelly roll. Bake in moderate oven (350°F.) until done, about 50 minutes.

KOENIGSBERGER KLOPS (Meat Balls)

2 slices bread	¼ teaspoon paprika
2 eggs, well beaten	½ teaspoon grated lemon rind
¾ pound ground beef	1 teaspoon lemon juice
¾ pound ground veal	1 teaspoon Worcestershire sauce
¼ cup onion, minced	5 cups boiling vegetable stock
Cooking fat or salad oil	Flour
5 tablespoons minced parsley	2 tablespoons capers or chopped
Salt and pepper	pickles

Soak bread in water to cover. Combine beaten eggs and ground meat. Sauté onion in 1 tablespoon fat until brown. Press water from bread and combine bread with meat, onion, 3 tablespoons parsley, 1½ teaspoons salt, paprika, lemon rind, lemon juice, and Worcestershire sauce. Mix well. Form into balls and drop into boiling vegetable stock. Cover tightly and simmer 15 minutes. Remove meat balls from liquid. Prepare a gravy from stock by using 2 tablespoons fat and 2 tablespoons flour for each cup of stock. Season to taste and simmer until smooth and thickened. Add capers or pickles and remaining parsley. Reheat meat balls in gravy. Serve, garnished with lemon slices. Serves 6.

MOCK CHICKEN LEGS

To 1½ pounds ground veal add 1 teaspoon salt, ¼ teaspoon pepper, and 1 slightly beaten egg. Shape like drumsticks on 6 skewers. Roll in seasoned breadcrumbs, then in egg diluted with 2 tablespoons water, and again in crumbs. Brown on all sides in hot fat. Cover, reduce heat, and cook slowly on top of stove for 30 to 45 minutes. Serves 4.

ARMENIAN WHEAT MEAT BALLS

2 tablespoons cooking fat	1 cup whole grain wheat
1 bunch parsley, minced	2 large, ripe tomatoes
5 medium onions, chopped	Salt and pepper
2 pounds ground beef	

Melt fat in saucepan. Add parsley, onions, and half the meat. When lightly browned, remove from fire and let cool. To remaining meat add whole grain wheat which has been soaked in water to cover for several hours (or use finely ground wheat, which does not require soaking). Shape into balls; flatten out very thin. Place 1 tablespoon of first mixture (onions and beef) in the center. Bring edges of flattened cake together to enclose filling and pierce each with a small hole. Half fill a deep pan with water. Add tomatoes and bring to boil. Add meat balls and cook gently until the wheat rather than meat is tender. Add salt and pepper, to taste. Serve hot with or without the liquid. Serves 6.

SYRIAN KIBBEE

1½ pounds lean ground lamb or beef
¾ pound ground wheat
2 small onions, ground fine
¾ pound lamb or beef, cut in
    small pieces

2 small onions, minced
¾ cup pine nuts
½ cup vegetable oil

Mix together the ground meat, wheat, and ground onion and put through grinder again, using a fine blade. Mix together the other meat, minced onion, and nuts and season to taste. Place second mixture in a frying pan without any fat and half cook it. Set aside until ready to use. Flatten pieces of first mixture between palms of hands to about ½ inch thickness, and cover bottom of greased casserole with them. Cover this with layer of second mixture. Repeat this process for the second layer. Smooth top by dipping hand in cold water and lightly working palm over meat mixture. Cut through into diamond shaped pieces. Cover with the oil. Bake in moderate oven (350°F.) 20 minutes, or until meat is brown on top and the edges shrink. Serves 6 to 8.

CAUCASIAN GRAPE LEAF ROLLS

Use a mixture of 1½ pounds ground beef, 1 cup rice, 1 teaspoon salt, a dash each of pepper and cinnamon. Place a tablespoon on each leaf. Fold in sides and roll up to ½ inch in diameter. Pack carefully in heavy pot. Add 2½ cups canned tomatoes and water to cover. Simmer 1 hour. Serves 6.

RUSSIAN MEAT BALLS

1 egg
1 teaspoon salt
¼ teaspoon pepper
3 tablespoons cooking fat
3 tablespoons minced onion

1 pound ground beef
1 cup tomato juice
1 green pepper, diced
¼ cup diced celery

Add egg, salt, pepper, and 1½ teaspoons minced onion to meat. Mix well. Form into balls and brown on all sides in hot fat. Place balls in greased baking dish with green pepper, celery, and remaining onion. Pour tomato juice over all. Cover and bake in moderate oven (350°F.) 1 hour. Serves 6 to 8.

SCRAPPLE

2 cups uncooked oatmeal
3 cups bouillon
1 teaspoon salt
1½ cups finely ground cooked veal

1 tablespoon grated onion
Pepper
¼ teaspoon powdered sage

Stir oatmeal into saucepan containing bouillon and salt, boiling rapidly. Sprinkle oats into bouillon slowly enough to keep water boiling. Add meat and seasoning. Reduce heat, cover, and cook 10 minutes or longer, stirring occasionally. Turn into a loaf pan which has been rinsed in cold water. Cool and chill until firm. Remove from pan and cut into ½-inch slices. Sauté in hot fat until brown on both sides. Serves 6.

lamb

How to cook lamb and mutton: All cuts of lamb are tender, therefore all may be cooked by dry heat: roasting, broiling, or pan-broiling. Lamb and mutton contain a very small amount of fat and very little moisture. If cooked too long or at too high a temperature the meat will dry and harden. The thin covering over the outside of the carcass, known as the "fell," does not affect the flavor of the lamb. Lamb should be cooked until medium done or well done. Always serve it very hot or cold. Never serve it lukewarm.

CROWN ROAST OF LAMB

Have crown prepared at market by tying together a side of lamb ribs from shoulder joint down and cutting down 2 inches between ribs and into other portion. Fill the center with favorite stuffing. Place roast on rack in open roasting pan. Roast in slow oven (300°F.), allowing 30 to 35 minutes per pound (including stuffing) or until meat thermometer inserted in thickest part of roast registers 175° to 180°F. To serve, cover bone ends with paper frills. Serve with pan gravy or mint sauce.

ROLLED SHOULDER OF LAMB

Season 5 to 6 pound lamb shoulder with salt and pepper. Place on rack in open roasting pan. Insert meat thermometer so that bulb reaches center of thickest part. Do not add water. Do not cover. Roast in slow oven (300°F.), basting every half hour with *FRENCH DRESSING* (use total of 1 cup). For medium-done lamb, meat thermometer should register 175°F., and 180°F. for well-done lamb. Allow 30 to 35 minutes to pound. Serves 10 to 12.

CUSHION LAMB SHOULDER ROAST

Use 3 to 4 pound square cut lamb shoulder. Have bones removed from side to form pocket. Wipe meat with damp cloth. Fill cavity with favorite stuffing. Fasten edges together by sewing or with skewers. Place fat side up on rack in roasting pan. Roast uncovered, without basting and without adding water, in slow oven (300°F.) until done. Allow 35 to 40 minutes per pound, or until meat thermometer registers 180°F.

ROAST LAMB BREAST

Have butcher remove shank and breast bone, and make deep pocket, cutting from flank end. Season and fill evenly with favorite stuffing. Place on rack in roasting pan, roast uncovered in slow oven (300°F.) about 2 hours, or until tender. Serves 6.

BROILED LAMB CHOPS

Preheat broiler to moderate (350°F.). Place chops in broiler about 3 inches from heat. If distance must be less, reduce temperature accordingly so that chops will broil at moderate temperature. When chops are browned on one side, season, turn, and finish cooking on the second side. Chops cut 1 inch thick require 12 to 15 minutes for broiling.

PAN-BROILED LAMB CHOPS

Rib, shoulder, or loin chops may be used. Place chops in heavy frying pan and brown on both sides. Reduce heat and cook to desired degree of doneness. Add no fat or water. Do not cover pan. Pour off excess fat as it collects in pan. Turn the chops frequently to cook uniformly. Sprinkle with salt. Serve at once on hot platter.

BREADED LAMB CHOPS

2 eggs	1 cup fine breadcrumbs
½ cup water	4 tablespoons cooking fat
6 lamb shoulder chops, cut ½ inch thick	Salt and pepper

Beat eggs slightly, mix with ¼ cup water. Dip chops in crumbs, in egg mixture, and in crumbs again. Brown in hot fat. Season and add remaining water. Cover and simmer 30 minutes, or until tender. Serves 6.

LAMB SMOTHERED IN TOMATOES

1½ pounds lamb shoulder steak	Poultry seasoning
1 cup breadcrumbs	2½ cups canned tomatoes
1 small onion	1 teaspoon pepper
1 teaspoon salt	

Wipe meat with damp cloth; spread with layer of breadcrumbs mixed with minced onion and other seasoning. Roll, tie with string, and place in casserole. Pour tomatoes over meat. Cover and cook in slow oven (300°F.), or on top of stove about 3 hours. If tomatoes do not cover meat, add a little boiling water. Serves 6.

ENGLISH COLYS

2 pounds lamb or veal (neck or shoulder)	½ teaspoon freshly ground pepper
2 tablespoons cooking fat	1 teaspoon marjoram
2 onions	2 tomatoes, cut in quarters
1 clove garlic	1 tablespoon chopped parsley
½ teaspoon salt	1 cup water
	2 cups diced potato or potato balls

Wipe meat well. Melt fat and sauté chopped onion and garlic. Add seasonings, tomatoes, and parsley. Turn into casserole. Add meat. Cover closely and simmer or bake 30 minutes. Add water and potatoes. Cover and cook 1½ hours longer. Serves 6.

LAMB PILAF

3 pounds lamb breast
3 large onions, sliced
Salt and pepper

4 cups hot water
1½ cups raw rice

Brown meat and onions in hot cooking fat or salad oil in heavy pot. Season with salt and pepper. Continue braising until meat is very dark, stir very often, scraping bottom of pan. Add hot water, rice, salt, and pepper. Cover and bake in a slow oven (300°F.) 2 hours. Serves 6 to 8.

Variations: Potatoes (as many as desired), 1 pound kidney beans soaked over night, or whole grain buckwheat may be substituted for the rice.

SHISH KEBAB

¼ cup olive oil
1 teaspoon salt
¼ teaspoon pepper
2 tablespoons wine (optional)
2 pounds lean lamb,
    cut in 1¼-inch cubes

2 large firm tomatoes, cut in
    thick slices or wedges
2 large onions, cut in thick slices
Small whole mushrooms
1 large green pepper, cut in
    1¼-inch squares
Cubed eggplant

Combine olive oil, salt, pepper, and wine, if desired. Spread over meat and vegetables. Let stand in cool place 2 to 3 hours. Arrange meat and vegetables alternately on skewers. If desired, rub skewers with cut clove of garlic. Broil slowly under moderate heat until tender, turning to evenly brown all sides. Serves 4.

SHASHLIK #1

3 pounds lean lamb
1 pound fresh mushrooms
Sliced onions
Pared eggplant, cut in 1¼-inch cubes

Firm tomatoes, cut in wedges
Salt and pepper
Cooked rice

Trim fat from meat and cut in 1¼-inch cubes. Clean mushrooms. If small, use whole. Remove stems and skin from large mushrooms. Wash and drain well. Alternate meat and vegetables on skewers. Season with salt and pepper. If desired, pour over a little melted fat. Broil under moderate heat, turning skewer to brown all sides. Total time 18 to 20 minutes. Serve at once with cooked rice. Serves 6.

SHASHLIK #2

4 pounds lamb, breast or steak
    Juice of 5 lemons
1 bunch parsley, chopped fine

1 bunch dill, chopped fine
2 cloves garlic
Salt and pepper, to taste

Cut meat into 1½-inch cubes. Place in deep dish or crock. Pour over mixture of lemon juice, parsley, dill, garlic, salt and pepper. Mix with meat so that each piece is seasoned. Cover and let stand in cool place 3 to 4 hours. Run skewers through pieces of meat. Broil about 12 minutes, turning so that all sides are evenly browned. If desired, alternate meat cubes with tomato wedges, mushrooms, and onion slices. Serves 8.

TURKISH TOMATO PILAF

1 pound mutton or lamb	Salt, cayenne, paprika
2 tablespoons cooking fat or salad oil	1 teaspoon sugar
1 cup rice, washed	Chicken fat
2½ cups canned tomatoes	Lemon juice

Cut meat in 2 pieces. Brown lightly on all sides in hot fat. When meat is half cooked, add rice and cook a few minutes until rice is coated and begins to puff. Add tomatoes (heated to boiling point), salt, and cayenne to taste, and sugar. Cook covered until rice has absorbed all liquid. Dry for a few minutes in moderate oven (350°F.) with door left ajar. Serve with sauce of melted chicken fat to which has been added a little lemon juice and paprika, to taste. Serves 4 to 6.

CAUCASIAN PILAF

2 pounds fat mutton, sliced	1 cup raw rice
1 onion, minced	2 bay leaves
4 cups stock	6 peppercorns
Salt and pepper, to taste	

Add onion to melted mutton fat in saucepan. When it starts to brown add pieces of meat. Add 1 cup stock, salt and pepper. Cover and simmer ½ hour. Scald and rinse rice. Add to meat with remaining ingredients. Cover and simmer 1½ to 2 hours. The rice should be tender but each grain should be separate. Serves 6 to 8.

BRAISED STUFFED BREAST

Lamb breast	2 cups fine breadcrumbs
Salt and pepper	½ cup mint leaves
3 tablespoons chopped celery	¾ teaspoon salt
1½ tablespoons chopped onion	¼ teaspoon pepper
2 tablespoons cooking fat	6 tablespoons salad oil

Have pocket cut into lamb breast from the large end. Sprinkle inside and out with salt and pepper. To make the stuffing, brown the celery and onions in hot fat. Add breadcrumbs, mint leaves, and seasoning. Mix well. Stuff pocket of roast. Fasten edges together with skewers. Brown breast on all sides in hot fat. Add ½ cup hot water and cover tightly. Cook slowly until done, about 1½ hours. Serves 4 to 6.

BARBECUED LAMB BREAST

2 pounds breast of lamb	¼ teaspoon red pepper
1 teaspoon salt	1 tablespoon vinegar
Pepper	1 cup water
½ cup chili sauce	1 medium onion, sliced

Cut lamb into serving pieces. Season with salt and pepper. Place in hot skillet and brown fatty sides. Mix chili sauce, red pepper, vinegar, and water; pour over lamb. Add onion to mixture. Cover. Simmer 1½ hours. Remove lid and cook on medium heat about 20 minutes, until barbecue sauce is almost absorbed. Serves 4.

SAVORY LAMB SHANKS

4 lamb shanks	½ teaspoon pepper
½ cup flour	½ teaspoon celery salt
1 teaspoon paprika	¼ teaspoon cloves
2 teaspoons salt	¼ teaspoon garlic salt
¼ teaspoon ginger	3 cups water

Wipe shanks with damp cloth. Dredge in flour. Brown on all sides in hot fat in large skillet. Place shanks in casserole. Pour off all but 2 tablespoons of fat. Add seasonings and balance of flour. Blend and add water. Cook slowly until slightly thickened. Pour over shanks. Cover and bake in moderate oven (350°F.) until tender, 1½ hours. Add more water if needed. Canned tomatoes may be substituted for water. Serves 4.

Savory lamb shanks with rice: Use ingredients in above recipe except flour. Brown shanks in large kettle. Add seasonings and water. Simmer gently for 1 hour. Then add 1 cup raw rice and simmer additional hour. Add more water if needed. Garnish with minced parsley. Serves 4.

LAMB CURRY

4½ to 5 pounds shoulder	½ teaspoon sugar
2 tablespoons cooking fat	2 chopped medium onions
3 teaspoons curry powder	½ cup chopped parsley (optional)
¼ teaspoon dry mustard	1 small chopped clove garlic
2½ teaspoons salt	1 #2 can tomatoes

Cut lamb into 1-inch cubes. Heat fat. Add all ingredients except meat and tomatoes. Fry gently until onions are soft. Add meat. Fry vigorously 20 minutes, stirring well. Add solid part of canned tomatoes. Cover and cook on low flame 1 hour, stirring occasionally. Add liquid from tomatoes, if necessary. Skim excess fat. Thicken to desired consistency with a little flour and water (or stock). Stir and gently cook for 25 minutes. Serve with boiled rice. Serves 8.

IRISH STEW WITH DUMPLINGS

2 pounds lamb or mutton	1 teaspoon salt
2 tablespoons cooking fat	¼ teaspoon pepper
3 cups boiling water	1 bay leaf
1 cup diced carrots	2 tablespoons minced parsley
1 cup diced turnips	2 tablespoons flour
1 teaspoon Worcestershire sauce	DUMPLINGS FOR STEW

Cut lamb into 2-inch squares. Brown in hot fat. Add hot water. Simmer, covered, for 2 hours. Add vegetables and seasonings. Cook ½ hour longer. Thicken liquid with flour blended with 2 tablespoons cold water. Drop dumplings on top. Cover and cook 12 to 15 minutes. Serves 8.

NORWEGIAN MUTTON STEW

2 pounds shoulder of mutton	2 tablespoons salt
2 tablespoons cooking fat	⅛ teaspoon pepper
2 small bunches carrots	Flour

Cut mutton in small pieces and brown in hot fat. Cover with water and simmer

1 hour. Add whole, scraped carrots, salt, and pepper. Cook, covered, until carrots are done, about 45 minutes. Thicken the gravy with flour. Serve with mashed potatoes. Serves 5.

SPANISH LAMB STEW

2 pounds breast of lamb	2 cups canned tomatoes
2 tablespoons cooking fat	½ cup raw rice
1 chopped onion	1 tablespoon salt
1 green pepper	¼ teaspoon pepper
2 cups canned peas	2 quarts hot water

Cut lamb in small pieces and sauté in fat. Add remaining ingredients. Simmer until meat is well done. Pour over following mixture: 1 beaten egg, 1 teaspoon olive oil, and ½ teaspoon vinegar. Serve at once. Serves 6.

BAKED LAMB STEW

2 pounds lamb shoulder	1½ cups sliced raw carrots
2 tablespoons cooking fat	1 cup diced celery
1 sliced onion	1 cup raw peas
Salt, to taste	¼ cup chopped parsley

Brown 1-inch cubes of meat in hot fat. Add onions and brown slightly. Add salt and vegetables, except parsley. Barely cover with water and bring to boiling point. Thicken with 2 tablespoons flour stirred to smooth paste with water. Pour into casserole. Cover and bake in slow oven (325°F.) until meat is tender, 1½ hours. Garnish with chopped parsley. Serves 4.

LAMB AND LIMA BEAN CASSEROLE

1½ pounds lamb	1 teaspoon salt
¼ cup flour	⅛ teaspoon pepper
3 tablespoons cooking fat	2 cups stewed tomatoes
1 cup boiling water	2 cups fresh lima beans

Use meat from neck or breast. Cut into 1-inch cubes, roll in flour, and sauté in fat until browned. Add water and seasonings. Simmer until meat is tender. Add tomatoes and beans. Bring to boil and turn into casserole. Bake covered, in moderate oven (350°F.), until beans are soft, about 30 minutes. Serves 6.

LAMB AND VEGETABLE CASSEROLE

4 onions, sliced	1 teaspoon paprika
2 tablespoons cooking fat	2 small potatoes, peeled
1½ pounds lamb, cubed	1½ cups canned or fresh string beans
3 green peppers, diced	1½ cups canned or fresh peas
1 teaspoon salt	1½ cups canned or fresh tomatoes

Fry onions in hot fat until brown. Place in casserole with lamb and green peppers. Season with salt and paprika. Bake in slow oven (325°F.) until lamb is tender, 30 to 45 minutes. Add potatoes, string beans, peas, and tomatoes. Cover and bake 20 minutes longer. If fresh vegetables are used, bake for 30 minutes. Serves 6 to 8.

GREEK LAMB WITH STRING BEANS

2 onions, minced
1½ pounds lamb, cut in small pieces
2 tablespoons cooking fat

1 pound string beans, diced
Salt and pepper

Sauté onions and lamb in hot fat for 20 minutes. Add string beans, ½ cup of hot water, and salt and pepper, to taste. Cover. Simmer until tender, about 30 minutes. Serves 4.

TURKISH MUTTON AND QUINCE

Peel, core, and slice 1 pound quinces. Boil in water to cover until tender. Drain. Cut 1 pound mutton or lamb into 1-inch cubes. Fry until brown in 2 tablespoons hot fat. When brown, add water to cover and simmer until tender. Add the quinces and cook 10 minutes longer. Add salt and pepper, to taste, and, if desired, add a little sugar. Cooking pears or apples may be substituted for the quinces.

LAMB WITH OKRA (Syrian Style)

2 pounds lamb shoulder
½ pound dried okra
¼ cup cooking fat
2 tablespoons minced parsley
1 small clove garlic, minced

1½ cups tomato sauce
2 cups meat stock
Juice of 1 lemon
Salt and pepper
Steamed rice

Simmer lamb in water to cover until tender, about 2 hours. Boil okra in salted water 20 minutes, then drain and brown in hot fat with parsley and garlic. Cut cooked lamb into small pieces and add to okra mixture with tomato sauce, stock and lemon juice. Serve hot with steamed rice. Serves 6.

LAMB ASPIC

2 packages lemon gelatin
2 cups hot water
2 cups cold water
30 stuffed green olives, sliced
4 cups diced cooked lamb

½ cup green pepper
4 tablespoons vinegar
4 tablespoons grated horseradish
3 teaspoons salt
½ teaspoon Worcestershire sauce

Dissolve gelatin in hot water. Add cold water. With some of the olives, make a design in bottom of a loaf pan (5x9 inches). Cover with thin layer of gelatin and place in refrigerator until set. Chill remaining gelatin until it begins to congeal. Add lamb, green pepper, seasonings, and remaining sliced olives. Pour over design in loaf pan. Chill until firm. Unmold on lettuce. Garnish with tomato slices. Serves 10.

veal

How to cook veal: Although veal is tender, it requires longer cooking than beef because of the large proportion of connective tissues. Roasting, braising, and stewing are the methods used in cooking veal. Veal chops and steaks cannot be satisfactorily broiled. They are usually browned in fat first, then covered and cooked slowly.

BRAISED VEAL SHOULDER

Brown rolled shoulder in hot fat. Season with salt and pepper. Place on rack in roasting pan. Add small amount of water. Cook in slow oven (300°F.) until tender, about 35 to 40 minutes per pound. Add vegetables for last 45 minutes of cooking.

ROAST ROUND OR ROLLED SHOULDER OF VEAL

Season meat with salt and pepper. Place roast on rack in an open pan. Lay thin strips of suet on top. Insert meat thermometer so that bulb is in center of roast. Roast in slow oven (300°F.) until thermometer registers 170°F. Without a thermometer allow 35 to 40 minutes per pound. Serve with pan gravy made from drippings.

STUFFED SHOULDER OF VEAL

5 pounds shoulder of veal
   Salt and pepper, to taste
2 onions, chopped
3 tablespoons cooking fat

2 cups soft breadcrumbs
3 cups chopped apples
½ pound prunes, cooked and
   chopped

Have a pocket cut in shoulder of veal. Sprinkle cavity with salt and pepper. Sauté onions in hot fat until transparent. Combine breadcrumbs, apples, and prunes. Season with salt. Add sautéed onions. Mix well. Stuff veal shoulder. Skewer or sew opening. Roast, covered, on rack in roasting pan in slow oven (325°F.) until done. Allow 25 to 30 minutes per pound. Baste occasionally with melted fat. Serves 8 to 10.

STUFFED BREAST OF VEAL

Have butcher bone and cut pocket in breast. Fill evenly with favorite stuffing. Place on rack in open roasting pan. Roast in slow oven (300°F.) until well done, allowing 30 to 35 minutes per pound.

STUFFED VEAL STEAK

2 pounds veal steak,
   cut ¼ inch thick
2 teaspoons salt
¼ teaspoon pepper

4 tablespoons flour
3 tablespoons cooking fat
2 cups tomato juice
Bread stuffing

Season veal steak with salt and pepper. Spread bread stuffing evenly over steak and roll. Fasten ends together with skewers or string. Roll in flour and brown in hot fat in skillet. Add ½ cup tomato juice, cover tightly, and simmer, 1 to 1½ hours, until meat is tender, turning occasionally. To serve, remove skewers or string, place on serving platter. Add remainder of tomato juice which has been mixed with flour to drippings and cook until thickened. Pour sauce over meat. Serves 6.

BRAISED CUTLETS OR CHOPS

Roll cutlets or chops in seasoned flour. Fry in hot fat until brown on both sides. Add 1 cup tomato juice or water. Cover and simmer ¾ to 1 hour. Remove meat to hot platter and keep hot. Thicken gravy by making a paste of 1½ tablespoons flour for each cup of liquid in pan.

BREADED VEAL STEAK

2 pounds veal, ½ inch thick
2 teaspoons salt
¼ teaspoon pepper
½ cup flour
2 eggs, slightly beaten

2 tablespoons water
1 cup breadcrumbs
About 6 tablespoons cooking fat
Stock

Cut meat into 6 pieces. Season with salt and pepper. Dip in flour, then in beaten eggs diluted with 2 tablespoons water, then dip into breadcrumbs. Chill 1 hour or more. Brown on both sides in hot fat. Add ½ cup stock. Cover closely and bake in slow oven (325°F.) until tender, about 50 to 60 minutes. Serves 6.

VEAL STEAK IN TOMATO SAUCE

Cut 2 pounds of veal steak (½ inch thick) into 6 pieces. Dredge in flour seasoned with salt and pepper. Brown on both sides in hot fat. Add 2 cups tomato juice. Cover. Simmer 1 hour. Serves 6.

PAPRIKA SCHNITZEL

2 pounds veal steak
Salt and pepper
Flour

2 tablespoons cooking fat
Paprika
3 onions, sliced

Cut steak into serving pieces. Sprinkle with salt and pepper. Roll in flour. Melt fat in a skillet. Add enough paprika to make it red. Fry onions until transparent. Add meat. Fry until golden brown all over. Cover and cook slowly for ½ hour. Add a little water or stock if necessary. Serves 6.

WIENER SCHNITZEL

Cut ½-inch-thick veal steak into serving pieces. Sprinkle with salt and pepper. Dip in beaten egg, then in breadcrumbs. Fry in hot fat until brown on both sides. Serve, garnished with lemon wedges, capers, and a fried egg, if desired, for each serving.

VEAL FRICASSEE

1½ pounds shoulder of veal
1 teaspoon salt
⅛ teaspoon pepper
Flour
2 tablespoons cooking fat

1 cup diced celery
12 white onions, peeled
6 carrots, scraped
1½ cups water

Cut veal into 1-inch cubes. Dredge with flour, salt and pepper. Brown in hot fat. Add vegetables, water, and seasonings. Cover. Simmer until meat is tender. Add potato dumplings. Cover tightly. Cook for 12 minutes. Thicken gravy slightly. Serves 6.

VEAL POT PIE

2 pounds veal
2 medium onions, sliced
2 teaspoons salt

½ teaspoon pepper
1½ tablespoons cooking fat
1½ tablespoons flour

End of ribs, neck meat, or knuckle may be used. Cut meat into small pieces. Cover with boiling water. Add 2 sliced onions, salt, and pepper. Simmer until tender, about 2 hours. Pour into a casserole. Melt fat and slowly blend in flour, and, when browned, add 1 cup veal stock, stirring constantly. Simmer until thickened, 5 minutes. Add to veal. Cover with biscuit dough cut in rounds. Bake in hot oven (400°F.) 20 minutes. Serves 6.

VEAL CHOPS AMBROSIA

6 loin veal chops
3 tablespoons flour
1 teaspoon salt
⅛ teaspoon thyme
⅛ teaspoon red pepper
1 clove garlic

3 tablespoons cooking fat
1 lemon
½ cup water
1 teaspoon Worcestershire sauce
1 bay leaf

Have chops cut ¾ inch thick. Dredge in flour, mixed with salt, thyme, and red pepper. Rub skillet with cut clove of garlic. Brown chops in hot fat. Cut lemon into 6 slices crosswise and place a slice on each chop. Add water, Worcestershire sauce, and bay leaf. Cover, and simmer 1½ hours or in moderate oven (350°F.) 1½ hours. Serves 6.

BREADED VEAL CUTLETS OR CHOPS

Simmer cutlets or chops in water about 45 minutes. Drain and season with salt and pepper. Dip in breadcrumbs, then in egg diluted with water and again in crumbs. Fry in hot fat until browned on all sides. Serve with brown or tomato sauce, made with veal stock.

VEAL CUTLETS IN BATTER

Cut thin slices of veal steak into serving pieces. Sprinkle with salt and pepper. Dip in fritter batter and fry slowly in deep fat. When brown, remove to platter. Dip large mushrooms in fritter batter and fry in deep fat. Serve wine sauce over steak and mushrooms.

SAVORY VEAL STEAKS

Cut 2 pounds of veal (1 inch thick) into 6 pieces. Sprinkle with salt and pepper. Mix together 1½ cups sifted cracker crumbs, ¼ teaspoon thyme, and ¼ teaspoon marjoram. Roll veal in seasoned crumbs, then in beaten egg diluted with 2 tablespoons of water and again in crumbs. Brown veal on both sides in fat. Cover skillet and cook over low heat for 30 minutes. Serve with brown or tomato sauce. Serves 6.

VEAL CUTLET MARENGO

2 pounds veal cutlet
3 tablespoons cooking fat or salad oil
2 tablespoons tomato purée
½ cup dry white wine
2 onions, minced
1 clove garlic, minced

2 tablespoons oil
1 cup canned tomato pulp
1 teaspoon salt
½ teaspoon pepper
1 cup sliced mushrooms

Brown veal well on both sides in a large frying pan. Add tomato purée and dry white wine. In another pan sauté onions and garlic in oil. Add tomato pulp, salt, and pepper. Heat thoroughly and pour over cutlet. Cover pan and simmer slowly for 2 hours. Just before serving add mushrooms which have been sautéed in hot fat for a few minutes. Serves 5 to 6.

VEAL CUTLETS IN WINE SAUCE

2 pounds veal cutlet
Salt and pepper
2 tablespoons olive oil or
salad oil
¼ cup chopped onion
¾ cup sliced mushrooms

1 tablespoon minced parsley
2 tablespoons flour
1½ cups stock or water
¼ cup wine
2 tablespoons lemon juice

Sprinkle cutlets with salt and pepper; fry in fat until browned on both sides. Place meat in a casserole. To fat in frying pan, add onions, mushrooms, and parsley and cook for a few minutes. Stir in and brown the flour. Add remaining ingredients. Cook until smooth and thick, stirring constantly. Pour over cutlets. Bake in slow oven (325°F.) 1 hour. Serves 6.

VEAL TIMBALES

2 tablespoons cooking fat
2 tablespoons flour
1 cup meat broth or thin gravy
2 eggs, well beaten

Salt and pepper, to taste
Lemon juice to taste
2 cups ground cooked veal
1 tablespoon chopped parsley

Make a sauce of fat, flour, and liquid. Add eggs, seasoning, and meat. Mix thoroughly. Pour into greased timbale molds or custard cups. Place cups in pan of water. Bake in moderate oven (350°F.) about ½ hour, or until set in center. Turn timbales out and serve hot sprinkled with parsley. Chicken, lamb, or left-over meat may be used instead of veal.

MEAT AND POTATOES IN TOMATO SAUCE (Greek Style)

½ cup olive oil
½ clove garlic, chopped
6 to 8 medium potatoes, sliced
1 large onion, minced
1 pound chopped veal or lamb
Black pepper, to taste

1½ teaspoons salt
¼ cup tomato paste
1 cup water
¼ cup red wine
Stick cinnamon, 1x2 inches
3 bay leaves

Heat olive oil in frying pan. Add garlic and cook until slightly browned. Remove from pan and reserve for later use. Lightly brown potatoes in the same oil, remove, and reserve. Make mixture of onion, garlic, meat, pepper to taste and salt. Add to oil and cook 3 minutes. Spread between alternate layers of fried potatoes in a greased baking dish. Mix together tomato paste, water, and wine and pour over top of potato and meat layers. Lay cinnamon and bay leaves on top. Pour the oil left in pan over all. Bake in moderate oven (350°F.) 45 minutes, or until browned. Remove cinnamon and bay leaves. Serve hot. Serves 6.

BRAISED VEAL PAPRIKA

4 onions, sliced	1 green pepper, diced
1 tablespoon cooking fat	1 cup water
1 teaspoon paprika	Salt and pepper, to taste
2 pounds veal steak	

Sauté onions in hot fat until light brown. Add paprika and veal, cut into 1-inch cubes. Brown meat on all sides. Add green pepper. Cover and cook 5 minutes. Add water and simmer until meat is tender, about 1½ hours. Add more water as needed to keep about 1 cup of gravy in kettle. Season to taste. Serves 6.

GERMAN VEAL STEW

Breast of veal	5 celery tops, minced
Salt	1 cup canned tomatoes
Powdered ginger	Hot water
2 tablespoons cooking fat	1 tablespoon flour
1 onion, sliced	Caraway seed
Minced parsley	

Sprinkle veal breast with salt and powdered ginger. Melt fat in frying pan. Add onion, 1 tablespoon parsley and minced celery tops. Fry until onion begins to color. Add veal breast and brown all over. Add tomatoes and a little hot water. Cover. Simmer 2 hours, turning meat several times while cooking. Thicken gravy with flour and a little water mixed to smooth paste. Add caraway seed and minced parsley, to taste. Bring to boil. Pour over meat. Serve hot. Serves 5 to 6.

BAKED VEAL WITH TOMATOES AND POTATOES

2½ pounds shoulder or neck of veal	½ teaspoon marjoram
Vinegar	¼ teaspoon each mace and thyme
Salt and pepper	Pinch of powdered dried bay leaves
2 onions, minced	1½ tablespoons chopped parsley
1 clove garlic, minced	2 cups diced potatoes
3 tablespoons cooking fat	1 cup beef stock
3 large fresh tomatoes, diced	

Season meat with a teaspoon of vinegar, then sprinkle with salt and pepper. Set aside. Fry onion and garlic in hot fat until transparent. Add tomatoes and simmer gently for 10 minutes, stirring frequently. Pour this mixture into a greased casserole. Season with marjoram, mace, thyme, bay leaves, and parsley. Mix well. Place meat over this and cover tightly. Bake in moderate oven (375°F.) 40 minutes. Turn meat once after 20 minutes of cooking. Add diced potatoes and stock. Cover and bake 45 minutes longer. Slice the meat and place on hot platter. Arrange potatoes and tomatoes around the meat. Pour gravy over all. Garnish with chopped parsley. Serves 6 to 8.

HUNGARIAN VEAL BIRDS

2 pounds veal steak
Salt, pepper, paprika, and thyme
2 cups soft breadcrumbs
1 tablespoon each minced parsley,
  onion, and mushrooms
¼ cup cooking fat

1 tablespoon minced sweet-sour
  gherkins
1 tablespoon minced olives
Flour
Melted shortening
Clove garlic
¾ cup boiling water or stock

Cut veal into servings ¼ inch thick. Season to taste with salt, pepper, paprika, and thyme. Combine breadcrumbs with parsley, onion, and mushrooms. Brown this mixture lightly in hot fat for 2 to 3 minutes, stirring constantly. Remove from fire. Stir in gherkins and olives. Season with salt and pepper. Divide this mixture evenly among the 6 portions of veal. Roll up and tie with string. Brush with melted shortening. Roll in flour and brown in 2 or 3 tablespoons shortening. Rub a casserole with garlic clove and grease it. Place meat birds in casserole. Add boiling water or stock. Bake, covered, in moderate oven (375°F.) 45 minutes. Turn birds once during baking process. Serves 6.

VEAL SUPREME WITH RICE

1 pound boneless veal
2 teaspoons salt
1 onion
Few celery leaves
6 whole black peppercorns
½ cup flour

⅛ teaspoon mace
Dash of cayenne
Salt to taste
2 tablespoons sherry (optional)
3 hard-cooked eggs

Cover veal with 1¾ cups water. Add salt, onion, celery leaves, and peppercorns. Simmer covered until meat is tender. Remove celery leaves and peppercorns. Cut meat into short strips. Thicken broth with flour and stir in meat. Add mace, cayenne, and salt to taste. Press egg yolks through fine sieve, cut egg whites lengthwise and add to meat. Cook until thickened; add sherry, if desired. Serve on steamed rice. Serves 5.

BAKED VEAL, RUSSIAN STYLE

2 pounds veal cutlet
Salt and pepper
Wine vinegar

Cooking fat
4 onions, sliced
5 tomatoes, sliced

Season veal with salt and pepper. Place in a deep bowl and add vinegar to cover. Marinate 1 hour. Drain, dry, and place in greased casserole. Brown in hot oven (450°F.). Brown onion and tomato slices in fat. Add to veal. Reduce heat to 300°F. and add stock or water to just cover. Bake 30 to 45 minutes longer. Serves 6.

JELLIED VEAL

Boil knuckle of veal in water to cover, about 2 quarts. Add a large slice of onion, turnip, carrot, a sprig of parsley, and 3 cloves. Simmer slowly until meat falls from bone. Remove meat, strain liquor through coarse cheesecloth. Return to fire. Season with salt, cayenne, and lemon juice. Reduce to ¼ by boiling uncovered. Cut veal in pieces. Arrange in mold. Pour liquid over all, filling mold. Chill until firm.

SCALLOPINE OF VEAL

1 pound veal cutlets
2 tablespoons olive oil
1 clove garlic

½ cup Sauterne or Chablis wine
½ cup water
2 teaspoons lemon juice

Cut ¼-inch-thick veal cutlets into small pieces. Roll in flour seasoned with salt and pepper. Heat oil with garlic in heavy frying pan. Sauté meat until browned. Remove garlic. Add wine, water, and lemon juice. Cover. Simmer until tender, about 30 minutes. A pinch of thyme or marjoram may be added. Serve with steamed rice. Garnish with minced parsley. Serves 4.

variety meats

The terms "meat specialties" or "variety meats" are applied to the organ meats that cannot be classified with the regular cuts. They include brains, hearts, kidneys, liver, oxtails, sweetbreads, tripe, and tongue. These meats are more perishable than other meats. They must be absolutely fresh, firm to the touch, and sweet in odor when bought. They should be made a part of your menus as often as possible because they are high in content of essential minerals and vitamins. Note that kidneys and oxtails are not included in Jewish cooking because they are not kosher. In accordance with the kosher food laws, liver has to be broiled before being used in other recipes. For chopped liver recipes see the *APPETIZER* and *SALAD* sections.

SAUTEED LIVER

Cut broiled liver into large cubes. Sprinkle with salt. Dredge in sifted cracker crumbs or flour. Sauté in hot melted shortening until lightly browned on all sides, about 8 to 10 minutes.

With mushrooms: If desired, add drained canned mushrooms or peeled fresh mushrooms to liver after it has cooked for a few minutes.

LIVER AND VEGETABLE CASSEROLE

1½ cups beef liver, cut in cubes
1 cup peas
½ cup carrots
1 teaspoon salt
Dash of pepper

1 tablespoon cooking fat
1 cup consommé
¼ cup chopped pimiento
¼ cup water

Arrange liver in casserole. Add peas, carrots, salt, pepper, cooking fat, and consommé. Cover and place in hot oven (425°F.) for 30 minutes. Heat pimiento in water and add to casserole, stirring slightly. Return to oven without cover for 10 minutes longer. Serve on mashed potato or hot rice. Serves 4.

LIVER FRICASSEE

1 pound sliced liver
½ teaspoon salt
⅛ teaspoon pepper
¼ cup flour
¼ cup cooking fat
2 cups canned tomatoes

2 medium green peppers, chopped
6 small white onions, chopped
½ teaspoon celery salt
½ teaspoon poultry seasoning
Cooked rice

Dredge liver with seasoned flour. Brown in hot fat. Add tomatoes, peppers, onions, and seasoning. Cover and simmer about 40 minutes. Serve with cooked rice. Serves 6.

BRAISED LIVER WITH VEGETABLES

1 pound sliced liver
About 2 tablespoons flour
1 green pepper, diced
4 small onions

4 carrots
Salt and pepper
⅓ cup water

Dredge liver with flour. Brown in hot cooking fat. Clean and dice green pepper, onions, and carrots. Arrange mixed vegetables over slices of liver. Season with salt and pepper. Add ⅓ cup water. Cover and cook slowly until liver and vegetables are tender. Beef liver will take about 45 minutes, lamb and veal liver about 30 minutes. Serves 5.

LIVER AND SCRAMBLED EGGS

1 pound liver
1 teaspoon salt
⅛ teaspoon pepper

½ cup flour
4 tablespoons cooking fat
6 eggs

Cut liver into strips 4x½ inches. Roll in seasoned flour and brown in hot fat. Cook slowly about 10 minutes. Remove liver from pan and scramble eggs in remaining fat. Serves 6 to 8.

SOUTH AMERICAN GOULASH

¾ pound beef liver
¼ cup chopped onion
⅓ cup chopped green pepper
3 tablespoons cooking fat
2 cups canned tomatoes
⅓ cup chopped celery

1 small clove garlic
2 teaspoons salt
⅛ teaspoon pepper
3 tablespoons flour
2 cups uncooked noodles

Cut liver into 1-inch cubes. Brown with onion and green pepper in hot fat. Add tomatoes, celery, garlic, and seasoning. Cook slowly for 25 minutes. Mix flour with a little water and add to mixture for thickening. Cook noodles in boiling salted water for 10 minutes. Drain. Serve goulash over hot noodles. Serves 5.

HOW TO COOK SWEETBREADS

Sweetbreads are the thymus gland of the calf, and may be sold separately or as a pair. The breast sweetbread or the round, compact half is somewhat more choice.

They are very perishable and should be cooked the day they are bought. Allow ½ to 1 pair sweetbreads per serving. Wash and simmer 20 minutes in water to cover, to which has been added 1 tablespoon vinegar and 1 teaspoon salt per quart of water. Drain, cover with cold water, and let stand until cool enough to handle. Remove membrane and tubes. Then broil, sauté, or prepare as desired.

BROILED SWEETBREADS

Place cooked sweetbreads on broiler rack. Brush with fat and broil slowly until brown on one side. Turn and brown on other side. Two pair beef sweetbreads serves 4.

FRIED SWEETBREADS

Slice cooked sweetbreads ½ inch thick. Dip in egg diluted with water and roll in seasoned breadcrumbs. Fry in hot melted fat until nicely browned on both sides. Two pair beef sweetbreads serves 4.

BRAISED SWEETBREADS

Use 2 pair to serve 4. Cut cooked sweetbreads lengthwise in ¼-inch-thick slices. Sauté in 2 tablespoons fat. Add 1 cup brown gravy (see BROWN SAUCES), 1 tablespoon ketchup, 2 teaspoons each of chopped onion and parsley, dash each of salt and pepper. Simmer slowly 10 to 15 minutes. Add ¼ cup sherry wine. Bring to a boil. Serve at once.

SWEETBREADS SUPREME

1 pound cooked sweetbreads
1 cup sliced fresh mushrooms or
   1 small can button mushrooms
4 tablespoons hot cooking fat
6 tablespoons flour

2 cups liquid from mushrooms
   and vegetable stock
Salt and pepper to taste
1 cup cooked or canned peas
8 slices toast

Break cooked sweetbreads into small pieces. Brown well drained mushrooms in hot fat. Stir in flour. Add liquid and seasonings. Cook until thick, stirring constantly. Add peas and sweetbreads. Serve on toast. Serves 8.

HOW TO COOK BRAINS

Brains of calf, lamb, and beef may be prepared, although calf's brains are the most delicately flavored. Soak brains in cold salted water for ½ hour. Remove membrane. Simmer in 1 quart water to which has been added 1 tablespoon vinegar or lemon juice and 1 teaspoon salt. Drain and break or slice into pieces. Brains may be substituted for sweetbreads in given recipes. Allow 1 pair brains per serving.

FRIED BRAINS

Cut drained, cooked brains in ½-inch-thick slices. Roll in fine breadcrumbs. Brown in hot fat. Season with salt and pepper.

SWEET AND SOUR CALF'S BRAINS

1 set calf's brains
1 onion, sliced
3 or 4 slices celery root
3 whole peppers
   About 3 tablespoons vinegar or
     lemon juice

½ teaspoon salt
¼ cup gingersnap crumbs
About 2 tablespoons brown sugar
¼ teaspoon cinnamon
¼ cup seedless raisins

Soak calf's brains in cold water to cover 1 hour. Drain. Remove membrane. Place brains, onion, celery root, and whole peppers in saucepan. Add water to just cover, to which has been added 1 tablespoon vinegar or lemon juice and ½ teaspoon salt. Bring to boil and simmer 20 minutes. Remove brains. Combine gingersnap crumbs, brown sugar, cinnamon, and seedless raisins and moisten with 2 tablespoons vinegar or lemon juice. Add to liquid in pan. Bring to boil and cook until blended and smooth, 10 minutes. Serve cold, garnished with lemon wedges. Serves 4.

BRAIN FRITTERS

½ pound cooked calf's brains
3 eggs
⅓ cup flour
   About 3 tablespoons cold water

¼ teaspoon salt
⅛ teaspoon pepper
Fat for frying

Slice cooked brains ¼ inch thick. Beat eggs, stir in flour, salt, pepper, and cold water to make thick batter. Dip sliced brains in batter. Fry in hot fat until browned on both sides. Serves 4.

SCRAMBLED BRAINS WITH EGGS

½ pound cooked brains
4 eggs
2 tablespoons ketchup
¼ teaspoon salt

Dash of Worcestershire sauce
4 tablespoons cooking fat
4 slices toast
2 tablespoons minced parsley

Cut cooked brains in ½-inch pieces. Beat eggs slightly and add seasonings and brains. Heat fat in frying pan. Pour in brain-egg mixture. Cook slowly, stirring enough to scramble. Serve on hot toast, garnished with parsley. Serves 6.

BRAINS A LA KING

1 pound cooked brains
2 chopped green peppers
2 teaspoons grated onion
½ cup diced celery
2 cups medium white sauce

2 tablespoons cooking fat
2 tablespoons chopped pimiento
½ teaspoon salt
⅛ teaspoon pepper
6 slices toast

Separate cooked brains into small cubes. Sauté green peppers, onion, and celery in fat. Add white sauce with pimiento, salt, and pepper. Add brains and heat thoroughly. Serve on toast. Serves 6 to 8. NOTE: Prepare the white sauce with chicken stock.

HEART FRICASSEE

Wash and trim 1 small beef heart. Cut crosswise. Dredge in flour and brown in hot fat. Season with 2 teaspoons salt and ¼ teaspoon pepper. Add ½ cup sliced onion and brown. Add 1 cup diced carrots and 1 cup canned tomatoes. Cover tightly. Simmer 1½ to 2½ hours, or until tender. Serves 6.

SWEET AND SOUR HEART

1 beef heart or	½ cup vinegar
2 veal hearts	¼ cup brown sugar
Cooking fat or salad oil	2 tablespoons flour
1½ cups canned tomatoes	1 teaspoon salt
¼ cup water	⅛ teaspoon paprika

Trim heart and cut into small cubes. Heat 3 to 4 tablespoons fat or oil in heavy saucepan. Add heart and sauté over moderate heat 10 minutes. Add tomatoes, water, vinegar, and sugar. Cover and simmer until heart is tender, 35 to 40 minutes. Add flour to 2 tablespoons fat melted in a skillet. Stir in ¼ cup sauce from hearts. Cook, stirring constantly, until smooth. Combine with hearts. Add more salt, if necessary, and paprika. Cook 5 minutes longer. Serves 6 to 8.

BRAISED HEART WITH APPLES

1 beef heart or	½ cup brown sugar
2 veal hearts	8 cloves
Salt and pepper, to taste	2 bay leaves, crushed
Flour	½ lemon, sliced
2 tablespoons cooking fat or salad oil	½ cup water
4 apples	

Wash and trim heart. Season with salt and pepper. Roll in flour. Brown in hot fat. Peel and quarter apples and arrange around heart. Sprinkle with brown sugar, cloves, and bay leaves. Arrange lemon slices on top and add water. Cover tightly and braise in a slow oven (300°F.), or simmer until heart is tender. A beef heart of ¾ pounds requires at least 4 hours. Veal hearts require 2 to 2½ hours. Serves 8 to 10.

BOILED BEEF TONGUE (Basic Recipe)

1 beef tongue	4 whole cloves
6 peppercorns	1 tablespoon vinegar

A 4-pound tongue serves 12. Fresh, corned, or smoked tongues may be used. Corned or smoked tongues are improved by soaking in cold water for several hours before cooking. Scrub tongue under running water. Place in deep kettle. Add seasonings and boiling water to cover. Boil 10 minutes, then simmer for 3 to 5 hours, or until a fork will penetrate readily to the center. Let tongue remain in water until cool enough to handle. Peel off outer skin. Cut out membranous portions of roots. Press into shape for serving. Serve hot with horseradish or raisin sauce, or slice and serve cold.

Baked fresh tongue: After peeling fresh cooked tongue, place in a shallow roasting pan. Rub with hot fat. Bake in a moderate oven (350°F.) about 50 to 60 minutes.

Beef tongue piquant: After peeling cooked fresh tongue, dust with flour seasoned with salt and pepper. Brown in hot fat. Combine ¾ cup tart grape jelly and 1 cup hot water. Mix thoroughly. Pour over tongue. Simmer about 40 minutes.

Fresh tongue with rice and spinach: Arrange sliced hot tongue on a platter with cooked spinach and rice.

Jellied tongue: Peel and trim cooked fresh tongue. Place in mold. Strain tongue liquid. Measure enough to fill mold. Add 2 tablespoons plain gelatin to measured liquid. Bring to boiling point. Pour over tongue. Chill until firm.

Tongue with cranberries: Place sliced cooked tongue in a pan. Combine ½ cup water or tongue liquid, ½ cup stewed cranberries, ¼ cup brown sugar, 2 tablespoons melted fat, and 3 slices lemon. Add to tongue. Simmer until heated through. Serve hot.

BEEF TONGUE WITH RAISIN SAUCE

1 fresh beef tongue	½ cup almonds, blanched and split
3 small onions	⅔ cup seedless raisins
2 small carrots	6 tablespoons cooking fat
4 stalks celery and leaves	3 tablespoons flour
6 sprigs parsley	¼ cup crushed gingersnaps
8 peppercorns	1 lemon, cut in small cubes
Salt and paprika	

Place tongue in a large kettle with onions, carrots, celery, and parsley. Add water to cover. Add peppercorns and salt. Simmer gently until tender, 3 to 5 hours. Drain. Reserve liquid. Skin tongue, remove roots, and keep hot until needed. Add almonds to 2 cups water and simmer ½ hour. Add raisins and simmer ½ hour longer. Drain. Reserve liquid. Melt fat and add flour and stir until blended. Gradually stir in reserved raisin and almond liquid and enough tongue liquid to make 3 cups in all. Add gingersnaps, almonds, raisins, and lemon cubes. Season with salt and paprika. Pour over sliced tongue. Serve hot.

SWEET AND SOUR TONGUE

1 cooked tongue	1 stick cinnamon
1 large onion, chopped	4 cloves
1 tablespoon cooking fat	¼ cup raisins
1 tablespoon flour	¼ cup brown sugar
2 cups hot tongue liquid	1 tablespoon molasses
½ teaspoon salt	Juice of 1 lemon
1 tablespoon almonds, finely chopped	

Peel and slice cooked tongue. Brown onion slightly in hot fat. Remove onion and set aside. Stir flour into hot fat and cook 3 minutes. Gradually add hot tongue liquid and salt and simmer gently until smooth and thickened, about 5 minutes. Add browned onions, almonds, cinnamon, cloves, and raisins. Mix well. Blend together the brown sugar, molasses, and lemon juice and stir into the mixture. Simmer about 10 minutes, stirring constantly. If desired, add more salt, sugar, and lemon juice to taste. Add sliced tongue and simmer until heated through. Serve hot with sauce.

RUMANIAN TONGUE WITH OLIVES

1 cooked beef tongue
1½ cups sliced olives
2 tablespoons melted cooking fat
2 tablespoons flour

1 onion, minced
2 cups tomato juice
Salt and pepper

Peel and slice cooked tongue. Place in baking pan. Cover with sliced olives. Melt fat in skillet and add flour, stirring until smooth. Add onion and tomato juice. Season with salt and pepper to taste. Boil until thickened. Pour over tongue. Bake in moderate oven (350°F.) 30 minutes. Serves 8 to 10.

BRAISED TONGUE WITH VEGETABLES

1 beef tongue, fresh, pickled, or smoked
1 cup carrots, diced
1 cup onions, sliced
1 cup celery, diced
¼ cup flour

¼ cup cooking fat
2 cups hot tongue liquid
2 cups strained canned tomatoes
Salt and pepper
Dash Worcestershire sauce

Partially cook tongue, about 2 hours, as in *BOILED TONGUE* recipe. Peel and trim roots. Place diced and sliced vegetables in a roasting pan. Place tongue over vegetables. Stir flour into hot melted fat in a pan and cook gently 3 minutes, stirring constantly. Gradually add hot tongue liquid. Simmer until mixture is smooth and thick, stirring constantly. Add tomatoes, seasoned with salt, pepper, and Worcestershire sauce. Pour over tongue. Cover and roast in slow oven (300°F.) until tender, about 2 hours. Serve with sauce.

TONGUE WITH POTATOES

1 beef tongue, fresh, pickled,
   or smoked
2 cups canned tomatoes
Juice of 1 lemon

¼ cup brown sugar
Salt and pepper
Small, peeled potatoes
2 cups hot tongue liquid

Partially cook tongue, about 2 hours, as in *BOILED TONGUE* recipe. Peel and trim cooked tongue. Place in roasting pan. Mix together the tomatoes, lemon juice, sugar, and salt and pepper to taste. Arrange as many small potatoes as desired around tongue and pour this mixture over all. Add hot tongue liquid. Cover and roast in slow oven (300°F.) until tender, about 2 hours. Turn tongue once while roasting. Baste occasionally with sauce.

TONGUE À LA MARYLAND

1 beef tongue
¼ cup melted cooking fat
½ teaspoon salt
1 bay leaf

¾ cup brown sugar
1½ cups canned or cooked cherries
1 cup tongue liquid
½ lemon sliced

Cook tongue as in *BOILED TONGUE* recipe. Trim and remove skin. Place in pan with melted fat, salt, bay leaf, brown sugar, cherries, tongue liquid and sliced lemon. Simmer until sauce thickens.

HOW TO COOK AND SERVE LUNG

Beef lung is used with soup meat and soup bones in making soup. When tender, it may be put through the food grinder with other cooked meats. It is then seasoned to taste and used as a filling for pirogen, piroshke, kreplach, strudel, or knishes. It may also be included with a pot roast.

LUNGEN STEW

1 beef lung, cubed	2 cups canned tomatoes
½ cup diced onions	About 4 teaspoons brown sugar
1 clove garlic, minced	1½ teaspoons salt
3 tablespoons cooking fat	¼ teaspoon pepper
1½ pounds lean beef, cubed	1½ cups diced carrots

Trim veins from lung before cutting into small cubes. Lightly brown onions and garlic in hot fat. Add beef and lung. Brown lightly on all sides. Add tomatoes, brown sugar, salt, and pepper. Cover. Simmer over moderate heat until meat is tender. Add carrots and, if desired, other diced or cubed vegetables after stew has cooked about 15 minutes. Total cooking time 40 to 50 minutes. Thicken stew with 1 tablespoon flour mixed to a paste with cold water. Blend with ½ cup stew sauce and then add to stew. Cook 5 minutes longer. Serves 6.

BAKED KISHKE (Stuffed Derma)

Beef casings bought at the market are only partially cleaned. Wash and clean casings thoroughly. For each cup of flour, use ⅓ cup fat, ¼ cup onion, ½ teaspoon salt, and ¼ teaspoon pepper. Mix well. Cut casings in 12-inch lengths. Fasten or sew one end of casings. Stuff. Fasten other end. Plunge into boiling water. Scrape until clean. Melt ¼ cup fat in a roasting pan and add 2 large sliced onions. Arrange kishke in pan. Bake in slow oven (325°F.) until well browned, 1½ to 2 hours. Baste frequently with drippings. Stuffed kishke may also be roasted with poultry or cooked with carrot tzimmes.

Boiled kishke: Prepare as for baked kishke. Boil 3 hours in water to cover in tightly covered pot. Drain well. Brown in hot fat in a covered deep skillet. Serve hot.

STUFFED POULTRY NECK (Gelfilte Helzel)

Remove skin from neck of goose, duck, or chicken in 1 piece. Stuff with filling as for KISHKE. Sew or skewer at both ends. Bake with poultry until well browned.

PITCHA OR SULZE (Calves Foot Jelly)

1 calf's foot	Juice of 1 lemon
1 onion	2 tablespoons white vinegar
1 clove garlic	2 eggs, hard-cooked
1 bay leaf	

Clean calf's foot thoroughly. Soak 1 hour in cold water. Drain. Cook 2 hours in water to cover. Add onion, garlic, bay leaf, lemon juice, and vinegar, cook 1 hour longer. Remove meat and cut half or all of it into small pieces. Strain liquid over it. Add sliced eggs. Chill until firm. If desired, part of the meat may be served hot.

GEFILTE MILTZ (Stuffed Spleen)

1 beef spleen   Salt and pepper
2 cups breadcrumbs   1 diced onion
2 eggs   2 tablespoons cooking fat

Have veins removed from spleen. Clean and make incision in center. Scrape out center and mix this meat with breadcrumbs, eggs, salt, and pepper. Brown onion in fat and add to mixture. Fill spleen and skewer or sew opening. Dot with fat. Bake in a greased pan or on rack in moderate oven (350°F.) until hard crust forms, about 2 hours. Baste occasionally with hot water.

TRIPE

Tripe is the lining of beef stomach. Honeycomb tripe is considered best. It is sold fresh or pickled. One pound serves 4. Wash well, cover with cold water. Bring to a boil. Drain. Cover with boiling water. Cover. Simmer until tender, 1 to 2 hours. If fresh tripe is used, add ½ teaspoon salt per pound when about half done. Use in recipes as indicated.

Broiled tripe: Dry boiled honeycomb tripe well. Brush with fat. Roll in fine breadcrumbs. Place on greased broiler rack. Broil under moderate flame until crumbs are browned, 2 to 3 minutes on each side.

Fried tripe: Dip boiled tripe in egg diluted with 2 tablespoons cold water. Roll in fine breadcrumbs. Repeat and fry in a little hot fat until brown on both sides.

Stewed tripe: Wash 1½ pounds fresh tripe. Cut in small strips. Brown in 3 tablespoons hot fat with ¼ cup onions or 1 clove garlic, minced. Slowly add and brown 2 tablespoons flour. Gradually stir in boiling water to cover. Simmer slowly until tender, 1 to 2 hours. Serve in sauce. Serves 6.

Tripe in sauce: Prepare SWEET AND SOUR sauce, TOMATO sauce, or CREOLE sauce. Reheat boiled tripe in sauce.

TRIPE IN BATTER

1 pound boiled tripe   1 teaspoon salad oil
1 egg, unbeaten   1 cup flour
½ cup cold water   ¼ teaspoon salt
1 teaspoon vinegar

Cut boiled tripe into small pieces. Combine egg, water, vinegar, and oil. Mix and sift in flour and salt. Beat until smooth. Dip tripe in batter. Fry in hot fat until browned on all sides. Serves 4 to 5.

pies, pastry and strudel

The fillings for pies are almost innumerable, but success in piemaking depends upon the attainment of the art of making tender, flaky pastry. A luscious fruit or rich, creamy filling won't disguise a poor crust beneath it. The development of skill in pastry-making may take a little practice to produce the perfect pie but it's a simple skill to acquire. Follow the basic recipe and you'll get the consistently good results that will give you the pride of accomplishment sought by every homemaker in making the great American dessert—the perfect pie.

Essential hints: All-purpose flour is generally used, although some cooks prefer a special pastry flour. Use chilled water and be very sparing with it. Don't overmix. Handle dough as little as possible and as lightly as possible. Chill after mixing. Plain pastry, made by the standard method, is tender and flaky. Hot water pastry is tender but has a tendency to crumble. It is somewhat difficult to handle, although some cooks consider it easier to make.

Necessary equipment: A board, rolling pin, a wire pastry blender or blending fork, a measuring cup, knife, and spoon are all that are necessary. If a pastry blender is not available, use two knives. A pastry cloth (medium-weight cotton canvas or duck) for the board and a stockinette for the rolling pin reduces flour needed to roll dough and makes handling of pastry easier, especially in hot weather.

About pie pans: A standard pie pan with a slanting rim is best. Pastry will brown more readily on the bottom in a glass baking dish or enamel pan, or in a tin that has grown dark from use than in a new tin or aluminum pan. Glass, of course, has the advantage that you can inspect the bottom to see if the crust is thoroughly baked, and it does make a more attractive serving dish.

PLAIN PASTRY (Basic Recipe)

¾ teaspoon salt
2½ cups sifted all-purpose flour

¾ cup shortening
About ⅓ cup ice cold water

Sift salt with flour. With pastry blender cut fat into flour until size of small peas. Sprinkle small amounts of cold water over flour-fat mixture and combine lightly with fork until dough holds together when pressed lightly. Chill, if time permits. Divide dough into 2 equal parts. Toss dough on lightly floured board and shape each part into a ball. Roll each crust ⅛ inch thick, rolling lightly in one direction only—not backwards and forwards. Roll from center to edges and use very little flour on board or rolling pin. Fold rolled crust in half, lift, and place in pan so that fold is along center. Unfold and fit carefully into pan so that no space is left between pan and pastry. Roll out top crust in same way and cut slits in a design near center to allow steam to escape during baking. Place filling in bottom crust. Moisten its edges with water. Cover with top crust. Press edges together. Trim off edge and press with floured tines of fork to seal. Bake in hot oven (450°F.) 10 minutes, then reduce to moderate (375°F.), and bake 30 to 40 minutes longer, or until filling is done and crust is browned. Yield: Pastry for two 9-inch shells, or 1 double-crust 9-inch pie, or 14 four-inch tart shells.

For 2-crust 8-inch pie: Use 2 cups flour, ½ to ⅔ cup shortening, ¾ teaspoon salt, and about ¼ cup ice cold water.

1-crust pie: Use ½ the basic recipe. Trim edge ½ inch larger than pan. Double the edge, making it stand up. Press into fluted shape all around with fingers or press edges with tines of fork. If the crust is to be baked without the filling, prick bottom and sides of crust before baking so that air can escape. Bake on inverted pie tin, in a hot oven (450°F.) 12 to 15 minutes. If the crust is to be baked with the filling, do not prick the crust.

Lattice crust: Roll half of dough as for a lower crust. Roll remaining dough thin, cut in strips ⅜ inch wide (about 14 to 16 strips). Place half the strips over top about 1 inch apart across one way, and half across the other way to give criss-cross effect. Place one strip all the way around the edge to hold strips in place. Press down with tines of fork. Bake as for 2-crust pie.

TART SHELLS

Prepare *PLAIN PASTRY* recipe and roll thin. Cut in 5 or 6-inch circles. 1. Fit into large muffin tins and press out all air bubbles. Double edges, making them stand up, and flute edges. Prick well with fork. 2. Fit pastry circles over inverted muffin pans. Pinch together at 4 corners and prick well with fork. Bake in hot oven (450°F.) about 15 minutes. Yield: 8 or 9 shells.

VARIATIONS OF PLAIN PASTRY

Cheese pastry: Prepare *PLAIN PASTRY* and add to portion reserved for upper crust ½ cup grated American cheese. Good with apple pie. If pastry is to be used for cheese wafers, straws, etc., add 1½ cups grated cheese and cut in with shortening.

Cream cheese pastry: Reduce shortening to ½ cup. Add ½ cup cream cheese and cut into flour with shortening.

Hot water pastry: Add ½ teaspoon baking powder and sift with flour. Substitute ⅓ cup boiling water for cold water and beat into shortening. Gradually stir in flour mixture and proceed as for *PLAIN PASTRY*.

Lemon pastry: Instead of all water, use 2 tablespoons lemon juice and 2 tablespoons or more of water in making *PLAIN PASTRY*. Add to sifted dry ingredients 1 teaspoon grated lemon rind and ½ tablespoon sugar. If desired, add for color 1 egg yolk beaten with lemon juice.

Nut pastry: Add ⅔ cup any finely ground nutmeats (almonds, pecans, walnuts, or black walnuts) to dough. Black walnuts are especially good with pumpkin pie.

Orange pastry: Use all orange juice instead of water. Add 1 tablespoon sugar and ½ teaspoon grated orange rind to sifted dry ingredients.

Sour milk pastry: Substitute thick sour milk for water, using enough to hold dough together. Add ¼ teaspoon soda and sift with dry ingredients.

Spiced pastry: Add to sifted dry ingredients 2 tablespoons powdered sugar and ⅛ teaspoon each cinnamon and nutmeg.

PATTY SHELLS

Roll out plain pastry ¼ inch thick. Cut with round, floured cutter. Remove centers from ½ these circles with a small cutter. Wet edges of the whole circles. Place the rings on them. Brush tops carefully with an egg slightly beaten with 1 tablespoon water. Take care not to moisten sides. Chill until stiff. Bake in hot oven (450°F.) 10 to 20 minutes. Bake small centers 10 minutes and use as tops after shells are filled.

CHEESE STICKS

Use CHEESE PASTRY recipe. Roll out ⅛ inch thick. Cut into strips about 3 to 4 inches long and ½ inch wide. If desired, sprinkle with paprika. Wrap in waxed paper and chill. Bake in hot oven (450°F.) 6 to 8 minutes. Or use leftover plain pastry and roll out ⅛ inch thick. Sprinkle heavily with grated cheese and paprika, if desired. Fold in half, sprinkle again and roll out. Repeat 2 more times. Cut in strips as above. Chill and bake.

QUANTITY PASTRY MIX

6 cups sifted all-purpose flour	2 cups shortening
1 tablespoon salt	

Sift flour with salt. With a pastry blender or 2 knives cut in shortening until the mixture is the consistency of small peas. Store in covered container in a cool place. For a 9-inch single-crust pie, use 1⅓ cups PASTRY MIX with 1 to 3 tablespoons water. For a double-crust pie use 2½ cups with 4 to 6 tablespoons water. Follow directions for handling pastry given in the recipe for PLAIN PASTRY.

ALMOND PASTRY

1½ cups sifted all-purpose flour	½ cup shortening
½ teaspoon salt	1 egg, beaten
¼ cup sugar	Ice cold water
¼ cup ground almonds	

Mix flour, salt, sugar, and almonds. Cut in shortening. Add egg and just enough cold water to make a stiff dough. Wrap in waxed paper and chill. Roll and bake as for PLAIN PASTRY.

SUET PASTRY

2 cups sifted all-purpose flour	1 cup minced beef suet (chilled)
1 teaspoon baking powder	About ½ cup ice cold water
¾ teaspoon salt	

Mix and sift flour, baking powder, and salt. Add well chilled suet and slowly add water, blending to make a smooth, firm dough. Wrap in waxed paper and chill thoroughly. Roll out and proceed as for PLAIN PASTRY. Use for meat pies, turnovers, etc.

MUERBE TEIG

1 cup sifted all-purpose flour	¼ cup butter
1 tablespoon sugar	1 egg yolk, slightly beaten
⅛ teaspoon salt	

Mix and sift flour, sugar, and salt. Cut in butter with pastry blender or 2 knives. Add egg yolk and mix thoroughly. Press into pie pan or spring form to ¼ inch thickness with hands. Fill with desired fruit filling. Bake in hot oven (425°F.) 10 minutes. Reduce to moderate (350°F.) and bake until fruit is cooked. Yield: one 9-inch shell.

VEGETABLE OIL PASTRY

2 cups sifted all-purpose flour
1 teaspoon salt

½ cup vegetable oil
¼ cup plus 1 tablespoon cold water

Sift together flour and salt. Combine oil and water in measuring cup. Beat with fork until thickened and creamy. To avoid separation, immediately pour (all at once) over entire surface of flour mixture. Toss and mix with fork. The dough will be moist. Form into ball. Divide dough in half. Before rolling, shape each half with hands into a flat round, making top and edges smooth. Roll on unfloured board. Do not use flour on board or pin. Roll lightly from center to edge. Continue to roll until dough no longer flakes off on pin and is smooth, or, if preferred, roll dough between two squares of wax paper. Lift edge of dough with spatula. Fold in half. Fit loosely into pie pan and unfold. If rolled between wax paper, remove top sheet, invert dough over pan, and peel off paper. Fit pastry into pan. Roll out top crust. Cut gashes for escape of steam. Fill pastry-lined pan with desired filling. Place top over filling and trim ½ inch beyond rim of pan. Seal edge by folding top crust under bottom crust. Flute edge. Bake at temperature required for filling used.

1-crust pie: Divide ingredients exactly in half and combine as directed above. Roll out. Fit into pie pan. Fold edge and flute. Prick entire surface of crust. Bake in hot oven (475°F.) 10 to 12 minutes.

SWEET PASTRY (Basic Recipe)

1½ cups flour
1 teaspoon baking powder
½ teaspoon salt
2 tablespoons sugar

½ cup shortening
1 egg yolk
4 tablespoons ice cold water

Sift dry ingredients together. Cut in shortening with pastry blender. Beat egg yolk and add water, then add to dry ingredients. Knead lightly. Chill thoroughly. Roll ⅛ inch thick and line pie pan. Crimp or flute edges. Use for peach, rhubarb, or berry pies. Bake shell 10 to 12 minutes in a hot oven (450°F.). Yield: 1 9-inch shell.

Flaky sweet pastry: Omit baking powder, egg yolk, and sugar. Add 1 slightly beaten egg white.

Sweet orange pastry: To FLAKY SWEET PASTRY add 1 teaspoon grated orange rind, using orange juice instead of water.

CRUMB CRUSTS

Zwieback crust: Combine 1¼ cups zwieback crumbs, ⅓ cup confectioners' sugar, and 3 tablespoons melted butter. Press into 9-inch greased pie pan. Chill.

Corn flake crust: Combine 1 cup crushed corn flakes with ¼ cup sugar and ⅓ cup melted butter. Press firmly into greased 9-inch pie pan. Chill. Crisp rice cereal may also be used.

Graham cracker crust: Crush 18 Graham crackers (1½ cups crumbs), blend with 1 teaspoon flour, ½ cup melted butter, ½ cup granulated sugar, and ¾ teaspoon cinnamon. Press firmly into greased 9-inch pie pan to a thickness of ¼ inch. Chill until set, about 40 minutes.

Almond graham cracker crust: Add about ½ cup finely ground almonds to crumbs before mixing with other ingredients.

Vanilla or chocolate wafer crust: Combine 1¼ cups crushed vanilla or chocolate wafers with ¼ cup melted butter. Press firmly into greased 9-inch pie pan. If desired, use only 1 cup crumbs and line sides of pan with whole wafers, cut in halves. Chill.

PUFF PASTE (Basic Recipe)

1 cup salted butter	½ cup ice cold water
2 cups sifted cake flour	

Wash butter by placing it in a mixing bowl, holding it under running water and squeezing and pressing with hands until it is pliable and waxy. Let ⅔ of butter become soft. Cut remaining butter into flour with pastry blender or 2 knives. Add cold water, using only enough to hold ingredients together. Roll out on a lightly floured board in a square sheet ¼ inch thick. Spread ⅔ of sheet with ¼ of softened butter. Fold unbuttered ⅓ over center ⅓. Fold remaining ⅓ over to cover first ⅓ with the buttered side down. This makes 3 layers of dough with butter between layers. Turn dough ¼ of way around on board. Roll out to ¼ inch thickness. Spread with butter again. Fold again in the same way. Chill thoroughly, about 25 minutes. Do not bring in direct contact with ice. Roll out and spread with butter. Fold and chill 2 more times. Chill the last time for at least 1 hour. Then roll and shape as directed in recipes for *PUFF PASTE*. Puff paste may be wrapped in waxed paper and kept a few days.

To bake puff paste: Shape, chill thoroughly. Arrange on baking sheets covered with 2 thicknesses of heavy brown paper. Bake in very hot oven (500°F.) and reduce heat 50° every 5 minutes down to moderate (350°F.). Turn as needed to brown evenly. Some pastry cooks like to bake puff paste at a uniform heat of 500°F., but in this case it has to be covered with heavy waxed paper after 10 minutes baking.

Cream horns: Roll paste out ⅛ inch thick. Cut in long strips ¾ to 1 inch wide. Brush with egg white diluted with water. Wrap paste around metal cream horn forms or form cornucopias from stiff brown paper and wind strips around cornucopias spiral fashion, letting edges of dough overlap a little. Chill well before baking. Bake as directed for *PUFF PASTE*. Remove from forms or cornucopias. Chill.

Patty shells: Roll *PUFF PASTE* ¼ inch thick. Cut into 3-inch rounds with floured cutter. Cut out centers from half of rounds with a smaller cutter. Moisten underside of each ring with cold water. Place 1 on each full round. Press down lightly. Bake smaller rounds to use as covers. Bake as directed for *PUFF PASTE*.

Bouchées: Follow method for patty shells, rolling pastry ⅛ inch thick and making cases smaller.

Vol-au-vent: Work with about ¼ of puff pastry, keeping remainder chilled until needed. Roll paste ⅓ inch thick. Cut an oval with floured mold or knife. Brush outer edge with water. Add a rim of pastry about ¾ inch wide. Prick several places with fork. Chill and bake. If desired, bake smaller ovals for covers, using the paste from center of outer rims. Watch carefully and cover with paper if it browns too quickly.

NAPOLEONS

Bake 3 sheets of *PUFF PASTRY*, pricking before baking. Spread cream filling between the sheets. Cover top with confectioners' frosting. Sprinkle with blanched and chopped pistachio nuts. Cut with a very sharp knife into pieces about 2½x4 inches.

CREAM PUFF SHELLS (Choux Paste) (Basic Recipe)

1 cup water	1 cup sifted all-purpose flour
½ cup butter	4 eggs
¼ teaspoon salt	

Place water, butter, and salt in heavy saucepan. Bring to boil. Add flour all at once, stirring vigorously with wooden spoon over flame until thick. When mixture forms a smooth ball and leaves sides of pan, remove from flame. Add unbeaten eggs, one at a time, beating thoroughly after each addition. Scrape rounded tablespoonfuls on greased baking sheet, allowing about 2 inches between puffs. Bake in hot oven (450°F.) 10 minutes. Lower temperature to moderate (375°F.) and bake 20 to 30 minutes longer, or until puffs are rigid enough to hold shape on removal from oven. Cool on wire rack. When cool cut a slit in the side of each. Fill puffs with cooked cream filling, whipped cream, fruit and whipped cream, ice cream, or use to serve creamed eggs, fish, or other creamed foods as entrees. Yield: 12 large puffs.

Chocolate cream puffs: Melt 1 square unsweetened chocolate with butter-water mixture.

Eclairs: Force paste through pastry bag and form into oblong shapes about 1 by 4 inches. Bake same way. Yield: 12 to 18.

Fried puff shells (queen fritters): Prepare basic *PUFF SHELL* mixture. Scrape mixture from tablespoon into deep hot fat (375°F.). Use one rounded tablespoon per puff. Fry until a nice crust has formed, turning frequently, about 12 minutes. Drain. Cut tops off shells. Fill with desired filling and replace tops. Yield: 12 large puffs.

Miniature puffs: Use about ¾ teaspoon paste. Scrape off end of spoon to make small puffs in rounds or oblongs. Bake about half the time. To serve with cocktails, fill with any desired savory filling. To serve as dessert fill with desired sweet filling and frost with butter frosting or confectioners' icing, tinting frosting in pastel shades. Yield: about 48 small puffs.

MERINGUE

¼ teaspoon salt	6 tablespoons granulated sugar
3 egg whites	1 teaspoon lemon juice or
¼ teaspoon baking powder (optional)	½ teaspoon vanilla (optional)

Add salt to egg whites. Beat until foamy, then add baking powder. Beat until stiff, then beat in sugar gradually. Add flavoring. Continue beating until sugar is well blended and mixture piles up fluffy. Spread meringue on pie, bringing it well out on the edge of crust. Unless it has something to cling to, it will shrink in the baking. Spread in careless strokes, leaving surface irregular. Bake in slow oven (325°F.) 12 to 15 minutes, or until golden brown.

MARSHMALLOW MERINGUE

¼ pound marshmallows
1 tablespoon milk
¼ teaspoon vanilla

2 egg whites
¼ teaspoon salt
¼ cup sugar

Combine marshmallows and milk and heat slowly, folding over and over until marshmallows are about half the original size. Remove from heat. Add vanilla and continue folding until mixture is smooth but light and fluffy. Beat egg whites with salt until stiff. Gradually add sugar, beating constantly. Fold in the slightly warm marshmallow mixture. Pile on pie and place under moderate broiler flame about 3 inches from flame. Broil until lightly browned, about ½ minute.

UNBAKED JELLY MERINGUE

Beat 4 egg whites until stiff. Add one 7 to 8 ounce glass of jelly (½ grape and ½ currant makes a colorful and tasty combination). Continue beating until fluffy. Spread on cake or to top desserts or custards. If desired, sprinkle with chopped nuts or coconut.

BROWN SUGAR GLAZE

Mix 1 tablespoon milk and 1 teaspoon light brown sugar. Brush on pastry before baking.

APPLE PIE (Basic Recipe)

1 recipe PLAIN PASTRY
6 to 8 tart apples, sliced
1 cup sugar
1 tablespoon lemon juice
2 tablespoons flour

⅛ teaspoon salt
½ teaspoon cinnamon or nutmeg (for spicy pie, use ½ teaspoon each)
1 tablespoon butter or margarine

Combine ingredients, except butter, and let stand while preparing pastry. Line pie plate with pastry. Add filling and dot with butter. Cover with top crust. Bake in hot oven (425°F.) 35 to 45 minutes, or until crust is golden brown and apples are tender.

Apple fruit pie: Use 4 apples, diced, and add 1 cup each cranberries and raisins. Add ¼ cup water and cook until apples are tender. Add remaining ingredients and additional sugar if not sweet enough. Proceed as directed for APPLE PIE.

Apple pie with melted cheese: After apple pie is baked, lay thin slices of cheese or grated cheese over the top. Put in slow oven (325°F.) until cheese is melted. Serve at once while cheese is warm. Either a freshly baked or cold pie may be prepared in this way.

Deep dish apple pie: Use double amount of filling for APPLE PIE. Bake in individual casseroles or an 8 or 9-inch baking dish 2 to 3 inches deep. Line sides but not bottom with pastry. Add filling. Sprinkle with a little water and cover with top crust. Bake in hot oven (425°F.) 35 to 40 minutes.

French apple pie: Prepare *PASTRY* for 1-crust pie. Fit into pan. Flute edge, chill, and fill with apples, etc., as usual. Then sprinkle with following: **Crumb topping:** Cream together ½ cup butter or margarine and ½ cup brown sugar. Cut in 1 cup flour. Bake as directed for plain *APPLE PIE.* Serve warm, with plain or whipped cream.

Open-face apple pie: Peel 6 to 8 tart apples. Core them and cut into eighths. The pieces of apple should be at least ½ inch thick. Apples should not be sliced thin, as this makes the pie very juicy. Combine 1 cup sugar and 4 tablespoons flour. Add the apples, 2 tablespoons lemon juice, and pour into crust. Add 1 tablespoon butter or margarine in small bits, also a few dashes of cinnamon or nutmeg. Cover top with strips of crust. Bake in hot oven (400°F.) 45 minutes.

BRANDIED APPLE PIE

1 recipe *PLAIN PASTRY*
4 cups sliced tart apples
½ cup brown sugar
1 teaspoon lemon juice

3 tablespoons brandy
1 tablespoon melted butter
American cheese

Roll pie dough out ⅛ inch thick and line pie plate. Fill with sliced apples. Sprinkle alternately with sugar, lemon juice, brandy, and melted butter. Cover with top crust and slash for escape of steam. Seal edges. Bake in hot oven (450°F.) 10 minutes, then reduce heat to moderate (350°F.) and bake 25 minutes longer. Serve hot or cold with American cheese.

SCOTCH APPLE PIE

6 to 8 apples
1½ cups dark brown sugar
1 cup water
2 teaspoons vinegar
4 tablespoons flour

⅛ teaspoon salt
1 teaspoon butter
1 teaspoon vanilla
1 recipe *PLAIN PASTRY*

Peel, core, and slice apples. Heat half of sugar with water and vinegar. Add apples and simmer until tender. Remove apples from syrup. Mix remaining sugar with flour and salt. Add slowly to syrup and cook until thickened. Remove from heat and add butter and vanilla. Fill the pastry lined pie pan with the apples. Pour over hot mixture. Cover with strips of pastry arranged in lattice form. Bake in a hot oven (425°F.) 10 minutes. Reduce heat to moderate (375°F.) and bake 25 to 35 minutes longer.

DUTCH APPLE PIE

½ recipe *PLAIN PASTRY*
6 to 8 apples
3 tablespoons flour
1 cup sugar

¼ teaspoon cloves
1 cup sour cream
½ teaspoon cinnamon
1½ tablespoons sugar

Line 9-inch pie pan with pastry. Pare apples and cut into thin slices. Arrange on unbaked pie shell. Mix flour, 1 cup sugar, and cloves. Add sour cream and mix thoroughly. Pour over apples. Sprinkle mixture of cinnamon and 1½ tablespoons sugar over top. Bake in hot oven (450°F.) 10 minutes. Reduce heat to moderate (350°F.) and bake 40 minutes longer. Serve warm or chilled.

APPLE PRUNE PIE

1 cup chopped stewed prunes	4 tablespoons flour
4 cups chopped apples	¼ cup prune juice
1 tablespoon grated orange rind	¼ cup molasses
⅓ cup orange juice	2 teaspoons melted butter
½ cup sugar	½ recipe *PLAIN PASTRY*
½ teaspoon salt	1 cup whipping cream, unsweetened

Mix together prunes, apples, orange rind and orange juice. Combine sugar, salt, flour, prune juice, molasses, and melted butter. Add to fruit mixture. Blend well. Pour filling into unbaked pie shell. Bake in hot oven (425°F.) 15 minutes. Reduce heat to moderate (350°F.) and bake 45 minutes longer. Serve with whipped cream.

COTTAGE CHEESE APRICOT PIE

½ recipe *PLAIN PASTRY*	1½ cups creamed cottage cheese
1 cup dried apricots	½ cup cream
2 eggs beaten	½ cup milk
¾ cup sugar	Cinnamon
½ teaspoon salt	

Line a 9-inch pie pan with pastry rolled out less than ⅛ inch thick. Wash apricots well and dry thoroughly. Cut fruit into small pieces and spread over bottom of crust. Combine eggs, sugar, and salt. Beat until well blended and foamy. Add cottage cheese, cream, and milk. Stir until mixed. Pour mixture over apricots. Sprinkle top with cinnamon. Bake in a hot oven (450°F.) 10 minutes. Reduce heat to slow (325°F.) and bake 1 hour, or until a knife inserted in the center comes out clean. Cool before serving.

FRESH BERRY PIE (Basic Recipe)

4 cups (1 quart) fresh berries	2 teaspoons quick-cooking tapioca
⅞ to 1 cup sugar	½ teaspoon cinnamon
1 recipe *PLAIN PASTRY*	1 tablespoon butter or margarine
4 tablespoons flour	

Use fresh ripe berries (strawberries, raspberries, blueberries, blackberries, or loganberries, etc.). Wash them, pick over, and remove stems and hulls. Drain and increase or decrease sugar in accordance with sweetness of fruit (up to 1½ cups sugar for 1 quart berries). Fill pastry-lined 9-inch pan with berries, sprinkling them with the sugar-flour mixture. Sprinkle tapioca over when half the berries are in the pan and again toward top. Sprinkle with cinnamon and dot with butter. If fruit is dry, sprinkle with 1 to 2 tablespoons water. Cover with top crust. Bake in hot oven (450°F.) 10 minutes, then in moderate oven (350°F.) about 30 minutes, until crust is nicely browned and berries are cooked through. Serve slightly warm, not hot.

FRESH CHERRY PIE

Make same as *FRESH BERRY PIE* except use pitted sour pie cherries in place of berries. Use about 1⅓ cups sugar for 9-inch pie and add a drop of almond flavoring. Cover with lattice top. Bake until nicely browned. Serve slightly warm, not hot.

FRESH PEACH (OR APRICOT) PIE

Make same as *FRESH BERRY PIE* except use sliced peaches (or apricots) in place of berries and leave out tapioca. Use ⅞ cup of sugar. Serve warm.

CONCORD GRAPE PIE

Skin 4 cups Concord grapes, saving skins. Put pulp in saucepan without water. Bring to a boil. While hot put through a strainer to remove seeds. Combine strained pulp and skins. Mix 1 cup sugar, 3 tablespoons flour, and ⅛ teaspoon salt together. Put about ¼ of this mixture on bottom of 9-inch pastry lined pan and mix remainder with grapes. Add 1 teaspoon lemon juice and turn into pie pan. Cover with top crust. Bake as *FRESH BERRY PIE*.

CANNED BERRY PIE (Basic Recipe)

2⅔ cups canned berries
½ to ¾ cup sugar
4 tablespoons flour
1 recipe *PLAIN PASTRY*

½ teaspoon cinnamon (optional)
1 tablespoon butter or margarine
½ cup juice from berries

Use only canned berries. Drain well. Taste juice and use minimum amount of sugar. Mix sugar and flour; sprinkle ½ of it over chilled pastry in 9-inch pan. Add berries, sprinkling remaining flour and sugar through them. Sprinkle with cinnamon. Dot with butter. Add juice. Quickly cover with top crust. Bake in hot oven (450°F.) 15 minutes, then about 20 minutes in moderate oven (350°F.) until nicely browned. Serve slightly warm, not hot.

CANNED CHERRY PIE

Make same as *CANNED BERRY PIE* except use sour, pitted red pie cherries instead of berries. Omit cinnamon. Add drop of almond flavoring. Cover with lattice top. Bake until nicely browned. Serve slightly warm, not hot.

BERRY GLACE PIE

1 quart strawberries or
  1 quart raspberries
1 9-inch baked *PASTRY SHELL*
¾ cup water

3 tablespoons cornstarch
1 cup sugar
1 teaspoon lemon juice
Whipped cream

Wash and drain strawberries. Line baked cool pastry shell with berries, reserving 1 cup for glaze. Simmer reserved berries and water in saucepan 3 to 4 minutes. Combine cornstarch and sugar and add to cooked fruit. Cook until syrup is thick and clear, stirring constantly. Add lemon juice and cool slightly. Pour over berries in pastry shell. Chill thoroughly. Decorate with border of sweetened whipped cream.

CRANBERRY PIE

2 cups cranberries
¾ cup raisins
⅓ cup water
2 tablespoons flour

¼ teaspoon salt
1 cup sugar
1 recipe *PLAIN PASTRY*

Cook cranberries and raisins in water about 10 minutes, stirring constantly to prevent scorching. Mix flour, salt, and sugar. Add to fruit. Stir and cook about 5 minutes. Cool. Place in pastry lined pan. Cover with lattice top. Bake in hot oven (425°F.) 25 minutes.

CRANBERRY RAISIN PIE

1 recipe *PLAIN PASTRY*
2 tablespoons flour
2 cups sugar
¼ teaspoon salt
⅔ cup water

3 cups cranberries
1 cup raisins
2 teaspoons grated lemon rind
2 tablespoons butter

Line pie pan with pastry. Blend together flour, sugar, salt, and water. Heat to boiling. Add cranberries, raisins, and lemon rind. Cook until cranberries begin to pop, about 10 minutes. Add butter. Cool before turning into pastry-lined pan. Cover with top crust or arrange strips of pastry to form a lattice. Bake in hot oven (450°F.) 10 minutes, reduce heat to moderate (350°F.), and bake 30 to 40 minutes longer.

EGGNOG PIE

4 egg yolks, slightly beaten
½ cup sugar
½ teaspoon salt
½ cup hot water
1 tablespoon plain gelatin
¼ cup cold water

4 egg whites, stiffly beaten
½ cup sugar
1 teaspoon grated nutmeg
2 teaspoons rum or rum flavoring
1 9-inch baked pie shell

Cook first 4 ingredients over boiling water, stirring constantly, until mixture coats spoon. Soften gelatin in cold water 5 minutes. Pour custard over gelatin mixture. Blend well and cool. When it starts to congeal, fold in stiffly beaten egg whites, blended with sugar, nutmeg, and rum. Pour mixture into baked pie shell. Chill until firm. If desired, spread with thin layer of whipped cream and sprinkle with nutmeg.

WINTER FRUIT PIE

1 cup dried apricots or peaches
1 cup raisins
¾ cup peach or apricot juice
2 tablespoons lemon juice
1 tablespoon grated lemon rind

2 tablespoons flour
½ cup sugar
1 cup chopped pecans
1 recipe *PLAIN PASTRY*
2 tablespoons butter

Simmer dried apricots or peaches and raisins in water until tender, about 15 minutes. Combine fruit juice, lemon juice, and rind and pour over drained fruit. Add remaining ingredients, stirring lightly until well blended. Turn into pastry-lined pan. Dot with butter. Cover with top crust. Bake in a hot oven (425°F.) 10 minutes. Lower heat to moderate (350°F.) and bake about 35 minutes longer.

GOOSEBERRY MERINGUE PIE

2 cups gooseberries
½ cup water
1 cup sugar
¼ cup flour

½ teaspoon salt
1 baked 9-inch pie shell
2 egg whites
4 tablespoons sugar

Cook gooseberries in water until tender. Mix 1 cup sugar, flour, and salt. Add to berries and cook until thick. Cool and pour into baked pie shell. Spread with meringue made by beating egg whites until they are peaky and then beating in 4 tablespoons sugar. Bake in moderate oven (350°F.) 12 to 15 minutes.

LEMON SPONGE PIE

½ recipe *PLAIN PASTRY*
¼ cup butter
1 cup sugar
3 tablespoons flour

3 eggs, separated
½ cup lemon juice
1 tablespoon grated lemon rind
1½ cups milk

Line 9-inch pie pan with pastry. Cream butter until soft and fluffy. Add sugar and flour gradually and mix thoroughly. Add egg yolks and beat well. Add lemon juice and rind. Slowly add milk, mixing well. Fold in egg whites beaten until stiff but not dry. Turn into pastry-lined pie pan. Bake in hot oven (425°F.) 12 minutes. Reduce heat to slow (325°F.) and bake 30 minutes longer.

MINCEMEAT PIE

Fill pastry lined pan with mincemeat. Cover with a top crust. Bake in hot oven (425°F.) about 25 minutes.

MINCEMEAT FOR PIE

4 pounds apples
2 pounds lean beef or
  veal, chopped fine
4 cups brown sugar, firmly packed
2½ pounds raisins
1¼ teaspoons nutmeg
½ teaspoon cloves
½ pound ground suet

1½ pounds currants
¼ pound ground citron
½ cup molasses
1½ teaspoons cinnamon
1 teaspoon mace
2 teaspoons salt
Cider, grape juice, or water

Peel, core and chop apples. Combine with remaining ingredients. Moisten with cider, grape juice, or water. Simmer gently until meats and fruits are tender and the flavors blended. Pack in sterilized jars and seal.

HASTY MINCEMEAT

1 cup chopped apple
½ cup chopped seedless raisins
½ cup currants
¼ cup suet, chopped fine
1 tablespoon molasses
1 cup sugar
1 tablespoon cider

1 teaspoon cinnamon
½ teaspoon ground cloves
½ nutmeg, grated
⅛ teaspoon mace
1 teaspoon salt
1 cup ground meat
2 tablespoons jelly

Combine and mix the ingredients except the meat and jelly. Moisten with a little stock. Simmer gently 1 hour. Add meat and jelly and simmer 15 minutes longer. Yield: about 3 cups.

MOCK MINCE PIE

1 cup chopped seedless raisins
4 tablespoons cracker crumbs
1½ cups sugar
1 cup molasses
⅓ cup lemon juice or
    ⅓ cup vinegar

½ cup butter
2 eggs, well beaten
1 teaspoon cinnamon
¼ teaspoon cloves
¼ teaspoon allspice

Combine all the ingredients. Mix thoroughly. Turn into pastry-lined pans. Cover with top crusts. Bake in hot oven (425°F.) about 25 minutes. Makes 2 9-inch pies.

DRIED PEACH OR APRICOT PIE

2 cups dried peaches or apricots
1½ cups water
1 recipe PLAIN PASTRY

¾ cup sugar
1 tablespoon butter

Soak dried fruit in water several hours or over night. Cook slowly without sugar until tender. Dredge prepared lower crust with flour. Fill with a layer of fruit; sprinkle generously with sugar. Alternate fruit and sugar until crust is filled. Dot with butter. Cover with top crust, moisten edges, and flute. Dredge top slightly with flour. Bake in moderate oven (375°F.) until well browned. Lattice strips may be substituted for top crust.

SOUR CREAM PEACH PIE

⅔ cup peach syrup
2 tablespoons tapioca
½ cup sugar
1½ cups thick sour cream

½ teaspoon vanilla
1 baked 9-inch pie shell
7 or 8 peach halves

Mix together peach syrup, tapioca, and sugar. Cook in double boiler until mixture thickens, 15 minutes. Cool. Mix sour cream with vanilla. Combine the two mixtures. Fill pie shell with half the mixture. Arrange peach halves. Pour over remaining cream mixture. Garnish with sliced peaches. Bake in moderate oven (350°F.) until set, about 40 minutes.

FRENCH PEACH PIE

½ recipe PLAIN PASTRY
3½ cups sliced fresh peaches
    (about 8 medium-size)
1 cup sugar
2 tablespoons all-purpose flour

1 egg, slightly beaten
1 cup heavy sweet cream
½ teaspoon vanilla
¼ cup shredded almonds

Line 9-inch pan with PLAIN PASTRY and fill with sliced peaches. Combine sugar and flour. Add egg and cream and mix well. Add vanilla. Pour mixture over peaches. Sprinkle with almonds. Bake in hot oven (450°F.) for 10 minutes. Reduce heat to moderate (350°F.) and bake until done, about 35 minutes longer. Serve cold.

HONEY PEACH PIE

Line an 8-inch pie pan with pastry. Fill with sliced fresh peaches. Sprinkle peaches with 1 tablespoon quick cooking tapioca. Drizzle over ⅓ cup honey. Lay twisted strips of pastry across the top. Fasten well at edges. Bake in a hot oven (425°F.) until delicately browned, about 35 to 40 minutes.

SPICED PEACH PIE

⅛ teaspoon allspice	1 recipe PLAIN PASTRY
⅛ teaspoon cloves	2 tablespoons cornstarch
¼ cup cider vinegar	¼ teaspoon cinnamon
1 large can peach halves	¼ cup brown sugar

Add spices to vinegar and dissolve. Combine with canned peaches and syrup. Simmer, covered, for 10 minutes. Line pie pan with pastry. Arrange peaches in pan, cut side up. If halves are very large, quarter. Mix cornstarch with ½ cup syrup in which peaches were cooked, and pour over. Cover top with strips of pastry in a lattice. Sprinkle with cinnamon and brown sugar. Dot with butter. Bake in hot oven (450°F.) until done, 15 to 30 minutes.

PECAN PIE

½ recipe PLAIN PASTRY	3 eggs, slightly beaten
⅓ cup butter	½ teaspoon salt
½ cup brown sugar	1 cup corn syrup
½ cup strong coffee	½ teaspoon vanilla
1 cup chopped pecans	

Line 9-inch pie pan with pastry. Cream butter and sugar. Add remaining ingredients and blend well. Turn into unbaked pie shell. Bake in hot oven (425°F.) 10 minutes, then reduce heat to moderate (350°F.), and bake 25 minutes longer, or until firm. Yield: 1-crust (9-inch) pie.

QUICK PINEAPPLE MERINGUE PIE

¼ teaspoon salt	⅔ cup drained crushed pineapple
Few drops almond extract	⅓ cup lemon juice
1 tablespoon grated lemon peel	6 tablespoons sugar
3 eggs, separated	¼ teaspoon salt
1 15-ounce can (1⅓ cups)	1 9-inch baked pie shell
sweetened condensed milk	

Add salt, almond extract, and grated lemon peel to egg yolks and beat slightly. Stir in condensed milk and add pineapple. Slowly add lemon juice, stirring until thick. Pour into baked pie shell. Prepare meringue by gradually beating 6 tablespoons sugar into stiffly beaten egg whites to which salt has been added. Spread unevenly over filling in pie shell. Bake in slow oven (325°F.) about 12 minutes, or until lightly browned and firm. Cool. Chill thoroughly in refrigerator before serving. If preferred, top pie with whipped cream instead of meringue. Decorate top with small mounds of drained crushed pineapple.

PUMPKIN PIE (Basic Recipe)

½ recipe PLAIN PASTRY	¼ teaspoon allspice
3 eggs	¾ teaspoon salt
¾ cup brown sugar	2 cups milk
1 teaspoon cinnamon	1½ cups cooked or canned pumpkin
1 teaspoon ginger	1 tablespoon molasses

Combine slightly beaten eggs, sugar, spices, and salt. Gradually add milk, then pumpkin and molasses. Blend lightly. Turn filling into unbaked pastry shell. Bake in hot oven (425°F.) 10 minutes, then in slow oven (325°F.) 20 to 25 minutes, or until knife inserted in center comes out clean. Serve with whipped cream.

Peanut pumpkin pie: Sprinkle ¼ cup finely chopped nuts over top of pumpkin mixture before baking.

Pumpkin coconut and nut pie: Stir ⅓ cup grated coconut and ¼ cup finely chopped nuts into pumpkin mixture before pouring into shell. Sprinkle top with additional coconut.

PUMPKIN PECAN PIE

½ recipe PLAIN PASTRY
⅓ cup dark brown sugar
½ teaspoon salt
1 teaspoon cinnamon
½ teaspoon ginger
¼ teaspoon nutmeg

¼ teaspoon cloves
⅓ cup corn syrup
2 eggs
1½ cups canned, or strained cooked pumpkin
¾ cup evaporated milk

PECAN CRUNCH TOPPING
¼ cup brown sugar
½ cup chopped pecans
1 to 2 teaspoons milk

Line pie pan with pastry. Combine ingredients and blend thoroughly. Pour into unbaked pie shell. Make a crunch topping by combining brown sugar and nuts, moistened with 1 to 2 teaspoons milk. Sprinkle over top of pie. Garnish with whole nutmeats if desired. Bake in hot oven (425°F.) 10 minutes. Reduce heat to moderate (350°F.) and bake 45 minutes longer, or until firm.

RAISIN PIE

3 cups raisins
¾ cup molasses
1 cup water
2 cups finely chopped apples
1 teaspoon cinnamon
¼ teaspoon nutmeg
¼ teaspoon ground cloves

½ teaspoon salt
2 tablespoons flour
½ teaspoon grated orange rind
¼ cup orange juice
1 recipe PLAIN PASTRY
2 tablespoons butter

Cook together raisins, molasses, and water until raisins are plump and tender. Remove from heat and add apples. Add sifted dry ingredients. Add grated rind and orange juice and mix well. Pour into pastry-lined pie shell. Dot with butter. Cover with lattice crust. Bake in moderate oven (350°F.) about 45 minutes.

Pocketbook raisin pies: Roll out dough ⅛ inch thick. Cut in 4-inch squares. On each place a mound of raisin mixture. Dot with butter. Fold pastry over top of mixture. Seal edges together. Prick tops to allow steam to escape. Bake in moderate oven (350°F.) 30 minutes.

SOUR CREAM RAISIN PIE

1½ cups sour cream
2 eggs, separated
1 cup sugar
½ teaspoon cinnamon
¼ teaspoon cloves
¼ teaspoon nutmeg

4 tablespoons flour
½ cup chopped raisins
1 teaspoon vanilla
1 9-inch baked pie shell
2 tablespoons sugar

Scald 1 cup of cream in double boiler. Mix egg yolks, 1 cup sugar, spices, flour, and remaining cream and add slowly to scalded cream. Cook 15 minutes. Add raisins and vanilla. Cool and pour into baked pie shell. Cover with meringue made from stiffly beaten egg whites and 2 tablespoons sugar. Brown in slow oven (325°F.) about 45 minutes.

RHUBARB PIE

2 eggs
3 cups rhubarb, diced
1 cup sugar
3 tablespoons flour

⅛ teaspoon salt
½ teaspoon cinnamon or nutmeg
½ recipe PLAIN PASTRY
1 tablespoon butter or margarine

Beat eggs with a fork, combine with remaining ingredients, except butter. Mix well. Put mixture into pastry lined pie plate. Dot butter over filling. Bake in hot oven (425°F.) 40 to 45 minutes.

STRAWBERRY CHEESE PIE

1 package (3 ounces) cream cheese
2 tablespoons milk
1 baked 9-inch pie shell
1 quart fresh strawberries
1½ cups water

Few drops red coloring
1 cup sugar
3 tablespoons cornstarch
½ pint whipping cream, whipped

Soften cheese with milk and spread over bottom of baked pie shell. Fill shell with the choicest berries, using about 1 pint. Cook remaining berries in water until soft. Put through a sieve or mash well and add red coloring. Combine sugar and cornstarch. Add to sieved fruit. Cook until thickened, stirring often. Pour over berries in pie shell. Chill and top with whipped cream.

SWEET POTATO PIE

2 cups mashed, hot sweet potatoes
3 tablespoons melted butter
1 teaspoon cinnamon
½ teaspoon nutmeg
½ teaspoon ginger
1¼ teaspoons salt

½ cup molasses
¼ cup orange juice
1 tablespoon grated orange rind
3 eggs, well beaten
1 cup milk
½ recipe PLAIN PASTRY

Mix together ingredients in order given. Turn into unbaked pie shell. Bake in hot oven (450°F.) 10 minutes, then reduce heat to moderate (350°F.). Bake until set, about 40 minutes. Cool. Serve with whipped cream flavored with a dash of cinnamon.

TROPICAL PIE

¾ cup sugar
⅓ cup flour
¼ teaspoon salt
1¼ cups milk
3 egg yolks
½ cup orange juice
2 tablespoons lemon juice

1 tablespoon grated orange rind
1 teaspoon grated lemon rind
1 baked 9-inch pie shell
3 egg whites
¼ cup sugar
Maraschino cherries
Shredded coconut

Combine sugar, flour, salt, and milk. Cook over hot water until thick, about 20 minutes. Beat egg yolks, and add a little of the hot milk mixture, stirring constantly. When thick, in about 5 minutes, remove from the heat and add orange juice, lemon juice, and rinds. Turn into baked shell. Cool and top with a meringue made by beating the egg whites with ¼ cup sugar until stiff enough to hold up in peaks. Decorate pie with maraschino cherries and coconut.

GELATIN CHIFFON PIE (Basic Recipe)

1 tablespoon plain gelatin
¼ cup cold water
4 eggs, separated
½ to 1 cup sugar, to taste
½ to 1½ cups liquid or crushed fruit
(according to strength of flavor)

¼ teaspoon salt
1 9-inch baked pie shell
1 cup heavy cream (optional)

Soak gelatin in cold water 5 minutes. Beat egg yolks well and add half the sugar and liquid or fruit. Cook in top of double boiler to custard consistency. Cool. Beat egg whites with remaining sugar and salt until stiff. Beat cream until stiff. Fold egg whites and cream into custard and pour mixture into baked pie shell. Chill before serving. If desired, the cream may be reserved to top the pie. Add 1 teaspoon vanilla and 2 tablespoons powdered sugar in whipping.

Apricot: Use 1 cup apricot pulp, ½ cup apricot juice, 2 tablespoons lemon juice, and ⅓ cup sugar. Eggs are not needed if whipped cream is used. If desired, reserve ¼ of cream for top, and sweeten with 2 tablespoons sugar.

Chocolate: Use 1 cup sugar. Add to egg yolk mixture 2 squares bitter chocolate or 6 tablespoons cocoa dissolved in ½ cup boiling water. Add 1 teaspoon vanilla. Omit cream from filling.

Lemon: Use 1 cup sugar, ½ cup lemon juice, and ½ teaspoon grated lemon rind.

Pineapple: Use ½ cup sugar, 1¼ cups canned crushed pineapple, and 1 tablespoon lemon juice.

Pumpkin: Use 1 cup sugar, 1¼ cups cooked pumpkin, ½ cup milk, and ½ teaspoon each cinnamon and nutmeg in custard mixture. Do not use whipped cream in mixture.

Strawberry: Use 1½ cups sliced strawberries soaked in ¾ cup sugar instead of cooked mixture. Add to it soaked gelatin, dissolved in ½ cup boiling water and 1 tablespoon lemon juice. If desired, use whipped cream.

BANANA CHIFFON PIE

1 tablespoon plain gelatin
¼ cup cold water
1 cup mashed banana
1 teaspoon grated lemon rind
4 tablespoons sugar
2 egg yolks

⅛ teaspoon salt
¼ cup lemon juice
2 egg whites
4 tablespoons sugar
1 baked pie shell

Soak gelatin in cold water. Place banana, lemon rind, 4 tablespoons sugar, beaten egg yolks, and salt in heavy saucepan. Put over low flame and stir constantly until thickened. Remove from heat. Blend in soaked gelatin and lemon juice. Cool. Beat egg whites until stiff, then beat in 4 tablespoons sugar. Fold into cold banana mixture. Fill baked pie shell. Cover with whipped cream. Sprinkle with chopped nuts or coconut, if desired. Yield: one 9-inch pie or 12 tarts.

BLACK BOTTOM CHIFFON PIE

1 tablespoon plain gelatin
2¼ cups milk
¾ cup sugar
1 tablespoon plus 1 teaspoon
   cornstarch
4 eggs, separated
1½ squares melted chocolate

1 9-inch baked pie shell
1 teaspoon vanilla
¼ teaspoon salt
¼ teaspoon cream of tartar
1 cup whipping cream, whipped
2 tablespoons confectioners' sugar
   Chocolate shavings (few sprinklings)

Soften gelatin in ¼ cup of the milk. Scald remaining 2 cups milk. Blend ½ cup of the sugar with cornstarch. Stir hot milk into this mixture and blend well. Add to beaten egg yolks and cook over hot water, while stirring, until smooth and thickened, about 15 minutes. Blend 1 cup of the mixture with melted chocolate. Cool and pour into baked pie shell. Add softened gelatin to remaining hot custard and stir to blend. Cool, but do not let stiffen. Add vanilla and blend. Beat egg whites with salt and cream of tartar until moist soft peaks form when beater is withdrawn. Add sugar gradually, beating until stiff and glossy. Fold custard into egg whites. Pour over chocolate layer in pie shell. Chill until set. Add confectioners' sugar to the whipped cream and blend. Cover top of pie with cream. Garnish with chocolate shavings.

COFFEE CHIFFON PIE

1 tablespoon plain gelatin
¼ cup cold black coffee
4 eggs, separated
⅓ teaspoon salt

¾ cup sugar
½ cup hot black coffee
1 tablespoon lemon juice
1 baked pie shell

Soften gelatin in cold coffee 5 minutes. Beat egg yolks in top of double boiler until thick and lemon-colored. Add salt, half of sugar, and hot coffee, stirring in carefully. Cook over boiling water until smooth and thick, stirring constantly. While still hot, add lemon juice and gelatin. Cool. When partly thickened fold in egg whites beaten with remaining sugar. Pour into baked pastry shell and chill. To serve top with whipped cream. Yield: 1-crust (9-inch) pie.

LEMON CHIFFON PIE (Basic Recipe)

1 tablespoon plain gelatin
⅓ cup cold water
4 egg yolks
1 cup sugar
¼ cup lemon juice

⅛ teaspoon salt
1 teaspoon grated lemon rind
4 egg whites
1 baked pie shell

Soften gelatin in water. Beat egg yolks. Add ½ cup sugar, lemon juice, and salt. Cook over simmering water, stirring constantly, until thickened. Add lemon rind and gelatin. Stir until gelatin is dissolved. Cool. Beat egg whites until foamy. Gradually add remaining sugar, beating constantly. Fold into lemon mixture. Pour into cooled, baked pastry shell. Chill until firm. Serve with whipped cream topping, or sprinkle with chopped nuts over top.

Lime chiffon pie: Substitute ⅓ cup lime juice for lemon juice and 1 teaspoon grated lime rind for lemon rind.

Orange chiffon pie: Substitute orange juice for lemon juice and 1 tablespoon grated orange rind for 1 teaspoon grated lemon rind.

Lemon or lime chiffon pudding: Mold mixtures in dessert dishes without pastry. Serve with whipped cream or chopped nuts or both.

NESSELRODE CHIFFON PIE

1½ tablespoons plain gelatin
¼ cup cold water
1 cup milk
1 cup thin cream
3 eggs, separated
¼ cup sugar or
   ¼ cup corn syrup

½ teaspoon salt
2 teaspoons vanilla
⅓ cup sugar
2 tablespoons chopped maraschino
   cherries
1 9-inch baked pie shell
2 tablespoons sweet chocolate, shaved

Soften gelatin in cold water 5 minutes. Scald milk and cream. Beat egg yolks slightly and add ¼ cup sugar or corn syrup and salt. Slowly add scalded milk and cream to egg mixture, stirring constantly. Cook over hot water, stirring constantly until mixture coats spoon, about 7 minutes. Remove from heat. Add gelatin and stir until dissolved. Cool and add vanilla. Chill in refrigerator until it thickens to consistency of soft custard. Beat egg whites until stiff but not dry and gradually fold in ⅓ cup sugar. Fold into gelatin mixture with maraschino cherries. Turn into baked pie shell. Sprinkle with chocolate. Chill until firm.

SHERRY CHIFFON PIE

1 tablespoon plain gelatin
¼ cup cold water
½ cup boiling water
½ cup sugar
½ cup sherry

1 cup evaporated milk, chilled well
2 tablespoons lemon juice
1 9-inch GRAHAM CRACKER
   CRUST

Soften gelatin in cold water. Add boiling water and stir until completely dissolved. Stir in sugar and sherry. Cool until it begins to thicken. Whip milk until stiff. Fold in lemon juice and then the thickened mixture. Pour into pie crust. Chill.

CREAM PIE (Basic Recipe)

1 cup sugar	3 eggs, separated
½ cup flour	2 tablespoons butter
½ teaspoon salt	1 teaspoon vanilla
2 cups scalded milk	1 9-inch baked pastry shell

Mix ⅔ cup sugar, flour, and salt. Gradually stir in milk and set over hot water. Stir until thoroughly thickened. Cover. Cook 10 minutes, stirring a few times to keep smooth. Blend a small amount of hot mixture into slightly beaten egg yolks. Combine with mixture in double boiler. Cook about 2 minutes, stirring constantly. Add butter and vanilla. Cool slightly. Pour into cooled, baked pastry shell. Cover with meringue made by gradually beating ⅓ cup sugar into stiffly beaten egg whites. Bake in moderate oven (350°F.) until lightly browned, about 15 minutes. Chill. Meringue may be omitted and pie served with whipped cream. If pie is made with only 2 eggs, reduce sugar to ¾ cup.

Almond cream pie: Substitute ⅓ teaspoon almond extract for vanilla. Add toasted slivered almonds to cooled filling just before pouring into pastry shell. Top with whipped cream. Garnish with toasted slivered almonds.

Banana cream pie: Alternate layers of sliced bananas and cream filling or add 1 cup mashed bananas to cooked filling.

Butterscotch cream pie: Substitute ½ cup firmly packed brown sugar for granulated sugar. Increase butter to 3 tablespoons.

Chocolate cream pie: Add 2 squares chocolate to milk. When melted, beat until smooth. Reduce flour to 6 tablespoons. Proceed as for *CREAM PIE.*

Chocolate sponge pie: Prepare *CHOCOLATE CREAM PIE FILLING.* Fold meringue into filling. Bake as for *CREAM PIE.* Chill. Serve with whipped cream.

Coconut cream pie: Stir ½ cup shredded coconut into cream filling. Cover with meringue and sprinkle with coconut before or after browning.

Fruit cream pie: Lightly stir 1 cup of fresh berries, ½ cup well drained crushed pineapple, 1 cup chopped dates, or 1 cup raisins into cooked filling just before turning into baked shell. Cover with meringue and brown.

CARROT CREAM PIE

½ recipe *PLAIN PASTRY*	⅛ teaspoon ginger
1½ cups raw ground carrots	¼ teaspoon salt
Salt	1 cup milk
¾ cup sugar	1½ tablespoons butter, melted
3 eggs, beaten	1 cup whipping cream
1 teaspoon cinnamon	½ teaspoon vanilla
1 teaspoon allspice	Shredded blanched almonds

Line 9-inch pie plate with piecrust rolled ⅛ inch thick. Cook ground carrots until tender with a little salt and as little water as possible. Cool. Force through potato ricer 4 times. Add and blend in sugar, eggs, cinnamon, allspice, ginger, salt, milk, and melted butter. Turn into lined pie shell, after brushing bottom with melted butter and sprinkling with a little flour. Bake 10 minutes in hot oven (450°F.). Reduce heat to moderate (350°F.) and bake 30 minutes longer. When cold, **top** with whipped cream flavored with vanilla and a little sugar, then dust with shredded blanched almonds or other nuts.

Variations: ½ cup chopped nuts may be substituted for ½ cup carrots.

With jam: Brush bottom of unbaked pastry with apricot jam, orange marmalade, prune jam, etc., before turning in filling.

With pineapple: Equal parts of drained pineapple and carrots may be used instead of carrots only.

RAISIN NUT CREAM PIE

½ cup seedless raisins	3 tablespoons lemon juice
1 cup water	¼ teaspoon cloves
½ cup sugar	½ teaspoon cinnamon
2 tablespoons butter	½ cup chopped nuts
2 tablespoons flour	1 9-inch baked pie shell
3 egg yolks	3 egg whites
1 tablespoon grated lemon rind	¼ cup sugar

Simmer raisins, water, and sugar over low heat until tender, about 10 minutes. Add butter. Mix a little of the raisin mixture into flour and return to low heat, stirring constantly until thickened, about 10 minutes. Remove from heat. Beat egg yolks slightly and add to raisins with lemon juice and rind, cloves, cinnamon, and nuts. Return to heat and simmer until well blended, about 3 minutes. Turn into baked pie shell. Cool and top with a meringue made by beating egg whites with sugar until stiff enough to hold in peaks. Brown in slow oven (325°F.) about 15 minutes.

CUSTARD PIE (Basic Recipe)

½ recipe *PLAIN PASTRY*	1 tablespoon flour
3 eggs	2⅔ cups scalded milk
½ cup sugar	1 teaspoon vanilla
½ teaspoon salt	¼ teaspoon nutmeg

Line a 9-inch pie pan with pastry. Flute edges. Chill. Beat eggs slightly. Combine sugar, salt, and flour; add to milk. Pour this mixture over eggs, stirring until well mixed and sugar is dissolved. Add vanilla. Pour into chilled pastry shell. Sprinkle with nutmeg. Bake in hot oven (425°F.) for 20 minutes, then 325°F. for final 20 minutes, or until a knife inserted in center comes out clean.

Caramel custard pie: Increase sugar to ⅔ cup. Caramelize ⅓ cup sugar and add to scalded milk.

Coconut custard pie: Add 1 cup moist shredded coconut to custard. Sprinkle some over top.

Custard nut pie: Increase sugar to ¾ cup. Add ¾ cup finely ground nuts to custard mixture.

LEMON MERINGUE PIE

1½ cups sugar	3 egg yolks
⅛ teaspoon salt	⅓ to ½ cup lemon juice
½ cup cornstarch	2 teaspoons butter
Grated rind 1 lemon	1 baked pie shell
2 cups boiling water	

Combine sugar, salt, cornstarch, and lemon rind in saucepan. Add boiling water, stir to blend well. Cook over very low heat for about 7 minutes, stirring constantly. When thickened, add egg yolks, which have been slightly beaten and combined with 2 tablespoons of hot filling. Blend in lemon juice and butter. Continue cooking for 5 minutes. Remove from heat, cool slightly, and pour into baked shell. Cover with meringue.

Lime meringue pie: Use lime in place of lemon and omit butter in recipe for LEMON MERINGUE PIE. Add a few drops of green coloring.

LEMON CREAM PIE

1 cup sugar	3 egg yolks
¼ teaspoon salt	2 tablespoons butter
6 tablespoons cornstarch	⅓ cup lemon juice
Grated rind of lemon	1 baked pie shell
2 cups scalded milk	

Proceed as for LEMON MERINGUE PIE. Add scalded milk instead of boiling water. Serve same day as baked.

PEACH CREAM CHEESE TARTS

3 cups sliced fresh peaches	1 package (3 ounces) cream cheese
¾ cup sugar	2 tablespoons cream
6 baked tart shells	¼ teaspoon nutmeg
(3½-inch diameter)	

Simmer peaches with sugar until done. Do not add liquid. Drain peaches and place in tarts. If desired, canned peaches may be substituted for fresh. Boil the syrup drained from the peaches until thick. Pour over the fruit in tart shells. Blend cream cheese, cream, and nutmeg. Place in pastry tube and decorate top of tarts. Bake in a moderate oven (350°F.) until topping browns slightly, about 5 minutes.

GLAZED CHERRY TARTS

1 quart pitted red cherries	1 tablespoon cornstarch
½ cup confectioners' sugar	8 baked tart shells
1 cup water	Whipped cream
½ to ¾ cup granulated sugar	

Mix 3 cups cleaned, pitted cherries with confectioners' sugar. Let stand at least 1 hour. Cook remaining cherries with water until tender. Rub through a sieve. Mix granulated sugar and cornstarch. Add to strained cherry juice and cook until clear. If desired, add red coloring. Arrange whole cherries in tart shells. Pour hot glaze over top. Cool and garnish with whipped cream. Yield: 8 tarts.

Variations: Stemmed, cleaned strawberries, gooseberries, or blueberries may be substituted for cherries. Omit coloring with latter two. Tart shells may be partially filled with CREAM PIE FILLING. When cool add berries and glaze.

BANBURY TARTS

1 cup chopped raisins	1 tablespoon bread or cracker crumbs
1 cup sugar	Juice and rind of 1 lemon
1 egg, slightly beaten	1 recipe PLAIN or PUFF PASTRY

Combine raisins, sugar, beaten egg, crumbs, and lemon. Roll *PLAIN* or *PUFF PASTRY* ⅛ inch thick and cut in pieces 3½x3 inches. Put 2 teaspoons of mixture on each piece. Moisten edges and fold over diagonally. Bake in hot oven (425°F.) 20 minutes. Yield: about 18 tarts.

CRANBERRY CREAM CHEESE TARTS

Pastry for 8 tart shells
2 cups cranberry sauce, strained
1 cup heavy cream
¼ cup confectioners' sugar

1 package cream cheese (3 ounces)
12 marshmallows, diced
½ cup walnut meats, chopped

Make 8 small tart shells by baking rounds of pastry on inverted muffin tins or aluminum star molds. Place thick cranberry sauce in a coarse sieve and let drain slightly. If desired, use canned, prepared cranberry sauce. Whip cream until stiff. Add sugar and smoothly mashed cream cheese. Fold in marshmallows. Gently mix together the walnuts, cranberries, and cream mixture. Fill the cooled tart shells. Yield: 8 small tarts.

GLAZED CHERRY TARTS
(*Using prepared pudding*)

2 cups pitted red cherries
¾ cup sugar
1 package cherry gelatin

2 cups hot water
1 package prepared vanilla pudding
8 baked tart shells

Combine cherries and sugar. Let stand 30 minutes. Dissolve gelatin in hot water. Chill until slightly thickened. Fold in cherries. Cook vanilla pudding according to directions on package and cool. Pour about ¼ cup pudding into each tart shell. Spread cherries in thickened gelatin on top of pudding. Chill until firm. Serve plain, or with whipped cream.

CRANBERRY STAR TARTS

Roll out plain pastry to ⅛ inch thickness. Cut with a floured star-shaped cutter. Place half of stars on ungreased baking sheet. Put about 1 tablespoon cranberry sauce on each star. Cut small holes in remaining stars. Place on top of other stars. Seal edge together. Bake in hot oven (450°F.) 12 to 15 minutes.

TURNOVERS (Basic Recipe)

Roll plain pastry ⅛ inch thick. Cut into 3 to 4 inch circles. Moisten the edge of half the circle. Place a teaspoon of preserves in center. Fold half the circle over the other, making edges meet. Press edges together firmly with tines of fork. Brush with beaten egg. Prick the tops. Chill. Bake in very hot oven (450°F.) 12 to 15 minutes. Sprinkle with sugar before serving. Full recipe for plain pastry makes about 15 to 18. For fillings, use any berry or fruit preserve, marmalade, or suggested fillings for cookies. Cooked dried fruits may be sweetened and also used.

FRIED APPLE PIES

1 cup applesauce
¼ cup brown sugar, firmly packed
¼ cup seedless raisins
½ teaspoon allspice

1½ teaspoons lemon juice
1 tablespoon melted butter
1 recipe *PLAIN PASTRY*

Combine applesauce, sugar, raisins, allspice, lemon juice, and butter. Roll pastry on a lightly floured board to ⅛ inch thickness. Cut into 3½-inch rounds. Place applesauce mixture in center of half the rounds. Moisten the edges with water. Cover with remaining rounds and press edges together with tines of fork. Fry in deep hot fat (375°F.) until brown. Drain on absorbent paper. Makes about 12.

HUNGARIAN JAM PASTRIES

2 cups sifted all-purpose flour	6 tablespoons butter
1¼ teaspoons baking powder	½ cup milk
2 teaspoons sugar	1 cup raspberry jam
½ teaspoon salt	Powdered sugar

Mix and sift flour, baking powder, sugar, and salt. Add butter and milk. Mix thoroughly. Roll dough out on a floured board until ¼ inch thick. Place in a square or oblong greased pan. Cover with raspberry jam. Make a lattice work of narrow strips of dough over the top. Bake in hot oven (400°F.) until evenly browned, about 30 minutes. Sprinkle with powdered sugar. Cut at once into small squares.

COTTAGE CHEESE PASTRIES

1 cup sifted all-purpose flour	½ cup creamed cottage cheese
¼ teaspoon salt	Preserves or jelly
½ cup butter	Confectioners' sugar

Mix and sift flour and salt. Cut in butter with a pastry blender until the mixture is the consistency of small peas. Mix in cottage cheese. Wrap in waxed paper. Chill in refrigerator until dough is firm enough to handle easily. Roll out to ⅛ inch thickness. Cut into 3½-inch squares. Place 1 teaspoon preserves or jelly in the center of each square. Moisten the edges. Gather up the corners and pinch them together. Bake in a moderately hot oven (400°F.) 20 minutes, or until lightly browned. Cool and sprinkle with confectioners' sugar. Yield: about 10 pastries.

EDINBURGH TEA SQUARES

1 cup butter	2½ cups rolled oats
1 cup sugar	½ teaspoon salt
1 cup sifted all-purpose flour	

Cream butter and sugar. Add flour, rolled oats, and salt. Stir until mixture holds together. Place half the mixture in an ungreased baking dish and smooth it. This should not be more than ¼ inch thick. Spread surface with cooled filling. Cover with remainder of pastry and bake. After removing from oven, mark into 2-inch squares. Cut when cold. These are delicious if chilled before serving.

Filling: Cook 1 cup pitted dates with 1 cup water over low flame until a paste is formed. When cool add 1 tablespoon lemon juice.

ORIENTAL BAKLAVA

PASTRY:
2 cups sifted all-purpose flour
1 teaspoon salt
½ cup shortening
1 egg and water to make ½ cup

FILLING:
2 cups slivered almonds
½ cup brown sugar, firmly packed
1 cup melted butter
1 teaspoon cinnamon
½ teaspoon nutmeg

Mix and sift flour and salt. Cut shortening into flour until it has consistency of corn meal. Blend egg and water with fork. Add to dry ingredients, mixing only until well moistened. Turn onto waxed paper and knead 8 minutes. Form into ball and let rest 30 minutes. Divide pastry into 4 portions. Roll out 1 portion at a time until almost paper-thin on lightly floured pastry cloth into a rectangle 8 by 16 inches. Cut rectangle in half to form two 8-inch squares. Place 1 square in bottom of 8-inch square pan. Spread 2 tablespoons filling over this. Add a second layer of pastry and filling. Continue to alternate layers until all are used, ending with a top layer of pastry. Cut into 8 or 16 servings. Pour 3 tablespoons syrup over all. Bake in moderate oven (375°F.) 35 to 40 minutes. Serve remaining cooled sauce over hot Baklava. Serves 8 to 16.

To make filling: Mix all ingredients.

To make syrup: Combine 1 cup water, 1 cup sugar, grated rind of 1 lemon, and grated rind of 1 orange in a saucepan. Boil 5 minutes.

BASIC STRUDEL PASTRY (Stretched Dough)

2 cups sifted all-purpose flour
⅛ teaspoon salt
1 egg, beaten

About ½ cup warm water or milk
1 tablespoon vegetable oil or
    melted shortening

Mix and sift flour and salt into a deep bowl. Combine the egg and lukewarm water or milk and add to flour. Combine ingredients quickly with pastry blender or two knives. Knead dough on board until it is elastic and no longer sticks to board. Place dough on floured board and cover with warm bowl for 30 minutes. Then work the oil into the dough. Cover a table with a floured cloth. Place dough in the center. Roll it out as thin as possible. To stretch, place both hands, palms down, under the pastry and work from the center toward the outer edges, all around the table until the dough is stretched evenly and paper thin, without breaking the dough. The thicker dough at edges may be cut away. Spread any of the juicy fillings such as apple, cheese, or prune in rows about 2 inches apart. Sprinkle generously with sugar and desired spices. Add a sprinkling of oil or melted shortening over all. Roll the dough over mixture on one side, then hold cloth high and the strudel will roll itself over and over as each row of filling is reached. Trim off the ends. Cut to fit a large, greased shallow baking pan. Roll strudel into it. Bake in moderate oven (375°F.) until nicely brown and crisp, 40 to 50 minutes, unless other time is indicated with filling. With most fillings, it is desirable to baste the strudel occasionally with melted shortening or oil, unless otherwise indicated in filling recipes.

ROLLED STRUDEL DOUGH (Basic Recipe)

2 cups sifted all-purpose flour
⅛ teaspoon salt
1 tablespoon sugar
1 egg

3 tablespoons vegetable oil or
    melted shortening
About 1 cup ice cold water

Mix and sift flour, salt, and sugar into a deep bowl. Make a well in center. Add egg and oil or melted shortening. Stir slowly to combine. Add cold water a little at a time until dough is firm enough to handle. Knead several minutes on a lightly floured board. With a floured rolling pin, roll out until very thin (about ⅛ inch), rolling from edges to center. Work around the dough, not from one side. Use any of the strudel fillings. Fill, roll up, and bake in moderate oven (375°F.) until brown and crisp, 45 to 50 minutes. This oven heat and baking time apply to all following strudel recipes, unless otherwise specified.

APPLE STRUDEL

3 cups thinly sliced tart apples
½ cup seedless raisins
½ cup currants
½ cup nuts, chopped

1 cup sugar
1 teaspoon cinnamon
¼ cup vegetable oil
STRUDEL DOUGH

Combine sliced apples, raisins, currants, nuts, sugar, and cinnamon. Spread over strudel dough. Sprinkle with vegetable oil. Roll and bake.

AUSTRIAN APPLE STRUDEL

1 cup breadcrumbs
½ cup melted butter
STRUDEL DOUGH
3 cups thinly sliced tart apples

½ cup seedless raisins
½ cup currants
1 cup sugar

Brown the breadcrumbs in melted butter. Brush strudel dough with melted butter. Sprinkle with fried breadcrumbs, then with sliced apples, raisins, currants, and sugar. Roll up and brush with melted butter. Bake.

APRICOT PRUNE STRUDEL

1½ cups dried apricots, cut fine
1½ cups dried prunes, cut fine
2 tablespoons lemon juice
2 tablespoons orange juice
Grated rind of 1 lemon

¼ cup honey
½ cup sugar
STRUDEL DOUGH
¼ cup fine breadcrumbs

Combine dried fruits with juices and grated rind. Heat honey slightly and add with sugar. Sprinkle strudel dough with crumbs. Spread mixture. Roll up and bake.

CABBAGE STRUDEL

1 medium head of cabbage
½ cup melted butter
½ cup seedless raisins
½ cup currants

2 cups sugar
½ cup chopped almonds, blanched
1 teaspoon cinnamon
STRUDEL DOUGH

Chop cabbage and combine with butter. Cook gently until cabbage is tender, stirring constantly, about 20 minutes. Cool. Add raisins, currants, sugar, almonds, and cinnamon and mix well. Spread and roll up. Baste with melted butter while baking.

CHEESE STRUDEL

1 tablespoon butter
6 eggs, separated
1 pound dry cottage cheese
1 cup sour cream
  STRUDEL DOUGH

½ cup sugar
Melted butter
½ cup breadcrumbs
½ teaspoon cinnamon
½ cup raisins

Cream together 1 tablespoon butter with egg yolks. Press cottage cheese through a ricer and mix the two together. Add sour cream and ¼ cup sugar. Mix well and fold in stiffly beaten egg whites. Sprinkle stretched strudel dough with melted butter, the remaining sugar, breadcrumbs, cinnamon, and raisins. Spread cheese mixture and roll up. Brush with melted butter and bake 1 hour.

CHERRY STRUDEL

2 quarts cherries, stemmed and
   pitted
½ cup breadcrumbs
   Grated rind of ½ lemon
1 cup sugar

½ teaspoon cinnamon
¾ cup chopped nuts
¼ cup vegetable oil
  STRUDEL DOUGH

Combine cherries, breadcrumbs, grated lemon rind, sugar, cinnamon, and nuts. Sprinkle vegetable oil over stretched dough. Spread cherry mixture and roll up. Baste with hot fat while baking.

CHOCOLATE STRUDEL

6 eggs, separated
6 tablespoons sugar
4 ounces sweet chocolate, grated
1 cup nuts, finely ground
1 teaspoon vanilla

STRUDEL DOUGH
Melted butter
½ cup breadcrumbs
½ cup raisins

Beat egg yolks and sugar until light. Add grated chocolate, nuts, and vanilla. Mix well. Fold in stiffly beaten egg whites. Sprinkle strudel dough with melted butter, breadcrumbs, and raisins. Spread chocolate mixture and roll up. Brush with melted butter. Bake 1 hour.

DRIED FRUIT STRUDEL

¾ pound of any dried fruit
   (apricot, pear, or peach)
1 orange, ground, including peel
1 lemon, ground, including peel
1½ cups sugar
1 cup walnuts, chopped

½ teaspoon cinnamon
1 cup white raisins
1 cup fine cake crumbs
1 tablespoon shortening
1 cup shredded coconut
  STRUDEL DOUGH

Wash dried fruit. Cover with boiling water and soak several hours or over night. Drain. Chop fine and add ½ the orange and lemon and ¾ cup of sugar. Mix until thoroughly blended. In another bowl combine remaining ground orange and lemon, walnuts, remaining sugar, cinnamon, raisins, cake crumbs, shortening, and coconut. Mix well and spread over strudel dough. Drip a little melted shortening over all. Spread dried fruit mixture and roll up. Slice in 1-inch pieces but do not cut completely through. Sprinkle lightly with cinnamon and sugar mixture. Bake in hot oven (400°F.) 1 hour. Remove from oven and complete slicing while still warm.

KASHA STRUDEL

¼ cup minced onion
4 tablespoons melted shortening
Salt and pepper to taste

STRUDEL DOUGH
2 cups cooked kasha
(buckwheat groats)

Fry onion in hot fat until lightly browned. Combine all ingredients and roll up. Baste with hot fat while baking.

LEMON STRUDEL

6 eggs, separated
1 cup sugar
Juice of 3 lemons
3 teaspoons cornstarch
⅓ cup cold water

⅛ teaspoon salt
Grated rind of 1 lemon
½ teaspoon baking powder
STRUDEL DOUGH
Melted butter

Beat egg yolks well with sugar and lemon juice. Dissolve cornstarch in cold water. Stir into yolk mixture and add salt. Cook over boiling water until thick. Add grated lemon rind. Cool. Beat egg whites with baking powder until stiff. Fold into cooled yolk mixture and blend well. Sprinkle strudel dough with melted butter. Spread filling and roll up. Bake in hot oven (400°F.) until golden brown, 1 hour. Remove from pan and cool before slicing.

LUNG STRUDEL

STRUDEL DOUGH
3 cups chopped, cooked lung
¼ cup chopped grieben (cracklings)

2 hard-cooked eggs, chopped
1 tablespoon grated onion
Salt and pepper to taste

Combine all ingredients. Spread and roll up. Baste with hot fat while baking.

NOTE: Be sure to use water (not milk) in the strudel dough when used with this or other meat fillings.

MANDEL (Almond) STRUDEL

4 egg yolks
½ cup sugar
Grated rind of 1 lemon

1 cup almonds, blanched and ground
¼ cup vegetable oil
STRUDEL DOUGH

Beat egg yolks and sugar together until light. Add grated lemon rind and almonds. Sprinkle vegetable oil over stretched dough. Spread with almond mixture. Roll up and bake. Baste with hot fat while baking.

NUT AND JELLY STRUDEL

STRUDEL DOUGH
1 cup ground nutmeats
1 cup seedless raisins
1 cup preserves

1 teaspoon cinnamon
1 tablespoon sugar
Melted shortening

Combine all ingredients except shortening. Sprinkle strudel dough with melted shortening. Spread mixture and roll up. Brush with hot fat and bake.

PINEAPPLE STRUDEL

Melted butter
½ cup breadcrumbs
STRUDEL DOUGH

2½ cups canned crushed pineapple
1 cup cherry preserve
Cinnamon and sugar

Sprinkle butter and breadcrumbs over strudel dough. Mix well-drained pineapple and cherry preserve. Spread and roll up. Brush with melted butter. Sprinkle with cinnamon and sugar. Bake.

PLUM STRUDEL

STRUDEL DOUGH
Melted butter
1 cup sugar and cinnamon

½ cup breadcrumbs
2 pounds freestone plums, halved
    and pitted

Brush dough with melted butter. Spread with sugar, cinnamon, breadcrumbs, and plum halves. Roll up and brush with melted butter. Bake.

POPPY SEED STRUDEL

½ pound finely ground poppy seed
1½ cups sugar
1 cup seedless raisins
    Grated rind of 1 lemon

STRUDEL DOUGH
Melted butter
½ cup cream
1 cup thinly grated tart apple

Grind poppy seed in food chopper with finest attachment. Mix together poppy seed, 1 cup sugar, raisins, and lemon rind. Brush STRUDEL DOUGH with melted butter. Sprinkle with remaining ½ cup sugar. Spread poppy seed mixture. Sprinkle with cream and grated apple. Sprinkle melted butter over top and roll up. Brush with melted butter and sprinkle with sugar. Bake.

RAHM (Sour Milk) STRUDEL

1 quart thick sour milk
STRUDEL DOUGH
1 cup fine breadcrumbs
2 cups sugar

1 cup chopped nuts
1 teaspoon cinnamon
1 cup raisins

Drip sour milk lightly over STRUDEL DOUGH. Sprinkle breadcrumbs over milk, then sugar, chopped nuts, raisins, and cinnamon. Roll up and place in a greased pan. Brush with melted butter. Bake.

RICE STRUDEL

½ cup rice
2 cups milk
1 tablespoon butter
1 cup sugar
6 eggs, separated
1 teaspoon vanilla

1 teaspoon cinnamon
½ cup seedless raisins
STRUDEL DOUGH
Melted butter
1 tablespoon breadcrumbs

Boil rice in milk until tender. Cool. Cream butter with sugar until light. Add egg yolks, 1 at a time, creaming well after each addition. Add vanilla, cinnamon, cooled rice, and raisins. Fold in stiffly beaten egg whites. Brush strudel dough with melted butter. Sprinkle with breadcrumbs. Spread rice mixture and roll up. Brush top with melted butter. Bake.

SOUR CREAM STRUDEL

1 tablespoon butter
5 eggs, separated
1 cup sour cream
  Melted butter

STRUDEL DOUGH
½ cup breadcrumbs
½ cup nuts, ground
1 cup raisins

Cream butter and add egg yolks, 1 at a time and mix well. Add sour cream and fold in stiffly beaten egg whites. Sprinkle strudel dough with melted butter, breadcrumbs, nuts, and raisins. Spread filling and roll up. Bake in hot oven (400°F.) until brown, 1 hour. Turn off heat and leave in oven for 5 minutes.

FRENCH FRUIT TART

About 1 ⅔ cups vanilla wafer
  crumbs, finely rolled
¼ cup butter or margarine, melted
1 tablespoon instant coffee
5 egg yolks
¾ cup sugar
3 tablespoons flour

2 cups milk
1 teaspoon vanilla
  Fresh peaches, pared and sliced
  Fresh strawberries, hulled and
  washed
  Fresh blueberries
½ cup red currant jelly

Combine vanilla wafer crumbs and melted butter into which the instant coffee has been stirred. Pour crumb mixture into a 9-inch pie plate pressing crumbs firmly against bottom and sides using an 8-inch pie plate. Bake in moderate oven (375°F.) 8 minutes. Cool. Beat egg yolks and sugar until thick and lemon-colored. Slowly beat in flour until well blended. Scald milk with vanilla and stir into egg mixture. Return custard to saucepan and cook over medium heat, stirring constantly, until custard thickens and boils. Boil for 1 minute. Cool in a bowl, covering the surface with wax paper to prevent a skin forming. Spoon into pie shell. Top custard with fresh fruit in any pattern you wish. Melt red currant jelly in a saucepan and brush over the fruit to glaze. Refrigerate until ready to serve. Makes 8 servings.

poultry

Feast day or any day, chicken, turkey, duck, and goose are favorites. Choose from many cherished dishes—golden roast chicken or turkey, chicken fried to a crispy turn, stewed chicken with dumplings, etc. How to cook any kind of poultry depends on the bird's age, weight, quality, and fatness. In general, plump young birds are best for broiling, frying, or roasting. Older birds or lean young ones are best braised, stewed, or steamed. How much poultry to buy per serving is found in the section on *SERVINGS AND POUNDS*.

PREPARING THE BIRD

Ready-to-cook birds should need no preparation before cooking. But you may have to remove a few pinfeathers. Wash and dry bird.

Dressed birds have been bled and picked but the head and feet and internal organs have not been removed. To prepare, start by removing pinfeathers. Singe off hairs, cut off head and feet, and cut out the oil sac on top of tail. Then scrub the bird. **Cut** circle around vent below tail, leaving it free to be removed with internal organs. Make a crosswise slit, large enough for drawing, between this circle and rear end of breastbone. Leave a band of skin between the two cuts. Draw out internal organs. Save heart, liver, and gizzard. Slit skin lengthwise at back of neck, leaving skin on bird. Slip skin down and remove crop and windpipe. Cut neck off short and save.

To clean giblets, cut blood vessels from heart and carefully cut away green gall sac from liver. Be careful not to break the gall sac. Gall is bitter and will spoil the flavor of any meat it touches. Cut through one side of gizzard to inner lining, remove lining and discard.

POULTRY COOKING RULES

Whether poultry is freshly drawn or frozen, two good rules are: (1) Cook at low to moderate temperatures; and (2) don't overcook. In roasting, birds should not be covered. The meat is more juicy and there is less shrinkage. Keep frozen birds frozen until time to thaw for cooking. To cook without thawing first, allow one and a half times as long as usual. If a chicken is to be used for soup, remove excess fat and render it. The fat and the cracklings may be used in other recipes.

HOW TO RENDER CHICKEN OR GOOSE FAT

If a chicken is to be used for soup, or if goose has excess fat, it is advisable to remove the excess fat and render it. The rendered fat and the cracklings (grieben) are used in a number of recipes given in this and other sections of the book. Cut the excess fat from the bird and, if cracklings are desired, also remove the fatty parts of skin. Cut into small (1-inch-square) pieces. Place in a heavy skillet. Add cold water to cover. Cover and bring to a boil. Cook about 20 minutes. Uncover and cook over low heat until all water has evaporated and only the melted fat and cracklings remain. Add 1 diced onion and continue cooking until the skin is crisp and well browned and the onion brown but not burned. Strain off the fat. Chill and use in cooking. Serve the cracklings with rye bread and crackers.

ROASTING GUIDE

Bird	Dressed weight	Ready-to-cook weight	Crumbs for stuffing	Oven temperature	Time
	Pounds	Pounds	Quarts	°F.	Hours
Chicken	3 to 4	2¼ to 3	¾ to 1	350	1½ to 2
	4 to 6	3 to 4½	1 to 2	325	2 to 3
Duck	5 to 7	4 to 5½	1 to 2	325	2 to 3
Goose	10 to 12	8 to 10	2½ to 3	325	3½ to 4½
Turkey	6 to 10	5 to 8½	1½ to 2	325	2 to 3
	10½ to 14	9 to 12	2 to 3	325	3 to 3½
	14½ to 18	12½ to 15½	3 to 4	325	3½ to 4½
	18½ to 24	16 to 21	4 to 5½	300	4½ to 6
	24½ to 30	21½ to 26	5½ to 7	300	6 to 7½

HOW TO COOK GIBLETS

Clean gizzard, heart, and liver. Cover gizzard and heart (neck may be included) with boiling water. Add ½ teaspoon salt, cover and simmer until tender, 1 to 2 hours. Add liver ½ hour before cooking is completed. Drain and reserve stock for gravy, etc. Chop giblets and use in stuffing, gravy, etc.

ROAST CHICKEN

Select a 3½ to 6 pound chicken, allowing ½ to ¾ pound per person. Wash carefully inside and out. Dry. Season cavity, stuff, and truss. Grease skin thoroughly with melted fat. Lay bird on flat or in V-shaped rack breast down. Cover with fat-moistened cheesecloth. Roast at constant oven temperature (325° to 350°F.). Turn breast up when ¾ done. Baste with melted fat (preferably rendered chicken fat) if bird appears dry. It is not necessary to sear bird or add water or cover pan. Allow about 25 minutes cooking time per pound. Weigh the stuffed bird so the total cooking time may be approximated. Cloth may be removed the last 15 to 20 minutes of the roasting time.

COUNTRY STYLE ROAST CHICKEN

Place chicken in an uncovered pan in hot oven (450°F.) and sear for 20 minutes, or until chicken is brown on all sides. Reduce heat to slow (275° to 300°F.) oven. Pour ¼ cup boiling water into pan. Cover pan and roast until bird is tender, allowing 25 to 30 minutes per pound. Do not baste. For a crisp crust, uncover during last 30 minutes. Prepare gravy from drippings.

JELLY GLAZED ROAST CHICKEN

Whip ½ cup currant jelly. Spread over ROAST CHICKEN last 30 minutes of cooking. Complete roasting uncovered. Baste frequently with jelly and drippings.

ROAST TURKEY

Allow ¾ pound per person. Wash carefully inside and out. Dry. Stuff and truss. Grease skin thoroughly with melted fat. Lay bird on flat or V shaped rack breast down. Cover with fat-moistened cheesecloth. Roast at constant oven temperature in preheated oven at 300°F. Turn breast up when ¾ done. Baste with melted fat (preferably rendered chicken fat) and pan drippings if bird appears dry. It is unnecessary to sear bird or add water or cover pan. Cut trussing cord 1 hour before total cooking time is completed. To crisp skin, remove cloth ½ hour before total cooking time is completed. Allow following times for various size turkey: for 8 to 10 pound allow 20 to 25 minutes per pound; for 10 to 16 pound allow 18 to 20 minutes per pound; for 16 to 25 pound allow 15 to 18 minutes per pound.

TURKEY HASH

To 2 cups chopped, cooked turkey (or chicken) add 1 cup diced, cooked potatoes and ½ cup gravy or stock. Brown slowly in fat.

ROAST HALF TURKEY

Wash, clean, and dry 10 pound half turkey. Cut off neck bone at base and fold neck skin back. Rub cavity with salt. Skewer skin to breast meat on keel bone edge. Tie leg just above knuckle joint to tail. Wing should be tied or skewered to breast. Place cut side down on flat rack in shallow pan. Brush with melted fat. Cover with piece of cheesecloth dipped in melted fat. Roast uncovered in slow oven (325°F.) allowing 20 to 25 minutes per pound. Add 1 teaspoon sage, 2 teaspoons thyme, 1 medium onion, chopped fine, 2 tablespoons chopped parsley, ½ cup chopped celery, 3 teaspoons salt, and 2 cups chopped Brazil nuts to 8 cups corn or white breadcrumbs. Use day old white bread and remove the crusts. Pour 2 tablespoons melted fat and ¼ cup boiling water over breadcrumbs and toss lightly with a fork. Mound stuffing on a well-greased double thickness of wax paper to approximate shape of cavity. When turkey is half done, 1½ to 2 hours, remove from pan and place paper with stuffing on rack. Fit half turkey over stuffing and roast until done. Serve stuffing in vegetable dish. Serves 12.

ROAST DUCK

Singe and clean as other poultry. Stuff, truss, and sprinkle with salt and pepper. Place duck on rack in roasting pan. Roast uncovered, basting occasionally with pan drippings. Turn breast side down if breast becomes too brown. Roast young ducks 12 to 15 minutes per pound at 450°F. in preheated oven. Roast older ducks 20 to 25 minutes per pound at 325°F. for entire period.

ROAST GOOSE

Stuff and truss. Rub goose with melted fat, salt, pepper, and flour. Place on rack in uncovered roasting pan without water. Prick skin several times. Roast in slow oven (325°F.) 20 to 25 minutes per pound.

ROAST SQUAB

Clean as other fowl. Rub insides with salt and pepper. Stuff. Roast uncovered in slow oven (325°F.) until done, about 45 minutes.

ROAST CAPON

Prepare as for roast chicken, allowing 20 to 25 minutes per pound.

ROAST GUINEA

Clean as other fowl. Stuff and truss. Place in uncovered roaster. Sear in hot oven (500°F.) 15 minutes. Reduce heat to 300°F. Cover. Roast until tender. Baste frequently. Allow 20 to 25 minutes per pound.

BOHEMIAN ROAST GOOSE POTATO STUFFING

5 large potatoes	1 egg
¼ cup grated onion	1 tablespoon melted poultry fat
1 tablespoon minced parsley	1 roasting goose
1 teaspoon caraway seed	Salt and pepper to taste

Wash potatoes. Boil with skins on. When done, peel, mash and add onion, parsley, caraway seed, egg, and fat. Mix well and season to taste. Wash and dry goose. Remove excess fat. Stuff and truss. Melt down excess fat in pan on top of stove. Rub melted fat into goose. Sprinkle with flour, salt, and pepper. Place on rack in roasting pan. Do not add water. Prick skin several times to let fat run out. Roast, uncovered, in slow oven (325°F.) 20 to 25 minutes per pound. Baste every 15 minutes.

Gravy: Remove all but 2 tablespoons fat from roasting pan. Sift into pan 3 tablespoons flour. Blend smoothly with fat. Add 3 cups water. Place pan over low flame and stir constantly until gravy thickens, blending in brown juice from bottom of pan. Season with salt and pepper.

GOOSE WITH BRAISED CABBAGE (Russian)

1 goose	1 medium red cabbage, shredded
Salt and pepper	1 tablespoon vinegar
Caraway seed	¼ cup cooking fat

Prepare goose for roasting. Rub outside well with pepper and caraway seed. Combine cabbage, vinegar, salt and pepper; mix well and braise in hot fat for 5 minutes. Use this to stuff goose. Roast goose in slow oven (325°F.) uncovered, 30 minutes per pound. Serve hot.

GOOSE GIBLETS WITH RICE (Ganseklein)

Goose giblets	¼ cup chopped onion
1 large onion, sliced	1 cup rice, washed
Salt, pepper, and paprika	Minced parsley
2 tablespoons cooking fat	

Put the giblets (wings, neck, gizzard, back, etc.) in a large pot. Add water to cover, sliced onion, and salt and pepper to taste. Simmer until tender, about 2 hours. There should be about 3 cups of stock. When giblets are almost done, melt fat in a pan. Add chopped onion and fry until transparent. To this, add washed, drained rice. Stir constantly until rice is golden brown. Over this pour the stock from giblets. Boil until rice is tender, about 30 minutes. Serve with giblets. Garnish with minced parsley and paprika. Serves 4 to 6.

CANTONESE DUCK

5 to 6 pound duckling,
   dressed weight
¼ cup sherry wine

¼ cup honey
Salt and pepper

With sharp pointed knife cut through duck skin along center of breast from neck to vent. Loosen skin by pulling away from flesh and at the same time running knife underneath. Cut skin where necessary, but keep flesh intact. Discard skin. Cut skinned duck in serving size pieces and place in bowl. Combine remaining ingredients and pour over duck meat. Cover and let marinate in cool place for 3 hours, turning occasionally. Place duck and marinade in large covered frying pan and cook over low heat until tender, about 45 minutes to 1 hour. Serve immediately or, if crisp brown crust is desired, place pieces of duck in uncovered baking dish and heat in moderate oven (350°F.) for at least 15 minutes. Serve hot or cold. Serves 4.

DUCK IN WINE SAUCE

5 to 6 pound duckling
1 teaspoon salt
2 tablespoons duck fat
½ clove garlic, minced
2 tablespoons flour
2 cups red wine

8 mushrooms, sliced
2 sprigs parsley
1 small bay leaf
⅓ teaspoon thyme
8 small white onions
8 small carrots

Remove skin and fat from duck. Cut duck into serving size pieces. Cover and cook skin and fat with giblets in 2 cups water and ½ teaspoon salt. Drain off liquid. Allow fat to rise to top, then pour it off. Melt 2 tablespoons duck fat in large frying pan. Brown pieces of duck in fat over moderate heat. Remove duck to 9-inch casserole. Add garlic to fat and cook 1 minute. Stir in flour. Add wine, mushrooms, parsley, bay leaf, thyme and salt. Bring to boil, stirring constantly, until sauce thickens. Place peeled onions, trimmed carrots and duck giblets in casserole with duck. Top with sauce. Cover tightly. Bake in moderate oven (350°F.) until duck and vegetables are tender, about 1¼ hours. Serves 4.

PINEAPPLE DUCK

5 to 6 pound duckling
4 cups water
2 teaspoons salt
3 tablespoons duck fat
½ clove garlic
1 cup duck broth
1 cup drained, diced canned
   pineapple

1 medium-sized green pepper
2 tablespoons cornstarch
¼ cup water
1 teaspoon salt
1 tablespoon lemon juice or
   vinegar
1 teaspoon kitchen bouquet or
   soy sauce

Have butcher cut duck in quarters. Place duck in 6 quart saucepan or Dutch oven with neck, giblets, water, and salt. Cook, covered, over moderate heat until tender, about 45 minutes to 1 hour. Or cook in pressure saucepan according to directions. Remove duck. Drain off liquid. Allow fat to rise to top, then pour it off. Removing skin, cut duck meat in pieces about 2 inches long, ½ inch square. Place 3 tablespoons duck fat in large frying pan or Dutch oven. Add garlic. Cook over low heat 2 minutes, then remove garlic. Add duck meat and cook over moderate heat 5 minutes, tossing lightly. Add broth, pineapple, and green pepper cut in 1-inch squares. Blend together and stir in cornstarch, water, salt, lemon juice, and kitchen bouquet. Add to broth. Cook, stirring lightly, until juice thickens. Serve with hot cooked rice. Serves 4.

POT ROAST OF DUCKLING WITH HERBS

5 to 6 pound duckling
2 tablespoons cooking fat
  Salt and pepper, to taste
1 medium onion, sliced
2 tablespoons fat
½ cup sherry

⅓ cup currant jelly
½ cup hot water
1 bay leaf
3 tablespoons coarsely chopped parsley

Clean duckling thoroughly. Singe carefully and remove pin feathers. Wash and dry. Brown in fat in frying pan. Place in deep casserole or baking pan with tight cover. Sprinkle with salt and pepper. Lightly brown onion slices in fat. Add sherry, jelly, water, and seasoning. Mix thoroughly and pour over duckling. Cover tightly and simmer 2½ hours or until tender, turning several times during cooking process. Serve on platter. Pour strained liquid from pan over duckling and garnish platter with stewed dried apricots and pitted prunes.

FRIED CHICKEN

Select young chicken. Disjoint and cut up for cooking. Mix ¼ teaspoon pepper, 1½ teaspoons salt, and 1½ tablespoons paprika with 1 cup flour for every 3 pounds of meat. Rub flour into pieces. Save left over flour for gravy. Melt fat in a heavy skillet to depth of ½ to ¾ inches. Brown meaty pieces first in the hot fat, slipping less meaty pieces in between as chicken browns. Avoid crowding, use two skillets if necessary. As soon as chicken begins to brown, about 10 minutes, reduce heat, and cook slowly until tender, 30 to 60 minutes, depending upon size of pieces. Cover tightly as soon as it is a light, uniform tan. Add 1 to 2 tablespoons water before covering if pan cannot be covered tightly or if bird is heavier than 3 pounds. Uncover last 15 minutes to brown. Turn several times to brown evenly.

To test: Cut thickest part of any piece to the bone. If done the meat should cut easily and no pink color be visible.

To fry giblets: Simmer gizzard until tender. Rub seasoned flour into giblets. Fry until browned, about 10 minutes.

SOUTHERN FRIED CHICKEN

Coat pieces of chicken heavily with seasoned flour to which has been added 1 teaspoon baking powder for each cup of flour. Brown on both sides in very hot fat to a depth of about 1½ inches. Reduce heat and cook slowly about 1 hour, turning pieces to brown evenly on all sides.

HONG-KONG FRIED CHICKEN

3 tablespoons soy sauce
5 tablespoons peanut oil
½ teaspoon salt
⅛ teaspoon black pepper
1 teaspoon ginger root, finely minced
1 young broiler, halved

2 cups chicken stock
1 cup hot water
2 tablespoons flour
½ cup fresh mushrooms
½ small can pimientos, minced
1 onion, minced

Mix together soy sauce, 2 tablespoons peanut oil, salt, pepper, and ginger root. Rub into chicken. Let stand overnight. Heat 3 tablespoons peanut oil in skillet. Add chicken and cook gently 20 minutes, turning frequently. Add chicken stock. Cover and cook 5 minutes. Remove chicken and keep hot. Mix water and flour together until smooth and add to hot gravy. Stir until well blended and thickened. Add chopped mushrooms, which have been sautéed in fat 5 minutes. Add pimiento and onion. Simmer 10 minutes longer. Serve chicken on hot platter with hot rice. Pour gravy over all. Serves 4 to 5.

MEXICAN FRIED CHICKEN

3½ pound fryer, cut up	1 onion, chopped
1 teaspoon salt	1 green pepper, chopped
½ cup flour	1 cup canned tomatoes
1 tablespoon chili powder	1 cup water
½ cup cooking fat or salad oil	½ cup rice

Dip pieces of chicken in mixture of salt, flour, and chili powder. Brown in fat. Remove from skillet. Add to drippings onion, green pepper, tomatoes, water, and uncooked rice. Season with salt and pepper, and a little more chili powder, if desired. Add chicken, cover, and cook gently until chicken and rice are tender, about 40 minutes. Add more water from time to time, if necessary. Whole ripe olives may be added for last 15 minutes. Serves 6.

OVEN FRIED CHICKEN

Prepare chicken as for *FRIED CHICKEN*. When pieces are uniformly and delicately browned, transfer to covered roasting pan or casserole. Add a little water if desired. Bake in slow oven (325°F.) until tender, 1 to 1½ hours. To crisp, remove cover the last 5 to 10 minutes of cooking.

BROILED CHICKEN

Select very young bird, weighing not over 2½ pounds. Place split chicken in shallow pan. Brush both sides with melted fat. Flatten chicken in pan, skin side down. Place pan on rack adjusted so that surface of chicken is about 4 inches from heat. Broil slowly. Regulate heat (or change rack position) so that chicken just begins to color lightly in spots at the end of 10 to 12 minutes. Turn and baste with fat about every 10 minutes, as browning increases. Cook until tender and evenly browned, 30 to 45 minutes, according to size. Season both sides with salt and pepper. Cut in half crosswise for 4 servings. Lift broiled chicken to hot platter. Pour pan drippings over bird.

Baking: Bake bird in an open pan in moderate oven (350°F.) 15 minutes. Sprinkle with salt. Brush with melted fat. Broil until evenly browned.

Barbecued chicken: Baste bird with *BARBECUE SAUCE* while broiling.

Parboiling: Large chickens may be parboiled about 10 minutes before broiling.

Steaming: Place bird on rack in shallow pan. Add enough water to reach just below bird. Cover and steam in moderate oven (350°F.) 30 minutes. Brush bird with melted fat. Sprinkle with salt. Broil in hot oven.

CHICKEN MARENGO (French Style)

1 chicken, young fryer	12 medium size mushrooms
Fat for frying	1 clove garlic
¾ teaspoon salt	1 small can tomatoes
¼ teaspoon pepper	1½ cups stock
12 small white onions	½ cup white wine

Cut chicken into serving pieces. Brown in fat. Add seasonings, onions, mushrooms, garlic, and tomatoes. Cover frying pan. Cook in moderate oven (350°F.) about 1½ hours. While cooking, add 1 cup stock and baste occasionally. When tender, remove to hot platter. Add ½ cup stock and ½ cup white wine to sauce in pan. Cook sauce until thickened. Remove clove of garlic. Pour sauce over chicken. Serves 4.

ARROZ CON POLLO (Latin American)

1 young 3½-pound chicken	3 cups canned tomatoes
½ cup olive oil	1 clove garlic
½ cup diced onion	1 bay leaf
1½ teaspoons salt	1 cup raw rice
Pepper, to taste	

Cut up and fry chicken in oil gently until evenly browned. Remove chicken. Cook onions lightly. Replace chicken. Add salt and pepper. Add tomatoes heated to boiling. Drop garlic clove and bay leaf on top. Add washed rice. Cook gently over low heat (or in moderate oven, 350°F.) until rice is tender and fluffy, about 1 hour. Lift and stir once after first 15 minutes. Remove garlic and bay leaf. Serve on warm platter, garnished with slivers of olives and green pepper rings. Serves 5 to 6.

Arroz de franzo: In Portugal, white wine is added.

Spanish arroz con pollo: In Spain, saffron and cummin seed are added.

ITALIAN CHICKEN CACCIATORE

1 young chicken, 2½ to 3 pounds	1 clove garlic
½ cup olive oil, scant	1 teaspoon salt
1 finely sliced onion	¼ teaspoon pepper
3½ cups canned tomatoes or	½ cup white wine, optional
8 medium tomatoes	

Disjoint and dry chicken. Cook gently in hot olive oil until delicately browned. Turn occasionally to brown evenly. Add onion and cook until onion is transparent and golden. Add tomatoes, garlic, salt, and pepper. Cover tightly. Simmer until chicken is tender and tomatoes are reduced to thick sauce, about ¾ hour. Add wine last 15 minutes of cooking. Remove garlic clove before serving. Serves 4 to 5.

CAUCASIAN CHICKEN WITH RICE (Pilaf)

1 stewing chicken (4 to 6 pounds)	2 cups rice
1 large onion, sliced	Boiling water
Cooking fat or chicken fat	Salt and pepper

Cut chicken into serving pieces and cover with water. Brown onion in hot fat. Add to chicken and cook until tender. Bring to a boil and skim well. Cover rice with boiling water and let stand 1 hour. Drain. Wash rice in cold water. Remove chicken. Add the rice to boiling chicken stock. Season with salt and pepper, to taste. Boil until rice is tender, 20 to 25 minutes. Serve hot. Serves 6 to 8.

CHICKEN PAPRIKASH

1 3-pound chicken	1 green pepper, minced
Salt and pepper	2 stalks celery, diced
2 large onions, minced	1 teaspoon paprika
2 tablespoons cooking fat	1 tomato, cut in eighths

Cut chicken into serving pieces. Season with salt and pepper. Fry onions in hot fat in a heavy skillet until golden brown. Add green pepper, celery, and paprika. Mix well. Add chicken and tomato. Cover and simmer gently until chicken is tender, 1½ to 2 hours. Turn occasionally to keep from burning, taking care to keep chicken intact. When done, remove chicken to hot platter. If more sauce is desired, add a little water and bring to boil. Pour over chicken. Serve with dumplings or rice. Serves 4 to 6.

STEWED CHICKEN AND NOODLES

2½ to 3 pound chicken	1 carrot
Salt and pepper, to taste	1 sprig of parsley
1 onion	2 cups dry noodles
1 bunch of celery tops	

Cut chicken into pieces. Add 4 cups water, 2 teaspoons salt, onion, and vegetables tied in bunch. Bring slowly to boil. Skim and simmer until chicken is tender. Remove vegetables. Add noodles to chicken. Simmer 15 minutes. Add ⅛ teaspoon pepper and more salt, if necessary.

CHICKEN WITH DUMPLINGS

Select plump chicken. Cut in pieces. Place in large utensil with tight-fitting cover. For a 4-pound chicken, add about 3 cups boiling water and 2 teaspoons salt. Cover. Cook on high heat until steaming, then turn heat low. Simmer slowly until chicken is tender, 3 to 3½ hours. Prepare dumplings. Be sure there is sufficient liquid to allow some for gravy. Dumplings absorb some liquid. Additional water may be added and brought to a quick boil before cooking dumplings. Serves 5.

BRUNSWICK STEW

1 4-pound chicken	Cayenne
¼ cup cooking fat or chicken fat	3 cups fresh lima beans
½ cup chopped onions	3 cups kernel corn
5 tomatoes, peeled and quartered	Salt
1 cup boiling water	2 teaspoons Worcestershire sauce
5 cloves	1 cup toasted breadcrumbs (optional)

Cut chicken into serving pieces. Sauté slowly in hot fat until light brown. Remove from pan. Brown onion in same fat. Place chicken, onions, tomatoes, boiling water, cloves, and a few grains cayenne in large pot. Cover and simmer until chicken is nearly tender, about 2 hours. Add lima beans and corn. Cover and simmer until vegetables are tender, about 45 minutes longer. Season with salt and Worcester-shire sauce. Stir in breadcrumbs. Serves 8.

Variations: Canned tomatoes may be substituted for fresh. If desired, 1 pound of brisket of beef may be combined with chicken.

CHICKEN À LA KING

4 tablespoons chicken fat	¾ cup sautéed mushrooms, diced
4 tablespoons flour	⅓ cup canned pimiento, diced
2 cups chicken or other stock	1 large egg yolk
1½ cups diced cooked chicken	Salt and pepper

Melt fat. Blend in flour and slowly add stock. When sauce is smooth and boiling, add chicken, mushrooms, and pimiento. Reduce heat. Add egg yolk and stir until slightly thickened. Season to taste. Serve at once. Serves 6.

Variation: Just before serving, add ⅓ cup blanched, slivered almonds and 1½ table-spoons sherry.

CHICKEN GIBLET FRICASSEE

¼ cup minced onion	½ teaspoon salt
1 cup diced celery	¼ teaspoon pepper
¼ cup diced green pepper	1 teaspoon paprika
2 tablespoons chicken fat	½ pound ground beef
Giblets from 2 chickens	1 tablespoon flour
2 cups water	

Sauté onion, celery and green pepper in hot chicken fat until tender. Add cut up giblets (wings, gizzard, neck, etc., may be used). Brown lightly; add water, salt, pepper, and paprika. Simmer 1 hour and add ground meat formed into small balls. Cover and simmer until chicken is tender, about 1 hour longer. Thicken gravy with flour mixed to a paste with 2 tablespoons cold water. Cook 5 minutes longer. Serve with noodles or boiled rice. Serves 4.

STEWED CHICKEN

Select a 3½ to 5 pound fowl. Leave whole or cut into pieces. Add hot water to cover and 2 teaspoons salt. Cover and cook slowly until tender, about 2 hours. For more flavor, add 1 stalk celery, 1 onion, 1 carrot, 1 whole clove, and 2 whole black peppers. Dumplings or noodles may be cooked in the stock.

CHICKEN FRICASSEE

Cut up fowl and cook as for *STEWED CHICKEN*. Roll pieces in well seasoned flour and sauté in chicken fat in a heavy skillet until browned. Thicken 1½ cups of the stock with 2 tablespoons flour blended into 2 tablespoons chicken or other fat. Or, mash the vegetables and use to thicken stock. Serve with rice, spaghetti, or noodles.

CHICKEN PIE

1 4-pound chicken
Salt and pepper
1 cup potato balls
10 small onions, boiled
½ cup carrots, diced
¾ cup canned peas

½ cup mushrooms, sliced
3 tablespoons chicken fat
3 tablespoons flour
2 cups chicken stock
2 egg yolks, beaten
PASTRY or *BISCUIT DOUGH*

Cut chicken in serving pieces. Combine with soup greens, add water to cover, and season to taste. Simmer until tender. Remove chicken from stock. Cut meat from bones in as large pieces as possible. Cook separately potato balls, onions, and carrots until tender. Place meat in large greased casserole. Drain and add cooked potato balls, carrots, onions, peas, and mushrooms. Melt chicken fat, blend in flour, and add chicken stock gradually. Cook until smooth and thick, stirring constantly. Season well with salt and pepper. Stir in beaten egg yolks and pour into casserole. Cover pie with thinly rolled dough (made with water, not milk). Prick in several places to let out steam, or, if biscuits are used, place them so that a little space is left between. Bake in moderate oven (375°F.) until nicely browned. Serves 6 to 8.

CHICKEN NOODLE CASSEROLE

2 cups noodles
½ pound mushrooms, sliced
2 cups diced, cooked chicken
1 cup dry breadcrumbs
¼ cup minced onion

1 teaspoon salt
⅛ teaspoon pepper
2 cups hot chicken stock
3 tablespoons chicken fat
2 sprigs parsley, chopped

Cook noodles in 2 quarts boiling salted water. Drain. Alternate noodles, mushrooms, and chicken in a well-greased casserole. Sprinkle each layer with breadcrumbs, minced onion, parsley, and salt and pepper. Top with crumbs. Pour hot stock over all. Dot with fat. Bake uncovered in moderate oven (350°F.) until top layer of crumbs is golden brown, about 30 minutes. Serves 6.

CHICKEN CHOP SUEY

1 cup shredded green pepper
1 cup shredded onion
3 tablespoons cooking fat or salad oil
2 cups diced, cooked chicken
2 cups shredded celery and tops

2 cups canned bean sprouts
1½ cups chicken broth
1 tablespoon cornstarch
1 cup toasted almonds
¼ cup soy sauce

Add the green pepper and onion to hot fat in skillet and allow to cook several minutes without browning. Add chicken and cook 5 minutes. Add celery, bean sprouts, and broth, reserving enough broth to make a paste with the cornstarch. Add paste to the chop suey and cook gently 10 minutes, stirring frequently. Lastly, stir in almonds and soy sauce. Serve with hot rice. Serves 8 to 10.

RUSSIAN CHICKEN CASSEROLE (Chochombili)

1 5-pound stewing hen
1 tablespoon chicken fat
3 onions, sliced

1 cup water
¾ cup tomato paste
Salt and pepper

Cut chicken into serving pieces. Brown in hot fat. Remove and brown onions in same fat. Place both in casserole. Add water, cover, and simmer 1 hour. Add tomato paste, salt, and pepper to taste. Cover and simmer until tender, 1 to 1½ hours. Serve with steamed rice. Serves 6.

Variation: Chicken and onions may be baked in moderate oven (350°F.) for 2 hours instead of simmering on top of stove.

CHICKEN IN WINE SAUCE

1 young chicken (3 pounds)
5 tablespoons olive oil
Salt and pepper, to taste
Parsley
1 bay leaf

1 small clove garlic
1 tablespoon flour
½ cup white wine
2 tablespoons tomato sauce
½ cup sliced mushrooms

Cut chicken into serving pieces. Brown on all sides in hot olive oil. Season with salt and pepper. Add a few sprigs parsley, bay leaf, and garlic. Cover and simmer until almost tender, about 1½ hours. Remove chicken. Sprinkle flour over gravy and stir until smooth. Stirring constantly, gradually add wine, tomato sauce, and mushrooms. Cook 10 minutes. Remove garlic. Serve chicken in hot sauce. Serves 6.

CHICKEN SMOTHERED IN WINE

1 young chicken (3 pounds)
3 tablespoons cooking fat or salad oil
8 small white onions
8 small carrots
1½ cups red wine
½ clove garlic, minced

2 tablespoons flour
12 mushrooms
2 sprigs parsley
1 bay leaf
⅛ teaspoon dried thyme
Salt and pepper, to taste

Quarter chicken and brown in fat. Remove and brown onions and carrots lightly. Add ½ cup wine and remaining ingredients. Return chicken to pan. Cover tightly and simmer until chicken and vegetables are tender, about 1 hour. Add balance of wine as liquid cooks down. Serves 4.

CHICKEN WITH PRUNES

1 stewing chicken (4 to 6 pounds)
4 onions, sliced
2 tablespoons cooking fat or chicken fat

1 teaspoon salt
⅛ teaspoon pepper
½ pound prunes

Cut chicken into serving pieces. Brown onions in hot fat. Add chicken. Season with salt and pepper. Cover, simmer in water to cover for 1 hour. Add prunes. Simmer until chicken is tender. Serves 6.

CHINESE PINEAPPLE CHICKEN (Boo Loo Gai)

2 young 1½-pound chickens
Flour and salt
Cooking fat or salad oil
1 cup bean sprouts
1 cup grated fresh pineapple

1 tomato, peeled and sliced
½ green pepper, shredded
2 teaspoons soy sauce
½ cup shredded almonds (optional)

Split chickens in halves and rub with flour and salt, to taste. Cook in fat until brown and tender. Remove from skillet and keep warm while preparing sauce. Add bean sprouts, pineapple, tomato, green pepper, and soy sauce to fat left in skillet. Heat, mix, and serve over chicken. Sprinkle shredded almonds over dish. Garnish with slices of green pepper and tomato wedges. Serves 4.

CURRIED CHICKEN AND NOODLES

6 tablespoons cooking fat	3 cups chicken stock or bouillon
¼ cup chopped onion	Salt
⅓ cup chopped celery	2 cups diced, cooked chicken
6 tablespoons flour	1 8-ounce package noodles
1 tablespoon curry powder	⅓ cup chopped peanuts

Melt fat in top of double boiler and add onion and celery. Cook until tender. Place over boiling water and add flour and curry powder. Stir until well blended. Gradually add chicken stock and cook, stirring constantly until mixture thickens. Season to taste with salt. Add chicken and reheat. Cook noodles in boiling, salted water until tender. Drain and rinse with boiling water. Place in casserole. Pour curried chicken into center of noodles. Sprinkle with chopped peanuts and serve. Serves 6.

CURRIED CHICKEN RING

1 8-ounce package wide noodles	1 cup water
½ teaspoon salt	2 tablespoons flour
1 tablespoon cooking fat	1 tablespoon curry powder
1 cup celery, chopped	⅛ teaspoon pepper
1 cup chicken gravy	2 cups chicken, diced

Cook noodles in boiling salted water until tender. Drain, add fat, and pack tightly into a greased casserole. Keep hot in oven. Cook celery in small amount of water 15 minutes. Heat chicken gravy and water, using any celery stock which is left. Mix dry ingredients with just enough cold water to make a smooth paste. Add a few tablespoons of diluted chicken gravy to flour and curry mixture, then pour into hot stock, stirring constantly until thickened. Add celery and chicken. Unmold noodles on platter. Pour curried chicken around noodles. Serves 4.

ARMENIAN CHICKEN PILAF

1 chicken (4 to 5 pounds)	FOR PILAF:
Salt and pepper, to taste	1 cup uncooked rice
1 cup chopped celery	½ cup fat
1 cup water	1½ teaspoons salt
2 tablespoons parsley, minced	½ teaspoon pepper
1 tablespoon cooking fat	2½ cups boiling water
2 tablespoons flour	3 tablespoons currants, washed
2 pounds spinach	2 chicken livers, coarsely chopped
	1 tablespoon almonds, blanched and halved

Season chicken with salt and pepper. Place in roasting pan. Add celery, water, parsley, and fat. Cover tightly and bake in moderate oven (350°F.) until tender, about 2 to 2½ hours. Baste occasionally. Thicken gravy with 2 tablespoons flour and enough cold water to make a paste. Cook 5 minutes and serve hot over chicken and rice. Serve with RICE PILAF and steamed spinach.

Rice pilaf: Wash and drain rice. Heat ½ cup fat in saucepan and add rice with salt and pepper. Cook until slightly puffed but not brown. Add boiling water. Simmer until liquid is almost absorbed. Add currants, chicken livers, and almonds. Cook until liquid is entirely absorbed. Remove from fire. Serve at once with the chicken. Serves 8.

CHICKEN-IN-THE-POT

1 3½ to 4 pound chicken, cut up
2 teaspoons salt
Dash of pepper
3 cups water
¼ cup chopped celery
12 small onions
8 small potatoes
12 small whole carrots
Flour
Water

Season chicken with salt and pepper. Brown in a little fat. Place in pot. Add water, cover and simmer until chicken is almost tender, about 45 minutes. Add vegetables. Cover and simmer until vegetables are cooked. Remove chicken and vegetables to a large casserole. Prepare gravy as follows: Skim off any surface fat. Measure chicken stock and return to pot. Add 2 tablespoons flour mixed to a smooth paste with ¼ cup cold water for each cup chicken stock. Simmer 5 minutes, stirring constantly. Add salt and pepper, if needed. Pour hot gravy over chicken and vegetables. Serve from casserole. Serves 6.

CHINESE CHICKEN WITH ALMONDS

1 cup rice
2½ quarts boiling water
1 tablespoon salt
1½ cups minced cooked chicken
3 cups cold chicken broth
4 teaspoons cornstarch
Salt, to taste
Pepper, to taste
½ cup toasted, shredded almonds

Cook rice in boiling, salted water until tender. Keep warm and when ready to serve arrange on plates in shape of squares. Pour over minced chicken made as follows: Mix broth and cornstarch thoroughly in top of double boiler. Place over boiling water. Cook, stirring constantly until mixture thickens. Add minced chicken. Season to taste with salt and pepper. Top each serving with a sprinkling of toasted almonds. Serves 6.

CHICKEN RING, MUSHROOM SAUCE

4 cups shredded stewed chicken
½ pound mushrooms, sautéed
1½ cups diced celery
2 cups chicken broth
2 eggs, unbeaten
1½ teaspoons salt
½ teaspoon black pepper
About 2½ cups soft breadcrumbs
2 cups medium white sauce
3 hard-cooked eggs

One large stewing chicken will yield 4 cups of cooked meat. Dice and sauté mushrooms. Combine chicken, celery, broth, eggs, seasoning, and crumbs. Add 1 cup sautéed mushrooms. Use enough crumbs to absorb excess moisture. Pack into greased ring mold. Bake in slow oven (325°F.) 45 minutes, or until firm and lightly browned. Turn carefully onto hot platter. Fill center of ring with medium white sauce combined with remaining mushrooms. Garnish with sliced hard-cooked eggs. Serves 10 to 12.

CHICKENBURGERS

2 cups cooked, minced chicken
1½ cups finely rolled cracker crumbs
¾ cup chicken stock

½ teaspoon minced onion
Salt and pepper, to taste
2 tablespoons cooking fat or salad oil

Combine ingredients, adding more liquid or crumbs for proper consistency, if necessary, to form into cakes. Fry in hot fat until brown on both sides. Serve with hot mushroom or pineapple sauce. Makes 6 cakes.

POTTED ROAST CHICKEN WITH VEGETABLES

1 large roasting chicken
8 small onions, peeled
8 small new potatoes
8 small carrots, quartered
1 cup hot water

1 cup peas
1 cup sliced green beans
1 cup sliced mushrooms
1½ teaspoons salt
Bread stuffing

Stuff chicken with bread stuffing, adding the chopped giblets to stuffing. Tie legs of chicken. Place in a large casserole. Bake uncovered in hot oven (425°F.) 15 minutes. Reduce heat to slow (325°F.). Add onions. Cover and bake 30 minutes longer. Add potatoes, carrots, and 1 cup hot water. Cover and cook 30 minutes. Add peas, beans, and mushrooms. Season with salt. Cover and bake 30 minutes. Remove chicken and vegetables to hot platter. Serves 4 to 6.

MEXICAN CHICKEN

2 chickens (2½ to 3 pounds)
Flour, seasoned with salt and
pepper
3 tablespoons cooking fat or salad oil
8 canned pimientos

1 large onion, chopped fine
2 cloves garlic, chopped fine
2 cups water
4 tablespoons flour
2 tablespoons cooking fat

Cut chicken into serving pieces. Dredge in seasoned flour. Brown in hot fat. Prepare sauce as follows: Drain pimientos and mash through a sieve. Mix well with onion, garlic, and water. Pour over chicken. Cover and cook slowly until chicken is tender, about 1½ hours. Remove chicken to serving dish and keep in warm place. Thicken sauce with paste made of flour blended into fat. Serves 6 to 8.

CHINESE SPICY CHICKEN

10 tablespoons salad oil
1 5-pound chicken, cut in pieces
Cornstarch
5 tablespoons soy sauce
2 teaspoons salt

1-pound can bamboo shoots, diced
7 large green peppers, diced
5 large onions, diced
2 cups diced canned pineapple
2 teaspoons brown sugar

Place 5 tablespoons oil in pan and heat. Dust chicken with cornstarch. Place chicken in pan with oil. Cover and cook until half done. Add soy sauce and salt. Cover and cook until very tender. Remove and set aside. Add 5 remaining tablespoons oil, the bamboo shoots, green pepper, onions, and pineapple to mixture in pan. Simmer 5 minutes. Add brown sugar and chicken. Heat through. Serve immediately with fluffy rice. Serves 8.

JELLIED CHICKEN LOAF

2 tablespoons plain gelatin
¼ cup cold water
1½ cups hot chicken stock or bouillon
1 teaspoon salt
   Dash of pepper
2 cups diced cooked chicken
⅓ cup chopped celery

⅓ cup shredded raw carrots
½ cup chopped green pepper
¼ cup cold tomato juice
1½ cups hot tomato juice
½ teaspoon Worcestershire sauce
1 cup cooked peas
2 tablespoons minced onion

Soften 1 tablespoon gelatin in cold water and dissolve in the hot chicken stock. Season with ½ teaspoon salt and pepper. Cool. When gelatin begins to thicken fold in 1 cup of chicken, celery, carrots, and green pepper. Pour mixture into a loaf pan which has been brushed with French dressing. Chill and allow to stiffen before adding second layer. Soften remaining 1 tablespoon gelatin in cold tomato juice and dissolve in hot tomato juice. Season with remaining ½ teaspoon salt and Worcestershire sauce. Cool. When mixture begins to thicken, fold in remaining chicken, peas, and onion. Pour into loaf pan over first layer. Chill 2 to 4 hours. Unmold onto platter of greens. Serve with mayonnaise. Serves 6.

KOREAN CHICKEN

½ cup olive oil
1 cup soy sauce
   Stalks of 5 green onions, chopped
1 large clove garlic, minced
½ teaspoon freshly ground black
   pepper

¼ teaspoon dry ginger
¼ teaspoon dry mustard
1 young fryer (about 3 pounds)
   Steamed rice

Combine all ingredients to make a sauce. Cut up chicken into serving pieces and marinate in the sauce from 1 to 3 hours. Turn the chicken several times so that all parts are thoroughly seasoned. Place chicken in shallow roasting pan. Pour over the sauce. Broil under moderate heat about 10 minutes on each side or until browned. Baste several times with the sauce in the pan while broiling. Serve with steamed rice. Serves 4.

CURRIED FOWL

1 4-pound fowl
2 quarts water
2 onions, sliced
3 stalks celery with leaves
1 tablespoon salt
   Pepper to taste

½ bay leaf
2 cups shredded carrots
3 tablespoons flour
½ teaspoon curry powder
½ cup shredded coconut (optional)
   Boiled rice

Cut fowl into serving pieces and put into kettle with water, onion, celery, salt, pepper, and bay leaf. Cover and heat to boiling point. Reduce heat and simmer until tender, 2 hours or longer. (If a pressure cooker is used, use only 2 cups water. Cook 20 minutes at 15 pounds pressure.) Remove chicken and strain broth. To 2½ cups broth, add carrots and cook until tender, about 7 minutes. Blend flour and curry powder with a small amount of remaining cool broth and stir into carrots-chicken stock mixture. Boil 1 minute, add chicken and reheat. To serve, sprinkle with coconut and surround with a border of boiled rice. Serves 5.

BREADED BAKED CHICKEN

1 roasting chicken (4 pounds)
Flour
Salt and pepper
1 egg, beaten

1½ cups dry breadcrumbs
⅓ cup salad oil
2 cups boiling water

Disjoint chicken as for fricassee. Dip each piece in seasoned flour, then in beaten egg, and last in breadcrumbs. Brown in hot oil in skillet. Arrange browned pieces in small roaster or large casserole; add boiling water. Cover and bake in moderate oven (350°F.) for 2 hours. Serve chicken on heated platter with gravy from bottom of casserole. Serves 5 to 6.

CHICKEN SAUTÉ SEC

1 frying chicken (about 3½ pounds),
    cut in pieces for serving
Flour, salt, and pepper
4 tablespoons pareve margarine
2 shallots or green onions, finely chopped

2 tablespoons chopped parsley
Sprinkling of thyme and basil
½ cup sauterne wine
1 4-ounce can sliced mushrooms

Dust pieces of chicken with flour seasoned with salt and pepper. Melt margarine in a large, heavy skillet; add chicken and sauté until golden brown, turning the pieces frequently and adding more margarine, if necessary. Add shallots, parsley, thyme, basil, and wine; cover tightly and simmer gently for 30 minutes. Drain mushrooms and add; continue cooking for 15 minutes, or until chicken is tender and no liquid remains in the pan. Serves 3 or 4.

CHICKEN CREOLE

1 frying chicken, 3½ pounds
1 teaspoon salt
Few grains black pepper
¼ cup olive oil
2 tablespoons pareve margarine
1 tablespoon flour
½ cup minced onion or
    6 chopped shallots
5 tablespoons chopped green pepper

1 No. 2 can tomatoes
Few grains cayenne
1 sprig thyme or ¼ teaspoon
    powdered thyme
1 tablespoon minced parsley
1 bay leaf
2 cloves garlic, minced
½ cup white wine
Cooked rice

Cut chicken in frying pieces. Sprinkle with salt and pepper. Brown on all sides in olive oil. In another pan, melt the margarine, blend in flour, and cook until brown. Add onion or shallots and green pepper and brown slightly. Add tomatoes, cayenne, thyme, parsley, bay leaf, and garlic. Cook over low heat until sauce is thickened, about 15 minutes. Add chicken, cover and simmer over low heat until chicken is perfectly tender, about 45 minutes. Add wine 15 minutes before cooking time is up. Serve over cooked rice. Garnish with parsley and avocado slices, if desired. Serves 4 to 6.

salads

Salads have become increasingly popular throughout the years and now play an important part in balancing meals. They are full of health-giving vitamins and minerals and add color, flavor, and texture to meals. The salad-wise homemaker will choose salads to fit the meal. If they accompany the main course of the dinner, she will choose a light salad. If served as a first course, the salad will be made up of tart fruits or seafood. A frozen salad or a fruit salad will be chosen for the dessert course. If a salad is chosen as the main course of the meal, it should have some protein-rich food such as meat, poultry, fish, eggs, or cheese as the main ingredient. For hints on the choice of correct dressings see the *SALAD DRESSING* section.

SALAD MAKING HINTS

1. Buy the freshest salad greens possible, wash them, dry thoroughly, and store in refrigerator in the vegetable compartment or bag or in a damp towel until ready to serve. Fresh, clean, crisp, tender greens are the basis of a good green salad.

2. All ingredients should be well drained before they are combined with the dressing, to avoid giving dressing a watery consistency. Dry greens thoroughly by patting with a towel.

3. Use a variety of greens. Try shredded cabbage, endive, watercress, and romaine as a change from head or leaf lettuce. Tear lettuce into bite-size pieces instead of cutting. Outer leaves of lettuce should be discarded only when they are bruised.

4. When mixing salads toss ingredients gently until mixed. Don't stir vigorously.

5. Add the dressing to salads at serving time to avoid wilting the greens, or, better still, serve the dressing from a separate bowl. People differ in the amount of dressing they prefer.

6. Use leftover vegetables in salad bowls.

7. The flavor of some salads, especially those containing cooked vegetables or meats, is improved by marinating the ingredients in French dressing. To do this, let foods stand in the dressing in a cool place until they are well seasoned. Drain before serving.

8. Wooden salad bowls should not be washed. Wipe clean with a cold damp cloth. Before using, season with warm salad oil, followed by rubbing the bowl with a cut clove of garlic.

9. Use a variety of dressings. It is not necessary to make a dressing for each salad. Most dressings keep well in the refrigerator.

10. Avoid too much garnish. Depend upon the natural color and flavor of foods for an attractive appetizing salad. Arrange salads lightly and attractively.

SALAD TRICKS AND GARNISHES

Suitable garnishings for meat and vegetable salads are: sliced cucumbers, quartered and sliced tomatoes, canned beets cut into cubes, sticks, or slices, sliced or quartered hard-cooked eggs, green and red pepper, pimiento, stuffed olives, carrot sticks, sliced or diced pickles, cheese strips, cubes, or slices, and other suggested garnishes. Fruit salads may be garnished with maraschino cherries, melon balls, mint leaves, herbs, strawberries, dark fruits, ripe olives, nuts, coconut, shredded dates, figs, and pitted prunes.

Asparagus tips: Marinate small cooked or canned tips in French dressing. Sprinkle ends with paprika.

Calla lilies: Pare a white turnip. Cut into thin lengthwise slices. Chill in ice water until they curl and resemble calla lilies. Form stems from carrot strips.

Carrot curls: Slice carrot paper thin lengthwise. Roll up each slice and fasten with toothpick. Crisp in ice water. Remove toothpick.

Carrot stick bundles: Slice carrot lengthwise into small strips. Cut pits from large olives. Push 3 or 4 strips through openings in olives.

Carrot strips: Wash and scrape young tender carrots. Cut into thin strips lengthwise. Chill in ice water.

Celery curls: Wash a bunch of celery and cut off leaves. Cut bunch lengthwise into 5 or 6 pieces—the more pieces the curlier the sections. Chill in ice water until ready to serve.

Cheese balls: Shape cream cheese into tiny balls. Sprinkle with paprika or roll in finely chopped nuts or olives.

Cucumber and onion slices: Peel and slice cucumbers and small white onions. Cover with equal amounts of vinegar and water. Let stand about 1 hour. Drain. Sprinkle with salt and water.

Cucumber balls: With a French vegetable cutter, cut large cucumbers into balls. Marinate in dressing. Sprinkle with paprika.

Cucumber boats: Remove seeds and pulp from a cucumber. Fill with cream cheese. Cool, slice again, if desired. Beets and carrots may be cooked until just done and then filled with cottage cheese.

Cucumber radish fans: Cut ends of 2 unpeeled cucumbers. Quarter lengthwise. Slash each quarter in ⅛-inch slices. Do not cut all the way through. Cut 8 large radishes crosswise into thin slices. Insert radishes between cucumber slices.

Cucumber strips: Peel cucumber and cut in half. Remove seeds and cut solid part into narrow strips about 3 inches long. Cover with damp cloth. Chill well before serving. Sprinkle with paprika.

Fluted cucumbers: Cucumbers may be left unpeeled or peeled. Run a fork down the length of the cucumber, repeating completely around the cucumber. Slice.

Green or red pepper rings: Cut off tops. Remove seeds and centers. Cut crosswise into thin slices. Crisp in ice water. Dry before using.

Lettuce cups: For lettuce cups to lie flat on the plate, cut each leaf up from the stem end about 2 or 3 inches. Fit 2 leaves together on each plate, interlocking the slits.

Onion juice: Peel and cut an onion in half. Holding one of the halves over a small bowl or cup, scrape downward with a knife until the desired amount of juice is obtained.

Onion rings: Cut large Bermuda or Spanish onion into thin slices. Crisp in ice water, then loosen rings and drain well.

Pickle fans: Cut pickle in very thin slices to within ¼ inch of the stem end. Spread slices slightly to resemble a fan.

Radish fans: Select firm and rather long radishes. With a thin, very sharp knite, cut thin slices crosswise almost through radish. Chill in ice water. The slices spread, fan shaped, as they chill.

Radish roses: Cut down thin strips of red peel of radishes almost through to stems to form petals. Place radishes in ice water, and as they chill the peel will curl back like petals.

Scallions: Trim washed green stalks, leaving about 3 inches. Trim onion if skin is loose or shriveled. Chill in ice water.

Sectioning oranges and grapefruit: Using a sharp knife, remove all of the peeling, including the white membrane, from oranges and grapefruit. Cut down on one side of each dividing membrane and bring the knife back up the other side so that each section slides out. When all sections have been removed, squeeze out remaining juice from the pulp. Use in salad, fruit salad dressings, or in a beverage.

Stuffed pickles: Core large pickles. Fill with cream cheese. Chill thoroughly and slice.

TOSSED VEGETABLE SALADS

This is the simplest of all bowl salads. Any number of fresh or cooked vegetables may be used. Choose one or several kinds of following greens: lettuce, chicory, romaine, endive, escarole, water cress, green dandelions, or raw spinach. Add any of following: sliced or chopped radishes, onions, celery, green pepper, cucumber, tomato, carrot and bits of leftover snap beans, beets, carrots, peas, sliced cauliflower, etc.

Be sure greens are crisp, clean, and dry. Wash them thoroughly in cold water, then dry by shaking in a towel. No salad should ever be watery. Break greens into desired pieces. Add chopped or sliced vegetables. Mix in salad dressing, using two forks, being sure not to break the vegetables. Serve on lettuce leaves or in individual salad bowls. For a suggestion of garlic or onion, rub bowl, before adding ingredients, with a freshly cut surface of either.

French salad bowl: Place a crust of bread rubbed with garlic in large bowl, while tossing the salad with dressing. The greens should be broken into pieces. Use any desired combination.

SPINACH TOSS SALAD

Clove of garlic
3 cups broken lettuce
¾ cup shredded fresh spinach
¾ cup shredded raw carrots
¼ cup diced celery

6 radishes, sliced
1 tablespoon minced onion or
   ¼ cup sliced green onion
¼ cup French dressing

Rub bowl with a clove of garlic (do not let garlic remain in bowl). Mix vegetables in bowl. Just before serving, pour French dressing over and toss until well mixed. Serves 6.

BERMUDA SALAD BOWL

2 cups sliced cauliflowerets	⅔ cup French dressing
½ cup sliced Bermuda onion	4 cups shredded lettuce
½ cup sliced stuffed olives	½ cup Roquefort cheese

Combine cauliflowerets, onion, and olives. Marinate in French dressing 30 minutes before serving. Just before serving, add lettuce and toss lightly. Break cheese into small pieces and add with lettuce. Serves 6.

COMBINATION SALAD

1 cup cooked snap beans	2 cups shredded lettuce
½ cup shredded raw carrots	1 hard-cooked egg
½ cup celery strips	French dressing

Combine snap beans, raw carrots, celery strips, and lettuce. Mix lightly. Arrange sliced eggs on vegetables. Serve with French dressing. Serves 5.

Vegetable and egg combination salad: Increase eggs to 3 and add ½ cup chopped green peppers to COMBINATION SALAD recipe.

MACEDOINE SALAD

Shredded lettuce	1 cup cooked potato cubes
1 cup cooked carrots, cut into strips	2 tablespoons chopped parsley
1 cup cooked string beans	French dressing

Arrange shredded lettuce on salad plates. Mix vegetables with French dressing and serve. Serves 6.

SPECIAL HEALTH SALAD

1 cup sliced raw cauliflower	⅓ cup chopped nuts (optional)
1 cup grated raw carrots	Evaporated milk dressing or
2 cups shredded lettuce	French dressing
1 bunch sliced radishes	

Combine vegetables and chill. Add nuts. Just before serving, add dressing and toss lightly. Serves 5.

CABBAGE SALADS

Cole slaw: Use fresh, tender cabbage. Mix 4 cups of finely shredded cabbage with 1 cup of cooked evaporated milk, sour cream, or vinegar dressing.

Cabbage and pepper slaw: Add ½ cup chopped green pepper to cabbage.

Red and white slaw: Use equal amounts of red and white cabbage.

Honey cole slaw: Beat 1 cup cold sour cream until thick. Add ¼ cup honey, 1 teaspoon salt, and 2 teaspoons celery salt. Pour over 4 cups finely shredded cabbage.

Hot slaw: Combine in saucepan 2 slightly beaten egg yolks, ¼ cup cold water, ¼ cup vinegar, 1 tablespoon butter or margarine, 1 tablespoon sugar, ½ teaspoon salt. Cook on low heat, stirring constantly until mixture thickens. Add 3 cups shredded cabbage and reheat. Serves 5.

Snappy cole slaw: Place in saucepan ½ cup vinegar and 1 tablespoon butter or margarine. Bring to boil. Remove from heat. Add ¼ cup sugar, ½ teaspoon salt, ½ teaspoon dry mustard, ¼ teaspoon celery seed, ⅛ teaspoon black pepper, and ⅛ teaspoon paprika. Cool. Pour over 3 to 4 cups finely shredded cabbage.

CABBAGE AND CARROT SALAD

1½ cups shredded carrots	2 teaspoons sugar
3 cups shredded cabbage	1 tablespoon vinegar
½ teaspoon salt	3 tablespoons mayonnaise

Combine carrots, cabbage, salt, sugar, and vinegar. Moisten with mayonnaise. Mix lightly. Arrange on crisp lettuce. Sprinkle with minced parsley or paprika. May be garnished with orange slices. Serves 6.

Cabbage and apple salad: Substitute 1½ cups thinly sliced unpeeled tart red apples for the carrots.

Cabbage, apple, and pickle salad: Combine 2 cups shredded cabbage, ⅛ teaspoon salt, 1 cup diced unpeeled apple, ¼ cup chopped sweet pickle, and 3 tablespoons pickle juice. Mix lightly. Serve at once. Serves 5.

Cabbage and onion salad: Shred cabbage. Cut the onions into very thin rings. Season with salt, celery salt, pepper, and paprika. Mix with mayonnaise or French dressing. Serve on cabbage leaf.

Cabbage, carrot, and celery salad: Decrease shredded cabbage to 2 cups. Add 1 cup thinly sliced celery.

CARROT SALADS

Carrot and apple salad: Coarsely dice 3 unpeeled apples. Combine with 2 cups grated carrots and 1 tablespoon finely minced onion. Add ½ cup sweet or freshly soured cream blended with 2 tablespoons lemon juice, ¾ teaspoon salt, and ⅛ teaspoon pepper. Mix well. Serve on lettuce. Serves 6.

Carrot and green pepper salad: Combine 3 cups shredded carrots with 1 cup chopped green pepper, and 3 mint leaves, chopped. Moisten with mayonnaise. Serve in lettuce cups. Serves 6.

Carrot and pineapple toss: Mix together 1 cup shredded raw carrot, 1 cup well-drained crushed pineapple, 2 cups shredded cabbage, and ⅓ cup French dressing. Serve in lettuce cups or on other salad greens. Serves 5.

Carrot and raisin salad: Combine 3 cups shredded carrots, ¼ teaspoon salt, and 1 cup seedless raisins. Add ½ cup mayonnaise and mix lightly. Serve on crisp lettuce. Serves 6.

Grated carrot salad: Wash young, tender carrots. Grate on fine grater. Using a fork gently combine with French dressing. Place on lettuce leaves. Serve at once. A bit of cheese may be grated with carrots.

VEGETABLE HEALTH SALADS

Chinese celery cabbage salad: Place 2 cups shredded Chinese celery cabbage on crisp outer leaves. Serve with *THOUSAND ISLAND* dressing or nippy mayonnaise. Serves 4.

Lettuce with sour cream dressing: Use head or leaf lettuce. Shred in medium fine pieces. With fork, gently blend in *SOUR CREAM* dressing.

Raw spinach and lettuce salad: Mix 3 cups shredded lettuce and 3 cups shredded spinach. Pour cooked dressing over salad just before serving. Serves 5.

Tomato leaf lettuce salad: Shred 4 cups leaf lettuce, combine with 2 large tomatoes, cut in small pieces, and 1 finely cut small onion. Before serving, pour over French dressing. Toss lightly. Serves 5.

Water cress salad: Wash 2 bunches water cress thoroughly. Remove yellow leaves. Mix with ½ cup French dressing and serve at once. Onion rings may be mixed with the water cress. Serves 4.

FARMER'S CHOP SUEY

Sour cream
Fresh tomatoes, cubed
Carrots, diced
Celery, diced
Green pepper, chopped

Lettuce, shredded
Green onions, cut up
Radishes, sliced
Peeled cucumbers, diced
Minced parsley

Combine serving portions of vegetables in individual bowls. Add sour cream. Garnish with minced parsley. Serve with buttered, thinly sliced pumpernickel bread. Any combination of crisp, diced vegetables may be used.

CHICKEN SALAD (Basic Recipe)

2 cups diced cooked chicken
1 cup chopped celery
2 hard-cooked eggs, sliced

Salt and pepper, to taste
Mayonnaise

Remove all gristle, skin, and hard, dry parts of chicken before dicing. Combine with celery. Season to taste. Moisten with mayonnaise.

With French dressing: Marinate chicken in French dressing. Chill. Drain and combine with other ingredients. Blend with mayonnaise, if desired. Season to taste. To serve, garnish with mayonnaise, sliced hard-cooked eggs, and capers. If desired pimiento strips, sliced olives, or sliced cucumbers, toasted almonds or marinated asparagus tips may be used for a garnish. Serves 4.

Chicken and avocado: Use 2 cups diced, cooked chicken, 1 cup diced avocado. Moisten with Russian dressing.

Chicken and mushrooms: Use 2 cups diced cooked chicken, ½ cup sautéed button or sliced mushrooms, and ½ cup diced celery. Moisten with desired dressing.

Chicken with nuts and olives: Use 2 cups diced, cooked chicken, ½ cup diced celery, ½ cup sliced ripe olives, and ½ cup sliced toasted almonds. Moisten with mayonnaise.

Chicken and sweetbreads: Use 2 cups diced cooked chicken, 1 cup diced cooked sweetbreads, and ½ cup chopped cucumber. Moisten with mayonnaise.

Chicken and tomato: Use 1 cup diced cooked chicken, ½ cup diced crisp cracklings, and 1 cup diced tomato. Moisten with desired dressing.

Chicken and tongue: Use 1 cup diced cooked chicken, 1 cup diced cooked tongue, ½ cup chopped celery, and ½ cup chopped stuffed olives. Moisten with dressing.

Chicken with fruit and nuts: Use 2 cups diced chicken, ½ cup chopped celery, ½ cup diced pineapple (or whole grapes or cherries), and ½ cup sliced toasted almonds. Moisten with mayonnaise.

Meat salad: Substitute any kind of diced, cooked meat for chicken. For large groups, veal may be economically combined with chicken. For 25 servings, use 3 quarts meat and/or fowl and 2 quarts diced celery.

CHICKEN SALAD ON THE HALF SHELL

1 cup diced cooked chicken
2 tablespoons French dressing
1 cup diced celery
¼ cup drained crushed pineapple

Salt and pepper
2 or 3 avocados
Boiled dressing or mayonnaise

Combine chicken and French dressing. Chill about 1 hour. Just before serving, mix chicken, celery, and pineapple with enough salad dressing to moisten. Season to taste. Cut avocados in half lengthwise and remove stone. Hollow out, if necessary, to make a nest for the salad, adding the diced pulp to salad mixture. Fill avocados with salad. Dot with additional dressing, or pipe dressing with pastry tube around the edge of each shell. Garnish with greens. Serves 4 to 6.

CHICKEN VEGETABLE SALAD

2 cups diced cooked chicken
½ cup cooked carrots, diced
½ cup cooked peas
½ cup cooked string beans

½ cup cooked beets
1 teaspoon salt
1 teaspoon paprika
1 teaspoon chopped parsley

Mix chicken and vegetables. Add salt, paprika, and parsley. Marinate in French dressing. Chill thoroughly. Arrange on lettuce leaves. Top with mayonnaise. Garnish with beets and asparagus tips. Serves 6.

RUSSIAN VEAL SALAD

2 apples, diced
1 large cucumber, pared and diced
1 very small dill pickle diced
3 small boiled potatoes, diced

2 cups cooked veal, diced
Mayonnaise
Salt and pepper

Combine all ingredients. Add mayonnaise and season with salt and pepper, to taste. Mix well and chill. Serve on salad greens. Serves 6.

ITALIAN PEPPER SLAW

1 clove garlic
2 cups finely shredded cabbage
¼ cup chopped green pepper
¼ cup chopped pimiento
½ teaspoon salt
½ teaspoon celery seed
    Dash of red pepper and paprika

1 tablespoon soft breadcrumbs
2 tablespoons tomato paste
2½ teaspoons water
¼ teaspoon salt
⅛ teaspoon sugar
2½ teaspoons salad oil
2 teaspoons cider vinegar

Rub salad bowl with garlic clove. Put vegetables, ½ teaspoon salt, celery seed, red pepper, and dash paprika in bowl. Mix remaining ingredients thoroughly. Pour over contents of salad bowl. Toss. Serves 6.

WIENER SALAD BOWL

2 cooked wieners, sliced
2 cups canned kidney beans
⅓ cup sliced pickles

¾ cup French dressing
½ large onion, sliced
1 head lettuce, broken in small pieces

Skin and slice wieners. Drain kidney beans. Add meat, pickles, and ½ cup French dressing. Chill. Just before serving, add remaining ingredients. Toss thoroughly. Serves 8.

SAILOR'S SALAD

2½ cups cooked halibut
    French dressing
1 cucumber, peeled and cubed
1 tablespoon chopped onion
¼ cup chopped capers
1 pimiento, chopped

1 tablespoon salt
¼ teaspoon pepper
⅛ teaspoon tarragon
1 cup mayonnaise
    Drained tomato cups
    Boston lettuce

Flake halibut, moisten with French dressing. Chill thoroughly. Combine chilled halibut with cucumber, onion, capers, pimiento, seasoning, and mayonnaise. Fill tomato cups with fish mixture. Garnish with cucumber slices and pimiento. Serve on crisp lettuce leaves. Serves 6.

LIVER AND EGG SALAD

3 onions, minced
3 tablespoons chicken fat or oil
½ pound chicken livers

4 hard-cooked eggs
2 stalks celery, minced
    Salt and pepper

Sauté onions in melted fat until lightly browned. Broil the livers. Chop livers with eggs and celery. Mix with browned onions. Season with salt and pepper. Moisten with fat in which onions were fried. Serve on salad greens.

ORIENTAL EGG SALAD

1 cup flaky hot boiled rice
1 large potato, hot mashed
4 hard-cooked eggs
⅓ cup salad dressing
1 tablespoon chopped onion

1 tablespoon chopped parsley
2 tablespoons chopped sweet
    red pepper or canned pimiento
1 tablespoon chopped green pepper
    Salt and pepper

Combine rice, potato, two eggs, forced through strainer, and salad dressing. Chill. Just before serving, add remaining ingredients. Season well. Serve with or without greens from large bowl. Garnish with remaining eggs, sliced or sieved. Serves 4.

SUNSHINE EGG SALAD

8 hard-cooked eggs
1 cup finely diced celery
¼ cup salad dressing
1 teaspoon Worcestershire sauce
1 tablespoon lemon juice
1 teaspoon scraped onion

Salt and pepper
6 thick slices of tomato
Salad greens
Paprika
Celery curls

Chop eggs coarsely. Add celery, dressing, and seasoning. Season to taste with salt and pepper. Press into molds and chill. Unmold on tomato slices placed in a bed of salad greens. Sprinkle with paprika. Garnish with celery curls and additional dressing if desired. Serves 6.

CAUCASIAN EGGPLANT SALAD

1 medium eggplant
Lemon juice to taste
Parsley, minced

1 minced onion
Olive oil to taste
2 hard-cooked eggs (optional)

Broil eggplant over or under a flame, turning slowly, until peel is black. Remove peel and stem. Mash with a wooden spoon. Add the other ingredients to taste. Serve on salad greens.

Rumanian eggplant salad: Broil and mash eggplant as above. Add 1 minced onion, 1 chopped green pepper, vinegar, and salt, to taste.

FISH SALADS

Use cooked or canned fish. Cut into ¼ to ½ inch cubes or flake. Toss lightly with mayonnaise or cooked salad dressing. Add salt, if necessary. Chill and serve in salad bowl or individual plates. Garnish with dressing, crisp greens, cooked or raw vegetables.

Apple and fish salad: Use 2 cups flaked fish and 2 cups diced tart apple.

Cucumber and fish salad: Use 2 cups flaked fish, ½ cup each of diced cucumber and celery, ½ shredded head lettuce, 1 finely chopped small onion, and a few diced radishes.

CHOPPED HERRING SALAD

2 herrings
2 small onions, minced
2 medium tart apples
¼ cup breadcrumbs

1 tablespoon sugar
¼ teaspoon salt
¼ teaspoon pepper
¼ cup mild vinegar

Soak herring over night. Drain. Remove skin and bones. Chop fine with onions and peeled and cored apples. Add remaining ingredients and mix well. Cover. Chill 30 minutes. Serve on salad greens. Garnish with black olives, parsley, and sliced tomatoes.

Variation: Add 2 hard-cooked eggs, chopped fine.

GREEK HERRING SALAD

1 large herring
1 mild onion, thinly sliced
2 tomatoes, diced
1 small head cabbage, shredded

1 large green pepper, shredded
Salt and pepper, to taste
About 2 tablespoons olive oil
About 2 tablespoons vinegar

Clean and fillet the herring. Cut into small pieces. Combine all ingredients. Season with salt and pepper to taste and toss with olive oil and vinegar. Garnish with black olives, sliced cucumbers, and spring onions.

MEAT SALAD BOWL (Basic Recipe)

¼ cup sliced onions
1 small head lettuce
2 tomatoes, cut in wedges
2 cups cooked or canned peas

¼ cup sliced, stuffed olives
1 cup cooked meat, cut in strips
1 teaspoon salt
1 cup French dressing

Separate onion rings. Break lettuce in bite-size pieces. Arrange vegetables and meat on lettuce. Sprinkle with salt. Add dressing. Toss lightly.

Variations: Tongue, beef, veal, lamb, duck, turkey, liver, or chicken may be used for the meat. Cabbage may be used in place of celery.

Tuna or salmon salad bowl: Use tuna or salmon in place of the meat. Omit onion. Add 1 cup chopped celery.

POTATO SALAD (Basic Recipe)

3 cups diced cooked potatoes,
   cooked in jackets
1 tablespoon grated onion
3 tablespoons French dressing

1 tablespoon minced parsley
1 teaspoon salt
¼ teaspoon paprika
Mayonnaise

Combine ingredients, except mayonnaise, tossing lightly with a fork. Chill 3 to 4 hours. Just before serving add mayonnaise, mixing carefully. Serve on lettuce or watercress. Serves 6.

Cornucopia salad: Roll thin slices of bologna to form cornucopias. Fill with potato salad.

Potato salad with celery: To basic recipe add 1 cup diced celery.

Potato egg salad: To basic recipe add 1 cup diced celery and 3 chopped hard-cooked eggs.

Savory potato salad: To basic recipe add ½ cup tartar sauce and ⅓ cup chow-chow and stuffed olives, minced.

Potato salad with carrots: To basic recipe, add 1 cup diced celery and 1 cup grated carrot.

Potato salad with cabbage: To basic recipe add 1 cup finely cut cabbage.

Potato salad with nuts: To basic recipe add 1 cup diced celery and ¾ cup salted peanuts, chopped Brazil nuts, or toasted filberts.

Potato salad with cucumber: To basic recipe, add 1 cup diced celery and 1 diced cucumber.

Potato salad ring: Pack potato salad into medium-size ring mold. Chill. Unmold on bed of greens. Garnish with assorted sliced cold meats, radish roses, and quartered tomatoes.

MACARONI SALAD (Basic Recipe)

3 cups cold cooked elbow macaroni	⅓ cup French dressing
½ minced green pepper	Lettuce
1½ tablespoons minced onion	Mayonnaise or
½ cup chopped celery	COOKED DRESSING

Combine macaroni, green pepper, onion, celery, and French dressing. Chill. Arrange on lettuce and garnish with mayonnaise or COOKED DRESSING.

With hard-cooked eggs: Slice and add 3 hard-cooked eggs.

With tuna fish: Use a little less macaroni. Add a 7-ounce can flaked tuna fish. Use additional mayonnaise.

With vegetables: Add 1 cup mixed cooked or canned carrots, peas, and diced string beans. If desired, marinate vegetables first.

Baked bean salad: Substitute cold baked beans for macaroni.

Brown bean salad: Substitute cold cooked brown beans for macaroni.

STUFFED TOMATO SALADS

To prepare tomatoes for stuffing: Select medium-size smooth tomatoes. Scald, remove skins. Cut a slice from top and remove some of the pulp. Sprinkle inside with salt, invert, and let stand 30 minutes to chill. Fill with stuffing. Serve on salad greens.

Avocado stuffing: Mix diced avocado with celery hearts. Moisten with French dressing.

Cabbage stuffing: Mix 1½ cups shredded cabbage, ¼ teaspoon celery seed, ¼ teaspoon salt, and 2 tablespoons French dressing.

Chicken stuffing: Mix diced cooked chicken, diced cucumber, chopped tomato pulp. Moisten with mayonnaise.

Cottage cheese and chives: Mix cheese and chopped chives. Stuff tomatoes. Top with a spoonful of desired dressing and stuffed olives.

Pineapple cheese stuffing: Combine finely chopped fresh or canned pineapple, tomato pulp, cream cheese, and minced water cress. Moisten with mayonnaise.

Other suggested stuffings: WALDORF SALAD, egg salad, tuna fish, or any meat salad.

FRUIT SALADS

Golden salad: Combine 1½ cups orange sections, 1½ cups shredded raw carrot, ½ cup raisins. Add ¼ cup French dressing and toss lightly. Serve on lettuce or shredded cabbage. Serves 5.

Grapefruit or orange salad: Peel orange or grapefruit. Remove seeds and white membrane. Separate sections by cutting close to membrane on each side. Arrange on lettuce. Serve with French dressing.

Peach or pear and cottage cheese salad: Use halved or sliced fruit. Place peach or pear in lettuce cup. Fill centers with ¼ cup cottage cheese. Top with salad dressing.

Quick and easy salad: Arrange 4 or 5 spinach leaves on each salad plate. Place a mound of cottage cheese in center. Surround with quarters of sliced orange or tangerine sections.

Waldorf salad: Combine 2 cups cubed apples, ¼ cup chopped nutmeats, and 1 cup cubed celery. Moisten with ½ cup mayonnaise. Mix lightly with 2 forks. Serve on lettuce. Serves 6.

Waldorf surprise salad: Combine 2 cups cubed, unpeeled apples, ½ cup chopped dates or raisins, and ½ cup chopped celery. Mix ¼ cup mayonnaise with 1 tablespoon horseradish. Add to fruit. Cover. Place in refrigerator. Let stand at least 1 hour before serving. Serves 6.

EASY FRUIT SALADS

Avocado: Cut unpeeled fruit in half lengthwise. Sprinkle with lemon juice. Allow half fruit to each person. Serve on bed of salad greens with French dressing.

Avocado and orange: Alternate sections of oranges with slices of peeled avocado. Serve with lemon wedges and French dressing.

Avocado ring: Cut avocado in half and peel thinly. Fill seed cavity with pineapple or pimiento cheese. Press halves together, wrap in waxed paper. Chill. Cut into slices ¼ inch thick. Arrange 2 or 3 slices in lettuce cup. Serve with French dressing.

Cranberry cheese: Combine 1½ cups cottage cheese with ¾ cup well-drained cranberry jelly and ¼ cup broken pecan meats. Serve with mayonnaise.

Orange mint: Arrange orange sections on bed of salad greens. Sprinkle finely chopped fresh mint leaves on top. Serve with French dressing.

Peach berry: Place peach halves on lettuce. Fill cavities with raspberries, blackberries, blueberries, or sweet cherries.

Pear: Use canned or fresh pears, placing one half, hollow side up, on a bed of greens. Fill with chopped nuts and maraschino cherries.

Minted peach salad: Place peach halves on bed of greens. Sprinkle with lemon juice and chopped mint. Serve with *WHIPPED CREAM DRESSING.*

WINTER FRUIT SALAD

Sprinkle sliced bananas with pineapple or lemon juice. Combine with equal quantities diced, unpeeled red apples and orange or tangerine sections. Add a few tablespoons chopped peanuts. Toss with shredded lettuce and a *FRUIT DRESSING.*

LUNCHEON FRUIT SALAD

Lettuce cups	Orange sections
Fresh or canned pears, sliced	Lemon juice
Seedless grapes	*FRENCH FRUIT DRESSING*
Melon balls	Salted nutmeats

Any fresh or canned fruit that gives a pleasing flavor combination may be used in place of the above. Arrange lettuce cups, placing one on each plate. Fill with peach and pear slices, orange sections, grapes, and melon balls. Sprinkle with lemon juice to prevent fruit from darkening. Serve with dressing. Place a few salted nutmeats on each plate.

ORANGE, PINEAPPLE, AND APPLE SALAD

3 oranges, peeled and diced
3 slices canned diced pineapple or
    1 cup tidbits
1 unpeeled red apple, diced
½ cup pitted dates, cut into small
    pieces (optional)

1 cup seedless grapes, cut in half
    (optional)
⅓ cup mayonnaise

Mix fruit with mayonnaise. Chill thoroughly. Serve on shredded lettuce. Serves 6.

FRUIT SALAD IN MELON RING

Cut cantaloupe in ¾-inch-thick crosswise slices. Remove rind and seeds. Arrange lettuce leaves on salad plates. Put melon rings on lettuce. Combine diced banana, diced pineapple, and pitted halved grapes and put inside melon rings. Serve with *FRUIT DRESSING*.

CHEF'S SALAD

2 bunches endive
3 small bunches water cress
3 small stalks celery
1 head lettuce

10 anchovies
3 tomatoes, peeled
3 hard-cooked eggs

Break salad greens into pieces and place in salad bowl. Arrange anchovies and quarters of tomato and egg on top. Serve with salad dressing. Serves 6.

MENORAH SALAD

Cut a banana in half crosswise. Stand upright in a round slice of canned pineapple on lettuce to form the candle. Place a maraschino cherry on top of banana to represent flame. Make handle from strip of green pepper looped into pineapple at base of candle. Pour a little mayonnaise down side of candle and base to represent dripping wax.

HEARTY SNACK SALAD

1 cup cooked tongue
2½ cups canned or cooked vegetables
1 cup thinly sliced celery
1 tablespoon chopped onion

2 tablespoons chopped sweet pickle
½ cup sharp mayonnaise
1 head lettuce
1 hard-cooked egg

Cut tongue in strips. Drain chilled vegetables. Combine tongue, vegetables, onion, and pickles with mayonnaise. Chill 1 hour to blend flavors. Serve in lettuce cups. Garnish each serving with a slice of egg. Serves 6.

Variations: Use cooked chicken, canned tuna, salmon, or other cooked meats or fish instead of tongue.

Snappy sauerkraut salad: Add 1 cup sauerkraut to *SNACK SALAD* with mixed vegetables.

VEGETABLE SALAD BOWL SUGGESTIONS

Beans and peas: 1 cup cooked string beans, ½ cup cooked peas, ½ cup sliced celery, ½ cup chopped apple, about 1 cup salad greens. Toss with French dressing.

Bean sprouts: 1 cup bean sprouts, ½ cup chopped celery, 1 sliced cucumber, ¼ cup sliced radishes, 4 or 5 rings of green pepper. Toss with French dressing seasoned with a little soy sauce.

Beet and cauliflower: 1½ cups cooked cauliflower, chilled and broken into flowerettes, ¼ cup chopped celery, ¾ cup diced beets, and a little grated onion, with thin dressing and lettuce.

Broccoli and egg salad: 1½ cups cooked broccoli, chilled, 4 chopped hard-cooked eggs, 4 tablespoons crumbled Roquefort cheese, thinned salad dressing.

Carrot, egg, and celery: 1½ cups cooked diced carrots, ¾ cups diced celery, 1 chopped hard-cooked egg, greens, and ½ teaspoon minced onion. Toss with thinned cooked dressing.

Corn: 2 cups drained whole kernel corn, 2 tablespoons chopped green pepper, 1 tablespoon minced onion, ½ chopped pimiento, 1 chopped hard-cooked egg. Toss with thinned cooked dressing and lettuce.

Corn and tomato salad: 2 tomatoes, cut in chunks, ½ cup whole kernel corn, 2 tablespoons chopped green pepper, about 1 cup salad greens. Toss with French dressing.

Cucumber and carrots: 1 cucumber, unpeeled and sliced, 1 green pepper, cut in strips, 3 grated carrots, ½ cup chopped celery, ½ small head of lettuce or other greens. Toss with thinned mayonnaise.

Kidney bean salad: 1½ cups kidney beans, ½ cup chopped celery, ¼ cup chopped pickles. Toss with lettuce and salad dressing thinned with sour cream.

Lima bean: 1½ cups cooked lima beans, ½ cup diced pickled beets, 2 tablespoons minced onion, 2 tablespoons chopped parsley. Toss with chopped lettuce and French dressing seasoned with Worcestershire sauce.

Navy bean and radish: 1½ cups well-seasoned boiled navy beans, ½ cup sliced radishes, about 1 cup of shredded lettuce or other greens and a few pitted olives. Toss with French dressing seasoned with onion juice.

Raw beet salad: 2 cups ground raw beets, ½ cup piccalili. Toss with French dressing or thin mayonnaise and a few salad greens.

String bean and radish: 2 cups slivered string beans, 1 teaspoon chopped chives, ½ cup thinly sliced crisp radishes tossed with a few greens and French dressing. If desired, add a few tablespoons crumbled Roquefort.

LEAF LETTUCE, SPINACH, AND SPRING ONION SALAD

Wash spinach and leaf lettuce carefully. If lettuce leaves are large, break into smaller sections. Slice spring onions thin. Toss onions through the spinach and leaf lettuce. Add radishes for a touch of color. Serve with evaporated milk dressing.

APPLE SALADS

Apple cups: Use red-skinned unpeeled apples. Wash apples. Cut off a thin slice from stem end. Core without cutting through bottom of apple. With spoon scoop out apple to form cup. Fill with any of the following. Serve on crisp greens.

1. Combine equal amounts of chopped celery, peas, and chopped nuts. Moisten with mayonnaise.

2. Mix fruit salad with French dressing.

3. Add chopped celery and nutmeats to any fruit-flavored packaged gelatin. Top with a sour cream dressing.

4. Combine minced chicken with halved red grapes, chopped celery and pecans, and mayonnaise. Top with dressing.

Apple cubes: Combine cubes of unpeeled red apples with orange and grapefruit sections. Moisten with French dressing. Serve on bed of shredded raw spinach.

Apple slices: (1) Combine apple with banana slices and red raspberries. Moisten with French dressing. Serve on nest of shredded red and white cabbage. (2) Combine apple slices with sliced peaches and pineapple cubes. Moisten with red-tinted mayonnaise. Garnish with water cress and chopped red cherries.

ORANGE AND VEGETABLE SALAD BOWL

1½ cups orange sections	3 cups shredded, raw cabbage
¾ cup diced, pared cucumber	½ cup French dressing
or chopped sweet pickle	½ head lettuce

Toss together all ingredients except lettuce. Arrange in lettuce-lined bowl. Serves 6.

salads—gelatin

VEGETABLE SALAD MOLD (Basic Recipe)

1 tablespoon plain gelatin	½ teaspoon salt
¼ cup cold water	2 tablespoons sugar
1 cup hot water	⅛ teaspoon pepper
¼ cup mild vinegar	1½ cups diced or shredded vegetables
1 tablespoon lemon juice	1 tablespoon minced onion

Use raw or cooked vegetables. Add more sugar if desired. Soften gelatin in cold water. Dissolve in hot water. Add vinegar, lemon juice, salt, sugar, and pepper. Cool until syrupy. Fold in vegetables. Turn into mold which has been rinsed in cold water. Chill until firm. Unmold on lettuce. Serve with desired dressing. Serves 6.

1. ½ cup diced celery, ½ cup diced cucumber, ¼ cup sliced radishes, 2 tablespoons chopped green pepper.

2. ½ cup raw cabbage, ½ cup grated raw carrots, ¼ cup diced apples, ¼ cup chopped nuts.

3. 1 cup raw shredded cabbage, ½ cup chopped celery and 2 tablespoons chopped green pepper or pimiento.

4. ½ cup each chopped celery, shredded raw carrots, and cooked peas.

5. 1 cup shredded raw cabbage and ½ cup sliced green olives.

6. ¾ cup each shredded raw cabbage and shredded carrots.

7. ½ cup each canned asparagus tips, green peas, shredded raw carrots, 2 tablespoons chopped pimiento.

8. ¾ cup each cubed pickled beets and chopped celery.

9. ½ cup each chopped celery, diced cooked beets, shredded raw cabbage.

10. ¾ cup each cooked peas and chopped roasted peanuts.

11. ½ cup each diced celery, canned lima beans, diced or shredded carrots, raw or cooked.

12. ½ cup each canned red kidney beans and peas, ½ cup chopped celery, ¼ cup chopped green pepper, 1 tablespoon grated onion.

FRUIT SALAD MOLD (Basic Recipe)

1 tablespoon plain gelatin	¼ cup sugar
¼ cup cold water	¼ teaspoon salt
1 cup hot fruit juice or water	1½ cups canned or fresh fruit
¼ cup lemon juice	

Soften gelatin in cold water. Add hot fruit juice or water and stir until dissolved. Add lemon juice, sugar, and salt. Chill until syrupy. Fold in diced fruits. Rinse mold in cold water. Line bottom with thinly sliced fruits. Pour in thickened mixture. Chill until firm. Unmold on lettuce. Serve with desired dressing. Serves 6.

1. ½ cup diced apples, ½ cup cut up orange segments, ¼ cup chopped dates, ¼ cup chopped nuts.

2. ½ cup each diced grapefruit, orange sections, diced canned pineapple.

3. ½ cup each diced orange sections, diced pears and peaches, fresh or canned.

4. ¾ cup diced apple, ½ cup chopped celery, ¼ cup chopped nuts.

5. ½ cup each diced canned pineapple, diced apple, sliced strawberries.

6. ½ cup each diced canned pineapple, shredded raw carrot, shredded cabbage.

7. ¾ cup each diced pears, fresh or canned, and diced cucumber.

8. ¾ cup each diced canned pineapple and diced raw cucumber.

9. ½ cup each sliced bananas, diced orange sections, white grapes.

10. ½ cup each sliced red cherries, diced melon, diced orange sections.

11. 1½ cups of cantaloupe and honeydew melon balls.

MOLDED MEAT SALAD (Basic Recipe)

3 cups hot stock	2½ cups cold diced chicken or veal
1 tablespoon plain gelatin	½ cup diced celery
2 tablespoons cold water	¼ cup chopped green pepper
2 teaspoons lemon juice or vinegar	¼ cup chopped pimiento
½ teaspoon salt	

Prepare stock by boiling beef shank or chicken in water to cover until tender. Strain. Add a bay leaf, 3 cloves, salt and pepper to taste. Simmer 10 minutes. Strain.

Soak gelatin in cold water. Dissolve over boiling water. Add lemon juice or vinegar and hot stock. Mix thoroughly. Cool. Mix and add other ingredients. Pour into mold which has been rinsed with cold water. Chill until firm. Unmold on lettuce. Garnish with olives, radish roses, celery curls, etc. Serves 6 to 8.

Jellied bouillon with frankfurters: Use beef stock in above recipe. When gelatin begins to thicken add frankfurters and sliced hard-cooked eggs.

TOMATO ASPIC (Basic Recipe)

2 tablespoons plain gelatin	1 teaspoon salt
½ cup cold water	4 peppercorns
2½ cups canned tomatoes	½ bay leaf
1 tablespoon minced onion	4 cloves
1 tablespoon sugar	2 tablespoons lemon juice

Soften gelatin in cold water. Cook tomatoes and seasonings (except lemon juice) 5 to 10 minutes. Strain. Pour 2 cups hot tomato mixture over softened gelatin. Add lemon juice and pour into molds rinsed with cold water. Chill. Unmold on lettuce. Serve with mayonnaise or COOKED DRESSING. Serves 6.

Tomato aspic ring: Pour into large ring mold or individual small molds. Chill until firm. Unmold. Fill center with chicken, tuna, or salmon salad.

Tomato aspic with celery and peas: Add 1 cup canned peas and 1 cup diced celery to thickened aspic.

Tomato aspic with cottage cheese: Fill molds ⅔ full of tomato aspic. When firm, complete filling molds with seasoned cottage cheese. Unmold with cottage cheese on the bottom.

Tomato aspic with cucumber: Add 2 cups diced cucumber to thickened aspic.

GRAPEFRUIT AVOCADO SALAD

1 tablespoon plain gelatin	½ teaspoon salt
¼ cup cold water	3 ounces cream cheese
1 cup hot water	1 medium avocado
¼ cup lemon juice	Salt, to taste
¼ cup granulated sugar	1 cup diced grapefruit

Soften gelatin in cold water. Dissolve in hot water. Add 3 tablespoons lemon juice, sugar, and salt and mix well. Cool. To half of gelatin mixture add cream cheese mashed with fork. Cover bottom of small loaf pan, or half fill individual molds. Chill until firm. Cut avocado in half, remove seed and skin, and cut into cubes. Sprinkle with salt and remaining lemon juice. Add avocado and grapefruit to remaining gelatin mixture. Pour over cream cheese layer and chill until firm. Serves 6.

LAYERED CHEESE AND APPLE SALAD

1 package lemon gelatin	1 diced red apple
2 cups boiling water	1 teaspoon sugar
2 tablespoons lemon juice	3 ounces cream cheese
½ teaspoon salt	½ cup broken nutmeats

Dissolve gelatin in boiling water. Add 1 tablespoon lemon juice and salt. Chill.

Combine apple, sugar, and remaining lemon juice. When gelatin mixture is slightly thickened, fold apples into half the mixture. Turn into mold and chill until firm. Place remaining gelatin mixture in a bowl of cracked ice and beat with a rotary beater until thick and fluffy like whipped cream. Fold in mashed cheese and nuts. Pour over gelatin-apple layer and chill until firm. To serve, cut in slices and arrange on lettuce leaves. Top with mayonnaise or any desired dressing. Serves 6.

TUNA FISH MOLD

1 tablespoon plain gelatin	¼ teaspoon paprika
¼ cup cold water	1½ tablespoons melted butter
2 egg yolks	¾ cup milk
1 teaspoon salt	2½ tablespoons vinegar
¼ teaspoon mustard	2 cups canned tuna fish, flaked

Soften gelatin in cold water. Beat egg yolks slightly. Mix with salt, mustard, and paprika. Add butter, milk, and vinegar. Cook over boiling water, stirring constantly, until thickened. Add softened gelatin and stir until dissolved. Add flaked fish. Turn into fish mold rinsed in cold water. Chill until firm. Unmold on lettuce. Serves 6.

Salmon salad: Substitute 2 cups canned salmon for tuna fish.

Stuffed cucumbers or tomatoes: Pare large cucumbers or tomatoes, and remove centers. Fill with fish-gelatin mixture. Chill. Cut in slices. Serve on lettuce.

Creamy salmon mold: Add ½ cup stiffly beaten whipped cream to salmon mixture. Turn into fish mold rinsed in cold water. Chill until firm. Unmold on crisp lettuce leaves. Garnish with ripe olives and cucumber slices.

CRANBERRY RING SALAD

1 package lemon gelatin	½ cup crushed canned pineapple
1½ cups boiling water	¾ cup cranberry sauce
½ cup chopped celery	

Dissolve gelatin in boiling water. Chill. When slightly thickened, add celery, pineapple, and cranberry sauce. Turn into ring mold rinsed in cold water. Chill until firm. Unmold on crisp lettuce and garnish with mayonnaise.

MOLDED SALAD SUGGESTIONS

Apple lime mold: Dissolve 1 package lime gelatin in 1 cup hot water. Add 1½ cups sweetened, unflavored apple sauce. Pour into molds and chill.

Asparagus and tomato mold: Simmer 2 cups tomato juice, bit of bay leaf, 1 clove, ½ teaspoon salt, and ½ onion, sliced, for 15 minutes. Add 1 tablespoon plain gelatin soaked in 4 tablespoons cold water. Dissolve. Strain and cool mixture. When slightly thickened add 1½ cups tender cooked or canned asparagus cut into ½-inch pieces. Turn into molds and chill.

Blueberry melon mold: Dissolve 1 package lemon gelatin in 1 cup hot water. Add 1 cup blueberry juice and cold water. Cool. When slightly thickened fold in 1 cup cantaloupe or honeydew melon balls and 1 cup blueberries. Chill until firm. Unmold. Sliced fresh or canned peaches may be substituted for melon balls.

Cherry olive mold: Dissolve 1 package cherry gelatin in 1 cup hot water. Add 1 cup cherry juice and cold water. When slightly thickened, add 1½ cups sour red cherries, slightly sweetened, ¼ cup chopped pickle, and ¼ cup sliced stuffed olives. Chill.

Cherry port nut mold: Dissolve 1 package cherry gelatin in 1 cup hot water. Add ½ cup port wine combined with ½ cup cherry juice. Fold in 1 cup pitted whole Bing cherries and ½ cup coarsely broken walnuts. Mold and chill until firm.

Cranberry lemon mold: Dissolve 1 package lemon gelatin in 1 cup boiling water. Run 1 cup raw cranberries through food chopper and add 1 cup orange juice and ½ cup sugar. Add to cooled gelatin. Pour into molds and chill.

Ginger ale grape mold: Dissolve 1 package lemon gelatin in 1 cup hot grape juice. Cool. Add 1 cup ginger ale. Turn into molds and chill.

Ginger ale lime mold: Dissolve 1 package lemon gelatin in ½ cup boiling water. When cool, add 1½ cups ginger ale. Chill until slightly thickened and fold in 1 cup diced mixed fruits (fresh or canned and drained), ¼ cup chopped celery, and ¼ cup chopped nuts. Pour into molds and chill.

Grapefruit lime mold: Dissolve 1 package lime gelatin in 1 cup hot water. Add 1 cup grapefruit juice and cold water. When cool, add 1 to 2 cups grapefruit sections. Pour into molds and chill.

Greengage lime mold: Dissolve 1 package lime gelatin in 1 cup hot water. Add 1 cup plum juice and water, and 2 cups greengage plums. Chill.

Lemon vegetable mold: Dissolve 1 package lemon gelatin in 1 cup hot water. Add 1 cup cold water and 1 tablespoon lemon juice. Cool. Add 1 cup shredded cabbage, ½ cup cooked peas, ½ cup cooked, diced carrots, ¼ teaspoon salt. Mix well. Pour into molds and chill.

Loganberry and banana mold: Dissolve 1 package raspberry gelatin in 1 cup hot water. Add 1 cup loganberry juice and cold water. When slightly thickened fold in 1 sliced banana and 1 cup loganberries.

Pineapple cottage cheese salad: Dissolve 1 package lemon or lime gelatin in 1 cup hot water. Add 1 cup cold water. Cool. Add 1 cup seasoned cottage cheese and ½ cup drained crushed pineapple. Pour into mold rinsed in cold water and chill until firm. Unmold on crisp lettuce and garnish with mayonnaise. Serves 6.

PERFECTION SALAD

1 tablespoon plain gelatin	¼ cup vinegar
2 tablespoons cold water	1 cup shredded cabbage
1 cup boiling water	¾ cup diced celery
2 tablespoons sugar	1 tablespoon chopped green pepper
1½ teaspoons salt	¼ cup chopped stuffed olives
Dash of pepper	Lettuce
¾ cup canned pineapple juice	Mayonnaise

Soften gelatin in cold water 5 minutes. Add boiling water, stirring until dissolved. Add sugar, ½ teaspoon salt, pepper, and pineapple juice. Chill. Add vinegar and remaining salt to vegetables and olives. When gelatin mixture begins to thicken, fold in vegetables. Turn into individual molds and chill. Unmold on lettuce and garnish with mayonnaise. Serves 6.

GINGER ALE FRUIT SALAD

1 tablespoon plain gelatin
2 tablespoons cold water
½ cup boiling water
1 tablespoon sugar
Dash of salt
1 cup ginger ale
2 tablespoons lemon juice
½ cup heavy cream, whipped

½ cup sliced oranges
½ cup diced, canned pineapple
½ cup berries
1 tablespoon chopped preserved ginger
½ cup chopped pecans
Lettuce
Mayonnaise

Soften gelatin in cold water. Add boiling water and stir until dissolved. Add sugar, salt, ginger ale, and lemon juice. Chill. When slightly thickened, fold in cream, fruits, berries, ginger, and nuts. Turn into individual molds and chill. Unmold on lettuce. Garnish with mayonnaise. Serves 6.

ROQUEFORT CHEESE SALAD MOLD

½ pound Roquefort or Blue cheese
6 ounces cream cheese

1 tablespoon plain gelatin
½ cup heavy cream, whipped

Mash cheeses to a smooth paste. Soften gelatin in ½ cup cold water and stir over hot water until dissolved. Add cheese paste to whipped cream and stir in gelatin. Turn into mold rinsed in cold water. Chill until firm. Serve with mayonnaise or French dressing. Serves 6 to 8.

GOLDEN GATE SALAD

1 tablespoon plain gelatin
¼ cup cold water
1¼ cups pineapple juice
½ teaspoon salt

¼ cup lemon juice
2 tablespoons sugar
1 cup canned pineapple, crushed
1 cup shredded raw carrot

Soak gelatin in cold water 5 minutes. Dissolve over hot water. Add pineapple juice, salt, lemon juice, and sugar. When partially set, fold in pineapple and carrots. Turn into mold rinsed in cold water. Serve on salad greens with mayonnaise. Serves 6.

Golden cheese salad: Substitute 1 cup shredded cheese for carrots.

MOLDED CUCUMBER SALAD

1 package lime gelatin
2 cups hot water
1 tablespoon lemon or vinegar
1 teaspoon scraped onion

½ teaspoon salt
Dash of pepper
1 cup finely chopped cucumber

Dissolve gelatin in 2 cups hot water. Add vinegar and seasoning. Chill. When slightly thickened, fold in cucumber. Turn into square pan and chill until firm. Cut into squares and serve on lettuce. Serves 4 to 6.

Pineapple and carrot: Use orange gelatin with shredded carrot and pineapple instead of cucumber.

Pineapple and cucumber: Substitute ½ cup crushed pineapple for ½ cup cucumber.

CHICKEN AND EGG MOLD

2 tablespoons plain gelatin
½ cup cold water
1 cup hot chicken broth
1 cup mayonnaise
1½ teaspoons curry powder
2 cups cooked chicken, finely chopped

6 hard-cooked eggs, chopped fine
3 tablespoons finely chopped green pepper
¼ cup finely chopped celery
1¾ teaspoons salt
Dash of pepper

Soften gelatin in cold water. Add hot broth, stir until gelatin is dissolved and cool. Mix mayonnaise with curry powder and combine with chicken, eggs, green pepper, celery, salt, and pepper. Add to gelatin mixture. Pour into mold rinsed in cold water and chill. Unmold chicken on bed of water cress. Garnish with avocado slices and radish roses. Serves 6 to 8.

MOLDED SEA FOOD SALAD

1 tablespoon plain gelatin
2 tablespoons cold water
1 cup BOILED SALAD DRESSING
2 cups flaked, cooked fish fillets
½ cup diced celery

1 pimiento, minced
Lettuce
Thinly sliced cucumber
Sour cream
Salt and paprika

Soften gelatin in cold water and dissolve over boiling water. Add to dressing. Fold in fish, celery, and pimiento. Turn into dampened mold. Chill. Unmold and garnish with lettuce cups filled with thinly sliced cucumber blended with seasoned sour cream. Serves 4. (Tuna fish or salmon may also be used for this salad.)

salads—frozen

FROZEN VEGETABLE SALAD

1 cup finely shredded cabbage
1 cup chopped celery
½ cup raw grated carrot
¼ cup shredded green pepper

1 teaspoon grated onion
¾ cup mayonnaise
Salt and pepper
½ cup heavy cream, whipped

Add mayonnaise to vegetables and mix well. Season with salt and pepper; fold in whipped cream. Turn into refrigerator tray. Freeze until firm. Serves 8.

FROZEN TOMATO SALAD

6 firm small tomatoes
1 cup cottage cheese
½ cup chopped cucumber
2 tablespoons minced onion
3 tablespoons chopped green pepper

2 tablespoons chopped pimiento
½ teaspoon salt
1 cup COOKED SALAD DRESSING
1 cup heavy cream, whipped

Wash tomatoes, plunge in boiling water one minute, then in cold, drain, and remove skins; cool. Scoop out center to form cups. Stuff with mixture of cheese, cucumber, onion, green pepper, pimiento, salt, and 3 tablespoons salad dressing. Arrange in refrigerator freezing tray cut side down, taking care not to spill filling. Mix remaining salad dressing with whipped cream; pour around tomatoes, almost covering them. Freeze about 2 hours, but do not allow to freeze too hard. Cut in squares so that each portion is a stuffed tomato in a square of frozen dressing. Serve on lettuce; top with more dressing. Serves 6.

ORIENTAL SALAD

3 ounces cream cheese
3 tablespoons mayonnaise
⅛ teaspoon salt
1 cup heavy cream, whipped
¼ cup chopped kumquats
¼ cup chopped dates
¼ cup chopped maraschino cherries
¼ cup crushed pineapple
1 tablespoon finely chopped preserved ginger
½ cup chopped blanched almonds

Mix cheese to smooth paste with mayonnaise; add salt. Fold in whipped cream and fruit and ginger mixture. Pour into refrigerator tray; sprinkle almonds over top. Freeze. Serve on crisp lettuce. Serves 8.

FROZEN FRUIT SUPREME

½ cup red cherries
½ cup pineapple
½ cup apricots
½ cup sliced bananas
¼ cup blanched shredded almonds
1 cup heavy cream, whipped
1 cup mayonnaise

Drain fruit; cut in small pieces. Blend whipped cream with mayonnaise. Combine all ingredients; freeze in refrigerator tray. Cut in squares; serve on crisp lettuce with mayonnaise. Serves 10 to 12.

Variations: Vary by combining equal portions of pears, peaches, preserved figs, chopped nuts, and crushed pineapple.

FROZEN FRUIT WITH COTTAGE CHEESE

1 cup cottage cheese
⅛ teaspoon salt
1 cup pineapple, finely diced
1 cup cherries, pitted
1 cup peaches, diced
2 oranges, diced
8 marshmallows, quartered
1 cup whipping cream
½ cup mayonnaise

Combine cheese, salt, fruits, and marshmallows, tossing together lightly with a fork. Chill. Whip cream until stiff and combine lightly with mayonnaise. Fold into cheese mixture. Freeze in refrigerator tray 3 to 4 hours. Serve on crisp lettuce. Garnish with mayonnaise combined with whipped cream. Serves 8.

FROZEN ROQUEFORT CHEESE SALAD

¼ pound Roquefort cheese
1 teaspoon lemon juice
2 tablespoons cream cheese
1 cup finely chopped celery
½ teaspoon chopped onion
Dash of paprika
½ cup whipping cream

Whip the cream. Combine with other ingredients. Freeze in refrigerator tray. Serves 6.

FROZEN FRUIT AND NUT SALAD

1 package cream cheese (3 ounces)	1 cup orange sections
3 tablespoons mayonnaise	1 cup chopped walnuts
1 cup canned sweet cherries	1 cup crushed pineapple, drained
½ cup maraschino cherries	½ pint whipping cream

Cream cheese and mayonnaise together. Cut sweet cherries and maraschino cherries in half. Cut orange sections in thirds. Combine cream cheese mixture with cherries, orange, chopped walnuts, and pineapple. Whip cream and fold into fruit mixture. Pour into 12 custard cups (5 ounce size). Set cups in freezing compartment of refrigerator until frozen (about 3 hours). When salad is frozen remove from refrigerator and unmold individual salads by slipping a small knife around salad next to glass. Serve on lettuce, watercress, or endive. Serves 12.

FROZEN PEACH SALAD

2½ cups canned peach halves	½ cup syrup from peaches
1 tablespoon butter	¼ cup orange juice
1½ tablespoons flour	1 egg white, stiffly beaten
1 tablespoon sugar	½ cup evaporated milk, whipped
¼ teaspoon salt	

Place 8 drained peach halves, cut side down, in refrigerator tray. Melt butter; add flour and blend. Add sugar, salt, peach syrup, and orange juice. Cook, stirring constantly, until thick and smooth. Fold in stiffly beaten egg white. Cool. Dice remaining peaches and add to mixture. Fold in whipped evaporated milk. Pour over peaches. Freeze until firm. Cut in squares and place in lettuce cups, peach side up. Place a maraschino cherry in center of each. Serves 8.

FROZEN GRAPEFRUIT SALAD

1 8-ounce cream cheese package	1 grapefruit, sectioned
1 cup sour cream	1 avocado, diced
¼ teaspoon salt	1 cup seedless white grapes, halved
½ cup sugar	½ cup pecan pieces

Soften cream cheese; blend in sour cream. Add salt and sugar and stir until well blended. Add grapefruit sections, avocado, grapes, and pecans. Pour into a 9x5-inch loaf pan and freeze until firm. Slice and serve on salad greens with French dressing. Serves 6 to 8.

CALIFORNIA FROZEN SALAD

1 3-ounce package cream cheese	¼ cup chopped maraschino cherries
3 tablespoons mayonnaise	¼ cup crushed pineapple
⅛ teaspoon salt	1 tablespoon finely chopped preserved
1 cup heavy cream, whipped	ginger
¼ cup chopped kumquats	½ cup chopped blanched almonds
¼ cup chopped dates	

Blend cream cheese smoothly with mayonnaise; add salt. Fold in whipped cream and fruit and ginger mixture. Pour into refrigerator tray; sprinkle almonds over top. Freeze. Serve on crisp lettuce. Serves 8.

salad dressings

WHAT KIND OF DRESSING?

What shall it be—sweet or tart, thick or thin—for the salad dressing? The answer lies in your family's taste. Main-dish salads made with meat, fish, poultry, eggs, beans, cheese, or potatoes usually call for a mayonnaise-type or cooked salad dressing. But some of these more substantial salads are good with tart French dressing—salad oil combined with lemon juice or vinegar plus seasonings.

Tart French dressing is the most likely choice for vegetable salads and vegetable-fruit combinations. But some vegetable salads may well take a mayonnaise or cooked dressing.

Reserve the sweet clear French dressings for fruit salads. Mayonnaise made milder with whipped cream or thinned and sweetened with fruit juice is good for fruit salads too.

COOKED DRESSING (Basic Recipe)

¼ tablespoon salt	2 eggs, slightly beaten
2 tablespoons sugar	2 tablespoons butter
1 tablespoon flour	¾ cup milk
¾ teaspoon dry mustard	¼ cup vinegar or lemon juice
Few grains cayenne	

Sift dry ingredients; add eggs, butter, milk and vinegar very slowly. Stir and cook over boiling water until mixture begins to thicken. Strain and cool. For a thinner dressing use one egg yolk. Store covered until ready to use.

Almond and cucumber dressing: Add ½ cup diced cucumber and ¼ cup blanched and shredded almonds. Serve with fruit salad.

Banana nut dressing: Add 3 tablespoons peanut butter and 1 mashed banana to ¼ cup cooked dressing. Thin with a little cream, if necessary. Serve with fruit salads.

Chutney dressing: Add 2 tablespoons chopped chutney and ¼ cup whipped cream to ¾ cup cooked dressing. Serve with fruit or vegetable salads.

Cream dressing: Omit butter, use 1 cup light cream instead of milk.

Fruit dressing: Increase flour to 2 tablespoons. Substitute 1 cup orange juice for milk.

Honey dressing: Substitute 2 to 4 tablespoons honey for sugar.

Peanut butter dressing: Blend ¼ cup peanut butter with hot dressing after removing from heat.

Sardine cooked dressing: Skin, bone, and mash 6 sardines. Mix with 1 tablespoon lemon juice. Add to 1 cup cooked dressing. Serve with fish or vegetable salad.

Sour cream dressing: Fold in 1 cup whipped sour cream when cool.

Toasted nut dressing: Add ⅓ cup toasted chopped nuts to 1 cup cooked dressing. Serve with potato, tomato, or plain fruit salads.

Whipped cream dressing: Fold in ¾ cup heavy cream, whipped, when cool.

FRUIT SALAD DRESSING

¼ cup sugar
1 tablespoon cornstarch
¼ teaspoon salt
1 cup pineapple juice

Juice of 1 lemon
Juice of 1 orange
2 eggs, separated
1 cup heavy cream, whipped

Mix sugar, cornstarch, and salt in top of double boiler. Combine fruit juices and add to dry ingredients. Cook for 20 minutes. Remove from fire. Add well-beaten egg yolks. Cook again for 5 minutes, stirring constantly. Remove from fire, add to stiffly beaten egg whites, then cool. Before serving fold in whipped cream.

FRUIT CHEESE DRESSING

3 egg yolks
¼ cup sugar
1 tablespoon butter
2 tablespoons lemon juice

2 tablespoons pineapple juice
¼ teaspoon salt
1 cup cottage cheese

In top of double boiler beat yolks until thick and light colored. Add sugar and cook over simmering water until sugar is dissolved. Add butter and fruit juices. Cook, stirring constantly until mixture thickens. Add salt and cheese just before serving. Makes 2 cups.

MAYONNAISE (Basic Recipe)

1 egg or 2 egg yolks
1 teaspoon dry mustard
1 teaspoon salt
1 teaspoon syrup
Pepper

Cayenne pepper
Dash of paprika
1½ cups cold salad oil
2 tablespoons vinegar or lemon juice

Beat thoroughly the first 7 ingredients. Add oil 1 tablespoon at a time, beating thoroughly after each addition, until half the oil has been added. Then add remaining oil in larger quantities, and lastly add vinegar or lemon juice. Makes 2 cups.

Caper mayonnaise: Add a scant ½ cup finely chopped well washed capers to 1 cup mayonnaise.

Caviar anchovy mayonnaise: Add 4 washed, dried, and finely chopped anchovy filets and 1 tablespoon caviar to 1 cup mayonnaise.

Caviar horseradish mayonnaise: Add 1 tablespoon each of drained horseradish and caviar to 1 cup mayonnaise.

Caviar mayonnaise: Add 1 tablespoon caviar to 1 cup mayonnaise.

Chili mayonnaise: Add ¼ cup chili sauce, 1½ tablespoons vinegar, ¾ tablespoon Worcestershire sauce, and ¼ teaspoon chopped chives to 1 cup mayonnaise. Serve with fish salads.

Chutney mayonnaise: Add 1½ tablespoons chopped chutney to 1 cup mayonnaise.

Cranberry mayonnaise: Add 2 tablespoons well beaten cranberry jelly and 1 teaspoon grated orange rind to 1 cup mayonnaise.

Cream mayonnaise: Fold mayonnaise into ⅓ cup heavy cream, whipped. Serve with fruit salads.

Creamy fruit mayonnaise: Fold into 1 cup mayonnaise ½ cup heavy cream, whipped, and ¼ cup each chopped almonds and currant jelly.

Green mayonnaise: Color with vegetable coloring or spinach juice.

Honey cream dressing: Blend ¼ teaspoon dry mustard with 1 tablespoon honey and ½ teaspoon lemon juice. Add to mayonnaise. Serve with fruit salads.

Horseradish mayonnaise: Add 3 tablespoons prepared horseradish to 1 cup mayonnaise. Serve with cold beef.

Ideal salad dressing: Add 2 tablespoons condensed tomato soup, ½ tablespoon lemon juice, 1 teaspoon Worcestershire sauce, and 1½ teaspoons powdered sugar to 1 cup mayonnaise.

Nippy mayonnaise: Add 3 teaspoons prepared horseradish, 3 teaspoons prepared mustard, and 1 small chopped sweet pickle to 1 cup mayonnaise. Serve with tomato salads, head lettuce, or salad bowl.

Piquante mayonnaise: Add 2 tablespoons each olives and pickles, finely chopped, and 1 teaspoon each chopped onion and chives to 1 cup mayonnaise.

Ravigotte mayonnaise: Mix and chop ½ cup watercress, ½ cup parsley, 2 teaspoons chives, 1 tablespoon capers, and 4 anchovies. Force mixture through fine sieve and add to 1 cup mayonnaise. Serve with fish and vegetable salads.

Red beet mayonnaise: Add 1 tablespoon strained beet juice and 2 tablespoons finely chopped cooked beets to 1 cup mayonnaise.

Red mayonnaise: Tint with red vegetable coloring.

Roquefort mayonnaise: Add 2 tablespoons crumbled Roquefort cheese, a few drops Worcestershire sauce, 1 tablespoon French dressing, and 1 tablespoon minced chives to 1 cup mayonnaise.

Rum cream mayonnaise: Add 1 teaspoon rum, mixed with ½ cup whipped cream, and add ¼ cup chopped toasted almonds to 1 cup mayonnaise. Serve with fruit salads.

Russian dressing: Add 1 chopped hard-cooked egg, ¼ cup chili sauce, 2 tablespoons chopped green pepper to 1 cup mayonnaise. Serve with head lettuce.

Savory mayonnaise: Add ¼ teaspoon each Worcestershire sauce, paprika, and dry mustard to 1 cup mayonnaise. Serve with fish, meat, or vegetable salads.

Thousand Island dressing: Add 2 tablespoons chili sauce, 2 tablespoons chopped green pepper, 2 tablespoons pimiento, 2 tablespoons chopped sweet pickle to 1 cup mayonnaise. Serve with vegetable salads.

EGGLESS MAYONNAISE

½ teaspoon salt
½ teaspoon dry mustard
¼ teaspoon paprika
¼ teaspoon granulated sugar
Few grains cayenne

3 tablespoons evaporated milk
¾ cup salad oil
2 tablespoons vinegar or
   1 tablespoon vinegar and
   1 tablespoon lemon juice

Mix dry ingredients thoroughly. Add evaporated milk and blend well. Beat in salad oil gradually. Add vinegar or vinegar and lemon juice and beat until mixture is smooth. Makes 1 cup.

CONDENSED MILK MAYONNAISE

¼ cup vinegar or lemon juice
½ cup salad oil or melted butter
⅔ cup sweetened condensed milk
1 egg yolk, unbeaten

½ teaspoon salt
Few grains cayenne
1 teaspoon dry mustard

Combine ingredients in pint jar in order listed. Cover tightly and shake vigorously for 2 minutes. Mixture will blend perfectly. If thicker consistency is desired, place jar in refrigerator to chill before serving.

FRENCH DRESSING (Basic Recipe)

¼ teaspoon dry mustard
⅛ teaspoon pepper
¾ teaspoon salt
¼ cup vinegar

¼ teaspoon paprika
1 teaspoon sugar or corn syrup
¾ cup salad oil

Measure all ingredients into mixing bowl or glass jar. Beat with rotary beater or shake to mix thoroughly. Shake or beat just before serving. Makes 1 cup dressing.

California French dressing: Use grapefruit juice instead of vinegar.

Chiffonade dressing: Add following finely chopped: 2 tablespoons parsley, 2 hard-cooked eggs, 2 tablespoons red pepper, 1 tablespoon each chopped olives and cucumber pickle and ¼ teaspoon paprika.

Chutney French dressing: Use half lemon juice and half vinegar. Add ¼ cup finely chopped chutney.

Cream French dressing: Add 2 tablespoons sweet or sour cream.

Cucumber French dressing: Add 1 cup well drained, grated cucumber. Serve very cold with fish salads.

Curry French dressing: Add ¾ teaspoon curry powder before beating.

Egg-cheese French dressing: Add 1 hard-cooked egg, chopped fine, 4 tablespoons grated American cheese, 1 tablespoon each chopped parsley and chives, and 1 tablespoon each chopped green pepper and pimiento.

Foamy French dressing: Fold into cream French dressing 1 egg white, beaten until dry but not stiff.

Fruit French dressing: Substitute ¼ cup orange juice for ¼ cup vinegar. Add 1 tablespoon lemon juice. May be sweetened with additional corn syrup or honey.

Garlic French dressing: Pare and rub clove of garlic over bottom of bowl. If desired, clove of garlic may be left in dressing for about 1 hour.

Ginger French dressing: Add 1½ tablespoons finely chopped preserved ginger. Use on fruit salads.

Gourmet French dressing: Add 2 tablespoons brandy, 2 tablespoons tarragon vinegar, 6 tablespoons olive oil, and salt and pepper to taste.

Honey French dressing: Omit mustard and pepper. Add ½ cup strained honey and beat until frothy. Use on fruit salads.

Horseradish French dressing: Add 2 tablespoons horseradish before serving.

Lemon dressing: Substitute lemon juice for vinegar.

Mint dressing: Add 1 tablespoon chopped mint.

Olive French dressing: Add ¼ cup chopped olives before serving.

Roquefort French dressing: Crumble ½ cup Roquefort cheese and add to dressing before serving.

Spicy French dressing: Add 2 tablespoons prepared mustard and 2 teaspoons Worcestershire sauce.

Tarragon French dressing: Use tarragon vinegar for a pleasing flavor.

Tomato French dressing: Add 2 teaspoons tomato juice and a few drops onion juice.

Vinaigrette French dressing: Before beating, add 1 tablespoon chopped pickles, 1 tablespoon minced capers, 1 tablespoon chopped green olives, 1 tablespoon chopped pimiento, 1 teaspoon minced onion, and 1 teaspoon dry mustard.

TOMATO SOUP FRENCH DRESSING

1 can tomato soup, condensed	1 teaspoon Worcestershire sauce
¾ cup vinegar	1 teaspoon salt
1½ cups oil	2 teaspoons mustard
¼ cup sugar	Paprika, as desired
Juice of 1 lemon	

Combine all ingredients in quart jar. Cover and shake thoroughly. Store in refrigerator.

SPECIAL FRENCH DRESSING

1 clove garlic, grated fine	1 small onion, grated
½ cup sugar	⅔ cup tomato ketchup
⅓ cup mild vinegar	1 teaspoon salt
1 teaspoon Worcestershire sauce	2 cups salad oil

Mix in order given and beat thoroughly. Pour into quart jar. Store in cool place.

HERB FRENCH DRESSING

1 teaspoon salt	¼ cup vinegar
½ teaspoon sugar	¾ cup salad oil
¼ teaspoon pepper	1 tablespoon mixed dried herbs
½ teaspoon dry mustard	½ teaspoon Worcestershire sauce
½ teaspoon paprika	

Measure all ingredients into jar in order given. Cover and shake well. Chill. Shake well again before serving. Makes 1 cup.

CREOLE FRENCH DRESSING

6 tablespoons salad oil
¼ cup ketchup
½ teaspoon Worcestershire sauce
1 tablespoon vinegar
1 tablespoon lemon juice

4 drops Tabasco sauce
1 teaspoon salt
1 teaspoon sugar
¼ teaspoon pepper
¼ teaspoon dry mustard

Measure ingredients into jar in order given. Cover and shake well. Chill. Shake well again before serving. Makes about 1 cup.

SAVORY HONEY FRENCH DRESSING

½ cup salad oil
¼ cup honey
1 tablespoon salt
1 teaspoon dry mustard

2 teaspoons paprika
¼ cup vinegar
2 tablespoons ketchup
2 tablespoons lemon juice

Blend honey with dry ingredients. Add ketchup, lemon juice, vinegar, and oil. Beat well with rotary beater.

REDUCERS' DRESSING

½ cup salad oil
¼ cup lemon juice
¼ cup water
½ teaspoon salt

¼ cup ketchup
1 teaspoon dry mustard
¼ teaspoon paprika
½ teaspoon Worcestershire sauce

Combine all ingredients. Beat with rotary beater until well mixed. Chill in covered jar. Shake well before serving. Yield: 1¼ cups.

EVAPORATED MILK DRESSING

½ cup sugar
⅓ cup vinegar

½ cup evaporated milk
½ teaspoon salt

Add sugar to vinegar. Stir until sugar is dissolved. Beat in milk until mixture thickens. Pour over salad. Use fork to blend dressing through salad ingredients.

Sour cream dressing: Use the following ingredients: ½ cup sour cream, ½ cup sugar, ⅓ cup vinegar, and ½ teaspoon salt. Mix as for *EVAPORATED MILK DRESSING*.

Vinegar dressing: Use the following ingredients: ⅓ cup vinegar, ½ cup sugar, 3 tablespoons water, and ½ teaspoon salt. Mix as for *EVAPORATED MILK DRESSING*.

VINAIGRETTE DRESSING

1 teaspoon salt
1 teaspoon sugar
¼ teaspoon pepper
Paprika

¾ cup salad oil
2 tablespoons cider vinegar
2 tablespoons chopped dill pickle
1 teaspoon chopped parsley

Combine and mix salt, sugar, pepper, and paprika. Add oil, vinegar, pickle, and parsley. Beat vigorously with rotary beater.

ITALIAN DRESSING (Basic Recipe)

1 clove garlic
½ teaspoon dry mustard
½ teaspoon salt

4 tablespoons wine vinegar
½ cup olive oil

Cut garlic clove in half. Mix mustard, salt, garlic, and vinegar thoroughly. Add oil and stir until all ingredients are blended. Store in covered jar in cold place. Shake well just before using.

Gorgonzola cheese dressing: Crumble 2 ounces cheese. Add to dressing just before using.

Italian roquefort cheese dressing: Crumble 2 ounces cheese. Add to dressing just before using.

Other variations: Most of the variations of *FRENCH* or *COOKED DRESSING* may be used.

SIMPLE HONEY DRESSING

¼ cup lemon juice
½ cup honey

¼ teaspoon salt
3 tablespoons crushed pineapple

Mix lemon juice and honey. Add salt and crushed pineapple.

WHIPPED CREAM DRESSING (Basic Recipe)

½ cup whipping cream
¼ teaspoon salt

2 tablespoons lemon juice or vinegar
Few grains pepper

Beat cream until stiff. Fold in other ingredients very slowly. Chill and add to salad just before serving. Whipped cream dressing may be used as a sweet or savory dressing by the addition of flavorings and seasonings. It may be delicately tinted with a very small amount of liquid or paste coloring.

Anchovy cream dressing: Add 3 anchovy filets, washed, dried, and minced fine, with 1 teaspoon lemon rind to 1 cup whipped cream dressing just before serving.

Caviar cream dressing: Add 1 tablespoon red or black caviar and a few drops onion juice to 1 cup whipped cream dressing just before serving.

Ginger cream dressing: Add 1 teaspoon chopped, candied ginger and 1 teaspoon grated lemon rind to 1 cup whipped cream dressing just before serving.

Gourmet cream dressing: Add ¼ teaspoon anchovy paste and a little minced parsley and chives to 1 cup whipped cream dressing just before serving.

Horseradish cream dressing: Fold 2 tablespoons grated fresh horseradish into 1 cup whipped cream dressing just before serving. Omit vinegar if bottled horseradish is used.

Jelly cream dressing: To 1 cup whipped cream dressing add ½ cup tart red jelly, such as currant, cranberry, or raspberry just before serving.

Mustard cream dressing: Beat in 1 tablespoon prepared mustard as cream begins to thicken. Add salt to taste.

Nut cream dressing: Add 3 tablespoons chopped nutmeats to 1 cup whipped cream dressing just before serving.

Oriental cream dressing: Add 1 tablespoon each chopped dates, figs, and raisins to 1 cup whipped cream dressing just before serving.

Pepper cream dressing: Add ⅓ cup minced green pepper and 2 tablespoons minced pimiento to 1 cup whipped cream dressing just before serving.

Savory cream dressing: Combine 1 tablespoon capers, well washed and finely minced, 1 tablespoon finely minced sweet-sour gherkins, and 1 teaspoon grated orange rind, and add to 1 cup whipped cream dressing just before serving.

SOUR CREAM DRESSING

½ cup sour cream
½ teaspoon salt
½ teaspoon sugar

½ tablespoon lemon juice
1 tablespoon vinegar
Few grains cayenne

The cream may or may not be whipped. Stir in seasonings gradually. If desired, add ¼ teaspoon celery seed.

Horseradish sour cream dressing: Add 1 to 2 tablespoons freshly grated or bottled horseradish to sour cream dressing. If bottled horseradish is used omit vinegar.

CHEESE DRESSING

Mix thoroughly 1 cup evaporated milk, 1 cup soft Roquefort or other nippy cheese, and salt to taste. Chill.

HONEY MERINGUE DRESSING

1 egg white
¼ cup honey

½ cup mayonnaise

Beat egg white until stiff. Add honey slowly, beating after each addition until honey is well blended. Continue beating until mixture is stiff and stands up in peaks. Fold into mayonnaise.

CRANBERRY SALAD DRESSING

Cream 1 package (3 ounces) cream cheese. Combine with 6 tablespoons cranberry sauce and 2 tablespoons mayonnaise. Fold in ½ cup heavy cream, whipped.

LEMON PEANUT SALAD DRESSING

Cream 2 tablespoons peanut butter. Combine with 2 tablespoons thick cream, 2 tablespoons lemon juice, ¼ teaspoon grated horseradish, ½ teaspoon powdered sugar, and ¼ teaspoon each paprika and salt. Beat until very light.

SHERBET DRESSING

Add ½ cup chopped minced pecans, almonds, walnuts, or pistachio nuts, to each ½ pint of lemon, orange, or pineapple sherbet.

FRUIT DRESSING

Beat 2 eggs with rotary beater until light. Combine ¾ cup sugar, ½ cup pineapple juice, and ⅓ cup lemon juice and stir into beaten eggs. Place on medium heat and stir constantly until thickened. Cool. Serve plain or fold in 1 cup cream, beaten stiff.

YOGHURT SALAD DRESSING

1 8-ounce carton yoghurt
1 teaspoon unsweetened lemon juice
2 to 3 teaspoons prepared mustard
¼ teaspoon onion salt
½ teaspoon liquid artificial sweetener

Combine ingredients in jar. Mix well. Cover and store in refrigerator. Serve with tossed greens or potato salad. Makes 1 cup.

Celery Seed Dressing: Add 1 teaspoon celery seed.

GREEN GODDESS DRESSING

1 cup mayonnaise
1 clove garlic, minced or grated
3 anchovies, chopped
¼ cup finely cut chives or green
  onions with tops
¼ cup chopped parsley
1 tablespoon tarragon vinegar
1 tablespoon fresh lemon juice
½ teaspoon salt
Pepper, coarsely ground
½ cup sour cream, whipped

Combine ingredients, folding in the whipped sour cream after the other ingredients have been blended. Makes 2 cups.

LOUIS DRESSING

½ cup chili sauce
½ cup mayonnaise or salad dressing
½ cup creamy French dressing
1 teaspoon Worcestershire sauce

Slowly stir chili sauce into mayonnaise. Add French dressing and Worcestershire sauce. Mix well. Serve with lettuce and tomato salads. Makes 1½ cups.

LORENZO DRESSING

½ cup French dressing
2 tablespoons chopped watercress
2 tablespoons chili sauce
1 teaspoon minced pimiento
1 teaspoon minced chives or onion

Blend ingredients thoroughly and serve over salad greens. Makes ¾ cup.

sandwiches

SANDWICH MAKING HINTS

Bread: A variety of breads and rolls may be used for sandwiches, including white, whole wheat, rye, raisin, nut, brown bread, gingerbread, soft buns, and crisp poppy seed rolls. To facilitate slicing and spreading of ordinary sandwiches use day-old bread. For rolled sandwiches use very fresh bread. For very thin, dainty sandwiches buy unsliced bread and cut with a razor-sharp knife into slices not more than ¼ inch thick. If many sandwiches are to be made sharpen knife frequently. For sandwiches without crust, cut the crust from the loaf before slicing. For fancy sandwiches to be cut with cooky cutter, slice the bread lengthwise.

Butter: Cream butter until softened before spreading. Never melt butter. To facilitate creaming keep butter at room temperature for about an hour. Butter prevents the sandwich from becoming soggy when a moist filling is used. For savory sandwiches soften butter with mayonnaise, for sweet sandwiches with a little cream or whipped cream.

Fillings: For additional sandwich fillings refer to spreads in the *APPETIZER* and *SALAD* sections. Use a variety of fillings for contrast in color, flavor, shape, and texture. Vegetables, such as cucumber, sliced tomato, and lettuce, should be prepared and added just before serving. Sliced fillings such as meat and cheese should be cut very thin and arranged to fit the sandwich. For color in fillings, add chopped pimiento, pepper, parsley, olives, or pickle.

To keep sandwiches: If possible, avoid making sandwiches with moist fillings in advance, since the bread tends to become soggy. If sandwiches must be made in advance, wrap in wax paper or slightly dampened cloth. To keep sandwiches for an hour or longer, wrap first in wax paper, then in a damp cloth, and place in refrigerator. To prevent an interchange of flavors from various fillings, wrap each variety of sandwich separately in wax paper. Ribbon, checkerboard, loaf, and other sandwiches, which have to be chilled or even frozen in the refrigerator, should always be well wrapped in wax paper to preserve the flavor and prevent drying out.

TEA SANDWICHES

Cut rounds from bread slices with a biscuit cutter. Spread rounds of bread with softened butter and top with cream cheese softened with honey. Over this spread red raspberry jam. Place a dot of cream cheese mixture or whipped cream in center.

Toasted tea sandwiches: Use rounds cut from bread as in above recipe. Toast until brown on both sides. Spread with honey butter. Sprinkle with chopped nuts. Place under broiler until nuts are slightly browned and serve while hot.

CHECKERBOARD SANDWICHES

Cut an unsliced white bread and an unsliced graham or whole-wheat bread in 3 slices lengthwise ½ inch thick. Remove crusts. Spread a slice of white bread with creamed butter or softened cream cheese and place a slice of graham on it. Spread this with creamed mixture. Place on it a slice of white bread, making dark bread the middle layer. Repeat this process beginning this time with a slice of dark so that a slice of white bread is the middle layer. Trim each pile evenly, and cut each pile into three 1-inch strips. Spread these strips with creamed mixture and put together in such a way that a white block will alternate with a dark one, forming a checkerboard at ends. There will be two checkered loaves. Wrap each loaf tightly in waxed paper and place in refrigerator. When ready to serve, slice about ¼ inch thick.

PINWHEEL SANDWICHES

Remove all crust from white and whole-wheat loaves of bread. Spread cut ends lengthwise with creamed butter or other soft filling, using contrasting colors for each. Cut a very thin slice from each loaf and put the two together. Spread top slice with filling and roll as for jelly roll. Fasten with toothpicks, wrap in wax paper, then in a damp cloth, place in refrigerator for about 1 hour. Just before serving, slice in ¼-inch slices.

RIBBON SANDWICHES

Spread creamed butter or other soft filling between slices of whole-wheat and white bread. Spread creamed butter or soft filling between each two sandwiches, alternating white and whole-wheat bread. Press firmly together. Wrap in wax paper, then with damp towel. Place in refrigerator under a light weight. Chill thoroughly. Remove crust and cut in thin slices.

LAYER SANDWICHES

Remove crust from a whole loaf of sandwich bread and slice the loaf lengthwise in ½-inch slices. A different filling may be used between each two slices or the same may be used throughout. Colored cream cheese makes the finished sandwich look like a slice of layer cake. Jam, peanut butter, chopped parsley in creamed butter and cheese may be used between the different layers if desired. Spread filling between each two slices and pile on top of each other. Wrap loaf in a damp towel and chill in refrigerator until firm, at least 2 hours. Just before serving, cut into thin slices. If loaf is to be sliced at the table, frost entire loaf with tinted cream cheese and decorate with rosettes of cream cheese, sliced stuffed olives, bits of pimiento, etc. Serve on platter and cut in thin slices.

NOISETTE SANDWICHES

Cut either graham or nut bread in thin slices, spread lightly with butter and then lightly with orange marmalade. Put two slices together, remove crusts and cut in triangles. Garnish each sandwich with a half pecan or walnut meat placed in the center of the top slice.

BLACK AND WHITE SANDWICHES

Spread a slice of white bread lightly with creamed butter to which chopped parsley or water cress and a few drops of lemon juice have been added. On top of this place a piece of whole-wheat or nut bread and press lightly together. Remove crusts and cut in finger-shaped pieces.

TART SANDWICHES

Cut one slice of bread with a doughnut cutter and a second with the same cutter, but with the hole removed. Butter the one slice lightly, place the other on top, and fill the hole with jam or jelly.

SALAD SANDWICHES

Slice a loaf of white bread lengthwise. Trim off crusts. Spread each slice with softened butter or a substitute. Place a large spoonful of salad (minced vegetable, chicken, Waldorf, etc.) near one end of each slice. Roll the slices lengthwise, just enough to hold the salad in place. Cover sandwiches with damp cloth for 5 to 10 minutes. To serve, garnish with pickles, olives, and radishes.

FRENCH TOASTED SANDWICHES

Make sandwiches of white bread. Any kind of filling may be used, but the following are especially good for this type of sandwich: cheese, peanut butter mixed with honey, minced olives, or any of the prepared sandwich spreads. Dip each sandwich into a milk and egg mixture made by combining 1½ cups milk, 1 well beaten egg, and ⅛ teaspoon salt. Fry the sandwiches in butter, letting them brown evenly at a moderate temperature. Serve hot. Garnish with broiled apricot or peach halves, with a spoonful of red jelly in each fruit half.

BRIDGE PARTY SANDWICHES

Spread thinly sliced bread with any desired sandwich filling. Cover with a second slice. Press together lightly. Cut out with cooky cutter in the form of hearts, diamonds, clubs, and spades. Garnish top with tiny pieces of pimiento cut in heart or diamond shapes with garnish cutter, or with ripe olives cut to form spades or clubs.

CORNUCOPIAS

Trim crusts from thin bread slices, forming perfect squares. Spread with soft butter. Fold edges to form cornucopias. Fasten with toothpicks. Place in shallow pan. Cover with damp cloth. Chill thoroughly. Fill with desired filling. Remove toothpicks before serving.

FROSTED SANDWICH LOAF

1 large loaf bread	½ green pepper, chopped
Mayonnaise and butter	1 cup grated raw carrots
1 small can salmon	½ cup chopped celery
3 tablespoons chopped pickle	¾ pound cream cheese
2 large tomatoes	1½ cups cream
Salt and pepper, to taste	

Remove crusts from bread. Cut into four slices lengthwise. Spread each slice with softened butter. Drain and flake salmon. Combine with chopped pickle, moisten with mayonnaise, and spread on first slice. Cover second slice of bread with sliced tomatoes. Season. Combine green pepper with mayonnaise. Spread over sliced tomatoes. Combine grated carrots and chopped celery. Season with salt and pepper, moisten with mayonnaise, and spread on third slice of bread. Put the four slices together, press into loaf shape, wrap tightly in wax paper. Chill. Spread top and sides with cream cheese softened with cream. Keep in refrigerator until ready to serve. Garnish with radish roses, parsley, carrot strips, stuffed olives, pimiento, etc. Cut into 1-inch-thick slices.

ASPARAGUS ROLLS

Cut fresh bread in very thin slices and remove crusts. Spread with mustard or mayonnaise. Roll each slice around an asparagus tip. Fasten with toothpicks. Place in shallow pan. Cover with damp cloth. Chill thoroughly. Remove toothpicks before serving.

CHEESE SANDWICH FILLINGS

Cottage cheese: Combine 1 cup well-seasoned cottage cheese, 1 cup finely chopped peanuts, ½ teaspoon salt, and 1 tablespoon mayonnaise.

Cottage cheese cucumber: Peel 1 large cucumber. Remove seeds. Grate or grind, mix with 1 tablespoon grated onion and ½ teaspoon salt, and put in a strainer. Let set over a bowl until just ready to make sandwiches. Mix well with 1 pint cottage cheese and dash of pepper. Additional salt to taste may be added. Makes 8 to 10 sandwiches.

Cottage cheese and green pepper: Cream until smooth ½ pound dry cottage cheese with ⅓ cup evaporated milk. Add 1 teaspoon salt, ⅛ teaspoon pepper, 3 tablespoons chopped green pepper, and 1 tablespoon minced onion. Mix well. Makes 5 sandwiches.

Cottage cheese olive pimiento: Mix creamed cottage cheese with chopped olives and chopped pimiento.

Cream cheese: Cream 1 3-ounce package cream cheese with 1 tablespoon mayonnaise. Spread on thin slices of bread or spread one slice of bread with filling, the other with jelly.

Cream cheese and carrot: Mix cream cheese with ⅓ as much grated raw carrot. Cover with watercress.

Savory grated cheese: Mix grated Parmesan or American cheese with onion juice, butter, and chopped parsley.

EGG SANDWICH FILLINGS

Deviled egg: Chop fine 3 hard-cooked eggs. Combine with 3 teaspoons chopped parsley, 3 teaspoons vinegar, ⅛ teaspoon dry mustard, ¼ teaspoon salt, and ⅛ teaspoon pepper.

Egg and anchovy: Cream yolks of hard-cooked eggs with butter and anchovy paste.

Egg and celery: Chop well 3 hard-cooked eggs. Season with salt and pepper. Mix with ½ cup finely chopped celery and mayonnaise or prepared sandwich spread. Makes 4 sandwiches.

Egg and frankfurter: Chop 2 hard-cooked eggs. Combine with 2 cooked frankfurters, ground, 1 cup finely cut celery, 1 teaspoon salt, and ⅓ cup salad dressing. Chill. Makes 1½ cups.

Eggs and ketchup: Moisten ground hard-cooked eggs with ketchup.

Eggs and liver: Combine 4 chopped, hard-cooked eggs with ½ cup minced cooked liver. Season with salt and pepper and prepared horseradish. Moisten with mayonnaise.

Eggs and spinach: Mix ground hard-cooked eggs with half the amount of spinach.

Egg and watercress: Mix chopped hard-cooked egg, watercress, and mayonnaise.

FISH SANDWICH FILLINGS

Flaked Fish #1: Combine 1 cup canned fish flakes, 1 tablespoon chopped celery, 1 tablespoon chopped pickle (sweet or sour), 3 tablespoons mayonnaise, ½ tablespoon horseradish, ¼ teaspoon salt, and ⅛ teaspoon pepper. Mix well.

Flaked fish #2: Mix flaked tuna with chopped celery and chopped nuts. Moisten with mayonnaise.

Flaked fish #3: Mix flaked tuna with chopped pickle and crushed pineapple. Moisten with French dressing.

Flaked fish #4: Combine 1 cup salmon, tuna, or other canned seafood with ½ cup chopped celery. Moisten with mayonnaise.

Sardine #1: Cream sardines with melted butter, flavored with salt, cayenne, and a generous amount of horseradish. Moisten with lemon juice.

Sardine #2: Combine 1 can of mashed drained sardines, ½ cup finely chopped peeled cucumber (seeds removed), and lemon juice to taste.

Sardine #3: Mix sardines with chopped hard-cooked eggs, grated cheese, butter and lemon juice. Season with curry powder.

Sardine and egg: Combine 1 can drained, mashed sardines and 2 chopped hard-cooked eggs. Moisten with lemon juice to taste.

Tuna and egg: Combine 1 cup flaked tuna, 2 chopped hard-cooked eggs, and ¼ cup chopped stuffed olives. Moisten with mayonnaise.

FRUIT AND VEGETABLE SANDWICH FILLINGS

Carrots with peanuts: Grind together finely ½ cup salted peanuts and 1 cup raw carrots. Combine with 3 tablespoons mayonnaise and ¼ teaspoon salt. Makes 4 sandwiches.

Carrots with raisins and peanuts: Grind together coarsely 1 cup raw carrots, 1 cup salted peanuts, and 1 cup seedless raisins. Add ½ teaspoon salt, 2 teaspoons lemon juice, 2 tablespoons mayonnaise. Mix well and store in refrigerator. Makes 10 sandwiches.

Celery and almonds: Mix chopped celery and chopped almonds. Moisten with mayonnaise.

Combination: Combine ½ cup seedless raisins, ½ cup shredded carrots, ½ cup cottage cheese, ⅛ teaspoon salt, and 1 tablespoon mayonnaise. Makes 4 sandwiches.

Cucumber and radishes: Slice cucumbers thin. Top with thinly sliced radishes. Moisten with mayonnaise.

Date and nut: Mix ground dates and chopped nuts. Moisten with orange juice.

Dried fruit and nut: Combine ½ cup finely chopped raisins, figs, and dates, ½ cup chopped nutmeats, ⅛ teaspoon salt, 5 teaspoons mayonnaise, and few drops lemon juice. Store in covered jar in refrigerator. Makes 4 sandwiches.

Raw vegetable: Mix together thoroughly 1 cup chopped raisins, ½ cup shredded cabbage, ½ cup shredded carrots, ½ cup chopped apple, 1 tablespoon lemon juice, and 4 tablespoons salad dressing. Makes 4 sandwiches.

MEAT AND POULTRY SANDWICH FILLINGS

Bologna and egg: Grind ½ pound bologna, mix with ¼ cup chopped pickles, ½ cup mayonnaise, ½ teaspoon minced onion, dash of Tabasco sauce, 2 tablespoons pickle juice, 3 chopped hard-cooked eggs, and ½ teaspoon salt. Makes 7 sandwiches.

Chicken and ripe olive #1: Combine 1 cup chopped chicken with ½ cup chopped celery and ¼ cup chopped ripe olives. Moisten with mayonnaise.

Chicken and ripe olive #2: Chop cold cooked chicken. Add chopped ripe olives. Moisten with mayonnaise.

Chicken or turkey: Moisten chopped, cooked chicken or turkey with mayonnaise or salad dressing. Season with salt and pepper. If desired, add finely chopped almonds.

Chopped meat: Mix together 1 cup chopped left-over meat, 2 chopped hard-cooked eggs, 1 teaspoon dry mustard, minced pickle. Moisten with mayonnaise. Makes 5 sandwiches.

Corned beef: Combine 1 cup chopped corned beef, ½ cup chopped celery, 1 tablespoon prepared mustard, and ¼ cup mayonnaise. Mix well.

Ground liver: Combine 1 cup ground, cooked liver, 1 teaspoon chopped pickle, 1 tablespoon pickle juice, 4 tablespoons mayonnaise, dash of Tabasco (optional), salt and pepper to taste. Mix thoroughly. Makes 5 sandwiches.

Meat loaf: Mix chopped cooked meat loaf with chili sauce.

Mock chicken: Combine 1 cup coarsely ground veal, ½ cup chopped or shredded raw carrots, ½ cup chopped celery, 2 tablespoons Chow Chow, 3 tablespoons mayonnaise, and salt to taste. Mix thoroughly. Makes 5 sandwiches.

Salami and egg: Combine chopped salami and hard-cooked egg. Top with sliced onion or tomato.

Tongue and olive: Combine 1 cup chopped cooked or canned tongue with ½ cup chopped stuffed olives. Moisten with mayonnaise or salad dressing.

HOT SANDWICHES

Baked beans and salami: Cut ¼ pound salami into small bits. Combine with 1½ cups canned baked beans with tomato sauce. Add 2 tablespoons each of chili sauce and prepared mustard and ½ teaspoon minced onion. Mash with a fork. Spread between slices of bread. Broil the sandwiches, turning to brown both sides.

Cranberry meat sandwich: Toast bread. Place a slice of broiled or roast meat on each slice of bread. Pour over gravy, if desired. Top with generous spoonful of hot cranberry sauce.

Grilled cheese sandwich: Toast bread on both sides under broiler. Butter one side of the toast. Cover with thin slices of sharp cheese. Place cheese under broiler so that it is about 5 inches from heat. Broil slowly until cheese is soft and melted. Serve hot.

Hot roast beef sandwiches: Make sandwiches with toasted bread and slices of roast beef. Serve on hot plates with hot gravy poured over the sandwiches. Garnish with a sprig of parsley and a pickle.

Salmon toastwiches: Spread softened butter on 10 slices white bread. Place 3 tablespoons salmon salad spread between each 2 slices. Combine 2 beaten eggs and ¼ cup milk. Dip each sandwich into egg-milk mixture, turning to coat both sides. Brown sandwich in hot fat in a skillet. Yield: 5 sandwiches.

Sautéed meat sandwiches: Moisten ground leftover meat with thick white sauce or gravy. Put between slices of bread. Brown on each side in hot fat.

Sautéed tomato and cheese: Spread slices of bread with nippy mayonnaise. Put a slice of tomato and a slice of American cheese between each 2 slices. Dip in an egg-milk mixture; fry as for French toast.

CHEESE BARBECUE

Grind together 1 pound cheddar cheese, ½ green pepper, 1 medium onion, 2 hard-cooked eggs, and 1 cup stuffed olives. Add ½ can tomato soup and 2 tablespoons melted butter. Mix well. Spread on bun halves or rye bread and broil.

CHEESEWICH

Cut day-old bread in ¼-inch slices. Cut thin slices of American cheese. Make sandwiches, seasoning with salt, paprika, and a light covering of mixed English mustard. Press sandwiches gently together and trim off crusts. Cut sandwiches in quarters or triangles. Melt some butter in frying pan. Fry sandwiches over very low heat until lightly browned, taking care in turning that they do not separate. Serve hot.

SOUFFLEED CHEESE SANDWICH

4 to 6 slices of bread	Dash of pepper
½ teaspoon salt	Dash of paprika
3 eggs, separated	½ cup grated sharp cheese

Toast bread (crust removed, if desired) on one side. Add salt to egg whites and beat until stiff, but not dry. Add pepper and paprika to yolks. Beat until light. Add cheese and fold into beaten egg whites. Heap on untoasted side of bread. Place on greased baking sheet. Bake in moderate oven (350°F.) for 15 minutes or until puffy and delicately browned. Serve at once. Yield: 4 to 6 sandwiches depending upon size of slice and thickness of egg mixture desired.

BARBECUE BURGERS

1 pound ground beef	2 tablespoons shortening
2 large onions, chopped	¼ cup ketchup
½ cup diced celery	1 cup canned tomatoes
1 cup sliced mushrooms	1 cup water

Fry meat, onions, celery, and mushrooms in hot fat until lightly browned. Add ketchup, tomatoes, and water. Season to taste with salt and pepper. If desired, 1 teaspoon chili powder may be added. Cover, and simmer 15 to 20 minutes. Add more water if necessary. Serve on hot toasted buns. Serves 6.

SALMON SANDWICH FONDUE

1 8-ounce can salmon	6 slices American Cheddar cheese
1 cup minced celery	3 beaten eggs
¼ cup mayonnaise	2½ cups milk
1 tablespoon prepared mustard	2 teaspoons Worcestershire sauce
¼ teaspoon salt	¼ teaspoon monosodium glutamate
12 thin slices whole wheat bread	(optional)

Drain salmon; flake, removing bones; add celery. Blend mayonnaise, mustard, and salt; add to salmon mixture; mix well. Spread between bread slices to make 6 sandwiches. Arrange sandwiches in shallow baking dish; top each with slice of cheese. Combine eggs, milk, Worcestershire sauce, and monosodium glutamate. Pour over sandwiches. Bake in slow oven (325°F.) 45 minutes. Makes 6 sandwiches.

FRENCH-TOASTED TUNA CHEESE SANDWICHES

1 7-ounce can tuna flakes	6 slices American cheese
1 teaspoon lemon juice	2 eggs, beaten
½ cup diced celery	½ teaspoon salt
3 tablespoons mayonnaise	1 cup milk
4 tablespoons butter or margarine	2 tablespoons butter or margarine
12 slices bread	

Combine tuna flakes, lemon juice, celery, and mayonnaise. Butter slices of bread on one side; spread 6 buttered slices with tuna mixture. Top each with a slice of cheese and place remaining slices on top; chill. Combine eggs, salt, and milk; stir to blend. Dip each sandwich in mixture to coat both sides. Melt butter in frying pan or on griddle over medium heat and lightly brown sandwiches on both sides, turning only once. Serve immediately. Serves 6.

sauces for desserts

BANANA SAUCE

1 tablespoon butter
1 tablespoon flour
¼ cup sugar
½ cup milk, scalded

1 egg yolk
1 banana, well mashed
½ cup heavy cream, whipped
    with a few grains salt

Cream butter. Add flour. Blend thoroughly, then add sugar gradually. Combine with scalded milk. Cook until thickened, stirring constantly. Add egg yolk, slightly beaten. Cook 3 minutes. Remove from heat. Add banana. Chill. Fold in whipped cream. Yield: about 1½ cups.

Variations: Substitute berries and other fresh or canned fruits for banana.

BRANDY SAUCE

⅓ cup sugar
½ tablespoon cornstarch
⅛ teaspoon salt

1 cup hot water
1 tablespoon butter
1 tablespoon brandy

Combine sugar, cornstarch, and salt in a saucepan. Add hot water slowly. Cook until clear, stirring constantly. Add butter and flavoring. Serve hot over mince pie or steamed pudding. Yield: 1 cup.

BUTTERSCOTCH SAUCE #1

1 cup brown sugar
2 tablespoons cake flour
    Dash of cinnamon
¼ teaspoon salt

1 cup boiling water
2 tablespoons butter
½ teaspoon vanilla

Sift together brown sugar, flour, cinnamon, and ¼ teaspoon salt. Add to boiling water. Cook 5 minutes, stirring continuously. Beat in butter and vanilla. Serve hot on ice cream, custard, or pudding.

BUTTERSCOTCH SAUCE #2

½ cup butter
2⅔ cups brown sugar

1 tablespoon lemon juice
½ cup heavy cream

Combine all ingredients. Cook in double boiler 1 hour, stirring occasionally. Yield: 3 cups. Add toasted almonds to sauce if desired.

CARAMEL SAUCE #1

¼ cup butter, melted
1 cup brown sugar
1 tablespoon cornstarch

1 cup cold water
2 teaspoons vanilla

Combine butter, sugar, and cornstarch dissolved in water in top part of double boiler. Bring slowly to boiling point, stirring to blend. Remove from heat. Add vanilla. Cover until ready to serve. Should mixture congeal, place over low flame, heat slowly, then thin to desired consistency with hot water, beat with spoon until smooth.

Brandy, rum, or lemon caramel sauce: Vary caramel sauce by substituting 2 tablespoons of any of these flavorings for vanilla.

CARAMEL SAUCE #2

Melt 1 cup sugar in heavy frying pan over low heat until light brown in color. Remove from heat and slowly add 1 cup boiling water. Boil 10 minutes or until caramel is dissolved. Yield: about 1 cup sauce.

RICH CHOCOLATE SAUCE (Basic Recipe)

½ cup light corn syrup
1 cup sugar
1 cup water

3 squares unsweetened chocolate
1 teaspoon vanilla extract
1 cup evaporated milk

Cook syrup, sugar, and water to soft ball stage (236°F.). Remove from heat. Add chocolate and stir until melted. Add vanilla. Slowly add evaporated milk, stirring constantly. Cool. Serve hot or cold. Store in covered jar in refrigerator. For hot fudge, reheat in top part of double boiler. Yield: about 3 cups sauce.

Chocolate whipped cream sauce: Fold an equal part of whipped cream into chocolate sauce.

Mint chocolate sauce: Substitute 2 drops oil of peppermint for vanilla.

Mocha sauce: Substitute strong, fresh coffee for all or part of water.

Orange chocolate sauce: Substitute orange juice for half or all of water; add grated rind of 1 orange.

Rum or brandy chocolate sauce: Add 1 tablespoon rum or brandy.

HOT FUDGE SAUCE

1 square unsweetened chocolate
1 cup sugar
2 tablespoons light corn syrup
⅛ teaspoon salt

⅓ cup water
1 tablespoon butter
½ teaspoon vanilla

Combine chocolate, sugar, corn syrup, salt, and water in saucepan. Heat slowly until chocolate is melted and sugar is dissolved. Boil, stirring constantly, until a small amount forms a soft ball in cold water (230°F.). Add butter and vanilla. Serve hot over ice cream, puddings, or plain cake.

SPECIAL FUDGE SAUCE

1¼ cups cocoa
¾ cup sugar
½ teaspoon salt
1 tablespoon cornstarch

½ cup white corn syrup
½ cup milk
2 tablespoons butter
2 tablespoons vanilla

Mix dry ingredients, add corn syrup and milk and mix thoroughly. Cook 15 minutes over hot water, stirring until thickened. Add butter. Cool and add vanilla. Yield: about 3 cups.

CHERRY SAUCE

2 cups sweet cherries, fresh or
  canned (drained)
1 tablespoon sugar

¼ cup orange juice
¼ cup water or cherry juice

If fresh cherries are used, cook in water until tender. Press through a sieve. Add sugar and juices to puréed or whole fruit mixture and serve cold. More sugar may be added for tart fruit. Makes 2½ cups.

Variations: Pineapple, strawberries, raspberries, peaches, apricots, etc., may be treated in a similar fashion.

HOT SPICED CHERRY SAUCE

2½ cups (#2 can) pitted sour
  red cherries
½ cup sugar

2 2-inch sticks cinnamon
16 whole cloves
2 teaspoons cornstarch

Drain cherries and reserve syrup. Measure syrup and add enough water to make 1 cup. Add sugar and spices and bring to boiling point. Cook 10 minutes. Strain out spices. Blend a little hot syrup with cornstarch. Add to hot mixture. Cook until slightly thickened, about 10 minutes. Add cherries and heat. Serve hot. Serves 4.

COFFEE SAUCE

1 tablespoon butter or margarine
1 tablespoon strong coffee
⅛ teaspoon salt

½ cup sifted confectioners' sugar
½ teaspoon vanilla
¼ cup heavy cream, whipped

Cream butter until soft. Work in coffee, salt, sugar, and vanilla. Beat until mixture is smooth. Lightly fold in whipped cream. Shaved blanched pistachio nuts are a nice garnish with this sauce. Yield: about ¾ cup.

CUSTARD SAUCE (Basic Recipe)

1 pint milk
¼ cup sugar

3 egg yolks
½ teaspoon vanilla

Heat milk, sugar, and few grains salt in top part of double boiler. Beat egg yolks slightly, add some of the heated milk, pour back into remaining milk. Place over hot, not boiling, water. Cook, stirring contantly until custard coats spoon. Remove at once, add vanilla, place pan in bowl of cold water. Stir occasionally until cool. Yield: about 2 cups sauce.

Almond custard sauce: Omit vanilla. Add ½ teaspoon almond extract.

Brandy custard sauce: Omit vanilla. Add 2 to 3 tablespoons fruit brandy and a dash of nutmeg.

Chocolate custard sauce: Melt 1 square unsweetened chocolate. Blend with 3 tablespoons sugar and add with vanilla.

Marshmallow custard sauce: Cut up 6 marshmallows and fold in last, leaving sauce somewhat lumpy.

Rum custard sauce: Omit vanilla. Add 2 to 3 tablespoons rum.

HARD SAUCE (Basic Recipe)

⅓ cup butter	½ teaspoon vanilla
1 cup confectioners' sugar	1 tablespoon boiling water

Cream butter until soft. Gradually add sugar, creaming well. Mix in vanilla and water few drops at a time, beating until fluffy. Pile lightly in serving dish. Chill until cold, but not hard. Yield: about ¾ cup (4 to 6 servings).

Apricot hard sauce: Omit vanilla. Beat in ½ cup strained apricot pulp with the sugar. Add 1 teaspoon apricot brandy.

Banana hard sauce: Omit vanilla. Beat in ⅓ to ½ cup mashed bananas.

Berry hard sauce: Omit vanilla. Beat in ½ cup crushed berries.

Brandy or rum hard sauce: Substitute 2 tablespoons brandy or rum for vanilla.

Butterscotch hard sauce: Substitute ½ cup firmly packed brown sugar for confectioners' sugar. Add 1 teaspoon vanilla and 1 tablespoon light cream.

Cherry hard sauce: Substitute 2 tablespoons cherry syrup for vanilla. Add ½ cup drained chopped cherries.

Cream hard sauce: Add ¼ cup heavy cream. Beat in thoroughly.

Fluffy hard sauce: Fold in 1 stiffly beaten egg white. Add vanilla to taste.

Ginger hard sauce: Omit vanilla. Add 4 tablespoons chopped preserved ginger.

Lemon hard sauce: Substitute 1 teaspoon grated lemon rind and 1 teaspoon lemon juice for vanilla.

Orange hard sauce: Substitute 2 teaspoons grated orange rind and 1 tablespoon orange juice for vanilla.

Royal hard sauce: Omit vanilla. Add 2 tablespoons liqueur or fruit flavored cordial.

Whipped cream hard sauce: Fold in ¼ cup heavy cream, whipped.

Wine hard sauce: Add 1 to 3 tablespoons sherry, Madeira or port to hard sauce.

Yellow hard sauce: Add 1 beaten egg yolk. Use any desired flavoring.

HONEY SAUCE

2 teaspoons cornstarch	½ cup honey
2 tablespoons melted butter	

Add cornstarch to melted butter and stir until smooth. Add ½ cup of honey and cook 6 minutes. Yield: ¾ cup.

JELLY SAUCE

Stir a glass of jelly into ¼ cup hot water. Add 1 tablespoon butter and cook in a double boiler for a few minutes. Thicken slightly with cornstarch smoothly blended with a little water before it is added to mixture in double boiler.

LEMON SAUCE (Basic Recipe)

½ cup sugar	Juice of ½ lemon
1 tablespoon cornstarch	Grated rind of ½ lemon
⅛ teaspoon salt	⅛ teaspoon nutmeg (optional)
1 cup boiling water	1 tablespoon butter

Mix together sugar, cornstarch, and salt. Gradually add boiling water; bring to boil. Cook over low heat until thickened and clear, about 15 minutes. Stir in lemon juice and rind. Add nutmeg and butter. Serve hot over puddings and other desserts. Yield: about 1¼ cups sauce.

Fluffy lemon sauce: Just before removing from heat, quickly stir in 1 slightly beaten egg yolk and cook 1 minute, stirring constantly. Remove from heat and fold in 1 stiffly beaten egg white.

Orange lemon sauce: Substitute fresh or canned orange juice for water.

Pineapple lemon sauce: Substitute pineapple juice for water.

Lime sauce: Omit nutmeg; substitute juice and rind of 1 lime for lemon.

Whipped cream lemon sauce: Fold together equal parts of lemon sauce and whipped cream.

Corn syrup lemon sauce: Substitute ¾ cup corn syrup for sugar. Use only ½ cup water.

MARSHMALLOW SAUCE

¼ pound marshmallows	¼ cup boiling water
1 cup confectioners' sugar	

Cut marshmallows into pieces. Melt in top part of double boiler. Dissolve sugar in boiling water and add to marshmallows. Stir until thoroughly blended. This mixture may be folded into 1 beaten egg white, if desired. Yield: about 2 cups.

MELBA SAUCE

1 cup pulp and juice of raspberries	½ cup sugar
½ cup currant jelly	½ tablespoon cornstarch
	1 tablespoon cold water

Add jelly and sugar to raspberries. Bring to boiling point. Add cornstarch mixed with cold water. Cook, stirring constantly until mixture becomes thick and clear. Cool and strain. Yield: about 2 cups.

MOLASSES SAUCE

1 cup molasses	⅛ teaspoon salt
1 tablespoon lemon juice	1 egg
2 tablespoons butter	

Simmer molasses 15 minutes or until quite thick. Add lemon juice, butter, and salt and pour mixture over well-beaten egg, beating while pouring. Then cook 3 minutes in top part of double boiler, stirring constantly. Yield: about 1½ cups.

FOAMY ORANGE SAUCE

⅓ cup butter or margarine	1 egg, separated
1 cup confectioners' sugar	¼ cup orange juice

Cream butter until soft, beat in sugar gradually, then egg yolk and orange juice. Just before serving fold in stiffly beaten egg white. For variety flavor with 1 table-spoon brandy, or substitute sherry for orange juice. Whipped cream may also be folded into the mixture. Yield: about 1½ cups.

PINEAPPLE SAUCE

2 cups crushed pineapple	1 tablespoon butter
¼ cup sugar	¼ teaspoon salt
1 tablespoon cornstarch	

Drain juice from crushed pineapple. Mix cornstarch and sugar. Add to juice. Cook over direct heat until sauce thickens, stirring constantly. Add drained fruit, butter, and salt. Cook a few minutes longer. Serve hot or cold over cottage pudding or plain cake. Yield: about 2 cups.

RUM SAUCE

4 tablespoons butter	½ cup cream
1 cup brown sugar	⅛ teaspoon salt
2 egg yolks, well beaten	3 tablespoons rum

Cream together butter and sugar. Add egg yolks, cream, and salt. Cook over boiling water until creamy and thickened. Remove from heat. Cool, add rum. Yield: 1 cup.

SHERRY SAUCE

2 eggs, separated	3 tablespoons sherry
1 cup powdered sugar	

Beat yolks until thick. Gradually beat in ½ cup sugar. Beat egg whites until stiff and add ½ cup powdered sugar gradually, beating until sugar disappears. Fold into yolk mixture. Flavor with sherry. Yield: about 1½ cups.

STRAWBERRY SAUCE

⅓ cup butter	1 egg white
1 cup powdered sugar	⅔ cup strawberries

Cream butter, add sugar gradually, then egg white with berries. Beat until fruit is mashed. Yield: about 1½ cups.

Variations: Almost any variety of fresh fruit may be substituted for strawberries.

VANILLA DESSERT SAUCE (Basic Recipe)

½ cup sugar	1 egg yolk
1 tablespoon cornstarch	2 teaspoons vanilla
⅛ teaspoon salt	2 tablespoons butter
1 cup boiling water	1 egg white

Mix sugar, cornstarch, and salt. Gradually add hot water. Cook over moderate heat in saucepan until thick, stirring constantly, 6 to 7 minutes. Add egg yolk. Cook 1 to 2 minutes, then add flavoring and butter. Cool slightly. Fold in beaten egg white. Yield: about 1½ cups sauce.

Chocolate sauce: Add 1 square grated chocolate with hot water.

Lemon sauce: Add 2 tablespoons lemon juice and 1 teaspoon grated lemon rind to sauce. Omit vanilla.

Marshmallow sauce: Cut up 6 marshmallows. Fold in last, leaving sauce somewhat lumpy.

Nutmeg sauce: Add ½ to ¾ teaspoon nutmeg to sauce.

Raisin nut sauce: Add ½ cup raisins and nuts, diced, and 1 teaspoon orange rind to sauce.

ZABAGLIONE

4 egg yolks	½ cup Sherry, Marsala,
3 tablespoons sugar	or Madeira wine

Beat yolks until light and thick. Add sugar. Continue beating until thoroughly blended. Slowly beat in wine. Cook in top of double boiler over hot, not boiling, water. Beat constantly until mixture leaves sides of pan. Remove from heat and beat 1 minute more. Serve hot or cold in sherbet glasses as a dessert, or over chilled fruits as a sauce.

WHITE SUGAR SYRUP (Basic Recipe)

1 cup sugar	Few grains salt
⅓ cup water	

Stir ingredients over low flame until sugar is dissolved. Boil 3 to 5 minutes, or until syrup is of desired consistency. Serve hot or cold on pancakes, waffles, etc.

Brown sugar syrup: Substitute brown sugar for white.

Caramel flavoring: Stirring constantly, heat 1 cup dry granulated sugar in a deep heavy pan until dark brown liquid forms. Let cool slightly. Add 1 cup boiling water very slowly to syrup. Simmer until thick. Store in covered jar in cool place. Keeps indefinitely.

Caramel syrup: Add 1 teaspoon CARAMEL FLAVORING to brown or white syrup.

COFFEE SYRUP

1 cup strong coffee
1 cup sugar

1 teaspoon vanilla
Few grains salt

Cook coffee and sugar together 5 minutes, add vanilla and salt. Cool. Keep in covered jar to use as needed. Makes about 1 cup.

ALL-PURPOSE FRUIT DESSERT SAUCE

This recipe is called "all-purpose" because it has so many uses. It may be used by itself or combined with whipped cream and served over waffles, ice cream, puddings, custards, etc., and its ingredients are available at any season of the year.

2 cups dried apricots
1¼ cups water

1½ cups sugar
5 cups canned crushed pineapple

Cook apricots in water in a wide-bottomed pan until the fruit is pulpy and disintegrates readily when stirred with a wire whisk. Add sugar and stir until dissolved, then add crushed pineapple. Bring to a boil. Pour into jars and cover. Store in refrigerator. Makes about 8 cups.

FRUIT JUICE SAUCE

1 tablespoon cornstarch
1 cup sugar
½ cup boiling water

2 tablespoons lemon juice
1 cup fruit juice, fresh or canned

Mix cornstarch and sugar. Add boiling water and boil 5 minutes. Cool and add fruit juice. If sweetened juices are used, the sugar may be reduced as desired. Makes about 2½ cups.

Variations: Any type of juice (strawberry, raspberry, pineapple, grape, peach, rhubarb, etc.) may be used.

LOW CALORIE WHIPPED TOPPING
(Use Instead of Whipped Cream)

½ cup ice water
1 tablespoon lemon juice
1 teaspoon vanilla

½ cup nonfat dry milk solids
3 tablespoons sugar

Put water, lemon juice, and vanilla in a bowl. Sprinkle dry milk on top. Beat until stiff with electric mixer or rotary beater, about 10 minutes. Beat in sugar; continue beating until stiff enough to hold soft peaks, about 5 minutes longer. Makes about 2½ cups.

Coffee Topping: Add 1 teaspoon instant coffee with vanilla.

sauces

SAUCES FOR FISH, MEAT, POULTRY AND VEGETABLES

The delightful finishing touch that distinguishes just an average cook from a master is the sauce. The choice of the right sauce will enhance a food and create new dishes out of old familiar recipes.

WHITE SAUCE (Basic Recipe)

	Butter or fat	Flour	Salt	Milk, cream, or stock
Thin:	1 tablespoon	1 tablespoon	¼ teaspoon	1 cup
Medium:	2 tablespoons	2 tablespoons	¼ teaspoon	1 cup
Thick:	3 tablespoons	3 to 4 table-spoons	¼ teaspoon or more	1 cup

Use methods 1, 2 or 3. Approximate yield: 1 cup sauce.

Uses: THIN SAUCE: Use as base for cream soups and other sauces.
MEDIUM SAUCE: Use for creamed and scalloped dishes, and gravies.
Stock may be substituted for milk in meat gravies.
THICK SAUCE: Use for croquettes and soufflés.

Method #1: Melt fat, stir in flour and salt. Cook until mixture bubbles. Remove from stove, add liquid, and stir until smooth. Return to stove. Cook in double boiler or over low flame until mixture thickens, stirring constantly or not at all.

Method #2: Melt fat and remove from flame. Add flour and salt. Stir until smooth. Add liquid gradually, stirring constantly over a low flame until mixture thickens.

Method #3: Stir enough liquid into flour and salt to form a thin smooth paste. Scald remainder of liquid in double boiler. Add flour paste to hot liquid, stirring constantly until mixture thickens. Cover and cook 20 minutes longer. Stir in fat just before serving. To keep hot and prevent crust from forming over sauce, place over hot water and cover tightly.

Caper sauce: Add 3 to 4 tablespoons chopped capers and 1 teaspoon lemon juice to white sauce. Serve with fish.

Cheese sauce: Add ½ to 1 cup chopped or grated American cheese and a dash of Worcestershire sauce or paprika (optional) to white sauce. Stir over hot, not boiling, water until cheese is melted. Serve with fish, eggs, macaroni, or rice.

Cheese olive sauce: Omit salt. Add ½ to 1 cup chopped or grated American cheese and ½ cup sliced stuffed olives to white sauce. Stir over hot, not boiling, water until cheese is melted. Serve with macaroni, rice, or vegetables.

Cheese tomato sauce: Use ½ cup tomato juice or strained tomatoes and ½ cup milk in preparing sauce. Add ¼ cup grated American cheese to hot sauce. Stir until melted. Serve over cauliflower.

Creole sauce: Use tomato juice or strained tomatoes for the liquid. Sauté minced onion, chopped green pepper, and minced celery in the butter before flour is added.

Curry sauce: Add ¼ to ½ teaspoon curry powder with dry ingredients. Serve with chicken, lamb, rice, or fish.

Egg sauce: Add 2 chopped hard-cooked eggs to white sauce, additional salt, and a dash of paprika. Serve with fish.

Horseradish sauce: Add 2 to 4 tablespoons prepared drained horseradish, and ¼ to ½ teaspoon prepared mustard to white sauce. Serve with boiled beef or corned beef.

Mock hollandaise sauce: To ½ cup well-seasoned white sauce add equal amount of mayonnaise and enough lemon juice to sharpen. Serve on asparagus and other green vegetables.

Mushroom sauce: Add ½ to 1 cup sliced cooked or canned mushrooms to white sauce. Serve with chicken or vegetables.

Mustard sauce: Add 1 tablespoon prepared mustard to white sauce. Serve with fish or tongue.

Paprika sauce: Add ½ to 1 teaspoon paprika with dry ingredients. Season with ¼ teaspoon onion juice, if desired. Serve with noodles, macaroni, or chicken.

Parsley sauce: Add 3 to 4 tablespoons minced parsley to white sauce. Serve with fish or vegetables.

Pimiento sauce: Add ¼ cup chopped pimiento to white sauce. ¼ cup chopped green pepper may be added, if desired. Serve with fish or vegetables.

Wine egg sauce: To 1½ cups white sauce, add 1 teaspoon Worcestershire sauce, 4 chopped hard-cooked eggs, and 2 tablespoons white wine. Blend thoroughly and serve hot on fish.

Yellow sauce: Add a little cold water to a slightly beaten egg yolk, and stir slowly into the white sauce. Cook for a minute over hot water, stirring constantly. Serve over vegetables, meat, or poultry.

BARBECUE SAUCE

1 medium onion, chopped	2 tablespoons vinegar
2 tablespoons cooking fat	2 tablespoons brown sugar
2 tablespoons lemon juice	1 cup ketchup
1 cup water	2 tablespoons Worcestershire sauce
½ cup chopped celery	⅛ teaspoon pepper
½ teaspoon dry mustard	1 teaspoon salt

Brown onion in hot fat. Add remaining ingredients and simmer gently 20 to 30 minutes. Pour over meat before cooking or baste meat during roasting. Use over baked or broiled chicken, frankfurters, braised beef, steaks, hamburgers, etc. Yield: about 2 cups sauce.

BROWN SAUCE (Basic Recipe)

4 tablespoons butter or cooking fat	1 teaspoon salt
5 tablespoons flour	⅛ teaspoon pepper
2 cups meat, vegetable, or fish stock	

Melt fat, blend in flour, cook until browned, stirring constantly. Gradually add stock, stirring constantly until mixture boils and thickens. Add salt and pepper. Boil 3 minutes longer, stirring constantly. Serve with meat, poultry, fish, or vegetables. Makes 2 cups.

Creole brown sauce: Sauté ¼ cup chopped onion and ½ cup chopped green pepper in fat before adding flour.

Dill sauce: Add to brown sauce 2 tablespoons wine or cider vinegar and chopped dill to taste. Serve with veal or lamb.

Giblet gravy: Substitute pan drippings for other fat. Add chopped cooked chicken or turkey giblets to gravy.

Mushroom brown sauce: Sauté 1 cup sliced mushrooms and 1 teaspoon chopped onion in fat before adding flour.

Pan gravy: Substitute pan drippings for other fat. Use water or stock.

Piquant brown sauce: Simmer together for a few minutes 2 tablespoons each tarragon vinegar and finely chopped green pepper, 1 teaspoon each chopped onion and chopped capers. Add to sauce with 2 tablespoons chopped pickle. Serve with fish, beef, veal, or tongue. If used with fish, use fish stock.

Port wine sauce: To 1 cup of brown sauce add 2 tablespoons port wine. Simmer about 5 minutes.

Savory horseradish sauce: Add 3 to 4 tablespoons prepared horseradish and 1 tablespoon prepared mustard to brown sauce.

Spanish brown sauce: Sauté ¼ cup chopped onion, ½ cup chopped green pepper, ½ cup sliced mushrooms in fat before adding flour. Substitute 1 cup tomato juice or stewed tomatoes for 1 cup stock. Serve with rice, spaghetti, or meat balls.

BUTTER SAUCES

Anchovy butter sauce: Add 1 tablespoon anchovy paste to MAITRE D'HOTEL SAUCE with the lemon juice.

Horseradish butter sauce: Combine 2 to 3 tablespoons horseradish with ½ cup melted butter.

Lemon butter: Combine 2 to 3 tablespoons lemon juice with ½ cup melted butter. Add 1 tablespoon chopped parsley and a dash of paprika.

Lemon chive butter sauce: Combine 1 tablespoon chives and 2 tablespoons lemon juice with ½ cup melted butter.

Maitre d'hotel butter: Cream ½ cup butter. Add 1 tablespoon chopped parsley and gradually blend in 3 tablespoons lemon juice, ½ teaspoon salt, and ⅛ teaspoon pepper. Serve with broiled fish. Yield: ⅔ cup sauce.

Mint butter sauce: Combine 2 to 3 tablespoons finely chopped mint with ½ cup melted butter.

Parsley butter sauce: Combine 2 to 3 teaspoons finely chopped parsley with ½ cup melted butter. Add 1 teaspoon lemon juice, ½ teaspoon salt, and ⅛ teaspoon pepper.

CAPER SAUCE FOR FISH

¼ cup melted butter or margarine
Juice of ½ lemon
1 tablespoon minced parsley

1 tablespoon minced capers
Fresh ground black pepper
Salt

Combine ingredients. Serve with steamed or boiled fish. Yield: about ½ cup.

GINGERSNAP SAUCE

4 gingersnaps
½ cup brown sugar
4 tablespoons vinegar

1 cup water
Juice of 1 lemon
¼ cup seedless raisins

Crush gingersnaps. Add remaining ingredients. Cook mixture until smooth, 10 to 15 minutes, stirring frequently. Serve over meat balls, tongue, lamb, etc.

HOLLANDAISE SAUCE (Basic Recipe)

½ cup butter
4 egg yolks
2 tablespoons lemon juice

¼ teaspoon salt
Dash of cayenne
¼ cup boiling water

Divide butter into 3 portions. Beat together egg yolks and lemon juice. Add 1 piece of butter and cook in double boiler, stirring constantly until mixture begins to thicken. Remove from stove, add second piece of butter, and stir rapidly. Then add remaining butter and continue to stir until mixture is completely blended. Add salt, cayenne, and boiling water. Return to double boiler; cook until thickened, stirring constantly. Serve at once.

NOTE: Sauce may separate if cooked too long, or at too high a temperature, or if permitted to stand too long before serving. To smooth beat in 1 tablespoon boiling water and a little lemon juice drop by drop, with a rotary beater.

Bearnaise sauce: Reduce lemon juice to 1½ tablespoons. Add 1 teaspoon each chopped tarragon and chopped parsley, 1 tablespoon tarragon vinegar, and 1 teaspoon onion juice or ½ teaspoon onion salt. Serve with baked or broiled fish.

Chive hollandaise sauce: Add 1½ tablespoons finely chopped chives to sauce. Serve with vegetables.

Cucumber hollandaise sauce: Add 1 cup drained, chopped cucumber to sauce. Serve with fish.

Dill hollandaise sauce: Add 1 tablespoon dill to sauce.

Mint hollandaise sauce: Add 1 tablespoon finely chopped mint to sauce.

EASY HOLLANDAISE

1 cup butter or margarine
2 eggs
¼ cup lemon juice

½ teaspoon salt
Few grains cayenne

Melt butter over hot water. Beat in remaining ingredients with rotary beater. Continue beating until thick. Remove at once from hot water. Yield: 1½ cups.

HOME PREPARED HORSERADISH

Wash horseradish root, scrape or cut off thick peel. Grate. Mix well with enough white vinegar to cover. Add sugar to taste and cover tightly to keep in strength.

With mayonnaise: Mix ¼ cup horseradish with 1 cup mayonnaise.

With russel: Wash, peel, and grate horseradish root. Mix with enough russel to cover and add sugar, to taste, and cover tightly.

With sour apples: Add grated sour apples and a few ground almonds to plain horseradish.

LEMON SAUCE FOR FISH

2 cups hot fish stock
Juice of 2 lemons
¼ cup chopped blanched almonds

3 egg yolks, beaten
Sugar to taste

Mix lemon juice, almonds, and fish stock. Cook over boiling water 15 minutes. Add a little cold water to the beaten egg yolks and stir slowly into the sauce. Serve at once, hot.

MINT SAUCE

2 to 3 tablespoons sugar
¼ cup hot water
½ cup mild vinegar

½ cup chopped fresh mint leaves
3 tablespoons lemon juice
½ teaspoon salt

Dissolve sugar in water. Add vinegar. Bring to boil. Pour over fresh mint leaves. Add lemon juice and salt. Let stand ½ to 1 hour before straining and serving with lamb. Makes about 1 cup sauce.

SPAGHETTI SAUCE

¼ cup diced onion
1 clove finely diced garlic
4 tablespoons olive oil
1 No. 2½ can Italian or American style tomatoes
1 chopped basil
¼ cup chopped parsley
2 crushed peppercorns

2 teaspoons salt
¼ teaspoon pepper
½ pound chopped lean beef
4 tablespoons olive oil
1 6-ounce can Italian style tomato paste
Mushrooms (optional)

Sauté onion and garlic slowly in olive oil. Put tomatoes through a food strainer and discard seeds. Add basil, parsley, peppercorns, salt, pepper, and tomatoes.

Simmer 30 minutes. Sauté beef and mushrooms in remaining olive oil in frying pan. Add beef and tomato paste to first mixture. Simmer 15 minutes more. Pour sauce over spaghetti. Serves 6 with 1 pound of spaghetti.

SPANISH SAUCE

1 tablespoon minced onion
1 tablespoon chopped green pepper
¼ cup sliced mushrooms
2 tablespoons cooking fat

2 cups canned tomatoes
½ teaspoon salt
½ teaspoon chili powder

Sauté onion, green pepper, and mushrooms in hot fat over low heat about 5 minutes. Add remaining ingredients and simmer until thickened. Yield: about 1½ cups sauce.

SWEET AND SOUR SAUCE #1

2 tablespoons vegetable oil
2 tablespoons flour
1 cup stock
½ teaspoon salt

⅛ teaspoon pepper
2 tablespoons brown sugar
Juice of 2 lemons

Heat oil. Blend in flour. Add stock gradually. Season with salt and pepper. Boil 5 minutes. Add sugar and lemon juice and cook 1 minute longer. Serve hot with vegetables or meat.

SWEET AND SOUR SAUCE #2

½ cup sugar
1 tablespoon flour
1½ cups boiling stock
¼ cup vinegar

½ teaspoon salt
⅛ teaspoon pepper
½ teaspoon paprika

Melt sugar in a pan and blend in flour. Very gradually add boiling stock. Stir in vinegar, salt, pepper, and paprika. Simmer 5 minutes. Serve hot.

TARTAR SAUCE

1 teaspoon minced onion
1 teaspoon chopped green olives
1 teaspoon chopped sweet pickle
1 tablespoon minced parsley

1 tablespoon minced capers
¾ cup mayonnaise
1 tablespoon tarragon vinegar

Drain first 5 ingredients thoroughly. Fold into mayonnaise. Add vinegar. Mix well. Chill. Serve with fish.

TOMATO SAUCE (Basic Recipe)

2 cups canned tomatoes
2 slices onion
1 teaspoon sugar
1 bay leaf
2 whole allspice

2 whole cloves
Flour
Butter or other fat
Salt and pepper

Simmer tomato, onion, sugar, and spices 10 minutes. Strain through fine sieve and measure the liquid. For each cup liquid blend 2 tablespoons flour and 2 tablespoons melted fat. Add to tomato juice with salt and pepper to season, and stir until thickened. Continue to cook over hot water 5 to 10 minutes. Serve hot over croquettes, meat loaf, or spaghetti.

Tomato cheese sauce: Add ½ cup grated cheese to tomato sauce. Cook until cheese is melted.

Tomato meat sauce: Brown tiny meat balls in fat before blending in flour. Serve with spaghetti or noodles in casserole.

Tomato wine sauce: Add ¼ cup sherry to tomato sauce.

SOUR CREAM SAUCE

2 egg yolks
¾ cup sour cream
1 tablespoon lemon juice

½ teaspoon minced parsley
⅛ teaspoon salt
¼ teaspoon paprika

Beat egg yolks and cream together in top part of double boiler. Place over simmering water and cook, stirring constantly, until mixture is of custard consistency. Remove from heat and add remaining ingredients. Serve at once with vegetables or fish.

BLENDER HOLLANDAISE SAUCE

½ cup butter
3 egg yolks (at room temperature)
2 tablespoons lemon juice

¼ teaspoon salt
Pinch of cayenne

Heat butter to bubbling but do not brown. Combine in the blender the egg yolks, lemon juice, salt, and cayenne. Blend these ingredients at low speed for a few seconds. Add hot butter gradually and blend a few seconds longer until the sauce is smooth and thickened. Makes about 1 cup.

FRENCH BUTTER PECAN SAUCE

½ cup butter, melted
2 tablespoons chopped chives
½ teaspoon salt
¼ teaspoon pepper

¼ teaspoon marjoram
2 to 4 tablespoons lemon juice
½ cup chopped pecans

Combine all ingredients; heat to blend flavors. Serve over cooked vegetables. Makes 1 cup or enough to sauce 4 10-ounce packages frozen vegetables.

SOUR CREAM-CUCUMBER SAUCE

½ cup thick sour cream
1 cup diced, unpeeled cucumber

½ teaspoon salt
4 drops onion juice

Whip sour cream until smooth; add cucumber, salt, and onion juice. Serve with fish. Makes 1¼ cups.

ALMOND BUTTER FOR VEGETABLES

To ¼ cup melted butter or margarine, add 2 tablespoons chopped salted almonds and 1 tablespoon lemon juice. Serve over green beans, Brussels sprouts, or broccoli.

soups

There are innumerable ways to vary soups and there are many enticing names but, basically, soups are divided into just a few groups. Soups made from white stock have veal or poultry as a base. Soups made from brown stock have dark meats as a base. Bouillon is a clear soup made from beef stock. Consommé is made from beef, chicken, veal, and vegetables. Chowders are thick soups made from fish, meat, and vegetables. Broth is the liquid resulting from meat which has been simmered slowly in water. The cream soups (purées and bisques) contain both milk and butter, as well as the vegetables after which they are named.

Soups should be an important part of any low-cost menus, not only because they are highly nutritious, but because to delicious soups may be added food ingredients which the average housewife may normally discard. The water in which meats, fish, and vegetables are simmered, as well as the liquids from canned vegetables, contain much of the precious vitamins and minerals and should be used as a liquid in the preparation of soups. They can be saved and stored in the refrigerator for future use. Scraps of raw or cooked vegetables, fish, meats, and bones should be used in soups together with the addition of the lower-priced cuts of meats. Inexpensive meat cuts have essentially the same nutritive values as the higher priced cuts. To obtain the full flavor from such soups, always simmer or boil these soups in closely covered kettles. A helpful hint to keep in mind is that soups made from these leftover ingredients may very often be improved with the addition of a can of prepared soup. Finally, remember that a little experimentation in combining various canned soups will result in many interesting soups with a minimum of effort.

BROWN SOUP STOCK (Basic Recipe)

4 to 5 pounds beef knuckle	3 quarts cold water
½ cup diced carrots	½ cup diced celery and leaves
½ cup onion diced	½ cup diced turnip
1 tablespoon salt	4 whole cloves
2 sprigs of parsley	1 bay leaf
6 to 8 peppercorns	¼ teaspoon marjoram

Cut meat into small pieces. Brown ½ of meat in marrow of bone or in 2 tablespoons fat. Add with remaining meat and bone to cold water. Heat to boiling. Simmer about 3 hours. Add vegetables and other ingredients; cook ½ to 1 hour longer. Strain and keep in cold place.

To clarify stock: Remove all fat from cold stock. Combine egg white and crushed shell of one egg with ¼ cup cold water. Add to cold stock and heat slowly to boiling. Remove from heat. Allow to stand 5 minutes then strain through double thickness of cheesecloth or fine wire strainer. When soup is too salty, add few pieces of raw potato while simmering and allow to cook for a few minutes. Remove potato.

Bouillon: Prepare brown stock. Cool, remove fat, heat, and clear.

Consommé: Substitute 2 pounds lean beef and 1½ to 2 pounds veal knuckle for beef knuckle. Chicken stock or chicken bones may be added.

Lamb or mutton stock: Substitute 4 to 5 pounds of lamb or mutton for beef. Do not brown. Remove any excess fat from meat before cooking.

White stock: Substitute 4 to 5 pounds knuckle of veal or fowl or combination of both for beef. Do not brown meat. Cover with cold water and proceed as directed. Marjoram may be omitted.

SOUPS FROM STOCKS

Barley soup: Soak ½ cup pearl barley for several hours. Cook in 1½ quarts of water until tender. Add 1½ quarts of any stock.

Julienne soup: To 1 quart of brown or white stock cut into long strips and add 2 small carrots, 1 small turnip, ¼ cup string beans, ¼ cup canned peas, and 1 tablespoon minced onion. Cook slowly until vegetables are tender.

Noodle soup: Add 1 cup cooked noodles to 1 quart desired stock.

Rice soup: Add 1 to 2 cups cooked rice to 1 quart desired stock.

Jellied consommé or bouillon: Add 2 tablespoons plain gelatin soaked in ½ cup cold water to 1 quart of consommé. Chill until firm and pile by spoonfuls in bouillon cups.

Consommé jardiniere: Cut vegetables into fancy shapes with vegetable cutters. Cook and serve in the hot consommé, allowing about 1 cup vegetables to 1 quart stock.

Consommé macedoine: Add cubed cooked vegetables in various colors to stock and reheat.

Consommé princess: Serve consommé with shredded chicken and new green peas.

Macaroni soup: Add cooked macaroni cut in small pieces to stock and reheat.

CHICKEN SOUP

1 fowl (4 or 5 pounds)	2 sprigs parsley
3 quarts cold water	1 small bay leaf
1 carrot, sliced	1 tablespoon salt
2 stalks celery	¼ teaspoon pepper

Cut fowl into pieces. Place in kettle with cold water. Cover and bring slowly to a boil. Add seasonings and vegetables. Simmer gently about 3 hours. Strain, chill, and remove fat. Strain again.

Chicken noodle soup: Heat 4 cups of chicken soup in top of double boiler. Add 1½ cups noodles and cook until noodles are tender, about 30 minutes. Serves 6.

Chicken rice soup: Follow same procedure as for chicken noodle soup, adding 1 cup rice instead of noodles. Cook until rice is fluffy, about 40 minutes.

BEEF NOODLE SOUP

2 to 3 pounds lean beef
1 soup or marrow bone
2½ quarts cold water
Salt and pepper
1 cup canned tomatoes
2 stalks celery
2 small onions

2 potatoes, diced
4 carrots
1 parsley root
3 sprigs parsley
1 parsnip
¼ cup lima beans
2 cups cooked noodles

Place meat in large pot. Add water, salt, and pepper. Bring to a boil and skim thoroughly. Add tomatoes, celery (cut in short lengths), onions, potatoes, carrots, parsley, parsley root, parsnip, and lima beans. Simmer until meat is tender, 2 to 3 hours. Add noodles and bring to boil. Serve immediately. Serves 8.

HOT BEEF BORSHT

8 medium beets
4 onions
2 pounds fat brisket of beef

About 2 tablespoons sugar
Juice of 2 lemons
Salt and pepper, to taste

Use dark red young beets. Wash, scrape, and grate. Simmer slowly with beef and onions in 2 quarts of water until meat is tender. Remove meat. Add sugar and lemon juice to taste to make the soup sweet and sour. Continue cooking 15 minutes. Season with salt and pepper. Serve hot.

COLD BEEF BORSHT

2 bunches young beets
2 quarts water
Salt and pepper, to taste

Juice of 1 lemon
Sugar to taste
2 eggs

Use dark red beets. Wash, peel, and grate. Add to water with salt and pepper, to taste. Cook until tender. Add lemon juice and about 1 tablespoon sugar. Cool. Soup should have distinctly sweet-sour taste. Since beets vary in sugar content, amount of seasonings is added accordingly. Beat eggs slightly and blend slowly with cooled borsht. May be served hot or ice cold topped with a tablespoon of sour cream. Sliced hard cooked eggs and chopped cucumber are also used as a garnish. A small sprig of fresh dill added to beets while cooking enhances flavor. If desired, serve with hot boiled potatoes.

SCHAV BORSHT (Sorrel or Sourgrass)

1 pound schav (sorrel)
1 quart water
1 small onion, chopped
½ teaspoon salt

2 tablespoons sugar
Juice of 2 lemons
2 egg yolks or sour cream

Wash leaves well, rinsing in several waters. Drain and chop fine. Add water and salt. Bring to boil. Add onion and simmer 15 minutes. Add sugar and lemon juice to taste. Simmer 5 minutes. Remove from heat. Cool, place in refrigerator. Thicken with beaten egg yolks or sour cream just before serving. Serves 4 to 5.

Spinach borsht: Substitute cleaned, chopped spinach for sorrel.

Spinach rhubarb borsht: Use 1 to 2 cups diced rhubarb for each pound of spinach. Cook the rhubarb in just enough water to cover and add to spinach borsht during last 5 minutes of cooking.

CABBAGE BORSHT

2 pounds soup meat
1 soup bone
1 onion
2 cups stewed or fresh tomatoes
6 cups cold water

1 head cabbage, shredded
½ cup raisins
Salt and pepper
Sugar and lemon juice

Add meat, bone, onion, and tomatoes to water in large kettle. Cover. Simmer gently 2 hours. Salt shredded cabbage thoroughly. Drench with hot water, chill with cold, drain, and add with raisins to soup. Simmer, covered, 30 minutes longer, or until meat and cabbage are tender. Season with salt and pepper. Add sugar and lemon juice to taste and simmer 15 minutes longer. Serve hot. Serves 6.

MEATLESS LENTIL SOUP

2 cups lentils
1 onion, diced
2 tablespoons cooking fat
1 carrot, diced
3 stalks celery, diced

1 teaspoon salt
¼ teaspoon pepper
2 quarts hot water
Minced parsley

Soak lentils overnight in cold water to cover. Drain and add diced onion browned in fat. Stir over fire 5 minutes. Add carrot, celery, salt, and pepper and 2 quarts hot water. Simmer slowly until lentils are tender, about 45 minutes. Rub through a sieve. Bring to boil and serve hot garnished with parsley. Serves 6 to 8.

Lentil and barley soup: Add ½ cup barley with the lentils.

Lentil soup with frankfurters: Slice frankfurters into pieces about ½ inch thick. Cook in a few cups of soup stock. Serve soup with sliced frankfurters.

Lentil soup with meat: Add soup bone and 1½ to 2 pounds soup meat. Simmer until meat is tender.

CHOLENT

3 to 4 pounds beef
1 pound dried lima beans
3 large onions, sliced
¼ cup chicken fat
Salt, pepper, and paprika
1 small clove garlic

3 pounds medium potatoes, peeled
A piece of bay leaf
2 tablespoons flour
⅛ teaspoon ginger (optional)
Boiling water to cover

For the meat use flanken, brisket, or short ribs. Soak beans overnight. Drain. Brown onions in hot fat in a heavy pot tightly covered. Remove onions. Rub meat with salt, pepper, paprika, and garlic. Brown in the hot fat. Add all ingredients, lastly sprinkling with flour. Add boiling water to cover. Cover tightly and bring to boil. To finish cooking place in a hot oven (400°F.) for about ½ hour. Then turn to very slow heat (250°F.) and cook overnight and until noon of the next day. If this method isn't practical, instead cook 3 to 4 hours over a low flame. If necessary, add a little water and place the pot on an asbestos pad over a very low flame and keep hot until the next day. Cholent should not be stirred while cooking.

NOTE: If available, the most practical way to cook cholent is in a small top-of-the-range oven.

Bean and barley cholent: Omit potatoes. Add 1 cup barley.

With kneidlach: Add several medium sized dumplings to cholent just before placing in oven or on asbestos pad.

MEATLESS VEGETABLE SOUP

1 large onion, minced	2 teaspoons chopped parsley
4 tablespoons butter	1 parsley root, diced
½ cup carrots, diced	1 parsnip, diced
⅓ cup cabbage, shredded	1½ cups diced potatoes
½ cup peas	6 cups boiling water
¼ cup string beans, diced	1 teaspoon sugar
¼ cup celery, diced	2 teaspoons salt
⅓ cup whole kernel corn	1 cup canned tomatoes

Sauté onion in melted butter in a large pot until transparent. Add remaining vegetables, except potatoes and tomatoes, and cook 10 minutes, stirring constantly. Add potatoes, water, seasonings, and tomatoes. Simmer until vegetables are tender. Serve hot. Serves 6 to 8.

MEATLESS TOMATO AND RICE SOUP

1 onion, chopped	1 tablespoon sugar
¼ cup diced celery	¼ cup cold water
1 tablespoon cooking fat	1 tablespoon flour
4 cups canned tomatoes	1 cup cooked rice
1 cup water	3 sprigs parsley, chopped
Salt and pepper	

Sauté onion and celery in fat in a soup pot until soft and slightly yellow. Add tomatoes, water, salt, pepper, and sugar. Cover and simmer 30 minutes. Press through sieve. Make a paste of cold water and flour, add small amount of hot soup, mix well, and combine with remaining soup, stirring until well blended. Simmer 15 minutes longer. Add cooked rice and reheat. Serve garnished with chopped parsley. Serves 4 to 6.

Tomato and rice soup (with meat): Add a soup bone and 1½ to 2 pounds soup meat when adding tomatoes. Do not fry onion and celery. Serve soup unstrained. Simmer soup until meat is tender. Meat may be sliced and served with horseradish.

MEATLESS SPLIT PEA SOUP

2 cups split peas
6 cups cold water
1 potato, diced
3 sprigs parsley, diced
1 parsnip, diced
1 large celery root, diced

1 small onion, diced
1 carrot, diced
1 small clove garlic
1 parsley root, diced
Salt and pepper
½ cup egg barley (farfel)

Pick over peas and wash thoroughly. Soak in cold water several hours. Add additional water to make up the 6 cups and bring to boiling point. Add remaining ingredients except egg barley. Simmer 2 hours, stirring occasionally. Remove garlic. Rub through sieve and add egg barley. Simmer 45 minutes longer. If desired, serve with croutons and omit egg barley. Serves 6.

MINESTRONE

1 cup navy beans
2 quarts water
¼ cup olive oil
1 cup diced celery
1 tablespoon minced onion
2 tablespoons minced parsley

2 cups canned tomatoes
1 clove minced garlic
2 cups shredded cabbage
1 tablespoon salt
½ cup elbow macaroni
¼ teaspoon pepper

Soak beans overnight. Heat olive oil in soup pot. Add celery, onion, parsley and garlic. Sauté lightly. Add remaining ingredients and simmer 2 to 3 hours. Serve sprinkled with grated Parmesan cheese. Serves 6 to 8.

CONSOMME MADRILENE

2 tablespoons plain gelatin
5 cups beef stock
3 tablespoons tomato paste
2 tomatoes, sliced (skins on)
¼ cup red wine

2 tablespoons tarragon vinegar
1 bay leaf
1 teaspoon salt
6 peppercorns
3 egg whites

Add gelatin to 1 cup stock and let stand 5 minutes. Add to remaining stock with tomato paste, sliced tomatoes, red wine, vinegar, bay leaf, salt, and peppercorns. Beat egg whites until stiff but not dry. Add to soup. Heat to boiling, stirring constantly, over low heat. Remove from heat. Let stand 10 minutes. Pour through a damp cloth. Chill until slightly thickened. Garnish with finely shredded tomato and chopped fresh mint. Serves 6.

QUICK CORN CHOWDER (Basic Recipe)

1 medium onion, chopped fine
3 tablespoons cooking fat
3 cups boiling water
3 medium sized potatoes, cubed

Dash of pepper
1½ teaspoons salt
1½ cups canned corn
3 cups scalded milk

Sauté onions in fat until lightly browned. Add boiling water, potatoes, and seasonings. Cook until potatoes are tender, about 15 minutes. Add corn and milk. Heat to boiling point, but do not boil. Serves 6.

Bean chowder: Substitute 1½ cups canned lima beans for corn and diced carrots for potatoes.

Fish chowder: Substitute 1½ pounds fish (haddock or cod) for corn. Add fish with potatoes and cook until both are tender. Then add milk, heat, and serve. Additional fish bones or heads may be used, if desired.

Potato soup: Omit corn. Cook 2 tablespoons chopped celery leaves with potatoes. Garnish each serving with a little butter and dash of paprika.

With dried beans: Soak dried beans in water for several hours and substitute for corn. Cook beans until half tender, then add carrots and cook until tender. Add milk, heat, and serve.

CORN AND LIMA BEAN CHOWDER

1 cup dried lima beans	1½ cups whole kernel corn
2 cups water	2 teaspoons salt
1 teaspoon salt	1 teaspoon sugar
2 tablespoons chopped onion	⅛ teaspoon pepper
¼ cup cooking fat	½ cup water
1 cup diced celery	3 cups milk

Soak beans in 2 cups water several hours. Add salt. Cook until tender. This should make 2 cups cooked beans. Lightly brown onion in hot fat; add celery, corn, salt, sugar, pepper, and water. Simmer ½ hour. Add 2 cups cooked dried lima beans and the milk. Heat thoroughly. Serves 6.

Advance preparation: Fix entire chowder with the exception of lima beans and milk. Cool and store in refrigerator. Just before serving, add the beans and milk. Heat thoroughly.

CARROT POTATO CHOWDER

1 white onion, minced	¼ teaspoon paprika
¼ cup butter	1 tablespoon flour
2 cups diced raw potatoes	2 cups milk, scalded
3 cups boiling water	2 carrots, diced and cooked
1 teaspoon salt	

Sauté onion in 2 tablespoons butter in large saucepan until lightly browned. Add potatoes, boiling water, salt, and paprika. Boil about 15 minutes or until potatoes are soft. Blend flour with remaining butter and gradually add milk stirring constantly until smooth and thickened. Add to potato mixture. Add carrots. Cook 5 minutes, stirring until smooth. Serves 6.

HADDOCK CHOWDER, GREEK STYLE

3 pounds whole haddock	3 eggs
6 cups water	Juice of 1 lemon
1 cup thinly sliced celery	Salt and pepper, to taste
½ cup rice	

Cook haddock in water gently until fish flakes. Strain off broth. Add celery and rice. Cook until rice is soft. Beat eggs lightly, add lemon juice and mix well. Pour 1 cup broth over egg mixture and add all to remainder of broth. Season to taste. Add large pieces of haddock with all skin and bones removed. Serves 6.

NOTE: Ocean perch, cod, or flounder fillets may be substituted for haddock.

POTATO AND SPINACH SOUP (Basic Recipe)

¼ cup onion, chopped
2 tablespoons cooking fat
3 cups water
1 teaspoon salt

2 cups potatoes, diced
2 cups spinach, chopped
1 tall can evaporated milk

Sauté onion in fat until yellow. Add water, salt, potatoes, and spinach. Cook until tender, about 20 minutes. Add milk. Reheat. Garnish each portion with minced parsley or a dash of paprika. Serve with toasted bread cubes. Serves 6.

Bohemian potato: Omit spinach. Add ½ cup diced celery and ¼ cup diced pimiento.

Potato and cabbage soup: Use chopped cabbage instead of spinach.

Turnip soup: Substitute 2 cups mashed turnips and 1 cup mashed potatoes for diced potatoes and spinach.

CREAM OF VEGETABLE SOUP (Basic Recipe)

1 to 1½ cups cooked finely
  chopped or puréed vegetable
1½ teaspoons salt
⅛ teaspoon pepper

1½ tablespoons flour
3 tablespoons melted butter
3 cups milk

Dice vegetables. Cook until soft in just enough boiling salted water to cover. Press through a sieve or chop very fine. Prepare thin white sauce of flour, butter and milk. Add vegetables, heat thoroughly, and season to taste. Stir until smooth. Serves 5.

Cream of asparagus soup: Use 1½ cups cooked asparagus pulp and liquid.

Cream of carrot soup: Use 1½ cups cooked carrot pulp and liquid.

Cream of celery soup: Use 1½ cups finely diced celery and liquid.

Cream of lima bean soup: Use 1½ cups cooked or canned lima beans and liquid.

Cream of onion soup: Use 5 medium sized onions and liquid.

Cream of pea soup: Use 1½ cups cooked or canned peas and liquid.

MUSHROOM BISQUE

1 pound mushrooms
3 cups water
1 slice onion
½ teaspoon salt
3 tablespoons butter
¼ cup flour

2 cups milk
Salt and pepper
Paprika
1 egg yolk
⅓ cup heavy cream, whipped

Clean and chop mushrooms. Add water, onion, and ½ teaspoon salt. Simmer ½ hour. Press through a medium sieve. Melt butter and blend in flour. Gradually add milk and cook over hot water, stirring occasionally until thick. Add the sieved mushrooms, season with salt, pepper, and paprika to taste. Beat egg yolk and gradually add to mushroom mixture. Serve with garnish of whipped cream. Serves 4 to 6.

CHICKEN SUB GUM SOUP

1 can mixed Chinese vegetables
6 cups canned chicken broth
3 eggs, beaten

Soy sauce
Pepper

Drain vegetables and chop. Add to boiling broth and cook 5 minutes. Pour eggs slowly into soup, stirring slowly until eggs form small "flowers." Season to taste with soy sauce and pepper. Serves 8.

CREAM OF TOMATO SOUP (Basic Recipe)

4 tablespoons butter
4 tablespoons flour
1½ teaspoons salt
2 cups milk
2 cups canned tomatoes

⅛ teaspoon pepper
½ bay leaf
2 cloves
1 tablespoon chopped onion

Melt 2 tablespoons butter. Add 2 tablespoons flour and 1 teaspoon salt. Add milk gradually and cook until slightly thickened. In another pot cook together tomatoes, ½ teaspoon salt, pepper, bay leaf, cloves and onion 10 minutes. Press through sieve. Reheat and stir hot tomato pulp gradually into hot *WHITE SAUCE*, stirring constantly. Add seasonings. Do not allow to come to boil. Serve at once. If soup curdles, beat with rotary beater until smooth. Serves 5.

Tomato cheese soup: Add ¾ cup grated strong American cheese just before serving.

CREAM OF MUSHROOM SOUP

½ pound mushrooms
2 cups milk
4 tablespoons butter

½ tablespoon flour
½ cup cream
Salt and pepper, to taste

Peel mushrooms and cut into very small pieces. Combine with milk in top of double boiler. Simmer slowly 2 hours. Then press mushrooms through a very fine sieve with wooden masher. Replace in double boiler. Blend butter and flour. Add to mushrooms with cream, pepper, salt, and milk in which mushrooms were cooked and stir well. Cook about 15 minutes longer. Serves 6.

BEAN AND BARLEY SOUP

1 cup dried lima beans
6 cups cold water
2 teaspoons salt
¼ teaspoon pepper
1 small carrot, diced

2 slices onion, minced
3 tablespoons barley
1 cup evaporated milk
2 tablespoons butter

Soak beans overnight. Drain and add cold water, salt and pepper. Cook until almost tender. Add carrots, onion, and barley. Cook until soft. Add milk and butter before serving. Serves 6.

Pea or lentil barley soup: Peas or lentils are substituted for beans.

SWEDISH FRUIT SOUP

1 cup each dried peaches, pears, apricots and prunes
½ cup raisins
4 quarts cold water
½ each lemon and orange, sliced very thin

1 cup sugar
¼ teaspoon salt
2 tablespoons red cinnamon candies
2 tablespoons cornstarch or
   2 tablespoons tapioca

Wash dried fruit and soak overnight in cold water. Bring to boiling point and simmer gently 1 hour. Add remaining ingredients and cook until clear, about 30 minutes. Stir gently several times. Serves 8 to 10.

SOUR CHERRY SOUP

2 cups sour cherries
1 teaspoon salt
2 tablespoons sugar

4 cups water
1 tablespoon flour
1 cup sour cream

Combine cherries, salt, sugar, and water. Boil 10 minutes if canned cherries are used, 20 minutes for fresh cherries. Make a paste of flour and a little cold water, gradually add to soup and boil 5 minutes longer. Remove from heat. Chill thoroughly. Stir in sour cream just before serving. Serves 6.

PLUM SOUP

Slice 1½ pounds plums and cook in 5 cups of water until fruit is soft, about 20 minutes. Press plums through a sieve. Thicken liquid with 1 tablespoon flour blended with a little cold water. Add sugar to taste and cook 5 minutes more. Chill. Serves 6.

CANNED SOUP COMBINATIONS

Many new soup flavors are made possible by combining 2 canned soups of different yet harmonizing flavors. Condensed soups must have water or milk added according to directions on label and need only to be heated. The addition of herbs, cream, or perhaps wine (Madeira or sherry), finely chopped onion, chives, parsley, etc., will improve the flavors as well as seasoning such as curry, Worcestershire or Tabasco sauce. Appetizing combinations result from personal experimentation and flavors. Canned soups are also used to enhance the flavor of homemade soups as well as in recipes requiring soup stock.

Asparagus mushroom: Combine 1 can each asparagus and mushroom soups. Dilute condensed soups with milk. Heat and garnish with chopped pimiento.

Celery chicken soup: Equal parts celery and chicken soup.

Chicken and mushroom soup: Equal parts mushroom and chicken soup.

Corn chowder berkshire: Equal parts corn chowder and cream of tomato.

Indian chowder: Equal parts corn chowder and onion soup.

Old fashioned mushroom soup: Equal parts mushroom soup and chicken noodle soup. Garnish with minced parsley.

Old fashioned vegetable soup: Equal parts vegetable soup and tomato soup.

Purée mongole: Equal parts cream of tomato and green pea soup, diluted with milk.

Quick borsht: Finely chop 2½ cups drained canned beets. Combine with canned beet juice, 1 teaspoon minced onion, 1 can condensed bouillon, and 1 cup water. Heat without boiling, about 5 minutes. Add 1 tablespoon lemon juice and ½ teaspoon salt. Serve hot, garnishing each portion with 1 teaspoon finely chopped dill pickles and finely chopped hard-cooked egg. For a chilled borsht to be served with sour cream omit the bouillon and water and add vegetable stock. Season to taste.

Tomato corn chowder: Combine 1 can tomato soup, 1 can milk, and heat. Add 1 cup canned cream style corn, ¼ teaspoon curry powder, 1 teaspoon sugar, and ¼ teaspoon salt.

soup accessories

SOUP ACCOMPANIMENTS

Almost everyone likes some sort of crisp accompaniment with soup. These include the numerous varieties of crackers spread with butter, sprinkled with paprika or grated cheese, and heated in the oven just before serving.

For chowders and meat soup: Bread sticks, oyster crackers, hard rolls, French bread and melba toast.

For clear soups: Thin wafers, cheese straws, butter-toasted fingers or rings, cheese-spread toast strips, and melba toast.

For cream soups: Salted crackers, croutons, a bowl of popcorn, small pretzels, and cheese crackers.

SOUP GARNISHES

The finishing touch—a bit of colorful garnish—is liked by everyone and should not be forgotten when serving soups. Here are some suggestions.

For chowders and meat soups: Chopped parsley, thin slices of lemon for fish chowders; thin slices of frankfurters in bean and pea soups. See other suggestions with specific recipes.

For clear soups: Finely minced parsley, chives, thin slices of lemon, balls or slices of avocado, thin cooked celery rings or celery leaves, sautéed mushroom slices, thinly sliced olive rings, julienned carrots, string beans, rice, macaroni in small shapes.

For cream soups: Salted whipped cream alone or with minced parsley or chopped nuts, toast croutons, chopped pimiento, chopped chives, puffed cereals, raw grated carrots, or thick sour cream.

HOMEMADE NOODLE DOUGH (Basic Recipe)

2 large eggs	2 cups sifted all-purpose flour
½ teaspoon salt	(about)

Beat eggs and salt slightly, add flour. Use more flour if needed to make a stiff dough. Knead well, until dough is soft and elastic (about 5 minutes). Roll out very thin and evenly on a slightly floured board. Remove the sheet of dough to a clean cloth until it is dry but not brittle or sticky. Roll up lightly in a flat roll, and with a sharp knife cut crosswise into very thin, threadlike strips. Toss the strips lightly to separate them. Let dry thoroughly before storing in a covered jar. Do not try to make noodle dough in damp weather. To cook in soup, drop by handfuls in boiling soup 10 minutes before serving.

Broad noodles: Follow recipe for noodles but cut strips wider, about ¼ inch across.

Noodle puffs (fingerhuetchen): Prepare dough and roll out as for noodles; let stand until almost dry. Fold dough in two and cut through both thicknesses with a small floured cutter (thimble size) pressing well so edges stick together. Fry in deep hot fat until brown. They should puff up like small balls. Serve in hot soup.

Noodle squares (plaetschen): Roll dough out thin as for noodles. When dry, cut into 3 inch strips. Place on top of each other and cut in ½ inch strips crosswise. Pile up again and cut to form ½-inch squares. Dry and store as for noodles. Cook in boiling soup for 15 minutes.

KASHE VARNISHKAS

Cut noodle dough into ½ to ¾ inch squares. Cook until tender in rapidly boiling salted water. Drain well and combine with prepared kashe (buckwheat groats).

KREPLACH

Use the *HOMEMADE NOODLE DOUGH* recipe. Roll out thin. Do not dry. Cut into 2-inch squares. Place 1 tablespoon of filling (see following 2 recipes) on each square. Fold crosswise into triangles, pressing edges together securely. Drop into boiling salted water or soup; cook 15 minutes. Serve in soup or with a rich tomato sauce or meat gravy.

Variation: Boil 10 minutes in salted water. Drain and fry in hot fat until brown and crisp on both sides. Serve in soup or as a side dish.

MEAT FILLING FOR KREPLACH

1 teaspoon onion juice	1 egg
1 teaspoon salt	1 pound ground beef, cooked
Pepper to taste	

Add seasonings and egg to meat; mix well. Fill kreplach.

Chicken filling: Use cooked chopped chicken meat in place of beef. Add 1 tablespoon minced parsley.

Chicken liver and egg filling: Combine cooked chicken livers and hard-cooked eggs. Chop together until smooth. Season as above.

CHEESE FILLING FOR KREPLACH

1 pound dry cottage cheese	1 teaspoon sugar
2 tablespoons melted butter	½ teaspoon cinnamon
1 egg	¼ teaspoon salt

Mix all ingredients. Fill kreplach. To cook, drop into boiling milk. When done, kreplach will rise to top. Remove from milk. Serve with melted butter.

Variation: Add grated rind of 1 lemon and 1 tablespoon chopped almonds.

PIROGEN OR PIROSHKE

1½ cups sifted all-purpose flour
¼ teaspoon baking powder
½ teaspoon salt
¼ teaspoon pepper

½ cup shortening
1 egg
¼ cup cold water

Mix and sift dry ingredients. Cut in shortening; add egg. Gradually add enough water to hold dough together. Roll out on floured board. Cut into 5-inch squares or rounds for pirogen, or into 3-inch rounds or squares for piroshke. Place a spoonful of filling (see next recipe) in center of each. Pinch edges together tightly to seal in filling. Brush with melted shortening or egg yolk diluted with equal amount of water. Triangles are formed from the dough, and half-moons from the rounds. Bake in moderate oven (375°F.) on greased pans 20 minutes or until brown. Serve with soups or meat. With a savory filling they may be served with cocktails.

Variations: Pirogen or piroshke may be made in any desired size from well-kneaded yeast dough or any of the pie crust doughs. If yeast dough is used, filled dumpling should be allowed to rise for 1 to 1½ hours.

FILLINGS FOR PIROGEN OR PIROSHKE

Beef and onion filling: Fry 1 pound chopped beef and 2 sliced onions lightly in hot fat. Remove and add 3 hard-cooked eggs, 1 teaspoon fennel leaves, salt and pepper to taste. Mix well.

Meat filling: Sauté minced onion in melted shortening; add 1 pound ground beef or veal and seasoning to taste. Brown slightly.

Rice and mushroom filling: Sauté a minced onion in melted shortening. Add ½ cup chopped canned or fresh mushrooms or ¼ cup dried chopped mushrooms which have been soaked in cold salted water. Add 1 cup cooked rice. Season to taste. Mix thoroughly.

Other fillings: Use chopped cooked poultry, lung, liver, or buckwheat groats (kashe). Season to taste with salt, pepper, and onion juice.

KNISHES (Basic Dough Recipe)

2 cups sifted all-purpose flour
1 teaspoon baking powder
½ teaspoon salt

2 tablespoons water
1 tablespoon vegetable oil
2 eggs, well beaten

Mix and sift flour, baking powder, and salt. Form a well in center; add water, oil, and eggs. Mix and form into a smooth dough. On a lightly floured board roll out to ⅛ inch thickness. Cut into rounds or squares or if desired leave whole. Fill with desired filling (see next 4 recipes). Moisten edges and fold over the filling. Press edges firmly together. Place in a pan greased with hot oil and bake in a moderate oven (350°F.) until browned and crisp. If the dough is uncut, fill and roll up like a jelly roll. The fillings given here are only a few suggestions. In fact, the methods for making knishes and the fillings are limited only by the imagination of the cook.

CHICKEN FILLING FOR KNISHES

2 cups chopped cooked chicken
½ cup bread crumbs or
   crumbled matzos

1 cup chicken gravy (about)
Salt and pepper

Combine all ingredients. Season to taste and use as filling.

MEAT FILLING FOR KNISHES

2 cups cooked ground meat
½ cup mashed potatoes
2 tablespoons melted cooking fat
1 small onion, minced

½ teaspoon salt
¼ teaspoon pepper
1 egg, beaten
Paprika (optional)

Combine all ingredients. Mix well.

LIVER FILLING FOR KNISHES

1 onion, minced
1 tablespoon chicken fat
½ pound cooked liver
¼ pound cook lung
½ pound cooked beef

1 egg
½ cup cooked kashe or
   ½ cup cooked rice
Salt and pepper

Fry minced onion in chicken fat until lightly browned. Grind liver, lung, and beef in food chopper. Combine with remaining ingredients.

CHEESE KNISHES

FOR DOUGH:

4 cups sifted all-purpose flour
2 teaspoons baking powder
½ teaspoon salt
2 eggs, well beaten
1 tablespoon melted butter
1 cup thick sour cream

FOR FILLING:

1 pound dry cottage cheese
½ cup thick sour cream
2 tablespoons bread or matzo crumbs
2 tablespoons melted butter
2 tablespoons sugar
2 tablespoons raisins
2 eggs, well beaten

Mix and sift flour, baking powder, and salt. Add eggs, butter, and sour cream. Knead into a soft dough, adding a little milk if necessary. Roll out on floured board to ¼ inch thickness. Cut into rounds or squares. Fill with cheese filling. Moisten edges. Fold over and pinch edges firmly together. Place in a greased baking pan. Bake in moderate oven (350°F.) until nicely browned.

VARENIKI WITH COTTAGE CHEESE

2 cups sifted all-purpose flour
1 egg yolk, unbeaten
2 tablespoons water, about

1 cup dry cottage cheese
1 egg, unbeaten
Salt and pepper

Mix flour, egg yolk, and water to make a dough. Knead well (about 5 minutes) and roll out very thin on a floured board. Cut into 4-inch squares. Mix cottage cheese, egg, salt and pepper to taste. Place a spoonful in center of each square. Bring the edges of the dough together and seal securely by pinching together with fork. Drop into boiling salted water. When done they should rise to the surface. Serve hot with melted butter, or sour cream, or a mixture of both.

Vareniki with fruit: Wash 2 pounds of plums, cherries, or blueberries. Cover with sugar and let stand 1 hour or more. Drain juice. Boil to a syrup. Place a tablespoonful of drained fruit on each square of dough. Dot edges with slightly beaten egg white, fold over, and seal by pinching together with fork. Cook as above. Serve with sugar, fruit syrup, or sour cream.

Vareniki with meat: Combine seasoned chopped meat with 1 raw egg per cup of meat and 1 medium-sized onion, minced fine. Mix and use as filling.

HOME-MADE EGG BARLEY (Farfel)

Beat slightly 1 egg with ¼ teaspoon salt. Add flour (about 1 cup) until mixture forms a stiff ball. Let stand about ½ hour. Grate dough on a coarse grater or chop in a wooden bowl. Spread out on a board to dry. Stir occasionally to facilitate drying. Let stand until thoroughly dry, at least several hours. Store in covered jar. Add to boiling soup. Cook 15 minutes.

Variation: Cook in boiling salt water 15 minutes. Drain and serve with butter or gravy as a side dish.

BAKED EGG BARLEY (Farfel)

Fry ½ cup minced onions in hot chicken or other cooking fat until golden brown. Add 2 cups egg barley. Fry until brown. Pour into a casserole. Add 3 cups soup stock or boiling water and gravy. Season with 1 teaspoon salt. Bake in moderate oven (350°F.) until liquid has been absorbed and egg barley is tender, about 1 hour. Serve as a side dish.

SOUP NUTS (Mandlech or Mandlen)

3 eggs, slightly beaten	1 teaspoon salt
2 tablespoons salad oil	2 cups sifted all-purpose flour (about)

Mix ingredients to make a soft dough, firm enough to roll with your hands. Divide into 2 or 3 parts, and with floured hands form into pencil thin rolls. Cut into ½-inch pieces. Bake in shallow, well-greased pans in moderate oven (375°F.) about 20 minutes, or until golden brown. Shake pans occasionally to brown evenly. When cold and dry these may be stored for several days. Heat just before serving in soup or with gravy.

EGG DROP FOR SOUP (Einlauf)

1 egg, beaten	3 tablespoons flour
Dash of salt	¼ cup cold water

Stir all ingredients together until smooth. Drop slowly from end of spoon into boiling soup. Cover. Cook 5 minutes and serve hot.

Variation: Pour well-beaten egg gradually into boiling soup just before serving.

EGG WAFERS (Eierkichel)

3 eggs
1 tablespoon vegetable oil
2 teaspoons sugar

¼ teaspoon salt
1⅔ cups all-purpose flour (about)
½ teaspoon baking powder

Beat eggs well. Add remaining ingredients. Knead until smooth (about 5 minutes). Roll out about ⅛ inch thick on floured board. Cut in large round, square, or diamond shapes. Brush lightly with oil. Bake on greased cooky sheet in moderate oven (375°F.) ½ hour or until light brown. Serve with soup or use as a canapé foundation.

Variation: Sprinkle with sugar and cinnamon before baking.

ONE BOWL PIROSHKE (No-Dissolve Yeast Method)

4½ to 5½ cups unsifted all-purpose flour
1 teaspoon sugar
1 teaspoon salt
1 package active dry yeast
½ cup (1 stick) softened pareve margarine

1 cup very hot tap water
3 eggs (at room temperature)
1 egg yolk, beaten
2 tablespoons water

In a large bowl thoroughly mix 1½ cups flour, sugar, salt, and undissolved active dry yeast. Add softened margarine. Gradually add very hot tap water to dry ingredients and beat 2 minutes at medium speed of electric mixer, scraping bowl occasionally. Add whole eggs and ¾ cup flour, or enough flour to make a thick batter. Beat at high speed 2 minutes, scraping bowl occasionally. Stir in enough additional flour to make a soft dough. Turn out onto lightly floured board; knead until smooth and elastic, about 8 to 10 minutes. Place in greased bowl, turning to grease top. Cover; let rise in warm place, free from draft, until doubled in bulk, about 1 hour. Punch dough down; divide into 3 equal pieces. On a lightly greased board, roll 1 piece into a 12x16-inch rectangle. Using a floured 4-inch cookie cutter or tumbler, cut into 12 circles. Reserve scraps of dough. Place 1 tablespoon of either filling (below) in center of each circle. Fold dough over filling to form semi-circle. Pinch seams well. Place on greased baking sheets. Repeat with remaining pieces of dough. Combine scraps; knead to form a smooth ball. Roll to a 12-inch square; cut into 9 circles. Proceed as before. Cover; let rise in a warm place, free from draft, until doubled in bulk, about 30 minutes. Brush with combined egg yolk and 2 tablespoons water. Using a fork, puncture each piroshke to allow steam to escape. Bake in a hot oven (400°F.) about 15 minutes, or until done. Remove from baking sheets and cool on wire racks. Best when served warm. Make 45 appetizers.

Meat filling: Sauté 1 pound ground beef and ½ cup chopped onion in 6 tablespoons pareve margarine until meat is browned. Blend in ¼ cup unsifted flour, 1 teaspoon dill weed, 1 teaspoon salt, and ¼ teaspoon pepper. Stir in ½ cup cooked rice; cool.

Cabbage filling: Cover 6 cups finely shredded cabbage (about 1¼ pounds) with boiling water; drain. Toss with 1½ teaspoons salt; drain 15 minutes. In a large skillet, sauté ⅓ cup chopped onion in 6 tablespoons pareve margarine. Stir in cabbage and cook slowly until tender, about 10 to 15 minutes. Mix in 1 finely chopped hard-cooked egg and ¼ teaspoon pepper. Cool.

stuffings and dumplings

BREAD STUFFING (Basic Recipe)

4 cups stale bread cubes
¼ teaspoon pepper
1 teaspoon salt
¼ teaspoon thyme or marjoram

½ to 1 teaspoon poultry seasoning
¼ cup finely chopped onion
¼ cup melted cooking fat

Combine bread, seasonings, and onion. Slowly add fat, tossing lightly with a fork until blended. For a more moist stuffing slowly add up to ⅓ cup hot water or stock. Makes about 4 cups stuffing. Allow 1 cup for each pound of poultry.

NOTE: Stuffings swell upon cooking and should not be tightly packed into the cavity of a bird, roast, or fish.

Celery stuffing: Add 1 cup finely chopped celery.

Chestnut stuffing: Add ½ cup finely chopped celery and 1 pound of boiled, chopped chestnuts.

Cornbread stuffing: Substitute cornbread crumbs for bread cubes.

Giblet stuffing: Add chopped, cooked giblets. Use giblet stock for moistening.

Mushroom stuffing: Sauté ½ cup sliced mushrooms in the fat and add.

Parsley stuffing: Add 2 to 3 tablespoons minced parsley.

Prune stuffing: Omit thyme or marjoram and prepare half of *BREAD STUFFING* recipe. Remove pits from 1 cup cooked prunes and add with 1 cup diced apple.

Raisin stuffing: Add ½ cup seedless raisins.

Sage stuffing: Omit thyme or marjoram. Add 1 tablespoon crumbled sage leaves.

APPLE STUFFING

½ cup chopped celery and leaves
½ cup chopped onion
¼ cup chopped parsley
2 to 3 tablespoons melted cooking fat

5 tart apples, diced
½ cup sugar
Salt and pepper, to taste
1 cup soft breadcrumbs

Cook celery, onion, and parsley for a few minutes in half of fat. Remove from pan. Put remaining fat in pan and add apples. Sprinkle apples with sugar. Cover and cook until tender. Remove lid, continue cooking until apples are candied. Combine with vegetables, breadcrumbs, and seasonings. Use with goose, duck, lamb, beef, or other meats.

CORN STUFFING FOR POULTRY

2 cups canned corn
2½ cups breadcrumbs
2 eggs
1 tablespoon finely minced
green pepper

½ cup chopped mushrooms
⅔ teaspoon salt
¼ teaspoon pepper
2 tablespoons cooking fat

Mix all ingredients thoroughly. If too dry, add a little stock. If too moist, add a few more breadcrumbs.

FISH STUFFING (Basic Recipe)

¼ to ½ cup melted butter
1 tablespoon grated onion
2 cups breadcrumbs or cubes
½ teaspoon salt

⅛ teaspoon pepper
1 tablespoon lemon juice
1 tablespoon chopped parsley
1 teaspoon capers (optional)

Amount of butter depends upon type of fish. Use smaller amount with lean fish, larger amount with fat fish. Add onion and crumbs to melted fat. Stir over low heat until crumbs brown slightly. Add and mix remaining ingredients. If desired, ¼ teaspoon sage or thyme may be substituted for capers. Yield: stuffing for 3 to 4 pound fish.

Cucumber stuffing: Reduce breadcrumbs or cubes to 1½ cups. Add 1 cup drained chopped cucumbers.

Pickle stuffing: Add ¼ to ⅓ cup chopped drained sweet or dill pickles.

FRUIT STUFFING

Soak 1 cup dried apricots or 1½ cups prunes in hot water for 20 minutes. Drain and chop. Combine, by tossing lightly with fork, with 4 cups soft breadcrumbs, ¼ cup melted cooking fat, 2 tart sliced apples, and ½ teaspoon salt. For more moist dressing use a little water from soaked fruit. Yields enough for 6 pound fowl.

MINT STUFFING

1½ tablespoons chopped onion
3 tablespoons chopped celery and
leaves
4 tablespoons cooking fat

½ cup fresh mint leaves
3 cups soft breadcrumbs
Salt and pepper to taste

Cook onion and celery for a few minutes in the fat. Then stir in mint leaves and breadcrumbs. Season with salt and pepper. Mix all ingredients together until hot. Makes enough for 3 to 4 pound cushion-style shoulder of lamb. For a rolled shoulder, use half the recipe.

ORANGE STUFFING FOR DUCK

3 cups dry breadcrumbs
1 cup diced apple
½ cup seedless raisins
4 tablespoons sugar

⅔ cup orange juice
¼ cup melted fat
Salt and pepper

Mix ingredients in order given. Season to taste with salt and pepper. Use more or less liquid as needed to moisten. Stuff duck lightly. Garnish with watercress or parsley and sections of orange dipped in thick sugar syrup. Serve with orange sauce made by adding ½ cup strained orange juice to 2 cups gravy.

PEANUT STUFFING

3 cups soft breadcrumbs
¾ cup chopped peanuts
½ teaspoon onion juice
1 teaspoon salt

⅛ teaspoon pepper
1 tablespoon chopped parsley
2 tablespoons melted cooking fat
½ cup stock or water

Combine breadcrumbs and peanuts. Add onion juice, salt, pepper, parsley, and fat. Moisten with hot stock or water. Toss lightly to mix. Yield: stuffing for 4-pound bird.

MASHED POTATO STUFFING

2 cups hot mashed potatoes
1 cup soft breadcrumbs
3 tablespoons melted cooking fat or
  salad oil

1 egg, lightly beaten
3 tablespoons chopped onion
1 teaspoon chopped parsley

Use white or sweet potatoes. Season well while mashing. Combine all ingredients. Moisten with stock if mixture is dry. Yield: 3 cups stuffing for veal or lamb breast or shoulder.

GRATED POTATO STUFFING

6 medium raw potatoes
1 onion, grated
2 eggs
½ cup flour
  Dash of pepper

1 teaspoon salt
  Minced parsley
½ cup hot melted cooking fat or
  salad oil

Peel and grate raw potatoes. Squeeze out excess water. Mix all ingredients, adding hot melted shortening last. Let mixture stand a few minutes before stuffing. Yield: stuffing for 4 to 5 pound breast of veal.

RICE STUFFING

2 tablespoons chopped onion
1 tablespoon chopped parsley
1 cup chopped celery and leaves
2 cups cooked rice

2 tablespoons cooking fat
½ teaspoon savory seasoning
Salt and pepper, to taste

Cook onion, parsley, and celery in fat a few minutes. Add rice and seasoning. Stir until well mixed and hot. Use as stuffing in chicken, duck, or other fowl or in boned cuts of meat. Any kind of rice, white, brown, or wild rice may be used in stuffing.

SPANISH RICE STUFFING

Prepare SPANISH RICE. Use for stuffing chicken or veal or lamb shoulder.

SAVORY STUFFING (Basic Recipe)

1 cup chopped celery	6 cups breadcrumbs
¼ cup chopped parsley	½ to 1 teaspoon salt
¼ cup chopped onion	⅛ teaspoon pepper
⅓ cup cooking fat	1 teaspoon savory seasoning

Cook celery, parsley, and onion in the hot fat for a few minutes. Add breadcrumbs and seasonings. Mix well. Approximate yield: stuffing for 5 to 6 pound fowl.

Chestnut savory stuffing: Add 1 pound of cooked, chopped chestnuts. To prepare chestnuts, boil in water for 15 minutes, peel off shells, and brown skin while still hot.

Cornbread savory stuffing: Use crumbled stale cornbread instead of breadcrumbs. Use for fowl, veal or other meats.

Hazelnut, filbert, pecan, or almond savory stuffing: Add 1 cup of any of these chopped nutmeats.

WILD RICE AND MUSHROOM STUFFING

2 cups wild rice	1 teaspoon salt
Dash of pepper	¾ cup sliced mushrooms
3 teaspoons chopped onion	¼ cup cooking fat or salad oil

Wash rice and cover with salted water. Bring to boil and cook until tender, about 20 minutes. Drain. Brown onion and mushrooms in hot fat. Mix with rice, salt, and pepper. Makes enough for 4 to 5 pound fowl.

Wild rice and chestnut stuffing: Omit mushrooms. Boil, peel, and chop ½ pound chestnuts. Mix with other ingredients.

BAKING POWDER DUMPLINGS (Basic Recipe)

2 cups sifted all-purpose flour	2 tablespoons shortening
1 teaspoon salt	¾ to 1 cup milk or
4 teaspoons baking powder	¾ to 1 cup water

Mix and sift flour, salt, and baking powder. Cut in shortening with pastry blender or 2 knives. Add liquid until a thick drop batter is obtained. Drop by tablespoonfuls into boiling soup or stew; cover tightly. Cook for 12 minutes. Serves 5.

Meat dumplings: Left-over cooked meat or cracklings may be added just before dropping into boiling soup or stew.

Parsley dumplings: Add ½ cup finely chopped parsley to flour mixture.

Puffy cheese dumplings: Reduce shortening to 1 tablespoon and add ½ cup grated sharp American cheese to flour mixture.

LIVER DUMPLINGS (Liver Kloesse)

1 cup chopped, cooked liver	⅛ teaspoon pepper
1 cup water	½ teaspoon grated onion
1 cup breadcrumbs	1 egg, slightly beaten
1 teaspoon salt	Grated lemon rind (optional)

Chicken, goose, beef, or calves liver may be used. Cook water and breadcrumbs to a paste, stirring to prevent burning. Cool. Add remaining ingredients. Mix well. Form into balls the size of walnuts. Drop into rapidly boiling salted water or boiling soup. Cook 5 to 10 minutes. Serves 6.

Chicken gizzard dumplings: Use cooked heart and tender part of gizzards with or without chopped liver.

Fried liver dumplings: Roll cooked dumplings in fine breadcrumbs and fry in hot fat.

Marrow dumplings: Substitute cooked or uncooked beef marrow for chopped liver and proceed as in *LIVER DUMPLINGS*.

PLAIN DUMPLINGS (Spatzen)

2 eggs, well beaten	1½ cups all-purpose flour
½ teaspoon salt	1 cup water or milk

Add salt, flour, and water to beaten eggs. Stir to stiff, smooth batter. Drop by teaspoons into boiling soup; cook 10 minutes before serving.

Variations: Cook plain dumplings in boiling salted water for 10 minutes. Drain. Serve with melted butter and fried onions, with scrambled eggs, gravy, or buttered crumbs.

MASHED POTATO DUMPLINGS (Kartoffell Kloesse)

1 cup bread cubes (¼ inch)	1 egg
1 tablespoon cooking fat	¾ cup sifted all-purpose flour
2 cups mashed potatoes	1½ teaspoons salt
1 tablespoon minced onion	½ teaspoon pepper

Fry bread cubes in hot fat. Add fat to hot mashed potatoes. Cool. Add onion and egg; mix well with fork. Sift in flour, salt, and pepper. Mix well. Shape into 12 balls, forming each around 4 or 5 fried bread cubes. Cook, covered, in boiling salted water 10 to 12 minutes. If desired, brown in melted fat before serving. Serves 6.

Potato meat dumplings: Leftover cooked meat may be added just before shaping in balls.

Savory potato dumplings: Add 1 teaspoon nutmeg and marjoram to dry ingredients.

With farina: Omit bread cubes; add ½ cup farina to flour and proceed as for *POTATO DUMPLINGS*.

With matzo meal: Omit bread cubes; use ¾ cup matzo meal in place of flour in dumplings.

GRATED POTATO DUMPLINGS

2 cups raw grated potatoes	½ teaspoon salt
⅔ cup all-purpose flour (scant)	½ teaspoon grated onion
1 egg	2 tablespoons breadcrumbs

Drain potatoes well; combine all ingredients to form a batter thick enough to shape into balls the size of a walnut. Drop into rapidly boiling soup or salted water; cook 20 minutes. When done, the dumplings will rise to top. If cooked in salted water, remove with a skimmer when done. Drain. Serve with gravy or soup. Serves 6.

ALMOND BALLS (Mandel Kloesse)

2 eggs, separated
⅛ teaspoon salt
⅛ teaspoon pepper
½ teaspoon parsley, minced

1 tablespoon blanched, grated almonds
½ teaspoon baking powder
1 to 1½ cups sifted flour

Beat egg yolks until very light. Add remaining ingredients and enough floor to make a stiff batter. Fold in stiffly beaten egg whites. Drop by spoonfuls into boiling soup; cook 10 minutes. First test in boiling salted water; if ball falls apart add more flour to batter.

EGG FOAM DUMPLINGS

3 eggs, separated
3 tablespoons flour

Dash of salt

Add salt to egg whites and beat until stiff. Add egg yolks one at a time; beating slightly after each addition. Fold in flour and pour into clear, boiling soup. Cook 5 minutes. Lift out of soup; cut into ovals with the side of a tablespoon. Serve with hot soup.

SPONGE DUMPLINGS

6 tablespoons milk
2 egg whites
4 tablespoons soft butter

⅔ cup all-purpose flour
¼ teaspoon salt
2 egg yolks

Combine milk, egg whites, butter, flour, and salt in a small pan. Cook over low heat, stirring constantly. When thick, remove pan from heat. Beat in egg yolks. When cool, drop by spoon into simmering soup. Simmer 5 minutes and serve. Serves 6.

RUMANIAN CHEESE BALLS

1⅓ cups dry cottage cheese
2 eggs, separated
½ teaspoon sugar

¼ teaspoon salt
Pinch of pepper
3 tablespoons flour

Force cheese through a sieve. Add egg yolks, sugar, salt, and pepper. Beat egg whites until stiff; sift flour over them and fold into first mixture. Dough will be very soft and hard to handle. If too soft, add another tablespoon flour. Flour a board thickly; spread dough out with floured hand. Cut off by spoonfuls and roll in flour, making small balls or rolls about 1 inch long. Drop into boiling soup. When balls rise to surface, lower flame and cover pot. Simmer 8 to 10 minutes or until light and fluffy. Serve with soup. Makes 24 small balls.

Variation for dessert: To serve as dessert, make balls slightly larger and boil in hot salted water. Drain. Place into a hot dish. Pour over melted butter. Sprinkle with buttered crumbs and sugar. Makes 8 large balls.

EGG BALLS

2 hard-cooked eggs
Dash each of salt and nutmeg

½ teaspoon melted butter
1 egg yolk, raw

Mash egg yolks well. Add salt, nutmeg, butter, and finely chopped egg whites. Add raw yolk and form into tiny balls. Cook 1 minute in boiling soup.

CORN MEAL DUMPLINGS

1 cup corn meal	2 slightly beaten eggs
1 teaspoon salt	½ teaspoon minced onion
1⅓ cups boiling water	¼ to ½ cup flour
1 teaspoon chopped parsley	

Combine corn meal and salt and gradually add to boiling water, stirring constantly. Remove from heat and stir until smooth. Cool. Add remaining ingredients except flour. Mix thoroughly. Drop by spoonfuls onto waxed paper heavily sprinkled with flour. Roll around on flour to form balls. Drop into boiling meat or chicken stew. Cover tightly. Cook 10 minutes. Serves 6.

SPATZEN OR SPAETZEL #2

2½ cups all-purpose flour	2 eggs, lightly beaten
½ teaspoon salt	½ cup milk
¼ teaspoon baking powder	½ cup water
Small grating of nutmeg, optional	½ cup melted butter

Combine flour, salt, baking powder, and nutmeg in a bowl. Mix together the eggs, milk, and water; gradually stir into the flour mixture. The consistency of the dough depends upon the method of shaping to be used. The dough may be made softer by the addition of a small amount of water or stiffer by adding more flour. The softer the dough, the lighter the dumplings; however, it must be firm enough to retain its shape. Spatzen should be light and delicate; try out a sample and if it is too heavy, add a little water to the dough. Cut or break off small bits of the dough with a spoon (about ¼x1 inch) and drop into 3 to 4 quarts rapidly boiling salted water. Cook 1 or 2 minutes. Or place the dough on a plate and cut shreds with a knife from the side of the plate into the water. Or the dough may be forced through a metal colander into the boiling water. When done, remove them with a slotted ladle to absorbent paper to remove excess water. Toss with melted butter. Serves 6.

Variations: (1) Place drained spatzen in a dish and cover with ¼ cup breadcrumbs which have been sautéed in ½ cup butter; (2) Toss spatzen with ¾ cup warm sour cream and a little butter; (3) Toss with ½ cup grated sharp Cheddar cheese and butter.

vegetables

Green, gold, red, and creamy white—whatever their hue, vegetables give the menu planner a wide selection. Vegetables are rich with vitamins and minerals. The skill of a good cook lies in cooking vegetables that are palatable with the greatest retention of these valuable nutrients. Properly cooked vegetables are attractive and colorful. Here are some basic rules:

1. Trim sparingly such greens as cabbage, head lettuce, chicory. Dark outer leaves are rich in iron, calcium, and vitamins. Use them.

2. Cook potatoes in their skins whenever possible for such dishes as boiled potatoes, hash-browned potatoes, potato salad, etc. Much of the nutrients are directly under the skin.

3. Cook vegetables quickly, as short a time as possible before serving. The longer vegetables are exposed to heat and air, the greater the loss of vitamin C.

4. Use little or no water for cooking. Any left-over liquid from cooking vegetables or from canned vegetables contains the dissolved minerals and vitamins and should be utilized in cooking soup, gravies, etc.

5. Heat canned vegetables as follows: Drain liquid into saucepan. Boil quickly, uncovered, to reduce amount. Add vegetable and heat quickly.

COOKING PERIODS

In using the Boiling Guide for Fresh Vegetables, remember that vegetables may require shorter or longer cooking periods than given, depending on variety and quality. The altitude at which you live will also affect boiling times. Cook frozen vegetables according to directions on the package. Commercially canned vegetables need only reheating. Home-canned vegetables should be brought to a rolling boil and boiled at least 10 minutes. Boil home-canned spinach and corn 20 minutes. Be especially careful not to overcook vegetables when using a pressure cooker. Even a few seconds' overcooking can lower eating quality and nutritive value. Follow the cooking times that come with your cooker. For very fresh and tender vegetables, you may be able to cut the time.

SCALLOPED VEGETABLES (Basic Recipe)

2 cups cooked or canned vegetables	2 tablespoons melted butter
1 cup medium WHITE SAUCE	½ to 1 cup soft breadcrumbs

Place alternate layers of drained vegetables and sauce in greased casserole. Mix butter and crumbs. Sprinkle over top. If desired, sprinkle with paprika. Bake in moderate oven (375°F.) until brown, about 25 minutes. Serves 4 to 6.

Scalloped vegetables with cheese: Substitute CHEESE SAUCE for WHITE SAUCE or sprinkle ½ cup grated cheese on top with the buttered crumbs.

BOILING GUIDE FOR FRESH VEGETABLES

VEGETABLE	Boiling time (minutes)	VEGETABLE	Boiling time (minutes)
Asparagus	10–20	Greens:	
		Beet, young	5–15
Beans:		Dandelion	10–20
Lima	20–30	Kale	10–25
Snap; 1-inch pieces	15–30	Turnip	15–30
Beets:		Kohlrabi, sliced	20–25
Young, whole	30–45	Okra, whole or sliced	10–20
Older, whole	45–90	Onions, whole or half	20–40
Broccoli, separated	10–20	Parsnips, whole	20–40
Brussels sprouts	10–20	Peas	8–20
Cabbage:		Potatoes, whole or half	25–45
Shredded	3–10	Rutabagas, pared, cut up	20–30
Quartered	10–15	Squash:	
Carrots:		Summer, sliced	10–20
Young, whole	15–25	Winter, cut up	20–40
Older, sliced	15–25	Spinach, whole	3–10
Cauliflower:		Sweet potatoes, whole	25–35
Separated	8–15	Swiss chard	10–20
Whole	20–30	Tomatoes, cut up	7–15
Celery, cut up	15–20	Turnips, cut up	15–20
Collards, whole	10–20		
Corn, on cob	5–15		

VEGETABLE SOUFFLE (Basic Recipe)

3 eggs, separated
½ cup thick *WHITE SAUCE*

1 cup chopped cooked vegetables
Salt and pepper

Beat egg yolks until thick and stir in *WHITE SAUCE.* Add vegetables. Season to taste. Fold in stiffly beaten egg whites and turn into greased baking dish. Set in pan of hot water and bake in slow oven (325°F.) 50 to 60 minutes. Serves 5 to 6.

CREAMED VEGETABLES (Basic Recipe)

Use any of the following vegetables: asparagus, broccoli, Brussels sprouts, cabbage, carrots, cauliflower, celery, corn, eggplant, green beans, leeks, lima beans, mushrooms, onions, peas, potatoes, or spinach. Combine 2 cups cooked or canned drained vegetables with 1 cup well-seasoned medium *WHITE SAUCE.* Heat in sauce or put vegetables in serving dish and pour over sauce. If desired, serve on toast. Garnish with a little chopped parsley. If desired, add a little grated onion to sauce.

VEGETABLE LOAVES OR TIMBALES (Basic Recipe)

Use 2 cups cooked and seasoned vegetables, mashed, puréed, or chopped. Stir in 2 well-beaten eggs. If desired, add 1 cup fine cracker crumbs and 2 to 4 tablespoons thin cream. Turn into well-greased loaf pan, ring mold, or timbale. Sprinkle with crumbs and bake in moderate oven (350°F.) until firm. For additional flavor, 2 tablespoons butter may be added to vegetable mixture. To bring out the flavor of any particular vegetable, add minced onion, hard-cooked egg, nutmeg, mace, or other herbs and seasonings, lemon juice, etc.

NUT ROAST

1 onion, minced	1 cup ground nutmeats
1 green pepper, seeded and chopped	1 egg, beaten
3 tablespoons butter	2 tablespoons parsley, minced
1 cup cooked rice	¾ teaspoon salt
⅓ cup breadcrumbs	¼ teaspoon paprika
1 cup tomatoes	Mashed potatoes

Sauté onions and pepper in melted butter until soft. Add rice, breadcrumbs, tomatoes, nutmeats, egg, and parsley. Season with salt and paprika. Place in a buttered casserole. Bake in moderate oven (375°F.) 30 minutes. Cover top with mashed potatoes. Dot well with butter and brown under broiler. Serve with hot tomato sauce. Serves 6.

ARTICHOKES

Artichokes globe: Select firm, green heads of even size (1 to a person). Wash, cut off stem and discolored outer leaves. Clip off 1 inch of top. Drop into enough lightly salted boiling water to cover and simmer 20 to 30 minutes. Serve with drawn butter or Hollandaise sauce in separate, individual dishes. To eat, pull off the leaves, one by one, and dip the lower part into the sauce. After all leaves have been pulled off, discard flower center or "choke," and eat the bottom, which is considered by many the choicest part of all.

Artichokes Jerusalem (1 pound serves 4): Wash, scrape, and soak in cold water about 1 hour. Drain; cook same way as GLOBE ARTICHOKES 20 to 30 minutes.

Artichokes Jerusalem en casserole: Select large, smooth artichokes. Scrape the tubers, and drop at once into cold water to keep from turning dark. Drain and pack into casserole. Sprinkle with salt and pepper. Dot with butter. Add no water. Cover and bake in moderate oven (350°F.) 45 to 60 minutes, or until tender. Serve in casserole.

ASPARAGUS

Select stalks that are straight, fresh, and green with closed tips. (1 pound serves 4.) Cut off tough ends of stalk. (Use tough ends of stalk in soup.) Scrub each stalk gently with vegetable brush. Tie loosely in serving bunches. Cook in covered pan, in boiling salted water with tips above level of water. Immerse tips when about ¾ done. Cooking time—15 to 20 minutes. Drain and serve with melted butter, salt and pepper, cheese sauce, or Hollandaise sauce.

Asparagus à la goldenrod: Cook 1 pound asparagus. Add 3 hard-cooked eggs, sliced in 1½ cups cheese sauce. Serve hot on buttered toast. If desired, add ¼ cup chopped ripe olives. Serves 6.

Asparagus au gratin: Follow recipe for SCALLOPED VEGETABLES with cheese.

Asparagus, cut: Cut into 2-inch pieces. Cook lower part 5 to 10 minutes before adding tips. Serve as cooked asparagus.

Asparagus in brown butter: Brown butter in skillet before pouring over cooked asparagus.

Asparagus soufflé: Follow recipe for VEGETABLE SOUFFLÉ.

Asparagus with pecan butter: Cook 1½ pounds whole asparagus. Season with melted butter in which 3 tablespoons chopped pecans (or slivered almonds) have been browned and to which 1 teaspoon lemon juice has been added. Serves 6.

Creamed asparagus: Cut cooked asparagus into 1-inch pieces. Heat in medium white sauce. Serve on toast. Diced hard-cooked eggs may be added to sauce. Garnish with minced parsley and pimiento strip.

French fried: Use well-drained cooked or canned asparagus tips. Dip in egg and fine crumbs or flour. Fry in deep fat (360°F.).

Scalloped asparagus: Follow recipe for SCALLOPED VEGETABLES using 2-inch lengths of cooked or canned asparagus. Add diced hard-cooked eggs and 1 or 2 tablespoons chopped pimiento.

BEANS—GREEN OR WAX (Snap Beans)

Select crisp beans of medium size. (1 pound serves 4.) Wash, cut off both ends and strings. May be cooked whole, cut into pieces, or sliced lengthwise. Cook in covered pan, with enough boiling salted water to cover, 20 to 30 minutes. Or cook uncovered, in very small amount of boiling salted water, 25 to 35 minutes. Serve with butter, salt, and pepper.

Creamed fresh snap beans: Wash and snap into 1-inch pieces. Place 2 tablespoons butter in skillet. Add 3 tablespoons water, salt, and pepper. Put in beans and cover tightly. Cook on high heat until steaming, then reduce to simmer heat. Cook 25 to 30 minutes. Before serving, add ½ cup cream or top milk, and bring to quick boil. Serve very hot.

In lemon rings: Cook 1½ pounds whole beans. Squeeze juice from 1 lemon, cutting skin into thin rings. Add part of juice to melted butter. Place bunches of beans through rings and pour butter over each bunch.

Italian style: Cook 1 pound beans until tender. Then simmer 10 minutes longer with 1 cup tomato soup, 1 clove garlic (to be removed at end of cooking period), 2 tablespoons butter, and salt and pepper to taste.

Sautéed beans: Cook and season 1½ pounds beans cut in strips. Cook in ¼ cup butter about 5 minutes, stirring frequently. Serve hot.

Scalloped snap beans: Follow recipe for SCALLOPED VEGETABLES.

Sweet and sour beans: Cook and season 1 pound beans. Prepare a sauce of 2 tablespoons butter, 2 tablespoons flour, 1 cup cooking water from beans, 2 tablespoons sugar, and 2 tablespoons vinegar. Add hot beans to sauce and serve hot.

BEANS—FRESH LIMA

To serve 5 buy 3 pounds unshelled or 1¼ shelled. Always keep shelled beans in refrigerator in covered utensil until ready to use. After shelling, wash and drain. Cook, covered in very small amount of boiling salted water, 20 to 30 minutes. Serve with butter, salt, and pepper.

Creamed fresh lima beans: Heat drained cooked beans in medium *WHITE SAUCE.*

Lima beans and frankfurters: Cook fresh lima beans. Add thin slices of frankfurters 10 minutes before beans are done.

Scalloped fresh lima beans: Follow recipe for *SCALLOPED VEGETABLES.*

Succotash: Combine equal parts cooked lima beans and cooked corn kernels.

CREAMED DRY LIMA BEANS

Soak 1½ cups dry lima beans in cold water several hours. Simmer beans until tender in water in which they have been soaked. Add ½ cup cream or top milk, 1 teaspoon salt, ¼ teaspoon pepper, and 1 tablespoon butter. Serves 6.

KIDNEY BEAN LOAF

2 cups dried kidney beans	½ cup cooking fat
2 cups water	1 egg
4 cups stale breadcrumbs	1½ teaspoons salt
2 cups grated cheese	½ teaspoon pepper
½ cup chopped onion	

Soak beans in water overnight. Bring to boil in same liquid, then simmer until beans are tender. Mash beans well. Add remaining ingredients, mixing well. Pack into loaf pan. Bake 1½ hours in slow oven (325°F.) (cold start). Baste occasionally with 1 tablespoon melted butter and ¼ cup water. Serves 6 to 8.

FRIJOLES

Soak 2 cups red kidney beans overnight. Cook until tender in salted water in top of double boiler. Drain. Brown ¼ cup each of sliced onion and minced green pepper in fat. Add beans. Serve hot with chili sauce.

BEETS

Cut off tops, leaving about 1 inch of stem. Scrub and wash thoroughly. Cover. Cook whole beets in enough boiling salted water to cover. Young beets 35 to 40 minutes, old beets 1 to 2 hours. Beets may also be pared and diced or shredded and cooked in a small quantity, boiling salted water about 15 to 20 minutes. Serve with butter, salt, and pepper.

Beets in orange butter: Wash 6 medium-size beets. Cook whole beets until tender, remove peel, and shred or chop fine. Place in casserole. Add 3 tablespoons butter, ¼ cup orange juice, 1 teaspoon grated orange rind, ½ teaspoon salt. Cover and bake in moderate oven (350°F.) until well heated. Serves 6.

Beets with celery butter: Cook 1½ pounds beets. Peel and dice. Serve with melted butter. Sprinkle with celery seed. Serves 6.

Boiled beet greens: Clean and wash thoroughly. Cook, covered or uncovered, in small amount of boiling salted water, turning greens frequently with fork. Serve with butter, salt, and pepper.

Harvard beets: Mix ½ cup sugar and 2 tablespoons flour; add ¼ cup water and ½ cup vinegar. Cook on medium heat until thick, about 10 minutes. Add ½ teaspoon salt, 2 tablespoons butter, then 3 cups cooked, diced beets. Cover and continue cooking about 10 minutes. Serves 4 to 5.

Honey buttered beets: Cook 1½ pounds beets. Peel and dice. Mix 1 teaspoon salt and 3 tablespoons honey and stir carefully into beets. Simmer 5 minutes. Add 1 tablespoon butter. Serve hot. Serves 6.

BEETS IN SPICY SAUCE

4 tablespoons butter	2 tablespoons grated onion
⅓ teaspoon dry mustard	1 tablespoon minced parsley
3 tablespoons tarragon vinegar	2 teaspoons Worcestershire sauce
½ teaspoon sugar	4 cups cooked beets, cubed
Dash of mace	

Combine all ingredients except beets. Bring to boil in top of double boiler. Stir frequently. Add beets. Toss together and heat thoroughly. To serve, garnish with chopped parsley. Serves 6 to 8.

BROCCOLI

Select stalks with dark green, tightly closed buds. Cut off tough part of stalk and coarse leaves. Wash carefully. Peel stalks. If necessary, cut in individual portions, split to make more attractive size and shape. Place in pan with ½ to ¾ cup water. Cover. Bring to boiling point on high heat, then reduce heat to simmer. Total cooking time about 25 minutes. Serve with melted butter and lemon wedges, with Hollandaise or cheese sauce.

Broccoli and cheese: Brush cooled broccoli with melted butter. Sprinkle with grated cheese. Heat slowly under broiler until cheese has melted.

Broccoli soufflé: Follow recipe for VEGETABLE SOUFFLÉ.

Broccoli with Parmesan cheese: Cook broccoli. Season with melted butter. Serve Parmesan cheese separately to be sprinkled over broccoli.

Broccoli with slivered almonds: Cook broccoli. Sauté slivered almonds in butter until browned. Add drained broccoli and heat thoroughly. Season and serve.

Creamed broccoli: Add 2 cups cooked broccoli to 1 cup medium WHITE SAUCE. Heat thoroughly.

Sautéed broccoli: Cook broccoli until almost tender. Drain and sauté in butter. Season and serve.

Scalloped broccoli: Follow recipe for SCALLOPED VEGETABLES.

BRUSSELS SPROUTS

Select fresh, green, compact heads. (1 pound serves 4.) Remove blemished leaves and tough portion of stem. Wash thoroughly. Cut small gashes lengthwise across stems so they will cook as quickly as heads. Place in pan with ½ cup water. Cover. Bring to quick boil, then simmer about 15 minutes. Drain. Serve with butter.

Brussels sprouts lyonnaise: Cook 1 quart Brussels sprouts. Sauté 1 medium sized onion, diced, in 3 tablespoons fat. Add ¼ cup bouillon and Brussels sprouts. Season to taste with salt and paprika. Simmer, stirring frequently until bouillon has evaporated. Sprinkle with 3 tablespoons chopped parsley and serve very hot. Serves 6.

Brussels sprouts with carrots: Combine Brussels sprouts with 1½ cups diced carrots. Cook together 15 minutes.

Brussels sprouts with celery: Combine equal amounts of diced celery and Brussels sprouts, cooked as directed.

Brussels sprouts with savory sauce: Cook 1 quart sprouts. Blend 2 tablespoons shortening with 1 tablespoon flour in hot skillet. Stir in ½ cup meat stock, juice of 1 lemon, and salt and pepper to taste. Let sauce cook slowly until smooth and thickened. Pour over hot drained sprouts. Serves 6.

French fried Brussels sprouts: Cook as directed for 10 minutes. Drain well and dip in egg and crumbs. Fry in deep fat (375°F.) until delicately browned. Drain on absorbent paper.

Scalloped Brussels sprouts: Follow recipe for SCALLOPED VEGETABLES.

CABBAGE—GREEN OR RED

Select crisp, solid head. (1 pound serves 3.) Pull off outer, wilted leaves. Cut into eighths, quarters, or shred. Wash well. Cook in covered pan, in boiling salted water (enough to cover) until tender. Young cabbage for 5 to 10 minutes, older cabbage 15 to 30 minutes. (Overcooking develops a strong flavor and odor.) Serve with butter.

Boiled red cabbage: To retain color, add 1 tablespoon lemon juice, vinegar, or a tart quartered apple to cooking water. Cook 15 to 20 minutes.

Cabbage cooked in milk: Cook 2 pounds cabbage in 2 cups milk 2 to 5 minutes. Make a paste of 3 tablespoons flour and 3 tablespoons melted butter and gradually add 1 cup thin cream. Combine with cabbage. Cook rapidly until thickened, stirring constantly. Season with salt and pepper. Serve hot. Serves 6.

Cabbage with tomatoes: Cook 1 pound cabbage. Mix 1 cup strained tomato pulp with 1 cup breadcrumbs, and 1 cup grated cheese. Season to taste. Arrange with cabbage in alternate layers in a casserole. Mix ½ cup crumbs and ½ cup grated cheese and sprinkle over top. Bake in moderate oven (350°F.) about 20 minutes. Serves 6.

Creamed cabbage: Follow recipe for CREAMED VEGETABLES.

Fried cabbage: Brown lightly in drippings.

Scalloped cabbage: Follow recipe for SCALLOPED VEGETABLES.

Tennessee cabbage: Melt 3 tablespoons butter in a skillet and allow to brown lightly. Add 5 cups shredded cabbage and stir well. Cover skillet tightly and simmer 5 minutes. Stir again and cook another 5 minutes. Add 1 teaspoon salt, ⅛ teaspoon pepper, and ½ cup cream. Cover and simmer 4 more minutes. It is very important not to overcook the cabbage. Total cooking time, 14 minutes. Serves 6.

VIENNESE CABBAGE

1 small head cabbage   ½ teaspoon salt
1 onion, minced   ¼ teaspoon paprika
1 tablespoon butter   1 cup sour cream

Shred cabbage and sauté lightly with onion in butter. Add salt and paprika; turn into greased casserole. Pour sour cream over all. Bake in moderate oven (375°F.) 20 minutes. Serves 4.

SWEET AND SOUR CABBAGE

1 medium cabbage, red or white   Boiling water
  Salt and pepper   2 tablespoons flour
3 small sour apples, sliced   3 tablespoons lemon juice
2 tablespoons cooking fat   4 tablespoons brown sugar

Shred cabbage very fine. Season with salt and pepper. Add cabbage and apples to melted fat in pan. Pour over boiling water to cover and simmer until tender. Sprinkle with flour, add lemon juice and sugar. Simmer 10 minutes longer. Vinegar may be substituted for lemon juice. If red cabbage is used, pour boiling water over several times before cooking. More sugar and lemon juice or vinegar may be added according to taste. Serves 6.

HUNGARIAN CABBAGE

1 large green cabbage   Dash of nutmeg
1 cup heavy sour cream, scalded   3 tablespoons butter
  Salt and pepper   1 teaspoon caraway seed

Shred cabbage coarsely. Cook uncovered 7 minutes or until tender. Drain thoroughly. Mix in sour cream. Season with salt and pepper to taste, and a dash of nutmeg. When ready to serve, stir in butter and caraway seed. Serves 8 to 10.

CABBAGE AND TOMATOES (Hungarian style)

2 onions, sliced   1 tablespoon paprika
1 medium head cabbage, chopped fine   6 large tomatoes, cubed
  Salt and pepper   2 tablespoons cooking fat

Brown onions and cabbage in melted fat. Season to taste with salt, pepper, and paprika. Add tomatoes. Cover and simmer 20 minutes. Serves 6.

CHINESE CELERY CABBAGE AND TOMATOES

¼ cup water   ½ cup canned tomatoes
1 teaspoon salt   1 small onion, finely chopped
⅛ teaspoon pepper   2 tablespoons butter
4 cups shredded Chinese cabbage

Add water, salt, and pepper to shredded cabbage. Bring to quick boil. Simmer 10 minutes. Add tomatoes and onions. Simmer until cabbage is tender, 10 minutes. Add butter. Serves 6.

CARROTS

Select firm carrots with fresh tops and bright orange in color. Young carrots are sweeter than large winter carrots. Wash and scrape. If carrots are very tender, it is not necessary to scrape them. A thorough scrubbing is sufficient. Leave whole, dice, slice crosswise or lengthwise, or cut in Julienne strips. Place carrots in a pot with tight-fitting lid. Add ½ to ⅔ cup water, 2 tablespoons butter, and a teaspoon salt. Bring to a quick steam, then reduce heat. If carrots are sliced thin, continue cooking 10 to 12 minutes. Cook young, tender carrots same length of time. Older whole carrots or large pieces should continue cooking 15 to 20 minutes. Serve carrots in remaining liquid after cooking.

Baked with roast: Scrape whole carrots and place around meat roast 1 hour before roast is done.

Carrot cups: Combine 2 cups grated raw carrot, ½ cup soft, fine breadcrumbs, 2 eggs, slightly beaten, 1 teaspoon salt, 2 tablespoons melted butter, ½ cup cream, 2 tablespoons finely chopped parsley. Mix well. Fill buttered custard cups ⅔ full. Set in shallow pan of hot water. Bake in slow oven (325°F.) until firm, about 50 minutes. Unmold and garnish with sliced stuffed olives. Serves 4 to 6.

Carrot soufflé: Follow recipe for *VEGETABLE SOUFFLÉ.*

Carrots with mint jelly: Simmer 1½ pounds cooked carrots slowly with 2 or 3 tablespoons butter and 1 tablespoon mint jelly. Serves 6.

Carrots with parsley butter: Toss 1½ pounds of cooked, sliced carrots in butter together with 2 or 3 tablespoons chopped parsley. Serves 6.

Carrots with peanut butter sauce: Add 1½ tablespoons peanut butter to 1 cup medium white sauce and combine with 1 pound cooked, sliced carrots. Serves 6.

Glazed carrots: Scrape 6 medium sized carrots and cut in long strips lengthwise. Cook until barely tender. Place carrots in baking dish. Combine 1 cup brown sugar, 3 tablespoons butter, and ½ cup water in a saucepan. Cook until sugar is dissolved and pour over carrots. Bake in moderate oven (350°F.) until glazed, basting occasionally, about 20 minutes.

Glazed mint carrots: Add 2 tablespoons fresh, chopped mint to melted butter, and follow recipe as for *GLAZED CARROTS.*

Golden glow carrots: Scrape carrots. Cut in half crosswise. Cook in salted water. Drain. Dip carrots in mayonnaise and roll in uncooked oatmeal. Sauté in butter until golden brown. Sprinkle with salt and pepper to taste.

Mashed carrots: Cook as directed and mash.

Sautéed carrots: Use cooked carrots cut into long thin strips. Dip in slightly beaten egg and cracker crumbs. Sauté in small amount of butter in hot skillet until well browned. Serve at once.

Scalloped carrots: Follow recipe for *SCALLOPED VEGETABLES.* Small cooked white onions may be added.

Sweet and sour carrots: Cook until tender, about 30 minutes, 1 pound sliced carrots in 2 cups water. Drain the liquid and add to it 1 tablespoon brown sugar, juice of 1 lemon, ½ teaspoon salt, and ⅛ teaspoon pepper. Melt 1 tablespoon butter or other cooking fat. Stir in 1 tablespoon flour, and a small amount of carrot liquid. Stir constantly until smooth. Add remaining liquid, stir well, and pour over carrots. Serve hot. Serves 4 to 6.

CARROT TZIMMES (Meatless)

8 large carrots	1 tablespoon lemon juice
½ teaspoon salt	3 tablespoons butter
¾ cup honey or sugar	3 tablespoons flour

Scrape and slice carrots ¼ inch thick. Place in heavy saucepan with cold water to just cover. Cook until almost tender. Add salt, honey, and lemon juice. Simmer gently about 20 minutes. Melt butter in skillet and blend in flour. Add to carrots, shaking pot to distribute evenly. Brown lightly under broiler before serving. Serves 6 to 8.

Variation: Two large sweet potatoes, cut into small pieces, may be combined with carrots.

CAULIFLOWER

Select white, tightly formed, spotless head with green leaves. 1 medium head serves 4. Remove heavy, outside leaves and woody base. Soak, head down, in cold, salted water 20 minutes. Drain and leave whole or separate into flowerets. Cook in covered pan in boiling salted water to cover. Whole 25 to 30 minutes, flowerets 10 to 12 minutes. Serve with butter, cheese, or Hollandaise sauce.

Cauliflower à la creole: Add 1 teaspoon salt and dash of pepper to 2½ cups canned tomatoes. Cook until most of liquid has evaporated. Place 4 cups cauliflower flowerets in buttered casserole. Pour over canned tomatoes. Sprinkle with 1 cup grated American cheese and ¼ cup soft breadcrumbs. Dot with butter. Bake in slow oven (325°F.) 12 to 20 minutes. Serves 5.

Cauliflower au gratin: Follow recipe for SCALLOPED VEGETABLES with cheese.

Cauliflower casserole: Alternate layers of cooked flowerets and sliced hard-cooked eggs in buttered casserole, using about 4 cups cooked cauliflower and 3 hard-cooked eggs. Sprinkle with buttered crumbs and paprika. Bake in moderate oven (350°F.) until well heated, about 20 minutes. Serves 4 to 6.

Cauliflower with breadcrumbs and parsley: Use a large head. Cook until tender. Serve over it 1 cup fresh breadcrumbs browned in a heavy skillet in ⅓ cup butter to which 1 finely chopped hard-cooked egg and 2 teaspoons minced parsley have been added. Serves 6.

Cauliflower with cheese crumb topping: Use large head of hot, cooked cauliflower. Sprinkle top with buttered crumbs, then a generous amount of grated American cheese. Place in oven or under moderate broiler to brown crumbs and melt cheese. Serves 6.

Cauliflower with cheese wine sauce: Cook a medium-size head until tender. Break into flowerets. Melt 1 cup processed, grated nippy cheese in top of double boiler with 1 tablespoon butter, 2 tablespoons flour, ½ teaspoon salt, and ¼ teaspoon pepper. Stir enough to blend ingredients, then gradually stir in 1 cup dry white wine. Continue cooking until thickened and creamy. Pour sauce over cauliflower. Serve on toast. Serves 6.

Cauliflower with mushrooms: Sauté ¼ pound mushrooms in butter. Add to cooked flowerets of 1 medium head. Serve on toast with cheese sauce. Serves 6.

Creamed cauliflower: Combine 1 cup medium WHITE SAUCE with about 2 cups cooked flowerets. Heat thoroughly and sprinkle with paprika.

French fried cauliflower: Dip cauliflower flowerets in fritter cover-batter. Fry in deep hot fat (375°F.) until delicately browned, 3 to 4 minutes.

Scalloped cauliflower: Follow recipe for *SCALLOPED VEGETABLES.*

CELERIAC (Celery Roots or Knobs)

Celeriac is a root with leaves that resemble and smell like celery. Select firm roots of uniform size (1 medium root per serving). Remove leaves and wash thoroughly. Leave whole or pare deeply and cut into cubes. Cook in covered saucepan with enough boiling, salted water to cover. Whole: cook 40 to 50 minutes, cubed 10 to 15 minutes. Drain and serve with butter or Hollandaise sauce.

Creamed celeriac: Combine with medium *WHITE SAUCE* (2 cups boiled celeriac to 1 cup sauce). Serve hot. Garnish with parsley.

Fried celeriac: Boil whole knobs. Drain and chill thoroughly. Dip into beaten egg and breadcrumbs. Fry in small amount of fat until browned on all sides. Season with salt and pepper.

CELERY

Select celery that is crisp with fresh leaves. Wash and scrub each stalk thoroughly. Serve hearts to be eaten raw. Cut stalks into 1-inch pieces. Cook in covered pan in boiling salted water to cover 15 to 20 minutes. Reserve cooking water and green leaves for soup.

Braised celery: Clean and cut 1 bunch celery into 3-inch pieces. Heat 2 tablespoons salad oil in skillet. Brown celery lightly. Add 1 cup meat stock or consommé. Cook slowly until stock is reduced about ½ cup. Season with salt and pepper.

Celery and snap beans: Place in a saucepan 2 cups cooked fresh snap beans or 2 cups canned snap beans, ½ cup cooked celery, ½ cup vegetable liquid or water, ½ teaspoon salt, dash of pepper, 1 tablespoon butter. Cook 10 minutes. Serves 5.

Celery au gratin: Follow recipe for *SCALLOPED VEGETABLES* with cheese.

Creamed celery: Combine with medium *WHITE SAUCE* (2 cups celery to 1 cup sauce). Serve hot. If desired, sprinkle with chopped toasted almonds.

CHESTNUTS

Boiled: Blanch in boiling water. Simmer, covered, in boiling salted water to cover until just tender, 10 to 20 minutes. Drain. Plunge into cold water. Remove shells and inner skins. Mash or rice and season with salt, pepper, and butter. Serve with medium *WHITE SAUCE* or use in stuffing.

Roasted: With a sharp knife make two crosswise slashes on the flat side of each chestnut. Melt some butter or oil in a saucepan (about 1 teaspoon for each cup of nuts). Drop in the nuts and keep shaking the pan over a hot flame until all nuts are coated with fat. Then bake them in a moderate oven (350°F.) until shells and inner skins can be removed easily, about 30 minutes. 1½ to 2 pounds serves 6.

CORN

Scalloped corn and celery: Melt 3 tablespoons butter, add 1½ cups fine breadcrumbs, and mix well. In buttered casserole place alternate layers of corn (cream style), 1 small minced green pepper, 1 cup diced raw celery, and buttered crumbs. Reserve enough crumbs for top. Scald 1 cup milk, add 1 teaspoon salt, and pour over vegetable mixture. Top with buttered crumbs. Cover and bake in moderate oven (350°F.) 25 minutes. Then uncover and bake until browned on top. Serves 4 to 6.

Scalloped corn and tomatoes: Alternate layers of cooked corn and stewed or canned tomatoes in a buttered baking dish. Sprinkle each layer with salt, pepper, and melted butter; cover with buttered crumbs. Bake in moderate oven (375°F.) until hot and crumbs are brown, 15 to 20 minutes.

Sautéed Mexican corn: Heat 2½ to 3 cups cooked corn, cut from the cob, and 1 tablespoon minced onion in 2 tablespoons butter. Add 1 tablespoon chopped pepper or pimiento, ½ teaspoon salt, and 1 teaspoon chili powder. Cook 10 minutes, stirring frequently. Serves 6.

CORN-ON-THE-COB

Select ears with fresh green husks, tender kernels. Corn should be husked just before it is cooked. Remove husks and strip off silks. Cook, covered in water to cover, 3 to 5 minutes for very young corn, 8 to 10 minutes for older corn. Do not salt water because salt tends to make corn tough. ½ teaspoon sugar per quart water may be added for older corn. Drain and place on napkin on platter. Cover with ends of napkin. Serve with butter, salt, and pepper.

Grilled corn: Drain boiled corn on the cob. Spread generously with butter. Place on rack in preheated broiler oven. Use high flame, turning ears to brown. Sprinkle with salt.

CORN FRITTERS

1 egg	2 teaspoons baking powder
½ cup milk	½ teaspoon salt
2 cups canned corn	Dash of pepper
1½ cups flour	2 teaspoons melted cooking fat

Beat egg. Add remaining ingredients and beat well. Drop by spoonfuls into hot fat (380°F.) until golden brown, about 3 minutes. Drain on absorbent paper. Makes 16 fritters.

CORN PATTIES (Mock Oysters)

2 egg yolks, well beaten	2 teaspoons cream
½ teaspoon salt	1 teaspoon butter
⅛ teaspoon pepper	2 teaspoons flour
1½ cups cooked fresh corn, cut from cob	2 egg whites, stiffly beaten

Combine all ingredients except egg whites. Mix thoroughly. Fold in the stiffly beaten egg whites. Drop by teaspoonfuls onto a hot greased griddle. Cook until brown on each side. Serve hot. Makes 24 small patties.

CORN PUDDING

3 eggs	1 teaspoon salt
2 cups fresh or canned corn	Pepper
2 tablespoons melted butter	2 cups milk

Beat eggs, add all other ingredients and more salt, if necessary. Turn into greased baking dish. Place in pan of hot water. Bake in moderate oven (350°F.) about 1 hour, or until set in center. Serves 6.

CUCUMBERS

Select firm, green, unwrinkled cucumbers, with long, slender shape. To boil: wash and pare, cut into cubes, strips, or thick slices. Cook in covered saucepan, in enough boiling salted water to cover, until tender, 10 to 15 minutes. Serve with butter, salt, and pepper.

Sautéed cucumbers: Pare and cut into ¼-inch slices or strips. Dip in egg and crumbs. Brown in butter or other fat.

BAKED CUCUMBERS

4 large cucumbers	1 cup breadcrumbs
2 tablespoons chopped onion	1 cup tomato pulp
2 tablespoons chopped parsley	1 teaspoon salt
4 tablespoons butter	Pepper

Wash and pare cucumbers. Cut in half lengthwise. Scoop out as much of seed portion as possible without breaking the fleshy part. Parboil cucumber shells in lightly salted water 10 minutes. Drain. Meanwhile cook onion and parsley in fat. Add other ingredients and cucumber pulp. Cook this mixture 5 minutes. Fill cucumber shells with hot stuffing. Place in shallow baking dish. Add a little water to keep them from sticking. Bake in moderate oven (350°F.) 15 minutes, or until stuffing has browned on top. Serve in baking dish. Serves 4 to 6.

EGGPLANT

Select eggplant that is light in weight for size, unwrinkled skin, smooth and shiny with rich purple color. One medium eggplant serves 4 to 5. Four cups pulp will serve 4 to 6. One large eggplant, stuffed, serves 6. Eggplant may be stewed, sautéed, broiled, or deep fried.

To broil: Pare and slice ½ inch thick. Season with pepper and lay slices on a preheated broiler. Spread each slice with ½ teaspoon vegetable oil and sprinkle with 1 teaspoon breadcrumbs. Broil in moderate oven (350°F.) without turning, until eggplant is tender.

To sauté: Pare and cut into ¼-inch slices. Season lightly with salt and allow to stand ½ hour. Drain and dry. Dredge with flour or dip in egg and crumbs. Sauté in a little hot fat until crisp and delicately browned, about 15 minutes.

To deep fry: Treat eggplant as above, then dip in beaten egg and breadcrumbs and fry in deep hot fat (375°F.).

To stew: Pare and slice or cut into cubes. Cook, covered in a small amount of salted water until just tender, about 10 minutes. Stewed eggplant is usually reheated with some other vegetable such as okra or tomato or both.

EGGPLANT STUFFED WITH BEEF

Cut in half lengthwise. Boil, unpared, in salted water to cover about 15 minutes. Hollow out and fill with stuffing made by browning 1 pound ground beef and 1 small onion in hot fat and combined with eggplant pulp, seasoned to taste. Refill eggplant shells and moisten well with fat. Bake in moderate oven (375°F.) until thoroughly hot. Serves 6.

STUFFED EGGPLANT (Greek Style)

1 eggplant	1 small onion, minced
2 small tomatoes, minced	1 tablespoon olive oil
1 tablespoon parsley, minced	Salt and pepper

Slice the top from eggplant and scoop out center into a bowl. Mash well and add remaining ingredients. Season to taste with salt and pepper and mix thoroughly. Stuff mixture into eggplant shell and replace top. Bake, upright, in hot oven (400°F.) 1 hour. Serves 4 to 6.

EGGPLANT CROQUETTES

1 medium eggplant	Pepper to taste
2 eggs	2 tablespoons breadcrumbs
1 teaspoon salt	Fat

Peel and dice eggplant. Cook, covered, in a very small amount of water. Drain. Add eggs, seasoning, and crumbs. Mix until smooth. Drop by spoonfuls into hot fat. Fry until brown on both sides. Serves 6.

SCALLOPED EGGPLANT

1 large eggplant	Pepper
4 tablespoons butter	4 cups canned or chopped
1 green pepper, chopped	raw tomatoes
1 small onion, chopped	1 cup breadcrumbs
2 teaspoons salt	

Pare the eggplant. Cut it into small, even pieces. Melt 2 tablespoons fat in a skillet and add green pepper and onion. Cook for a few minutes. Add tomatoes, eggplant, salt, and pepper. Cook 10 minutes. Place mixture in shallow greased baking dish. Melt remaining fat in a skillet; stir in breadcrumbs. Sprinkle crumbs over eggplant. Bake in moderate oven (375°F.) 15 minutes, or until eggplant is tender and crumbs are browned. Serves 6.

GREENS

Allow ¼ to ⅓ pound of greens per person. Leaves of mustard, kale, dandelion, beet tops, escarole, spinach, chard, chicory, and turnip tops may be used. Look over, remove all discolored and bruised leaves. Cut off roots and any tough stems. Select fresh, tender, crisp leaves with bright color. Wash in several waters, first two rather warm, to remove sand and dirt. Remove from last water, sprinkle with salt, and place in kettle without water other than what clings to leaves. Cover. Steam or cook until tender—about 10 to 30 minutes, depending on type of greens, being careful not to overcook. Spinach should not be cooked longer than 10 minutes.

KOHLRABI

Select leaves that are pale green and crisp, knobs about the size of a medium-size onion. 1 bunch serves 4 to 5. Trim off leaves, pare bulbs, and cut into ½-inch cubes. Cook, uncovered, in boiling salted water to cover, for 25 to 30 minutes. Drain, season with melted butter, cream, and salt and pepper, or serve with medium *WHITE SAUCE* or *HOLLANDAISE SAUCE*.

LEEKS

Select leeks with lower part white, upper part green. 1 bunch serves 4. Remove roots and wilted leaves. Wash and cook whole or cut into 1-inch pieces. Cook, uncovered, in boiling salted water to cover, for 15 to 20 minutes. Serve with melted butter.

HUNGARIAN LENTILS

½ pound lentils	1 tablespoon sugar
1 onion, minced	1 teaspoon salt
2 tablespoons cooking fat	2 tablespoons vinegar
2 tablespoons flour	Hot buttered toast
¼ cup cold water	

Pick over and wash lentils well. Soak overnight in cold water to cover. Drain and cover again with cold water. Simmer until tender. Sauté onion in hot fat until lightly browned. Blend in flour. Add water, sugar, salt, and vinegar. Mix well. Cook until smooth and thickened, about 2 minutes. Pour over lentils. Serve very hot on toast. Serves 6.

LETTUCE—BOILED

Allow 2 medium heads or 3 bunches to serve 6. Remove wilted leaves from leaf or head lettuce. Wash under running water. Cut heads in quarters. Add small amount of water to head lettuce, no water to leaf lettuce and cook until just tender, 5 to 10 minutes. Cover kettle for first 5 minutes and turn lettuce several times. Drain and season with salt, pepper, and melted butter.

MUSHROOMS

Select medium sized mushrooms with creamy white tops. Clean by brushing or washing in small amount of water (do not soak). Cut off tip of stem. If large and tough, peel mushrooms by paring from edge to center. If stems are large and tough, cut off and cook in small amount of water and use in stock or sauces.

Broiled mushrooms: Prepare as above, removing stems. Chop stems and season with salt and pepper. Place caps, gill side down, under flame of broiler 2 to 3 minutes. Turn and season with salt and pepper. Fill hollows with chopped seasoned stems and dot with butter. Broil under flame a few minutes longer. Lift carefully from broiler so that juices are not lost. Serve on buttered toast.

Creamed canned mushrooms: Use 2 cups canned mushrooms to 1 cup medium *WHITE SAUCE*. Heat thoroughly. Serve very hot on toast.

Creamed mushrooms: Proceed as for frying, using 2 tablespoons flour for each ½ pound mushrooms. Add 1 cup light cream when half done.

Fried mushrooms: Melt 3 tablespoons butter in skillet for each ½ pound mushrooms. Slice or quarter mushrooms. Sprinkle with flour and add to melted butter. Cover and cook until tender, 8 to 10 minutes.

MUSHROOMS WITH SOUR CREAM À LA RUSSE

1 pound fresh mushrooms	Pepper
2 tablespoons butter	2 teaspoons flour
1 small onion, chopped fine	1 cup sour cream
½ teaspoon salt	Dash of Worcestershire sauce

Do not peel mushrooms. Wash, drain, and slice them. Heat butter in saucepan. Add chopped onion and mushrooms. Sauté until almost done. Season and dredge with flour. Mix thoroughly. Lower heat, cover, and simmer a few minutes. Stir in sour cream, a little at a time. Do not let mixture boil. And Worcestershire sauce. Turn into greased casserole. Cover and bake in moderate oven (350°F.) 20 minutes. Serves 4.

BAKED STUFFED MUSHROOMS

12 large mushrooms	1 tablespoon ketchup
2 tablespoons butter	1 teaspoon finely chopped parsley
1 teaspoon grated onion	Salt and pepper
2 cups soft, fine breadcrumbs	

Wash mushrooms. Remove stems and chop fine. Melt butter and add chopped stems and grated onion. Fry gently. Add crumbs, ketchup, and parsley. Mix well. Sprinkle inside of caps with salt and pepper and stuff with crumb mixture, heaping up well. Place on greased baking sheet. Bake in hot oven (425°F.) until stuffing is browned, about 15 minutes. Garnish with strips of pimiento if desired. Serves 4 to 6.

OKRA OR GUMBO

Select fresh, young okra, pods crisp to the touch that break easily. I pound serves 4. Wash and remove stems carefully. Slice ½ inch thick. Cook in covered pan, in enough boiling, salted water to cover, until tender, 15 to 25 minutes. Drain and add 3 to 4 tablespoons melted butter for each pound. Season with salt and pepper and lemon juice, if desired.

Fried okra: Wash and dry okra thoroughly before cutting into ½-inch pieces. Heat 3 or 4 tablespoons fat in heavy skillet. Add okra, cover and cook 10 minutes, stirring frequently to prevent burning. Remove cover and cook until tender and lightly browned. Serve at once.

Okra and tomatoes: Sauté ½ cup minced onions in hot fat until brown. Add 1 pound sliced okra. Sauté 5 minutes. Add 2½ cups canned tomatoes, 1 teaspoon salt, ½ teaspoon paprika, ¼ teaspoon curry powder, and 2 teaspoons brown sugar. Cover, simmer until okra is tender. Cooked or canned corn kernels and chopped green pepper may be added.

ONIONS

Select onions of uniform size, unsprouted, firm to the touch. Peel under water. Leave whole, quarter, or slice. Cook in covered pan, in enough boiling salted water to cover. If small, sliced or quartered, cook 20 minutes. If large, about 30 to 40 minutes. Serve buttered, creamed, or scalloped.

GLAZED ONIONS

Peel 10 to 15 small white onions. Add enough boiling salted water to cover. Cook, uncovered, until almost tender. Drain. Melt 4 tablespoons butter and 2 tablespoons sugar in skillet. Add onions, ⅛ teaspoon salt, and a few grains pepper. Cook over low heat, 10 to 15 minutes, turning to brown on all sides. Serves 5 to 6.

FRENCH FRIED ONIONS

6 or 8 medium-size onions	1 egg
1 cup flour	¼ teaspoon salt
1 cup milk	Cooking fat

Skin the onions. Slice very thin and separate into rings. Dip into a batter made from the flour, milk, egg, and salt. Drain well. Fry in deep hot fat (360° to 375°F.) until golden brown. Drain on absorbent paper. Sprinkle with salt.

CREAMY FRIED ONIONS

Skin and cut 4 medium-size onions into ⅛-inch slices. Heat 3 tablespoons drippings in skillet. Add onions and cook on medium heat 15 minutes or until golden brown. Sprinkle 3 tablespoons flour over onions. Add ¾ cup water, 1 teaspoon salt, and a few grains pepper. Lastly add ¾ cup evaporated milk. Cook slowly for 2 minutes. Serves 5.

STUFFED ONIONS

5 large mild onions	2 tablespoons chopped parsley
3 tablespoons butter or	2 cups breadcrumbs
other fat	1 teaspoon salt
½ cup chopped celery	Pepper

Skin the onions. Cut in half crosswise. Simmer in salted water until almost tender. Drain. Remove centers without disturbing outer layers and chop fine. Melt 2 tablespoons fat in a skillet. Add chopped onion, celery, and parsley. Cook a few minutes. Push vegetables to one side. Melt remaining fat and add to it the breadcrumbs, salt, and pepper, then combine with vegetables. Fill onion shells with stuffing. Cover and bake in moderate oven about 30 minutes, or until onions are tender. Remove cover from baking dish during last 10 minutes to brown. Serves 5.

PARSNIPS

Select small to medium size, firm roots. 1½ pounds serves 5. Wash. Peel or scrape and cut into ½-inch slices or in half lengthwise. If tough, remove cores. Cook in covered pan, in enough boiling salted water to cover, 30 to 45 minutes. Drain and salt to taste.

Baked parsnips: Scrape and cut into strips ¼ inch thick. Place in buttered casserole. Add salt to taste and a tablespoon hot water to each 5 or 6 parsnips. Cover and bake in moderate oven (350°F.) until tender, 10 to 15 minutes. To sweeten, add 1 tablespoon dark molasses before baking.

French fried parsnips: Cut raw parsnips into very thin slices. Fry in deep hot fat (380° F.) until delicately brown, 7 to 8 minutes.

Glazed parsnips: Cook 12 medium-size parsnips until nearly tender. Heat 2 tablespoons butter, ⅓ cup sugar, and 1 tablespoon water in skillet. Add parsnips and cook until glazed and golden brown.

Mashed parsnips: Mash boiled parsnips or press through ricer. For 3 or 4 cups parsnips add ½ cup hot milk, 3 to 4 tablespoons butter, salt and pepper to taste. Beat until fluffy.

Pan fried parsnips: Heat drippings in skillet. Sauté cooked parsnips. May be rolled in seasoned flour before sautéing.

Scalloped parsnips: Follow recipe for *SCALLOPED VEGETABLES.*

PEAS–GREEN

One pound peas (unshelled) serves 2. Do not shell until ready to cook. However, if necessary to prepare in advance, store in covered utensil in refrigerator to preserve vitamin content. Shell and wash. Cook in covered pan in very small amount of boiling salted water, 10 to 20 minutes. Drain. Add butter and salt to taste.

Creamed peas: Follow recipe for *CREAMED VEGETABLES.*

Minted peas: Add sprigs of mint to boiling water with peas. When cooked, remove mint. Drain and season with salt and butter.

Peas and onions: Combine hot cooked peas with small cooked white onions.

Peas with peanut butter and parsley: Melt 1 tablespoon butter in saucepan. Add 3 cups cooked peas, salt and pepper to taste. Dot top with 1 tablespoon peanut butter. Stir occasionally until peanut butter is melted. Add 1 tablespoon minced parsley. Serve hot. Serves 6.

DRIED SPLIT PEAS

One cup serves 4 to 5. Wash and soak overnight in 4 times as much water as peas. Cook in covered pan in boiling salted water about 1½ hours. Salt to taste after ½ hour of cooking.

BOILED CHICK PEAS (Nahit)

Soak dried peas in water to cover for 12 hours. Drain and rinse in cold water. Add fresh water to cover and cook, covered, 30 to 40 minutes. Add salt to taste and continue cooking until tender. Drain and sprinkle lightly with salt. Serve hot or cold.

CHICK PEA (Nahit) CASSEROLE

1 pound chick peas	2 tablespoons cooking fat
1 tablespoon salt	2 tablespoons flour
2 pounds brisket of beef	2 tablespoons brown sugar

Soak peas in salted water to cover for 12 hours. Drain. Cover with boiling water and cook 15 minutes. Add meat. Simmer until peas are tender. Thicken gravy by melting fat, blending in flour and brown sugar, and adding 1 cup liquid from peas. Cook until thick and brown. Place peas and meat in a casserole and add gravy. Bake in moderate oven (350°F.) about ½ hour. Serves 6.

STUFFED PEPPERS (Basic Recipe)

Cut off stem ends of pepper. If very large, cut into half lengthwise. Remove seeds and inner white ribs. Parboil by dropping into boiling water. Remove from fire and let stand in the water about 5 minutes. Drain well, stuff with desired filling, and bake as directed.

MEAT AND RICE STUFFED PEPPERS

1 cup cooked rice	Salt and pepper
2 cups cooked meat	6 green peppers
1 tablespoon minced onion	Crumbs
1 egg, beaten	

Combine and mix rice, chopped meat, onion, and egg. Season to taste. Stuff prepared peppers. Cover with crumbs and dot with fat. Place upright in baking dish. Surround peppers with water or stock about ¼ inch in depth. Bake until peppers are tender and tops browned, 30 to 40 minutes. Serves 6.

Variation: Substitute 1 cup canned or cooked corn for 1 cup meat.

CHEESE STUFFED PEPPERS

6 green peppers	2 tablespoons olive oil
Cottage cheese	1 cup hot tomato sauce
Salt and pepper	3 eggs, separated
Flour	

Parboil peppers, remove outer skins. Season cottage cheese with salt and pepper to taste. Stuff peppers. Roll in flour and place in baking dish. Heat olive oil until smoking hot and pour into dish. Pour hot tomato sauce over peppers. Bake in moderate oven (350°F.) until tender, about 20 minutes. Combine slightly beaten yolks with stiffly beaten whites, season with salt and pepper, and pour over peppers. Bake 20 minutes longer. Serve hot. Serves 6.

SALMON STUFFED PEPPERS

6 green peppers	¾ cup milk
1 1-pound can salmon	1 teaspoon salt
1 onion, grated	1 egg, beaten
¾ cup soft breadcrumbs	2 teaspoons lemon juice

Combine all ingredients. Mix well. Stuff prepared peppers. Top with buttered breadcrumbs. Bake in moderate oven (375°F.) until just tender, 15 to 20 minutes. Do not allow peppers to brown.

POTATOES—BOILED

Wash and scrub with brush if potatoes are to be boiled in their skins. Cook in boiling salted water in covered pan until tender, 20 to 40 minutes. Drain and shake in pan over low heat until potatoes are dry and mealy.

Boiled new potatoes: Scrub with brush or scrape, but do not pare. Cook as above for 25 to 30 minutes.

Cheese potatoes: Cover hot boiled potatoes with cheese sauce or sprinkle grated cheese over potatoes. Add cream and heat.

Parsley potatoes: For each 5 or 6 potatoes, sprinkle 3 tablespoons chopped parsley and 2 tablespoons melted butter or chicken fat over cooked, pared potatoes.

Potatoes and carrots: Cook an equal amount of sliced carrots and potatoes together until done. Season and add cream and butter.

Potatoes and onions: Cook an equal amount of sliced or whole onions and potatoes together until done. Season with cream and butter.

Potatoes and peas: Cook whole new potatoes with new peas. Serve creamed.

Quick browned potatoes: Sprinkle hot boiled potatoes with flour. Brown in hot fat.

Savory potatoes: Season hot boiled potatoes with cream and paprika.

CREAMED POTATOES (Franconia)

Use cooked sliced or diced potatoes. Prepare thin WHITE SAUCE. If potatoes are cold reheat in sauce. Add chopped pimiento and sprinkle with chopped parsley.

MASHED POTATOES (Basic Recipe)

Boil potatoes. Force through a ricer or mash well. Season to taste with salt and pepper. Add ⅓ cup hot milk or potato liquid and 3 tablespoons butter, chicken fat, sour cream, or sour milk for every 5 potatoes. Beat well until light and fluffy. To keep hot set over pan of hot water or pile lightly in casserole and place in slow oven (325°F.).

Baked potato puff: Add 1 egg yolk to 2 cups riced potatoes. Beat well. Fold in 1 stiffly beaten egg white. Place on greased baking pan and bake in moderate oven (350°F.) until browned.

Cheese potatoes: Add ½ cup grated cheese to 2 cups mashed potatoes. Sprinkle grated cheese and paprika on top. Brown in moderate oven (350°F.).

Duchess potatoes: Add 2 tablespoons butter, ½ teaspoon salt, and 2 slightly beaten egg yolks to 2 to 3 cups hot riced or mashed potatoes. Mix thoroughly, Shape into patties or croquettes. Place in greased shallow baking dish. Brown in hot oven (450°F.). Serves 4 to 6.

Mashed potato cakes: Combine 2 cups seasoned, mashed potatoes with one egg. Shape into four patties. Dip in flour. Fry until well browned in hot shortening about ¼ inch deep in heavy skillet. Serves 4.

Mashed potatoes with fried onions: Prepare mashed potatoes. Before serving cover with sliced fried onions.

Parsley mashed potatoes: Beat finely chopped parsley into mashed potatoes.

Pimiento potatoes: Add diced pimiento to hot mashed potatoes.

Potato cakes with meat: Add ½ cup ground left-over meat to 2 cups cold mashed potatoes. Form into cakes. Fry until browned.

Potato nests: Make a cavity in center of mashed potato mound. Fill with creamed carrots or peas.

Yellow mashed potatoes: Rice or mash together boiled potatoes and boiled carrots

POTATOES—BAKED

Scrub potatoes, dry, rub skins with soft butter or chicken fat. Bake in preheated hot oven (450°F.) until tender, 45 to 60 minutes. Remove from oven, cut 2 crossed slits on one side, and pinch potato until it opens at slit. Put a lump of butter or chicken fat in opening, sprinkle with paprika.

Baked stuffed potatoes: Bake as above, then cut in half lengthwise. Carefully scoop out potato without breaking skin. Mash potato with butter or chicken fat, salt, pepper, and enough milk or potato water to give a fluffy texture. Pile mixture into shell, sprinkle with grated cheese and paprika. Return to oven to brown.

Baked stuffed potatoes with egg: For every potato add 1 chopped, hard-cooked egg to the mixture.

Baked stuffed potatoes with meat, fish, or vegetables: Omit milk. Combine potato with any leftover creamed fish or vegetables, or cooked poultry or meat moistened with fat.

Baked stuffed potatoes with mushrooms: For every potato add 1 tablespoon chopped or sliced sautéed mushrooms to the mixture.

FRENCH FRIED POTATOES

Wash, pare, and cut potatoes into lengthwise strips, about ½ inch thick. Soak in cold water 1 hour. Drain, dry thoroughly between towels. Heat kettle of deep fat, hot enough to brown a small piece of bread in 60 seconds (375°F.). Fry about a cupful of sliced potatoes at one time until lightly browned. Drain on absorbent paper. Just before serving return to hot fat (385°F.) and fry until crisp and brown. Drain on absorbent paper and sprinkle with salt. Serve at once.

Lattice potatoes: Cut potatoes with a lattice vegetable cutter. Fry as above.

Potato balls: Cut potatoes into tiny balls with ball cutter. Fry as above.

Potato chips: Cut potatoes into thin slices. Fry as above.

Saratoga chips: Cut potatoes into very thin slices. Soak in cold water, drain, and plunge into boiling water. Drain, dry, and fry as above.

SOUFFLEED POTATO SLICES

Select medium-size Idaho potatoes of uniform size. Pare and cut on slant in slices about ⅛ inch thick. Dry between towels. Fry, a few at a time, in medium hot deep fat (275°–300°F.) 5 minutes, keeping potatoes in motion. Then lift basket and plunge quickly into very hot deep fat (400°–425°F.) 1 to 2 minutes, or until puffed and browned, keeping potatoes moving. They should puff at once when dropped into kettle of very hot fat. Hold basket over kettle for fat to drip, then turn out on absorbent paper to drain. Sprinkle with salt. Serve at once. The type of potato and the quick changes from a medium hot to a very hot fat are important in making these slices.

COTTAGE FRIED POTATOES

Cook potatoes in jackets. Remove skins and slice or dice. Fry in hot fat, turning frequently, until brown and crisp. Season with salt and pepper.

Lyonnaise potatoes: Proceed as in *COTTAGE FRIED POTATOES*, frying thinly sliced onions with the potatoes.

HASH BROWNED POTATOES

Use a medium-size skillet. Heat 3 tablespoons shortening. Add 3 cups diced, cooked potatoes, salt and pepper to taste, and sufficient milk to moisten (about ¼ cup). Cover. Cook slowly, stirring only until milk is absorbed. Turn once.

ESCALLOPED POTATOES

3 tablespoons butter	1 teaspoon salt
¾ cup fine dry breadcrumbs	1½ cups milk
6 raw sliced potatoes	Paprika
3 large onions, sliced	

Melt butter, add dry crumbs, and mix well. Arrange alternate layers of potatoes and onions in a buttered casserole. Sprinkle with buttered crumbs. Add salt to milk and pour over all. Top with remaining crumbs and sprinkle with paprika. Cover and bake 30 minutes in preheated oven, then uncover, and bake until browned on top and potatoes are tender. Total baking time in hot oven (400°F.) 50 to 60 minutes, in slow oven (275°F.) 3 hours. Serves 4 to 6. Two and a half tablespoons flour may be substituted for crumbs. Sprinkle flour between layers and add butter in small bits.

Au gratin potatoes: Sprinkle grated cheese between layers and over top in above recipe.

POTATO CHEESE PUFFS

3 cups hot mashed potatoes	⅓ cup grated American cheese
½ cup heavy cream, whipped	

Mash potatoes with salt and butter to taste, and enough milk to give a light fluffy consistency. Place in buttered custard cups. Whip cream, add cheese, and mix well. Spread over potatoes. Bake in moderate oven (350°F.) about 15 minutes, or until browned. Serves 6.

POTATO CROQUETTES (Basic Recipe)

2 cups hot riced potatoes	Few grains cayenne
2 tablespoons butter	Few drops onion juice
½ teaspoon salt	1 egg yolk
⅛ teaspoon pepper	1 teaspoon finely chopped parsley
¼ teaspoon celery salt	

Mix ingredients in order given and beat thoroughly, shape, dip in crumbs, egg and crumbs again. Fry 1 minute in deep fat (365° to 380°F.) and drain on absorbent paper. Croquettes are shaped in a variety of forms. The most common way is first to form a smooth ball by rolling one rounding tablespoon of mixture between hands. Then roll on a board in shape of cylinder of desired length. Serves 6 to 8.

Potato and cheese croquettes: Add ⅓ cup grated cheese.

Potato and nut croquettes: Add ⅓ cup chopped nutmeats.

POTATO PANCAKES (Latkes)

6 medium size potatoes
1 small onion (optional)
2 eggs, slightly beaten
3 tablespoons flour

¼ teaspoon pepper
1 teaspoon salt
½ teaspoon baking powder

Peel and grate potatoes and onion. Let stand 10 minutes so that liquid will rise to top. Remove liquid. Stir in eggs. Add other ingredients. Drop by spoonfuls into a hot well-greased skillet. Brown on both sides. Drain on absorbent paper. Serve hot with apple sauce, sugar, or sour cream.

Potato cakes with meat: Add ½ cup diced, cooked meat or cracklings. Substitute breadcrumbs or matzo meal for flour. Fry same as *POTATO PANCAKES*.

Potato cupcakes: Bake potato pancake mixture in well-greased custard cups in moderate oven (350°F.) until brown, about 40 minutes. Serve hot.

Potato kugel #1: Prepare potato pancake mixture and bake in a shallow greased casserole in a moderate oven (350°F.) until brown, about 40 minutes. Serve hot.

POTATO KUGEL (Potato Pie) #2

6 medium size potatoes, peeled
2 eggs
½ cup flour
½ teaspoon baking powder

1½ teaspoons salt
⅛ teaspoon pepper
1 large onion, chopped fine
¼ cup fat

Grate potatoes quickly so they will not discolor. Squeeze out excess liquid. Add eggs and mix well. Sift together dry ingredients. Add to potatoes. Sauté onion in hot fat until lightly browned. Add both to batter. Stir well. Pour into greased baking pan. Bake in moderate oven (350°F.) until brown and crisp at edges, about 1 hour. Serve hot. Serves 6.

Variation: Turn into well-greased small custard cups. Bake in moderate oven (350°F.) about 45 minutes.

POTATOES O'BRIEN

Combine 2 cups cooked, chopped potatoes, ¼ cup each of minced green pepper and onion, and 1 tablespoon diced pimiento. Fry until golden brown in hot fat about ¼ inch deep in heavy skillet. Serves 4.

BROWNED POTATOES

Pare potatoes of uniform size. Parboil potatoes about 10 minutes, if desired, then place in pan in which meat is roasting. Bake until soft, about 40 minutes, basting occasionally with drippings in pan. Turn several times.

POTATOES IN SOUR CREAM

12 small new potatoes
  Salt and pepper
3 tablespoons butter

2 teaspoons flour
1 cup sour cream
1 tablespoon chopped parsley

Scrape skins from potatoes and rub with salt. Wash in cold water. Drain and place in a heavy pan. Season with salt and pepper. Cook, covered with a small amount of water over low heat 10 minutes. Shake to avoid scorching. Drain off excess liquid. Blend butter and flour and add to potatoes. Stir in sour cream. Mix well and cook, covered, over very low heat until potatoes are tender. Add more sour cream if necessary. Sprinkle with parsley. Serve hot. Serves 6.

ANNA POTATOES

8 cooked potatoes, cold
2 tablespoons grated American
  cheese

2 tablespoons breadcrumbs
1 tablespoon butter
Paprika, if desired

Cut cold potatoes into thin round slices. Place in a baking dish and sprinkle with grated cheese and fresh breadcrumbs. Dot with butter and bake in a moderate oven (375°F.) until golden brown, 10 to 15 minutes. A sprinkling of paprika may be added, before baking. Serves 6.

BRONZE POTATOES

Wash 5 medium-size potatoes, do not peel. Cook in boiling salted water until just tender. Drain. Cut with skins on, into 1/4-inch slices. Sauté in 1/4 cup hot fat until nicely browned on both sides, being careful not to break the slices. Sprinkle with salt and pepper and serve at once. Serves 6.

CHEESE POTATO SOUFFLE

2 cups mashed potato
3 eggs, separated
1/2 teaspoon salt

1/8 teaspoon white pepper
3/4 cup grated cheese

Combine hot mashed potato, well-beaten egg yolks, seasoning, and 1/2 cup grated cheese. Lastly fold in stiffly beaten egg whites. Turn into greased pan. Sprinkle remaining cheese over top. Place baking dish in a pan containing an inch of hot water. Bake in moderate oven (375°F.) 25 to 30 minutes. Serve at once. Serves 6.

SWEET POTATOES

Boiled in jackets: Wash and scrub sweet potatoes. Cook whole in boiling salted water, covered, about 30 minutes or until tender. Drain. Peel, and season with butter or meat drippings, salt and pepper to taste.

QUICK MASHED SWEET POTATOES

Peel hot cooked sweet potatoes (6 medium size make 6 servings). Mash thoroughly and quickly. Add seasoning and butter. Beat in hot milk a little at a time until sweet potatoes are fluffy and smooth.

Variations: #1. Shape seasoned mashed sweet potatoes into mounds with small well in center. Brown in hot oven (425°F.). Fill well with cranberry sauce or jelly, and serve hot.

#2. Use orange juice in place of milk, add a little grated orange rind, butter, and a few raisins. If desired, place in baking dish, top with meringue, and brown lightly in moderate oven (350°F.). Serve hot.

BAKED SWEET POTATOES

Select medium-size or large sweet potatoes. Scrub thoroughly, removing any imperfections, and rub skins all over with a little cooking fat of any kind. Place in a baking pan or on the grate of a moderate oven (350°F.). Bake until potatoes are soft, from 40 to 60 minutes, according to size. Remove from stove and cut lengthwise, then crosswise to allow steam to escape. Pinch the potatoes, pressing up the pulp so that it will show. To save time in baking sweet potatoes, they may be parboiled for 15 minutes. Serve plain, or with a dusting of paprika and a small butter ball, or a cube of butter on each potato.

STUFFED SWEET POTATOES

Cut large baked sweet potatoes in half lengthwise. Carefully scoop out inside, leaving a little of sweet potato as a lining for shell. Mash as for plain mashed sweet potatoes, adding seasoning and hot milk. Stuff back into shells. Brush top with melted fat. Reheat in hot oven (425°F.).

Variations: Add chopped left-over cooked meat or chopped peanuts. Or add a tablespoon of peanut butter for each sweet potato in place of fat, or a little grated orange rind and orange juice in place of milk.

PAN-FRIED SWEET POTATOES

Boil sweet potatoes in jackets, peel, and slice. Add salt and pepper to taste. Fry in hot fat in large skillet, turning occasionally until nicely browned.

SCALLOPED SWEET POTATOES

With apples: Place alternate layers of sliced cooked sweet potatoes and sliced raw apples in a greased baking dish. Sprinkle apple layers with sugar and a little salt. Dot with fat. Add just enough hot water to cover bottom of dish. Apples and sweet potatoes do not take up liquid. Bake covered in a moderate oven (375°F.) 30 to 40 minutes, or until apples are tender. If desired, uncover the dish for last 15 to 20 minutes of cooking and top with crushed dry breakfast cereal or breadcrumbs mixed with a little fat. Sliced raw sweet potatoes may be used but require a longer baking period.

Variations: Substitute peeled orange slices, cranberry sauce (not jelly), or sliced fresh pears for apples. With pears, use brown sugar instead of granulated for added flavor. Top with breadcrumbs and bake 20 to 30 minutes.

With orange juice: Omit apples and water in recipe above. Pour over sweet potatoes ⅓ to ½ cup orange juice containing a little grated orange rind. Top with breadcrumbs, and bake about 20 minutes.

With peanuts: Substitute chopped roasted peanuts for apples. Omit fat and crumbs, and, if nuts are salted, omit salt. Bake 20 to 30 minutes.

SWEET POTATOES WITH MARSHMALLOWS

Boil 4 to 6 medium-size sweet potatoes until tender, but not soft. Drain, peel, and put through ricer or mash with fork. Add milk, butter, 4 tablespoons chopped walnut meats, brown sugar, and salt to taste. Turn mixture into buttered baking dish, allowing enough room between layer of potatoes and top of dish for a layer of marshmallows, which swell and spread during cooking. Bake in slow oven (325°F.) until marshmallows are puffed and browned. Serve in baking dish. Serves 6.

SWEET POTATOES CANDIED WITH BROWN SUGAR

Combine and bring to boil ¾ cup brown sugar, ⅓ cup water, ½ teaspoon salt, and 2 tablespoons butter. Place halves of 6 cooked medium-size sweet potatoes in greased baking dish and pour over mixture. Bake in moderate oven (350°F.) 15 to 20 minutes, basting frequently with syrup. Serves 6.

GLAZED SWEET POTATOES

Pare sweet potatoes and cut in halves. Drop into enough boiling salted water to just cover. For each sweet potato add 1 to 2 tablespoons honey (corn or maple syrup, or molasses), and 1 teaspoon butter. Cover and boil until sweet potatoes are tender. If liquid has not cooked down enough by the time they are tender, remove cover and boil rapidly until a syrup is formed. Baste sweet potatoes occasionally with the syrup.

CANDIED SWEET POTATOES

6 medium-size sweet potatoes, peeled	¼ cup orange juice
	1 cup dark corn syrup
2 tablespoons flour	3 tablespoons butter

Parboil sweet potatoes in salted water. Drain. Cut in halves lengthwise. Place in a greased baking dish. Combine flour with orange juice. Add syrup and mix well. Pour over sweet potatoes. Dot with butter. Bake, uncovered, in moderate oven (375°F.) 1 hour. Serves 8.

SWEET POTATO PUFF

5 or 6 medium-size sweet potatoes	2 tablespoons hot milk
2 eggs, separated	1 teaspoon salt
2 tablespoons melted butter	

Cook sweet potatoes until tender. Drain, peel, and press through a potato ricer. There should be about 1 quart of pulp. Beat yolks and whites of eggs separately. Combine sweet potato with egg yolks, butter, milk, and salt. Beat well and fold in stiffly beaten whites. Pile mixture lightly into a greased baking dish. Bake in moderate oven (350°F.) 45 minutes, or until light and fluffy and browned on top. Serves 6.

SWEET POTATO PATTIES

Shape cold mashed sweet potatoes into small patties. Roll in breadcrumbs or crushed dry breakfast cereal. Brown on both sides in a little fat.

Variation: Add to the sweet potatoes chopped, cooked left-over meat, or finely chopped apple.

SWEET POTATOES IN ORANGE CUPS

3 large oranges	½ teaspoon salt
3 cups mashed sweet potatoes	1 tablespoon brown sugar
½ cup cream	6 marshmallows

Cut oranges in half. Remove pulp, discarding the white membrane. Cut pulp into small pieces. Combine and mix together sweet potatoes, cream, salt, brown sugar, and orange pulp. Fill orange cups with potato mixture and top with marshmallows. Arrange orange cups on baking sheet. Bake in moderate oven (350°F.) until marshmallows are golden brown, 20 minutes. Serves 6.

SWEET POTATO PUDDING

1¼ cups mashed sweet potato	½ cup boiling water
¼ teaspoon nutmeg	½ cup sugar
¼ teaspoon allspice	2 eggs, beaten
½ teaspoon salt	1 cup evaporated milk

Scrub and boil 2 medium-size sweet potatoes. Peel and mash. Mix spices and salt. Add water slowly. Combine sweet potatoes, spice mixture, sugar, and beaten eggs. Blend well and add milk. Turn into custard cups or baking dish and bake in slow oven (325°F.) until set, about 1 hour. If a deep baking dish is used, set in pan of hot water to bake. Serve hot or cold with *WHIPPED LEMON SAUCE*. Serves 6.

Whipped lemon sauce: (Prepare *WHIPPED LEMON SAUCE* when ready to serve pudding.) Chill ½ cup evaporated milk until icy cold. Whip milk until stiff. Add 1 tablespoon lemon juice and whip just enough to blend. Fold in ½ cup sifted confectioners' sugar and ½ teaspoon grated lemon rind.

SWEET POTATO CROQUETTES

2 cups mashed sweet potatoes	¼ cup hot cream
3 eggs	Pinch of salt
¾ cup pecans, chopped fine	Cracker crumbs, powdered

Press potatoes through ricer. Add 2 well-beaten eggs, nuts, cream, and salt. More or less cream may be needed, depending on the consistency of the potatoes. Shape into flat rounds. Dip lightly in beaten egg, then in crumbs. Fry in deep fat (375°F.). Serves 6.

RUTABAGAS AND TURNIPS

Wash, pare, and slice, dice, or quarter. Cook, covered in boiling salted water until tender, 20 to 30 minutes. Drain. Serve with melted butter, season to taste.

Mashed rutabagas or turnips: Prepare as above. Cook with only enough salted water so that the water can be mashed with the vegetable. Bring to steam rapidly, then turn heat to low. Cook until tender, mash, season with butter, salt, and pepper.

Glazed turnips: Cook 8 small or 2½ cups diced turnips until tender. Drain. Place in skillet with 3 tablespoons butter, 3 tablespoons corn syrup, and 1 blade of mace. Cook slowly until lightly browned, turning often. Serves 6.

Mashed with potatoes: Mash equal quantities of potatoes with turnips and rutabagas. Season with butter, salt, and pepper.

Rutabaga au gratin or turnips au gratin: Follow recipe for SCALLOPED VEGE-TABLES WITH CHEESE.

Rutabagas or turnips creamed: Follow recipe for CREAMED VEGETABLES.

SALSIFY (Oyster Plant)

Wash, scrape, and cut into small pieces. Place in cold water, adding 1 teaspoon vinegar to 1 quart of water to prevent turning dark. Drain. Cover with boiling salted water. Cover and cook until tender, 20 to 30 minutes. Drain and add melted butter, and season with salt and pepper to taste.

Creamed salsify: Boil salsify and drain. Prepare a sauce of 2 tablespoons butter, 2 tablespoons flour, 1 cup milk, ½ teaspoon salt, and a dash of pepper. Pour over cooked salsify. Reheat and serve with 1 tablespoon chopped parsley sprinkled over top.

Sautéed salsify: Boil salsify and drain. Dredge in seasoned flour. Sauté in fat until brown, 7 to 10 minutes.

SAUERKRAUT AND APPLES

3 apples	½ teaspoon salt
2 cups sauerkraut	1 tablespoon sugar
¼ cup cooking fat	1 teaspoon caraway seed
¼ cup water	2 small potatoes, grated
1 small onion, sliced	

Core and quarter the apples. Combine with sauerkraut, fat, water, and onion. Cook gently until apple is tender. Add salt, sugar, caraway seed, and grated potato. Cook until potato is done, about 5 minutes. Serves 6.

SPINACH

One pound serves 3. Pick over carefully, discard wilted leaves, cut off stem ends, and wash in several waters to remove grit. If young and tender, cook in water that clings to leaves. Start the cooking at moderate heat, cover the kettle at first, turn the spinach once or twice until thoroughly wilted, then remove cover, and stir frequently. Cook 10 to 15 minutes (a quantity of 2 pounds), chop fine, season with pepper, salt, and butter, and serve. Spinach cooked this way will retain its attractive green color and flavor. Older spinach is better if cooked in a small quantity of water for about 20 minutes, then drained, chopped, and seasoned with butter, pepper, and salt.

Spinach ring: Cook as above. Pack into greased ring mold. Keep in a pan of hot water until ready to serve. Unmold on hot plate. Fill center with any desired sauce or creamed eggs. Sprinkle spinach with chopped hard-cooked egg.

Dutch style spinach: Cook 2 pounds of spinach. Just before serving add 3 tablespoons butter, 1 or 2 rusks, finely crumbled, and a dash of nutmeg. Serves 6.

SCALLOPED SPINACH WITH CHEESE

1½ pounds fresh spinach	1 cup hot milk
1½ teaspoons salt	⅛ teaspoon pepper
4 tablespoons butter	½ cup grated cheese
2 tablespoons flour	½ cup soft breadcrumbs

Wash spinach well and cook with 1 teaspoon salt until tender, 8 to 10 minutes. Melt over low heat 2 tablespoons butter. Blend in flour and slowly stir in hot milk. Season with remaining ½ teaspoon salt and pepper. Add cheese. Stir until melted. Place alternate layers of spinach and cheese sauce in a greased 2-quart baking dish. Cover with breadcrumbs mixed with remaining butter. Bake in moderate oven (375°F.) 20 minutes. Serves 6.

HUNGARIAN SPINACH

Chop enough boiled and drained spinach to make 2 cups and keep warm. Melt 1 tablespoon butter and add 2 tablespoons flour, salt and pepper to taste, ½ teaspoon paprika, and 1 cup milk. Simmer until thick, stirring constantly. Place the hot spinach in a dish. Arrange 4 sliced hard-cooked eggs on top. Pour over the hot sauce. Serve at once. Serves 6.

SPINACH IN CREAM

2 pounds spinach	1 cup cream
2 tablespoons butter	½ teaspoon salt

Wash spinach thoroughly in running water until free from grit. Press into saucepan. Add a very small quantity of water, or cover pan and cook spinach with water which clings to leaves. Cook about 10 minutes, or until wilted, and stir occasionally, so that it cooks evenly. Drain and chop very fine. Melt butter in a saucepan. Add cream and salt, and when hot add chopped spinach but no liquid. Simmer a few minutes longer. Add more salt, if needed. Serve at once. Serves 6 to 8.

SPINACH TIMBALES

3½ cups chopped cooked spinach	2 tablespoons melted butter
3 eggs, slightly beaten	½ teaspoon salt
¼ cup cream	¾ cup soft, fine breadcrumbs

Combine ingredients and mix well. Fill buttered custard cups ⅔ full. Place in shallow baking pan of hot water. Bake in moderate oven (350°F.) about 40 minutes, or until firm. Unmold. Serve with WHITE SAUCE. Place a slice of hard-cooked egg on top of each timbale. Serves 6.

SUMMER SQUASH

Select young, firm, thin-skinned squash with no soft spots. Wash squash and dice, quarter, or slice. Do not remove seeds if squash is young and tender. Place in very small amount boiling salted water. Cover and boil until almost tender, 10 to 15 minutes. Uncover and boil rapidly a few minutes to evaporate liquid. Mash. Season to taste.

Baked squash: Cut squash in half. Remove seeds and membrane. Cut as desired. Bake 1½ hours at 400°F. or 3 hours at 300°F. in a covered pan. Do not add water. Before serving, top each piece with a lump of butter. If desired, scoop from shell and mash before serving.

Panned summer squash: Select young, tender squash. Wash well, and remove tips from each end. Cut into small pieces, leaving skin on unless it is very tough. Melt 3 tablespoons butter in a skillet until slightly brown. Put in 1½ quarts diced squash. Sprinkle with 1½ teaspoons salt and ⅛ teaspoon pepper. Cover and cook 10 to 15 minutes at moderate heat. Remove cover and cook a little longer for liquid to evaporate.

WINTER SQUASH

Scrub squash. Cut in halves lengthwise. Remove seeds and stringy portions. Pare and cut into small serving pieces. Cook rapidly in small amount boiling salted water, covered, until tender, 20 to 30 minutes. Drain, mash, and season to taste with salt, pepper, and butter.

Steamed winter squash: Prepare as above. Steam over boiling water until tender, 30 to 40 minutes. Press through sieve or potato ricer. Beat well. Season with salt, pepper, and butter.

Baked winter squash #1: Select a medium-size squash. Wash well and cut in pieces about 3 inches square. Remove seeds and stringy portion. Place in a greased shallow pan. Sprinkle with salt and pepper. Pour melted butter or other fat over top. Cover and bake in moderate oven (350°F.) 1 hour, or until squash is tender. Serve hot.

Baked winter squash #2: Prepare as for *BAKED SQUASH* above but place unseasoned in greased baking dish and bake 45 minutes. Remove from oven. Turn squash over. Spread with 1 tablespoon butter and sprinkle with 1 teaspoon mixed salt, pepper, nutmeg, and 2 tablespoons brown sugar. Return to oven and bake 20 to 30 minutes longer.

STUFFED BAKED TOMATOES

Select medium tomatoes of uniform size. Scald and peel. Scoop out the pulp, leaving a thin shell, and stuff with desired filling. If possible add at least part of the scooped out pulp to the stuffing.

STUFFINGS FOR BAKED TOMATOES

Broccoli: Dip cooked broccoli tips in melted butter. Top with buttered crumbs. Bake in moderate oven (350°F.) until top is brown.

Corn: Fry gently 1 tablespoon chopped onion and 1 tablespoon green pepper in 2 tablespoons butter. Add 2 cups drained whole kernel corn, ½ cup fine breadcrumbs, 2 well-beaten eggs, and ½ teaspoon salt. Fill tomatoes. Bake.

Corn and green pepper: Use corn cut from cob. Mix with cooked, chopped green pepper, season with salt, pepper, and onion. Top with buttered crumbs. Bake in moderate oven (350°F.) until top is brown.

Creole rice: Sauté minced onion in butter. Add cooked rice, tomato pulp and seasoning to taste. Top with buttered crumbs. Bake in moderate oven (350°F.) until browned.

Peas: Fry gently 1 tablespoon grated onion and ¼ cup finely cut celery in 2 tablespoons butter. Add 2 cups cooked peas and the pulp which has been scooped out of the tomatoes. Mix well. Fill tomatoes. Bake.

Vegetable jardiniere: Chop left-over cooked vegetables (cucumber, onion, green pepper, peas, cauliflower, etc.). Mix with a little cream sauce or cheese sauce. Top with buttered crumbs. Bake in moderate oven (350°F.) until browned.

BROILED TOMATOES

Wash tomatoes, remove stem ends and cut in half. Put in a greased shallow baking dish. Season with salt, pepper, and melted butter. Broil under moderate heat until tomatoes are cooked and browned, 20 to 30 minutes. Serve on buttered toast. Garnish with parsley.

FRIED TOMATOES

6 or 8 firm tomatoes	Finely sifted breadcrumbs
1 egg	Salt and pepper
1 tablespoon cold water	1 tablespoon chopped parsley

Wash tomatoes. Remove a thin piece from stem end. Cut into slices about ½ inch thick. Beat egg slightly. Add water. Dip tomatoes in egg and roll in breadcrumbs which have been seasoned to taste with salt and pepper. Allow coated tomatoes to dry out somewhat before frying. Heat fat in heavy skillet. Brown coated tomatoes in hot fat on one side, then turn carefully. Reduce heat so that tomatoes will have sufficient time to cook before browning. Lift from skillet to hot platter. Garnish with chopped parsley. Serve at once.

SCALLOPED TOMATOES

2 cups canned or cooked tomatoes	1 teaspoon grated onion
2 cups soft breadcrumbs	1 teaspoon sugar
4 tablespoons butter	¾ cup tomato juice, strained
¾ teaspoon salt	from tomatoes

Drain tomatoes and reserve ¾ cup of juice. Sauté breadcrumbs in butter. Place half the crumbs in bottom of greased 3-quart casserole. Mix tomatoes, salt, onion, and sugar. Pour over breadcrumbs. Add tomato juice. Sprinkle remaining crumbs over top. Bake uncovered in moderate oven (375°F.) 20 minutes. Serves 6.

STEWED TOMATOES

1 No. 2 can tomatoes	1 teaspoon sugar
2 tablespoons butter	Salt and pepper, to taste

Place tomatoes in a saucepan. Cover. Turn heat to high to bring to steaming point. Simmer 5 minutes. Add butter, salt, pepper, and sugar.

Variation #1: Add bread cubes or cracker crumbs for thickening, or 1 tablespoon flour blended with the butter.

Variation #2: Add 2 tablespoons thick sweet cream just before serving.

PANNED ZUCCHINI

Slice tender zucchini. Cut slices in quarters. Cook in very little water with just a little butter or vegetable oil added. Cook, covered, until tender. Season to taste.

LYONNAISE ZUCCHINI

For each cup of sliced cooked zucchini, sauté in butter ¼ cup sliced onions until lightly browned. Add hot zucchini to onions. Sauté together until zucchini are browned. Add salt and pepper to taste. Allow ½ cup zucchini per serving.

ZUCCHINI—STUFFED

6 medium-size zucchini
3 cups soft breadcrumbs
½ cup grated Parmesan cheese
1 small onion, chopped fine
2 tablespoons parsley, chopped fine

1 teaspoon salt
⅛ teaspoon pepper
2 eggs, well beaten
2 tablespoons butter

Wash the zucchini. Cut off ends but do not pare. Cook in salted boiling water 5 minutes. Cut in halves lengthwise. Remove pulp and combine with crumbs, cheese, onion, parsley, seasoning, and eggs. Fill the shells. Place in a baking dish. Dot with butter and sprinkle with a little cheese. Bake in moderate oven (350°F.) 30 minutes. Serves 6.

ZUCCHINI WITH CHEESE

3 small zucchini
⅔ cup grated American cheese
¼ cup milk

1 egg, well beaten
4 tablespoons butter

Cut washed zucchini into ¼-inch slices. Cook in very little water until tender. Place in a casserole and cover with a mixture of other ingredients. Bake in hot oven (400°F.) until cheese is melted and top browned. Serves 4.

POTATO KNISHES

1 cup mashed potato
1 egg
Flour to make a stiff dough

1 tablespoon pareve margarine or
     chicken fat
Salt to taste

Combine ingredients thoroughly; form into 2 mounds. Brush with diluted egg yolk or evaporated milk. Bake in moderate oven (350°F.) until delicately browned, or about 20 minutes.

Variations: The same proportions may be used in making larger quantities. Fillings may be added. Make a depression in the center of each mound and fill with 1 tablespoon of cooked leftover meat or chicken or a combination of chopped liver and hard-cooked eggs. Or fill with pot cheese seasoned to taste with salt and pepper and combined with 1 egg per cup of cheese. Then bake.

TZIMMES WITH PRUNES AND POTATOES

½ cup diced onion
2 tablespoons pareve margarine or
     chicken fat
2 pounds white potatoes, peeled
1¼ teaspoon salt
2 small marrow bones

2½ cups liquid (juice from prunes
     plus water)
¼ cup sugar
1 teaspoon paprika
1 tablespoon lemon juice
1-pound jar stewed prunes

Sauté onion until tender in fat in a 4-quart saucepan. Cut potatoes into quarters if they are large; leave whole if small. Add to onions the potatoes, salt, marrow bones, prune juice and water, sugar, paprika, and lemon juice. Simmer uncovered over low heat for 1¼ hours. Add drained prunes and cook ½ hour longer, stirring occasionally. Serves 6.

jams, jellies and preserves

Jams, jellies, and preserves are fruit products preserved by cooking with sugar. The following definitions will help the homemaker to understand recipes for "spreads" made with fruit. For successful results fruit should be well-ripened but not overripe.

Conserves: Made of 2 or more fruits, one of them usually a citrus fruit with nut-meats, raisins, or both added.

Fruit Butters: Made from strained fruit pulp cooked with sugar and spice to a thick, smooth consistency. The pulp of some fruits from which the juice has been extracted for jelly is often used if it has enough flavor and pectin.

Jams: Made from crushed fruits cooked with sugar until the mixture is homogeneous and thick.

Jelly: Made by cooking extracted fruit juices with sugar. A transparent, quivery product which holds its shape when unmolded. Is delicately tender but not syrupy or gummy.

Marmalades: Made from pulpy fruits, usually one or more citrus fruits being used and cut into comparatively large pieces cooked so as to hold their shape in a thick jellied transparent syrup.

Preserves: Contains whole fruits or distinct pieces of fruit preserved in a heavy sugar syrup.

JELLY MAKING HINTS

In order to "jell" a fruit must contain the right amount of pectin and acid. The amount and quality of pectin in fruits varies according to the stages of ripeness. A combination of fruits low in pectin and one rich in pectin will often bring about satisfactory results, or a commercial pectin (which can be bought in powder or liquid form) may be added. Carefully follow the manufacturer's directions given with these products.

Fruits rich in pectin: Sour apples, crabapples, unripe grapes, blackberries, currants, cranberries, gooseberries, huckleberries, plums, and quinces.

Fruits low in pectin: Sweet apples, cherries, peaches, pears, pineapple, rhubarb, strawberries, and some others. With these added pectin is required or combination with one rich in pectin.

To test for pectin: To 1 teaspoon cooked juice, add 1 teaspoon grain alcohol and stir slowly. Wood or denatured alcohol may be used, but do not taste, as these are poison. A large mass (solid) indicates a large amount of pectin. If moderately rich there will be a few pieces of gelatin, and if poor in pectin, only a small flaky sediment.

Jelly tests: The jelly is done when two drops of the syrup will run together and "sheet off" as one from the side of a spoon. With a thermometer cook syrup until it registers between 216° and 220°F.

APPLE OR CRABAPPLE JELLY

Wash 15 pounds tart apples and quarter without peeling. Place in preserving kettle, just cover with cold water, and simmer gently until soft and tender. Drain through jelly bag. Shift pulp occasionally to keep juice flowing. Measure 4 cups juice into 12-quart kettle and boil 5 minutes. Add 3 cups sugar and boil 5 to 8 minutes longer, or until a drop jells on a cold plate. Turn into hot sterilized glasses. Cover with melted paraffin and lid. Continue cooking 4 cups at a time until all juice is used. Use pulp for apple butter.

Mint apple jelly: Cook a few sprigs of fresh mint with apples when preparing to extract juice. (1 or 2 drops of mint extract may be used if fresh mint is not available.) Add a few drops green vegetable coloring and mint extract just before pouring into the glasses. Avoid adding too much flavoring and coloring.

Spiced apple jelly: Tie a few whole spices in a piece of muslin. Drop into juice at the beginning of cooking and let remain until jelly is poured into the glasses.

BERRY JELLY

Blackberries, blueberries, and loganberries are but a few of the many which may be used for jelly. Select firm fruit, using a mixture of ripe and slightly underripe fruit. Pectin is most abundant in slightly underripe fruits. Ripened fruits give the best flavor. Wash and stem the berries. Drain, then mash to release some of the juice. To every quart of berries, add ¼ cup water. If the berries are very juicy, do not add any water. Boil gently from 10 to 15 minutes, pour into a jelly bag and drain. Measure juice. Place in large preserving kettle and let boil for 5 minutes. Add ¾ cup sugar for each cup juice. Stir until sugar dissolves, then boil rapidly without stirring or skimming until liquid forms a jelly when cool. Skim and pour into hot, clean glasses. Seal.

CURRANT JELLY

Pick over currants. Do not remove stems. Wash. Drain. Place in preserving kettle. Mash with potato masher. Add ½ cup water to about 2 quarts fruit. Bring to a boil, simmer until currants appear white. Strain through jelly bag. Measure juice. Add ¾ cup honey and ¾ cup sugar for every 2 cups juice. Cook only 4 cupfuls juice at a time. Stir until sugar dissolves. Cook until a drop jells on a cold plate and jelly sheets from edge of spoon. Fill hot, sterilized glasses. Cover with paraffin.

GRAPE JELLY

Pick over and wash 4 pounds Concord grapes. Crush and boil together with 1 pint water for 20 minutes. Press through a jelly bag and allow to drain. Use ¾ to 1 cup sugar for each cup of grape juice. Bring grape juice to boil. Add sugar and stir until sugar is dissolved. Continue boiling until jelly stage is reached and jelly sheets from edge of spoon. Remove from heat and skim. Pour into hot, sterilized glasses. Cover with hot paraffin at once. For grape jelly at its best, use canned unsweetened juice. Fresh grape juice contains tartaric acid crystals which form readily in jelly. Canned unsweetened grape juice has much of the acid in crystal form removed.

APRICOT-PINEAPPLE JAM

Pit 5 pounds apricots. Cut into pieces. Combine with 5 cups shredded pineapple and 7½ cups sugar. Simmer until thick and clear, stirring frequently to prevent scorching. Pour into clean, hot glasses. Seal when cool.

BLACK CURRANT JAM

6 cups black currants   6 cups sugar

Wash, stem, and measure currants. Place in a large kettle. Cook 15 minutes. Add sugar and cook until mixture is thick and clear, about 15 minutes. Pour into sterilized jars. Seal.

Currant rhubarb jam: Substitute 2 cups rhubarb for 2 cups currants.

Red currant jam: Substitute red currants for black currants.

CHERRY JAM

4 cups chopped cherries   4 cups sugar
½ cup lemon juice

Wash and drain cherries. Remove stems and pits. Put cherries through food chopper using coarse knife and saving all juice. Measure 4 cups chopped cherries and juice into 10 or 12-quart kettle. Add sugar. Let stand 4 hours. Place over flame. Bring slowly to full rolling boil and boil hard for 12 minutes, stirring occasionally. Add lemon juice and again bring to full rolling boil, then boil 2 minutes longer. Skim. Turn into hot sterilized jars, filling to ½ inch from top, and seal at once. Yield: 1 to 1½ pints.

NOTE: It takes almost 2 quart boxes of cherries to make 4 cups after they are stemmed, pitted, and put through food chopper.

HUCKLEBERRY JAM

Pick over the berries. Measure. For each cup of fruit add ⅔ cup sugar. Stir over heat until sugar dissolves and mixture comes to a boil. Boil rapidly to preserve color and flavor of the fruit. Cook until thick and clear and a drop hardens on a cold plate. Cool slightly and pour into sterilized glasses. Fill to within ½ inch of top. Seal.

Elderberry jam: Follow *HUCKLEBERRY JAM* recipe.

Huckleberry rhubarb jam: Rhubarb may be used in equal amounts with the berries (by weight) without a noticeable change in texture or flavor.

PEACH JAM

4 pounds peaches   1½ oranges
5 cups sugar

Peel, stone, and slice peaches. Mix with sugar. Put oranges through food chopper. Add to peaches and sugar. Mix well. Bring slowly to boiling point and cook gently 20 minutes, stirring constantly. Turn into hot, sterilized jars filling to ½ inch of top. Seal at once. Yield: 6½ pints.

Cherry peach jam: Add ½ cup sliced maraschino cherries with peaches and sugar.

DAMSON PLUM JAM

4 quarts plums   Sugar
1 quart water

Wash and drain plums. Cut in halves. Add water, bring to boiling point, and simmer 15 minutes. Cool slightly. Remove pits. Measure pulp and juice and add ¾ cup sugar for each cup. Stir until thoroughly mixed. Bring slowly to boiling point and boil gently until clear and thick, about 20 minutes, stirring constantly to prevent burning. Pour into hot, sterilized jars, filling to ½ inch of top. Seal at once.

QUINCE JAM

Wash, pare, and remove core from 4 pounds quinces. Chop into very small pieces. Add 8 cups sugar, ¼ pound chopped crystallized ginger and juice, and grated rind of 2 lemons. Cook until thick and clear. Pour into sterilized jars. Seal.

BLACK OR RED RASPBERRY JAM

Wash raspberries, crush, and measure. If berries are sour add equal measurements of sugar. If sweet use ¾ as much sugar as berry mixture. Cook in own juice until thickened, stirring to prevent burning. Boil rapidly because long cooking tends to darken the fruit. Pack while boiling hot into hot jars and seal immediately.

STRAWBERRY JAM

1 quart strawberries (4 cups)   ½ cup unstrained lemon juice
4 cups sugar

Wash; drain, and hull berries. Measure 4 cups. Crush berries in large kettle. Place in layers in 12-quart preserving kettle covering each layer with sugar. Let stand 4 hours. Place over flame. Bring slowly to full rolling boil and boil vigorously 8 minutes. Add lemon juice and again bring to full rolling boil. Then boil 2 minutes longer. Skim. Turn into hot, sterilized jars, filling to ½ inch of top, and seal at once. Yield: 3½ pints.

GRAPE PRESERVES

Wash grapes. Press pulp from skins. They are especially nice if seeded. Weigh and use ½ cup water and ½ pound sugar for each pound of prepared fruit. Boil sugar and water 10 minutes. Add fruit and cook until mixture is clear and thick. Pour into hot, clean jars. Seal.

PEACH PRESERVES

2 pounds peaches   3 cups sugar

Scald peaches. Dip into cold water and peel. Remove pits. Cut into halves, quarters, or thick slices. Make a heavy syrup of sugar and water. Cook peaches in syrup until mixture is thick and clear. Pour into hot, sterilized jars and seal.

PLUM PRESERVES

1 quart plums   1½ cups sugar
1 cup water

Wash fruit and prick skins. Make a syrup of water and sugar. Add fruit and cook gently until it is tender and clear. Cool rapidly, and let plums stand for 1 hour in the syrup to plump. Remove plums to jars. Reheat the syrup to boiling and pour over plums. Seal.

NOTE. The syrup will thicken upon standing, so care should be taken not to cook plums longer than necessary.

PEAR AND QUINCE PRESERVES

6 pounds pears
3 pounds quinces

3 lemons, juice and grated rinds
5 to 6 pounds sugar

Pare, quarter, and core fruit. Squeeze over it the juice of 2 or 3 lemons to keep from turning dark. Stew the cores and parings in water to cover, until soft, then strain. Slice fruit and add to strained mixture. Add water to almost cover fruit. Cook until soft. Mash, then add sugar and grated rind of lemons. Continue cooking 1 hour longer, stirring carefully to prevent scorching. Test from time to time until syrup is thickened and sheets like jelly. Pour in jars and seal.

RASPBERRY PRESERVES

Mix thoroughly equal amount of raspberries and sugar. Cook slowly and stir until mixture boils. Boil gently for 6 minutes. Pour into clean, hot jars. Seal at once.

STRAWBERRY PRESERVES

2 cups strawberries
2 cups sugar

½ lemon, juice and rind

Carefully wash and hull strawberries. Add sugar and lemon. Heat, stirring gently, until mixture boils. Then boil 10 minutes. Skim, pour out on a large platter, and let stand until next day, turning over several times so that berries will become plump and well mixed with juice. Next day pack cold into sterilized jars and seal. The addition of the lemon puffs up the berries. Yield: 1 pint jar.

SUN-COOKED STRAWBERRY PRESERVES

Hull berries and wash well. Weigh, then place in shallow enameled pans, allowing 1 to 2 pounds of fruit to a pan. Spread sugar evenly over fruit, allowing ¾ pound sugar to every pound of berries. Cover pan and set aside for several hours or overnight. The sugar draws some of the juice from berries and after standing most of the sugar will be dissolved in the juice. Set pans over a low fire and stir gently until sugar is all dissolved. Then bring to a boil and boil for 1 minute, stirring occasionally. Remove pan from fire and cool. Cover pans with panes of glass. Place in a sunny window or in the sun outdoors. Let stand for 2 to 3 days until syrup is of a jelly-like consistency. Stir several times each day. Pack in clean, hot jars. To prevent any spoilage it is wise to process the filled jars (with covers adjusted) in a hot water bath for 2 or 3 minutes.

Variations: Currants, red raspberries, or firm, ripe cherries may be preserved the same way.

TOMATO PRESERVE

2 quarts tomatoes   4 cups sugar
3 lemons

Scald red or yellow tomatoes and peel. Cut into small pieces and drain in colander or sieve. (Use juice for soup, sauce, or can for future use.) Measure 2 quarts pulp. Place in preserving kettle with thinly sliced lemons. Cook gently uncovered 40 minutes or until lemon skins are tender. Add sugar, continue cooking 15 minutes, stirring occasionally. Turn into hot, sterilized jars and seal at once.

GRAPE CONSERVE

6 cups grapes, measured after   ½ pound seedless raisins
   removing stems   2 cups water
6 cups sugar   ¼ pound walnuts, chopped
Juice of 3 oranges

Remove pulp from grapes. Save skins. Add water to pulp and cook until seeds settle. Strain out seeds. Combine pulp with skins and remaining ingredients, except walnuts. Cook until few drops jell on a cold plate. Add nuts. Pour into hot, clean jars. Seal.

Cranberry or plum conserve: Follow above recipe, substituting cranberries or plums for grapes and adding juice of 3 lemons.

PEACH CONSERVE

Peel and pit peaches, and cut into thin slices. Measure. To each cup of prepared peaches add ¾ cup sugar and ½ lemon (juice and grated rind). Cook until thick and clear. Pour into hot, clean jars. Seal.

PEAR CONSERVE

4 pounds pears   3 pounds sugar
1 pound dates   ½ teaspoon cinnamon
1 pound seedless raisins

Pare and core pears. Put through food chopper with dates and raisins. Add sugar and cinnamon to mixture. Cook until thick, about 20 minutes. Pour into clean, hot glasses. Seal.

PINEAPPLE CONSERVE

1 quart pineapple, pulp and juice   2 oranges
3 cups sugar   1 lemon

Pare the pineapples and put them through food chopper. Steam until tender. Add sugar, grated rind, and pulp of oranges and lemon. Cook mixture rapidly until it is thick. Pour into glasses. Seal.

PLUM CONSERVE

2 cups plum pulp   ½ orange, juice and grated rind
1 to 1½ cups sugar   1 cup seedless raisins
½ lemon, juice and grated rind   ½ cup nutmeats

Wash Damson plums. Put through grinder and measure. Mix ingredients, except nutmeats. Cook mixture until thick and clear. Add nutmeats. Pack in clean, hot jars. Seal.

STRAWBERRY AND RHUBARB CONSERVE

Cut 1 quart rhubarb into ½-inch pieces, being careful not to peel. Mix together 1 quart strawberries, the rhubarb, and 6 cups sugar. Cook mixture slowly until it is thick and clear. Pour into clean, hot jars. Seal.

CHERRY AND PINEAPPLE MARMALADE

Wash, drain, and pit cherries. Put through food chopper. Peel and grind or shred pineapple. Mix pineapple and cherries, using ¼ as much pineapple as cherries. To fruit mixture, add ⅔ as much sugar as fruit and juice. Cook mixture until it is thick and clear. Pour into clean, hot jars. Seal.

ORANGE MARMALADE

8 oranges   Water
2 lemons   Sugar

Wash and dry fruit. Cut unpeeled oranges and lemons into quarters lengthwise. Slice very thin crosswise. Measure sliced fruit. Add twice as much water as fruit and juice. Let stand overnight. Next morning place over flame. Cover kettle, bring to boiling point, and cook 1 hour. Then set aside for 24 hours. Stir well and measure out 2 cups juice and fruit. Put into a 4 or 6 quart kettle. Add 2 cups sugar. Bring to full rolling boil and boil 9 minutes only, or to temperature of 220°F. Pour into hot, sterilized jelly glasses or jars. When cold, cover with melted paraffin and lid. Continue cooking 2 cups fruit and juice with 2 cups sugar, as given above, until all fruit is cooked. Approximate yield: 10 6-ounce glasses.

Amber marmalade: Follow method for ORANGE MARMALADE, using 1 grapefruit, 1 orange, 1 lemon, sugar, and water.

PEAR MARMALADE

Peel fresh pears. Slice and cover with sugar, using ¾ cup sugar to each cup of fruit. Let stand until it forms a syrup. Boil slowly until thick. When fruit is partly cooked, add ½ (No. 2) can shredded pineapple for every 8 cups pears. Pour into sterilized jars. Seal.

PINEAPPLE MARMALADE

1 pineapple   3 lemons
3 cups sugar   2 cups raisins

Pare pineapple, saving all juice. Cut into small cubes. Add sugar and grated rind, and juice of lemons and pineapple. Cook 30 minutes or until thick. Add raisins. Cook 5 minutes longer. Pour into sterilized jars. Seal. Yield: about 6 ½-pint jars.

RHUBARB MARMALADE

Rhubarb used for making marmalade should be tender and fresh. Cut without peeling into 1-inch lengths. Measure. Allow ¾ cup sugar to each cup rhubarb. Combine rhubarb and sugar in a preserving kettle. Heat very slowly to a boil. Cook until thick and clear. Pack into clean, hot jars. Seal.

APPLE BUTTER

10 pounds cooking apples	1½ teaspoons ground cloves
3 cups water	3 teaspoons cinnamon
4 cups sweet cider	1½ teaspoons nutmeg
8 cups sugar	1½ teaspoons allspice

Wash and core apples. Cook in water until soft and press through sieve. Boil cider down to 2 cups. Combine cider, apples, sugar, and spices in preserving kettle and cook slowly until it sheets from spoon. Stir about 3 or 4 times. Pour into hot, sterilized jars. Seal and adjust lids. Process 10 minutes in boiling water bath. Yield: 6 pints.

APPLE AND PLUM BUTTER

4½ pounds apples	6 cups sugar
3 pounds plums	1 teaspoon cinnamon
2 cups water	

Wash and cut apples and plums, including peels and cores. Add water and cook until fruit is tender. Press through a sieve. Add sugar and cinnamon. Cook until thick and clear. Stir occasionally to prevent sticking. Fill sterilized glasses. Seal. Makes 6 glasses.

GRAPE BUTTER

Use 1 pound sugar to 4 pounds grapes. Wash and stem grapes. Cook in a small amount of water until skins are soft. Press pulp through strainer to remove seeds and skins. Add sugar and cook until thick and clear. Pour into hot, clean glasses. Cool and seal.

PEACH BUTTER

4 pounds peaches	2 teaspoons cinnamon
2 cups water	1 teaspoon cloves
Sugar	

Peel peaches. Remove pits and spots. Place in kettle with water and cook until tender. Rub through sieve and measure. To each cup of pulp, allow ⅔ cup sugar. Add spices. Cook until thick, stirring frequently. Pour into sterilized hot jars. Seal.

PLUM BUTTER

Wash fruit. Place in kettle. Add 2 cups water to 4 pounds of plums. Cook slowly until pulp separates from pits. Press pulp through sieve. Measure. If pulp is thin, cook until thick enough to round up on spoon. Add sugar, allowing ⅔ cup sugar to each cup of pulp. Cook rapidly, stirring constantly to prevent scorching. Pour into clean, hot jars. Seal.

CURRANT BAR-LE-DUC

Add ¾ pound sugar to 1 pound large currants, washed and stemmed. Boil slowly for 5 minutes. Pour while hot into hot, clean glasses. Seal.

QUINCE HONEY

1 pint raw quince, coarsely grated   1 quart sugar
1 pint water

Boil together sugar and water 5 minutes. Add quince, and boil until translucent, about 10 minutes. Pour into sterilized jars, filled to overflowing. Seal.

PLUM BUTTER OR POVIDLE

Wash 4 pounds of purple plums. Remove stems, cut into halves, and remove pits. The water that clings to plums will be sufficient moisture in which to cook the fruit over low heat until very tender. Put through a sieve or food mill. Measure the purée: add sugar in equal proportions (1 cup of sugar for each cup of purée), and stir well. Cook over moderate heat, stirring constantly, until the mixture becomes very thick. This plum butter or povidle should be of a denser consistency than the usual fruit butters. Pour into glass containers. Use as filling for cookies, small cakes, or hamantaschen. Makes about 3 pints, depending upon the ripeness of the plums and the length of cooking.

FROZEN STRAWBERRY JAM

Thaw 2 10-ounce packages frozen strawberries, then put through food mill or mash. Add 3½ cups sugar and mix well. Let stand 20 minutes, stirring occasionally. When sugar has dissolved, add ½ of 6-ounce bottle liquid fruit pectin and stir 3 minutes. Ladle into jelly glasses, ½-pint jars, or freezer containers and let stand 24 hours, or until set. Seal with paraffin. Store up to 6 weeks in refrigerator or up to 1 year in freezer. Makes 4 ½-pint jars.

BLUEBERRY-RASPBERRY JAM

Wash and crush 1 quart each of fresh blueberries and fresh red raspberries. Measure 4 cups, filling last cup with water if necessary, into a large saucepan. Add 7 cups sugar; heat to full rolling boil; boil hard 1 minute, stirring constantly. Remove from heat. Stir in ½ of 6-ounce bottle liquid fruit pectin. Skim. Pour into hot scalded 8 ½-pint jars. Seal at once.

pickles and relishes

HINTS FOR GOOD PICKLES

For success in pickling use fresh, firm cucumbers. Use a good clear standard vinegar, free from sediment, containing 4 to 6 per cent of acetic acid. Use pure granulated salt, if possible. Table salt may be used, but you may not get as good results because of the carbonates added to table salt to prevent lumping. Whole spices in most cooked pickles keep the flavor longer.

Cloudy pickles: Are caused by a weak brine and a weak vinegar solution.

For a bright colored pickle: Use an enamel, aluminum, or stainless steel kettle to heat acid pickling liquids. Iron utensils darken pickles, copper ones impart an undesirable greenish hue. A stronger vinegar than recommended may give a darker color than desired. To give pickles a fresh, green color, add spinach or grape leaves.

Hollow or limp pickles: Result from overripe or imperfect vegetables or when vegetables have been standing too long before pickling.

Soft pickles: May result from too weak a brine solution or from neglecting to cover pickles completely in the brine.

Tough or shriveled pickles: May be caused by excessive salt, or sugar, or excessively strong vinegar. If very sour or very sweet pickles are desired it is best to put them in a weak solution at first and increase the strength later. Hurrying the processes of cooking or brining may cause shriveling.

KOSHER STYLE PICKLES (Easy Method)

Use medium-size cucumbers averaging about 3½ inches in length. Wash and drain cucumbers. Pack tightly in upright position into quart jars. Pack a generous bunch of dill including seed heads into each jar. Add 1 tablespoon coarse salt, 4 cloves garlic, and ½ teaspoon mixed pickling spices. Fill jar with cold water, making sure there are no air bubbles. Seal tightly. Ready in 2 weeks.

SLICED CUCUMBER PICKLES

24 medium-size cucumbers	2 cups sugar
12 onions	1 tablespoon turmeric
1 cup salt	2 teaspoons celery seed
8 quarts water	2 teaspoons mustard seed
1 quart vinegar	

Wash, clean, and slice cucumbers. Peel and slice onions. Soak sliced cucumbers and onions 2 hours in salt brine, made of salt and water. Drain. Combine vinegar, sugar, turmeric, celery seed, and mustard seed and bring to a boil. Remove from heat, add cucumbers and onions. Bring to boiling and cook 10 minutes. Pack into hot, sterilized jars, filling to within ½ inch of top. Seal at once.

DILL PICKLES

36 cucumbers	3½ quarts water
Dill	2 cups vinegar
Garlic	¾ cup salt

Wash cucumbers. Pack into hot, sterilized jars with pieces of dill. Add a clove of garlic to each jar. Boil water, vinegar, and salt 5 minutes. Pour hot over cucumbers, filling jars to ½ inch from top. Seal at once.

OIL PICKLES

100 small cucumbers	2 quarts vinegar
1 quart small onions	¼ pound ground mustard
¾ cup coarse salt	¼ pound white mustard seed
1 pint olive or other salad oil	1 tablespoon black pepper
1 ounce celery seed	

Slice cucumbers and onions. Place in layers in earthenware crock. Add salt to each layer. Cover with weighted plate on top, and let stand overnight. Drain. Mix seasonings and oil. Add vinegar slowly and pour over cucumbers and onions. Mix well. Pack into jars. Seal and store.

MUSTARD PICKLES

20 medium cucumbers, sliced	1 cup flour
2 small heads cauliflower, separated into flowerets	½ ounce turmeric
	1 quart vinegar
6 green peppers, diced	1 quart water
1 cup salt	1 quart tiny onions
8 cups sugar	2 quarts green tomatoes, cut
¼ pound (1¼ cups) dry mustard	into pieces

Place vegetables in separate containers and sprinkle with salt. Let stand overnight. Mix sugar, mustard, flour, and turmeric. Add vinegar and water and heat to boiling. Add vegetables and cook until tender and sauce has thickened. Seal in clean, hot jars.

SWEET CUCUMBER PICKLES

25 to 30 small cucumbers	1 teaspoon grated horeradish
1 quart vinegar	1 3-inch stick cinnamon
1 cup sugar	¾ teaspoon mustard seed
2 teaspoons whole black pepper	½ teaspoon whole cloves

Wash and drain cucumbers. Cover with weak brine, made by adding 1 cup salt to 1 gallon water. Let stand 24 hours. Drain, rinse in fresh water, drain again, and cover with vinegar mixed with sugar and spices. Bring to a boil and simmer for 3 minutes. Turn into sterilized jars, filling to overflowing. Seal at once.

ICICLE PICKLES

6 pounds medium-size cucumbers	Mustard seed
Ice water	White vinegar
Pickling onions	Sugar
Celery	Salt

Cut cucumbers into 4 to 8 pieces lengthwise. Soak in ice water for 3 hours. Drain. Pack into sterilized jars. Add 6 pickling onions, 1 piece of celery and 1 teaspoon mustard seed to each quart jar. Bring to a boil 3 quarts vinegar, 3 cups sugar, and 1 cup salt. Pour over cucumbers. Seal jars. Yield: 6 quarts.

CHUNK PICKLES

1 quart cucumbers	½ tablespoon stick cinnamon
1 cup vinegar	½ tablespoon celery seed
1 cup water	½ tablespoon whole allspice
1½ cups brown sugar	½ tablespoon mustard seed

Select fresh, crisp cucumbers. Cover with brine made by dissolving 2 tablespoons salt in 1 quart water. Let stand overnight. Drain, wash, and soak again overnight in clear water. Wipe dry and cut into chunks. Cook in diluted vinegar until tender. Pack loosely in clean, hot jars. Cover with hot pickling syrup made from water, vinegar, sugar, and spices. Seal at once.

MIXED PICKLES

2 cups pickling onions	1 quart cider vinegar
1 quart small cucumbers	2 cups carrots, cut into 2-inch pieces
4 tablespoons white mustard seed	2 red peppers, seeds removed
4 tablespoons salt	2 cups celery, cut into 2-inch
1 cup sugar	pieces

Cover onions and cucumbers separately for 24 hours with brine (1 cup salt to 4 quarts water). Drain. Soak in cold water 2 hours, and drain again. Add spices, salt, sugar, and vinegar; let stand overnight in covered pan. Drain off vinegar and heat it. Add vegetables and simmer for 15 minutes. Pour into clean, hot jars and seal.

SOUR CUCUMBER PICKLES

Wash ½ bushel of cucumbers. Sprinkle with 2 cups coarse salt and cover with boiling water. Let stand 24 hours. Drain and repeat twice. The fourth day place cucumbers in jars. Add to each quart jar ½ teaspoon each brown sugar, ground cinnamon, and ground cloves, and 1 teaspoon horseradish. Fill jar with cold vinegar. Seal.

CASSIA BUD PICKLES

2 quarts cucumbers	1 tablespoon celery seed
1 quart sliced small white onions	1 tablespoon mustard seed
½ cup salt	½ tablespoon ginger
2¾ cups sugar	½ teaspoon turmeric
2¾ cups vinegar	¼ teaspoon pepper

Wash and slice cucumbers, do not peel. Slice onions. Sprinkle cucumbers and onions with salt and let stand for 1 hour. Drain off brine, rinse with clear water, drain again. Mix together remaining ingredients. Heat to boiling. Add cucumbers and onions, and heat to boiling. Turn into hot, sterilized jars. Yield: 4 pints.

BREAD AND BUTTER PICKLES

25 medium cucumbers, sliced
12 onions, sliced
½ cup salt
2 cups sugar
2 teaspoons turmeric

2 teaspoons cassia buds
1 quart vinegar
2 teaspoons mustard seed
2 teaspoons celery seed

Soak cucumbers and onions in ice water with salt for 3 hours. Combine remaining ingredients and heat to boiling. Add cucumbers and onion and heat for 2 minutes. Do not allow to boil. Fill clean jars. Seal at once.

GREEN TOMATO PICKLES

1 peck green tomatoes, sliced
12 onions, sliced
1½ ounces black pepper
1 ounce whole allspice

¼ pound ground mustard
1 ounce whole cloves
1 ounce mustard seed
½ cup coarse salt

Arrange tomatoes and onions in layers, sprinkling salt between layers. Let stand overnight. Drain. Add remaining ingredients. Cover with vinegar and simmer gently for 15 minutes. Pack into clean, hot jars. Seal at once.

PICCALILLI (Spanish Pickle)

1 peck green tomatoes
1 head cabbage
8 large onions
3 red or green peppers
1 cup salt
2 cups brown sugar
2 tablespoons cinnamon

1 tablespoon cloves
2 tablespoons ginger
2 quarts vinegar
½ pound mustard seed
2 tablespoons black pepper
1 tablespoon allspice
¼ teaspoon cayenne pepper

Chop and mix tomatoes, cabbage, onions, and peppers. Add salt. Let stand overnight. Drain and add other ingredients. Boil for 30 minutes, stirring frequently. Pour into clean, hot jars. Seal at once.

PICKLED WATERMELON

3½ pounds watermelon rind
½ cup salt
2 quarts water
2½ pounds sugar

1½ cups cider vinegar
¼ teaspoon oil of cloves
¼ teaspoon oil of cinnamon

Remove outer skin from watermelon rind and cut into thin even slices. Soak overnight in brine made of salt and water. Drain, cover with cold water, and cook gently until tender, about 1½ hours. Drain well. Boil together sugar, vinegar, oil of cloves, and oil of cinnamon for 10 minutes. Add cooked rind. Bring slowly to boiling point. Remove from fire. Let stand over night. Reheat for 3 consecutive days. After reheating for the last time, turn into hot, sterilized jars. Seal at once.

CRANBERRY ORANGE RELISH

1 pound raw cranberries, ground
2 oranges, ground

2 cups sugar

Grind berries and whole oranges. Mix well with sugar. Seal in clean jars. Serve with meat and fowl.

CORN RELISH

1 dozen ears sweet corn	3 tablespoons mustard seed
8 green peppers	1 quart vinegar
4 red peppers	⅓ cup salt
4 ripe tomatoes	1 tablespoon turmeric
12 ripe tomatoes	1 cup sugar
1 quart onions	2 cups honey
5 tablespoons celery seed	1 cup dark corn syrup

Cook corn. Cut from cobs. Chop remaining vegetables or put through food chopper. Add remaining ingredients. Cook until thick, 1 to 1½ hours. Turn into hot, sterilized jars, filling to within ½ inch from top. Seal at once. Yield: 4 quarts.

NOTE: If desired, substitute 6 cups canned kernel corn, drained, for 1 dozen ears of corn.

INDIA RELISH

12 large green tomatoes	1 cup dark corn syrup
1 red pepper	1 cup vinegar
1 green pepper	1 tablespoon mustard seed
4 large onions	1 tablespoon celery seed
1 tablespoon salt	

Put through food chopper using coarse knife tomatoes, peppers, and onions. Drain well, reserving juice for soup or beverage. Add remaining ingredients and mix well. Cook gently until vegetables are tender and mixture is thick, about 15 minutes. Turn into hot, sterilized jars, filling to ½ inch from top. Seal at once. Yield: 3 pints.

PEPPER RELISH

12 green peppers	2 cups vinegar
12 red peppers	2 cups sugar
12 onions	3 tablespoons salt

Chop peppers and onions. Cover with boiling water and let stand 5 minutes. Drain. Add vinegar, sugar, and salt. Boil for 5 minutes. Pour into clean, hot jars. Seal at once.

FRUIT RELISH

3 large cooking pears	¾ cup sugar
3 large peaches or 6 canned peach halves	1½ cups vinegar
3 small onions	2 teaspoons salt
4 medium-size red tomatoes	Dash of cayenne
1 green pepper	Dash of cinnamon
	Dash of cloves

Peel fruits and vegetables. Cut pepper in half. Remove core and seeds. Put all through food chopper, using medium knife. Add sugar, vinegar, salt, and cayenne. Cook slowly until mixture thickens, about 2 hours. Add spices, turn into clean, hot jars, and seal. Yield: 3 pints.

PICKLED PEPPERS

8 medium-size green peppers (1½ pounds)	2 cups vinegar
	¾ cup honey

Wash peppers and cut a slice from stem end of each. Remove seeds. With a pair of scissors cut peppers into ⅜ to ½ inch rings. Cover with boiling water. Let stand 2 minutes. Drain and put at once into ice cold water. After 5 minutes, drain and pack tightly into hot sterilized jars. Boil vinegar and honey 5 minutes. Pour boiling hot over peppers, filling jars to ½ inch of top. Seal at once. Yield: 2 pints.

PICKLED ONIONS

Peel small white onions. Cover with brine, allowing 4 tablespoons salt to 1 quart boiling water. Let stand 2 days. Drain, cover with more brine, and let stand 2 more days. Drain. Prepare brine again and heat to boiling. Add onions and boil 3 minutes. Put onions in jars, interspersing with bits of mace, white peppercorns, cloves, bits of bay leaf, and slices of red pepper. Fill jars to overflowing with vinegar scalded with sugar, allowing 4 cups sugar to 2 quarts vinegar. Seal while hot. Allow about 1 pound onions for each quart jar to be filled.

PICKLED BEETS

2 cups cider vinegar
2 cups water
1 teaspoon salt
2 cups sugar
1 tablespoon white mustard seed

1 teaspoon allspice
1 teaspoon cloves
1 tablespoon cinnamon
Small whole cooked beets

Combine vinegar, water, salt, sugar, and spices which have been tied in a muslin bag. Use whole spices. Boil for 5 minutes. Skin beets, add and simmer 15 minutes. Remove spice bag. Fill clean jars and seal.

SWEET AND SOUR PICKLED BEETS

Cook 3 bunches beets in salted water and cool. Peel, slice, and place in a jar. Cover with 1 cup vinegar, juice of 2 lemons, 1 teaspoon salt, ⅛ teaspoon pepper, 1½ tablespoons sugar, and 3 or 4 bay leaves. Cover jar tightly and store in refrigerator.

APPLE CHUTNEY

12 sour apples
 2 minced green peppers
 1 minced red pepper
 1 cup seeded raisins, chopped
 1 pint vinegar
½ cup currant jelly

2 cups sugar
Juice of 4 lemons
1 tablespoon ground ginger
½ teaspoon cayenne
1 tablespoon salt

Pare, core, and chop apples. Mix ingredients in order given and simmer until thick. Pour into hot, clean jars. Seal.

TOMATO CHUTNEY

24 medium-size ripe red tomatoes
 6 medium-size onions
 3 red peppers
 3 green peppers
12 tart apples

1 pound seedless raisins
1 cup celery, cut fine
2 quarts vinegar
3 cups sugar
Salt

Chop together vegetables and apples. Add remaining ingredients. Cook until thick and clear. Pour immediately into clean, hot jars. Seal.

PICKLED CHERRIES

1 quart cherries, stems on	Vinegar
1 tablespoon salt	Water

Select large, perfect, sour cherries. Wash well. Do not remove stems. Pack into sterilized jars and to each quart add 1 tablespoon salt. Fill jars with solution of equal parts of vinegar and cold water. Seal at once.

WHOLE PICKLED GRAPES

Select bunches of grapes of the same size and ripeness. Any type of grape may be used, but they should not be overripe. Leave grapes on stems and, after washing and drying, pack the bunches closely into clean glass jars. To avoid bruising do not pack tightly. Prepare syrup of 1½ cups sugar to each cup white vinegar. Boil 5 minutes. Pour over grapes to fill jars. Seal.

SPICED BLUEBERRIES

4 quarts blueberries	1 tablespoon whole allspice
6 cups brown sugar	2 sticks cinnamon
2 cups vinegar	1 teaspoon whole cloves

Wash and drain berries. Boil sugar, vinegar, and spices (tied in bag) 5 minutes. Cool. Add berries. Simmer until tender. Let stand overnight. Pack berries into hot jars. Boil syrup 1 minute. Pour over berries. Seal.

Spiced elderberries: Substitute elderberries for blueberries.

SPICED FRUIT

½ peck fruit	3 pounds brown sugar
Whole cloves	1 ounce stick cinnamon
3 cups vinegar	

Use peaches, pears, crabapples, or apples. Select fine, firm fruit. Remove skin from peaches or pears, leaving the fruit whole. With crabapples the skin and stem should be left on but the fruit carefully washed and cleaned. Remove skin from apples. Cut into quarters or eighths, depending on size of apples. If using more than one variety of fruit do not combine. Pickle each kind separately. Place 3 or 4 cloves in each piece of fruit. To help retain shape of fruit cook until tender a few pieces at a time in vinegar, sugar, and cinnamon syrup. Place in sterilized jars. Fill with syrup. Seal.

PICKLED STRING BEANS

Cooked string beans	1 teaspoon allspice
2 cups water	2 cups vinegar
1 tablespoon cinnamon	2 cups sugar
1 teaspoon cloves	1 lemon, sliced thin

Select tender beans without string, if possible. Snip off ends and remove strings, if any, keeping full length. Cook beans until tender. Tie spices in cheesecloth bag and combine with other ingredients. Cover string beans with mixture. Simmer 15 minutes. Seal at once in hot sterilized jars. Allow about 1½ pounds beans for each quart jar.

Wax beans: Substitute wax beans for string beans.

Pickled carrots: Substitute carrots for string beans.

TOMATO KETCHUP

6 quarts sliced red tomatoes (about 9 pounds)	1 cup cider vinegar
4 red peppers	1½ cups sugar
5 large onions	2 tablespoons salt
1 stalk celery	¼ cup whole mixed pickling spices

Simmer sliced tomatoes until soft, about ½ hour. Place in sieve or colander. Drain off juice. Put peppers, onions, and celery through food chopper. Add to tomato pulp. Simmer 1 hour and press through fine sieve. Add vinegar, sugar, salt, and spices tied in a cheesecloth bag. Simmer 1½ to 2 hours, or until thick. Turn into hot, sterilized jars. Seal at once. Yield: about 2 pints. Use drained juice for beverage or bottle for future use.

CHILI SAUCE

2 dozen red tomatoes (about 10 pounds)	1 cup sugar
3 green peppers	2½ tablespoons salt
3 onions	2 cups vinegar
5 tablespoons mixed whole pickling spices	

Scald, peel, and put tomatoes, peppers, and onions through a food chopper; drain off juice. Tie spices loosely in a cheesecloth bag and add with remaining ingredients to tomatoes in large kettle. Cook slowly 3 hours, or until thick. Remove spice bag. Turn into hot, sterilized jars, filling jars to ½ inch from top. Seal at once. Yield: 2 pints.

CHILI COCKTAIL

Juice drained from tomatoes, peppers, and onions put through food chopper for ketchup and chili sauce may be canned and used for soup or beverage. Pour juice into hot, sterilized jar and process in boiling water bath. When serving, a few drops of Worcestershire sauce may be added.

MOCK MINCE MEAT (with Green Tomatoes)

2 cups chopped green tomatoes	2 teaspoons cinnamon
3 cups chopped tart apples	1 teaspoon each of salt, allspice, and cloves
3 cups sugar	¼ cup vinegar
1 pound raisins	

Combine all ingredients. Bring to a rapid boil, then simmer until thick. Pour into clean hot jars. Seal. Use as a relish or filling for pie.

SAUERKRAUT

Select large heavy heads of cabbage. Remove outer leaves, cut into quarters. Shred fine on large cabbage cutter. Pack tightly and full into 1-quart jars. Add 1 teaspoon salt to each jar and fill with boiling water. Seal. From time to time it is necessary to screw the caps tighter as fermentation causes loosening. Kraut is ready in about 3 weeks.

PICKLED PEACHES

½ peck peaches
Whole cloves
1½ pounds light brown sugar

3 cups cider vinegar
1 ounce stick cinnamon

Scald peaches. Dip in cold water for 1 minute. Peel. Place 4 or more whole cloves in each piece of fruit. Prepare syrup of sugar, vinegar, and cinnamon. Add peaches and cook gently until tender. Pack into hot, sterilized jars. Cover with syrup. Seal at once.

Pickled pears or apples: Substitute pears or apples for peaches.

BRANDIED CHERRIES

Select ripe, large white or red cherries. Wash and drain. Cut stems short. Pack into wide-mouthed quart bottles. To each quart container, allow ¼ cup granulated sugar, alternating layers of cherries and sugar until the jars are ¾ full. Fill to brim with brandy, using about 1 cup for each quart. Seal securely. Turn jars upside down, and turn them end up again every hour for 4 consecutive hours, so as to mix sugar and brandy. Then store in cool, dry, dark place at least 3 months before using.

PICKLED CRABAPPLES OR SECKEL PEARS

7 pounds crabapples or seckel pears
1 quart white vinegar
8 cups sugar

¼ cup whole cloves
1 stick cinnamon
1½ teaspoons whole ginger

Wash and remove blossom ends from fruit. Prick each piece several times. Heat vinegar and sugar to boiling. Add spices tied loosely in a cheesecloth bag. Add fruit and boil gently until tender but not broken. Remove spice bag. Quickly pack one hot sterilized jar at a time. Fill to ⅛ inch from top. Be sure vinegar solution covers the fruit. Seal each jar at once. Makes 6 pints.

canning

PRINCIPLES OF CANNING

Canning is a method of food preservation by the use of heat and airtight containers with retention of the maximum amount of flavor, texture, and food value. Successful canning is based on a knowledge of the methods by which food spoiling may be prevented. Tiny organisms—molds, yeasts, and bacteria—are normally present in fruits, vegetables, and meats, and will eventually cause fresh foods to spoil. The aim in canning is to destroy or inactivate by heat the action of the microorganisms. Molds, yeasts, and bacteria are present at all times in the air, water, and soil. In the canning process fruits and vegetables are heated sufficiently to stop the action of these tiny organisms with the exception of some types of bacteria. There are certain heat-resistant bacteria that go through a spore phase in their life cycle, a form in which they are very difficult to kill. In canning foods high in acid, like fruits, tomatoes, and pickled beets, the spores are readily destroyed at the boiling temperature in a reasonable length of time. In all vegetables other than tomatoes it may take 12 to 15 hours or more to destroy or inactivate the spores at the boiling temperature. If cooked at 10 pounds pressure in a steam pressure cooker, these same spores are destroyed in less than 1 hour. On the other hand the enzymes are useful to a degree in that they are responsible for the normal ripening process of fruits and vegetables. They will, however, cause decay after the normal ripening point has been reached if their action is not stopped. Extreme heat or extreme cold will inhibit and delay the action of enzymes.

BOILING WATER BATH METHOD

This method is used for fruits and acid vegetables (tomatoes). Any big, clean vessel will do for a boiling-water canner, if it's deep enough to let water boil well over tops of the jars at least 2 inches, has a tight-fitting lid, and a rack to keep the jars at least ½ inch from the bottom of the vessel. Place rack in canner. Fill with boiling water. Jars must be hot when placed in the canner. If necessary, heat in hot water. Bring water to a rolling boil. If necessary, add water to keep jars covered 2 inches. When processing time is completed, open cover by tilting toward you so that steam will not come in contact with face and hands. Remove jars one at a time. Complete seal. (See directions.)

High altitude processing in boiling water bath: For altitudes over 1,000 feet, increase processing time 20 per cent for each additional 1,000 feet.

STEAM PRESSURE METHOD

Use only this method for processing all non-acid vegetables and meats. Follow manufacturer's directions carefully for use and care of cooker. Each time cooker is used, be sure it contains enough water to come just below the level of rack (1 to 2 inches of water). Place jars on rack, leaving ample space between jars for free circulation of steam. Adjust cover and fasten on securely. Air must be exhausted by leaving petcock open until a steady stream of steam escapes for 5 to 10 minutes. Close petcock. Allow pressure to rise to specified point, counting pressure time when gauge reaches desired pressure. Maintain constant pressure by regulation of heat. When processing time is completed remove cooker from heat. DO NOT OPEN COOKER UNTIL PRESSURE GAUGE REGISTERS ZERO. Cool slowly until zero point is registered. Slowly open petcock until all steam has escaped. To open cover, tilt toward you, so escaping steam will not burn face or hands. Let jars stand a few minutes before removing one at a time. Complete seal (see directions).

High altitude processing with pressure cooker: For altitudes over 2,000 feet, add 1 pound of pressure for each additional 2,000 feet.

CANNING TOOLS

Gather together tools needed for canning before beginning to work. Use good cooking utensils with tight-fitting lids, measuring cups, a wire basket, or plenty of cheesecloth, bowls, a colander, large spoons, a ladle, a sharp knife or two, plenty of clean towels, dishcloths, and pot holders. A wide-mouthed funnel, wire clamps, or tongs for removing hot jars from pressure canner or water bath are helpful aids.

Checking jars and covers: Inspect jars carefully for possible defects, cracks, chips, or dents. Have ample supply of jar tops, new rubbers, or self-sealing lids. Make sure they fit. Do not reuse rubber rings or self-sealing lids. Zinc screw lids have no loose linings. Clamp lids must be tight. If necessary, remove top clamp, bend down in center, and bend in sides to tighten.

Preparing jars and covers: Wash jars, caps, and rubber rings in soapy water. Rinse with clear hot water. Sterilize by placing jars, caps, and rings in pan of hot water with a rack or cloth on the bottom of it. Bring to a boil just before ready to fill jars. Do not boil metal caps with self-sealing compound. Just dip in boiling water before using.

Packing jars: Remove 1 jar at a time from water. Pack hot jars as quickly as possible and seal immediately. Keep jars in hot water or on cloth or several layers of paper while packing. Don't pack food too solidly or heat will not penetrate thoroughly. Using knife blade, work out any air bubbles formed in jar. When packed always wipe food particles with clean damp cloth from rim of jar and from rubber ring.

Cooling jars: Never invert jars of any type after processing—even for a moment. Place jars on several thicknesses of cloth or newspaper. Avoid drafts. Leave air space between jars. Never cover jars while cooling.

Labeling jars: After jars have cooled for 24 hours, wipe clean, label with name, date, and with lot number, if more than one lot is prepared.

Storing jars: Store jars upright in cool, dry, dark place. Handle jars a minimum amount.

Checking jars: Examine jars after week or ten days for signs of spoilage. Remove and dispose of spoiled jars of food immediately.

Opening jars: To open glass-top or zinc screw lids, pull out jar rubber with a pair of pliers. To open self-sealing metal lids puncture top and lift up. On opening canned foods, odor should be characteristic of product with no outrush of air or liquid. Never taste to test for spoilage. Before every serving, all home-canned meats and vegetables (except tomatoes) should be cooked at boiling temperature for at least 10 minutes (spinach and other leafy vegetables for 15 minutes) in a covered container even when they are to be served cold.

HOW TO CLOSE LIDS

Metal self-sealing lids: Use only on jars with smooth, even top edges. Put lid in place with sealing compound touching rim of jar, attach screw band, then hold your index finger on lid so it won't slip while you screw band down firmly without exerting unusual force. Don't invert, move, or handle jars for at least 24 hours after processing. Screw bands may then be removed and reused. Test seal by tapping lids gently with a spoon. If properly sealed, they will sound a clear, ringing note, and the lid will have a slight dip caused by the vacuum inside. If lids bulge upward and give off a dull sound when tapped, the seal is imperfect. If seal is imperfect open and use the food at once or immediately replace the lid with a new one and reprocess the jar for half the original time.

Glass top self-sealing lids: Use on jars with smooth, even rims, free of nicks, cracks, or sharp edges. Leave 1 inch of space in top of jar regardless of type of food being canned. Fit wet rubber ring around projection on underside of glass lid. Place lid so rubber lies between lid and top edge of jar. Turn bands tight, then loosen slightly (about ¼ turn). Bands must fit loosely during processing. Immediately after processing, screw bands tightly to complete seal. Remove bands 24 hours after canning, and test seal by pulling on lid gently with the finger tips. If screw bands are not replaced on jars, handle jars gently to prevent breaking the seal. Do not turn filled jars upside down.

Clamp lids: Place rubber on ridge. Fasten top clamp only. Process. Then snap down side clamp. Do not invert jars.

Zinc screw lids: Place rubber ring on sealing shoulder of jar. Screw lid down until lid and rubber ring just touch. After processing, tighten lids the moment jars are removed. Do not invert jars after processing.

SYRUPS FOR CANNING FRUITS

Thin syrup: 1 part sugar, 3 parts juice or water. Bring to a boil, keep hot. Use on apples, blueberries, huckleberries, pears, pineapple, sweet cherries.

Medium syrup: 1 part sugar, 2 parts juice or water. Bring to a boil. Keep hot. Use on apricots, blackberries, peaches, plums, raspberries, strawberries, gooseberries, sour cherries, rhubarb.

Thick or heavy syrup: 1 part sugar, 1 part juice or water. Bring to a boil. Keep hot. Use on larger sour fruits.

Variations: Honey may be used to replace as much as half the sugar required. Corn syrup may be used to replace as much as ⅓ of the sugar required. Do not use sweeteners that have a strong flavor, such as brown sugar or sorghum.

GENERAL DIRECTIONS

Use only the very best fresh foods for canning. The finished product will not be any better than what went into it. Fruits and vegetables should be canned while they are fresh and at their best. The fresher the fruits and vegetables the higher their vitamin content and the lower the bacteria count. Most vegetables are best before they are fully matured so choose young, fresh vegetables. Select fresh, firm, ripe fruits. Remove any spots and bruises which may cause spoilage. Sort and wash carefully, removing all traces of sand and dirt. To keep apples, peaches, and pears from turning dark after peeling, place in a solution of 2 tablespoons each of salt and vinegar to 1 gallon of water. Scald peaches and tomatoes in boiling water for 1 minute to loosen skin, then dip into cold water ½ minute and remove skin.

CANNING FRUITS AND VEGETABLES IN BOILING WATER BATH

Apples: Wash, pare, and cut apples into pieces of desired size. Prepare only as many as can be processed at one time. Boil in thin syrup 5 minutes. Pack hot into jars. Cover with boiling syrup. There is less shrinkage by this method and the jars are better filled. Process in boiling water bath pint or quart jars or No. 2½ cans 15 minutes. No. 2 cans 10 minutes. Allow 2 to 3 pounds of apples for each quart jar.

Apricots: Wash, cut into halves, and remove pits. (If they are to be peeled, scald in boiling water to loosen skins before cutting.)

Cold pack: Pack apricots in glass jars. Cover with boiling syrup. Process in boiling water bath pint or quart jars 30 minutes.

Hot pack: Simmer 3 to 5 minutes in thin or medium syrup. Pack apricots hot into containers. Cover with boiling syrup. Process in boiling water bath pint or quart jars or No. 2½ cans 20 minutes, No. 2 cans 15 minutes.

Beets, pickled: Select tender beets. Wash thoroughly. Cook in boiling water, or steam 10 minutes or until skins slip easily. Remove skins. Leave small beets whole. Cut large beets into sections. Pack quickly into containers before beets cool. Add ½ teaspoon salt, 1 teaspoon or more of sugar, and 3 to 6 whole cloves, if desired, to each pint. Cover with boiling vinegar (unless vinegar is very strong, use it full strength). Process in boiling water bath pint or quart jars 30 minutes.

Cherries: Wash and pit cherries.

Cold pack: Pack into jars. Cover with boiling syrup. Process pint jars in boiling water bath 20 minutes, quart jars 25 minutes.

Hot pack: Add ½ to 1 cup sugar to each quart of cherries. Bring slowly to boiling point. Boil 2 minutes. Pack hot into glass jars or sanitary R–enamel cans. Cover with boiling syrup. Process in boiling water bath pint or quart jars or No. 2 or 2½ cans 15 minutes. Allow 1½ to 2 quarts cherries for each quart jar.

Gooseberries: Wash berries and remove stems.

Cold pack: Pack into containers. Cover with boiling syrup. Process in boiling water bath pint or quart jars 20 minutes.

Hot pack: Cover with boiling medium syrup. Boil 1 or 2 minutes. Pack into jars or cans. Process in boiling water bath pint or quart jars or No. 2½ cans 15 minutes, No. 2 cans 10 minutes. Allow 1½ to 2 quarts fresh berries for each quart jar.

Peaches: Select ripe, firm peaches. Plunge into boiling water to loosen skins. Remove and plunge into cold water. Peel. Prepare only as many as can be processed at one time.

Cold pack: Pack peaches into glass jars. Cover with boiling syrup. Process in boiling water bath pint or quart jars 30 minutes.

Hot pack: Simmer 3 to 5 minutes in syrup. Pack peaches into containers. Cover with boiling syrup. Process in boiling water bath pint or quart jars or No. 2 or 2½ cans 20 minutes. Allow 2 to 2½ pounds fresh fruit for each quart jar.

Pears: Wash, peel, cut in half, and remove core. Prepare only as many as can be processed at one time. Drain. Boil in thin or medium syrup 4 to 8 minutes, according to size and softness. Pack pears into containers. Cover with boiling syrup. Process in boiling water bath pint or quart jars or No. 2 or 2½ cans 20 minutes. Allow 2 to 2½ pounds fresh pears for each quart.

Pineapple: Peel, core, and remove "eyes." Slice or cut in pieces. Boil pineapple in thin syrup 5 minutes. Pack into containers. Cover with boiling syrup. Process in boiling water bath, pint, or quart jars, or No. 2½ cans 30 minutes, No. 2 cans 25 minutes. Allow 1 large pineapple for each quart jar.

Plums: Wash. Prick each plum to prevent bursting of skin.

Cold pack: Pack plums into glass jars. Cover with boiling syrup (medium or thick). Process pint jars 20 minutes, quart jars 25 minutes, in boiling water bath.

Hot pack: Simmer in medium syrup 5 minutes. Pack plums into containers. Cover with boiling syrup. Process in boiling water bath, pint or quart jars, or No. 2 or 2½ cans 15 minutes. Allow 2 to 2½ pounds for each quart jar.

Raspberries (black): Wash carefully, remove caps, and drain.

Cold pack: Fill glass jars, shaking or jarring against hand to make a more solid pack. Cover with boiling syrup (medium or thick). Process in boiling water bath, pint or quart jars 20 minutes.

Hot pack: Boil berries in medium syrup 2 minutes. Pack into containers. Cover with boiling syrup. Process in boiling water bath, pint or quart jars, or No. 2½ cans 15 minutes, No. 2 cans 10 minutes. Allow ½ to 2 quarts fresh berries for each quart jar.

Raspberries (red): Wash berries, being careful not to crush them. Drain. Pack into glass jars or sanitary R–enamel cans, alternating berries and boiling red syrup until containers are filled. Process the same as black raspberries. To prepare red syrup, use overripe or soft berries not firm enough for canning. Heat slowly to boiling point using ½ cup water to 1 cup berries. Extract juice by straining through fine sieve or cheesecloth. To each cup of juice add ½ cup sugar. Bring slowly to boiling point. Allow 1½ to 2 quarts fresh berries for each quart jar.

Rhubarb: Select young, tender rhubarb. Wash, cut into ½-inch lengths, but do not skin. Boil rhubarb in water or syrup until soft. Pack boiling hot into glass jars. Process in boiling water bath, pint or quart jars 10 minutes. Allow 1½ to 2 pounds for each quart jar.

Strawberries: Wash, cap, and drain fresh, firm berries.

Heat immediately: Add ½ to 1 cup sugar to each quart berries. Heat slowly to boiling point and let stand several hours or over night. Reheat slowly to boiling point. Pack berries hot into containers. Process in boiling water bath, pint or quart jars, or No. 2½ cans 15 minutes, No. 2 cans 10 minutes.

Heat later: Add ½ to 1 cup sugar to each quart of berries, alternating layers of berries and sugar. Let stand several hours or over night. Heat slowly to boiling point. Pack berries hot into containers. Process same as above. Allow 1½ to 2 quarts fresh berries for each quart jar.

Tomatoes: Select firm, well-ripened tomatoes. Wash. Scald, plunge in cold water to peel, and remove cores. Quarter.

Cold pack: Pack tomatoes solidly into containers. Add ½ teaspoon salt to each pint. When packing tomatoes in glass jars, leave 1 inch head space. When using tin cans, leave ¼ inch head space. Set in boiling water and keep there until contents in center of container are at least 160°F. Partially seal glass jars. Seal tin cans. Process in boiling water bath, pint jars 35 minutes, quart jars 45 minutes, No. 2 or No. 2½ cans 45 minutes.

Hot pack: Heat slowly to boiling point. Boil 2 minutes. Pack into containers. Process in boiling water bath, pint or quart jars, or No. 2 or 2½ cans 10 minutes. Allow 2½ to 3 pounds for each quart jar.

Tomato juice: Select firm, ripe tomatoes. Wash well, remove cores, and cut into small pieces. Season, if desired. Simmer until soft. Put through a fine sieve. Bring to boiling point. Fill jars or tin cans. Process in boiling water bath, pint or quart jars, or No. 2 or 2½ cans 15 minutes.

CANNING VEGETABLES IN PRESSURE COOKER

Asparagus: Select fresh, tender asparagus. Sort. Wash thoroughly, and trim off scales.

Long pieces: Cut stalks into lengths to fit upright in container. Tie in bundles. Place upright in kettle, with boiling water to cover lower part of stalks. Cover tightly. Boil 3 minutes. Pack hot, removing string as asparagus slips into containers. Add ½ teaspoon salt to each pint. Cover with fresh boiling water. Process at 10 pounds pressure: pint jars 25 minutes, quart jars 55 minutes, No. 2 and No. 2½ cans 20 minutes.

Short pieces: Cut stalks into 1-inch lengths. Cover with boiling water and boil 3 minutes. Pack hot into containers. Add ½ teaspoon salt to each pint and cover with boiling water. Process same as above. Allow 2 to 3 pounds for each quart.

Beans (lima): Select young, tender beans. Shell and wash. Cover with boiling water and bring to a boil. Pack hot. Add ½ teaspoon salt to each pint and cover with boiling water. Process at 10 pounds pressure: pint jars 35 minutes, quart jars 60 minutes, No. 2 and No. 2½ cans 40 minutes. Allow 4 to 5 pounds beans (in pods) for each quart jar.

Beans (fresh green soybeans): Cover shelled beans with boiling water and boil 3 or 4 minutes. Pack hot, and add ½ teaspoon salt to each pint. Cover with fresh boiling water. Process at 10 pounds pressure: pint jars or No. 2 cans 60 minutes, quart jars 70 minutes. Allow 4 to 5 pounds beans (in pods) for each quart jar.

Beans (snap): Wash thoroughly, trim off ends, and remove strings if stringy. Cut into pieces (½ to 1 inch) or cut lengthwise or leave whole. Cover with boiling water and boil 5 minutes. Pack hot. Add ½ teaspoon salt to each pint and cover with fresh boiling water. Process at 10 pounds pressure: pint jars 20 minutes, quart jars and No. 2 cans 25 minutes, No. 2½ cans 30 minutes. Allow 1½ to 2 pounds for each quart.

Beets: Select tender baby beets. Trim off tops, leaving 1 inch of stems. Wash thoroughly. Cook in boiling water about 15 minutes or steam until skins slip off easily. Skin and trim. Or peel beets before boiling them. Leave small beets whole. Cut large beets in sections. Pack quickly into containers before beets cool. Add ½ teaspoon salt to each pint. Cover with fresh boiling water (1 teaspoon vinegar added to each pint will help to retain the red color). Process at 10 pounds pressure: pint jars 25 minutes, quart jars 55 minutes, No. 2 and No. 2½ cans 30 minutes. Allow 2½ to 3 pounds fresh beets (without tops) for each quart jar. (Pickled beets may be processed in boiling-water bath.)

Carrots: Select tender carrots. Wash thoroughly. If desired, remove skins by scraping. Leave small carrots whole. Cut large carrots into lengthwise quarters or cubes. Cover with boiling water. Boil 5 minutes. Pack hot into containers. Add ½ teaspoon salt to each pint. Cover with boiling water—the same water in which the carrots were cooked. Process at 10 pounds pressure: pint jars and No. 2 cans 20 minutes, quart jars and No. 2½ cans 25 minutes. Allow about 2½ pounds fresh carrots (without tops) for each quart jar.

Corn: Use freshly picked corn in the milk stage. Work with small quantities at a time and complete the whole canning process as quickly as possible. Husk and silk the corn, using a stiff brush, if necessary, to remove the silk. Cut corn from cob so that kernels are whole. Do *not* scrape the cob. Add ½ as much boiling water as corn. Heat to boiling point. Pack into pint glass jars, or No 2 C—enameled tin cans. Add ½ teaspoon salt and ½ to 1 teaspoon sugar, if desired, to each pint. Process at 10 pounds pressure: pint jars 55 minutes, quart jars 85 minutes, No. 2 and No. 2½ cans 60 minutes. Allow 8 to 12 ears for each quart jar.

Peas: Select young, tender peas. Wash pods and shell only enough to fill containers to be processed at one time. Wash shelled peas. Cover with boiling water and bring to boiling point. Pack hot into pint jars or No. 2 cans. Add ½ teaspoon salt and ½ teaspoon sugar, if desired, to each pint. Cover with boiling water. Process at 10 pounds pressure: pint and quart jars 40 minutes, No. 2 and 2½ cans 30 minutes. Allow 2 to 2½ pounds unshelled peas for each pint jar.

Pumpkin and squash: Wash and peel pumpkin and winter squash; do not peel summer squash. Cut into 1-inch cubes. Boil or steam until tender and press through colander. Heat to simmering (190°F.). Pack hot. Add ½ teaspoon salt to each pint if desired. Process at 10 pounds pressure: pint jars 60 minutes, quart jars 80 minutes, No. 2 cans 75 minutes, No. 2½ cans 90 minutes. Allow 2 to 2½ pounds fresh pumpkin or squash for each quart jar.

Spinach or other greens: Look over and wash greens carefully. Discard imperfect leaves and tough stems. Heat greens in covered kettle containing small amount of water until completely wilted. Pack into pint jars or No. 2 cans, being careful not to pack too solidly. Add ½ teaspoon salt to each pint and cover greens with boiling water. Process at 10 pounds pressure: pint jars 45 minutes, quart jars 70 minutes, No. 2 cans 60 minutes, No. 2½ cans 75 minutes. Allow 2 to 3 pounds for each quart jar.

freezing & frozen food cookery

Having a freezer and making proper use of it can be like having an extra pair of hands in the kitchen or like having an extra day in every week. Begin by thinking of your freezer as more than just a place for food storage. Think of it as part of your daily cooking equipment, plan around it, and rely on it every day to help you.

However, to enjoy the advantages of a freezer to the fullest, you'll find it wise in the very beginning to take a little time to learn the facts about freezing—how to prepare, package, freeze, store, and cook frozen foods properly.

BASIC PRINCIPLES OF SUCCESSFUL FREEZING

Frozen foods are attractive, flavorable, and high in nutritive value when carefully prepared with strict attention to basic principles of freezing. There is a great difference, however, between frozen foods of quality and foods that are merely safe to eat because they have been frozen. Carelessness in any of the basic steps may easily produce foods that are entirely safe, yet whose quality is so diminished that you will have little pleasure in eating them.

1. Choose high quality foods. The frozen product will be no better than the food in its original state. Freezing does not improve the flavor or quality of any food.
2. Process foods carefully. Follow instructions about blanching vegetables, cutting and trimming meat and poultry, cooking and chilling prepared foods. Speed in handling is essential at all stages.
3. Package foods properly. Choose only freezer packaging materials which will protect food from air. Wrap tightly and seal with freezer tape. When air reaches food during storage, the result is loss of moisture accompanied by a change in flavor. This is the condition known as "freezer burn."
4. Label all foods accurately. Label each package with date, name of product, weight (if meat) and number of pieces or servings. It is helpful to add an "expiration date" to the label—the maximum storage time. All foods should be used before their expiration date.
5. Freeze at 0°F. or lower. Foods should always be frozen as rapidly as possible. Put unfrozen foods in the fastest freezing area or in direct contact with freezer walls or shelves and away from already frozen foods. Place packages so air can circulate between them.
6. Do not overload freezer with unfrozen foods. Put in only as much food as your freezer will freeze without unduly raising the temperature of foods already stored there. Overloading also keeps the new items from freezing quickly enough for optimum quality. Follow the directions with your freezer to determine how much food may be frozen at one time. If you have more than recommended amounts, have food frozen at a central locker plant, then store at home.
7. Store foods at 0°F. Keep a thermometer in the storage compartment, and make sure the temperature remains at zero or below. Foods stored at temperatures above zero lose flavor and nutritive value rapidly. Ice or snow inside the package usually indicates fluctuation of temperatures above zero.
8. Avoid long storage. No food remains at top quality indefinitely even though

frozen. Freezing retards bacterial and enzymatic action greatly but cannot stop it entirely, and it is best to plan on normal seasonal turnover of foods. Foods frozen first should always be used first.

FREEZING FRUITS

Fruits are especially easy to freeze, so allow ample space in your freezer for a complete variety. Most fruits have a high sugar content and, for best results, should be frozen quickly.

Which fruits to select: Most fruits, berries and melons can be frozen satisfactorily, but some freeze better than others. In the same manner, certain varieties of each fruit freeze better than others. Directions for freezing specific fruits rate varieties as to suitability for freezing. If in doubt about freezing certain fruits, consult your local nurseryman, county agent or State Agricultural College for further information. Whole citrus fruits should not be frozen, but serving slices, sections and juices are delicious and easy to freeze. Red raspberries are delicious when frozen.

When to gather fruits: The ideal time to freeze most fruits is at the height of maturity. It is best to allow most fruits to reach this stage on the vine, bush, or tree. However, fruits like peaches, plums, and figs are apt to become soft on the plant and are easily bruised in handling. Gather such fruits in the "firm ripe" stage and store overnight . . . insures more even ripening and, with peaches, they are easier to peel. Gather fruit in the cool of the morning. Sun-heated fruit may bruise excessively from handling and result in an inferior frozen product. Gather no more fruit than can be quickly pepared, packaged, and frozen at one time. While speed of handling is not so critical with fruits as with vegetables, the shorter the holding time after gathering for most fruits, the better the frozen fruit will be.

Wash fruit thoroughly: This is one of the most important steps in preparing fruits for freezing. Low-growing fruits and all wild fruits should be washed twice or more to remove sand and dust. Wash no more than one quart of small fruit (berries or cherries) at one time. This can be done in a colander, using a spray when possible. Never allow fruit to stand in water more than one minute as water-soaked fruit will not freeze successfully. After washing, drain fruit thoroughly. Spread fruit carefully on a tray or large utility dish on which several thicknesses of absorbent paper toweling have been placed. If possible, set tray in refrigerator about one hour to cool and firm the fruit.

Stem fruits carefully: Never squeeze the stems off berries. The stems of raspberries, dewberries, and gooseberries may be lifted off with the fingers. Use a sharp knife to stem strawberries.

Peel fruits rapidly: Apples, apricots, peaches, nectarines, and pears oxidize and discolor rapidly after the skin is removed. To prevent this, peel and slice fruit directly into a solution of 3 tablespoons lemon juice (or 3 tablespoons salt OR 4½ teaspoons citric acid) to each gallon of cold water. Don't allow fruit to remain in solution longer than one minute, so do no more than one package at a time. Rinse in cold water and drain before packaging. Then continue to peel, slice, and package until all fruit has been prepared.

Remove seeds carefully: Fruits with seeds (plums, prunes, peaches, apricots, and nectarines) must have the seed removed before freezing. Avoid bruising fruit.

Pulp: Fruit to be pulped (puréed) may be cooked before forcing through a purée strainer or electric food blender. Such fruits as strawberries, grapes, raspberries, peaches, and plums may be forced through purée strainer or food blender without cooking.

Sweeten fruits properly: Many fruits retain better flavor if sweetened before freezing. There are two methods of sweetening fruit: dry sugar method and syrup method.

Dry sugar method—Method #1: After the fruit has been washed, drained, and cooled, carefully transfer fruit to a bowl. Sprinkle sugar over fruit. Sweeten one quart at a time to avoid bruising. A clean flour sifter will give more even distribution of sugar. To mix sugar through fruit, use wooden slotted spoon and gently lift fruit through sugar. Package at once.

Method #2: Wash, cool, and drain fruit. Fill package about ¼ full. Sprinkle in ¼ of sugar, about one or two tablespoons. Continue filling container in this way. Container may be shaken occasionally to distribute sugar, but avoid pressure on container. Seal at once.

Syrup method: Syrup is the most satisfactory sweetening agent if fruit is to be used for sauce. Syrup is preferable for apricots, pears, and figs. The simplest way to add the syrup to the fruit is to first fill the container with fruit and then add syrup to cover. Seal at once. The syrup must always be cold before using . . . a good idea is to make the syrup a day in advance and store it in a covered container in the refrigerator.

Sugar syrup: Add sugar to boiling water and cook until sugar is thoroughly dissolved. The sweetness desired in the frozen fruit should govern the syrup to be used. See specific directions for recommended syrup with each particular fruit.

Very thin: 1 cup sugar to 4 cups boiling water.

Thin: 1 cup sugar to 3 cups boiling water.

Medium: 1 cup sugar to 2 cups boiling water.

Heavy: 1 cup sugar to 1 cup boiling water.

Package fruits carefully: Polyethylene bags are excellent, but care should be taken when sealing and handling the bag before the fruit is frozen. Rigid cartons, tin cans (if lacquered inside), and special glass freezing jars may be used. Containers must also be moisture-vaporproof because air leakage causes destruction of vitamins and minerals and also spoils the appearance of the fruit.

Package according to use: Decide how the frozen fruit is to be used and then package the fresh fruit accordingly. For instance, fruits to be used for pies or jams need not be sweetened before freezing, with the exception of apricots and peaches which sometimes discolor unless sugar or syrup is added. As a sauce, a pint carton of fruit will serve 3 or 4. A pint will make a skimpy 8-inch pie but a quart will make four generous individual shortcakes. But if used as a topping over ice cream, a pint of strawberries will serve 5 or 6. Select package sizes that adequately take care of a meal, with no save-overs. Frozen fruits lose their flavor if left standing several hours after thawing. **Never refreeze fruit.**

Allow for expansion and seal carefully: Package fruit firmly but do not use pressure or crush the fruit. If using a rigid container, there should be sufficent air space to allow for some expansion. Fill container to within ½ inch of top for dry sugar packs and ½ to ¾ inch for syrup packs. Make packages airtight.

Label clearly and freeze at once: After sugar or syrup has been added to fruit in container, package should be sealed, labeled clearly, and placed immediately on quick-freeze shelf with the sealed side up to prevent leakage. If this is not practical, place packages in freezer compartment of refrigerator until ready to load the freezer.

A hint for mothers of small children: When sorting fruits for freezing, use only those which are firm and ripe. Those which are overripe but still usable can be puréed for the baby and young children. Peaches, apples, apricots, plums, and pineapple are easy to purée and will save both time and money in the preparation of the children's meals.

How it's done: Peel (or pare) the fruit and then cook thoroughly . . . be careful not to overcook. You may want to add a bit of sugar as the fruit cooks. Then force it through a sieve or food mill or put it through an electric food blender. Cool thoroughly. After the fruit is cool, pour into refrigerator ice cube tray with the dividers in place. Freeze. When cubes are firmly frozen, remove them from the tray and package one or two cubes, enough for an individual serving, in small polyethylene bags. To serve: Let cubes stand at room temperature until suitable for serving.

HOW TO PREPARE FRUITS FOR FREEZING

Apples for sauce: Varieties suitable for freezing: good—Baldwin, Greening, Northern Spy, and Yellow Transparent. 1¼ pounds yield approximately 1 pint. Peel and core the apples. Cut into eighths. Place in saucepan and add only enough water to start the apples cooking. Bring to a quick boil. Reduce heat to simmer and cook about 10 minutes until apples are mushy. Add sugar to taste and stir. Some apples cook to a fine mush without straining, but if straining is necessary, force the sauce through a purée strainer. Cool thoroughly. Package in polyethylene bags. Freeze.

Apples for pie: Varieties suitable for freezing: good—any high-acid variety. 1 pound yields about 1 pint. Freeze enough in one container for a pie . . . a quart container holds apples for a 9-inch pie. **Do not freeze apples which have turned brown on the inside or have started to mold.** Peel and core the apples. Cut into slices for pie. Apples discolor rapidly after the skin has been removed, so slice apples directly into a solution of 3 tablespoons lemon juice (or 3 tablespoons salt OR 4½ teaspoons citric acid) to 1 gallon cold water. Never allow apples to remain in solution more than one minute. Rinse in cold water before draining. Place slices on a tray covered with several thicknesses of absorbent paper toweling. Place tray in refrigerator and allow to drain. Thorough draining before packaging makes slices easier to separate for making pies. Immediately after draining, pack into polyethylene bags and freeze. Add sugar, if desired, in the proportion of 1 part sugar to 4 parts apples.

Apricots: Varieties suitable for freezing: good—any tree-ripened variety. ¾ to 1 pound yields approximately 1 pint.

With skins: Select firm, fully ripened fruit of bright apricot color, with no traces of green. Wash thoroughly. Remove stem. Cut in half and remove pit. Dip pitted halves in a solution of 1 tablespoon lemon juice and 1 quart water. Drain by placing cut side down on a tray covered with several thicknesses of absorbent toweling. Place in polyethylene bags or rigid containers. Cover with cold, medium syrup. Seal. Freeze at once.

Without skins (Preferred): Place about 20 apricots in a wire basket. Plunge into boiling water to cover for 1 minute. Remove and plunge into cold water to cover for 1 minute . . . or until cool. Remove skin. Cut in half and remove pit. Dip pitted halves in a solution of 1 tablespoon lemon juice to 1 quart water. Drain by placing cut side down on a tray covered with several thicknesses of absorbent toweling. Place in polyethylene bags or rigid containers. Cover with cold, medium syrup. Seal. Freeze at once.

Blackberries: Variety suitable for freezing: fair—Wild Eldorado. 1 quart berries yields about 1 quart frozen fruit. Select firm, fully matured fruit. Immature blackberries, even though a good black in color, turn reddish black when frozen. Wash carefully in cold water, never more than 1 quart of berries at a time. Gently move the berries through the water by hand, then lift them to a tray covered with several thicknesses of absorbent paper toweling. Spread them only one layer thick. Place immediately in refrigerator to cool before packaging. If you wish to add sugar to berries, use the same method as for red raspberries. Package in polyethylene bags, seal and freeze. For use as a sauce, pack berries in polyethylene bags or rigid containers and cover with a thin or medium syrup. Seal and freeze immediately.

Blueberries: Variety suitable for freezing: excellent—any small-seeded variety. 1 pint berries yields approximately 1 pint frozen fruit. Carefully remove leaves, foreign matter and immature berries. Wash thoroughly. Remove stems. Drain on absorbent paper toweling. Place in bowl. Add sugar in proportion of 2 tablespoons sugar to 1 cup berries. Stir gently to avoid bruising the fruit. Package in polyethylene bags or rigid containers. Seal. Freeze.

Cantaloupe: Variety suitable for freezing: good—any fully ripened, deep yellow variety. 1 cantaloupe yields approximately 3 pints. Good for fruit cups or salads during the winter months. Select firm, fully ripened cantaloupe. Cut in half and remove seeds. A French potato ball cutter is ideal for scooping out the cantaloupe. If one is not available, remove rind, cut melon in slices and cube. Drain before packaging. Package in polyethylene bags. Seal and freeze. Once thawed, cantaloupe must be used immediately.

Cherries, sour: Variety suitable for freezing: excellent—Montmorency. 1 quart cherries yields about 1 pint frozen fruit. Wash thoroughly and quickly. Remove from water at once. Remove stems. Place on tray covered with several thicknesses of absorbent paper toweling. Set tray in refrigerator until cherries are firm again. Then remove pits. A salad fork or three-pronged kitchen fork is excellent to do this. With the fork, gently press prong into stem end and lift out the pit. Squeezing the pit out bruises the fruit. Work with only 1 quart at a time because juice accumulates and the cherries may have to be drained again. Add 2 tablespoons sugar to 1 cup cherries and package in polyethylene bags. Freeze. Cherries for pies may be frozen without sugar.

Cherries, sweet: Varieties suitable for freezing: fair—Bing and Lambert. 1 quart cherries yields about 1 pint frozen fruit. Select fully tree-ripened cherries. Proceed as for sour cherries. A medium syrup may be used if the sweet cherries are to be used as a sauce. Package in polyethylene bags or rigid containers. Seal and freeze at once.

Citrus juices: Select juicy, well-matured oranges and grapefruit. Extract juice. Remove seeds and strain, if desired. Pour into rigid containers. Seal. Freeze at once.

Cranberries: Variety suitable for freezing: excellent—Howes. ½ pound yields approximately 1 pint. Sort berries carefully. Remove stems and all spongy or poorly formed cranberries. Wash berries carefully. Drain. Package in polyethylene bags. Freeze. Cranberries do not need sugar for successful freezing.

Currants: Varieties suitable for freezing: good—any large variety. ¾ pound yields about 1 pint. Wash and drain currants before removing from stem. Then remove stem and place currants in a bowl. Mix with sugar in proportion of 1 part sugar to 4 parts currants. Place in polyethylene bags. If currants are to be used as a sauce, place in rigid containers and cover with medium syrup. Seal and freeze.

Dewberries: Variety suitable for freezing: fair—Boysenberries. 1 quart berries yields about 1 quart frozen fruit. Same procedure as for blackberries.

Figs: Varieties suitable for freezing: excellent—Magnolia, Brown Turkey, and Celestial. Gather figs that are completely ripe but not bruised or softened. Figs may be frozen with or without skin.

Peeled figs: Wash thoroughly. Remove stem. Using a sharp knife, peel very thin. Package according to size of family, allowing 4 or 5 figs per serving. Freeze. Place figs in polyethylene bags. When bag is ¼ filled, sprinkle sugar over figs. Continue alternating figs and sugar. Use 1 part sugar to 4 parts figs. Seal and freeze. Prepared this way, figs are delicious served with cream. Or fill container. Cover figs with a medium syrup. Seal and freeze. If figs are to be used as a topping over ice cream, use a heavy syrup.

Unpeeled figs: Sprinkle 6 quarts of figs with 1 cup baking soda. Pour 6 quarts boiling water over them. Let stand 10 minutes. Rinse in clear, cold water. Drain thoroughly on absorbent paper toweling on a tray. Set tray in refrigerator to chill. Package in polyethylene bags. Add medium syrup. Seal and freeze.

Gooseberries: Varieties suitable for freezing: excellent—wild, any large-sized variety. 1 pint fresh berries yields approximately 1 pint frozen fruit. Frozen gooseberries are excellent for pie. Select fully matured green gooseberries. Wash thoroughly. Remove stem and blossom end. Drain. Place berries in bowl. Add sugar, if desired, in proportion of 2 tablespoons sugar to 1 cup gooseberries. Package. Freeze.

Grapefruit and orange sections: Chill fruit thoroughly. Then, peel and section the fruit, making sure all skin and membrane are removed. Drain on absorbent paper toweling. Prepare only enough for 3 or 4 packages at one time as a protection against vitamin loss. Package in polyethylene bags with rounds of waxed paper between layers. Seal and freeze. Sugar may be added to grapefruit sections, if desired.

Huckleberries: Same procedure as blueberries.

Nectarines: Practically all varieties suitable for freezing. Same procedure as for peaches.

Peaches: Varieties suitable for freezing: Yellow, excellent—Hale Haven, J. H. Hale, and Red Haven. White, excellent—Golden Jubilee and Georgia Belle. 1 to 1½ pounds yield approximately 1 pint. Select tree-ripened peaches. Peel, rather than scald peaches . . . doing only a few at a time. Slice peaches directly into the polyethylene bag in which they are to be frozen. Add sugar alternately with the peaches in proportion of 2 tablespoons sugar to 1 cup peaches. Seal and freeze. This method helps to retard browning or oxidation of peaches. Or, you may peel and slice about one quart at one time. Place in a bowl and sprinkle 1 tablespoon lemon juice over them to retard discoloring. Add sugar in proportion of 2 tablespoons sugar to 1 cup peaches. Turn peaches over and over in bowl with wooden spoon. **Handle gently.** If you desire, peaches may be packed in medium syrup in polyethylene bags or rigid containers.

Note: Sometimes, due to growing season and the variety of peaches selected for freezing, the peaches may discolor in spite of anything that can be done.

Pears: (Not especially recommended for freezing.) Varieties suitable for freezing: fair—Kieffer and Baldwin. 1 to 1¼ pounds yield approximately 1 pint. Select tree-ripened fruit. Wash, peel and cut into desired sizes. Place peeled and cored fruit in a solution of 1 tablespoon lemon juice (or 1 tablespoon salt OR 1 teaspoon citric acid) to 1 quart of cold water. Drain on tray covered with several thicknesses of absorbent paper toweling. Set tray in refrigerator to chill pears. Pack in polyethylene bags or rigid containers. Add medium syrup to completely cover pears. Seal and freeze.

Pineapple: Excellent for freezing. 1 pineapple yields approximately 3 pints or 12 to 14 slices. An easy way to peel pineapple is to lay the fruit, side down, on a good cutting board. Grasp the stem end with one hand. With a sharp knife, cut bottom end off pineapple. Place pineapple upright on cutting board and, while holding by stem, remove peeling by slicing downward. When peeling is removed, return pineapple to its side and cut in ½-inch slices. Discard stem when last piece is sliced. Remove any "eyes" remaining in each slice. Cut out core. These slices may be frozen whole. Place in freezer foil (use drugstore wrap) or in polyethylene bags. Pineapple may be shredded and 2 tablespoons of sugar added to each cup. Or, a thin syrup may be used. Place in polyethylene bags or rigid containers. Seal. Freeze.

Note: If frozen pineapple is to be used in gelatin dessert, it must be brought to the boiling point and cooked a minute or two before using, otherwise gelatin will not congeal.

Plums: Varieties suitable for freezing: Plums, very good—Damson and Red June. Prunes, very good—Italian. 1¼ pounds yield approximately 1 pint. Select fully ripened fruit, not yet brown around the pit. Wash, sort, stem and cut in half, removing the pit. Drain on tray with several thicknesses of paper toweling. Set tray in refrigerator to chill fruit. Place fruit in bowl. Add sugar in proportion of 1 cup sugar to 5 cups fruit or use medium syrup. Package in polyethylene bags. Freeze.

Red raspberries: Varieties suitable for freezing: excellent—Cuthbert, Latham, and Viking. 1 pint fresh berries yields approximately 1 pint frozen ones. Raspberries are exceptionally fragile. Great care should be used in washing them, as they bruise easily. If possible, wash raspberries in water which has been cooled, with ice, to about 40°F. Wash only a few berries at a time and do not allow them to remain in the water more than 30 seconds. Use the same procedure as strawberries (see page 541). Drain thoroughly. Then place berries on tray covered with several thicknesses of absorbent paper toweling. Set tray in refrigerator to cool and firm the fruit . . . about one hour. Package raspberries in polyethylene bags or rigid containers. When container is ¼ filled with berries, add ¼ of the sugar (use proportion of 2 tablespoons sugar to 1 cup raspberries). Continue alternately adding berries and sugar until container is filled. Seal. Freeze immediately. Raspberries make their own syrup when sugar is added. A pint of raspberries makes 4 servings. Purple varieties may also be frozen by this procedure.

Rhubarb: Variety suitable for freezing: excellent—Victoria. 1¼ pounds yield approximately 1 pint. Freeze rhubarb as early in the spring as possible, before the rhubarb becomes tough and stringy. Wash under running water. Remove stem and leaf end. Cut in 1-inch pieces (cuts much easier with scissors). Drain. Package in polyethylene bags. Seal and freeze. Rhubarb keeps beautifully without sugar or syrup. A quart makes one 9-inch pie.

Strawberries: Varieties suitable for freezing: excellent—Marshall, Sparkle, Gem, Senator Dunlap, and Fairfax. ⅔ quart yields approximately 1 pint. Do not remove cap from fruit until after berries are washed. Sort and place in colander. Wash strawberries with fine spray, if possible. If not, dip colander in large container filled with very cold water. Gently lift colander up and down in water two or three times. Drain thoroughly. To remove cap, use a sharp paring knife. Do not squeeze cap off with fingers. Slip knife directly under the cap, taking care not to cut through into the center of the fruit. Pry cap off. Place fruit on tray covered with several thicknesses of absorbent paper toweling and put tray in refrigerator to chill the strawberries. Strawberries may be frozen in syrup or by adding sugar. Add sugar in proportion of 2 tablespoons sugar to 1 cup strawberries. The drained and cooled strawberries may be placed in a bowl and the sugar sprinkled over them, or they may be sweetened in container in which they are to be frozen. When container is ¼ full, add ¼ of the sugar, repeating until container is filled. Package in polyethylene bags or rigid containers. Seal and freeze at once.

Watermelon: Variety suitable for freezing: any variety is fair for freezing if thoroughly ripened. Centers of melons are best to use. Same as for cantaloupe.

Note: The freezer is an ideal place for quickly cooling a watermelon for picnics. Place whole melon in freezer for 3 or 4 hours.

How to prepare frozen fruits for serving: Always thaw fruit in the container in which it was frozen. This usually requires about 2 to 3 hours at room temperature. Do not open the container until the fruit is nearly thawed . . . since frozen fruit, once thawed, collapses quickly. Remove from freezer only the quantity of fruit you plan to use at one time. Frozen fruit cannot satisfactorily be refrozen once it is thawed.

FREEZING VEGETABLES

When to gather or buy vegetables: Select only those which are in prime condition for freezing. In general, immature vegetables have not fully developed all their sweetness and flavor. Overripe vegetables will neither taste good nor keep satisfactorily. The best time to gather vegetables is in the cool of the morning when the dew is gone. Never pick vegetables at night and keep them in the refrigerator until the next day . . . they lose that garden-fresh flavor. If you do not raise your own vegetables, buy freshly picked ones from local gardens or nearby farms. The vegetables you buy are satisfactory for freezing only if you **arrange to get them within an hour or two after picking.** Vegetables which have stood longer will not be as tender, nutritive or well-flavored as garden-fresh ones. Freezing captures and preserves the flavor and goodness but it cannot improve them. Frozen foods come from the freezer only as good as when they were frozen.

Speed is essential: Gather only as many vegetables as can be completely processed and placed in the freezer within two hours. The **"2 hours from vine to freezer"** rule is an excellent one to remember. Wash, sort, scald, chill, drain, package, and freeze without wasting any time between steps. Having all your supplies and materials ready before you begin is a big step toward accomplishing this "2-hour" rule. Learn these steps, follow them closely and results will be excellent. Have all packaging materials ready before you start freezing. It saves valuable time.

1. Gather vegetables in the cool of morning, selecting the choice grades and only quantities that can be handled speedily.
2. Wash and sort vegetables carefully.
3. Scald according to directions for each vegetable.
4. Cool and drain quickly.
5. Pack in airtight containers.
6. Freeze at once.
7. Enter item in your freezer inventory file.

Which vegetables to select: Most vegetables can be frozen satisfactorily. Exceptions: salad greens, celery, radishes, and whole tomatoes. Certain varieties of vegetables freeze better than others. Directions for freezing specific vegetables rate varieties as to suitability for freezing. For success of freezing other varieties, consult your local seed company, county agent or State Agricultural College.

Wash and sort vegetables carefully: Vegetables are prepared for freezing in much the same manner as for cooking. Wash carefully and thoroughly. While washing, sort for size and discard all inferior vegetables. For the best frozen vegetables, freeze only the choice fresh vegetables. Size-sorting of many vegetables (peas, beans, etc.) is important because you can obtain better uniformity.

Scald vegetables properly: Scalding is a must . . . never to be omitted! It regards enzymatic action, thus holds back the "growing process." Scalding "locks in" color, preserves flavor and saves vitamins so that, when served, the vegetable is as fresh as it was when taken from the garden. Scald only one pound of any vegetable at a time. Live steam cannot penetrate evenly through larger amounts. Too many vegetables scalded at once may cause an inferior product.

Live steam scalding: This is the preferred method.

Necessary equipment: Any large utensil with a tight-fitting cover, a trivet or rack, and a fine-mesh wire basket. If a wire basket is not available, a colander with small perforations may be used. It must not interfere with the cover's tight fit. If neither basket nor colander is available, loosely tie the vegetables in cheesecloth.

Procedure: Place rack in utensil. Add sufficient water to keep the utensil from boiling dry during scalding, but not enough to touch the vegetables. Keep this water boiling vigorously throughout the entire scalding period. Place vegetables into basket. When water is boiling violently, set basket in utensil and cover at once. Start counting scalding time when the lid is replaced.

Water bath scalding:

Necessary equipment: Large utensil with tight-fitting lid (deep well cooker in electric range is ideal), fine mesh wire basket or cheesecloth.

Procedure: Boil at least a gallon of water in the cooker or utensil. Have water boiling briskly so that temperature will not drop when vegetables are added. Place vegetables in wire basket or tie loosely in cheesecloth. Lower basket into rapidly boiling water and cover immediately. Start counting scalding time from the moment vegetables are placed in the boiling water.

Cool and drain quickly: Quick, effective cooling makes better frozen products. Draining is also most important. Moisture clinging to the vegetables when they are packed will form ice crystals and make it difficult to separate frozen vegetables when ready to cook.

Necessary equipment: Large pan or sink filled with ice water, clean dish towels or absorbent paper toweling.

Procedure: Immediately after scalding, cool vegetables quickly in ice water. With small vegetables (peas, beans, etc.) leave vegetables in container used during scalding and immerse it in ice water. Move basket back and forth to speed the cooling. Drain thoroughly by placing several thicknesses of absorbent toweling on a tray. Carefully spread the vegetables on toweling. Shake tray slightly to bring all sides of vegetables in contact with toweling.

Package in convenient quantities: Determine the size package that will best suit your family's needs. For instance, a pint carton of vegetables will usually serve 3 large or 4 small portions. A quart carton will serve from 6 to 8 portions. Containers larger than pints and quarts are not recommended for average-sized families because they waste valuable freezer space. Also food not eaten at one meal may be wasted as it is never advisable to refreeze thawed vegetables. If freezing for a family of two, freeze in one bag just enough to serve two persons and enclose several of these bags in a larger one. Mark number of smaller bags on outside of larger one.

Never skimp on packaging: Buy only packaging materials that are both moisture-proof and vaporproof. Glass freezing jars and outer cardboard cartons may be used over and over again. Polyethylene bags may be washed and reused providing they are free from pricks and holes. Plain tin cans, which can be sealed airtight, may also be used except for asparagus and New Zealand spinach, which require enamel or lacquer-lined cans. **Freezing always results in expansion of the food;** therefore it is necessary to leave head space to allow for this expansion. Pint cartons: ½-inch head space. Quart cartons: ¾-inch head space. Glass jars: 1- to 1½-inch head space. Tin cans: 1-inch head space.

Seal carefully: Be sure all packages are airtight! To close polyethylene bags: Put food in polyethylene bag. Then, starting at the bottom, **gently** press all the air out the bag. When the top of the food is reached, twist the bag tightly several times. Loop the top of the bag over and secure tightly with either a piece of string or an acetate band. Rubber bands do not hold at low temperatures.

Freeze at once: When packages are filled, sealed and labeled, place them immediately in the freezer. If this is not practical, place packages in freezer compartment of refrigerator until you are ready to load the freezer. Never allow filled packages to stand at room temperature.

A hint for mothers of small children: When sorting vegetables such as green beans, peas, carrots, or beets, you will find some that are too mature for freezing. Set these aside until after you have frozen the rest. These can be cooked, puréed, frozen, and used later for the baby and young children. Here's how it's done: Steam the vegetable until it is well cooked . . . not overcooked. Purée in an electric food blender or by forcing through a food mill. Thoroughly cool the puréed vegetable. After vegetable is cool, pour into refrigerator ice cube tray with the dividers in place. Freeze. When cubes are firmly frozen, remove them from the tray and package one or two cubes, enough for an individual serving, in small polyethylene bags. To serve: Heat cubes in a covered saucepan. Start with low heat until food is thawed.

HOW TO PREPARE VEGETABLES FOR FREEZING

Asparagus: (Do not use iron utensil . . . will discolor asparagus.) Varieties suitable for freezing: excellent—Mary Washington and Martha Washington. 1½ pounds yield approximately 1 pint. Scalding time:

Small spears: By steam, 5 minutes. By boiling water, 3 minutes.

Large spears: By steam, 6 minutes. By boiling water, 4 minutes.
Wash thoroughly. Discard all woody portions. Sort by size of butt end. Cut stalks correct length to fit polyethylene bag—usually about 5 inches for quart-sized bag. If you are planning to wrap asparagus in freezer foil, it is not necessary to cut all stalks a specific length. Remove all scales by slipping sharp knife under scale and snipping off. Sand collects under these scales. Also, sweetness of frozen product is much improved if scales are removed. Do not bruise stem. When scalding stand asparagus with tips up. Cool and drain. Pack stalks parallel in polyethylene bags or freezer foil, placing heads in opposite directions. Freeze at once.

Beans, green snap or yellow wax: (Do not use iron utensil . . . will discolor beans.) Varieties suitable for freezing: Green snap, excellent—Tendergreen, Stringless Green Pod, Kentucky Wonder. Yellow wax, fair—consult your local seed man. ⅔ to 1 pound yields approximately 1 pint. Scalding time: By steam, 5 minutes. By boiling water, 3 minutes. Wash thoroughly. Sort for size. Remove the stem end. Leave blossom end on, it is particularly rich in vitamins and minerals. For quick preparation, grasp as many beans as can be easily held in one hand. With small, sharp knife held in other hand, snip off stem end. Cut in 1-inch pieces, or in French style. Do not scald small and large beans together. Cool, drain, pack and freeze. Package in polyethylene bags.

Beans, lima: Varieties suitable for freezing: excellent—Fordhook (bush) and King of the Garden (pole). 2 to 2½ pounds in pods yield approximately 1 pint. Scalding time:

Baby lima beans: By steam, 5 minutes. By boiling water, 3 minutes.

Large Fordhook: By steam, 6 minutes. By boiling water, 4 minutes.

Wash pods, shell beans. Sort for size. Overmatured beans are not recommended for freezing. Scald, cool and drain. Package in polyethylene bags. Freeze. Lima beans still in their pods may be scalded in boiling water for 1 minute longer than shelled beans. Then cool, shell, drain, sort and package.

Beets: Variety suitable for freezing: good—Detroit Dark Red. 1¼ pounds, without tops, yield approximately 1 pint. Scalding time:

Young tender beets, up to 1½ inches in diameter, 3 minutes submerged in boiling water. **All other beets,** cook until tender. Wash thoroughly before scalding or cooking. Immediately after scalding, cool beets and remove skin. Small beets may be frozen whole. Large beets may be sliced, diced or quartered. Cool, drain on absorbent paper toweling, pack in polyethylene bags. Freeze.

Broccoli: Variety suitable for freezing: excellent—Italian Green Sprouting. 2 pounds yield approximately 1 pint. Scalding time:

Medium-sized pieces: By steam, 5 minutes. By boiling water, 3 minutes.

Large pieces: By steam, 6 minutes. By boiling water, 5 minutes.

Select compact heads of uniform color. Immerse broccoli for ½ hour in a solution of salt water to remove any insects. Use 1 cup salt to 1 gallon of water. Wash carefully. Remove woody portions. Separate heads in convenient size for packaging. Scald, cool and drain. Package in freezer foil or polyethylene bags. Freeze.

Brussels sprouts: Variety suitable for freezing: excellent—Long Island Improved. 1½ pounds yield approximately 1 pint. Scalding time: By steam, 5 minutes. By boiling water, 4 minutes. Sprouts should be firm and dark green in color. Immerse in salt water as for broccoli. Remove stem. If wilted, remove the outer leaves. Scald, cool, drain, package in polyethylene bags. Freeze. Allow 5 to 6 sprouts to a serving.

Carrots: Varieties suitable for freezing: excellent—Chantenay, Red Cored, Half Long. 1¼ to 1½ pounds yield approximately 1 pint. Scalding time:

Sliced: By steam, 4 minutes. By boiling water, 2 minutes.

Whole: By steam, 5 minutes. By boiling water, 3 minutes.

Select only young, small carrots. Never attempt to freeze carrots which have grown to full maturity. Wash and scrape. Sort for size. Scald, cool, drain and package in polyethylene bags. Alternate top and tip of whole carrots when packaging. Package. Freeze.

Cauliflower: Variety suitable for freezing: good—Snowball. 1 pound yields approximately 1 pint. Scalding time: By steam, 4 minutes. By boiling water, 3 minutes. Select compact, tender white heads. Trim and cut in pieces about 1 inch thick, or break small flowerets in medium-sized pieces. Sometimes it is necessary to immerse cauliflower in a salt solution (as for broccoli) to remove insects. Allow 5 to 6 medium pieces for each serving. Scald, cool, drain and package in polyethylene bags. Remove as much air as possible from the package. Freeze.

Corn on the cob: (Follow directions and corn will be just like fresh-picked.) Varieties suitable for freezing: excellent—Golden Bantam Hybrids, Golden Cross Bantam, Cherokee, DeKalb Hybrid. Scalding time: By boiling water—ears 1½ to 2 inches at base, 8 minutes. Larger ears require 11 minutes. Select corn with kernels well formed, while milk is thin and sweet. With sharp knife, cut a section about ½ inch wide from both ends. Husks will come off easier. Husk corn and remove silk. If necessary, wash corn. Sort for size. Scald for length of time indicated and cool in ice water the same length of time. Drain. Package in freezer foil or polyethylene bags according to your family's serving needs . . . with not more than 6 ears to a package. Freeze.

Corn, whole kernel: Varieties suitable for freezing: Same as corn on the cob. 6 ears yield approximately 1 pint when cut from cob. Scalding time: Same as for corn on the cob. Scald corn. Cool. To remove kernels from cob: Impale base end of cob on large nail driven through a board. Place in flat dish or on two thicknesses of waxed paper. Cut corn from cob, holding knife not flat but at a sharp angle. Examine kernels carefully, removing any bits of silk. Package in polyethylene bags. Freeze.

Eggplant: Variety suitable for freezing: good—Black Beauty. 1½ to 2 pounds yield approximately 1 pint. Scalding time: By steam, 5 minutes. By boiling water, 4 minutes. Select mature eggplant. Peel and cut into about ½-inch slices. If boiling water method of scalding is used, add 4½ teaspoons pure citric acid to 1 gallon of water. If steam method is used, add same amount of citric acid, or 3 tablespoons lemon juice, to cooling water. Put through another cold water rinse. Drain. Place waxed paper between each slice. Package in polyethylene bags or aluminum foil. Freeze.

Greens (spinach, kale, Swiss chard, mustard greens, and turnip tops): Varieties suitable for freezing: Spinach, good—King of Denmark. Kale, excellent—Dwarf Green

Curled. Swiss chard, excellent—Fordhook. Mustard, good—Mammoth. 1 to 1½ pounds yield approximately 1 pint.

Spinach, kale, Swiss chard: Scalding time: By steam, 2½ minutes. Best method: Use wire basket, if possible. By boiling water, 2 minutes.

Mustard greens and turnip tops: Scalding time: By steam, 3 to 3½ minutes. By boiling water, 2 minutes.

Use 2 gallons of water for each pound of greens. Select young, tender greens. Discard all bruised leaves and cut off stems before washing. Wash through several waters. **Lift** leaves from one pan of water to the other . . . don't pour off water . . . it may leave sand on the leaves. Scald only a small amount of greens at one time, and wire basket is preferable. This is particularly true of spinach. Drain. Complete draining of spinach is impossible, some water will remain in leaves. If these suggestions are followed, there will be little matting of greens. Do not use pressure when packing. Polyethylene bags are excellent for greens of all kinds. Freeze.

Mushrooms: Scalding time:

Button size: Steam 3 minutes.

Medium size: Steam 4 minutes.

Sliced: Steam 3 minutes.

Warning: Unless you are completely familiar with wild mushrooms and can accurately identify edible ones, never attempt to freeze them. Mushrooms must be handled quickly to prevent blackening. Wash thoroughly. Remove tough portion of stem. Scald, cool quickly and drain. Package in polyethylene bags. Start freezing immediately to avoid darkening.

Okra: Varieties suitable for freezing: good—Clemson Spineless, White Lightning. 1½ pounds yield approximately 1 pint. Scalding time:

Small to medium pods: Steam 2 minutes. This is the only method recommended for okra.

Select young, tender pods. Scrub thoroughly. Rinse. Remove stem end but do not cut into seed section. Care in cutting prevents the sticky juice from oozing out. Scald, cool and drain. Pack compactly in polyethylene bags . . . alternating top and tip ends. Freeze.

Peas: Varieties suitable for freezing: Green, excellent—Thomas Laxton and Alderman. Field, very good—Crowder and Black Eye. 1½ to 2 pounds yield approximately 1 pint. Scalding time: By steam, 3 minutes. By boiling water, 1 minute. Select peas that are tender and are not fully matured. Wash pods before shelling. Discard all immature and wrinkled peas while shelling. If pods are very full and difficult to shell, plunge pods in boiling water for 1 minute, then cool at once in ice water. Scalding the pods does not take the place of scalding the peas. Scald, cool, drain and package in polyethylene bags. Freeze at once.

Pimientos and green peppers: Varieties suitable for freezing: Pimientos, excellent—Perfection. Green peppers, very good—California Wonder.

Sliced or diced: Do not scald! Wash carefully, remove stem end and seeds. Slice or dice and package in small polyethylene bags in amounts you will use at one time. Several small bags may be packaged in pint or quart carton. Freeze at once.

Halved for stuffing: Cut green pepper in half, lengthwise. Remove stem end and seeds. Scald in boiling water 2 minutes. Cool in ice water, drain well. When packaging, separate halves with waxed paper, place in polyethylene bags. Freeze immediately.

Squash: Variety suitable for freezing: excellent—Yellow Summer. 1 pound yields approximately 1 pint. Scalding time: By steam, 3 minutes. Select squash not fully matured. Outer skin should be easily punctured with fingernail. Wash thoroughly. Use a vegetable brush to remove dirt lodged in crevices. Remove stem end. Do not peel. Cut in ½- to 1-inch slices. Do not remove seeds. Scald. Cool 1½ to 2 minutes. To avoid longer soaking, use quantities of ice in the water. Drain carefully. Package in polyethylene bags. Freeze.

Succotash: Prepare corn and lima beans as given under directions for each. Use baby beans only. Steam corn first, and while it is cooling and being cut from cob, scald and cool the beans. Mix together in equal portions. Package in polyethylene bags. Freeze.

HOW TO PREPARE FROZEN VEGETABLES FOR SERVING

All vegetables . . . **except** corn on the cob and eggplant . . . are best cooked from the frozen state. Break frozen vegetables into 3 or 4 chunks before placing in pan. Add about ¼ cup of water. Salt to taste. Cook about ⅓ to ½ of the time recommended for fresh vegetables. Frozen vegetables are scalded before freezing, so need less cooking time. Corn on the cob and eggplant should be thawed before cooking. Thaw at room temperature. Thawing requires about 20 minutes for eggplant; 2 hours for corn on the cob. Cook corn in boiling water 4 to 5 minutes. Prepare eggplant according to your favorite method.

Caution: Do not overcook vegetables . . . either frozen or fresh. Overlooking causes loss of color and flavor, as well as vitamins.

FREEZING MEATS

Most meats, including variety meats, may be frozen satisfactorily if properly wrapped, frozen quickly, and kept at 0°F. or below. The following pointers will help insure good quality in frozen meats:

1. Freeze meat while it is fresh and in top condition. Meat will be no better in quality when it is removed from the freezer than when it was put in.
2. Select proper wrapping materials. Choose a moisture-vaporproof wrap so that air will be sealed out and moisture locked in. When air penetrates the package, moisture is drawn from the surface of the meat and the condition known as "freezer burn" develops. There are several good freezer wraps on the market. Pliable wraps such as aluminum freezer foils and transparent moisture-vaporproof wraps and certain types of plastic bags are good for wrapping bulky, irregular-shaped meats, since these wraps may be molded to the meat. Freezer papers and cartons coated with cellophane, polyethylene, or wax; laminated freezer paper; plastic bags and certain types of waxed cartons are suitable for some cuts of meat. Casserole dishes containing meats are sometimes frozen in the dish in which they will be reheated or baked.
3. Prepare meat for freezing before wrapping. Trim off excess fat and remove bones when practical to conserve freezer space. Meat should not be salted as salt shortens freezer life. Wrap in "family-size" packages. When several chops, pat-

ties, or individual pieces of meat are packaged together, place double thickness of freezer wrap between them for easier separation during thawing.

4. Wrap tightly, pressing out as much air as possible. Two of the more popular methods of wrapping are either the "drug store wrap" or the "butcher's wrap." Fasten the loose ends securely with freezer tape.

5. Label properly. Indicate name of cut and date of package. If content is not obvious, it is helpful to indicate the weight or approximate number of servings.

6. Freeze at once at −10°F. or lower, if possible. Place packages next to a refrigerated surface in freezer. Allow space for air between packages during initial freezing time. Try to avoid freezing such a large quantity of meat at one time that the freezer is overloaded and the temperature thereby raised undesirably. Separate unfrozen food from food already frozen.

7. Maintain freezer temperature at 0°F. or lower during freezing storage. Higher temperatures and fluctuations above that temperature impair quality.

8. Frozen meat will be of best quality if used before the maximum time indicated. (Storage times in freezer at 0°F. or lower.)

> Beef (fresh), Roasts and steaks, 6 to 12 months.
> Veal (fresh), Roasts, 4 to 8 months; chops, 3 to 4 months.
> Lamb (fresh), Roasts, 6 to 9 months; chops, 3 to 4 months.
> Ground Beef, veal, and lamb, 2 to 3 months.
> Variety meats, 2 to 4 months.
> Luncheon meats, Freezing not recommended.
> Frankfurters, 1 month.
> Beef, corned, 2 weeks.
> Leftover cooked meat, 2 to 3 months.

COOKING FROZEN MEAT—GENERAL HINTS

Frozen meat may be cooked satisfactorily either by defrosting prior to or during cooking. Commercially frozen products should be prepared according to package directions.

When defrosting meats before cooking, the most practical methods are, (1) in the refrigerator, and (2) at room temperature. The meat should be defrosted in its original wrapping and should not be allowed to remain at room temperature after defrosting. Defrosting in water is recommended only if the meat is to be cooked in liquid. After meat is defrosted, it should be cooked in the same way as other fresh meat.

When cooking meat from the frozen state, it is necessary to allow additional cooking time. Frozen roasts require approximately a third to a half again as long for cooking as roasts which have been defrosted. The additional time for cooking steaks and chops varies according to the surface area and thickness of the meat, as well as the broiling temperature.

Thick frozen steaks, chops, and ground meat patties must be broiled farther from the heat than defrosted ones in order that the meat will be cooked to the desired degree of doneness without becoming too brown on the outside. When steaks or chops are to be coated with eggs and crumbs or with batter, the meat should be partially defrosted so the coating will adhere to the meat.

When panbroiling frozen steaks and chops, a hot frying pan should be used so that the meat has a chance to brown before defrosting on the surface, retarding browning. The heat should be reduced after browning and the meat turned occasionally so it will cook through without becoming too brown.

FREEZING POULTRY

Poultry may be frozen either whole or cut up. Select high quality birds. Dress, draw, clean and wash; drain well. Chill 12 hours before packaging. Disjoint and cut up poultry or leave whole. Wrap and freeze giblets separately. Wrap whole birds or pieces in moisture-vaporproof material. Seal, label, and freeze. **Never** freeze stuffed poultry.

Storage times: Chicken, 12 months; duck, goose, turkey, 6 months; giblets, 3 months. To cook, thaw in refrigerator, in original wrap.

FREEZING FISH

All fish should be frozen as soon as possible after catching. If delay is unavoidable, pack in crushed ice. Clean and dress fish as for immediate cooking. Generally, freeze small fish whole, large fish in steaks or fillets. When packaging individual fillets or steaks, use double thickness of wax paper to separate pieces. Dip in solution of ⅔ cup salt to 1 gallon of water for 30 seconds. Wrap in moisture-vaporproof material. Seal, label, and freeze.

Storage time at zero: 6 to 9 months. Thaw in refrigerator in original wrap or cook frozen allowing extra cooking time.

FREEZING EGGS

Only liquid eggs are frozen. They may be frozen as whole eggs, whites alone, or yolks alone. When freezing whole eggs, wash the eggs, break into a bowl. Stir with fork just to break yolks and mix well with whites. Do not whip in air. To each cup of eggs, add 1 tablespoon corn syrup or sugar **or** 1 teaspoon salt. Mix and sieve, then pack in freezer containers in amounts intended for use; for example, one meal, a cake, or scrambled eggs. Skim air bubbles off surface. Leave ½-inch headspace for expansion in pints. Seal and label with date, measure, number of eggs, **and** intended use. Freeze.

Egg yolks: Separate into a bowl. Stir with fork to break yolks. To each cup of yolks, add 2 tablespoons corn syrup or sugar **or** 1 teaspoon salt. Blend carefully, without whipping in air. Sieve and package as above.

Egg whites: Do not stir or add anything to whites. Package same as for whole eggs above.

Storage time: 6 to 8 months. Thaw completely in unopened containers; use promptly. Allow for corn syrup, sugar, or salt. Otherwise use the same as fresh eggs. About 2½ tablespoons whole egg equal 1 egg; about 1 tablespoon egg yolk equals 1 yolk; about 1½ tablespoons egg white equal 1 egg white.

FREEZING BUTTER OR MARGARINE

Select fresh, high quality butter. Wrap in moisture-vaporproof material using double thickness of material to avoid transfer of odor. Seal, label, and freeze.

Storage time for butter or margarine: 3 to 6 months. Thaw in unopened package and use the same as fresh. It is not advisable to freeze more than two pounds in any one package.

FREEZING ICE CREAM

Seal in freezer container or overwrap original carton with moisture-vaporproof material, then seal, label, and freeze. Homemade ice cream becomes grainy when stored. Commercial ice cream should not be stored more than 3 weeks. Remove from freezer shortly before serving. Ice cream in the half-gallon or gallon container is often a "specially-priced" item. To keep ice cream at its quality peak, place a piece of plastic wrap directly on the remaining ice cream each time some of it is dipped out to prevent the formation of ice crystals. Overwrap the outer container, and use within a short time.

FREEZING WHIPPED CREAM

Whip whipping cream, season, and flavor cream as usual. Spoon out in serving-size portions or mounds onto cooky sheet that has been covered with waxed paper. Set cooky sheet in freezer. When whipped cream is frozen solid, remove cream with a spatula, and place in freezer containers. Seal, label, and freeze immediately.

Storage time: about 3 months. Remove from freezer shortly before serving.

FREEZING BREADS AND ROLLS

Freezer-weight aluminum foil is ideal for packaging all breads and rolls. Can be placed directly in oven for reheating without removing wrapping.

Yeast breads: Bake as usual and cool quickly. Wrap one loaf to a package and seal. Storage time: 2 months. Thaw in package at room temperature about 3 hours. Use at once.

Yeast rolls: Use either plain or sweet dough recipes. Bake as usual and cool quickly. Wrap in foil and seal. Freeze at once. Storage time: 2 months. Thaw baked rolls in package at room temperature or in a very slow oven (250°–300°F.) about 15 minutes. Use at once.

Or, partially bake in slow oven (325°F.) about 25 to 30 minutes; do not let brown. Cool, wrap, and seal at once. Thaw partially baked rolls 10 to 15 minutes at room temperature. Then unwrap and bake in very hot oven (450°F.) 5 to 10 minutes. Serve at once.

Baking powder biscuits: Bake as usual, cool, wrap in foil, and seal. Storage time: 2 months. Thaw in package in very slow oven (250°–300°F.) about 20 minutes.

Pancakes and waffles: Bake as usual. Cool and separate by waxed paper before wrapping. Storage time: not over 2 months. To use, remove wrapping, reheat in automatic toaster set to "light" degree. Put through toasting twice to heat thoroughly.

Doughnuts: Fry as usual, cook wrap, and seal. Storage time: 2 to 4 weeks. Reheat in oven.

Muffins: Bake as usual. Cool, wrap in foil, and seal, or seal in freezer containers. Storage time: 2 months. Thaw wrapped, in very slow oven (250°–300°F.), or thaw in package at room temperature about 1 hour.

FREEZING CAKES

Cakes may be frozen either frosted or unfrosted, as preferred. Both are satisfactory, although, in general unfrosted cakes freeze better. Frosted and filled cakes may become soggy. While the uncooked batter may be successfully frozen, we prefer to freeze the cake after it has been baked. It saves considerable time when the cake is needed. Also, it does not tie up the cake pans because a piece of cardboard covered with aluminum foil can be used to support the cake.

Cake frostings and fillings may be prepared in advance and frozen; however those recommended for freezing are frostings with confectioners' sugar and fat, cooked candy type frostings with corn syrup or honey, fudge, fruit, nut, or penuche. They should be packed in suitable portions in freezer containers and sealed. Storage time: 2 months. To use, thaw in the refrigerator. Those not recommended for freezing are cream fillings, 7-minute frostings, boiled frostings, and soft frostings.

Unfrosted layer cakes: Bake as usual, remove from pan, cool thoroughly. Layers may be wrapped separately, or if two or more are to be frozen together, layers should be separated by a double thickness of plastic wrap before wrapping. Storage time: 6 months. Thaw in wrapping at room temperature, 2 to 3 hours for a large cake; 1 hour for layers.

Frosted cakes: These should be frozen before wrapping to prevent damaging the soft icing. Bake the cake, frost it, put it in the freezer for a couple of hours, then wrap and seal. This is particularly advisable for special birthday cakes with ornamental decorations. Storage time for frosted cakes: about 2 months. Frosted cakes must be unwrapped immediately after removing from freezer to prevent frosting from sticking to wrapping. Frosted and filled cakes should be thawed loosely covered in the refrigerator.

Cupcakes: Bake as usual and cool. Unfrosted cupcakes freeze better; however if you frost them, freeze before wrapping or sealing in freezer containers. Storage time: 2 months. To serve, thaw frosted cupcakes loosely covered in the refrigerator; thaw unfrosted cupcakes at room temperature about 40 minutes.

Sponge, angel food, and sunshine cakes: Bake as usual, cool thoroughly. If cake is frosted, freeze before wrapping, then wrap and seal. If desired, place in sturdy container. Storage time: about 1 month. Thaw unfrosted cake in container at room temperature about 2 to 3 hours. Thaw frosted cake, loosely covered in refrigerator.

Fruit Cake: Bake as usual, cool, wrap, and freeze. Storage time: 6 to 12 months. To serve, thaw in wrappings. Requires about 2 hours for 2 pounds of cake.

FREEZING COOKIES

Cookies may be satisfactorily frozen baked or unbaked.

Baked cookies: Bake as usual. Cool thoroughly. Pack in freezer containers with wax paper between layers and in air spaces. Seal, label, and freeze. Storage time: 6 to 12 months. To serve, thaw in package at room temperature.

Unbaked cookie dough: Almost all cookie dough freezes well except meringue type cookies. Pack cookie dough in freezer containers, seal, label, and freeze. Storage time: 6 to 12 months. To use, thaw in container at room temperature until dough is soft enough to be rolled or dropped. Bake as usual.

Unbaked refrigerator cookies: Shape into rolls, wrap, and seal. Freeze. Storage time: 6 to 12 months. To use, thaw slightly at room temperature. Slice rolls and bake as usual.

Unbaked bar cookies: Spread dough in baking pans. Wrap, seal, and label. Storage time: 6 to 12 months. To use, bake without thawing.

Unbaked drop cookies: Drop cookie dough may be dropped as usual onto cookie sheets, and placed in the freezer. When frozen the unbaked cookies can be packaged in cartons with two layers of wax paper between each layer. To bake, remove from carton without thawing, and immediately bake just as you would the freshly made product.

Unbaked rolled cookies: Roll out dough and cut out cookies. Stack cookies with 2 pieces of wax paper between layers to keep them from freezing together. Bake without thawing.

FREEZING PIES

You may freeze pies before or after baking. The majority of taste testers at the Institute voted for pies frozen *after* baking. When properly thawed, it is almost impossible to tell them from freshly baked pies.

Not all pies freeze to advantage. Mince pies and pies made with fruit or berries are most satisfactory. Double-crust pies freeze best.

Chiffon pies, especially chocolate and lemon, freeze satisfactorily; however storage time is short, about 2 weeks. These should be thawed in the refrigerator.

Custard or cream-filled pies tend to become grainy, and are not good for freezing. Meringues toughen during freezing and should not be used.

In making berry pies, it is essential to add extra thickening since freezing develops more juice in the fruit. Otherwise, the pies will be too "runny." See recipes for fillings.

Such fruits as apples, peaches, and apricots do not generally require a great deal of thickening. However, especially in the case of apples, it is necessary to judge whether the fruit is juicy or dry and to add thickening accordingly. Even with the juiciest fruits, 4 tablespoons of flour or cornstarch are sufficient.

To freeze baked fruit pies: Bake as usual in glass or metal pie pans. Cool thoroughly. Cover each with inverted paper plate. Wrap, seal, and label. If desired, place in a sturdy container. Freeze at once. Recommended storage time: baked fruit or berry pies may be stored up to 4 months; baked mince pies for 4 months. To serve, thaw pie in the package at room temperature or in slow oven (300°F.).

To freeze unbaked fruit pies: Treat light-colored fruits with ascorbic acid color keeper to prevent darkening. In general, prepare pies for freezing in the same way as for baking, but do not cut openings in the top crust. Use glass or metal pie pans. Cover each with an inverted paper plate. Wrap, seal, and label. If desired, place in a sturdy container. Storage time for most unbaked fruit pies: 2 months. To serve fruit pies, unwrap; cut slits in top crust. Without thawing, bake in very hot oven (450°F.) 15 to 20 minutes, then in moderate oven (375°F.) until done.

Berry, cherry pies: Unwrap, cut slits in top crust. Without thawing, bake in hot oven (400°F.).

Apple, unbaked: Use firmer varieties of apples. Steam slices 2 minutes, cool and drain; or treat with ascorbic acid color keeper. Prepare and package as above. Storage time: 2 months. To serve, unwrap; cut slits in top crust. Bake in hot oven (425°F.) about 1 hour.

Peach pie, unbaked: Treat fruit with ascorbic acid color keeper to keep color bright Prepare and package as above. Storage time: 2 months. To serve, unwrap; cut slits in top crust. Without thawing, bake in hot oven (400°F.) about 1 hour.

Deep-dish fruit pies, unbaked: Use deep pie pans. Bake or thaw in the same way as 2-crust pies above. Storage time: 2 months.

Pie pastry: Both pie pastry and graham cracker pie shells freeze satisfactorily. Roll out pie dough and fit into pie pans. Bake, if desired. Wrap, seal, and label. Storage time: about 2 months. To use, thaw baked pastry in slow oven (325°F.) 8 to 10 minutes. Bake unbaked frozen shells the same as fresh.

FREEZING MAIN DISHES

HINTS ABOUT INGREDIENTS IN MAIN DISHES

- In general, fried foods do not freeze successfully. French-fried potatoes and French-fried onion rings are the exceptions.
- Crumb or cheese toppings should be added when the food is reheated for serving.
- Rice is a good binder in casseroles and freezes well. "Converted" rice is preferable to the quick-cooking variety.
- Add unblanched or thawed uncooked peas to casseroles, stews, and soups to be frozen. The peas will cook during the reheating time.
- Do not include potatoes in stews and other dishes unless the product is to be consumed in a very short time. Potatoes tend to become soft and have a poor flavor when frozen. Add during reheating.
- Sauces containing a large amount of milk frequently separate during freezing and thawing but often may be stirred or beaten smooth again.
- Meat pies and turnovers are best frozen uncooked.

EFFECT OF FREEZING ON SPICES AND SEASONINGS

Pepper, cloves, and synthetic vanilla have a tendency to get strong and bitter. Onion also intensifies tremendously under freezing, and many commercial firms have turned to dried onions successfully to combat this. Celery seasonings also become strong, and curry sometimes develops a musty off-flavor. Salt loses flavor and may tend to increase rancidity of any items containing fat.

Consequently, it is best to season foods very lightly before freezing, and add flavoring as needed during the reheating.

MAIN DISHES WHICH FREEZE WELL

Examples include meat loaves; pot roast of beef with vegetables; hash; stuffed peppers; veal fricassee; veal birds; chicken loaf with sauce; roast turkey or chicken slices packed in gravy; stewed chicken; fish loaves; chop suey; Hungarian goulash; baked beans with tomato sauce; roast beef and other roast meats or poultry, sliced or in pieces.

The storage time of all of the above is generally at least 2 to 3 months. Cooking and thawing instructions for some specific dishes follow.

Be sure to cool all foods before freezing. Partially cool in the cooking utensil in which the food was cooked and finish cooling the food in the refrigerator.

Spanish rice: Use converted rice; cook until tender but not mushy. Storage time: 2 to 3 months. To serve, heat in top of double boiler, about 40 to 50 minutes. Add small amount of water, if needed.

Meat pies: Cook meat until tender. Cook vegetables until almost tender. Cool quickly and put in baking dishes. Top with pastry. Wrap, seal, label, and freeze.

Storage time: 2 to 3 months. To serve, bake frozen pies in hot oven (400°F.) for 45 minutes for pints and 1 hour for quarts, or until hot and crust is lightly browned.

Casseroles of poultry, meat, or fish with vegetable and/or cereal product. Storage time: 2 to 4 months. To serve, if frozen in ovenproof container, uncover, and bake in hot oven (400°F.) until food is heated or about 1 hour for pints, 1¾ hours for quarts. Or, steam over hot water in top of double boiler.

Creamed dishes such as creamed chicken or turkey, fish. Freeze any except those containing hard-cooked egg white. Use fat sparingly when making sauce since this helps to prevent separation of sauce when reheating. Don't overcook. Storage time: 2 to 4 months. To serve, heat in top of double boiler from the frozen state, stirring occasionally. Beat with a fork or spoon during reheating, if sauce separates. Allow about 30 minutes for thawing and reheating 1 pint of creamed mixture.

Meatballs in sauce: To serve, heat over low heat, stirring often, or in top of double boiler, stirring occasionally. Or, defrost overnight in refrigerator and heat thoroughly in saucepan. Storage time: 2 to 3 months.

Spaghetti sauce: Heat over low heat, stirring often, or in top of double boiler, stirring occasionally. Storage time: 2 to 3 months.

Stews of beef or veal: To prepare, select vegetables that freeze well. Omit potatoes. Onions lose flavor. Green pepper and garlic become more intense in flavor. Omit salt and thickening if stew is to be kept more than 2 months. Do not completely cook vegetables. Storage time: 2 to 4 months. To serve, heat quickly from frozen state. Do not overcook. Separate with fork as it thaws. Do not stir enough to make the mixture mushy.

FREEZING SOUPS

Soups with a milk base do not freeze satisfactorily. Vegetable, chicken, lentil, and other dried legume soups are excellent when frozen. When making any of these soups which require long, slow cooking, make an extra amount and freeze whatever is not used immediately. Be sure to cool soups before starting to freeze them.

Clear broths (chicken, turkey, or beef) freeze well. Do not add noodles or rice when planning to freeze clear broths; add when the broth is reheating.

How to package: When cool, soups may be poured into ice cube trays, frozen, and cubes removed and packaged in plastic bag.

Or, package in glass jars suitable for freezing or plastic containers. Storage time: Not over 4 months. To reheat, remove from package; heat in covered saucepan on low heat. Three of the frozen cubes will make one serving of soup when heated.

Caution: When packaging soups, sauces, or other liquids, leave at least one inch of head space in the container to allow for expansion during freezing.

FREEZING SANDWICHES

These sandwich filling ingredients freeze well: hard-cooked egg yolk; peanut butter; cream cheese; sliced or ground cooked meat; poultry; canned meat; tuna; salmon; Roquefort or Bleu cheese; nut pastes; olives; pickles.

Spread slices of bread generously with softened butter or margarine; add filling; cover with second buttered bread slice. Wrap tightly, seal, label with contents and date; freeze. Storage time: 2 weeks.

Not recommended: mayonnaise, jelly, whites of hard-cooked eggs; tomatoes; cucumber; celery; watercress.

To serve, thaw sandwiches in wrapping at room temperature 2 to 3 hours. Serve immediately.

PARTY FARE FROM YOUR FREEZER

When you are planning a large entertainment and have space available, freezing most or all the foods to be served is worthwhile. You can be elaborate as you like with your most imaginative canapés and sandwiches when you prepare them at leisure days before the party. Canapés or open-face sandwiches should be frozen first and wrapped as soon as filling or topping is firm. Canapés may be stored in freezer containers in layers with a sheet of freezer wrap between each layer and then overwrapped. Separate the layers when thawing so that fillings will not be damaged as they thaw.

HINTS ABOUT COMMERCIALLY FROZEN FOODS

Correct handling of commercially frozen foods is equally as important as handling of home-processed frozen foods if quality is to be maintained.

The greatest threat to quality lies in permitting temperatures to rise above zero. This is most likely to occur from time foods are selected at the supermarket until placed in the freezer at home. These four precautions will help you prevent excessive temperature changes:

1. Make frozen foods the final items selected at the store.
2. Place them in the insulated bags provided for this purpose before putting them in the shopping cart.
3. Avoid allowing frozen foods to stand for long periods in a heated car or one parked in summer sun.
4. Do not let frozen foods stand on the kitchen counter unnecessarily before being put in the freezer.

The higher the temperature to which a package of frozen food is allowed to rise, the greater the speed with which unfavorable changes in quality take place. Even products stored for a full year at 0°F. without fluctuation will be of considerably better quality than those which rise as high as 25°F. for only one day due to careless handling.

Squeezing a package of frozen foods is not a reliable way to find out if the food is cold enough. Many packages feel frozen hard at temperatures as high as 15 or 20°F. Although foods will not "spoil" at those temperatures, serious losses of quality, including discoloration, losses of nutritive value, and off flavors already are occurring rapidly.

WHEN THE POWER FAILS

Keep the freezer tightly closed. If the freezer is full when the power goes off, food will stay frozen at least 48 hours; if half full, about 24 hours. Some manufacturers may tell you in their instruction booklets how long power can be off without food damage.

Check with your utility company to see when service will be restored. If the interruption will be more than a reasonable length of time, you have two alternatives: (1) put dry ice into the freezer, or (2) transfer the food to another freezer or commercial locker plant which has standby power.

SHOULD THAWED FOODS BE REFROZEN?

In general, frozen foods which have been thawed should not be refrozen. Frozen meat which has been thawed may be held in the refrigerator for a limited time, or it may be cooked and frozen again. This is not actually refreezing.

If you suspect a food has been thawed too long and are in doubt about your ability to recognize spoilage, do not take a chance on using it.

HINTS ABOUT FROZEN FOOD IN THE REFRIGERATOR

Many homemakers ask whether frozen foods can be stored in the freezer section of their conventional refrigerators. The answer is NO for long time storage, YES for short time storage only.

The freezer sections of conventional refrigerators usually carry a temperature of about 15°F. This is not cold enough to quick-freeze foods, but foods already frozen may be stored there for a few days with safety.

The combination refrigerator-freezer having two separate doors operates on two different thermostats, one designed to hold a temperature of 35 to 40°F. in the fresh food section and the other, zero in the freezer compartment. This latter compartment is suitable both for quick freezing and storing of frozen foods over longer periods of time.

Keep a refrigerator-freezer thermometer in either type of freezer compartment to be certain of correct storage temperatures.

nutrition up to date

Nutrition is the food you eat and how the body uses it.

People differ in how much they want to know about nutrition, but everyone needs to know a few facts about food and health as a basis for selecting the foods to eat.

You need food to get energy for work and play, to move, to breathe, to keep the heart beating—just to be alive. Children and youths need energy from food for growth.

Food also provides a variety of substances—nutrients—that are essential for the building, the upkeep, and the repair of body tissues, and for the efficient functioning of the body.

Everyone needs the same nutrients throughout life but in different amounts. Proportionately greater amounts are required for the growth of a body than just for its upkeep. Boys and men need more energy and nutrients than girls and women. Large people need more than small people. Active people require more food energy than inactive ones. People recovering from illness need more than healthy people.

You and your family can get all the nutrients you need from foods, but no one food contains all the nutrients in the amounts required for growth and health. Only a variety of different kinds of foods will supply all you need.

A GUIDE TO EAT BY

Nutrition scientists have translated knowledge of the nutrient needs of people and the nutritive values of foods into an easy-to-use guide for food selection.

The daily food guide that follows sorts foods into four groups on the basis of their similarity in nutrient content. Each of the broad food groups has a special contribution to make toward an adequate diet.

Here are some of the reasons different food groups are emphasized in the guide and the names of some of the nutrients these foods provide.

Meat, poultry, fish, and eggs from the meat group and their alternates—dry beans, dry peas, and nuts—are valued for their protein. This is needed for the growth and repair of body tissues—muscle, organs, blood, skin, and hair. These foods also contribute iron and the B-vitamins—thiamine, riboflavin, and niacin.

Vegetables and fruits from the vegetable-fruit group are valuable sources of vitamins and minerals. In the guide, this group is counted on to supply most of the vitamin C and a large share of the vitamin A value in the diet. Choices are directed toward the citrus fruits and some other foods that are among the better sources of vitamin C; and toward the dark-green and deep-yellow ones for vitamin A value.

Vitamin C is needed for healthy gums and body tissues. Vitamin A is important for growth, normal vision, and a healthy condition of the skin and other body surfaces.

Foods from the milk group are relied on to meet most of the calcium needs for the day. Milk is the leading source of the mineral calcium, which is needed for bones and teeth.

Milk also provides protein, riboflavin, vitamin A, and many other nutrients. Cheese and ice cream also supply these nutrients, but in different proportions.

The bread-cereal group, with its whole-grain and enriched bread and other cereal products, furnishes important amounts of protein, iron, several of the B-vitamins, and food energy.

Fats, oils, sugars, and sweets are not emphasized in the guide because they are common in every diet. Some of the fats and oils provide certain of the vitamins, and some furnish essential fatty acids, but the chief nutritional contribution of these foods is energy value.

HOW TO USE THE GUIDE

Homemakers who follow the guide will find it flexible enough to use in choosing foods for families.

Food choices within the groups are wide enough to allow for a variety of everyday foods. Meals can be planned to include family favorites, foods in season, and foods to fit the family budget.

The size of servings can be suited to the needs of family members—small servings for children and for those wanting to lose weight; extra large servings (or seconds) for very active adults, teenagers, and those wanting to gain weight. Pregnant and nursing women also need more food.

Foods from the daily food guide fit easily into a three-meals-a-day pattern of eating. Foods from each group often appear in each meal—but this isn't essential. The important thing is that the suggested number of servings from each food group be included sometime during the day.

Many people want and need more food than the minimum servings suggested from the four food groups. To round out meals and satisfy appetites, you can include additional foods from the four groups as well as other foods not listed in these groups.

MEAT GROUP

Foods included: Beef; veal; lamb; pork; variety meats, such as liver, heart, kidney.
Poultry and eggs.
Fish and shellfish.
As alternates—dry beans, dry peas, lentils, nuts, peanuts, peanut butter.

Amounts recommended: Choose 2 or more servings daily.
Count as a serving: 2 to 3 ounces of lean cooked meat, poultry, or fish—all without bone; 2 eggs; 1 cup cooked dry beans, dry peas, or lentils; 4 tablespoons peanut butter.

VEGETABLE-FRUIT GROUP

Foods included: All vegetables and fruits. This guide emphasizes those that are valuable as sources of vitamin C and vitamin A.

Sources of vitamin C: Good sources: Grapefruit or grapefruit juice; orange or orange juice; cantaloupe; guava; mango; papaya; raw strawberries; broccoli; Brussels sprouts; green pepper; sweet red pepper.
   Fair sources: Honeydew melon; lemon; tangerine or tangerine juice; watermelon; asparagus tips; raw cabbage; collards; garden cress; kale; kohlrabi; mustard greens; potatoes and sweet potatoes cooked in the jacket; spinach; tomatoes or tomato juice; turnip greens.

Sources of vitamin A: Dark-green and deep-yellow vegetables and a few fruits, namely: apricots, broccoli, cantaloupe, carrots, chard, collards, cress, kale, mango, persimmon, pumpkin, spinach, sweet potatoes, turnip greens and other dark-green leaves, winter squash.

Amounts recommended: Choose 4 or more servings every day, including:

1 serving of a good source of vitamin C or 2 servings of a fair source.

1 serving, at least every other day, of a good source of vitamin A.

If the food chosen for vitamin C is also a good source of vitamin A, the additional serving of a vitamin A food may be omitted.

The remaining 1 to 3 or more servings may be of any vegetable or fruit, including those that are valuable for vitamin C and for vitamin A.

Count as 1 serving: ½ cup of vegetable or fruit; or a portion as ordinarily served, such as 1 medium apple, banana, orange, or potato, half a medium grapefruit or cantaloupe, or the juice of 1 lemon.

MILK GROUP

Foods included: Milk: fluid whole, evaporated, skim, dry, buttermilk. Cheese: cottage; cream; Cheddar-type, natural or process. Ice Cream.

Amounts recommended: Some milk every day for everyone.

Recommended amounts are given below in terms of 8-ounce cups of whole fluid milk:

Children under 9 .... 2 to 3	Adults .... 2 or more
Children 9 to 12 ...... 3 or more	Pregnant women .... 3 or more
Teen-agers .... 4 or more	Nursing mothers .... 4 or more

Part of all of the milk may be fluid skim milk, buttermilk, evaporated milk, or dry milk.

Cheese and ice cream may replace part of the milk. The amount it will take to replace a given amount of milk is figured on the basis of calcium content. Common portions of cheese and of ice cream and their milk equivalents in calcium are:

1-inch cube Cheddar-type cheese	=	½ cup milk
½ cup cottage cheese	=	⅓ cup milk
2 tablespoons cream cheese	=	1 tablespoon milk
½ cup ice cream	=	¼ cup milk

BREAD-CEREAL GROUP

Foods included: All breads and cereals that are whole grain, enriched, or restored; check labels to be sure.

Specifically, this group includes: Breads; cooked cereals; ready-to-eat cereals; cornmeal; crackers; flour, grits; macaroni and spaghetti; noodles; rice; rolled oats; and quick breads and other baked goods if made with whole grain or enriched flour. Bulgur and parboiled rice and wheat also may be included in this group.

Amounts recommended: Choose 4 servings or more daily. Or, if no cereals are chosen, have an extra serving of breads or baked goods, which will make at least 5 servings from this group daily.

Count as 1 serving: 1 slice of bread; 1 ounce ready-to-eat cereal; ½ to ¾ cup cooked cereal, cornmeal, grits, macaroni, noodles, rice, or spaghetti.

OTHER FOODS

To round out meals and meet energy needs, almost everyone will use some foods not specified in the four food groups. Such foods include: unenriched, refined breads, cereals, flours; sugars; butter, margarine, other fats. These often are ingredients in a recipe or added to other foods during preparation or at the table.

Try to include some vegetable oil among the fats used.

MAINTAINING DESIRABLE WEIGHT

It is best to maintain desirable weight for one's height at all ages, even during childhood. Here are two principles that you can use:

Reduce food intake as you become less active. Exercise and activity use up energy—or calories. If you cut down activity but not food, you are providing more energy than the body needs. The excess is stored as fat.

Reduce food intake as you—as an adult—get older. As adults grow older, less energy is needed to keep the body functioning.

To reduce food intake without shortchanging the body of essential nutrients, follow the pattern of choices suggested by the daily food guide. Weight watchers need the same types of food for health as everyone else. Crash diets and food fads are not the answer and may be dangerous to health.

Cut down on food, but don't cut out any important kinds of foods.

Snacks are counted as part of the day's total food. Sensible snacking can help meet nutritional needs, but indiscriminate eating between meals usually leads to more calories than are wanted, less of some nutrients than are needed.

TIPS ON MEAL PLANNING

Keep these points in mind when you plan meals for your family:

- Include a variety of foods each day and from day to day. Introduce a new food from time to time.
- Vary flavors and textures. Contrast strong flavor with mild, sweet with sour. Combine crisp textures with smooth.
- Try to have some meat, poultry, fish, eggs, milk or cheese at each meal.
- Make a collection of nutritious recipes that the family enjoys and serve them often.
- Brighten food with color—a slice of red tomato, a sprig of dark greens, or other garnish.
- Combine different sizes and shapes of food in a meal, when possible.

useful information

HOW TO FOLLOW A RECIPE SUCCESSFULLY

1. Read the recipe carefully.
2. Check your supplies to see that you have the necessary ingredients.
3. Assemble the ingredients and equipment needed for measuring, mixing, cooking, or baking—spoons, cups, bowls, pans, etc.
4. Light the oven if a preheated oven is necessary.
5. Use level measurements; measure the ingredients accurately.
6. Follow the procedure given for combining ingredients.
7. Follow directions given for cooking and baking. Use as nearly as possible the size pan indicated. Follow cooking time or baking time and temperatures given; also test for doneness by physical means since oven heat varies. Thermometers for baking, deep fat frying, and candy making make for successful products.
8. Handle finished product as indicated. Follow directions for removing from pan, molding, chilling, etc.
9. In making substitutions in a recipe, follow the rules for substitution and equivalents carefully.
10. To reduce a recipe choose a recipe in which the ingredients may be divided easily. Measure smaller quantities carefully. It is not practical to reduce successfully certain recipes as boiled frosting, steamed puddings, etc.
11. To increase a recipe, it is best not to exceed doubling the quantities of ingredients at one time. When the recipe is doubled, the cooking time is not necessarily increased since the larger quantity may be baked in two pans or a larger pan of no greater depth.

HOW TO MEASURE ACCURATELY

Use standard measuring cups and spoons. Measure dry ingredients before measuring liquids to save extra dish.

Part of cup: Use tablespoons or the smaller measuring cups—½, ⅓, ¼—for greater accuracy.

White sugar: If lumpy, sift before measuring. Do not pack down; lift lightly into cup. Level off with spatula or straight knife.

Brown sugar: Pack firmly into cup or spoon, so that when turned out it will hold shape of cup or spoon. If lumpy, roll and sift before measuring.

Syrup and molasses: Rinse spoon or cup in cold water before measuring.

Solid fats: When fat comes in 1-pound rectangular form, 1 cup or fraction can be cut from pound which measures about 2 cups. Or measure cupful by packing firmly into cup and leveling off top with spatula or straight knife. Water method may be used for part of cup. To measure ½ cup fat, for instance, put ½ cup cold water in 1-cup measure. Add fat, pushing under water until water level stands at 1-cup mark. Pour out water and remove fat.

White flour: Sift once. Lift lightly into cup. Level off top with spatula or straight knife.

Other flours, fine meals, fine crumbs, dried eggs, dry milk: Stir instead of sifting. Measure like flour.

Baking powder, cornstarch, cream of tartar, spices: Stir to loosen. Dip measuring spoon into can, bring up heaping full, level with spatula or edge of knife.

TABLE OF STANDARD MEASUREMENTS

Measurements in all recipes are level and based on standard measuring spoons, cups, etc.

Dash	⅛ teaspoon	12 tablespoons	¾ cup
3 teaspoons	1 tablespoon	16 tablespoons	1 cup
2 tablespoons	1 fluid ounce	1 cup	½ pint (8 oz.)
2 tablespoons	⅛ cup	2 cups	1 pint
4 tablespoons	¼ cup	2 pints or 4 cups	1 quart
5⅓ tablespoons	⅓ cup	4 quarts (liquid)	1 gallon
8 tablespoons	½ cup	8 quarts (solid)	1 peck
10⅔ tablespoons	⅔ cup	4 pecks	1 bushel

CONTENTS OF STANDARD CAN SIZES

8 ounces	1 cup	No. 2½	3½ cups or 28 ounces
Picnic	1¼ cups or 10 ounces	No. 3	4 cups or 32 ounces
No. 1 (tall)	2 cups or 16 ounces	No. 10	13 cups or 6 pounds, 10 ounces
No. 2	2½ cups or 20 ounces		

COMMON FOOD EQUIVALENTS

	Unit	Approximate Measure
Breadcrumbs	3 oz.	1 cup
Butter or shortening	1 lb.	2 cups
Cheese	1 lb.	4 cups grated
Chocolate	1 oz.	1 square
Coconut—shredded	1 lb.	6 cups
Cottage cheese	1 lb.	2 cups
Cranberries	1 lb.	4 cups
Cream cheese	3 oz. package	6⅔ tablespoons
Currants	1 lb.	3 cups
Dates, pitted	1 lb.	2½ cups
Eggs, whole	4–6	1 cup
Eggs, whites	8–10	1 cup
Eggs, yolks	12–14	1 cup
Flour:		
All-purpose	1 lb.	4 cups unsifted
Cake	1 lb.	4½ cups unsifted
Whole wheat	1 lb.	4 cups
Marshmallows	1 lb.	4 cups (64)
Molasses	1 lb.	1½ cups

Nutmeats	1 lb.	4 cups, shelled
Raisins	1 lb.	2 cups, packed
Rice	1 lb.	2 cups, uncooked; about 6 cups, cooked
Sugar:		
Brown	1 lb.	2 cups, firmly packed
Confectioners'	1 lb.	4 cups sifted
Granulated	1 lb.	2 cups
Whipping cream	½ pint	2 cups when whipped

HOW TO SUBSTITUTE ONE INGREDIENT FOR ANOTHER

Instead of	**You may use these**
1 whole egg, for thickening or baking	2 egg yolks. Or 2 tablespoons dried whole egg plus 2½ tablespoons water.
1 cup butter or margarine	⅞ cup rendered fat, with ½ teaspoon salt. Or 1 cup hydrogenated fat (cooking fat sold under brand name) with ½ teaspoon salt.
1 square (ounce) chocolate	3 or 4 tablespoons cocoa plus ½ tablespoon fat.
1 teaspoon double-acting baking powder	1½ teaspoons phosphate baking powder. Or 2 teaspoons tartrate baking powder.
Sweet milk and baking powder, for baking	Equal amount of sour milk plus ½ teaspoon soda per cup. (Each half teaspoon soda with 1 cup sour milk takes the place of 2 teaspoons baking powder and 1 cup sweet milk.)
1 cup sour milk, for baking	1 cup sweet milk mixed with one of the following: 1 tablespoon vinegar. Or 1 tablespoon lemon juice. Or 1¾ teaspoons cream of tartar.
1 cup whole milk	½ cup evaporated milk plus ½ cup water. Or 4 tablespoons dry whole milk plus 1 cup water. Or 4 tablespoons nonfat dry milk plus 2 teaspoons fat and 1 cup water.
1 cup skim milk	4 tablespoons nonfat dry milk plus 1 cup water.
1 tablespoon flour, for thickening	½ teaspoon cornstarch, potato starch, rice starch, or arrowroot starch. Or 1 tablespoon granulated tapioca.
1 cup cake flour, for baking	⅞ cup all-purpose flour.
1 cup all-purpose flour, for baking breads	Up to ½ cup bran, whole-wheat flour, or corn meal plus enough all-purpose flour to fill cup.

DEEP FAT FRYING

The selection of fat and the care given it is important in deep fat frying. Hydrogenated fats, corn oil, and cottonseed oil are used for deep-fat frying since they can be heated to a high temperature without smoking or burning. If particles of flour or crumbs remain in the fat it will smoke at a lower temperature than normal. The absorption of fat in the fried food increases as the smoking point is lowered. It is therefore important to avoid heating fat to the smoking point, and to clarify fat after it has been used. To reclaim fat, cook sliced raw potatoes in it to absorb flavors and strain through a cheesecloth or fine sieve to remove any particles.

A deep heavy kettle is best to use. A frying basket is convenient to lower the food into the fat and lift it out. A slotted spoon may be used. A thermometer is an aid although the bread cube test is practical for temperature determinations. Drop a 1-inch cube of stale bread into the hot fat. If bread browns in 60 to 70 seconds the temperature is satisfactory for uncooked mixtures (350°–370°F.); if it browns in 40 to 50 seconds, it is right for cooked mixtures (365°–380°F.); and if it browns in 20 to 30 seconds, it is hot enough for most cold foods (380°–390°F.).

Procedure: Fill kettle about ⅔ full of melted fat. Heat to desired temperature. Drain food on absorbent paper and lower gently into the hot fat, a few pieces at a time. Do not fry too much at one time because the temperature of the fat may be lowered too greatly, which would increase the cooking time and also cause the food to absorb more fat. As soon as food rises to surface of the fat, turn it several times for even browning. Do not crowd the pieces. When a golden brown, lift food out with wire basket or slotted spoon, allowing fat to drain over the kettle. Transfer to pan lined with absorbent paper so that excess fat will be absorbed.

The length of time required for frying depends upon the kind of food, size of pieces, and temperature of the fat.

Fat which is reclaimed each time after using may be used over and over again. Keep fat in a cool place away from light. When fat smokes it has been overheated and changed, and is no longer as desirable for deep fat frying.

HIGH ALTITUDE COOKING

Air becomes lighter with increased elevation, and its pressure upon the earth's surface becomes less. Because of the decreased atmospheric pressure, adjustments are necessary in many standard cookery methods. Baking of batters and doughs are particularly involved because the leavening power of baking powder is affected by altitude. Liquids boil at a lower temperature as the elevation increases. A pressure cooker is useful for foods that require long boiling. Baking guides for cooking at high altitudes may be obtained from the United States Bureau of Home Economics or from your state experimental station.

COMMON CAUSES OF FAILURE IN BAKING

BISCUITS

Rough biscuits: Caused from insufficient mixing.

Dry biscuits: Caused from baking in too slow an oven and handling too much.

Uneven browning: Caused from baking in dark surface pan (use a cookie sheet or shallow bright finish pan), too high a temperature, and rolling the dough too thin.

MUFFINS

Coarse texture: Caused from insufficient stirring and baking at too low a temperature.

Tunnels in muffins, peaks in center, and a soggy texture: Caused from over-mixing.

PIES

Pastry crumbles: Caused by over-mixing flour and fat.

Pastry is tough: Caused by using too much water and over-mixing the dough.

Pies do not brown: For fruit or custard pies use a glass pie pan or an enamel pan and bake at 400°–425° constant temperature.

BREADS, YEAST

Yeast bread is porous: Caused by over-rising or baking at too low a temperature.

Crust is dark and blisters: Caused by under-rising. The bread will blister just under the crust.

Bread does not rise: Caused by over-kneading or by using old yeast.

Bread is streaked: Caused by under-kneading and not kneading evenly.

Bread bakes uneven: Caused by using old dark pans, too much dough in pan, crowding the oven shelf, or baking at too high a temperature.

OVEN TEMPERATURES

Very slow	250° and 275°F.	Hot	400° and 425°F.
Slow	300° and 325°F.	Very hot	450° and 475°F.
Moderate	350° and 375°F.	Extremely hot	500° and 525°F.

TO TEST OVEN TEMPERATURES WHEN YOU DON'T HAVE A THERMOMETER

Sprinkle a little flour on a pan or use a piece of white tissue paper instead of flour. Place in heated oven. For slow oven—turns delicately brown in 5 min. For moderate oven—turns medium brown in 5 min. For hot oven—turns deep dark brown in 5 min. For very hot oven—turns deep dark brown in 3 min.

KOSHER GELATIN

A number of manufacturers produce kosher gelatin which is made of a vegetable base and may, therefore, be used with dairy products, fish, meat, or fruit and vegetable combinations. Flavored as well as plain gelatin is available. Ordinary gelatin is not kosher because it is generally made of non-kosher meat products.

HOW TO UNMOLD GELATIN DESSERTS, SALADS AND ENTREES

1. Lower mold quickly into bowl of hot (not boiling) water. Do not allow water to come over top of mold.
2. Lift mold from water and, with point of small knife, loosen jelly from sides of mold.
3. Place plate or serving dish over top of mold.
4. Hold plate and mold tightly together.
5. Turn upside down, so plate is on the bottom. Keep a firm hold on mold and plate and set plate gently down on the table.
6. Lift mold from jelly—shaking gently, if necessary. If jelly does not at once come out easily, remove from plate and dip mold again in hot water.

HOW TO WHIP CREAM

Chill cream thoroughly. Pour into a chilled bowl, and whip with a rotary beater until stiff. When whipped, cream approximately doubles in bulk.

HOW TO WHIP EVAPORATED MILK

Method 1: Heat milk over hot water until a film forms on the surface. Do not remove film. Stir until blended. Pour into a bowl and chill thoroughly. Beat with a rotary beater until stiff.

Method 2: Put unopened cans in a saucepan. Cover cans with cold water. Bring to a boil and cook 5 minutes. Chill the cans thoroughly. Pour the milk into a chilled bowl and whip with rotary beater.

HOW TO CARAMELIZE SUGAR

Heat sugar in a heavy frying pan or saucepan, stirring constantly until a golden brown syrup is formed. Remove from fire immediately.

HOW TO BLANCH NUTS

Pour boiling water over the shelled nuts. Let stand until the skins wrinkle (about 3 to 5 minutes). Drain and rub with the fingers or the dull edge of a knife to remove the skins. Dry well on absorbent paper or in a very slow oven (250°F.) or less.

HOW TO RENDER SUET

Place chopped suet in saucepan over medium heat. As it melts, pour into bowl. Don't overheat melted suet or it will turn dark and have a strong flavor. Store in a cool place until ready to use.

HOW TO SLICE BRAZIL NUTS

Cover nuts with cold water and bring slowly to boiling. Simmer 2 to 3 minutes. The nuts can then be sliced without breaking.

HOW TO MAKE CROQUETTES

Separate the food material into fine shreds or grind it. Prepare a thick, well-seasoned white sauce. (See the sauce section.) Add 1 cup sauce to each 3 cups of prepared food. Mix until well blended. The mixture should be as soft as can be handled. Cool. Form the croquettes with 2 spatulas on a lightly floured board into balls, cones, or cylinders. Make them uniform in size. Allow 1 to 2 tablespoons for each croquette. Dip into slightly beaten egg, diluted with 1 tablespoon water, roll in crumbs, and dip again in egg. Fry in deep hot fat (usually 365°F.) until brown. Drain on absorbent paper.

HOW TO CREAM FOODS

Use freshly cooked, canned, or leftover fish, meat, poultry, or vegetable. Leave whole or cube as desired. Prepare a medium white sauce. (See the sauce section.) Add sauce to food that is to be creamed and mix lightly, or add sauce to the food after it has been placed in the serving dish. Allow ½ to ¾ cup sauce for each cup of prepared food.

HOW TO SCALLOP FOODS

Use finely chopped or shredded cooked meat and fish, or diced and sliced uncooked or cooked vegetable. Fill a well-greased baking dish with alternate layers of food and medium white sauce. Cover the top with buttered crumbs. (For meats use a butter substitute.) Bake in moderate oven (375°F.) until the food is thoroughly cooked. Uncover and allow to brown.

HOW TO MAKE SOUFFLES

Use finely shredded or chopped fish, meat, poultry, vegetable, or grated cheese. Prepare a thick, well-seasoned white sauce. (See the sauce section.) Add ½ cup food to approximately ¾ cup of the sauce. Add the well beaten yolks of 3 eggs. Stir until blended. Fold in the stiffly beaten egg whites. Pour into a well-greased baking dish. Bake in a moderate oven (350° to 375°F.) until a knife inserted in center comes out clean.

SERVINGS AND POUNDS (HOW MUCH TO BUY)

How much meat to buy for dinner? How many servings will come from a pound of fresh beans, a No. 2½ can or a frozen package? The food shopper with an eye to thrift and good management learns to buy carefully just what she can use.

The figures below and on the following pages can help you decide how much to buy and, when reading market ads, you can use these figures to help decide what are real bargains. The amount of meat, poultry, and fish per serving varies with the amount of bone and fat. It also varies with the amount of extenders—such as stuffing, potatoes, rice—used with the meat.

Size of serving for each fruit and vegetable is given for whichever way it is most commonly served—cooked or uncooked. Size of serving for dry beans and peas and for cereals and cereal products—except flaked and puffed—is given for the cooked form.

MEAT, POULTRY, FISH

MEAT	Amount to buy per serving
Much bone or gristle . . .	½ to 1 pound
Medium amounts of bone	⅓ to ½ pound
Little bone	¼ to ⅓ pound
No bone	⅙ to ¼ pound

POULTRY
dressed weight[1]
Chicken:

Broiling	¼ to ½ bird
Frying and roasting . . .	¾ to 1 pound
Stewing	⅓ to ¾ pound
Ducks	1 to 1¼ pounds
Geese	¾ to 1 pound
Turkeys	⅔ to ¾ pound

POULTRY	Amount to buy per serving
ready-to-cook weight[1]	
Chicken:	
Broiling	¼ to ½ bird
Frying, roasting	⅔ to ¾ pound
Stewing	¼ to ⅔ pound
Ducks	¾ to 1 pound
Geese	⅔ to ¾ pound
Turkeys	About ½ pound

FISH

Whole or round	1 pound
Dressed, large	½ pound
Steaks, fillets	¼ pound

[1] Number of servings obtained from a bird depends on the kind, weight, age, sex, grade, and fatness of the bird and the way it is prepared.

VEGETABLES AND FRUITS

FRESH	Size of serving	Servings per pound[2]
Asparagus:		
Cut	½ cup	4
Spears	4–5 stalks	4
Beans, lima	½ cup	[3] 2
Beans, snap	½ cup	6
Beets, diced	½ cup	4
Broccoli	2 stalks	3–4
Brussels sprouts	½ cup	5–6
Cabbage:		
Raw, shredded	½ cup	7–8
Cooked	½ cup	4–5
Carrots:		
Raw, shredded	½ cup	8
Cooked	½ cup	5
Cauliflower	½ cup	3
Celery, cooked	½ cup	3–4
Collards	½ cup	2
Corn, cut	½ cup	[4] 2
Eggplant	½ cup	4
Onions, cooked	½ cup	4
Parsnips	½ cup	4
Peas	½ cup	[3] 2
Potatoes	½ cup	4–5
Spinach	½ cup	3–4
Squash	½ cup	2–3
Sweet potatoes	½ cup	3–4
Turnips	½ cup	4

[2] As purchased. [3] In pod. [4] In husk.

FRESH	Size of serving	Servings per pound[2]
Apricots	2 medium	5–6
Berries, raw	½ cup	4–5
Cherries, pitted, cooked	½ cup	2
Plums	2 large	4
Rhubarb, cooked	½ cup	4

For apples, bananas, oranges, and pears, count on about 3 to a pound; peaches, 4 to a pound.

DRY	Size of serving	Servings per pound[2]
Dry beans	¾ cup	9
Dry peas, lentils	¾ cup	7

CANNED	Size of serving	Per can
8-ounce can	½ cup	2
No. 2 can	½ cup	4–5
No. 2½ can	½ cup	6–7
No. 3 cylinder (46 oz.)	½ cup	11–12

FROZEN	Size of serving	Per package
Family-size packages	½ cup	3–4
Juices, concentrated, 6 fluid ounces	½ cup	6

CEREALS AND CEREAL PRODUCTS

	Size of serving	Servings per pound
Flaked corn cereals	1 cup	18–24
Other flaked cereals	¾ cup	21
Puffed cereals	1 cup	32–38
Corn meal	¾ cup	16
Wheat cereals:		
Coarse	¾ cup	12
Fine	¾ cup	16–22

	Size of serving	Servings per pound
Oatmeal	¾ cup	13
Hominy grits	½ cup	20
Macaroni and noodles	¾ cup	12
Rice	½ cup	16
Spaghetti	¾ cup	13

WAYS TO USE LEFT-OVERS

If it's good food, don't throw it away. Little left-overs, or big ones, fit into many dishes. A switch in recipes here or a novel dessert there—and your left-overs are put to work in interesting ways. Egg yolks can substitute for whole eggs, for example. If bread is a bit dry, then it's just right for French toast. Other left-overs have a way of adding food value or a fresh new touch—such as fruit in muffins or vegetables in omelets. Listed below are some of the dishes in which left-overs may be used.

Egg yolks, in
Cakes
Cornstarch pudding
Custard or sauce
Pie filling
Salad dressing
Scrambled eggs
Egg whites, in
Custard
Fruit whip
Meringue
Souffles
Hard-cooked egg or yolk, in
Casserole dishes
Garnish
Salads
Sandwiches
Sour milk, in
Cakes, cookies
Quick breads
Cooked snap beans, lima beans, corn, peas, carrots, in
Meat and vegetable pie
Soup
Stew
Stuffed peppers
Stuffed tomatoes
Vegetables in cheese sauce
Cooked leafy vegetables, chopped, in
Creamed vegetables
Meat loaf
Meat patties
Omelet
Souffle
Soup
Cooked or canned fruits, in
Fruit cup
Fruit sauces
Jellied fruit
Quick breads
Shortcake
Upside-down cake
Yeast breads

Sour cream, in
Cakes, cookies
Dessert sauce
Pie filling
Salad dressing
Sauce for vegetables
Cooked meats, poultry, fish, in
Casserole dishes
Hash
Meat patties
Meat pies
Salads
Sandwiches
Stuffed vegetables
Cooked potatoes, in
Croquettes
Fried or creamed potatoes
Meat-pie crust
Potatoes in cheese sauce
Stew or chowder
Cooked wheat, oat, or corn cereals, in
Fried cereal
Meat loaf or patties
Sweet puddings
Cooked rice, noodles, macaroni, spaghetti, in
Casseroles
Meat or cheese loaf
Timbales
Bread
Slices, cubed for croutons
Slices, for French toast
Dry crumbs, in
Brown betty
Croquettes
Fried chops
Soft crumbs, in
Meat loaf
Stuffings
Cake or cookies, in
Brown betty
Ice-box cake
Toasted, with sweet topping, for dessert

CARVING A ROLLED RIB ROAST

1. Place roast on platter with the larger cut surface down. Slice across the grain from the far right side. Cut slices ⅛ to ⅜ of an inch thick. Cut each cord only as you come to it. Cut, loosen with fork and let the cord drop to the plate.

2. Lift each slice to serving dish as it is cut.

CARVING A CROWN ROAST

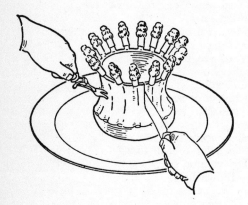

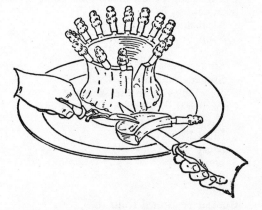

1. Slice down between ribs.

2. Allow one rib to each slice. Lift out on knife blade with fork to steady it.

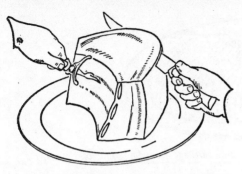

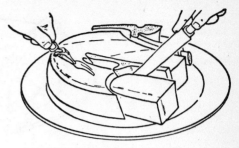

1. *Separate a section by running the knife between two muscles.*

1. *Have the butcher separate the backbone from the ribs. Put the roast on the platter with the larger cut surface down and with the ribs to the carver's left. Insert fork between the two top ribs. Cut slices ⅛- to ⅜-inch thick. Slice from the far outside edge across the grain.*

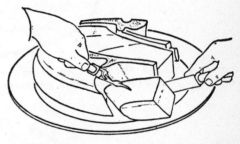

2. *Turn the section so the grain runs parallel with platter.*

2. *Cut along rib with tip of knife to free each slice.*

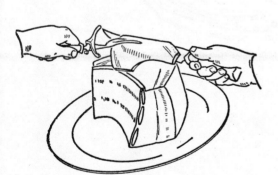

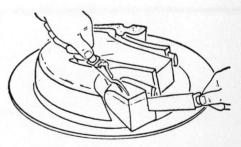

3. *Lift each slice to the side and slice enough for everyone before putting meat on individual plates.*

3. *Cut each section across the grain. Serve 2 or 3 slices to each person.*

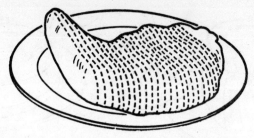

To carve beef tongue, remove excess tissue and cartilage from large end of tongue. Cut thin even slices.

To carve beef brisket, have round side away from you when placed on platter. Trim off excess fat. Then slice in rotation from each of three sides as pictured.

To carve cushion lamb shoulder, make thin slices through meat and stuffing as shown in illustration.

dictionary of culinary terms

à la carte: [French] By the bill of fare. To order thus is to choose from the menu, dish by dish with a separate price for each item, and not from a set combination.

à la creole: [French] After the fashion of the Creoles, i.e., prepared with tomatoes and highly seasoned.

à la diable: [French] Deviled, or seasoned with spicy condiments.

à la king: Served in a rich white sauce containing diced mushrooms, pimientos, and green peppers.

à la mode: [French] In the fashion: applied to ways of serving certain dishes, as pie with ice cream, or braised beef cooked in a sauce of vegetables.

à la Newburg: [French] Served in a sauce of butter, cream, egg yolks, and wine.

antipasto: [Italian] A dish of salted fish, cold cuts, olives, etc., served as an appetizer.

aspic: A jelly of meat juice, tomato juice, etc., used as a relish or a mold for meat, fish, etc.

au gratin: [French] Made with grated cheese or a lightly browned crust of breadcrumbs.

au jus: [French] Served in its natural juice or gravy: said of meat.

bake: To cook by dry heat in an oven.

barbecue: To cook (meats or poultry) on a spit or rack over coals or in a broiler, and baste with a piquant sauce.

baste: To moisten (meats or poultry) with melted fat, drippings, etc., while roasting.

batter: A mixture of flour, liquid, etc., of such a consistency that it can be poured or dropped from a spoon.

beat: To mix by stirring or striking repeatedly with a utensil.

bisque: A thick, strained, creamed vegetable soup.

blanch: To place (fruits, tomatoes, nuts, etc.) in boiling water 1 to 5 minutes, then drain and rinse in cold water, for the purpose of removing skins easily.

blend: To mix (two or more ingredients) until smooth.

boil: To cook (in a liquid) at boiling temperature, with bubbles rising continually and breaking on the surface.

boiling point: The temperature at which a liquid boils. The usual boiling point of water is 212° F.

bombe glacé: [French] A frozen dessert molded in a round, melonlike shape, usually containing two or more frozen mixtures.

bouchée: [French] A small patty of light pastry usually filled with a savory fish or meat mixture.

bouillabaisse: [French] A chowder made of two or more kinds of fish and sometimes seasoned with wine.

bouillon: A clear soup made from lean beef.

braise: To brown (meat) in fat, then simmer in a covered pan with a small amount of liquid over low flame.

bread: To cover (food) with breadcrumbs, usually by dipping first into slightly beaten egg or milk and then into seasoned crumbs.

brew: To cook in hot liquid until flavor is extracted.

brioche: A light, slightly sweetened yeast bread originated in France.

brochette: French word for skewer. **En brochette:** Broiled on a skewer.

broil: To cook by exposing to direct heat on a rack placed under the source of heat or over an open fire or grill.

cabob or **kabob:** Seasoned pieces of meat roasted on a skewer.

café au lait: [French] Coffee with hot milk.

canapé: [French] A small piece of toasted bread or a cracker spread with spiced meat, sardines, cheese, etc., served as an appetizer, often with drinks.

candy: To cook (fruit or vegetables) in sugar or sirup so as to glaze.

caramel: [French] Burnt sugar or sugar melted until it turns brown, used to color or flavor food.

caramelize: To heat (sugar) slowly until it melts and develops a golden-brown color and characteristic flavor.

casserole: A covered earthenware or glass dish in which food can be baked and served; food so prepared is said to be **en casserole.** The term is also used for the food itself,

573

specifically for a mold of rice, mashed potatoes, etc., baked with a filling of vegetables, meats, etc.

caviar: A salty relish made of the eggs of sturgeon, salmon, or certain other fish.

champignon: [French] The common edible mushroom.

charlotte: A pudding or dessert made of fruit, gelatin, etc., in a mold of bread, cake, or graham-cracker crumbs.

chill: To allow to become thoroughly cold but not frozen.

chop: To cut into small bits with a knife or chopper.

chutney: A spicy relish made of fruits, spices, and herbs.

coat: To cover entire surface of (food) with flour, breadcrumbs, etc.

coats spoon: When a thin even film of cooking mixture forms on spoon.

cobbler: A deep-dish fruit pie with no bottom crust and a thick top crust of biscuit dough.

coddle: To cook gently, as an egg, by heating in water just below the boiling point.

combine: To mix together.

compote: [French] A dish of stewed fruits in sirup.

condiment: A seasoning or relish for food, as pepper, mustard, sauces, etc.

consommé: A clear soup made by boiling meat, etc., in water.

court bouillon: [French] Stock in which fish was cooked.

cracklings: The crisp residue of fat after the fat has been removed by frying.

cream: To beat until smooth and creamy, as a sugar, shortening, and egg mixture.

crêpes suzette: [French] Very thin pancakes rolled up and sprinkled with sugar, sometimes served with a flaming brandy sauce.

crisp: To make firm or brittle in cold water, as vegetables, or in moderate dry heat, as crackers.

croquette: A small, rounded or cone-shaped mass of chopped meat, fish, or vegetables, fried in deep fat until browned.

croustade: [French] A baked form such as a toast case; a hollowed-out piece of fried bread or a patty shell, used to hold creamed foods.

crouton: One of the small, crisp pieces of toasted or fried bread often served in soup.

cruller: A rich fried doughnut usually made with the dough twisted or curled.

crumpet: An unsweetened batter cake baked on a griddle, somewhat like a pancake. It is usually toasted and buttered before serving.

cube: To cut into small or medium-sized squares.

curry: A powder prepared from turmeric and various spices and herbs, used as a seasoning in cooking, especially in the East Indies. The term is also used for various sauces or stews made with this powder.

cut in shortening: To combine firm shortening and flour with a pastry blender or with two knives.

demitasse: A small cup of or for after-dinner black coffee.

devil: To prepare (food, usually finely chopped) with hot seasoning.

dice: To cut into cubes of ¼ inch or smaller.

dissolve: To melt or liquefy.

dot: To cover surface of (food) with small pieces of butter, cheese, etc.

dough: A mixture of flour, liquid, etc., worked into a soft, thick mass that can be kneaded or rolled for baking into bread, pastry, etc.

drawn butter: Melted butter, sometimes thickened, used for a sauce.

dredge: To sprinkle (food) thickly with flour, sugar, or meal.

drippings: The fat and juices that drip from meat or poultry while roasting.

dust: To sprinkle lightly (on).

éclair: A small, oblong pastry shell filled with whipped cream or flavored custard and covered with frosting.

entree or entrée: The main course of a meal; sometimes, in large, formal dinners, etc., a dish served before the roast or between the main courses.

escalop or escallop: To bake with crumbs or in a ceam sauce.

farce: A forcemeat or stuffing for a fowl.

filet mignon: [French] A round cut of lean beafsteak, as from the beef tenderloin, broiled, usually with mushrooms and bacon.

fillet or filet: A boneless, lean piece of meat or fish. To fillet is to bone or slice (meat or fish).

fines herbes: [French] A mixture of chopped herbs used for seasoning, stuffing, or garnish.

finnan haddie: Smoked haddock.

fish and chips: A favorite British dish of deep-fat-fried fillets of fish and French fried potatoes.

flake: To separate into small pieces with a fork.

flapjack: A large pancake or griddlecake.

flour: To cover with a thin film of flour.

fold in: To add (ingredients, as whipped cream or beaten egg whites) gently without loss of air.

fondant: A soft, creamy paste made of sugar, used especially as a filling for candies.

fondue: A fluffy baked food made of eggs, butter, cheese, and milk, often thickened with bread or cracker crumbs.

forcemeat: Meat chopped up and seasoned, usually for stuffing.

frappé: [French] A dessert made of partly frozen beverages, fruit juices, etc., or a drink made of some beverage poured into a glassful of shaved ice.

fricassee: Poultry, veal, or lamb, cut up, stewed, and served in a sauce of its own gravy. **To fricassee** is to prepare (meat) by this method.

frijoles: Literally, beans; specifically, a Mexican dish consisting of beans cooked with oil, tomatoes, and chili.

frizzle: To cook in a small amount of fat until food is crisp and curled at the edges.

frosting: A mixture of sugar, water, or other liquid, flavoring, and sometimes whites of eggs, etc., for covering a cake; icing.

fry: To cook in a small amount of hot fat or oil in a pan over direct heat. In deep-fat frying, enough fat or oil is used to cover the food being cooked.

garnish: To decorate (food) with parsley or other vegetables to add color or flavor.

gherkin: A small, prickly variety of cucumber or the immature fruit of the common cucumber, used for pickling.

glacé: [French] Glazed or iced.

glaze: To coat with a thin sugar sirup icing or jelly.

goulash: A thick Hungarian stew made of beef or veal and vegetables seasoned with paprika.

grate: To grind (food) into shreds or particles by rubbing on a grater.

grill: To broil on a gridiron.

grind: To put (food) through a food chopper.

gumbo: A thick soup made with okra pods and other vegetables, and, sometimes, chicken.

hors d'oeuvre: Small relishes and appetizers, as olives, anchovies, etc., served usually at the beginning of a meal.

ice: A frozen dessert, usually made of water, fruit juice, egg whites, and sugar.

icing: The same as frosting.

infusion: The liquid extract obtained when a substance is steeped in water.

jerked beef: Beef preserved by slicing it into strips and drying these in the sun or over a fire.

julienne: Cut into thin strips: said of vegetables.

junket: A dessert of milk, curdled with rennet, and sweetened and flavored.

kisses: Small cookies (meringues) made of whites of eggs and powdered sugar.

knead: To mix and work (dough) into a smooth, plastic mass by folding over, pressing, and squeezing.

kumiss or **koumiss:** Fermented mare's or camel's milk, or imitations of it made of milk, sugar, and yeast.

lard: To cover uncooked lean meat or fish with strips of fat, or to insert strips of fat with a skewer.

legumes: The fruit or seed of leguminous plants, as of peas, beans, etc.

lyonnaise: Prepared with finely sliced, fried onions: said especially of potatoes.

macédoine: [French] A mixture of fruits or vegetables, cut into small, uniform pieces and served as a salad, cocktail, etc., often in jelly.

marinade: An oil-acid mixture, sometimes with added herbs and wine, in which meat, fish, or salad is soaked to give the food added flavor and tenderness.

marinate: To soak (food) in marinade.

marron: A large, sweet European chestnut, often used in confectionery.

marzipan: A confection of ground almonds, sugar, and egg white made into a paste and variously shaped: also called **marchpane.**

mask: To cover completely with a thick sauce, mayonnaise, or jelly.

melt: To dissolve with heat.

mince: To cut or chop into very small pieces.

minestrone: [Italian] A thick vegetable soup.

mix: To combine ingredients until evenly distributed, usually by stirring or beating.

mocha: A flavoring made of coffee infusion or coffee and chocolate: from the name of a variety of coffee grown originally in Arabia.

mousse: [French] A frozen dessert of whipped cream, white of egg, sweetening, and flavoring, sometimes with gelatin added. The term also refers to certain hot dishes of smooth texture.

mulligatawney soup: An East Indian soup made of meats, curry, and other spices.

musaca: An oriental dish made of lamb and vegetables.

napoleons: Thin pastry strips with jam, cream filling, and frosting.

Nesselrode: A mixture of preserved fruits, chopped nuts, etc., used in ice cream, pudding, or the like.

Newburg: Served in a specially prepared sauce. See **à la Newburg.**

pan-broil: To cook (meat) in a preheated skillet that has been rubbed with fat.

pan-fry: To cook in a skillet in a small amount of fat.

paprika: The dried ripe fruit of various mild red peppers, or the mild, red condiment ground from it.

parboil: To drop (food) in rapidly boiling water and cook until partially done.

pare: To cut or trim away the rind, skin, or covering, as potatoes, apples, etc.

paste: A soft, smooth mixture.

pâté: [French] A pie or paste.

pâté de foie gras: [French] A paste made of the livers of fattened geese.

patty: A pastry shell filled with a creamed mixture of food. The term is also used for a small, flat cake of ground meat, fish, etc., usually fried.

peel: To cut or trim away the outer skin or rind.

peppercorn: The dried berry of the black pepper plant.

petits fours: [French] Small cakes, usually frosted.

pièce de résistance: [French] The main dish in a meal.

pilau, pilaf, pilaff, *or* **pilaw:** Rice cooked with meat, poultry, or fish, and spices.

pimiento *or* **pimento:** Red, sweet, Spanish pepper pod.

pit: To remove pits from (fruits).

pizza: An Italian pastry of raised dough covered with tomato sauce, anchovies or sausage, cheese, etc.

plank: To broil and serve (meat or fish) on a board made for the purpose.

poach: To cook slowly in simmering (not boiling) water, or in a small receptacle put over such water.

pot-au-feu: [French] Beef stew with vegetables.

praline: A crisp candy made of pecans, almonds, or other nuts browned in boiling sugar.

preheat: To heat (oven, etc.) to desired temperature before cooking food.

purée: Food prepared by straining the boiled pulp through a sieve. **To purée** is to prepare (food) in this way. The term is also used for a thick soup with purée in it.

ragout: A thick, rich, highly seasoned stew.

ramekin: An individual baking dish.

ravioli: Small squares of noodle dough pressed together over a filling of chopped meat, cheese, or spinach, cooked in stock and served with a sauce.

remolade *or* **rémoulade:** A spicy sauce made with the yolks of hard-cooked eggs, vinegar, oil, etc., and served with cold dishes or as a salad dressing.

render: To melt (fat trimmed from meats and fowl) by heating slowly at a low temperature.

rennet: A substance, prepared from the stomach of calves, and used to curdle milk, as in making cheese or junket.

rissole: A small ball or roll of minced fish, meat, or poultry enclosed in pastry and fried.

roast: To cook (meat, etc.) by dry heat, usually in an oven.

rotisserie: A restaurant featuring broiled and barbecued meats.

roux: A mixture of melted butter (or other fat) and browned flour, used for thickening sauces, soups, gravies, etc.

sago: A starch foodstuff made from the pith of certain palm trees, used in granulated form chiefly in puddings and fillings.

sauté: To fry quickly and turn frequently in a little fat.

scald: To heat milk or liquid to just below the boiling point.

scallion: A green onion.

scallop: To cut (food) into small pieces and bake with a sauce in a casserole, often with a topping of breadcrumbs.

scone: A kind of tea cake, often resembling a baking powder biscuit, usually baked over a hot fire on a griddle, and served with butter.

score: To cut narrow grooves or gashes in the outer surface of (meat, etc.).

scramble: To cook (eggs) by mixing the white and yoke together, as with milk or butter.

sear: To brown the surface of (meat) quickly in a skillet by intense heat.

shallot: An onionlike plant whose clustered bulbs, resembling garlic but milder, are used for flavoring.

sherbet: A frozen dessert of fruit juice, sugar, and water, milk, or egg white.

shirr: To bake (eggs) with crumbs in small buttered dishes.

shred: To cut with a knife or shredder into thin narrow strips.

sift: To put fine dry ingredients as flour, sugar, etc., through a sifter.

simmer: To cook (foods) gently in liquid

just below the boiling point (180°—200° F.).

skewer: To pierce or fasten (meat or poultry) with long, wooden or metal pins to keep in position during cooking.

smörgåsbord *or* **smorgasbord:** An assortment of appetizers, especially as served buffet style at a long table.

soufflé: A delicate, fluffy, baked dish made light by the addition of stiffly beaten egg whites before baking.

spit: A thin, pointed rod or bar on which food is placed and held to be broiled or roasted over a fire.

sponge: A bread dough made with yeast.

spoon bread: A kind of bread, usually of corn meal, that remains doughy after baking and must be served with a spoon.

spumoni *or* **spumone:** An Italian frozen dessert made of various layers of smooth ice cream, often containing candied fruits and pistachio nuts.

squab: A young pigeon.

steam: To cook in double boiler or steamer by heat from boiling water.

steam-bake: To cook in the oven in a pan set over a container of hot water.

steep: To soak in boiling liquid to extract flavor.

sterilize: To free from living microorganisms by application of intense heat.

stew: To simmer or boil slowly in a small amount of liquid until tender.

stock: Water in which fish, meat, poultry, or vegetables have been cooked, used as a base for soup, gravy, etc.

stuff: To fill (a chicken, turkey, etc.) with seasoning, breadcrumbs, etc., before roasting.

succotash: A dish of corn kernels and shelled lima beans cooked together.

sweetbread: The pancreas (*stomach sweetbread*) or the thymus (*neck, or throat sweetbread*), especially of a calf, when used as food.

Tabasco: A very hot sauce made from a kind of pepper: a trade-mark.

table d'hôte: A complete meal with courses as specified on the menu, served at a restaurant or hotel for a set price.

tamale: A Mexican dish of minced meat and corn meal, highly seasoned with red pepper, wrapped in corn husks, dipped in oil, and steamed.

timbale case: A type of fried pastry shell, filled with a cooked food.

toast: To brown by direct heat.

torte: A rich, cakelike dessert usually made from crumbs, eggs, and nuts.

tortilla: A thin, flat, unleavened Mexican cake prepared from coarse corn meal and hot water, and baked on hot griddle or slab of stone.

toss: To mix lightly, as salad ingredients.

trifle: A dessert made of spongecake or macaroons soaked in fruit juices and wine, and topped with jam, whipped cream, custards, etc.

tripe: A part of the stomach of calf or steer, used as food.

truffle: A kind of fungus, similar to mushrooms, that grows some inches below the surface of the ground and is used in seasonings and as a garnish.

truss: To skewer or bind the wings, etc., of (a fowl) before cooking.

try out: To render fat. See **render.**

turnovers: Pastry or puff paste filled with meat or fruit, folded, and baked.

tutti-frutti: A preserve, candy, or ice cream made with a mixture of fruits or fruit flavorings.

Welsh rabbit: A dish of melted cheese, often mixed with ale or beer, served on crackers or toast: also called **Welsh rarebit.**

whip: To beat (eggs, cream, etc.) into a froth with a fork or egg beater.

Wiener Schnitzel: A breaded veal cutlet served with anchovy fillets and a slice of lemon.

wurst: [German] Sausage.

Yorkshire pudding: A batter pudding baked in the drippings of roasting meat.

supplement: yeast bread

The recipes in this yeast bread supplement follow the no-dissolve yeast method. In this newly developed method you just mix the active dry yeast with the other dry ingredients. Then add the warm liquids. There is no need to worry about temperature of the liquids. Detailed instructions are given in each recipe. If you still prefer to make some or all of these yeast breads or sweet goods using the conventional method of dissolving yeast in water, here's all you need do to adapt these recipes:

1. Measure recipe amount of warm water (105°–115°F.) into large warm bowl.
2. Sprinkle in yeast; stir until dissolved.
3. Add lukewarm milk or other liquid called for in recipe. Add margarine.
4. Gradually stir in dry ingredients.
5. Proceed with kneading, raising, and baking as directed.

Note: If recipe liquid is other than water, substitute ¼ cup water for ¼ cup other liquid and dissolve as above.

TEMPERATURE IS ALWAYS IMPORTANT IN RISING

Doughs and batters that rise in the conventional way need an even temperature of about 80° to 85°F. to properly activate the yeast. Here's how the yeast works: The growth of yeast produces a gas that is held in bubbles; these expand and the dough is said to "rise." A high temperature will kill yeast; a low temperature retards growth. In summer, this means you have to be careful about too much heat, and in winter, find a way to keep the batter or dough warm and cozy. There are several ways to provide the steady warmth that must be maintained during the rising period:

1. Place the bowl of dough on the center rack of cold oven with a large pan of hot water beneath it. Change the water as necessary.
2. Fill a large pan two-thirds full with hot water; place a wire rack on top and the bowl of dough on the rack.
3. Warm the bowl before putting dough into it by filling with hot water, pouring it out, drying it thoroughly; then grease it.
4. Set the bowl in a deep pan of water; test the water to see that it is warm, not hot.
5. Put the bowl in a draft-free place near (not on) the warm range or a radiator.
6. Turn on the oven at 400°F. for a minute. Then, turn off the oven and place the bowl of dough on the center oven rack, oven door closed.

ONE BOWL CHALLAH (No-Dissolve Method)

4½ to 5½ cups unsifted all-purpose flour	1 cup very hot tap water
2 tablespoons sugar	Pinch of saffron
1½ teaspoons salt	4 eggs (at room temperature)
1 package active dry yeast	1 teaspoon cold water
⅓ cup softened margarine	¼ teaspoon poppy seeds

In a large bowl thoroughly mix 1¼ cups flour, sugar, salt, and undissolved active dry yeast. Add softened margarine. Gradually add very hot tap water to dry ingredients and beat 2 minutes at medium speed of electric mixer, scraping bowl occasionally. Add 3 eggs, 1 egg white, and ½ cup flour, or enough flour to make a thick batter. Beat at high speed 2 minutes, scraping bowl occasionally. Stir in enough additional flour to make a soft dough. Turn out onto lightly floured board; knead until smooth and elastic, about 8 to 10 minutes. Place in greased bowl, turning to grease top. Cover; let rise in warm place, free from draft, until doubled in bulk, about 1 hour. Punch dough down; turn out onto lightly floured board. Divide dough in half. Form ½ of dough into a 12-inch roll; cut into 6 equal pieces. Roll each piece into a 14-inch rope. Place the 6 ropes side by side and seal together at the farthest end. Shape loaf as follows: 1. Bring up and diagonally cross the outer 2 ropes so that the right rope goes over the left rope. 2. Cross the outer right rope (formed by Step No. 1) back down over 2 ropes. 3. Cross the second from the left rope over and up to the extreme right. 4. Cross the outer left rope back down over 2 ropes. 5. Cross the second from the right rope over and up to the extreme left. Repeat the shaping pattern from Step No. 2 until all the dough is used. Seal ends securely together. Repeat with remaining piece of dough to form second loaf. Place on large greased baking sheets. Beat together the remaining egg yolk and cold water; brush loaves with egg mixture. Sprinkle with poppy seeds. Let rise, uncovered, in warm place, free from draft, until doubled in bulk, about 1 hour. Bake in hot oven (400°F.) about 30 minutes, or until done. Remove from baking sheets and cool on wire racks. Makes 2 loaves.

ONE BOWL WHITE SALT-FREE BREAD (No-Dissolve Method)

2¾ to 3¼ cups unsifted all-purpose
    flour
  1 tablespoon sugar

1 package active dry yeast
1 cup very hot tap water
2 tablespoons peanut oil

In a large bowl thoroughly mix 1 cup flour, sugar, and undissolved active dry yeast. Gradually add very hot tap water and peanut oil to dry ingredients and beat 2 minutes at medium speed of electric mixer, scraping bowl occasionally. Add ¼ cup flour, or enough flour to make a thick batter. Beat at high speed 2 minutes, scraping bowl occasionally. Stir in enough additional flour to make a soft dough. Turn out onto lightly floured board; knead until smooth and elastic, about 8 to 10 minutes. Place in greased bowl, turning to grease top. Cover; let rise in warm place, free from draft, until doubled in bulk, about 45 minutes. Bake in hot oven (400°F.) about 30 minutes, or until done. Remove from pan and cool on wire rack. Makes 1 loaf. Punch down dough; turn out onto lightly floured board. Shape into a loaf and place in greased 9x5x3-inch loaf pan. Cover; let rise in warm place, free from draft, until doubled in bulk, about 45 minutes.

ONE BOWL WHEAT GERM CASSEROLE BREAD
(No-Dissolve Method)

2¾ to 3¼ cups unsifted all-purpose flour
  2 teaspoons salt
  ½ cup wheat germ
  2 packages active dry yeast

2 tablespoons softened margarine
1⅓ cups very hot tap water
2 tablespoons molasses (at room
    temperature)

In a large bowl thoroughly mix 1 cup flour, salt, wheat germ, and undissolved active dry yeast. Add softened margarine. Gradually add very hot tap water and molasses to dry ingredients and beat 2 minutes at medium speed of electric mixer, scraping bowl occasionally. Add ½ cup flour, or enough flour to make a thick batter. Beat at high speed 2 minutes, scraping bowl occasionally. Stir in enough additional flour to make a stiff batter. Cover; let rise in warm place, free from draft, until doubled in bulk, about 45 minutes. Stir batter down. Beat vigorously, about ½ minute. Turn into a greased 1½-quart casserole. Bake in moderate oven (375°F.) about 45 minutes, or until done. Remove from casserole and cool on wire rack. Makes 1 loaf.

ONE BOWL LOW CHOLESTEROL BREAD (No-Dissolve Method)

7 to 8 cups unsifted all-purpose flour
2 tablespoons sugar
2 teaspoons salt
1 package active dry yeast
1 tablespoon softened margarine
2½ cups very hot tap water

In a large bowl thoroughly mix 2½ cups flour, sugar, salt, and undissolved active dry yeast. Add softened margarine. Gradually add very hot tap water to dry ingredients and beat 2 minutes at medium speed of electric mixer, scraping bowl occasionally. Add ¾ cup flour, or enough flour to make a thick batter. Beat at high speed 2 minutes, scraping bowl occasionally. Stir in enough additional flour to make a soft dough. Turn out onto lightly floured board; knead until smooth and elastic, about 8 to 10 minutes. Place in greased bowl, turning to grease top. Cover; let rise in warm place, free from draft, until doubled in bulk, about 1 hour. Punch dough down; turn out onto lightly floured board. Divide dough in half; shape each half into a loaf. Place in 2 greased 9x5x3-inch loaf pans. Cover; let rise in warm place, free from draft, until doubled in bulk, about 1 hour. Bake in hot oven (400°F.) about 40 to 45 minutes, or until done. Remove from pans and cool on wire racks. Makes 2 loaves.

WHITE BREAD (No-Dissolve Method)

5½ to 6½ cups unsifted all-purpose flour
3 tablespoons sugar
2 teaspoons salt
1 package active dry yeast
1½ cups water
½ cup milk
3 tablespoons margarine

In a large bowl thoroughly mix 2 cups flour, sugar, salt, and undissolved active dry yeast. Combine water, milk, and margarine in a saucepan. Heat over low heat until liquids are warm. (Margarine does not need to melt.) Gradually add to dry ingredients and beat 2 minutes at medium speed of electric mixer, scraping bowl occasionally. Add ¾ cup flour, or enough flour to make a thick batter. Beat at high speed 2 minutes, scraping bowl occasionally. Stir in enough additional flour to make a soft dough. Turn out onto lightly floured board; knead until smooth and elastic, about 8 to 10 minutes. Place in greased bowl, turning to grease top. Cover; let rise in warm place, free from draft, until doubled in bulk, about 1 hour. Punch dough down; turn out onto lightly floured board. Cover; let rest 15 minutes. Divide dough in half and shape into loaves. Place in 2 greased 8½x4½x2½-inch loaf pans. Cover; let rise in warm place, free from draft, until doubled in bulk, about 1 hour. Bake in hot oven (400°F.) about 25 to 30 minutes, or until done. Remove from pans and cool on wire racks. Makes 2 loaves.

RYE BREAD (No-Dissolve Method)

2½ cups unsifted rye flour
2½ cups unsifted white flour (about)
1 tablespoon sugar
1 tablespoon salt
1 tablespoon caraway seeds (optional)
1 package active dry yeast
1 cup milk

¾ cup water
2 tablespoons honey
1 tablespoon margarine
¼ cup corn meal
1 egg white
2 tablespoons water

Combine flours; in a large bowl thoroughly mix 1⅔ cups flour mixture, sugar, salt, caraway seeds, and undissolved active dry yeast. Combine milk, ¾ cup water, honey, and margarine in a saucepan. Heat over low heat until liquids are warm. (Margarine does not need to melt.) Gradually add to dry ingredients and beat 2 minutes at medium speed of electric mixer, scraping bowl occasionally. Add 1 cup flour mixture, or enough flour mixture to make a thick batter. Beat at high speed 2 minutes, scraping bowl occasionally. Stir in enough flour mixture to make a soft dough. (If necessary, add additional white flour to obtain desired dough.) Turn dough out onto lightly floured board; knead until smooth and elastic, about 8 to 10 minutes. Place in greased bowl, turning to grease top. Cover; let rise in warm place, free from draft, until doubled in bulk, about 1 hour. Punch dough down; turn out onto lightly floured board. Divide in half; form each piece into a smooth ball. Cover; let rest 10 minutes. Flatten each piece slightly. Roll lightly on board to form tapered ends. Sprinkle 2 greased baking sheets with corn meal. Place breads on baking sheets. Combine egg white and 2 tablespoons water; brush breads. Let rise, uncovered, in warm place, free from draft, 35 minutes. Bake in hot oven (400°F.) about 25 minutes, or until done. Remove from baking sheets and cool on wire racks. Makes 2 loaves.

WHOLE WHEAT BREAD (No-Dissolve Method)

4½ cups unsifted whole wheat flour
2¾ cups unsifted white flour (about)
3 tablespoons sugar
4 teaspoons salt
2 packages active dry yeast

1½ cups water
¾ cup milk
⅓ cup molasses
⅓ cup margarine

Combine flours; in a large bowl thoroughly mix 2½ cups flour mixture, sugar, salt, and undissolved active dry yeast. Combine water, milk, molasses and margarine in a saucepan. Heat over low heat until liquids are warm. (Margarine does not need to melt.) Gradually add to dry ingredients and beat 2 minutes at medium speed of electric mixer, scraping sides of bowl occasionally. Add ½ cup flour mixture, or enough flour mixture to make a thick batter. Beat at high speed 2 minutes, scraping bowl occasionally. Stir in enough additional flour mixture to make a soft dough. (If necessary, add additional white flour to obtain desired dough.) Turn dough out onto lightly floured board. Knead until smooth and elastic, about 8 to 10 minutes. Place in greased bowl, turning to grease top. Cover; let rise in warm place, free from draft, until doubled in bulk, about 1 hour. Punch dough down; turn out onto lightly floured board. Divide in half. Shape into loaves. Place in 2 greased 8½x4½x2½-inch loaf pans. Cover; let rise in warm place, free from draft, until doubled in bulk, about 1 hour. Bake in hot oven (400°F.) about 25 to 30 minutes, or until done. Remove from pans and cool on wire racks. Makes 2 loaves.

100% WHOLE WHEAT BREAD (No-Dissolve Method)

8¾ to 9¾ cups unsifted whole
    wheat flour
4 teaspoons salt
2 packages active dry yeast

1½ cups milk
1½ cups water
½ cup honey
6 tablespoons (¾ stick) margarine

In a large bowl thoroughly mix 3 cups flour, salt, and undissolved active dry yeast. Combine milk, water, honey, and margarine in a saucepan. Heat over low heat until liquids are warm. (Margarine does not need to melt.) Gradually add to dry ingredients and beat 2 minutes at medium speed of electric mixer, scraping bowl occasionally. Add 1 cup flour, or enough flour to make a thick batter. Beat at high speed 2 minutes, scraping bowl occasionally. Stir in enough additional flour to make a soft dough. Turn out onto lightly floured board; cover dough with bowl and let rest for 10 minutes. Then knead until smooth and elastic, about 8 to 10 minutes. Place in greased bowl, turning to grease top. Cover; let rise in warm place, free from draft, until doubled in bulk, about 50 minutes. Punch dough down; turn out onto lightly floured board. Divide dough in half; shape each half into a loaf. Place in 2 greased 8½x4½x2½-inch loaf pans. Cover; let rise in warm place, free from draft, until doubled in bulk, about 50 minutes. Bake in moderate oven (375°F.) about 35 to 40 minutes, or until done. Remove from pans and cool on wire racks. Makes 2 loaves.

BUTTERMILK BREAD (No-Dissolve Method)

5½ to 6½ cups unsifted all-purpose
    flour
3 tablespoons sugar
2½ teaspoons salt
¼ teaspoon baking soda

1 package active dry yeast
1 cup buttermilk
1 cup water
⅓ cup margarine

In a large bowl thoroughly mix 2 cups flour, sugar, salt, baking soda, and undissolved active dry yeast. Combine buttermilk, water, and margarine in a saucepan. Heat over low heat until liquids are warm. (Margarine does not need to melt.) Mixture will appear curdled. Gradually add to dry ingredients and beat 2 minutes at medium speed of electric mixer, scraping bowl occasionally. Add 1 cup flour, or enough flour to make a thick batter. Beat at high speed 2 minutes, scraping bowl occasionally. Stir in enough flour to make a soft dough. Turn out onto lightly floured board; knead until smooth and elastic, about 8 to 10 minutes. Place in greased bowl, turning to grease top. Cover; let rise in warm place, free from draft, until doubled in bulk, about 1 hour. Punch dough down; turn out onto lightly floured board. Divide dough in half. Shape each half into a loaf. Place in 2 greased 8½x4½x2½-inch loaf pans. Cover; let rise in warm place, free from draft, until doubled in bulk, about 1 hour. Bake in moderate oven (375°F.) about 35 minutes, or until done. Remove from pans and cool on wire rack. Makes 2 loaves.

CINNAMON BREAD (No-Dissolve Method)

4½ to 5½ cups unsifted all-purpose
    flour
¼ cup sugar
1 teaspoon salt
1 package active dry yeast
1¼ cups milk

¼ cup (½ stick) margarine
2 eggs (at room temperature)
    Melted margarine
⅓ cup sugar
1½ teaspoons ground cinnamon

In a large bowl thoroughly mix 1¾ cups flour, ¼ cup sugar, salt, and undissolved active dry yeast. Combine milk and ¼ cup margarine in a saucepan. Heat over low heat until liquid is warm. (Margarine does not need to melt.) Gradually add to dry ingredients and beat 2 minutes at medium speed of electric mixer, scraping bowl occasionally. Add eggs and ½ cup flour, or enough flour to make a thick batter. Beat at high speed 2 minutes, scraping bowl occasionally. Stir in enough additional flour to make a soft dough. Turn out onto lightly floured board; knead until smooth and elastic, about 8 to 10 minutes. Place in greased bowl, turning to grease top. Cover; let rise in warm place, free from draft, until doubled in bulk, about 1 hour. Meanwhile, combine ⅓ cup sugar and cinnamon. Punch dough down; turn out onto lightly floured board. Divide dough in half. Roll ½ the dough into a 12x8-inch rectangle. Brush lightly with melted margarine. Sprinkle with ½ the cinnamon-sugar mixture. Roll tightly from the 8-inch side as for jelly roll. Seal ends of loaf and fold underneath. Place loaf, seam side down, in greased 8½x4½x2½-inch loaf pan. Repeat with remaining dough. Cover; let rise in warm place, free from draft, until doubled in bulk, about 1 hour. Bake in a moderate oven (350°F.) about 30 minutes, or until done. Remove from pans and cool on wire racks. Makes 2 loaves.

RAISIN CASSEROLE BREAD (No-Dissolve Method)

4½ to 4¾ cups unsifted all-purpose flour	1 cup milk
	½ cup water
½ cup sugar	¼ cup (½ stick) margarine
1 teaspoon salt	1 egg (at room temperature)
2 packages active dry yeast	1 cup seedless raisins

In a large bowl thoroughly mix 1½ cups flour, sugar, salt, and undissolved active dry yeast. Combine milk, water, and margarine in a saucepan. Heat over low heat until liquids are warm. (Margarine does not need to melt.) Gradually add to dry ingredients and beat 2 minutes at medium speed of electric mixer, scraping bowl occasionally. Add egg and 1 cup flour, or enough flour to make a thick batter. Beat at high speed 2 minutes, scraping bowl occasionally. Stir in enough additional flour to make a stiff batter. Cover; let rise in a warm place, free from draft, until doubled in bulk, about 1 hour. Stir batter down. Beat in raisins, about ½ minute. Turn into 2 greased 1-quart casseroles. Bake in moderate oven (350°F.) about 40 to 45 minutes, or until done. Remove from casseroles and cool on wire racks. Make 2 loaves.

CHEESE CASSEROLE BREAD (No-Dissolve Method)

4¾ to 5½ cups unsifted all-purpose flour	1 cup milk
	1 cup water
3 tablespoons sugar	2 tablespoons margarine
1 tablespoon salt	1½ cups grated sharp Cheddar cheese
2 packages active dry yeast	1 egg (at room temperature)

In a large bowl thoroughly mix 1¾ cups flour, sugar, salt, and undissolved active dry yeast. Combine milk, water, and margarine in a saucepan. Heat over low heat until liquids are warm. (Margarine does not need to melt.) Gradually add to dry ingredients and beat 2 minutes at medium speed of electric mixer, scraping bowl occasionally. Add cheese, egg, and ½ cup flour, or enough flour to make a thick batter. Beat at high speed 2 minutes, scraping bowl occasionally. Stir in enough additional flour to make a stiff batter. Beat until well blended. Cover; let rise in warm place, free from draft, until doubled in bulk, about 40 minutes. Stir batter down. Beat vigorously, about ½ minute. Turn into 2 greased 1-quart casseroles. Bake in moderate oven (375°F.) about 40 to 50 minutes, or until done. Remove from casseroles and cool on wire racks. Makes 2 loaves.

WHITE BATTER BREAD (No-Dissolve Method)

4 to 4½ cups unsifted all-purpose flour
3 tablespoons sugar
1 tablespoon salt
2 packages active dry yeast

1 cup milk
1 cup water
2 tablespoons margarine

In a large bowl thoroughly mix 1½ cups flour, sugar, salt, and undissolved active dry yeast. Combine milk, water, and margarine in a saucepan. Heat over low heat until liquids are warm. (Margarine does not need to melt.) Gradually add to dry ingredients and beat 2 minutes at medium speed of electric mixer, scraping bowl occasionally. Add 1 cup flour, or enough flour to make a thick batter. Beat at high speed 2 minutes, scraping bowl occasionally. Stir in enough additional flour to make a stiff batter. Beat until well blended. Cover; let rise in warm place, free from draft, until doubled in bulk, about 40 minutes. Stir batter down. Beat vigorously, about ½ minute. Turn into a greased 9x5x3-inch loaf pan. Bake in moderate oven (375°F.) about 40 to 50 minutes, or until done. Remove from pan and cool on wire rack. Makes 1 large loaf.

Herb Batter Bread: Combine ¼ teaspoon basil leaves, ¼ teaspoon oregano leaves, and ¼ teaspoon thyme leaves with the 1½ cups flour, sugar, salt, and yeast. Then proceed with recipe as directed. Make 1 large loaf.

ONE BOWL DINNER ROLLS (No-Dissolve Method)

2¾ to 3¼ cups unsifted all-purpose flour
¼ cup sugar
½ teaspoon salt
1 package active dry yeast

5 tablespoons softened margarine
⅔ cup very hot tap water
1 egg (at room temperature)
Melted margarine

In a large bowl thoroughly mix ¾ cup flour, sugar, salt, and undissolved active dry yeast. Add softened margarine. Gradually add very hot tap water to dry ingredients and beat 2 minutes at medium speed of electric mixer, scraping bowl occasionally. Add egg and ½ cup flour, or enough flour to make a thick batter. Beat at high speed 2 minutes, scraping bowl occasionally. Stir in enough additional flour to make a soft dough. Turn out onto lightly floured board; knead until smooth and elastic, about 8 to 10 minutes. Place in greased bowl, turning to grease top. Cover; let rise in warm place, free from draft, until doubled in bulk, about 1 hour. Punch dough down; turn out onto lightly floured board. Proceed according to directions for desired shape. Cover; let rise in warm place, free from draft, until doubled in bulk, about 1 hour. Carefully brush rolls with melted margarine. Bake in a hot oven (400°F.) about 10 to 15 minutes, or until done. Remove from baking sheets and cool on wire racks. Makes 2 or 3 dozen rolls.

Pretzels: Divide dough into 2 or 3 equal pieces.* Then divide each piece into 12 pieces. Roll each into a pencil-shaped 16-inch roll. Shape into pretzels and place on greased baking sheets, about 2 inches apart.

* Divide dough into 2 pieces to make family-size rolls or divide into 3 pieces to make smaller dinner rolls.

Curlicues: Divide dough into 2 or 3 equal pieces.* Roll out each piece into a 9x12-inch oblong. Brush generously with melted margarine. Cut into 12 strips (about 1 inch wide). Hold one end of each strip firmly and wind dough loosely to form coil; tuck end firmly underneath. Place on greased baking sheets, about 2 inches apart.

Parkerhouse Rolls: Divide dough in half. Roll each half into a ¼-inch thick circle. Cut into rounds with a 2½-inch biscuit cutter. Crease each round with dull edge of knife to one side of center. Brush each round to within ¼-inch of the edges with melted margarine. Fold larger side over smaller so edges just meet. Pinch well with fingers to seal. Place on greased baking sheets so rolls are almost touching.

ONE BOWL CHEESY ONION BURGER BUNS
(No-Dissolve Method)

5¾ to 6¾ cups unsifted all-purpose flour
3 tablespoons sugar
1½ teaspoons salt
2 packages active dry yeast

2 tablespoons softened margarine
2 cups very hot tap water
1½ cups grated sharp Cheddar cheese
¼ cup finely chopped onion

In a large bowl thoroughly mix 2 cups flour, sugar, salt, and undissolved active dry yeast. Add softened margarine. Gradually add very hot tap water to dry ingredients and beat 2 minutes at medium speed of electric mixer, scraping bowl occasionally. Add 1 cup flour, or enough flour to make a thick batter. Beat at high speed 2 minutes, scraping bowl occasionally. Stir in cheese, onion, and enough additional flour to make a soft dough. Turn out onto lightly floured board; knead until smooth and elastic, about 8 to 10 minutes. Place in greased bowl, turning to grease top. Cover; let rise in warm place, free from draft, until doubled in bulk, about 1 hour. Punch dough down; turn out onto lightly floured board. Divide dough into 20 equal pieces. Form each piece into a smooth ball; place balls 2 inches apart on greased baking sheets. Cover; let rise in warm place, free from draft, until doubled in bulk, about 45 minutes. Bake in hot oven (400°F.) about 15 to 20 minutes, or until done. Remove from baking sheets and cool on wire racks. Make 20 buns.

BISCUIT ROLLS (No-Dissolve Method)

3¼ to 4¼ cups unsifted all-purpose flour
1 tablespoon sugar
1½ teaspoons salt
2 teaspoons baking powder

1 package active dry yeast
1 cup milk
½ cup water
⅔ cup shortening

In a large bowl thoroughly mix 1¼ cups flour, sugar, salt, baking powder, and undissolved active dry yeast. Combine milk, water, and shortening in a saucepan. Heat over low heat until liquids are warm. (Shortening does not need to melt.) Gradually add to dry ingredients and beat 2 minutes at medium speed of electric mixer, scraping bowl occasionally. Add ½ cup flour, or enough flour to make a thick batter. Beat at high speed 2 minutes, scraping bowl occasionally. Stir in enough additional flour to make a soft dough. Turn out onto lightly floured board; knead about 20 to 25 times to form a round ball. Roll dough out to ½-inch thickness. Using a 2-inch biscuit cutter, cut dough in circles and arrange in 3 ungreased

* Divide dough into 2 pieces to make family-size rolls or divide into 3 pieces to make smaller dinner rolls.

8- or 9-inch round cake pans. Cover; let rise in warm place, free from draft, about 1 hour. Bake in a hot oven (400°F.) about 20 minutes, or until done. Remove from pans and cool on wire racks. Best when served hot. Makes about 3 dozen rolls.

ONE BOWL HARD ROLLS (No-Dissolve Method)

4½ to 5½ cups unsifted all-purpose flour
2 tablespoons sugar
2 teaspoons salt
1 package active dry yeast
3 tablespoons softened margarine

1½ cups very hot tap water
1 egg white (at room temperature)
Corn meal
½ cup water
1 teaspoon cornstarch

In a large bowl thoroughly mix 1⅓ cups flour, sugar, salt, and undissolved active dry yeast. Add softened margarine. Gradually add very hot tap water to dry ingredients and beat 2 minutes at medium speed of electric mixer, scraping bowl occasionally. Add egg white and 1 cup flour, or enough flour to make a thick batter. Beat at high speed 2 minutes, scraping bowl occasionally. Stir in enough additional flour to make a soft dough. Turn out onto lightly floured board; knead until smooth and elastic, about 8 to 10 minutes. Place in greased bowl, turning to grease top. Cover; let rise in warm place, free from draft, until doubled in bulk, about 45 minutes. Punch dough down; turn out onto lightly floured board. Cover; let rest 10 minutes. Divide in half. Form each half into a 9-inch roll. Cut into nine 1-inch pieces. Form into smooth balls. Place about 3 inches apart on greased baking sheets sprinkled with corn meal. Cover; let rise in warm place, free from draft, until doubled in bulk, about 45 minutes. Slowly blend remaining ½ cup water into cornstarch. Bring mixture to a boil. Cool slightly. When ready to bake, brush each roll with cornstarch glaze. Slit tops with a sharp knife criss-cross fashion. If desired, sprinkle with sesame or poppy seeds. Bake in a very hot oven (450°F.) about 15 minutes, or until done. Remove from baking sheets and cool on wire racks. Makes 1½ dozen rolls.

CROISSANTS (No-Dissolve Method)

¾ cup (1½ sticks) margarine
¼ cup unsifted all-purpose flour
2½ to 3 cups unsifted all-purpose flour
3 tablespoons sugar
1 teaspoon salt
1 package active dry yeast

¾ cup milk
¼ cup water
2 eggs (at room temperature)
1 tablespoon milk
Sugar

Cut margarine into ¼ cup flour until mixture is smooth paste. Place between two sheets of wax paper and roll into a 10x4-inch rectangle. Chill 1 hour. When margarine mixture is chilled, prepare dough. In a large bowl thoroughly mix 1 cup flour, 3 tablespoons sugar, salt, and undissolved active dry yeast. Combine ¾ cup milk and water in a saucepan. Heat over low heat until liquids are warm. Gradually add to dry ingredients and beat 2 minutes at medium speed of electric mixer, scraping bowl occasionally. Add 1 egg and ½ cup flour or enough flour to make a thick batter. Beat at high speed 2 minutes, scraping bowl occasionally. Stir in enough additional flour to make a soft dough. Turn out onto heavily floured board. Roll out to a 12-inch square. Carefully peel wax paper from chilled margarine mixture; place over center ⅓ of dough. Fold an outside ⅓ of dough over margarine slab; then cover with remaining ⅓ of dough. Give dough a quarter turn. Roll out to 12-inch square. Fold as above. Turn dough, roll and fold as above 3 more times. Wrap in wax paper and chill 2 hours. Divide dough into 3 pieces and shape 1 piece at a time, refrigerating the remainder. Roll 1 piece of dough out on floured board into a 12-inch circle. Cut into 8 pie-shaped pieces. Beat together 1 egg and 1 tablespoon milk. Brush point of each piece with egg mixture. Roll each piece up tightly, beginning at wide end. Seal points. Place on greased baking sheets with points underneath. Curve to form crescents. Brush with egg mixture and sprinkle with sugar. Repeat with remaining dough, egg mixture, and sugar. Let rise, uncovered, in warm place, free from draft, until light, about 30 minutes. Bake in moderate oven (375°F.) about 12 minutes, or until done. Remove from baking sheets and cool on wire racks. Best when served warm. Makes 24 rolls.

CHEESE HERB BUFFET LOAVES (No-Dissolve Method)

6 to 7 cups unsifted all-purpose flour
2 tablespoons sugar
2 teaspoons salt
2 packages active dry yeast
1 cup milk
1 cup water
¼ cup (½ stick) margarine

½ cup grated Parmesan cheese
½ cup finely chopped parsley
½ teaspoon oregano leaves
½ teaspoon garlic salt or seasoned salt
1 egg white, slightly beaten
2 tablespoons water

In a large bowl thoroughly mix 2 cups flour, sugar, salt, and undissolved active dry yeast. Combine milk, 1 cup water, and margarine in a saucepan. Heat over low heat until liquids are warm. (Margarine does not need to melt.) Gradually add to dry ingredients and beat 2 minutes at medium speed of electric mixer, scraping bowl occasionally. Add ¾ cup flour, or enough flour to make a thick batter. Beat at high speed 2 minutes, scraping bowl occasionally. Stir in enough additional flour to make a soft dough. Turn out onto lightly floured board; knead until smooth and elastic, about 8 to 10 minutes. Place in greased bowl, turning to grease top. Cover; let rise in warm place, free from draft, until doubled in bulk, about 30 minutes. Meanwhile, combine cheese, parsley, oregano, and garlic or seasoned salt. Punch dough down; turn out onto lightly floured board. Divide dough in half; let rest 5 minutes. Roll out ½ the dough into 8x15-inch rectangle. Sprinkle with half the cheese mixture. Cut into 3 rectangles, 8x5 inches. Tightly roll each from the 8-inch side; pinch seams to seal. Pinch ends and fold underneath. Place loaves, seam side down and ¼-inch apart, on half of the greased baking sheet. Repeat with remaining dough and filling; place loaves on same baking sheet. Cover; let rise in warm place, free from draft, until doubled in bulk, about 30 minutes. Bake in hot oven (400°F.) 10 minutes. Remove from oven; brush with egg white which has been combined with 2 tablespoons water. If desired, sprinkle with sesame seeds. Bake 15 minutes, or until done. Remove from baking sheet and cool on wire rack. To serve, separate loaves and slice each into ½-inch slices. Makes 6 small loaves.

RUSSIAN BLACK BREAD (No-Dissolve Method)

4 cups unsifted rye flour
3 cups unsifted white flour
1 teaspoon sugar
2 teaspoons salt
2 cups whole bran cereal
2 tablespoons caraway seed, crushed
2 teaspoons instant coffee
2 teaspoons onion powder
½ teaspoon fennel seed, crushed

2 packages active dry yeast
2½ cups water
¼ cup vinegar
¼ cup dark molasses
1 square (1 ounce) unsweetened
    chocolate
¼ cup (½ stick) margarine
1 teaspoon cornstarch
½ cup cold water

Combine rye and white flours. In a large bowl thoroughly mix 2⅓ cups flour mixture, sugar, salt, cereal, caraway seed, instant coffee, onion powder, fennel seed, and undissolved active dry yeast. Combine 2½ cups cold water, vinegar, molasses, chocolate, and margarine in a saucepan. Heat over low heat until liquids are warm. (Margarine and chocolate do not need to melt.) Gradually add to dry ingredients and beat 2 minutes at medium speed of electric mixer, scraping bowl occasionally. Add ½ cup flour mixture, or enough flour mixture to make a thick batter. Beat at high speed 2 minutes, scraping bowl occasionally. Stir in enough additional flour mixture to make a soft dough. Turn out onto lightly floured board. Cover dough with bowl and let rest 15 minutes. Then knead until smooth and elastic, about 10 to 15 minutes (dough may be sticky). Place in greased bowl, turning to grease top. Cover; let rise in warm place, free from draft, until doubled in bulk, about 1 hour. Punch dough down; turn out onto lightly floured board. Divide dough in half. Shape each half into a ball, about 5 inches in diameter. Place each ball in the center of greased 8-inch round cake pan. Cover; let rise in warm place, free from draft, until doubled in bulk, about 1 hour. Bake in moderate oven (350°F.) about 45 to 50 minutes, or until done. Meanwhile, combine cornstarch and ½ cup cold water. Cook over medium heat, stirring constantly, until mixture boils; continue to cook, stirring constantly, 1 minute. As soon as bread is baked, brush cornstarch mixture over tops of loaves. Return bread to oven and bake 2 to 3 minutes, or until glaze is set. Remove from pans and cool on wire racks. Makes 2 loaves.

SOUR DOUGH BREAD (No-Dissolve Method)

Starter:
1¾ cups unsifted all-purpose flour
1 tablespoon sugar
1 tablespoon salt
1 package active dry yeast
2½ cups warm water

Dough:
5 to 6 cups unsifted all-purpose flour
3 tablespoons sugar
1 teaspoon salt
1 package active dry yeast
1 cup milk
2 tablespoons margarine
1½ cups starter

To make starter, combine flour, sugar, salt, and undissolved active dry yeast in a large bowl. Gradually add warm water to dry ingredients and beat 2 minutes at medium speed of electric mixer, scraping bowl occasionally. Cover; let stand at room temperature (78°-80°F.) 4 days. Stir down daily. To make dough, combine 1 cup flour, sugar, salt, and undissolved active dry yeast in a large bowl. Combine milk and margarine in a saucepan. Heat over low heat until liquid is warm. (Margarine does not need to melt.) Gradually add to dry ingredients and beat 2 minutes at medium speed of electric mixer, scraping bowl occasionally. Add 1½ cups starter and 1 cup flour, or enough flour to make a thick batter. Beat at high speed 2 minutes, scraping bowl occasionally. Stir in enough additional flour to make a soft dough. Turn out onto lightly floured board; knead until smooth and elastic, about 8 to 10 minutes. Place in greased bowl, turning to grease top. Cover; let rise in warm place, free from draft, until doubled in bulk, about 1 hour. Punch dough down; turn out onto lightly floured board. Let rest 15 minutes. Divide dough in half. Shape each half into loaf and place in greased 9x5x3-inch loaf pan. Cover; let rise in warm place, free from draft, until doubled in bulk, about 1 hour. Bake in hot oven (400°F.) about 30 minutes, or until done. Remove from pans and cool on wire racks. Makes 2 loaves.

To Reuse Starter: Add 1½ cups lukewarm water, ¾ cup unsifted all-purpose flour, and 1½ teaspoons sugar to unused starter. Beat for 1 minute at medium speed of electric mixer. Cover and let stand until ready to make bread again. Stir down daily.

PUMPERNICKEL BREAD (No-Dissolve Method)

9 cups unsifted white flour
3 cups unsifted rye flour
2 tablespoons salt
1 cup whole bran cereal
¾ cup yellow corn meal
2 packages active dry yeast
3½ cups water

¼ cup dark molasses
2 squares (1-ounce each) unsweetened chocolate
1 tablespoon margarine
2 cups mashed potatoes (at room temperature)
2 teaspoons caraway seeds

Combine white and rye flours. In a very large bowl thoroughly mix 2 cups flour mixture, salt, cereal, corn meal, and undissolved active dry yeast. Combine water, molasses, chocolate and margarine in saucepan. Heat over low heat until liquids are warm. (Margarine and chocolate do not need to melt.) Gradually add to dry ingredients and beat 2 minutes at medium speed of electric mixer, scraping bowl occasionally. Add potatoes and 1 cup flour mixture, or enough flour mixture to make a thick batter. Beat at high speed 2 minutes, scraping bowl occasionally. Stir in caraway seeds and enough additional flour mixture to make a soft dough. Turn out onto lightly floured board; cover dough with bowl and let rest 15 minutes. Then knead until smooth and elastic, about 15 minutes. Place in greased bowl, turning to grease top. Cover; let rise in warm place, free from draft, until doubled in bulk, about 1 hour. Punch dough down; let rise again 30 minutes. Punch dough down; turn out onto lightly floured board. Divide into 3 equal pieces. Shape into round balls. Place in 3 greased 8- or 9-inch round cake pans. Cover; let rise in warm place, free from draft, until doubled in bulk, about 45 minutes. Bake in moderate oven (350°F.) about 50 minutes, or until done. Remove from pans and cool on wire racks. Makes 3 loaves.

ONE BOWL ANADAMA BREAD (No-Dissolve Method)

5½ to 6½ cups unsifted all-purpose flour
2½ teaspoons salt
1 cup yellow corn meal

2 packages active dry yeast
¼ cup (½ stick) softened margarine
2 cups very hot tap water
½ cup molasses (at room temperature)

In a large bowl thoroughly mix 2½ cups flour, salt, corn meal, and undissolved active dry yeast. Add softened margarine. Gradually add very hot tap water and molasses to dry ingredients and beat 2 minutes at medium speed of electric mixer, scraping bowl occasionally. Add ½ cup flour, or enough flour to make a thick batter. Beat at high speed 2 minutes, scraping bowl occasionally. Stir in enough additional flour to make a soft dough. Turn out onto lightly floured board; knead until smooth and elastic, about 8 to 10 minutes. Place in greased bowl, turning to grease top. Cover; let rise in warm place, free from draft, until doubled in bulk, about 1 hour. Punch dough down; turn out onto lightly floured board. Divide dough in half and shape into loaves. Place in 2 greased 8½x4½x2½-inch loaf pans. Cover; let rise in warm place, free from draft, until doubled in bulk, about 45 minutes. Bake in moderate oven (375°F.) about 35 minutes, until done. Remove from pans and cool on wire racks. Makes 2 loaves.

BARM BRACK (No-Dissolve Method)

4½ to 5½ cups unsifted all-purpose flour
½ cup sugar
1½ teaspoons salt
1 teaspoon grated lemon peel
3 packages active dry yeast

¾ cup water
½ cup milk
¼ cup (½ stick) margarine
2 eggs (at room temperature)
1¼ cups golden seedless raisins
⅓ cup chopped mixed candied fruits

In a large bowl thoroughly mix 1½ cups flour, sugar, salt, lemon peel, and undissolved active dry yeast. Combine water, milk, and margarine in saucepan. Heat over low heat until liquids are warm. (Margarine does not need to melt.) Gradually add to dry ingredients and beat 2 minutes at medium speed of electric mixer, scraping bowl occasionally. Add eggs and ¾ cup flour, or enough flour to make a thick batter. Beat at high speed 2 minutes, scraping bowl occasionally. Stir in enough additional flour to make a soft dough. Turn out onto lightly floured board; knead until smooth and elastic, about 8 to 10 minutes. Place in greased bowl, turning to grease top. Cover; let rise in warm place, free from draft, until doubled in bulk, about 40 minutes. Punch dough down; turn out onto lightly floured board. Knead in raisins and candied fruits. Divide in half. Shape into loaves. Place in 2 greased 8½x4½x2½-inch loaf pans. Cover; let rise in warm place, free from draft, until doubled in bulk, about 50 minutes. Bake in moderate oven (375°F.) about 30 to 35 minutes, or until done. Remove from pans and cool on wire racks. Makes 2 loaves.

COFFEE BREAKERS OR CINNAMON ROLLS
(No-Dissolve Method)

4½ to 5½ cups unsifted all-purpose flour
½ cup sugar
1½ teaspoons salt
2 packages active dry yeast

½ cup milk
½ cup water
¼ cup (½ stick) margarine
2 eggs (at room temperature)

In a large bowl thoroughly mix 1⅔ cups flour, sugar, salt, and undissolved active dry yeast. Combine milk, water, and margarine in a saucepan. Heat over low heat until liquids are warm. (Margarine does not need to melt.) Gradually add to dry ingredients and beat 2 minutes at medium speed of electric mixer, scraping bowl occasionally. Add eggs and ½ cup flour, or enough flour to make a thick batter. Beat at high speed 2 minutes, scraping bowl occasionally. Stir in enough additional flour to make a soft dough. Turn out onto lightly floured board; knead until smooth and elastic, about 8 to 10 minutes. Place in greased bowl, turning to grease top. Cover; let rise in warm place, free from draft, until doubled in bulk, about 1 hour. Punch dough down; turn out onto lightly floured board. Divide in half and shape as desired according to one of the following shapes.

Coffee Breakers: While dough is rising prepare pans. Melt ½ cup (1 stick) margarine in a saucepan. Add ⅔ cup firmly packed light brown sugar and 2 teaspoons light corn syrup; bring to a rolling boil. Immediately pour into two 15½x10½x1-inch jelly roll pans. Sprinkle with ¾ cup chopped pecans. Roll out half the dough into a 12-inch square. Brush with melted margarine. Combine ½ cup firmly packed light brown sugar and 2 teaspoons ground cinnamon. Sprinkle center ⅓ of dough with ¼ the cinnamon mixture. Fold ⅓ of dough over center third. Sprinkle with ¼ the cinnamon mixture. Fold remaining ⅓ of dough over to make a 3-layer 12-inch strip. Cut into twelve 1-inch pieces. Hold the ends of each piece and twist in opposite directions, 2 or 3 times. Seal ends firmly. Place in prepared pan about

1½ inches apart. Repeat with remaining half of the dough and filling. Cover; let rise in warm place, free from draft, until doubled in bulk, about 1 hour. Bake in hot oven (400°F.) about 15 to 20 minutes, or until done. Invert rolls onto plates or wire racks to cool. Best when served warm. Makes 24 rolls.

Cinnamon Rolls: Roll each half into an 18x9-inch oblong. Brush with melted margarine. Combine 1½ cups sugar, ⅔ cup seedless raisins, and 2 teaspoons ground cinnamon. Sprinkle ½ over each piece of dough. Roll each up as for jelly roll to make 18-inch rolls. Seal edges firmly. Cut each roll into 12 pieces, about 1½ inches wide. Place, cut side up, in 2 greased 9-inch round cake pans or 2 greased 8-inch square pans. Cover; let rise in warm place, free from draft, until doubled in bulk, about 1 hour. Bake in moderate oven (350°F.) about 25 minutes, or until done. Remove from pans and cool on wire racks. Serve plain, or if desired, frost with confectioners' sugar frosting. Makes 24 rolls.

KOLACKY #2 (No-Dissolve Method)

2¾ to 3¼ cups unsifted all-purpose flour
¼ cup sugar
1 teaspoon salt
1 package active dry yeast
⅓ cup milk
⅓ cup water
2 tablespoons margarine
2 eggs (at room temperature)

In a large bowl thoroughly mix 1 cup flour, sugar, salt, and undissolved active dry yeast. Combine milk, water, and margarine in a saucepan. Heat over low heat until liquids are warm. (Margarine does not need to melt.) Gradually add to dry ingredients and beat 2 minutes at medium speed of electric mixer, scraping bowl occasionally. Add eggs and ½ cup flour, or enough flour to make a thick batter. Beat at high speed 2 minutes, scraping bowl occasionally. Stir in enough additional flour to make a soft dough. Turn out onto lightly floured board; knead until smooth and elastic, about 8 to 10 minutes. Place in greased bowl, turning to grease top. Cover; let rise in warm place, free from draft, until doubled in bulk, about 1 hour. Punch dough down; turn out onto lightly floured board. Roll out to ½-inch thickness. Cut circles with a 2½-inch biscuit cutter. Place about 2 inches apart on greased baking sheets. Cover; let rise in warm place, free from draft, until doubled in bulk, about 1 hour. Press an indentation in the center of each bun, leaving a rim about ¼-inch wide. Fill with Raisin Filling (below). Bake in hot oven (400°F.) about 10 minutes, or until done. Remove from baking sheets and cool on wire racks. If desired, sprinkle with confectioners' sugar. Makes about 20 buns.

Raisin Filling: Combine 2 cups of seedless raisins, 1 cup firmly packed light brown sugar, 3 tablespoons cornstarch, 1 teaspoon ground cinnamon, ½ teaspoon ground allspice, ¼ teaspoon ground cloves, and 1⅓ cups water in a saucepan. Bring to a boil, stirring constantly. Cook 1 minute longer. Remove from heat; stir in ½ cup chopped English walnuts. Cool.

KULICH (No-Dissolve Method)

2¼ to 2¾ cups unsifted all-purpose flour
¼ cup sugar
1 teaspoon salt
1 teaspoon grated lemon peel
1 package active dry yeast
½ cup milk
¼ cup water
2 tablespoons margarine
1 egg (at room temperature)
¼ cup chopped blanched almonds
¼ cup seedless raisins
Confectioners' sugar frosting
Colored sprinkles

In a large bowl thoroughly mix ¾ cup flour, sugar, salt, lemon peel, and undissolved active dry yeast. Combine milk, water, and margarine in a saucepan. Heat over low heat until liquids are warm. (Margarine does not need to melt.) Gradually add to dry ingredients and beat 2 minutes at medium speed of electric mixer, scraping bowl occasionally. Add egg and ½ cup flour, or enough flour to make a thick batter. Beat at high speed 2 minutes, scraping bowl occasionally. Stir in enough additional flour to make a soft dough. Turn out onto lightly floured board; knead until smooth and elastic, about 8 to 10 minutes. Place in greased bowl, turning to grease top. Cover; let rise in warm place, free from draft, until doubled in bulk, about 1 hour. Punch dough down; turn out onto lightly floured board. Knead in blanched almonds and raisins. Divide dough in half. Shape each half into ball; press each into a greased 1-pound coffee or shortening can. Cover; let rise in warm place, free from draft, until doubled in bulk, about 1 hour. Bake in moderate oven (350°F.) about 30 to 35 minutes, or until done. Remove from cans and cool on wire racks. When cool, frost tops with confectioners' sugar frosting and decorate with colored sprinkles. Makes 2 cakes.

BOBKA (No-Dissolve Method)

2 cups unsifted all-purpose flour	¼ cup (½ stick) margarine
¼ cup sugar	3 eggs (at room temperature)
1 package active dry yeast	¼ cup mixed candied fruits
½ cup milk	¼ cup seedless raisins

In a large bowl thoroughly mix ¾ cup flour, sugar, and undissolved active dry yeast. Combine milk and margarine in a saucepan. Heat over low heat until liquid is warm. (Margarine does not need to melt.) Gradually add to dry ingredients and beat 2 minutes at medium speed of electric mixer, scraping bowl occasionally. Add eggs and ½ cup flour, or enough flour to make a thick batter. Beat at high speed 2 minutes, scraping bowl occasionally. Add remaining flour and beat 2 minutes at high speed. Cover; let rise in warm place, free from draft, until bubbly, about 1 hour. Stir in candied fruits and raisins. Turn into greased and floured 2-quart Turk's Head pan or tube pan. Let rise, uncovered, in warm place, free from draft, for 30 minutes. Bake in moderate oven (350°F.) about 40 minutes, or until done. Before removing from pan, immediately prick surface with fork. Pour Rum Syrup (below) over cake. After syrup is absorbed, remove from pan and cool on wire rack. When cool, if desired, frost with confectioners' sugar frosting. Makes 1 cake.

Rum Syrup: Combine ½ cup sugar, ⅓ cup water and 2 teaspoons rum extract in a saucepan; bring to a boil.

STOLLEN (No-Dissolve Method)

5½ to 6½ cups unsifted all-purpose flour	⅔ cup margarine
	3 eggs (at room temperature)
½ cup sugar	¾ cup chopped blanched almonds
1¼ teaspoons salt	¾ cup mixed candied fruits
2 packages active dry yeast	⅓ cup golden seedless raisins
¾ cup milk	Confectioners' sugar frosting
½ cup water	

In a large bowl thoroughly mix 2 cups flour, sugar, salt, and undissolved active dry yeast. Combine milk, water, and margarine in a saucepan. Heat over low heat until liquids are warm. (Margarine does not need to melt.) Gradually add to dry ingredients and beat 2 minutes at medium speed of electric mixer, scraping bowl occasionally. Add eggs and ½ cup flour, or enough flour to make a thick batter. Beat at high speed 2 minutes, scraping bowl occasionally. Stir in enough additional flour to make a soft dough. Turn out onto lightly floured board; knead until smooth and elastic, about 8 to 10 minutes. Place in greased bowl, turning to grease top. Cover; let rise in warm place, free from draft, until doubled in bulk, about 1½ hours. Combine blanched almonds, candied fruits, and raisins. Punch dough down; turn out onto lightly floured board. Knead in nut and fruit mixture. Divide dough into 3 equal pieces. Roll each piece of dough into a 12x7-inch oval. Fold in half length-wise. Place on greased baking sheets. Cover; let rise in warm place, free from draft, until doubled in bulk, about 45 minutes. Bake in moderate oven (350°F.) about 20 to 25 minutes, or until done. Remove from baking sheets and cool on wire racks. Frost with confectioners' sugar frosting while warm. If desired, decorate with blanched almonds and candied cherries. Makes 3 stollens.

DANISH PASTRY (No-Dissolve Method)

3½ to 4 cups unsifted all-purpose flour
½ cup sugar
1½ teaspoons salt
2 tablespoons cornstarch
1½ teaspoons grated lemon peel
2 packages active dry yeast
¾ cup milk
½ cup water
¼ cup (½ stick) margarine
2 eggs (at room temperature), separated
1½ cups (3 sticks) margarine
1 tablespoon water
Confectioners' sugar frosting
Colored sprinkles

In a large bowl thoroughly mix 1¼ cups flour, sugar, salt, cornstarch, lemon peel, and undissolved active dry yeast. Combine milk, water, and ¼ cup margarine in a saucepan. Heat over low heat until liquids are warm. (Margarine does not need to melt.) Gradually add to dry ingredients and beat 2 minutes at medium speed of electric mixer, scraping bowl occasionally. Add 2 egg yolks, 1 egg white (reserve remaining egg white), and ¾ cup flour, or enough flour to make thick batter. Beat at high speed 2 minutes, scraping bowl occasionally. Add enough additional flour to make a stiff batter; stir just until blended. Cover tightly with aluminum foil; chill about 1 hour. On wax paper, spread 1½ cups margarine into a 10x12-inch rectangle. Chill 1 hour. On a lightly floured board, roll chilled dough into a 12x16-inch rectangle. Place margarine slab on ⅔ of dough. Fold uncovered third over middle section; cover with remaining third. Give dough a quarter turn; roll into a 12x16-inch rectangle; fold as above. Turn, roll and fold once more; chill one hour. Repeat procedure of 2 rollings, foldings, turnings, and chillings two more times. Then refrigerate overnight. On a lightly floured board, divide dough in half. Roll ½ the dough into a 15x6-inch rectangle. Cut 12 strips, 15x½-inch. Twist each strip and form into a circle, sealing ends well. Place on greased baking sheets. Repeat with remaining piece of dough. Cover lightly with plastic wrap; refrigerate overnight. Combine reserved egg white with 1 tablespoon water. Brush rolls with egg white mixture. Bake in moderate oven (375°F.) about 15 to 20 minutes, or until done. Remove from baking sheets and cool on wire racks. Frost with confectioners' sugar frosting and decorate with colored sprinkles. Makes 2 dozen rolls.

CINNAMON ORANGE CRESCENTS (No-Dissolve Method)

4 to 5 cups unsifted all-purpose flour
½ cup sugar
2 teaspoons salt
1 tablespoon grated orange peel
2 packages active dry yeast
¾ cup milk
½ cup water

½ cup (1 stick) margarine
1 egg (at room temperature)
Melted margarine
¾ cup sugar
1 tablespoon ground cinnamon
Confectioners' sugar frosting

In a large bowl thoroughly mix 1½ cups flour, ½ cup sugar, salt, orange peel and undissolved active dry yeast. Combine milk, water, and ½ cup margarine in a saucepan. Heat over low heat until liquids are warm. (Margarine does not need to melt.) Gradually add to dry ingredients and beat 2 minutes at medium speed of electric mixer, scraping bowl occasionally. Add egg and ½ cup flour, or enough flour to make a thick batter. Beat at high speed 2 minutes, scraping bowl occasionally. Stir in enough additional flour to make a soft dough. Turn out onto lightly floured board; knead until smooth and elastic, about 8 to 10 minutes. Place in greased bowl, turning to grease top. Cover; let rise in warm place, free from draft, until doubled in bulk, about 1 hour. Punch dough down; turn out onto lightly floured board. Divide dough into 8 equal pieces. Roll 1 piece of dough into an 8-inch circle. Brush with melted margarine. Combine ¾ cup sugar and cinnamon. Sprinkle circle with about 1½ tablespoons cinnamon-sugar mixture. Cut into 8 pie-shaped pieces. Roll up tightly, beginning at wide end; seal points firmly. Place on greased baking sheets with points underneath. Curve to form crescents. Repeat with remaining pieces of dough and cinnamon-sugar mixture. Cover; let rise in warm place, free from draft, until doubled in bulk, about 1 hour. Bake in moderate oven (350°F.) about 12 minutes, or until done. Remove from baking sheets and cool on wire racks. Frost with confectioners' sugar frosting. Makes 64 small rolls.

BLUSHING CREAM CONES (No-Dissolve Method)

2 to 2½ cups unsifted all-purpose flour
¼ cup sugar
¾ teaspoon salt
1 package active dry yeast
¼ cup milk
¼ cup water
2 tablespoons margarine
1 egg (at room temperature)

2 packages (3 ounces each) cream cheese, softened
2 tablespoons sugar
1 egg yolk
¼ teaspoon almond extract
¼ cup blanched almonds, toasted
¼ cup chopped candied cherries

In a large bowl thoroughly mix ¾ cup flour, ¼ cup sugar, salt, and undissolved active dry yeast. Combine milk, water, and margarine in a saucepan. Heat over low heat until liquids are warm. (Margarine does not need to melt.) Gradually add to dry ingredients and beat 2 minutes at medium speed of electric mixer, scraping bowl occasionally. Add egg and ¼ cup flour, or enough flour to make a thick batter. Beat at high speed 2 minutes, scraping bowl occasionally. Stir in enough additional flour to make a soft dough. Turn out onto lightly floured board; knead until smooth and elastic, about 8 to 10 minutes. Place in greased bowl, turning to grease top. Cover; let rise in warm place, free from draft, until doubled in bulk, about 1 hour. Cream together cheese and 2 tablespoons sugar until fluffy. Beat in egg yolk and almond extract. Stir in toasted blanched almonds and cherries. Refrigerate until ready to use. Punch dough down; turn out onto lightly greased board. Roll dough into a 15-

inch square. Cut into twenty-five 3-inch squares. Place about 2 teaspoons cheese mixture in center of each square. Overlap 2 opposite corners. Seal seams tightly to form cones. Place on greased baking sheets. Cover; let rise in warm place, free from draft, until doubled in bulk, about 1 hour. Bake in hot oven (400°F.) about 12 minutes, or until done. Remove from baking sheets and cool on wire racks. If desired, frost with confectioners' sugar frosting. Makes 25 rolls.

ONE BOWL PECAN CINNAMON BARS (No-Dissolve Method)

1¼ to 1¾ cups unsifted all-purpose
    flour
2 tablespoons sugar
½ teaspoon salt
1 package active dry yeast
½ cup (1 stick) softened margarine

½ cup very hot tap water
1 egg yolk (at room temperature)
1½ cups chopped pecans
½ cup sugar
1½ teaspoons ground cinnamon

In a large bowl thoroughly mix ½ cup flour, 2 tablespoons sugar, salt, and undissolved active dry yeast. Add softened margarine. Gradually add very hot tap water to dry ingredients and beat 2 minutes at medium speed of electric mixer, scraping bowl occasionally. Add egg yolk and ¼ cup flour, or enough flour to make a thick batter. Beat at high speed 2 minutes, scraping bowl occasionally. Stir in enough additional flour to make a stiff batter. Cover bowl tightly with aluminum foil. Refrigerate 2 hours or if desired, chill overnight. Combine pecans, ½ cup sugar, and cinnamon. Sprinkle about ¼ of pecan-sugar mixture over lightly floured board. Turn dough out onto board; sprinkle with more pecan-sugar mixture. Roll dough to small rectangle; sprinkle with more pecan-sugar mixture. Fold ends over center. Repeat until all pecan-sugar mixture is used. Roll out to make an 8x10-inch rectangle. Carefully place dough onto greased baking sheet. Bake in a hot oven (400°F.) about 15 to 20 minutes, or until done. Remove from baking sheet and cool on wire rack. Cut into bars to serve. Makes about 20 bars.

TINY LEMON STICKY BUNS (No-Dissolve Method)

4½ to 5½ cups unsifted all-purpose
    flour
1½ cups sugar
2 teaspoons salt
1 tablespoon grated lemon peel
2 packages active dry yeast
¾ cup milk

½ cup water
½ cup (1 stick) margarine
1 egg (at room temperature)
1 cup chopped blanched almonds
½ teaspoon ground nutmeg
Melted margarine

In a large bowl thoroughly mix 1½ cups flour, ½ cup sugar, salt, lemon peel, and undissolved active dry yeast. Combine milk, water, and ½ cup margarine in a saucepan. Heat over low heat until liquids are warm. (Margarine does not need to melt.) Gradually add to dry ingredients and beat 2 minutes at medium speed of electric mixer, scraping bowl occasionally. Add egg and ½ cup flour, or enough flour to make a thick batter. Beat at high speed 2 minutes, scraping bowl occasionally. Stir in enough additional flour to make a soft dough. Turn out onto lightly floured board; knead until smooth and elastic, about 8 to 10 minutes. Place in greased bowl, turning to grease top. Cover; let rise in warm place, free from draft, until doubled in bulk, about 1 hour. Sprinkle blanched almonds into 3 greased 9-inch round cake pans. Prepare Lemon Topping (below) and pour over almonds. Combine remaining 1 cup sugar and nutmeg. Punch dough down; turn out onto lightly floured board. Divide in

3 equal pieces. Roll each piece into a 20x8-inch rectangle. Brush with melted margarine. Sprinkle with sugar and nutmeg mixture. Roll each up from long side as for jelly roll. Seal edges firmly. Cut into 1-inch slices. Place, cut side up, in prepared pans. Cover; let rise in warm place, free from draft, until doubled in bulk, about 1 hour. Bake in moderate oven (350°F.) about 20 to 25 minutes, or until done. Invert buns onto plates or wire racks to cool. Makes 5 dozen buns.

Lemon Topping: Combine 1½ cups sugar, ½ cup (1 stick) margarine, ½ cup light corn syrup, ¼ cup water, and 3 tablespoons grated lemon peel in a saucepan. Bring to a boil. Cook 3 minutes, stirring constantly.

SUGAR CRISP ROLLS (No-Dissolve Method)

2 to 2½ cups unsifted all-purpose flour	¼ cup water
1¼ cups sugar	¼ cup (½ stick) margarine
½ teaspoon salt	1 egg (at room temperature)
1 package active dry yeast	1 cup chopped pecans
¼ cup milk	Melted margarine

In a large bowl thoroughly mix ¾ cup flour, ¼ cup sugar, salt, and undissolved active dry yeast. Combine milk, water, and ¼ cup margarine in a saucepan. Heat over low heat until liquids are warm. (Margarine does not need to melt.) Gradually add to dry ingredients and beat 2 minutes at medium speed of electric mixer, scraping bowl occasionally. Add egg and ¼ cup flour, or enough flour to make a thick batter. Beat at high speed 2 minutes, scraping bowl occasionally. Stir in enough additional flour to make a soft dough. Turn out onto lightly floured board; knead until smooth and elastic, about 8 to 10 minutes. Cover; let rise in warm place, free from draft, until doubled in bulk, about 1 hour. Punch down and let rise an additional 30 minutes. Combine remaining 1 cup sugar and pecans. Punch dough down; turn out onto lightly floured board. Roll dough to a 9x18-inch rectangle. Brush with melted margarine. Sprinkle dough with half the sugar mixture. Roll up from long side as for jelly roll; seal edges. Cut into 1-inch slices. Roll each slice of dough into a 4-inch circle using remaining sugar mixture in place of flour on board, coating both top and bottom of each circle. Place on greased baking sheets. Cover; let rise in warm place, free from draft, until doubled in bulk, about 30 minutes. Bake in moderate oven (375°F.) about 10 to 15 minutes, or until done. Remove from baking sheets and cool on wire racks. Makes 1½ dozen rolls.

ELECTION CAKE (No-Dissolve Method)

4 to 4½ cups unsifted all-purpose flour	2 packages active dry yeast
1 cup sugar	¾ cup (1½ sticks) softened margarine
1 teaspoon salt	1½ cups very hot tap water
1½ teaspoons ground cinnamon	2 eggs (at room temperature)
½ teaspoon ground nutmeg	1½ cups seedless raisins
¼ teaspoon ground cloves	¾ cup chopped pecans
¼ teaspoon ground mace	¼ cup chopped citron

In a large bowl thoroughly mix 1¾ cups flour, sugar, salt, cinnamon, nutmeg, cloves, mace, and undissolved active dry yeast. Add softened margarine. Gradually add very hot tap water to dry ingredients and beat 2 minutes at medium speed of electric mixer, scraping bowl occasionally. Add eggs and ¾ cup flour, or enough flour to make a thick batter. Beat at high speed 2 minutes, scraping bowl occasionally. Add raisins, pecans, citron, and enough flour to make a stiff batter. Stir until well combined. Turn into greased 10-inch tube pan. Cover; let rise in warm place, free from draft, until doubled in bulk, about 1½ hours. Bake in moderate oven (375°F.) about 45 minutes, or until done. Remove from pan and cool on wire rack. Makes 1 cake.

LINCOLN LOG (No-Dissolve Method)

4 to 5 cups unsifted all-purpose flour	2 eggs (at room temperature)
¾ cup sugar	1 package (8-ounce) cream cheese, softened
1½ teaspoons salt	
2 packages active dry yeast	1 egg yolk
½ cup milk	Chocolate frosting (your favorite recipe)
½ cup water	
¼ cup (½ stick) margarine	

In a large bowl thoroughly mix 1¼ cups flour, ½ cup sugar, salt, and undissolved active dry yeast. Combine milk, water, and margarine in a saucepan. Heat over low heat until liquids are warm. (Margarine does not need to melt.) Gradually add to dry ingredients and beat 2 minutes at medium speed of electric mixer, scraping bowl occasionally. Add eggs and ½ cup flour or enough flour to make a thick batter. Beat at high speed 2 minutes, scraping bowl occasionally. Stir in enough additional flour to make a soft dough. Turn out onto lightly floured board; knead until smooth and elastic, about 8 to 10 minutes. Place in greased bowl, turning to grease top. Cover; let rise in warm place, free from draft, until doubled in bulk, about 1 hour. Meanwhile, prepare filling. Cream the cheese with ¼ cup sugar until light and fluffy. Blend in egg yolk. Punch dough down; turn out onto lightly floured board. Divide dough in half. Roll ½ the dough into a 10x14-inch rectangle. Spread with half the cheese filling. Roll up, as for jelly roll, to form 14-inch roll. Seal edges. Place on greased baking sheet. Cut slits ¾ through log at 1-inch intervals. Repeat with remaining dough and filling. Cover; let rise in warm place, free from draft, until doubled in bulk, about 1 hour. Bake in moderate oven (350°F.) about 20 to 25 minutes, or until done. Remove from baking sheets and cool. Frost with chocolate frosting. Makes 2 cakes.

MARTHA WASHINGTON'S FAN (No-Dissolve Method)

6 to 7 cups unsifted all-purpose flour	⅔ cup softened margarine
½ cup sugar	1¼ cups very hot tap water
1¼ teaspoons salt	3 eggs (at room temperature)
2 tablespoons instant nonfat dry milk solids	Melted margarine
	Confectioners' sugar frosting
2 packages active dry yeast	

In a large bowl thoroughly mix 2 cups flour, sugar, salt, dry milk solids, and undissolved active dry yeast. Add softened margarine. Gradually add very hot tap water to dry ingredients and beat 2 minutes at medium speed of electric mixer, scraping bowl occasionally. Add eggs and ½ cup flour, or enough flour to make a thick batter. Beat at high speed 2 minutes, scraping bowl occasionally. Stir in enough additional flour to make a soft dough. Turn out onto lightly floured board; knead until smooth and elastic, about 8 to 10 minutes. Place in greased bowl, turning to grease top. Cover; let rise in warm place, free from draft, until doubled in bulk, about 1 hour. Meanwhile, prepare Coconut-Butterscotch Filling (below). Punch dough down; turn out onto lightly floured board. Divide dough into 3 equal pieces; let rest 5 minutes. Roll 1 piece of dough into a 6x20-inch rectangle. Brush ⅔ of the length of the dough with melted margarine; sprinkle the margarine-covered dough with ⅓ of the prepared filling. Fold unspread dough over ½ of the spread dough. Then fold again, making 3 layers of dough and 2 layers of filling. Seal edges and end. Place on greased baking sheet. Using scissors, start 1-inch from sealed end and cut 8 strips, leaving the opposite side uncut to about 1-inch from the edge. Separate the strips slightly and twist so that the filling shows; then pinch ends into points. Repeat with remaining pieces of dough and filling. Cover; let rise in warm place, free from draft, until doubled in bulk, about 45 minutes. Bake in moderate oven (350°F.) about 20 to 25 minutes, or until done. Remove from baking sheets and cool on wire racks. Frost while warm with confectioners' sugar frosting. Makes 3 coffeecakes.

Coconut-Butterscotch Filling: Combine 1 can (4-ounce) shredded coconut, 1 cup chopped pecans, and ½ cup firmly packed light brown sugar. Blend in 3 tablespoons margarine, melted.

OATMEAL BANNOCKS (No-Dissolve Method)

2½ to 3 cups unsifted all-purpose flour	½ cup milk
⅓ cup sugar	½ cup water
¾ teaspoon salt	¼ cup (½ stick) margarine
1 cup uncooked old fashioned rolled oats	1 egg (at room temperature)
2 packages active dry yeast	½ cup currants

In a large bowl thoroughly mix ¾ cup flour, sugar, salt, rolled oats, and undissolved active dry yeast. Combine milk, water, and margarine in a saucepan. Heat over low heat until liquids are warm. (Margarine does not need to melt.) Gradually add to dry ingredients and beat 2 minutes at medium speed of electric mixer, scraping bowl occasionally. Add egg and ½ cup flour, or enough flour to make a thick batter. Beat at high speed 2 minutes, scraping bowl occasionally. Stir in enough additional flour to make a soft dough. Turn out onto lightly floured board; knead until smooth and elastic, about 8 to 10 minutes. Place in greased bowl, turning to grease top. Cover; let rise in warm place, free from draft, until doubled in bulk, about 45 minutes. Punch dough down; turn out onto lightly floured board. Knead in currants. Divide dough in half; roll each half into an 8-inch circle. Place in 2 greased 8-inch round cake pans. With a sharp knife, cut each circle into 8 wedges, cutting almost through to bottom. Cover; let rise in warm place, free from draft, until doubled in bulk, about 30 minutes. Bake in moderate oven (375°F.) about 20 minutes, or until done. Remove from pans and cool on wire racks. Makes 2 cakes.

APRICOT BRAID (No-Dissolve Method)

2½ to 3 cups unsifted all-purpose flour	1 cup boiling water
¼ cup sugar	1 cup firmly packed light brown sugar
1 teaspoon salt	⅓ cup unsifted all-purpose flour
1 package active dry yeast	2 tablespoons sugar
¾ cup milk	½ teaspoon ground cinnamon
¼ cup (½ stick) margarine	1 egg yolk
1 egg (at room temperature)	2 tablespoons milk
1½ cups dried apricots	

In a large bowl thoroughly mix ¾ cup flour, ¼ cup sugar, salt, and undissolved active dry yeast. Combine ¾ cup milk and 2 tablespoons margarine in a saucepan. Heat over low heat until liquid is warm. (Margarine does not need to melt.) Gradually add to dry ingredients and beat 2 minutes at medium speed of electric mixer, scraping bowl occasionally. Add egg and ¼ cup flour, or enough flour to make a thick batter. Beat at high speed 2 minutes, scraping bowl occasionally. Stir in enough additional flour to make a soft dough. Turn out onto lightly floured board; knead until smooth and elastic, about 8 to 10 minutes. Place in greased bowl, turning to grease top. Cover; let rise in warm place, free from draft, until doubled in bulk, about 1 hour. Meanwhile, combine apricots and boiling water in a saucepan. Bring to a boil. Reduce heat and simmer, uncovered, until liquid is absorbed and apricots are tender, about 25 minutes; sieve. Stir in brown sugar until dissolved. Cool. Punch dough down; turn out onto lightly floured board. Divide in half. Roll out each half into a 14x8-inch rectangle. Place on greased baking sheets. Spread ½ of the apricot filling down the center ⅓ of each rectangle. Slit dough at 1-inch intervals along each side of filling. Fold strips at an angle across filling, alternating from side to side. Cover; let rise in warm place, free from draft, until doubled in bulk, about 1 hour. Combine ⅓ cup flour, 2 tablespoons sugar, and cinnamon. Cut in remaining 2 tablespoons margarine until mixture is crumbly. Brush cakes with combined egg yolk and 2 tablespoons milk. Sprinkle each with half of crumb mixture. Bake in moderate oven (350°F.) about 20 minutes, or until done. Remove from baking sheets and cool on wire racks. Makes 2 coffeecakes.

BRIOCHE BRAID (No-Dissolve Method)

1¾ to 2¼ cups unsifted all-purpose flour
¼ cup sugar
¼ teaspoon salt
1 package active dry yeast
¼ cup milk

¼ cup water
⅓ cup margarine
2 eggs (at room temperature)
½ teaspoon lemon extract
Melted margarine

In a large bowl thoroughly mix ¾ cup flour, sugar, salt, and undissolved active dry yeast. Combine milk, water, and ⅓ cup margarine in a saucepan. Heat over low heat until liquids are warm. (Margarine does not need to melt.) Gradually add to dry ingredients and beat 2 minutes at medium speed of electric mixer, scraping bowl occasionally. Add eggs, lemon extract, and ½ cup flour, or enough flour to make a thick batter. Beat at high speed 2 minutes, scraping bowl occasionally. Add enough additional flour to make a stiff batter. Beat by hand 5 minutes. Brush top of dough with melted margarine. Cover; let rise in warm place, free from draft, until doubled in bulk, about 1 hour. Stir batter down; cover tightly with aluminum foil and refrigerate overnight. Turn out onto a heavily floured board. Divide into 3 pieces; roll each piece into a 20-inch roll. Braid the rolls together; pinch ends to seal. Place on large greased baking sheet. Cover; let rise in warm place, free from draft, until doubled in bulk, about 1 hour. Bake in moderate oven (375°F.) about 20 to 30 minutes, or until done. Remove from baking sheet and cool on wire rack. Best when served warm, either plain or frosted with Sugar Glaze (below). Makes 1 coffeecake.

Sugar Glaze: Combine ¾ cup unsifted confectioners' sugar, 1 tablespoon water, and ½ teaspoon lemon extract. Beat until smooth.

ONE BOWL DUTCH HUSTLE CAKE (No-Dissolve Method)

1 to 1½ cups unsifted all-purpose
  flour
¼ cup sugar
½ teaspoon salt
1 package active dry yeast
2 tablespoons softened margarine
½ cup very hot tap water
1 egg (at room temperature)

1½ cups drained canned or cooked
  apple slices
2 tablespoons brown sugar
¼ teaspoon ground cinnamon
¼ teaspoon ground nutmeg
2 tablespoons margarine
Confectioners' sugar frosting

In a large bowl thoroughly mix ½ cup flour, sugar, salt, and undissolved active dry yeast. Add 2 tablespoons softened margarine. Gradually add very hot tap water to dry ingredients and beat 2 minutes at medium speed of electric mixer, scraping bowl occasionally. Add egg and ½ cup flour, or enough flour to make a thick batter. Beat at high speed 2 minutes, scraping bowl occasionally. Stir in enough additional flour to make a stiff batter. Spread batter evenly in greased 9-inch square pan. Arrange apple slices on top. Sprinkle with mixture of brown sugar, cinnamon and nutmeg. Dot with remaining 2 tablespoons margarine. Cover; let rise in warm place, free from draft, until doubled in bulk, about 1 hour. Bake in hot oven (400°F.) about 25 minutes, or until done. Remove from oven; let stand 10 minutes before removing from pan. Cool on wire rack. Drizzle with confectioners' sugar frosting. Makes 1 cake.

FROSTED PINEAPPLE SQUARES (No-Dissolve Method)

½ cup sugar
3 tablespoons cornstarch
¼ teaspoon salt
1 egg yolk, slightly beaten
1 can (1-pound 14-ounce) pineapple
  chunks
3¾ to 4¼ cups unsifted all-purpose
  flour

1 teaspoon sugar
1 package active dry yeast
½ cup milk
½ cup water
1 cup (2 sticks) margarine
4 egg yolks (at room temperature)
Confectioners' sugar frosting

Mix ½ cup sugar, cornstarch, and salt together in saucepan. Stir in slightly beaten egg yolk and undrained pineapple chunks. Cook over medium heat, stirring constantly, until mixture comes to a boil. Set aside to cool. In a large bowl thoroughly mix 1⅓ cups flour, 1 teaspoon sugar, and undissolved active dry yeast. Combine milk, water, and margarine in a saucepan. Heat over low heat until liquids are warm. (Margarine does not need to melt.) Gradually add to dry ingredients and beat 2 minutes at medium speed of electric mixer, scraping bowl occasionally. Add egg yolks and ½ cup flour, or enough flour to make a thick batter. Beat at high speed 2 minutes, scraping bowl occasionally. Stir in enough additional flour to make a soft moist dough. Divide dough in half. Roll out ½ the dough on floured board to fit the bottom of ungreased 15½x10½x1-inch jelly roll pan. Spread with cooled pineapple filling. Roll remaining dough large enough to cover filling. Seal edges together. Snip surface of the dough with scissors to let steam escape. Cover; let rise in warm place, free from draft, until doubled in bulk, about 1 hour. Bake in moderate oven (375°F.) about 35 to 40 minutes, or until done. Let cake cool in pan. Frost while warm with confectioners' sugar frosting. Cut into squares to serve. Makes 1 large cake.

CHERRY-GO-ROUND (No-Dissolve Method)

3½ to 4½ cups unsifted all-purpose flour
½ cup sugar
1 teaspoon salt
1 package active dry yeast
1 cup milk
¼ cup water
½ cup (1 stick) margarine

1 egg (at room temperature)
½ cup unsifted all-purpose flour
½ cup chopped pecans
½ cup firmly packed light brown sugar
1 can (1-pound) pitted red sour
    cherries, well drained
Confectioners' sugar frosting

In a large bowl thoroughly mix 1¼ cups flour, sugar, salt, and undissolved active dry yeast. Combine milk, water, and margarine in a saucepan. Heat over low heat until liquids are warm. (Margarine does not need to melt.) Gradually add to dry ingredients and beat 2 minutes at medium speed of electric mixer, scraping bowl occasionally. Add egg and ¾ cup flour, or enough flour to make a thick batter. Beat at high speed 2 minutes, scraping bowl occasinoally. Stir in enough additional flour to make a stiff batter. Cover bowl tightly with aluminum foil. Refrigerate dough at least 2 hours. (Dough may be kept in refrigerator 3 days.) When ready to shape dough, combine ½ cup flour, pecans, and brown sugar. Turn dough out onto lightly floured board and divide in half. Roll ½ of the dough to a 14x7-inch rectangle. Spread with ¾ cup cherries. Sprinkle with ½ the brown sugar mixture. Roll up from long side as for jelly roll. Seal edges. Place sealed edge down in circle on greased baking sheet. Seal ends together firmly. Cut slits ⅔ through ring at 1-inch intervals; turn each section on its side. Repeat with remaining dough, cherries, and brown sugar mixture. Cover; let rise in warm place, free from draft, until doubled in bulk, about 1 hour. Bake in moderate oven (375°F.) about 20 to 25 minutes, or until done. Remove from baking sheets and cool in wire racks. Frost while warm with confectioners' sugar frosting. Makes 2 coffee-cakes.

FRECKLE BREAD (No-Dissolve Method)

4¾ to 5¾ cups unsifted all-purpose
    flour
½ cup sugar
1 teaspoon salt
2 packages active dry yeast
1 cup potato water or water

½ cup (1 stick) margarine
2 eggs (at room temperature)
¼ cup mashed potatoes (at room
    temperature)
1 cup seedless raisins

In a large bowl thoroughly mix 1½ cups flour, sugar, salt, and undissolved active dry yeast. Combine potato water or water and margarine in a saucepan. Heat over low heat until liquid is warm. (Margarine does not need to melt.) Gradually add to dry ingredients and beat 2 minutes at medium speed of electric mixer, scraping bowl occasionally. Add eggs, potatoes, and ½ cup flour, or enough flour to make a thick batter. Beat at high speed for 2 minutes, scraping bowl occasionally. Stir in raisins and enough additional flour to make a soft dough. Turn out onto lightly floured board; knead until smooth and elastic, about 8 to 10 minutes. Place in greased bowl, turning to grease top. Cover; let rise in warm place, free from draft, until doubled in bulk, about 1 hour and 15 minutes.* Punch dough down; turn out onto lightly floured board. Divide dough into 4 equal pieces. Shape each piece into a slender loaf, about 8½ inches long. Put 2 loaves, side by side, in each of 2 greased 8½x4½x2½-inch loaf pans. Cover; let rise in warm place, free from draft, until

* Note: If plain water is used, rising time will be about 1 hour 45 minutes.

doubled in bulk, about 1 hour. Bake in moderate oven (350°F.) about 35 minutes, or until done. Remove from pans and cool on wire racks. Makes 2 loaves.

SALLY LUNN (No-Dissolve Method)

3½ to 4 cups unsifted all-purpose flour
⅓ cup sugar
1 teaspoon salt
1 package active dry yeast

½ cup milk
½ cup water
½ cup (1 stick) margarine
3 eggs (at room temperature)

In a large bowl thoroughly mix 1¼ cups flour, sugar, salt, and undissolved active dry yeast. Combine milk, water, and margarine in a saucepan. Heat over low heat until liquids are warm. (Margarine does not need to melt.) Gradually add to dry ingredients and beat 2 minutes at medium speed of electric mixer, scraping bowl occasionally. Add eggs and 1 cup flour, or enough flour to make a thick batter. Beat at high speed 2 minutes, scraping bowl occasionally. Stir in enough additional flour to make a stiff batter. Cover; let rise in warm place, free from draft, until doubled in bulk, about 1 hour. Stir batter down and beat well, about ½ minute. Turn into a well-greased and floured 9-inch tube pan. Cover; let rise in warm place, free from draft, until doubled in bulk, about 1 hour. Bake in slow oven (325°F.) about 45 to 50 minutes, or until done. Remove from pan and cool on wire rack. Best when served warm. Makes 1 bread.

BABA AU RUM (No-Dissolve Method)

1¾ to 2¼ cups unsifted all-purpose
    flour
¼ cup sugar
1 package active dry yeast

½ cup milk
¼ cup (½ stick) margarine
3 eggs (at room temperature)

In a large bowl thoroughly mix ⅔ cup flour, sugar, and undissolved active dry yeast. Combine milk and margarine in a saucepan. Heat over low heat until liquid is warm. (Margarine does not need to melt.) Gradually add to dry ingredients and beat 2 minutes at medium speed of electric mixer, scraping bowl occasionally. Add eggs and ½ cup flour. Beat at high speed 2 minutes, scraping bowl occasionally. Stir in enough additional flour to make a thick batter. Cover; let rise in warm place, free from draft, until bubbly, about 1 hour. Stir down batter. Turn into well-greased and floured 2-quart Turk's Head pan or ring mold. Cover; let rise in a warm place, free from draft, 30 minutes. Bake in moderate oven (350°F.) about 30 to 35 minutes, or until done. Before removing from pan, immediately prick surface with fork. Pour Rum Syrup (below) over cake. After syrup is absorbed, remove from pan. Makes 1 cake.

Rum Syrup: In a saucepan, combine ½ cup sugar and ¼ cup water; bring to a boil. Remove from heat and stir in ¼ cup orange juice and 1 tablespoon rum extract.

Index

matzo meal, (*continued*)
  mendelach, 6
  muffins, 17
  omelet, 5
  pancakes, 9, 10
mayonnaise, dunk, pink, 34
  see salad dressings, mayonnaise
mead, 22
meal planning, 560
measurements
  accurate, 561
  table of standard, 562
meat
  Armenian wheat meat balls, 328
  balls, *see* meat balls
  Bavarian pot roast, 315
  beef, 312
    brisket
      sweet and sour, 320
      with beans #1, #2, 319
      with cabbage and sweet potatoes, 320
      with prunes and sweet potatoes, 320
      with sauerkraut, 318
    eggplant and, 327
    ground in cabbage leaves, #1, #2, 321, 326
    macaroni goulash, 323
    miroton, 323
    pot roast, 315
    ragout, 322
    stew, 317, 322, 323
    sweet and sour
      meat balls, 322
      pot roast, 320
      sauce, 325
      stuffed peppers, 325
      with cabbage, 318
    tongue, 347, 348, 349
  birds casserole, 316
  blintzes, 9, 108
  boiled dinner, 318
  brains, 345, 346
  braised short ribs of beef, 316
  brine for corned beef, 318
  calves foot jelly, 350
  canapé spreads, 328
  carnatzlach, 326
  carving, 570–572
  Caucasian dolma, 327
  Caucasian grape leaf rolls, 329
  chili con carne, 526
    with lima beans, 526
  chremslach filling, 11
  croquettes, 326
  derma, 350
  dolma, 327
  duckling pot roast, 387
  dumplings, baking powder, 473

meat, (*continued*)
  Dutch pot roast, chuck and vegetables, 321
  English beef stew, 322
  essic fleisch, 321
  frankfurters, 323
  freezing, 547–548
  gelfilte helzel, 350
  gefilte miltz, 351
  goulash, 317, 323, 344
  Greek musaca, 327
  hamburgers, Rumanian broiled, 326
  heart, 347
  helzel, gefilte, 350
  Hungarian goulash, 317
  jellied meat loaf, 322
  kishke, 350
  knishes, 467
  Koenigsberger klops, 328
  kreplach, 465
  lamb, 317, 327, 330–336, 340
    how to cook, 330
    uses of, 312
  liver, 343–344
    knishes, 467
  loaf, 324
  lung, 350
  meat balls, 303, 325, 328, 329
    freezing, 554
  miltz, gefilte, 351
  musaca, Greek, 327
  mutton, 330, 334, 336
  neck, stuffed poultry, 350
  New England boiled dinner, 318
  Norwegian beef birds, 321
  nutrition information, 558–559
  patties, 327
  pickling brine for corned beef, 318
  pie, 317
    freezing, 553
  pirogen, 466
  pitcha, 350
  pot roast duckling with herbs, 387
    see meats, beef
  ragout of beef, 322
  rolled rib roast, 315
  Russian meat balls, 329
  salad
    bowl, 408
    gelatin, 414
  sandwich fillings, *see* sandwiches, meat and poultry filling
  sauces, *see* sauces for fish, meat, poultry, vegetables
  sauerbraten, 316
  scrapple, 329
  servings and pounds, 567
  shepherd's pie, 317